Statistics, Knowledge and Policy

KEY INDICATORS TO INFORM DECISION MAKING

 OECD

ORGANISATION FOR ECONOMIC CO-OPERATION AND DEVELOPMENT

ORGANISATION FOR ECONOMIC CO-OPERATION AND DEVELOPMENT

The OECD is a unique forum where the governments of 30 democracies work together to address the economic, social and environmental challenges of globalisation. The OECD is also at the forefront of efforts to understand and to help governments respond to new developments and concerns, such as corporate governance, the information economy and the challenges of an ageing population. The Organisation provides a setting where governments can compare policy experiences, seek answers to common problems, identify good practice and work to co-ordinate domestic and international policies.

The OECD member countries are: Australia, Austria, Belgium, Canada, the Czech Republic, Denmark, Finland, France, Germany, Greece, Hungary, Iceland, Ireland, Italy, Japan, Korea, Luxembourg, Mexico, the Netherlands, New Zealand, Norway, Poland, Portugal, the Slovak Republic, Spain, Sweden, Switzerland, Turkey, the United Kingdom and the United States. The Commission of the European Communities takes part in the work of the OECD.

OECD Publishing disseminates widely the results of the Organisation's statistics gathering and research on economic, social and environmental issues, as well as the conventions, guidelines and standards agreed by its members.

This work is published on the responsibility of the Secretary-General of the OECD. The opinions expressed and arguments employed herein do not necessarily reflect the official views of the Organisation or of the governments of its member countries.

Foreword

Statistics are a fundamental input for individual and collective decision-making, both at national and international levels. Over the past decade, there has been an increasing interest in complementing policy decisions with the latest statistical information and to set quantitative targets for the policy itself. In addition researchers, the media, civil society and business leaders are demanding more and more information to assess current trends and evaluate the results of various policies and decisions.

In today's complex and diverse societies, limitations on resources along with conflicting demands necessitate good decision making and the setting of priorities. In a democracy we assume that these choices are made by citizens, both directly through their civic and political participation and indirectly through their choice of electoral representation. In order for both citizens and their elected officials to make choices that will best address the people's needs, high quality, shared, accessible information about how the nation, smaller community or population group is doing on a variety of dimensions is absolutely essential.

This is not to imply that societies or policy makers are lacking information. An overabundance of data is readily available in the press and especially on the Internet. Several private data providers now play a role in the "Market of Information" and compete daily with official sources to capture the attention of media, businesses, households and individuals. In some cases, this competition is based on serious efforts to produce data not available elsewhere, but in other cases, surveys carried out by private institutes on a few units and/or econometric estimates are presented and commented on as indisputable fact. As a result, because of the unprecedented range and number of sources available, users are unable to navigate through them or assess their quality: the final result is a certain degree of confusion.

Furthermore, the international dimension of problems and policies, the development of benchmarking techniques to compare the relative position of each country with other countries of similar degrees of development, and the surveillance mechanisms developed by the international community require comparable statistics. At the same time, individual businesses, not only multinationals, need good quality statistics to evaluate and compare the dynamics of actual and potential markets, domestic and international prices, etc. Unfortunately, international comparability of statistics is still a concern.

While the United Nations Millennium Development Goals (and related indicators) provide a framework for evaluating the progress of developing countries, there exists no co-ordinated worldwide effort to study the development and implications of these large-scale systems of public information for developed countries. Therefore, the OECD has decided to act as a catalyst to convene and promote research and information sharing among countries, allowing them to compare strategies intended to measure and assess the overall "position" and "progress" of a certain political entity *vis-à-vis* other similar entities.

It is with this in mind that the OECD decided to organise "Statistics, Knowledge and Policy", the first OECD World Forum on Key Indicators. This Forum allowed statisticians, policy makers, journalists, academics and representatives from business and civil society to discuss the development of institutional frameworks and research projects to identify key indicators to assess the economic, social and environmental progress or state of a political entity. The Forum, held in Palermo (Italy) 10-13 November 2004, was sponsored by the Italian Government and other primary public and private institutions. It attracted 540 experts from forty-three countries. In addition, several thousand people from all over the word followed the plenary sessions through a live Web-cast.

These two volumes contain the proceedings of the Forum, organised by sessions. In particular, they contain keynote speeches, invited papers presented in various sessions and papers presented at the technical workshops. This introduction is meant to provide the reader with an overview of the themes discussed at the Forum, with a special focus on the key messages emerged from various sessions.

The OECD is grateful to all speakers, chairpersons, discussants and delegates for their contribution to the Forum. A special acknowledgment goes to the Italian Government (especially the Ministry of Economy and Finance, the Ministry of Environment and Land Protection, the Ministry of Labour and Welfare, the Ministry of Innovation and Technologies, and the Ministry of Foreign Affairs), the Italian National Statistical Office (Istat), the Bank of Italy, and the Union of Chambers of Commerce, Industry, Handicraft and Agriculture for their support. SAS, Telecom Italia, GRTN and Credito Siciliano sponsored the event. Finally, the OECD is grateful to the Municipality of Palermo and its Mayor for their effort in organising the Forum in such a magnificent venue, the *Teatro Massimo,* and for the warm hospitality shown to all participants.

Enrico Giovannini

Chief Statistician of the OECD

Table of Contents

Additional Resources including the Knowledge Base are available Online at:
www.oecd.org/oecdworldforum

The First World Forum on Key Indicators

Enrico Giovannini

Chief Statistician of the OECD

This first World Forum on Key Indicators was organised in order to share experiences rather than to develop a comprehensive set of international indicators or reports. Its objectives were to share existing experiences and to evaluate the possibility to develop:

- project-based collaborative research: to conduct a comparative analysis of experiences already available in OECD countries in this domain, deriving lessons learned and topics for discussion that will help build knowledge on how meaningful indicators systems are developed and used to frame issues taken up by OECD countries;

- an organised community of practice: to establish an ongoing international forum where individuals from various sectors would meet periodically to analyse best practices and new developments in the area of quantitative assessment of overall performance of various political or administrative entities.

Advance work for the first objective included the creation of a knowledge base containing roughly 200 reports on national and international key indicators experiences developed by private and governmental institutions. Users can access these reports either by topic or theme and it can be found on the Forum website at www.oecd.org/oecdworldforum.

More than 150 speakers were invited to contribute to the Forum, organised into both plenary and parallel sessions including:

- Plenary sessions with presentations on best practices from the United States, Australia, Ireland and Italy.

- A plenary session on the international dimension of the development of key indicators systems.

- Plenary sessions with keynote speakers Jean-Claude Trichet, President of the European Central Bank, David M. Walker, Comptroller General of the Government Accountability Office, and Donald J. Johnston, Secretary-General of the OECD.

- Groups of four parallel sessions covering:

    - Information domains – how to deal with the measurement of emerging phenomena in the economy, society, and the environment.

- Process building – how to build indicators sets involving various domains of society (policy makers, statistical and research networks, the business community, media, and civil society).

- Advocacy and numeracy for key indicators – how to support the dissemination of indicators sets, prepare users to use them and advocate their use in decision-making processes.

- Uses of indicators for policy making – how to use such data for benchmarking analysis, for allocating funds, for strategic planning etc.

• Roundtable sessions – to discuss the role of the institutions of the media, national audit offices and central banks in developing, using and promoting indicators systems.

Workshops highlighting the OECD's work on indicators were also conducted, whose papers are included in the second volume of the proceedings.

Keynote Speeches

Donald J. Johnston, Secretary-General of the OECD made the distinction between information and knowledge with the following analogy: "Statistics represent the raw material for the creation of knowledge, just as steel represents the raw material for the manufacture of automobiles. But it is knowledge that takes steel and turns it into an automobile, and it is knowledge which takes the raw material of statistics and turns it into knowledge, and in a further stage into policy." Building knowledge is not an easy task especially in light of the overwhelming number of sources, both official and unofficial, the manipulation of figures to support specific causes, and the lack of statistical literacy amongst most of the public and even the media. However, as Mr. Johnston pointed out, we must be making progress on this front because twenty years ago we referred to the "Information Society" while today we speak of "Knowledge-Based Societies". The OECD understands the importance of knowledge-building for policy making because that is the role it serves for its member countries. Although the OECD does not have any legislative powers, through its collection and dissemination of statistics, consultations with stakeholders representing various sectors of society through its committees, analysis of economic and social policy, and comparisons of various experiences, the OECD arms its member countries with knowledge to make the best policy choices. In conclusion, he quoted Benjamin Franklin, who said *"An investment in knowledge pays the best interest"*, stressing that the OECD is committed to contribute to such investment through events such as the Forum and inviting all participants to maximise the short and long term revenues from this investment.

Jean-Claude Trichet, President of the European Central Bank (ECB) highlighted the importance of an integrated set of data for the work of central bankers and other economic policy makers. As the economy is never at rest, monetary decisions must be taken amidst financial shocks where the future can never be foreseen. Macroeconomic models or synthetic indicators are not sufficient tools to make the kinds of decisions required to stabilise such a complex economy and often fall victim to obsolescence in the rapidly changing economic environment. While all central banks need a comprehensive source of data, this is especially true for the ECB who is in charge of monetary policy for a completely new economy. Mr. Trichet pointed to the fact that ten years ago statistics for the Euro area were nonexistent, but now compare favourably with other major countries in many respects. The success factors and the lessons learned are outlined in his speech.

Of the most important is that of providing for the necessary checks and balances to ensure the independence of statistical institutes, which is the key to having data of quality and integrity.

Improving national progress and increasing accountability was the theme of the speech given by David M. Walker, Comptroller General of the United States. Are citizens able to hold their elected officials accountable? Are they getting results with the resources they have been allotted and can they prove the progress they are claiming? Are our nations fighting corruption and making the best use out of taxpayers' money? In his view, a national key indicators system would provide the electorate with answers to these questions, in turn building public trust as well as the effectiveness of public policy. Mr. Walker also compared the ideals of an indicators system to the work of the Government Accountability Office (GAO), the supreme audit institution in the U.S. Among other roles, the GAO serves as the "congressional watchdog" because of its responsibility to oversee the U.S. federal government. To this end, GAO reports must be objective, fact based, non-ideological, non-partisan, fair and balanced. Those developing an indicators initiative should approach the task with the same goals in mind. Mr. Walker also urged other supreme audit institutions to use their position as independent professional service organisations with expertise in statistics to encourage the development of a key indicators project in their country.

National Case Studies

The national case studies presented at the Forum each detailed the process and design of indicators initiatives tailored to meet their particular needs and national interests. The main conclusion from these presentations is that there is no "one-size-fits-all" or magic formula to create a working indicators system, but these four cases constitute "success stories" from which other countries aspiring to their own initiatives can gain valuable insight.

The United States case study presentation highlighted the Key National Indicators Initiative (KNII). The conceptual basis for the KNII is a broad-based comprehensive indicators system that would integrate key topic areas and selected indicators into a single system that aggregates, organises, and disseminates information products and services. It will be a source that essentially provides "one-stop shopping" for high-quality information, selected from the governmental, commercial, and scientific sectors, that is a fully democratised, transparent source of information, and one that is easily accessible. The key features of the initiative are the following: building on current practice, theoretical framework, public involvement in the choice of indicators, criteria for indicator selection, quality control, identification of data sources and accessibility to users. Authors concluded welcoming the Forum as a timely opportunity to move the United States' initiative and noting that, as the construction of indicators must be based on the co-operation of citizens and establishments, the KNII initiative can help in overcoming the present concerns about privacy and confidentiality.

A national success story is the initiative launched by the Central Statistical Office of Ireland. The report "Measuring Ireland's Progress", containing 108 indicators and covering 48 domain themes, was published for the first time in 2003. The purpose of this publication is to present a manageable set of indicators which, when taken together, would broadly summarise the progress being made in Ireland in achieving desirable outcomes for society. The paper discusses the political environment necessary to get the needed support for the initiative, the process used to identify indicators, the policy outcomes and the future of the project. Clearly this is challenging territory for national statistical offices (NSOs) and the institutional position and independence of the NSOs has to be very strong in order to minimise any risks to its credibility. Yet, in most OECD countries, the statistical office would be accepted by the public as an "honest broker" in relation to the publication of information on the delivery of services and the apparent societal outcomes - so from the point of view of informing society, statisticians should not avoid being pro-actively involved.

The Italian case was focused on territorial indicators, in light of persisting economic and social regional disparities especially in relation to the North and South. A large share of policies are now being aimed at enhancing the competitiveness of certain regions increasing the demand for better data on a regional and local level. A twofold approach has been adopted in the use of indicators – a soft and a hard use - in order to tackle the problems resulting both from the incompleteness of information, that prevents turning desired outcomes into verifiable indicators, and from the fuzziness of causality links between policy actions and objectives. A *soft use* of context indicators has been adopted for ultimate policy outcomes when both problems were very prevalent and could not be overcome. A *hard use* of indicators, to which rewards and sanctions are linked, has been adopted for intermediate policy objectives concerning institution building, - an essential precondition for the effectiveness of regional policies – when both problems could be more effectively addressed. Though both experiences examined in the paper have been successful, the *hard use* of indicators has insofar proved to be more effective. However, the *soft use* of indicators in the case of ultimate outcomes for citizens and firms has certainly allowed for better focusing of some projects and of policy monitoring. Finally, the paper stressed the strong role "political judgment" plays on the use of indicators. In a world where policy evaluation is important, there is room for a less ambitious, but fundamental role of indicators in terms of accountability: to enhance the general communication to the public of policy objectives, revealing policy makers' preferences and results in order to improve policy making.

"Measuring Australia's Progress" is a yearly publication of the Australian Bureau of Statistics (ABS) containing a suite of indicators combining economic, environmental and social aspects. The annual publication is outlined in the paper and the challenges in compiling it are discussed. Specifically, some challenges included the complicated process of selecting the indicators and finding the delicate balance between the various domains as well as the handling of subjective measurements (i.e. measuring happiness). Particularly important was the selection of the "primary concept" among "progress", which considers whether various aspects of life - environmental, social and economic - are improving, one's "quality of life". This is strongly linked to (sometimes synonymous with) wellbeing and can also be used in a collective sense to describe how well a society satisfies people's wants and needs, "wellbeing or welfare", which is generally used to mean the condition of being healthy, contented and satisfied with life. It typically includes material, physical, social and spiritual aspects of life, and "sustainability", which considers whether an activity or condition can be maintained indefinitely. The choice of focusing on progress was based on several considerations: first, measuring progress meant considering whether things were moving in the right direction or not, without evaluating whether a certain level or pattern of activity is sustainable. Second, a focus on progress allowed ABS to give more prominence to the health of the economy and environment than would usually be covered in a project focused on wellbeing or quality of life.

Cross-Country Comparisons

An important opportunity for the statistical community to raise awareness of the importance of quantitative data in decision making was the development of the Millennium Development Goals. This high profile United Nations initiative involved setting 18 targets for 8 goals to be reached by 2015. All targets specify exact objectives and define in numerical terms how far countries need to go in order to achieve the goals. These indicators are being used in national, regional and international programmes to monitor and evaluate the implementation of policy initiatives. They are also increasingly being used in the design and management of national policy. However, continuous efforts are needed by the international statistical community to further strengthen their co-ordination and collaboration to avoid duplication, ensure consistency and overcome problems of comparability across different sets of data. The international availability of comprehensive, reliable and well-documented statistics and indicators on the Millennium Development Goals must be further improved and the data on indicators, together with the methodologies, should be made as widely available as possible.

On the European level are the Lisbon Objectives to make the EU "the most competitive and dynamic knowledge-based economy in the world, capable of sustaining economic growth with more and better jobs and greater social cohesion". The annual report on the movement towards this target relies heavily on the use of "Structural indicators" which are made available to the public on the Eurostat Website. Also adopted by the European Lisbon Council is the "Open Method Co-ordination" (OMC) which involves establishing timetables to achieve defined goals; using indicators and benchmarking to determine best practice; translating the European guidelines into specific policy at the regional and national levels; and monitoring, evaluating and holding peer reviews on the impact of these decisions. The increased use of the OMC has encouraged a more systematic use of statistical information and more explicit reference to quantitative information in the justification of policy initiatives. On the other hand, the experience of "structural indicators" is evidence of the need for actions from the statistical institutions in order to respond jointly to the information demands of policy makers. Finally, use of indicators for long term perspectives like in the Lisbon agenda calls for sustainable systems that can be best provided within the official statistics framework.

Since the late 1980s, OECD member countries have been co-operatively developing a range of internationally comparable education statistics and indicators. These are now published annually by OECD in *Education at a Glance*. In addition to the 30 OECD countries, this work is now extended to 20 other countries through *the World Education Indicators Programme* undertaken jointly by OECD and the UNESCO Institute for Statistics with support from the World Bank. In the mid-1990s, the countries decided to include direct measures of student learning through what became the *Programme for International Student Assessment (PISA)*. All 30 OECD countries and a growing number of others are involved - 28 having currently signed on for PISA 2006.The presentation prepared by the OECD (the paper is not included in these proceedings) illustrated the framework that guides the indicators development and described the strategies used to improve the comparability of statistics and indicators, as well as ways in which the indicators have informed national policy debates.

Measuring Economic, Social and Environmental Phenomena

In the session on measuring economic phenomena, J.P. Cotis, OECD Chief Economist, demonstrated the usefulness of internationally comparable indicators in trying to answer the question "Is Europe really in decline?" In looking past our common perceptions such as "Europeans are lazy" and looking at the indicators we learn the real reasons that productivity has been lagging behind the U.S. over the past 20 years and which policies could reverse this trend. On the other hand, J. Grice presented the UK initiative to better measure the output of Government services. For this purpose, a team led by Sir Tony Atkinson, one of the UK's most eminent economists was established to recommend principles for the measurement of government output, inputs and productivity. It sets out a work programme for improving measures of output in Health, Education, Public Order and Safety and Social Protection. Finally, G. Wagner highlighted the importance of microdata to examine economic and social dynamics, but up to now, there have been very few international microdatabases available that allow easy handling of microdata for a large number of countries. Therefore, the author discussed problems of setting up internationally comparable microdata sets.

Social issues are arguably the most challenging to measure yet some of the most important and relevant to policy makers and the society at large. G. Esping-Andersen demonstrated why headcounts are not sufficient, but that dynamic indicators taking into account life stages are crucial to understanding the true state of society and creating the appropriate policy measures. B. Hvinden described good social indicators as those able to quantify and qualify social exclusion in terms of both relation and distribution. Is one able to fully participate in social arenas and live a fully human life? If not, what are the key factors and can policy measures work to overcome this? Also outlined are the pre- and post- institutional/political and scientific/statistical basis that must be present in order for a suite of indicators to be successful in guiding decision-making and to avoid being "still-born" (scientifically successful but never finding the intended policy application). Finally, K. Tallis discussed how the institutional/political and scientific/statistical bases are fundamental to have a suite of indicators that can truly guide policy, rather than just providing general contextual information for community discussion of social issues. In particular, he discussed the question of what conditions must be established to ensure that an investment in social indicators will be fruitful.

However, while there are generally accepted and used composite indicators for the economic (GDP) and the social (Human Development Index HDI) domains, there is no such indicator for the environmental realm. Several environmental composite indicators that have been proposed were outlined in the papers presented at the Forum. In particular, W. Radermacher, by using case studies from the environmental domain, showing the problem of short-lived indicators and of disregarding an actor involved, developed an optimistic construction process for indicator-building taking account all relevant actors (in statistics, science, and politics) and of the complexity of their work systems. The analysis of the case studies also shows that indicator-building cannot be a linear process but is rather an iterative decision-making process where satisfactory sub-solutions are found and sub-targets are met.

Involving various domains of society

In order for an indicators initiative to gain wide-spread support and eventual use, a genuine community of interest must be established from the onset of the project.

Several papers presented at the Forum addressed this fundamental issue. Because the statistical indicators will provide information to be of use to not only policy makers at the local, national and international levels, but also to the public at large including the civil society, business leaders, scientific community, international and non-profit organisations, advocacy groups, academics and the media, their involvement in the design and implementation of the project is essential. Sessions highlighting the role of several of these groups of stakeholders are summarised below.

Arguably the most important role of indicators is to be an agent of change. In order for an initiative to be able to do this, involving civil society is of the utmost importance for various reasons. Civil society organisations are lead by some of the nations' leading thinkers and experts whose participation will help to ensure that the indicators are not limited to the narrow perception of a statistician or bureaucrat. As civil society organisations are often active advocates of societal change, it is essential to have their involvement from the onset of the project to ensure their use of the findings as a document of reference which can be used in debate and in the advancement of various causes.

Although the decision to include the media in an indicators initiative is straightforward, the relationship between the media and statistics is quite complicated as the journalists present at the Forum highlighted. The media depend on numbers to make their stories more credible and depend on credibility to sell newspapers or convince people to watch their programming. However, the media is constantly under the pressure of time constraints and if the official source cannot provide the statistics on time, the media will go to other, perhaps less serious sources to obtain them. Furthermore, even serious sources are sometimes more interested in being quoted than maintaining the accuracy that only time-consuming work can ensure. Some may argue that we now have a credibility crisis. Where numbers were once accepted as fact, they are now being called into question and debated just as much as the words on the page.

The relationship between indicators and their use by policy makers is also quite complex requiring constant dialogue between statisticians and policy makers. In today's globalised environment policy makers necessitate reliable indicators and international benchmarking techniques to help them make fully informed decisions. However, along with the increased need for comparability, the other aspects of quality (timeliness, clarity, comprehensiveness, etc) are complicated and rendered more difficult. One must not forget that one of the most important functions of a transparent indicators system is to provide the public with a tool with which to hold their elected officials accountable. Therefore, certain safeguards must be taken to ensure that the statistical institutions are sufficiently independent from political pressures, yet that the policy makers are still charged with setting priorities and making the decisions.

The business sector is an area where relevant indicators can have a significant influence on decision making and economic evolution. Although the business sector has rarely been asked to be involved in the definition of statistical indicators, as potential users with a real need for relevant statistics, it is important that they be incorporated as stakeholders from the beginning of any indicators initiative. Business leaders have expressed a strong desire, especially in light of the increasingly globalised business environment, for internationally comparable statistics and benchmarks; and there is a particular need among Small and Medium Enterprises who often do not have the resources or availability to collect the needed information in order to make the most savvy business choices. Business leaders also point to the often obsolete statistical classifications by industry, sectors and product areas which are no longer relevant in the rapidly changing, dynamic process of industrial and technological transformation. In addition, convincing the business community that participating in indicators initiatives as well as providing the needed input information, even when time consuming, will have significant benefits is also a part of the challenge.

Central bankers, like other policy makers, in such a constantly changing, complex economic environment require a comprehensive set of data in order to make sound monetary policy decisions. This need was emphasised especially in light of financial stability policy decisions which often involve individual conflicts of interest. For example, authorities may have to rescue a failing private bank with public funds. Policy measures such as this necessitate objective statistics to allow the authorities to claim fairness.

Superior Audit Institutions (SAIs) also have a unique role to play in the development and implementation of indicator systems. Although SAIs do not have a direct role in the collection and dissemination of data, because of their independent status, they can promote the accuracy and effectiveness of these indicators as well as uncover inconsistencies or errors. A widely accepted system of indicators would also provide a common set of criteria in performance auditing of the effectiveness of public policies and reduce diverging conclusions.

Advocacy, Numeracy and Dissemination

As it stands, the media are the link between producers of statistics and the users and public at large. Although the media are integral to the success of indicators systems in terms of communicating its uses and implications to the public, because of their deadlines and time and space constraints, they are often not the most appropriate medium to inform the public of in-depth issues. For an individual looking for comprehensive information on the state of his/her society, the mainstream media will not suffice.

Although there is a wealth of information contained in databases, in today's statistical environment, the individual will most likely be faced with intimidating formats and spread sheets and will likely have to pay an access fee. The current statistical distribution method ignores the fact that the ICT tools needed to make statistics understandable and interesting to non-experts already exist, and that the younger generation is already highly computer literate and quite capable of using these technologies. Gapminder, a software developed for interactive animated visualisation of development statistics, is one example of how statistics can be made accessible to the public. This project is described in these proceedings. The key challenge is not only to make the public and the media more statistically literate, but also to apply contemporary advances in information technology to existing statistical databases to make statistics a part of school curricula and an attractive source of information for public users.

Conclusions and further actions

During the wrap-up session, chaired by the Deputy Secretary-General H. Schlögl, three speakers were asked to summarise the main points coming out of the Forum representing the Council (US Ambassador to the OECD, Hon. C. Morella), the OECD Committees (J. Rosted, Chair of the OECD Committee on Industry and Business Environment) and the Secretariat (E. Giovannini, Chief Statistician of the OECD). During that session several people also took the floor, commenting on the speakers' remarks.

According to speakers' view, this OECD initiative addressed a key issue for the development of modern democracies. The transparency and accountability of public policies; the people's capacity for understanding the characteristics and the evolution of the economies and societies in which they are living in order to decide for themselves whether life is getting better; the role of the media in contributing to the development of a common facts-based knowledge among citizens: all these issues require a special effort by modern societies to develop high quality statistics, to use them, among other things, to develop a shared knowledge about the state and the development of the society and to build accountable decision-making processes based on reliable statistical evidence.

The experts who attended the Forum, representing constituencies that had not previously met in a single international event to discuss these issues, openly acknowledged the usefulness of the Forum to address these issues. The Forum demonstrated that there was a need for a catalyst able to allow national constituencies to learn from other countries' experiences and that many good practices are already available in OECD countries.

As far as the development of "key indicators" within countries is concerned, the Forum demonstrated that various approaches are feasible. There is not a unique way to develop "key indicators", nor a unique set of indicators, and each country should choose the best approach taking into account cultural and institutional environments. Statistical, political, technical and organisational issues must be addressed, but the success of such an initiative mainly relies on the capacity to involve various sectors of society in a co-operative effort, a process which is worthwhile in itself for the positive spill-over effects it can bring to society as a whole.

The Forum also demonstrated the existence of a potential community of interest on the issue of "key indicators" in almost all OECD countries and in several non-member economies. On the other hand, a strong leadership is required to bring forward such a process within a country. Among the candidates for launching "key indicators" initiatives are NSOs or central authorities in charge of promoting the accountability of public policies or trying to 'join up' government to improve its effectiveness; for at sub-national levels the situation can vary significantly.

In conclusion, delegates asked the OECD to:

- launch a medium-term process on key indicators, through electronic discussion groups, specialised workshops, etc.;

- organise a second World Forum in two-three years time.

Therefore, the OECD Secretariat has developed a research project, which will be implemented in the near future. Contacts have also been established with some member countries to organise a second World Forum in 2007.

Keynote Speeches

The ECB's Use of Statistics and Other Information for Monetary Policy

Jean-Claude Trichet

President of the European Central Bank

Introduction

The links between statistics, knowledge and policy are of crucial importance for policy-makers and for society as a whole. I can only congratulate the organisers for the impressive programme they have drawn up and I am sure that we shall all leave Palermo full of ideas on how statistical knowledge can be better used to face current and future economic and social challenges.

Central bankers, like all other policy-makers, operate in an environment of high uncertainty regarding the functioning of the economy as well as its prevailing state and future development. In addition, the second half of the 1990s and the first years of this century have been characterised by structural changes, some of them on a global scale, others confined to Europe, all of which have added to the "normal" sources of uncertainty. At the global level, the fall of the Soviet empire, the conversion of emerging Asia to market economics, accelerating advances in science and innovation in information technology and a deepening and widening of globalised financial markets have all been, or are, part of the powerful phenomenon of globalisation. At the European level, the adoption of the euro by 12 countries, structural reforms in goods and labour markets and the enlargement of the Union are some of the key developments in this respect. Therefore, disentangling the shocks that continually hit the euro area economy and assessing their impact on the risks to price stability in real time remains a very demanding task, in spite of the progress made in statistical data compilation, economic theory and econometrics over the past decades.

In such a complex environment, a single model or a limited set of key indicators is not a sufficient guide for monetary policy. Instead, an encompassing and integrated set of data is required. The development of statistics for the euro area and the future priorities for further enhancements reflect this requirement. A rich set of timely statistical data is a necessary but insufficient precondition for sound monetary policy-making. Only if the information is structured and analysed in a consistent way will monetary policy makers be in a position to take the most appropriate decisions to obtain their policy goals.

Let me elaborate a bit more on these three themes: the need for an encompassing and integrated set of data, the achievements of, and outlook for, euro area statistics and the ECB's framework for analysing this information.

Monetary policy and the need for an encompassing and integrated set of data

If we lived in the world of macroeconomic textbooks, a few simple models with a limited set of variables would be a sufficient basis for monetary policy-making and the statistical requirements could be kept to a minimum. As we all know, the real world is much more complex and, therefore, information needs are much more elaborated. In such a world, a rich and integrated set of data is needed because macroeconomic models, synthetic indicators and unconnected statistical indicators are often too rough a guide to the current and likely future development of the economy.

As mentioned before, central banks have to take decisions under conditions of constant uncertainty. The economy is never at rest. A multitude of disturbances of diverse nature affect the economy all the time: financial shocks, demand shocks, supply shocks etc., and these cannot easily be distinguished in real time, let alone foreseen.

In their attempts to identify disturbances and track how they spread through the economy, central banks are assisted by models. But too often, existing models are not sufficiently sophisticated instruments to identify shocks. For one thing, their focus may be too narrow, in a way that makes them unduly selective. A partial representation of the economic structure can only partially help in monetary policy decision-making, notably in real time. For instance, it is very difficult to find empirical models that allow for an integral view of both non-financial ("real") and monetary-financial phenomena. So, it may be impossible to arrive at a convincing explanation of the origin and propagation of a significant financial shock, say, on the basis of sets of equations that do not elaborate on the role of the financial sector or account for only tenuous links between that sector and the rest of the economy.

Another example is provided by the many pitfalls that come with using "synthetic" indicators of inflationary pressure. The most famous of these "synthetic" indicators is the so-called "output gap". The "output gap" can be defined as a measure of the deviation of the aggregate output of an economy from the maximum level that would be consistent with price stability. This maximum level is then the "potential output". When current output is above potential, the pressure on the scarce resources should then translate into an increase in prices, that is, inflation.

In the real world, the monetary authority constantly faces the challenge of observability and measurement. Unfortunately, we cannot "assume" to know the "potential output". The best we can do is to try to "estimate" the output gap by using observations of many other correlated variables. We all know how imprecise and model-dependent this "estimated" measure can be. It would then be dangerous to derive monetary policy decisions from such an indicator. In my view, the example of the "output gap" demonstrates that theoretical economic models and monetary policy practice are, at times, quite far apart.

A second reason why models – and the synthetic theoretical constructs that accompany them – may often be elusive guides for policy lies in the fact that they are subject to rapid obsolescence as the structure of the economy is subject to permanent change. We, central bankers, like private agents, need to learn constantly about the environment in which we operate.

In the face of structural changes we are like "sailors in uncharted seas". Under these conditions we cannot afford to rely on a few sources of information nor can we simply use the "old navy maps" that are incorporated in existing models – even those that provided valuable information in the past. What used to be a key indicator under the "old regime" might not be so useful under the "new regime". What used to suffice in order to describe the old data-generating process might be insufficient for an accurate description of the new environment.

If this is of the essence for all central banks, this is particularly true for the ECB, which has been put in charge of the monetary policy of a totally new economic entity.

The creation of EMU represents a major structural change for the European economy and a great challenge to policy-makers. Nobody could tell, at the outset, to what extent the introduction of the single currency would affect the functioning of the single market of goods and services, or the very nature of financial markets or price and wage-setting behaviour across the euro area. Indeed, times of institutional change are arguably times in which private expectations may fail to converge on a focal point. The widely-held assumption has been that the statistical patterns emerging from an aggregation of pre-EMU data may not reveal much about the structure of the new economic entity, and any inference drawn on its basis may – in extreme cases – even be misleading. This is all the more likely when we consider the fact that, as far as monetary and financial convergence in the future euro area was concerned, it was based upon a concept of "benchmarking", namely convergence towards the best performers, which suggests that aggregation of the EMS data might be even less predictive. Such a situation has called for a cautious interpretation of model results and, even more importantly, for a broad information basis in order to cross-check the interpretation of various pieces of information. This implies a need for detailed and high-quality statistics for the euro area.

The construction of a comprehensive statistical support has confronted the ECB with a number of practical issues, to which I now turn.

Statistics for the euro area: achievements and outlook

Over the past ten years, major progress has been achieved in developing statistics for the euro area. Less than a decade ago, we did not even have the statistical *requirements* for the Monetary Union, let alone the statistics themselves for the euro area. Today, euro area statistics compare favourably with those of other major countries in many respects. A concrete example is the monthly balance of payments for the euro area and the availability of a timely, flash estimate of the euro area Harmonised Index of Consumer Prices (HICP). Moreover, the ECB compiles an elaborate and timely set of monthly statistics on monetary developments in the euro area and interest rates.

Statistical preparations had to start early, due to the long lead times involved. On average, it takes around 18 months from inception to delivery of a new set of statistics that involves the collection of additional information from economic agents.

While there is still room for improvement, which I will explain later on, I feel confident that the ECB has now at its disposal a solid set of statistics of sufficient quality for the conduct of monetary policy. Let me share with you some of the success factors and "lessons to learn" from this development process.

First and foremost, the achievements have been possible thanks to the intensive and fruitful cooperation and coordination with other statistical agencies. In particular, the efficient and effective coordination between the statistical departments of the ECB and of the national central banks within the ECB's Statistics Committee has been very conducive to the development of the comprehensive set of euro area statistics that is disseminated by the ECB. Equally, the cooperation between Eurostat and the ECB's Directorate General Statistics is very intensive and fruitful, and is based on the allocation of tasks laid down in the Memorandum of Understanding signed in March 2003.

Secondly, I would like to stress the importance of close cooperation with users, which should guarantee that the statistics are "fit for purpose". At the same time, with the right institutional arrangements in place, responsiveness to user needs in the design and accessibility of statistics should not undermine the independence of statistics and statisticians, which is an essential factor.

A third important "success factor" in the design of statistical systems is a strong legal basis. Article 5 of the Statute of the ESCB and of the ECB states that "in order to undertake the tasks of the ESCB, the ECB ... shall contribute to the harmonisation, where necessary, of the rules and practices governing the collection, compilation and distribution of statistics within its fields of competence". As a consequence, the ECB developed a legal framework for the collection of statistics and for ensuring compliance with these legal acts. Legal instruments are necessary to achieve satisfactory standards and equal treatment across Member States.

Fourthly, the setting-up of euro area statistics from scratch has required an intensive process of harmonisation of the methodologies used by the various countries for the collection and production of statistics. This enables us, for example, to compile meaningful area-wide aggregates. The need for the harmonisation of statistical concepts also applies at an international level. The application of the international standards is, first of all, a way to ensure that the statistics remain independent of the policy users. Secondly, application of the international standards allows for meaningful comparisons and aggregation. Given that cross-country comparability of official statistics is key to their usefulness and credibility, all countries across the globe should want to implement worldwide standards in their statistics.

Take, for example, balance of payments statistics. Countries will only be able to achieve a common analysis of their bilateral economic and financial relationships if their mutual external statistics mirror each other. A recent study by the ECB comparing the mirror data for direct investment between the euro area, the UK, the US and Japan shows that, in all cases, sizeable asymmetries in these data still exist. Eliminating these asymmetries requires not only an adherence to international standards, but also good worldwide cooperation between the statisticians involved and probably an exchange of micro-data for statistical purposes.

Finally, perhaps the most important lesson of all, the independence of statistical institutes is key to the quality and integrity of the underlying statistics. Recent incidents involving government finance statistics have demonstrated this very clearly. The compilation and reporting of statistics must not be vulnerable to political and electoral cycles. Countries should consider the quality and integrity of their statistics as a priority matter, to ensure that a proper system of checks and balances is in place when compiling these statistics, and should apply minimum standards, reinforcing the independence, integrity and accountability of national statistical institutes.

Despite the significant achievements and the good quality of euro area statistics in general, further improvements and enhancements are planned. Ongoing economic transformation has to be accommodated in a forward-looking manner and statistical gaps identified by users inside and outside the ECB have to be filled in as far as possible. Given the long lead times which characterise statistical projects, the Directorate General Statistics of the ECB has established medium-term priorities in this field. Important items on this agenda are: a full system of euro area quarterly accounts for each institutional sector[1], more comprehensive statistics for the monitoring and analysis of financial

---

1   The financial and non-financial accounts would cover the following sectors in principle: households (including non-profit institutions serving households), non-financial corporations, financial corporations, government and the rest of the world.

stability, the further development of external statistics, promoting the compilation of Principal European Economic Indicators, including the application of the first-for-Europe principle, and an increasing focus on the various quality dimensions of European statistics. Let me elaborate a bit more on the first two items. Progress in these areas is expected to have a major influence on policy analysis.

The work currently undertaken by the ECB and Eurostat on quarterly euro area accounts aims at a fully integrated system of sectoral financial and non-financial accounts. Having such a system in place may lead over time to major progress in both the structural analysis of the euro area and the assessment of the current economic situation. Fully integrated sectoral accounts provide the ideal framework for analysing the structure of the economy and its changes over time as well as the propagation of shocks through the system. This helps to gain further insights into the monetary policy transmission mechanism and the relative importance of the various transmission channels. At the same time, monitoring a wide range of key indicators in a single macroeconomic accounting framework provides a coherent picture of the current economic situation. This is particularly important in the context of the ECB's monetary policy strategy, which takes into account a broad range of indicators.

Integrated financial and non-financial sector accounts provide a framework for analysing the link between the financial and the real economy – an issue notoriously difficult to analyse on the basis of the currently available analytical framework. An integrated system of quarterly sector accounts would also provide a powerful information basis for forecasting, allowing what is nearly impossible today, namely the integration of monetary and financial variables in macro-econometric models. Of course, many of these uses will only be possible once an integrated system of sectoral accounts has been available for quite a number of years and with an appropriate timeliness. But being forward-looking and developing visions is of great importance in the field of statistics.

Another highly relevant area of statistical work for central bankers concerns statistics and indicators for financial stability analysis. In the aftermath of the Asian crises, which brought to the fore the importance of financial stability analysis, the related conceptual framework was strengthened and progress in understanding the genesis and propagation of financial instability was made.

Central banks have an interest in financial stability issues particularly, but not exclusively, because financial stability supports sustainable price stability in the medium and long run. This implies that financial stability indicators – whether in the form of key balance sheet ratios for monetary financial institutions or leverage indices for non-financial corporations – may acquire an important status in the data set on which the central bank bases its assessment of the risks to price stability over extended horizons. The forward-looking nature of the ECB's monetary policy strategy allows an extension of the policy-relevant horizon sufficiently into the future to factor in the likely effects of financial imbalances that may be forming. At the same time, obtaining a comprehensive and timely statistical view of the financial system helps to identify the sources of such risks.

This is the rationale for central banks' keen interest in financial stability analysis. But financial stability analysis is complex and, hence, information-intensive. Data are needed not only on the financial situation of banks, but also on that of other financial corporations, such as insurance corporations. Moreover, the financial position of non-financial corporations and households has to be carefully assessed. Finally, not only financial markets but also other asset markets, such as real estate markets, have to be monitored closely.

Currently, financial stability issues in the euro area are analysed on the basis of existing data collected for monetary policy or supervisory purposes. Evidently, the coverage and definitions of data collected for monetary policy purposes do not always fulfil the needs of financial stability analysis. In addition, the data from supervisory sources are not harmonised across countries.

The development of harmonised bank profitability, asset quality and capital adequacy data is a big challenge for a multinational economy such as the euro area. The same applies to the much needed enhancement and harmonisation of information on insurance corporations and on the financial situation of firms and households. Moreover, this work should exploit synergies with the initiatives of other international organisations, in particular the work of the IMF on financial soundness indicators.

The need for a comprehensive analytical framework

Statistics as well as additional information such as synthetic indicators, model forecasts and anecdotal evidence provide economic analysts with the raw material to derive a consistent and timely judgment about the true prevailing economic circumstances and the position of the economy in its business cycle. At the same time, just as a good meal not only requires high-quality ingredients but also an excellent cook and recipe, high-quality monetary policy analysis also requires excellent staff and an appropriate analytical framework. The importance of the latter can hardly be overstated. While central bankers around the world are "data fiends" in their heroic attempts to minimise errors of inference and to make robust decisions amidst uncertainty about the true structure of the economy, the availability of a vast wealth of raw data from diverse sources may mean that policy-makers become constantly bombarded by conflicting signals. Amidst such a flood of information, policy runs the risk of losing its bearings and of over-reacting to the latest indicator.

It is against this background that the ECB decided to adopt an analytical framework within which all possible sources of information – statistical as well as judgemental – can be brought together in a coherent fashion while at the same time allowing for alternative and diverse models and perspectives of the workings of the economy. In our view, this framework enables a wealth of information to be "digested" routinely without compromising the ultimate objective: to maintain a clear sense of direction.

In order to give a structure to the diverse sources of information, a structure that is consistent with our view of the monetary policy transmission mechanism, we have organised our analytical framework into "two pillars". These consist of two complementary perspectives on the determination of price developments.

One perspective, which we refer to as the "economic analysis", is grounded on the belief that price developments over the short to medium term are largely influenced by the interplay of supply and demand in the goods, services and factor markets.

As a means of cross-checking, we have equipped ourselves with another perspective, which we refer to as the "monetary analysis" and that is grounded on the belief that medium to long-run price developments can be attributed to the growth rate of the stock of money.

Each of these "pillars" is, in turn, characterised by a rich and comprehensive analysis of a large amount of data. For example, within the "economic analysis" we monitor the developments in prices and unit costs, overall output, aggregate demand and its components, government finance accounts, capital and labour market conditions, exchange rates, financial markets, balance sheets of households and firms, etc. The ECB's "economic analysis" has been significantly extended and enriched over time. This is largely thanks to the progress made in the production of euro area general economic and financial statistics and in the analytical processing of such information. As mentioned above, the inaugural publication of integrated financial and non-financial quarterly accounts for the euro area, hopefully in 2006, will be another milestone.

The ECB and the national central banks use a variety of models for macroeconomic analysis and forecasting. The macroeconomic projections by Eurosystem staff constitute an important input into the monetary policy decisions, because they are a way of organising a large amount of information and they help to create a consistent picture of possible future developments. However, the economic projections cannot encompass or even reflect all the complexities, conditioning factors, nuances and the multi-dimensional nature of a comprehensive assessment of the risks to price stability on which monetary policy decisions need to be based. While the information synthesised from various indicators serves as an important input into the decision-making process, the Governing Council of the ECB does not take decisions only on the basis of projections. The Governing Council's "judgement" must eventually come into play in order to assess the likelihood of the alternative scenarios suggested by the economic analysis. This is particularly important when it is quite unclear how a certain situation will evolve, as is the case sometimes with sharp movements in asset prices.

Related to this, attempts to base monetary policy decisions solely on inflation forecasts would involve significant limitations. Notably, they would entail an inefficient use of information, since every forecast, or any composite index of indicators, is based on one possible scenario and one combination of assumptions. In the end, monetary policy requires judgement on the part of the policy-maker to assess not only the plausibility of all possible scenarios, but also the nature of the shocks and the best policy reaction in order to deal with this uncertain environment. Just focusing on one or a few forecast figures would make it difficult for policy-makers to transmit the complexity of monetary policy deliberations to the public in a precise and transparent manner.

Over a medium to long-term horizon, inflation forecasts based on statistical analysis become very inaccurate. Yet, medium to long-run inflation expectations are crucial in guiding the consumption and investment decisions of private agents. In order not to lose sight of the low frequency developments that may influence inflation over longer horizons than are used in the forecasts, the ECB has reinforced its analytical framework with a monetary perspective. This "pillar" looks at price formation from a medium to long-term standpoint and is intended to purge monetary policy from the risk of becoming unduly short-sighted and overreacting to the latest economic news. By constantly reminding the central bank that in the long run prices and money stock increases are correlated, the monetary pillar is a standing support to the ECB's commitment to price stability at all horizons that are relevant for economic decisions.

Taking decisions and evaluating their consequences on the basis not only of the shorter-term indications from the analysis of economic and financial conditions, but also of money and liquidity considerations, allows a central bank to see beyond the transient impact of the various shocks and to maintain a more steady policy course. Looking back over our first six years of operations, monetary analysis has helped to underpin the medium-term orientation of our monetary policy conduct.

Allow me also to stress that the analysis of monetary indicators at the ESCB consists of an articulated process, whereby a detailed study of all the components and counterparts of M3 provides a detailed picture of the latest monetary developments, alongside the broad picture of the underlying trends.

As I said, a world in which policy is conducted in a "data-rich environment" – to quote an article by Ben Bernanke[2] – can be one in which both central bankers and other economic agents become captive to the latest macroeconomic indicator and may lose direction. In such a world, a central bank will only be successful in delivering price stability if it provides an anchor for the inflation expectations of the public and if it is as transparent as possible about its ultimate policy objective.

For this reason, the ECB decided to be fully transparent about the numerical definition of its goal, price stability, that the Treaty on European Union assigned to it. As you know, in 1998, when taking up its monetary policy tasks, the Governing Council of the ECB defined price stability as a year-on-year increase in the euro area Harmonised Index of Consumer Prices of below 2% and close to 2%.

The definition of price stability not only has the advantage of helping to anchor inflation expectations and to enhance the transparency and accountability of the European Central Bank. It has also been very instrumental in preserving continuity during the transition from the national currencies to the euro. The euro was given the same definition of price stability as the one attributed to the most credible national currencies, which benefited from the lowest market interest rates at the time. As a consequence, from day one onwards, the euro was given the best yield curve available in the economies of the euro area.

The European Central Bank has played a leading role in the general trend towards greater transparency and openness. It has in fact set standards of transparency in the practice of monetary policy. The ECB was the first major central bank to display its diagnosis immediately after its decisions and to hold regular press conferences after each of its monetary policy meetings. It is still the only one that does so. In those press conferences, we give a full and detailed explanation of our analysis and of the reasons underlying our policy decisions. In addition, the ECB's Monthly Bulletin gives the public the full set of detailed assessments and data underlying our policy decisions only a few days after they are taken.

To sum up, I trust that the success of the ECB and of the Eurosystem in firmly anchoring medium and long term inflation expectations at a level below 2% and close to 2% from day one of the existence of the euro is due to the careful gathering of all necessary conditions for such a prowess.

I see at least six such necessary conditions: the **institutional independence** of the ECB; the clarity of its Treaty mandate – **price stability** -; **the accountability** vis à vis public opinion, including through the hearings before the European Parliament; **the comprehensive nature of its monetary policy concept**, with an economic and a monetary pillar; **its medium term perspective** and, last but not least, its **transparency.**

---

2   B. Bernanke and J. Boivin: "Monetary policy in a data-rich environment," Journal of Monetary Economics, Volume 50, Issue 3 (2003).

We are displaying publicly our monetary policy concept. Not all central Banks do that. We are displaying our definition of price stability. Not all central Banks do that. We were the first important central Bank, in January 1999, to publish in quasi real time after our decisions our diagnosis and the reasons for our action and to hold a press conference. Not all central banks do that, even today. We are making public the quarterly projections of the staffs of the ECB and of the Eurosystem. And I profoundly trust that it is this substantial level of transparency which has also contributed to make the ECB's policy decisions highly predictable for the market as academic research has documented.

A last remark. As already mentioned, all what I have said presupposes that data are reliable and credible. It is absolutely imperative that figures are not influenced by political interference and by electoral cycles. The ECB's Governing Council strongly encourages countries to tirelessly improve the professionalism and independence of the relevant institutions. It would also strongly support the European framework to be further enhanced with full capacity to check without restrictions facts and figures including through missions on the spot.

Key National Indicator Systems: An Opportunity to Maximize National Progress and Strengthen Accountability

David M. Walker

Comptroller General of the United States

The aim of this conference is, in many ways, unprecedented. A worldwide community of leaders from government, private industry, and academia has taken time out from their busy schedules to assemble here with a single purpose. That purpose is to share knowledge on how to develop independent, fact-based, balanced, reliable and transparent systems of key national indicators that span several domains, including economic, social, environmental, and security. Such indicators would have several potential benefits, including helping policymakers and the public better assess, both on absolute and relative bases, the position and progress of nations on issues ranging from the economy to the environment. Although we represent diverse, and sometimes even conflicting points of view, our success here in Palermo depends on our willingness to work together to address common challenges and achieve a common goal.

I'd like to focus on a central theme that links every topic being discussed at this conference. On its surface, this theme appears straightforward, even simple, but its many complexities should not be underestimated. The theme I'm talking about is how best to improve national progress and strengthen accountability in the 21st century.

Maximizing national progress and strengthening accountability in the 21st century will require both reflection and action. To begin and sustain this process, we'll need to answer and continually improve our answers to several basic questions.

First, and at the most basic level, are we as individuals, and for many of us as public servants, doing what we can to maximize our contributions to society? Would our consciences be clear tonight if we knew we were going to be held to account for our contributions tomorrow?

Second, are our public institutions, including government, guiding progress in a responsible way? Are they getting real results with the resources and authorities they have been given and can they prove the progress they claim?

Third, are our nations doing everything they can to fight corruption and make the best possible use of taxpayer dollars? Are policymakers pursuing worthwhile public policy goals in a way that avoids shifting an unfair burden of debt or other adverse consequences onto our children and grandchildren?

Finally and more broadly, how can the many societies, races, and religions that share this planet work together to pursue a greater good that benefits all mankind? In a world that grows smaller every day, it seems to me that every human being – whether it's a factory worker in China, a banker in Brazil, a farmer in France, or an auditor in America – is increasingly linked by issues of mutual concern.

As Comptroller General of the United States, I head the U.S. Government Accountability Office, more commonly known as "GAO." GAO is an independent agency in the legislative branch of our federal government. Among other things, we're the supreme audit institution (SAI) in the United States.

GAO is sometimes called the "investigative arm of Congress" or the "congressional watchdog" because GAO helps Congress oversee the rest of the U.S. federal government. For more than 80 years, GAO has worked to fight corruption, speak truth to power, improve performance, promote transparency, and assure accountability in how government does business. Simply stated, we try to make government work better for all Americans. To this end, GAO provides the U.S. Congress with oversight of agency operations, insight into ways to improve government services, and foresight about future and emerging challenges facing our nation and its citizens.

GAO is in the knowledge and information business, so we are very familiar with the subject of national indicators. In fact, GAO's approach to conducting its work may be instructive for developing and promulgating a portfolio of key national indicators. For example, GAO reports have credibility because the information they contain is professional, objective, fact based, nonpartisan, non-ideological, fair, and balanced. GAO reports have impact because policymakers in Washington know they can count on the facts and analyses presented in our work. Our agency operates under strict professional standards, including independence criteria. From cover to cover, every GAO report is thoroughly checked for accuracy before it's issued. GAO also has a set of core values that form the foundation for what we do and how we do it. These core values — accountability, integrity, and reliability — supplement the professional standards we follow and represent a higher calling for our institution and all the individuals who compose it. In my view, these core values are also relevant to any key national indicator initiative.

Although every nation has its own approach to ensuring accountability at various levels, including government, I think each of us here tonight would agree that a set of meaningful and reliable key national indicators can be indispensable to that effort.

After all, timely, useful, reliable and transparent information is the single most important and powerful tool we have to facilitate strategic planning, assess progress, inform decision-making and strengthen accountability. Supreme audit institutions have a special role to play in developing this information.

As independent professional services organisations with extensive expertise in statistics, many SAIs are well positioned to encourage the development of such systems and suggest ways to ensure the reasonableness and reliability of the related processes and resulting information. While SAIs are well positioned to help in connection with key national indicators, why should they or anyone else care? Frankly, how a nation keeps score, counts. Keeping score is the only way to maximize performance and ensure accountability. Facing facts is essential. If a nation doesn't keep score, how will it know what it's trying to achieve? If a nation doesn't keep score, how will it know how it's doing? If a nation doesn't keep score, how can it find the best solutions and get the best results with limited resources? After all, while our dreams may be unlimited, our resources are not.

From a broader perspective, keeping a nation informed is essential to any culture that values accountability and progress. Honest and transparent reporting also helps to build public trust and confidence both in government and all sectors of society.

This bedrock principle of informing a nation and its citizens is nothing new. It's a matter of common sense that's been around for centuries. But as we enter a period of new national and global challenges, the need for an informed citizenry has acquired a renewed importance and meaning.

Today, information is collected and shared at the speed of light. Through the Internet, massive amounts of data are now available to anyone, anywhere, anytime. But this information is often fragmented, provided by multiple sources with wide variations in quality, scalability, and comparability. Each of our key national indicator efforts must recognize this reality.

Key national indicators can help us to better understand which programs, policies, functions, and activities are working and which are not. When seen in the aggregate and as part of a broader portfolio, key national indicators can provide a fuller and fairer view of how well a nation is doing as well as whether and, if so, how its political leaders are planning for the future. Such information can educate policymakers and the public about the appropriateness, affordability, and sustainability of a nation's current path. Key national indicators can also help elected officials make tough but necessary policy choices including facilitating better targeting of government actions while ensuring long-term fiscal, social and environmental sustainability as well as the intergenerational equity of existing and proposed government policies and programs.

There's simply no substitute for understanding the big picture — that is, the position and progress of a nation as a whole. The challenge and the opportunity before us is to build sophisticated information resources and key indicator systems that yield vital insights that transcend specific economic sectors, public and private institutions, and national borders.

There are many areas in which the stakes are high and better knowledge is needed. In the case of the United States, these areas include ensuring fiscal sustainability, enhancing homeland security, stimulating economic growth, creating productive and fulfilling jobs, improving education and innovation, delivering quality and affordable health care, strengthening competitiveness, protecting the environment, and promoting quality of life.

With access to solid facts and results-based information, we increase our chances of developing well-framed questions, conducting appropriate analyses, making good decisions, arriving at effective solutions, and creating accountability for results. In my view, statisticians, SAI's, political leaders, the press, and the public throughout the world have a vital interest in seeing that key indicator systems are developed, promoted and used.

Key indicator systems are already in place in several sectors in the United States and in other countries. During the conference, we'll be hearing more about these systems. Despite this progress, I'm sorry to say that the United States still lacks a key indicator system at the national level. As a result, in some areas U.S. policymakers are flying blind, like an airplane pilot at night and without an instrument panel. This must change if we expect to maximize government's performance and ensure its accountability. Stated differently, the U.S. leads in many things but not in all things. The U.S. is lagging behind other Nations in connection with key national indicators. As a result, we need and want your help!

But change does seem to be on the way in the U.S. As you heard this morning from Katherine Wallman and Kenneth Prewitt, the U.S. key national indicators initiative is moving ahead. Also, during the past two years, GAO has been working with the U.S. Congress; executive branch agencies; and prominent professional groups, such as our National Academies, to study the key national indicator systems of selected cities, regions, states, nations, and supranational institutions.

During this effort, our GAO team learned from many of you in this room. Tonight, we'd like to return the favor by sharing with you the results of our first wide-ranging study of key indicator systems in the United States and around the world. The report is called "Informing Our Nation: Improving How to Understand and Assess the USA's Position and Progress." Yesterday, we issued this report to the U.S. Congress and posted it publicly on the Internet. My staff brought a limited number of printed copies and compact discs to this conference, but you can also download the report from GAO's website at www.gao.gov. If you don't have time to read the entire report, there's a one-page summary that highlights the key findings and conclusions at the front of the report.

This report answers three main questions. First, what is the state of the practice in key indicator systems? Second, what are the implications for the United States? And third, what options are available to the United States to implement such a system? My hope is that the answers to these questions will contribute to the discussion here in Palermo and will help to spur international action on key indicator systems once the conference is over.

By adopting key national indicator systems, we'll be able to generate quality information that can help individuals, institutions, and nations accelerate progress and make better choices when it comes to their futures. We'll also create knowledge that both informs and constrains the exercise of power and ensures that no one is above the law and everyone is accountable for results.

In summary, key national indicators systems can serve to inform strategic planning, enhance performance and accountability reporting, and facilitate effective policy analysis and program evaluation in ways that can benefit many countries and generations. They can also help to inform the public, stimulate public debate and help to assure that nations have an informed electorate.

Achieving success in developing key national indicator systems that are reasonably comprehensive, relevant, reliable, recognized, credible, comparable, transparent, accessible, useful and used will require the combined efforts of many parties over an extended period of time. Let us start here in Palermo! By doing so, we can help to maximize both national and global progress while strengthening accountability around the globe. I, along with my other GAO colleagues, look forward to working together with each of you and others to partner for progress in this and other important areas of mutual interest and concern.

Thank you for your time and attention as we say in America, let's do it!

Building Knowledge

Donald J. Johnston

Secretary-General, Organisation for Economic Co-operation and Development

I wish to address the general theme of this conference: statistics, knowledge and the measurement issues associated with social and economic progress.

Statistics - Quality

Now, statistics is information. But information is not knowledge as Einstein famously observed not so many years ago. Ideally, statistics should be unassailable facts upon which knowledge is based.

If I may use an analogy, statistics represent the raw material for the creation of knowledge, just as steel represents the raw material for the manufacture of automobiles. But it is knowledge that takes steel and turns it into an automobile, and it is knowledge which takes the raw material of statistics and turns it into knowledge, and in a further stage into policy.

Let me offer a specific example which will serve as a reference point for that conclusion.

You are no doubt familiar with the concept of NAIRU, that is, the non-accelerating inflation rate of unemployment. The theoretical underpinning of this formulation is that when unemployment declines to a certain level, the pool of available labour shrinks and workers have more leverage to obtain wage increases, with the result of upward pressure on inflation. This formulation is not universally endorsed it well illustrates the paradigm we are discussing here, namely, statistics or information, contributing to knowledge and in turn to policy. One begins with data on inflation and the level of unemployment. This is the raw material for developing knowledge about the relationship between them: the NAIRU. As unemployment falls, central bankers will provide a policy response when they believe the NAIRU is being reached. Normally this will mean a tightening of monetary policy to control anticipated inflation.

The reality is that policy responses will vary from country to country. But at the outset it is essential to ensure the quality of the raw material, namely the statistics from which knowledge is derived. If the unemployment or inflation numbers are wrong, the knowledge will be flawed and the policy response inappropriate.

To quote from Joel Best's book "Damned lies and Statistics": "While some social problems statistics are deliberate deceptions, many -- probably the great majority -- of bad statistics are the result of confusion, incompetence, innumeracy, or selective self righteous efforts to produce numbers that reaffirm principles and interests that their advocates consider just and right".

I imagine that this sophisticated group of experts would look at many statistics, especially social statistics with a critical eye to assess their source, quality and purpose. But this is not true of the general public and perhaps not of the media. Published statistics seem to acquire a life of their own even if their source is close to a guesstimate. And we face the problem as well of what Best describes as mutant statistics, namely statistics which in the course of repetition mutate. In this context Best cites an amusing example to illustrate the point.

Serving on a student's dissertation committee he read the following in the student's prospectus.

"Every year since 1950, the number of American children gunned down has doubled."

He checked the Journal from which the statistic was taken and indeed the same sentence appeared. The compounding element of doubling every year brought the number of children gunned down in 1995 to 35 trillion!

The Author of this remarkable statement claimed to have obtained it from the Children's Defence Fund yearbook of 1994 where the following was said:

"The number of children killed each year by guns has doubled since 1950".

Since the population had increased by 73% over the same period, the number was not a stunning surprise. But that subtle change of wording was probably accepted by many without question.

This digression is simply to underscore the importance of objective critical assessment of statistics which risk the propagation of false knowledge.

Indeed, if it is not done now, I believe education systems should teach our youth to carefully assess the validity of such data because they will encounter masses of it in today's world of statistical wars and much of it will influence their behaviour and even their careers.

That is why the quality of statistics is so critical where public policy could take a wrong turn through bad information and hence flawed knowledge.

And, in the globalizing world of today, it is critical that we reach broad consensus on the methodology underlying many statistics with global implications, beginning with macro economic data of major economies which impact on exchange rates, trade and investment flows.

And, in this 21st century, I see two areas where data will be essential to international planning and cooperation, namely climate change and demography. We must work from the same data and that data must be accurate.

Statistics - Quantity

One of the priorities of today's global society is gathering and disseminating information. Some still believe that with more information we are better prepared to confront the challenges of the 21st Century. In 2004, the US Federal Government alone spent 4.7 billion dollars for financing statistical programmes. Is the volume of information with which we are all inundated improving decision-making, governance, business strategies, and standards of living?

Many of us feel overwhelmed by the volume of statistics inundating us via television, print or the Internet. And we are producing more statistical information than ever before. Politicians strive to insert figures in every speech. Businesses use micro and macro data to make their decisions about investments and future production. NGOs and special interest groups parade statistics in front of the public every day in support of their cause of choice. How reliable are these statistics which so many marshal in support of their arguments?

Just as important, how can we know what information we should pay attention to? This conference has brought together people who are trying to help our societies answer that question – by devising agreed frameworks of information and common, shared knowledge that will help them assess progress.

Building Knowledge

Albert Einstein had it right when he said *"Information is not knowledge"*.

Information is structured and formatted data, whereas knowledge empowers its possessors with the capacity for intellectual and physical action. I believe our thinking has evolved in the right direction over the past 20 odd years because, when I was Minister responsible for Science and Technology in Canada, we spoke of the "Information Society". You remember that. Now we speak of "Knowledge-based Societies". We have learned that increasing information alone does not ensure any improvement in decision-making or in policy development. The knowledge economy is a system where knowledge has become the most important factor of production and the most important type of capital.

The OECD is a knowledge building organisation. Our 150 committees and working groups, composed essentially of officials from all the member countries, develop new statistics and also collect and disseminate these basic raw materials of knowledge. The committees, often in consultation with other stakeholders such as business, labour, parliamentarians or public interest groups, also investigate policy challenges that face governments across the full range of economic and social policy. They analyse and compare experiences in order to build knowledge about the policies that work and the ones that don't work. This knowledge is often codified in OECD recommendations or guidelines. And the OECD is sharing knowledge and experience with a growing universe of non-member countries so that our partnership is indeed becoming more global.

The OECD does not have any regulatory power, nor the legal authority to impose concrete implementation of its recommendations and policy advice. Nevertheless, the OECD is widely recognized as one of the most influential international bodies in arming policy makers and public opinion with the information and guidance needed to face current and future challenges. What makes the OECD capable of advising the international community on such a wide range of issues? In short, I would answer: reliable statistics, strong analytical skills, good networking, serious international benchmarking, open minded policy dialogue and transparency. All of these elements are equally necessary and they can only be maintained over time thanks to the professionalism of staff working in the OECD Secretariat and the co-operation of experts from member countries.

As an illustration, I would cite one of the OECD's most successful and well known initiatives - the PISA programme - aimed to measure the performance of students and of school systems. A first round of results covering 43 countries and focussing on reading literacy was published in 2000; a second round covering 41 countries and emphasising mathematics will be published in few weeks time. Statistical results have been used both by the OECD and by other national and international users to develop analytical studies. In several countries in-depth reviews of the strengths and weaknesses of national education systems have been conducted after the publication of PISA results. Concrete initiatives have been undertaken to address the most serious problems, looking to those countries with the most positive results as examples. The PISA results generated an incredible amount of media coverage and stimulated public awareness about the quality of their students and school systems, also fostering the development and the use of statistical indicators to assess the performances of individual education institutes.

This example demonstrates how a serious research programme, well sustained by relevant and reliable statistical information, can mobilize an incredible amount of resources, increase the quality of policy debate, help individual countries develop their own strategies to address key challenges, improve the public's understanding of real problems, and, in short, to facilitate the chain "Statistics, knowledge and policy".

This successful story, which, of course, is not unique, also demonstrates the importance of partnerships and networking amongst different parties, both at international and national levels. As far as national networks are concerned, the key players are: the civil society, the business community, policymakers, the academic community and the media.

Measurement of Economic and Social Progress

The example of the PISA project also illustrates a well know statement of Niels Bohr that *"Nothing exists until it is measured"*.

I wish to come back to the measurement question, but this time in terms of <u>what</u> nations, the OECD or the international community at large should measure.

Many still harbour simplistic views of economic and social progress focusing on GDP. But what does GDP really tell us about economic and social progress? Not much.

Some years ago, I attended a conference of Women Leaders from all over the globe. I well remember the plea of a young woman from a developing country who said: *"We are told that our country is developing at a remarkable rate, with GDP growth of 8%, but is this progress when we cannot drink the water, we breathe polluted air, raw sewage in the gutters and our streets are not safe?"*

Clearly, GDP is a useful yardstick for some purposes. But today, our societies expect a more comprehensive understanding and measurement of progress. We need to refine our indicators to express what is important to people and what makes up their quality of life.

The late Robert Kennedy, in referring to the impressive GNP of the United States in the 1960s pointed out that *"it counts air pollution and cigarette advertising and ambulances to clear our highways of carnage. It counts special locks for our doors and the jails for those who break them. It counts the destruction of our redwoods and the loss of natural wonder in chaotic sprawl. It counts napalm and the cost of nuclear warheads, armoured cars for police who fight riots in our streets, and so on. An indicator like GNP does not capture the health of our children, the quality of their education, or the joy of their play -- it measures everything, in short, except that which makes life worthwhile."*

We must extend the concept of growth to that of progress of our society as a whole. The great OECD family of partnership has over many decades, promoted the sharing of knowledge in order to increase not only the per capita incomes of member countries, but also the growth of healthy societies. I like to describe progress in terms of a triangle paradigm: anchored at one side by economic growth and on the other by social stability or social cohesion, with good governance ensuring the transfer of the benefits of growth to society as a whole. The synergies in this triangular paradigm are self-evident: it is clear that economic growth is not sustainable unless it is accompanied by sustainable social development, and the latter is not sustainable without economic growth. In brief, every economic policy must have a social objective. The paradigm itself must rest on a foundation of a sustainable physical environment – the biosphere.

This places an important responsibility on governments which must design and adapt policies to enable sustainable progress on all fronts. To build economic growth, governments must ensure the right environment for entrepreneurial activities, regulations supporting healthy financial sectors, fair taxation, competition policy, and so on. But in our knowledge-based economies, the most important capital, as I mentioned a few minutes ago, is human capital. The social cohesion side of the triangle must ensure education of the young and continuing, life-long learning for the no longer young. It must also provide an effective and efficient health system, pensions, flexible labour markets, and so on. And the natural capital of a healthy environment must not be depleted and where it has been, it must be restored.

However, all of this begs the question: how are we to measure progress on economic, social and environmental fronts? Some might recast this by saying, how do we measure the sustainable development of all these areas? It most assuredly cannot be done by GDP growth which would be akin to measuring the water in a deep well with a one meter rod.

Once we are able to agree on a common knowledge base in each area derived from reliable statistics, then we can move on to the substantive issue: what do we mean by progress, the quantity we intend to measure?

While there is much truth in that, and undoubtedly in physics, progress is a concept which varies according to the approach used to measure it. Nevertheless, progress on sustainable development encompasses, at least, three broad domains: the economy, the environment and society.

Even if there are disagreements on a definition of progress, there is broad consensus that GNP is not an acceptable measurement of it (although it remains the ready reference for economic success in the minds of many).

In the Measuring Australia's Progress (MAP) initiative, for example, progress is "not only improvement in the material standards of living, or other changes in the economic aspects of life, but also changes in social and environmental areas. Progress encompasses the major direct influences on the changing well-being of the Australian population, the structure and growth of the Australian economy and the environment – important both as a direct influence on the well-being of Australians and their economy, and because people value it in its own right."

Several countries have started measuring progress towards sustainable development using indicators systems which seem quite similar to those developed within "key indicators" initiatives.

Taking into account the literature developed over the last few years, I could continue for hours to discuss what "progress", "development", "well-being", and "happiness" mean. But this would not be very useful. What I learned from the documents prepared for this Forum is that these initiatives do not try to provide an "official" definition of progress valid for all and over all time, which is something that by nature cannot be assessed through figures and charts. What they attempt to do is develop a "coherent framework" covering various domains to allow for evaluation that is always driven by the "values" of that particular society at that particular point of time. The decision about the choice of indicators must be made by individual communities.

This brings me to discuss the role that different sectors of the society should to play in developing a common knowledge base derived from reliable statistics which are developed from agreed upon methodology.

The Role of Different Stakeholders

It would be too simple to say that all sectors of society must be involved in the development of key indicators systems or in any other initiative aimed to identify fact-based agreed upon common knowledge. But if knowledge is to be used, it must be "common knowledge" or knowledge that society will recognise as addressing its concerns. Ultimately society must choose what to include as measures of progress.

As far as national networks are concerned, the key players are: the civil society, the business community, policymakers, the academic community and the media. The specific role and contribution of each group varies remarkably across projects, but strong partnerships are imperative in developing "key indicators" initiatives. This is crucial because if the initiative is not perceived as well- balanced in terms of goals, participation of various institutions, willingness to accept different points of view, scientific seriousness, and transparency vis-à-vis the outside world, the risk of failure becomes very high.

These recommendations do not apply only to national communities. As a result of globalisation international and supranational organisations must also contribute to this effort. International organisations, like the OECD, have to create global networks to allow local communities to discuss, share knowledge and identify best practices. They also have to promote the co-operation between countries in order to facilitate international benchmarking and comparisons. A major undertaking to define international progress, in which the OECD participated with the United Nations, the World Bank and the IMF, are the Millennium Development Goals. The OECD continues to work with these organisations to measure progress defined in these terms as well as to apply its shared knowledge to making progress on the goals.

Let me conclude with a quote from Benjamin Franklin, who said *"An investment in knowledge pays the best interest"*. The OECD is committed to contribute to such investment, and this Forum is a wonderful example of what is meant by investment in knowledge. It is now up to all of us to maximise the short and long term revenues from such investment.

National Case Studies

Developing Key National Indicators for the United States

Katherine Wallman, Chief Statistician, U.S. Office of Management and Budget, Executive Office of the President

Kenneth Prewitt, Carnegie Professor of Public Affairs, Columbia University, United States

Susan Schechter, U.S. Office of Management and Budget, Executive Office of the President[1]

Introduction

In large, diverse societies like the United States, public life revolves around making individual and collective choices. These choices generally are made in the context of either implicit or explicit aspirations. For example, few citizens, business or community leaders, or government officials would disagree that decent wages, safe schools, and clean air are worthy goals. However, finite time and resources necessarily require that individuals, communities, and the nation as a whole choose among competing needs, making difficult decisions regarding which of the many problems to attend to, how best to address them, and what portion of limited resources to devote to them. While hard choices are a fact of private and public life, the ways these choices are made can vary. In democracies such as ours, the presumption is that priorities are set by citizens, both directly through their civic and political participation and indirectly through their market choices and selection of elected representatives. In turn, the policies set by the institutions of commerce, government, and the nonprofit sector are both responsive to and guide the main engines for implementing the public will.

Many factors complicate this process, including competing interests and values that lead well-intentioned people to reach different conclusions about which issues are most important and which solutions are most likely to produce results. Such tensions are not only a fact of life, but also a strength of a diverse nation, ideally producing enhanced problem solving, clearer accountability, and, ultimately, choices and results that best represent the collective interests of the public through the open exchange of ideas.

Crucial to ensuring that this decision-making process--whether by citizens or by economic, civic, and political leaders--is simultaneously responsive and responsible is the availability of comprehensive, high quality, shared, accessible information about how the nation or a smaller community or population group is doing on a variety of dimensions. Such information is key for policy making in government, investment and product decisions in business, citizen involvement in electoral politics, charting directions in the

---

1   The views expressed in this paper are those of the authors and do not represent the views of the U.S. Office of Management and Budget or Columbia University. This presentation draws from materials of the KNII Steering Committee, and attempts to reflect the views of the Committee. However, the authors are solely responsible for the formulation of those views in this paper.

nonprofit sector, and even the life decisions of individuals. In and of itself, objective information about such things as unemployment rates, air and water quality, patterns of immigration and assimilation, or trends in public safety or health cannot ensure good decisions or positive results. But information is fundamental to framing and achieving these goals, and thus the health, vibrancy, and effectiveness of the nation's democracy. This is especially true in today's complex national and global environment, which often is characterized by increasing demands and decreasing resources to meet them effectively.

Although different types of information are needed for making effective individual and collective choices, one important category--national indicators--has increasingly been receiving attention. We understand an indicator to be a statistical measure that tracks change over an extended period of time. A snapshot of a social, economic, or environmental condition at a single point in time, however important or useful in its own right, would not qualify as an indicator. Statistical indicators, so understood, systematically extend understanding beyond the realm of personal experience, and in this way are indispensable to democratic governance in large and complicated societies. Indicators offer a numerical foundation to the narrative of progress and improvement we each hope for in our countries.

National indicators themselves are not new in the United States, and we have evidence of their effectiveness in particular areas. For example, the current system of economic indicators (e.g., the gross domestic product, unemployment rates) is well-established and integrated into decision making and public dialogue. At the present time, 38 indicators produced by eight agencies within our Departments of Agriculture, Commerce, Labor and the Treasury, as well as the Federal Reserve Board, are designated as the United States' Principal Economic Indicators. Their scheduled release dates are included in a calendar published prior to the beginning of each year, and data are released by the producing agency according to that calendar. The history of our principal economic indicators extends back at least 70 years. Over that period, new indicators occasionally have been introduced; a quarterly services indicator recently designated to be published beginning in 2005 will be the first addition to our principal economic indicators in almost two decades. Older indicators that have been superseded by more timely information have been removed from the system as appropriate. These United States' principal economic indicators, official statistics that derive from federal government investments, now routinely influence choices ranging from individual careers and institutional hiring to capital investment, microeconomic strategy, and macroeconomic policy.

As successful as these economic indicators have been, however, they are limited in scope and remain open to refinement. Our economy-related measures, by definition, do not describe the numerous noneconomic issues (e.g., safety, health, the environment) that citizens, business leaders, and government officials need to make effective decisions. Moreover, various sources of data for indicators on high profile issues such as unemployment make common understanding a challenge even for sophisticated audiences. And while much of the raw data necessary for creating a more comprehensive set of indicators is available, the data are seldom arranged in ways that facilitate personal and collective decision making. In an age of unprecedented information flows, the common understanding necessary for informed public discourse even with respect to the economy, for which we have a fairly sophisticated indicator system, is inadequate; for other areas of importance, such understanding is even less adequately grounded.

Therefore, a broad consortium of leading institutions in the United States is now planning for a new, more comprehensive national indicator system, under the working title "Key National Indicators Initiative" (KNII).

Need for the KNII

The United States, in its governmental, economic, and scientific activities, strives to base most of its decisions on quantitative data. Corporate leaders await the latest economic indicators with intense anticipation, basing their investment and production decisions on movement in their values. The executive and legislative branches of the federal government use statistics on the health and welfare of the population as the focus of debates on future policy and assume the data are accurate enough to develop sophisticated funding formulas used to allocate resources. The judicial branch uses statistics to guide judgments in a wide variety of arenas (e.g., environmental damage, safety performance of vehicles, and so on). In social science and medical science, quantitative measurements about the society are used to identify phenomena that need more study.

While the society is committed to quantitative decision making, information is too balkanized to make this straight-forward. The country needs a tool that can easily retrieve and combine information in a manner responsive to diverse users' interests, permitting them to probe below the national level. We need a source that essentially provides "one-stop shopping" for high-quality information, selected from the governmental, commercial, and scientific sectors. And, we need a fully democratized and transparent source of information that is easily accessible. This is not to say that this kind of initiative has not been needed in the past. However, a number of factors now make the need for a new initiative more salient and more likely to succeed.

First, the increasing complexity of the policy process, coupled with the growing interconnectedness of local, national, and even international issues and the ever-expanding demands placed on limited resources, require improved decision tools. Second, the unprecedented multiplication of both the range and the sources of available data, often resulting in information overload and difficulties in assessing the quality of information, heightens both the opportunities for creating a comprehensive, reliable database and the urgency for doing so. Third, new information and communication technologies now make it more possible to build such a database in a form that allows maximum flexibility of use and broad accessibility for multiple audiences, as well as to take advantage of huge economies of scale. And fourth, our approach to creating the KNII is designed to ensure maximum public involvement in the process of selecting topic areas and indicators to build legitimacy; trust in the quality of the data used to develop the indicators; credibility in the indicators used to measure conditions and trends; flexibility in who uses the indicators and for what purposes; accessibility of the indicators to a wide range of users; and relevance of the information to actual individual and collective decisions.

Key Features of the KNII

1. Building on Current Practice. At present the United States has a number of robust sector-specific national indicators as well as various city and state-wide indicator programs. The KNII National Coordinating Committee and its Steering Committee have examined many of these indicator systems in order to build on their success and to gain from lessons learned. One of the prototypes that the KNII effort has studied

closely is the Federal Interagency Forum on Child and Family Statistics. In 1997, this Forum was called upon to develop priorities for collecting enhanced data on children and youth, improve the reporting and dissemination of information on the status of children to the policy community and the general public, and produce more complete data on children at the state and local levels. The Forum, which now has participants from 20 federal government agencies as well as partners in private research organisations, fosters coordination, collaboration, and integration of federal efforts to collect and report data on conditions and trends for children and families.

The Forum's primary product is a recurring report entitled *America's Children: Key National Indicators of Well-Being*. The report presents an accessible compendium of 25 indicators on important aspects of children's lives drawn from official federal statistics. These indicators are easy to understand by broad audiences, objectively based on substantial research, balanced so that no single area of children's lives dominates the report, measured regularly so that they can be updated to show trends over time, and representative of large segments of the population rather than one particular group. *America's Children* includes a Population and Family Characteristics section and key indicators in four domains–Economic Security, Health, Behavior and Social Environment, and Education. A Special Feature section provides the opportunity for new data or data on a specific area of interest to be presented.

A similar cross-cutting indicator portrait is provided by *Older Americans: Key Indicators of Well-Being*; the second edition of this report is being released in November 2004. But most social and demographic indicators in the United States have been presented in reports that focus on specific topical areas, such as health, education, and science and engineering. For example, *Healthy People 2010: Understanding and Improving Health* provides a comprehensive set of disease prevention and health promotion objectives for the nation to achieve in the first decade of the 21st century, and presents indicators with which to measure them. Ten leading health indicators highlight major health priorities. The Healthy People initiative represents a participatory process to stimulate broad multi-sector involvement by federal, state, local, and community agencies as well as the private sector.

In another example, *Science and Engineering Indicators*, first released in 1972 and published biennially since, provides a broad-based set of quantitative information about U.S. science, engineering, and technology. Data are grouped under eight topical headings (e.g., Science and Engineering Labor Force, and Industry, Technology and the Global Marketplace) and within those areas, specific indicators reside. Similarly, *The Condition of Education* presents indicators of important developments and trends in American education. The report presents 38 indicators on the status and condition of education and often includes special analyses (such as the 2004 report's analysis of changes in undergraduate student financial aid). The 38 indicators are grouped into six main areas such as enrollment trends, student achievement, and societal support for learning.

Most recently, the United States has endeavored to develop an improved, cross-cutting set of environmental indictors. As a first step, the Environmental Protection Agency (EPA) issued *EPA's Draft Report on the Environment 2003*, designed to describe what the agency knows--and does not know--about the current state of the environment at the national level, and how the environment is changing, as well as to identify measures that can be used to track the status of and trends in the environment and human health, and to define the challenges in improving those measures. The EPA report is organized around five core topics: three describe the current state of air, water, and land, and two present indicators on human health and ecological conditions. Important next steps in this initiative include working with state, tribal, and local governments, non-governmental organisations, and the private sector to develop integrated local, regional, and national environmental indicators. Along with other cross-cutting and topical indicators activities in the United States, EPA's emerging efforts will contribute to the KNII.

2. Framework. The conceptual basis for the KNII is a broad-based comprehensive indicator system that would integrate key topic areas and selected indicators into a single system that aggregates, organizes, and disseminates information products and services. For each topic area and for specific indicators, comparisons could be displayed to show differences and trends by race or ethnicity, age, gender, income, geography, and other variables, whenever possible as suggested by target audiences.

Topic areas covered by the KNII generally are expected to fall into one of three categories – the economy, the people, and the environment. This tripartite framework enjoys two attributes: its simplicity and its wide use by a majority of developed nations, especially in Europe. It also maps well to developing frameworks at the state, local, and national levels in the United States. Furthermore, it takes account of a tremendous body of existing data in the economic arena, a wealth of information on the U.S. population, and emerging work on environmental indicators. Within each of these three areas, more specific topics--each with its own set of indicators--can be considered.

The Economy	The People	The Environment
Employment	Health	Land
Consumption	Shelter	Water
Productivity	Education	Air
Infrastructure	Safety	Ecosystems
Money	Families	
Business	Civic Engagement	
Government	Culture	

In many cases, we expect that indicators on particular topics will be available from ongoing efforts; in other cases, we anticipate that indicators may need to be refined or developed in the coming years.

3. Public Involvement. To populate the KNII indicator framework, the initiative will reach out to target audiences, including the public; local, state, and federal governments; the private sector; non-profit organisations; international organisations; and the media. This outreach is expected to involve roundtable discussions with reporters and editors, public relations and marketing experts, and leaders in the various target audiences. Plans include conducting a series of large focus groups or town hall meetings that will be supplemented by national polling to gather broad public input on the overall concept and key topic areas. Designed from the start with wide and deep involvement from stakeholders--businesses, governments, non-profit organisations, advocacy groups, and citizens--as well as experts in data collection, management, and dissemination, the KNII, when fully realized, will represent an unprecedented private-public collaboration by more than 200 diverse individuals and organisations committed to a single goal: improving the quality of information-based public discourse in the United States and in doing so, strengthening democracy and improving the quality of life.

4. Criteria for Indicator Selection. A critical underpinning for the KNII will be the establishment of strict criteria to guide the inclusion of indicators in the system. Specifically, any indicator included as part of the KNII must have:

- relevance to needs of the users, which prompts initial interest in an indicator;

- credibility, which reflects objectivity and freedom from real or perceived manipulation;

- accuracy appropriate to the phenomenon of key interest to the users, which consists of precision or stability, lack of variation unrelated to real change in the phenomenon, freedom from bias, and absence of consistent overestimation or underestimation;

- completeness, which reflects the degree of match between what the indicator measures and the real phenomenon of interest;

- timeliness for needs of users, which provides the users with information current to their needs;

- transparency, which reveals how the indicator was obtained;

- comparability, which indicates whether, over time, space, populations, or other key variables, the indicator values can be compared;

- understandability, which means the indicator is easily and accurately comprehended by large numbers of people, from citizens to policymakers; and

- accessibility, which reflects the ease of acquiring values of the indicator for the purposes of the user.

In addition to tracking the state of the country as a whole, whenever possible indicators should allow comparisons with other nations, as well as within the country at low levels of geography and across a variety of demographic characteristics.

5. Quality Control. Statistical indicators gain their importance in a sequence of judgments by the users about attributes of the indicators. While indicators may be of interest to some users because of relevance alone, they usually have very limited value if they are not judged desirable on the latter features listed above. However, users vary in the value they place on each of these criteria, or possibly assign value to other attributes or dimensions that could govern indicator selection. Further, some of the dimensions may, in fact, oppose or contradict one another (e.g., timeliness versus completeness). For these reasons, the lasting success of an indicator system depends on wise selection of indicators that meet minimally acceptable quality levels across all dimensions. A quality control process for the KNII is considering a number of questions:

- If an indicator is available only years after the phenomenon was measured, should it be included? What if only limited trend data will be produced?

- Should the portfolio of indicators include subjective measures of attitude and opinion?

- If an indicator series is available only for some parts of the country, should it be included?

- If an indicator undergoes substantive changes (e.g., data collection methods, sponsorship, measurement design), should it be dropped?

- If there is little or no documentation on how the indicator is produced, should it be included?

- If the indicator is prone to instability because of small sample sizes, should it be included?

- If there are two indicators purporting to measure the same phenomenon, should both be included? Related to this, how should different measures (or, differences in measures) of the same phenomenon be reconciled or explained?

6. Data Sources. In the United States, official federal statistics are produced by a highly decentralized national statistical system, comprising more than 70 agencies, or organisational units within agencies, that collect statistical information. While a number of these agencies have statistical work as their principal mission, many more develop statistics in conjunction with responsibilities to provide benefits to individuals or jurisdictions or to regulate an industry or product. (It may be relevant to note that even in countries with a single, centralized statistical office, the collection, analysis and/or dissemination of statistics on health, education, crime, and so forth often take place in the relevant ministries.) A central office in the United States Office of Management and Budget, located within the Executive Office of the President, provides oversight, coordination, and guidance for these statistical activities; identifies priorities for improving federal statistical programs; establishes government-wide statistical policies and standards; and promotes the quality, integrity, and efficiency of federal government statistical programs. Much effort is devoted to improving the relevance, accuracy, timeliness, and availability of federal statistics while protecting the integrity of statistical information products, respecting pledges of confidentiality, and minimizing both reporting burden on the public and the statistical systems' use of federal resources.

   In addition to the federal statistical system, a large number of states (but not all of them) have sophisticated statistical operations, as do some counties and cities. And there is of course a sizeable private data collection industry, including market research and opinion polling. Planners of the KNII recognize the value of statistical information produced outside the federal statistical agencies. While the majority of KNII indicators will be derived from federal data sources, current planning is to also include indicators from other sources. This will be particularly relevant in the flexibility of the KNII system to provide national as well as local area data, and to provide data for specific population groups of interest.

7. Accessibility to Users. The heart of the KNII would be a highly visible, web-based information source providing easily understood, objective indicators. Available 24 hours a day, 7 days a week, the KNII website would provide citizens, journalists, researchers, and business, civic, and political leaders with direct access or links to the highest quality, most well-organized, most up-to-date information on the health of their community, state, region, and nation. The website would allow individuals to tailor and retain customized sets of information they want to follow.

   In addition to overseeing and maintaining the website, the KNII would encourage and facilitate the use of the information available in the system through e-mail alerts, fact sheets and reports, presentations to various private and public groups, and occasional conferences. Complementary products, such as a periodic publication featuring high level indicators across domains, might be developed to focus attention on the broader system. While the structure and content of the KNII website will evolve over time, the guiding principles underlying the selection of indicators would remain the same.

Our working assumption is that the KNII system would be used by:

- Citizens interested in assessing the relative health of their communities and nation

- Elected officials and candidates for office

- Civic leaders and non-profit organisations

- Private and public service providers

- Business leaders

- Policy makers and their staffs

- Interest and advocacy groups

- Scholars and researchers

- Educators and students

- Journalists and reporters

Clearly, the KNII cannot equally serve the diverse needs of each of these constituencies. In general, we would expect that the media and the public might find most useful the "high level" indicators, while scholars will continue to need far more detailed data to address research questions. The KNII database would be designed to ensure that each of these constituencies could either directly access the indicators of most substantive interest to them or gain needed assistance in their searches for data at a level of detail appropriate to their specific needs.

Unresolved Issues

The KNII is a work-in-progress; its planners are addressing a number of key design issues and challenges. Some relate to the organisation and funding of the KNII, and are not reviewed here. Other design issues are conceptual, and it is these that we believe will be of most interest to the participants in the OECD World Forum.

1. Breadth and Degree of Coverage. A more inclusive indicator set avoids the difficulty of selection and the risk of disappointing important constituencies who do not find "their" indicator in the set. Persons interested in the cultural life of the society, for example, will want detailed expenditures on and rates of participation in cultural institutions, and may give little attention to indicators focused on economic and social welfare trends. The credibility of an indicator set will be questioned if it does not provide appropriate coverage to match the complexity of the entity it purports to assess, but, conversely, the value of an indicator set can be diminished if it is too large or unwieldy for effective user interaction. We want the KNII to be robust and yet avoid creating just another "almanac." By key indicators we have in mind an agreed and limited set, chosen through a collaborative process that promises to have the greatest visibility across many sectors and levels of society. The test is whether a periodic indicator report will stimulate a broad public discussion integrating many key issues and will thereby strengthen the contribution of the KNII to democratically

guided public choices. Indicators that do not become part of this more exclusive set will of course still be accessible via the KNII web site, as will the back-up data from which the key indicators were constructed.

2. Adaptation and Evolution. Trend data are valuable because they are based on repeated measures across time, thereby placing a premium on constancy in the measurement instrument. In tension with this value is whether an indicator system can innovate, that is, capture new conditions that emerge in any dynamic society. Fixed race and ethnicity categories, for example, inherited from the 19th century, do not capture the complexity of a multicultural society and the growth of inter-marriage across racial and ethnic lines.

Another aspect of the balance between constancy and currency arises when measurement methods are improved, as recently illustrated in the United States when a new industry classification was introduced (in cooperation with Canada and Mexico). Although time-series data were disrupted, measurement methods for industry and commerce designed for the mid-20th century became progressively flawed with the rapid growth of the service industry and the arrival of information technologies. The United States has now added to its economic indicators measures of three dimensions of the service industry, with more in the planning stage. A challenge for any indicator program is balancing the value of constancy against the need to be current.

3. Level of Geographic and Demographic Detail. In a nation as politically decentralized as the United States, there is much interest in an indicator set that offers information at the community, city, state, and regional levels. Equally important to many potential users is information disaggregated by variables such as employment status, age, race, gender, educational achievement, and so forth. There is an understandable concern that national numbers might show overall improvement but mask problems in some local areas or for some demographic groups. For example, national numbers might show economic conditions to be improving, but leave undetected the fact that inner cities are not better off than a decade ago.

The degree and scope of disaggregation is of course constrained by sample size and, when drawing from multiple sources, by data comparability. It has been suggested that the KNII might solve the sample size problem by incorporating local data sets that meet appropriate quality standards. Although this approach has the advantage of flexibility and responsiveness to local needs, it leads to indicators that do not mean the same thing in all parts of the nation. This could weaken the capacity of the KNII to support a shared civic discourse in which the entire nation can simultaneously participate. Comparability at both the regional and supra-national levels will be an ongoing challenge.

4. Legitimacy and Constituency Involvement. As noted above, we want the KNII to be responsive to and enjoy the support of a variety of constituencies, a goal no doubt shared by indicator programs in all OECD countries. One way to achieve this is to incorporate constituency views in the design and implementation of the KNII. This, obviously, becomes a process of constituency involvement that itself has to be managed. There can be winners and losers in the sense that some constituencies might be better served than others as the profile of particular indicators is raised while that of others is not. There can be widely varying judgments about what constitutes an acceptable quality threshold, with statisticians often arguing for higher standards than advocacy organisations. More generally, as noted above, KNII planning has

stressed the value of public-private partnership in the governance and funding of the effort, but the institutionalisation of this partnership poses issues not yet resolved.

5.   Indicators and Values. Perhaps no challenge is more vexing than simultaneously ensuring that key indicators are both apolitical *and* relevant to the policy-making process. It is easy to say that the indicators will be insulated from the often intense conflicts that today characterize American political life. It is easy to say that the KNII will be used to make hard choices about allocating resources across competing social needs. What is not easy is bringing those two sentiments together. The KNII effort will not itself set goals for American society, and certainly will not be designed to assign blame or credit as trend lines move up or down. It is not a political report card. Yet the KNII will measure issues that are differently valued by various groups in society, and thus be drawn into political debate. We offer a simple example. For many citizens, climbing divorce rates indicate there is a problem to be corrected by policy incentives that will encourage long-lasting marriages. For other citizens, divorce rates indicate greater freedom than in the past for spouses to exit a non-working relationship. In this example, the task of the KNII would be to provide the best measures available of trends showing how Americans join in and separate from marital relations and civil unions, and thereby assure common evidence for debates about values and alternative policy proposals.

The KNII is sensitive to the fact that numbers – especially trend numbers purporting to describe progress (or its absence) – carry political weight, and is not naïve about the pressures that can be put on statistics to reflect well, or poorly, on those responsible for the well-being of the society. The KNII's planners place a high premium both on a truly bi-partisan endorsement of its basic design features and on an ensuing non-partisan administration of the key national indicators system.

Although this list is not exhaustive, it is sufficient to justify describing the United States' effort as a "work-in-progress." We stand to gain much by working with, learning from, and contributing to efforts of our OECD partners and other nations around the world. We welcome this Forum as a timely opportunity to move the United States' initiative forward by drawing on the accumulated wisdom of those countries that have already resolved the array of conceptual and organisational challenges we face. To the degree possible, as we learn through our own national experiences, we also stand ready to contribute to the emerging community of practice this body represents.

We are committed to solving these challenges, and to securing in America's public life an effective indicators program. The KNII is a way to offer something back to citizens for their cooperation in providing the responses that are the platform on which statistical indicators are constructed. A national statistical system is, finally, nothing more than the aggregation of boxes ticked, questions answered, and forms filled in by millions upon millions of citizens. We can construct indicators only because citizens and establishments have cooperated with censuses and surveys in the past. But in the present period of heightened concerns about privacy and confidentiality, citizens are growing less cooperative when asked to provide information. One way to earn the levels of cooperation necessary for high quality social, economic, and environmental statistics is to give to citizens the means to understand and shape their society. In this deep sense, the KNII is a public good to which government and citizens alike must contribute.

Measuring for Decision Making: Soft and Hard Use of Indicators in Regional Development Policies

Fabrizio Barca[1]

Head of Department for Development Policies, Ministry of Economy and Finance, Italy

Introduction: EU regional policy and territorial indicators

Persisting social and economic regional disparities within countries, in the global context of increased movements of goods, capital and labour, have called for a greater role of policies aimed at enhancing the competitiveness of specific regions. In Europe, new development strategies have emerged that move away from sectoral interventions and subsidies to compensate for territorial gaps, towards integrated place-based policies, focusing on the provision of public goods (or collective services under-produced by markets) to increase indirectly the productivity of private investments in areas with unused potential[2].

The implementation of new strategies for regional development is accompanied by major changes in the locus of decision making. Since the 90s, several countries have decentralised a large share of their policies to regional and local governments; cooperation and networks among different levels of government (local, regional, national, supra-national) and between public and private agents are replacing traditional top-down decision-making in the design of policies and projects.

This policy shift raises a strong challenge in terms of knowledge and information needs. Devising and delivering public goods and making networks truly useful to local needs is a knowledge-intensive process. Furthermore, most of the knowledge needed to implement policy is dispersed among several agents, at local and central levels. Policy actions designed for specific territories require therefore a high degree of vertical and horizontal co-ordination among administrations and improved co-operation between public and private bodies.

As a result, in the process of decision making, institutions that convert scattered private information into collective knowledge come to play a fundamental role.

In Italy, regional development policies involve four levels of government: the European level, setting general rules and objectives; the central State, adapting those rules to the national context, monitoring their implementation, providing technical assistance to regions and allocating rewards and sanctions; Regions, with a fundamental role in selecting projects, allocating resources among them and monitoring their implementation;

---

1   Written collectively with Monica Brezzi, Flavia Terribile and Francesca Utili.

2   See OECD (2003).

counties and municipalities, pooling together local actors, designing projects and promoting their implementation. This institutional set-up has two implications. First, the efficiency of the decision making process heavily relies on the capacity of interaction, both formally and informally, among institutions. Second, the implementation of new governance tools – whereby general policy targets and the "rules of the game" are set by an upper level through technical and political consultation with the lower levels, and the specification and implementation of these targets require continuous diagnostic monitoring through partnership network[3] - hinges on the exchange of reliable, timely and meaningful, quantitative information.

In implementing in Italy this new policy framework a very relevant role is being played by EU regional policy. EU policy provides a toolbox of measuring instruments (e.g. statistical tools; quality standards and guidelines for evaluating and monitoring development programmes; sanctions and rewards systems for the allocation of funds; additionality rules; etc.) allowing Member States to use a common language for evaluating the territorial dimension of phenomena at stake and design appropriate policies[4].

Since the late 90s, Italy has promoted and refined this EU-originated toolbox to support the implementation of the new development strategy for the Southern regions, characterised by a serious historical output gap. Within the Community Support Framework (CSF) 2000-2006 for the Italian South, institutions for developing comprehensive information systems were established and different sets of territorial indicators were used to evaluate the geographical dimension of phenomena and assess the quality of policy action[5]. These represent major steps forward in the development of a new regional policy.

The principles underlying the selection and construction of territorial indicators reflect their specific purpose: to support and guide policy making. In performing this task, two main interrelated problems, affecting the use of indicators for decision making, were to be tackled.

First (problem 1), in an "incomplete information framework", policy objectives - whether intermediate or final ones - are difficult to translate into quantitative and verifiable measures (where for verifiability we intend the possibility of evaluating *ex post*

---

3   See Barca F. (2001, 2003).

4   It should be noted that in the current negotiation on the reform of EU regional policy for the period 2007-2013, the Commission and several Member States agree to develop this common toolbox (e.g. definition of a common lexicon, common objectives and quantitative targets, reliable statistical tools) thereby increasing the level of synergy between regional, national and community policies and the Lisbon and Gothenburg agendas. Some net-contributing countries – namely some of those advocating a significant reduction of community resources for cohesion policy – have suggested to restrict the use of this toolbox to what is below called a "soft" use, linked to the adoption of an "open method of co-ordination" for regional policy; see HM Treasury, Department for Trade and Industry, Office of the Deputy Prime Minister (2003). As it will be clear from section 3, this restriction would likely weaken the effectiveness of policy as well as pushing some other net-contributing countries to reduce their contributions.

5   Within the Community Support Framework 2000-2006, around 22 billion Euros of EU funds – to be matched by the same amount of national resources - were assigned to the six Objective 1 regions in the South of Italy (Basilicata, Calabria, Campania, Puglia, Sardegna and Sicilia) and one phasing-out region (Molise). These resources represent about thirty percent of all public capital spending in the area in this period. Within the CSF, more than four million Euro were assigned to develop the statistical infrastructure. Most of the rules and incentive mechanisms agreed by central and regional administrations under the CSF were subsequently extended to all public investment policies in the South.

the achievement of objectives), since the knowledge needed to do so is partly held by the agents implementing the policy, and is partly produced through policy implementation. Second (problem 2), the causality link between actions and objectives is very hard to be established, since many variables and noise influence the achievement of objectives.

The use of indicators is linked to the relevance of these two problems and the way they were solved. In particular the Italian CSF 2000-2006 implemented indicators in two very different ways, which we describe here as "soft" and "hard".

On the one hand, a set of territorial indicators was chosen that describes final objectives (e.g. in terms of well-being, desired characteristics of regional economic systems, quality of services, etc.). Different aspects of the same phenomenon (e.g. social exclusion) are captured by a variety of indicators (e.g. financial poverty, accessibility to services, quality of housing, etc.). These indicators, denominated "context indicators" were aimed at a "soft use": better targeting of policy actions and broadly assessing their effectiveness. The choice of a soft use is explained by the fact that problems 1 and 2 were very relevant and no tool was available to reduce them enough.

On the other hand, indicators that describe intermediate process objectives were chosen to capture policy targets in terms of institution building. While easier to monitor, these "process indicators" are strongly affected by problem 1, since what is a good measure of effectiveness of institution building depends on the institutional context itself and it is often revealed only in the very process of implementation. In order to make a "hard use" of these indicators, a "knowledge revealing mechanism" had to be established, both before and after the definition of the targets, by which indicators could be more clearly specified during the monitoring process. Sanctions and rewards could then be attached to these indicators and citizens could judge their local governments with relatively homogenous standards.

The process of definition of indicators is necessarily a dynamic one, responding to new policy challenges and objectives. Lessons learned from the Italian experience can have relevance in the framework of the political negotiations on the reform of EU cohesion policy 2007-2013.

This paper examines the technical and institutional basis on which the two set of territorial indicators were selected, and the implications for policy making. The following section reviews "context indicators", the involvement of different institutions in the selection process, the different uses of indicators to guide decision making. The third section analyses the group of "performance indicators", the consensus-building process underlying their selection, the role of partnership mechanisms at the foundation of the rewards and sanctions' system, the limits of this system. Problems in establishing commonly agreed indicators to guide decision making are summarised in the conclusions and possible solutions are identified.

Soft use of indicators: the case of measuring final objectives

The task

Within the priorities of the CSF 2000-06 for the Italian South[6], a large set of variables called "context indicators" and measuring well-being, quality of services, supply of

---

6   The CSF is arranged around six priorities: natural resources, cultural resources, human resources, local development, urban development, material and information network.

infrastructure, labour market conditions, etc. - has been identified to describe strengths and weaknesses of areas targeted by policy and to assess policy impact. These indicators represent, with different degrees, the strategic choices of the CSF, as they are defined to measure final objectives of regional policies within specific policy areas.

The two general problems, of translating the policy objectives into quantitative and verifiable measures and establishing a direct link between policy actions and the dynamics of context indicators, were very clear at the time when context indicators were chosen.

The first problem – how to find clear-cut indicators to represent policy objectives in an incomplete information framework – was addressed by involving all the relevant actors in the choice of indicators and by choosing more than one indicator for each phenomenon[7]. As for the second problem - the difficulty in establishing a direct link between policy actions and objectives - it was decided not to build a causality model.

Given these limitations, context indicators were aimed at a "soft use": targeting policy actions and broadly assessing their effectiveness. The mistake was avoided to use them for a sharp evaluation of policies.

More specifically, the use of context indicators for decision making was aimed at three tasks:

1. *Pinning down regional weaknesses and strengths* (such as, which is the offer of tourist attractions in the South and what share of visitors are drawn to the South? In recent years was there any difference in the delivering of public services among regions? And which is the perception of citizens? Which is the trend of the gender gap in the participation to labour market?). The clarification is especially important in an asymmetric information framework, where the central administration in charge of setting the general strategy and monitoring the implementation of the CSF does not hold all the relevant information and needs to involve sector experts and all the administrations responsible for the implementation of the strategy. The participation of relevant stakeholders in the selection process of indicators is aimed at reinforcing their bottom-up nature.

2. *Reducing the degree of fuzziness of regional policy objectives*. The interaction among different levels of government (central government, coordinating the process, and regional and central administrations, implementing it) in defining the context indicators and, in some cases, quantifying targets to be aimed at within few years, helps to focus the objectives, and provide some direction for policy.

3. *Increasing the accountability of all the stakeholders involved in decision making:* administrations responsible for policy implementation are pressed to explain possible deviations from the expected dynamics; policy makers have a political incentive to realise the announced objectives. Communication to the public – through the revelation of policy preferences – is the necessary condition for policy effectiveness.

The following paragraph describes the basic features of context indicators; the section entitled "water, information society and social exclusion: supporting decision making" shows, through examples for water management, social exclusion and information

---

7   As a result, the data base includes almost 90 indicators, while when it was built at the end of 1999 less than 60 indicators had been defined.

society, how context indicators were identified and used in decision making and to what extent the three above-mentioned tasks were addressed. The section "targeting context indicators" recounts the choice of setting targets for some of the context indicators; the meaning and use of targets are discussed in relation to the problems presented.

Selection and use of context indicators

During the ex-ante evaluation of the CSF, context indicators were identified for each strategic area of the programme. The effort was made to ensure indicators satisfying the following basic features: unambiguous measure of weaknesses or strengths of an area, either in terms of well-being or in terms of development opportunities; availability at regional level (for all the regions); timeliness (the delay is limited on average to one year); availability of time-series and updates; uncontroversial quality of data.

The choice of indicators was conducted by the Department for Development Policies (DPS) of the Ministry of Economy and Finance together with central and regional administrations responsible of policy implementation and other relevant public and private actors. The aim of DPS was to select bottom-up indicators through partnership and co-decision. While enabling central and regional administrations to better understand the potential and weaknesses of each territory and to agree on the overall strategy of the CSF, this process allowed DPS to increase its knowledge on how the strategies could be implemented in the different regions, by extracting "local" information held by regional decision-makers.

After the approval of the CSF by the European Commission (August 2000), the need to improve the statistical information available and to obtain more detailed information led to a formal agreement with the National Statistical Office (Istat) to finance the production of statistical information at territorial level within the CSF. The agreement was constantly supervised by a scientific committee, monitoring the improvements in the availability and quality of information at the territorial level. Technical assistance was supplied in order to better measure available information (choice of indicators, sources, updates, etc.). Inter-institutional working groups were established to detect the information gaps to be filled and to define adequate indicators both in specific sectors not previously covered (for example water supply and regional poverty estimates) and in strategic sectors not adequately described by statistical information (for example innovation and information society). In order to obtain better information, *ad hoc* surveys were carried out and collaboration was offered to improve existing data.

So far, 96 indicators have been selected and are being measured, of which 89 have spatial and temporal values available. Table 1 contains a sample of the indicators organized by CSF priority: the last available values for both Centre-North and South are presented, with the value for Italy equal to 100. The actual database includes, for each indicator, yearly values (generally starting from 1995) for each region and macro area. The database is of public domain on the web site of the National Statistical Office and updated versions are released twice a year.

Table 1: A sample of Context indicators data base (Italy =100)

Sector	Indicator	last available year	Centre-North	South	Italy
Priority I "Natural Resources"					
Water	Water distribution irregularities (as perceived by households)	2003	61,1	180,4	100,0
Water	Km of swimming-forbidden seashore	2002	84,5	105,3	100,0
Electricity	Frequency of long stoppages of electric power service	2002	77,4	136,5	100,0
Pollution and waste	Urban recycled waste over total urban waste	2001	134,9	27,0	100,0
Priority II "Cultural Resources"					
Cultural resources	Per capita average expenses for theatre and concerts	2003	127,7	50,4	100,0
Cultural resources	Tickets sold for theatre and concerts per 100 people	2003	124,6	55,8	100,0
Priority III "Human Resources"					
Labour	Unemployment rate of youth (age 15-24)	2003	14,4	49,1	27,1
Labour	Gender difference between labour participation rates	2003	21,0	35,0	26,1
Education	Drop-out rate (students who left school over total enrolled students) in the first year of high school	2002	13,6	16,8	15,1
Research	Expenditure of the public and private enterprises for R&D (percentage over GDP)	2001	121,0	36,0	100,0
Priority IV "Local development"					
Local development	Industry added value (over labour equivalent units of the sector)	2002	102,4	88,1	100,0
Local development	Added value in the turistic sector (over labour equivalent units of the sector)	2002	101,2	95,8	100,0
Local development	Net birth rate of enterprises (new enterprises, minus cancelled ones at year t, over stock of enterprises at year t-1)	2003	91,4	119,5	100,0
Priority V "Urban development"					
Urban development	Difficulty to reach grocery stores (as perceived by households)	2003	96,3	107,6	100,0
Urban development	Number of air monitoring devices per 10.000 inhabitant	2002	127,8	50,4	100,0
Urban development	Share of public transportation use to work places over total transportation to work places	2003	100,7	98,5	100,0
Priority VI "Material and information network"					
Transportation	Passengers in airports over regional population	2002	122,3	60,3	100,0
Transportation	Air pollution due to transportation (tons of carbone dioxide due to road transportation per inhabitant)	2002	103,9	93,1	100,0
Information society	Percentage of population in municipalities connected to SAIA (system of exchange of administrative information)	2001	122,4	60,4	100,0
Information society	Percentage of families with internet connection	2003	106,9	87,7	100,0

Source: DPS-ISTAT, Context Indicators Database

Water, information society and social exclusion: supporting decision making

A first example is provided by the case of context indicators for water management. It clearly shows the three main tasks introduced in the paragraph entitled "the task".

One of the objectives of the Natural Resource priority of the CSF is to "guarantee adequate water supply"; the achievement of this objective depends on several aspects partly linked by causal links (density of population along the coast, use of water for agriculture, maintenance and improvement of cleaning systems, improvement of urban dwellings, implementation of the sector law - "Galli" law 36/94 - etc.). These aspects and their links were taken into account when designing the programme strategy, and deciding the financial effort[8]. The sector strategy underscored the necessity to build efficient management systems in order to pursue the objective.

Different indicators were available which can give measure of the progress in "guaranteeing adequate water supply": infrastructure indicators, effectiveness of the water system, reform implementation. As context indicator the *"percentage of families perceiving irregularities in the water distribution"* (see figures 1 and 2)[9] was finally chosen. This indicator ensures the basic features of context indicators: together with availability, to capture well being in a non ambiguous way.

Figure 1 shows[10] that the gap between the South and the rest of Italy is still significant, and it has actually worsened between 1998 and 2001. A closing of the gap has taken place in 2002-2003, while a target has been set for year 2008 which brings this indicator for the South at the Italian level for year 2000[11]. Strong differences exist among Regions (fig. 2).

The negative results of the period 1996-2001 have indeed led to strengthen the effort to adequate the water system to the national and European standards and to increase public investment in the sector. At the same time the cooperation among different levels of government in defining the CSF's strategy has helped administrations to refine the objective and to explicit the critical aspects[12].

In designing the strategy for the water sector, important aspects that affect and blur the final objective of guaranteeing adequate water supply were identified, such as the amount of liberalisation of the water sector, the level of efficiency in the management, the degree of implementation of the sector law ("Galli" law 36/94). The CSF clearly identified the responsibilities for necessary intermediate steps towards a sound management of water systems. In particular, except for the first two years, only actions directed to integrated water systems within ATO could be funded.

It should be noticed that in the reform process some of these institutional steps were so clearly and unambiguously identified, that they could indeed be turned into "hard"

---

8   Ten per cent of the total CSF funds plus almost 900 millions of euro of national resources earmarked to the under-utilised areas are devoted to the implementation of integrated water systems.

9   The source of data is the "Indagine multiscopo" conducted by the National Statistical Office yearly; the survey is addressed to a panel of more than 22.000 families.

10   The source of all the pictures in par. 2 is the DPS-ISTAT Context Indicator Database.

11   It is important to notice that this indicator comes from a customer satisfaction survey, therefore its values can be the result of features of the service as well as of changes in the families' expectations.

12   For example, through this process the lack of the fundamental information about the organisation of the sector in "optimal areas" (ATO) became clear – for details see DPS (2004).

indicators and be therefore targeted for the allocation of sanctions and rewards. An indicator which measures the pace with which Regions accomplish the sector reform, was then chosen, and an incentive scheme for the achievement of the desired target by 2003 was designed (see the third section "Hard use of indicators: the case of measuring intermediate objectives").

Figure 1: Families perceiving irregularities in water distribution (as a percentage of total families): Southern Italy and Italy

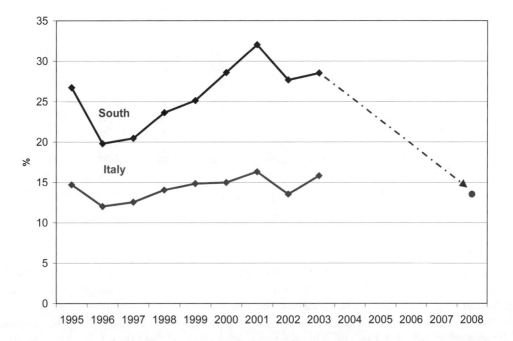

The availability of regional data helped to increase the accountability of regional decision makers, creating an incentive for administrations to intervene and address actions (for example a new survey was conducted in Basilicata on different aspects of water supply and the acceleration of the investment plan in the ATO in many regions).

A second example shows how co-operation among administrations in the choice of indicators for decision-making can lead to the improvement of existing statistics and to the provision of information for actually appraising policy: the case of indicators for the "Material and information network" priority of the CSF.

The target of this priority is to strengthen the modernisation of public administrations, in particular the regional and local ones, delivering better services to citizens and firms in order to increase the competitiveness of the area. When the CSF was designed, the strategy for promoting information society and the use of information and communication technologies in the public administration was quite generic. The choice for context indicator reflected this early stage, as well as the lack of statistical information on the theme: "*percentage of municipalities with electronic administrative database*". Besides the fact that it was a measure of internal management innovation, it did not guarantee the reliability and updating of data.

Figure 2: Families perceiving irregularities in water distribution (as a percentage of total families) by regions (South)

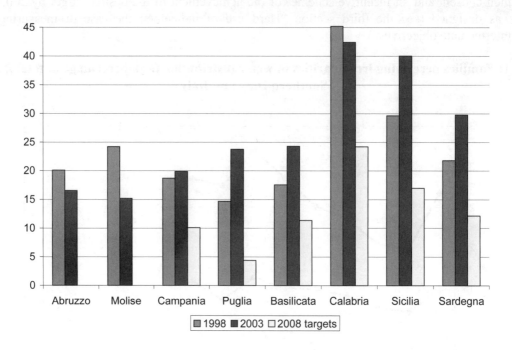

In the following years, a clear e-government strategy has been developed and objectives for the innovation of regional and local administrations have been established[13] and embraced in the CSF during its mid-term evaluation. In the meantime, the context indicator was changed to also measure the evolution of local administrations towards technological services for citizens: "*percentage of municipalities connected to the on-line database for the exchange of administrative information*" (see figure 3). This context indicator is nevertheless not completely satisfactory to measure local e-government, since it considers only municipalities and only a specific activity (not necessarily the most relevant one) that can benefit citizens. More focused information to monitor the progress of local administrations in the area of e-government are needed (timely official surveys at regional level are still not available), and the recent agreement between the National Statistical Office and the Ministry for Innovation to develop an information system on e-government is an important step in this direction. Co-ordination among Regions and central administrations in charge of developing and monitoring the information society within the working groups of the CSF has helped to focus the regional priorities and the subsequent territorial indicators.

A third example concerns the problem of multi-dimensionality in the measurement of well-being and policy effectiveness. For most features of well-being, one-dimension measures do not offer adequate understanding of how backward one area is, nor do they offer much guidance for policy. This is the case of social exclusion.

---

13   See E-government Plans in local and central government offices: www.innovazione.gov.it/ita/egovernment/entilocali/egov_Fase2.pdf

Figure 3: Percentage of municipalities connected to on-line database for the exchange of administrative information

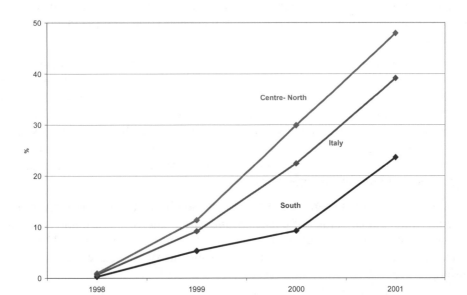

Together with the growth of GDP, the reduction of social exclusion in the South is one of the general objectives of the CSF. In the implementation of this goal, one is presented with two very relevant problems. First, a wide-spread belief exists that social disadvantage in the South is much less serious than what traditional measures of poverty show: the percentage of families in the South whose per person expenses are lower than the national average (called the relative poverty line[14]) is in 2002 equal to more than 22%, compared to around 6% in the Centre-North, but most argue that the comparison between the two macro does not take into account the lower cost of living and the relevance of the black economy in the South[15]. This belief affects both the actual political consensus for policy targeted to the South and the South's convictions and confidence in claiming for this policy.

Second, poverty in monetary terms does not provide much guidance for policy-making. By *de facto* calling for redistributive measures, it completely obscures problems of access to services and opportunities that no redistributive measure can indeed address.

Both problems can be correctly faced by making use of a multidimensional approach. This approach can capture signals of economic well-being as well as the possibility for individuals to have access to adequate social services such as quality of housing and area of residence, access to medical services, availability of child care, etc. This approach can first allow checking whether the extent of social exclusion is well captured by monetary poverty. It can then provide indications, region by region, for what service gap actually affect social exclusion.

---

14   Poverty is estimated on the basis of the number of families whose expenses are under a certain level. This level is computed as the average monthly expenses per person and it is equal to 823,45 euro in 2002. This level represents the relative poverty line for a two people family.

15   The updated data for 2003 substantially confirm 2002 situation with a slight improvement for the South. Nevertheless, since the exclusion indicators have not been updated, this paper refers to the year 2002.

Within the agreement with the National Statistical Office to improve territorial statistics for better monitoring and evaluation of the impact of the CSF, DPS financed for 2002 edition of the Households Budget Survey[16] both (i) a new set of questions addressed to families regarding different aspects of their living condition, and (ii) the availability of these indicators and of that on monetary poverty at regional level.

The information available on regional monetary poverty first confirms previous results on poverty distribution[17]. While a decrease is shown in the percentage of families in the South under the poverty line between 2001 and 2003, a strong gap between the Centre-North and the South of Italy persists: in 2002, 66 out of the 100 poor families live in the South, which includes only 33% of all the families. At the same time a significant variability among regions in the South is observed and, even if to a much smaller extent, also in the Centre-North[18]. But, the more interesting results concern the comparison of monetary and multidimensional measures.

First, a strong gap between Centre-North and South of Italy is confirmed also when considering the regional values of exclusion indicators: the two distributions are always distant and recognisable, except in the case of the child-care indicator. The monetary indicator is then confirmed to be very relevant in synthetically describing social exclusion.

On the other hand, all exclusion indicators present high variability among regions, especially in the South. Monetary indicator of poverty appears to be a very poor measure of well-being, since it covers up for very different situations. Only exclusion indicators can illustrate specific situations of perceived disadvantage and therefore offer indications on where to address policy actions[19], thus orienting the action of policy makers at different levels of government (see figure 4 for one example).

Regional ranking within the two macro areas is different for the exclusion indicators, showing that they are able to capture different aspects of social conditions (see table 2). For example Basilicata, Calabria and Molise which have the three highest values for monetary poverty, do perform better, relatively to the other southern regions, with regard to some of the indicators of social exclusion. Similar things happens in Trentino Alto-Adige and Friuli Venezia-Giulia.

Finally, consumption expenses do not directly reflect difficulties that families face to buy necessary goods. The exclusion indicator which measures the percentage of families who perceive difficulties in paying food, medical expenses and utilities offers a better description of a family's conditions. The variability among the Southern regions for this indicator is statistically significant, but at the same time the distribution of this indicator twinned with the monetary poverty shows that in the Southern regions monetary difficulties can be perceived as less serious than in the Centre-North (see figure 5).

---

16   This is the traditional source of official information on poverty in Italy; see ISTAT "Indagine sui consumi delle famiglie italiane", various years.

17   It is important to remind that, due to the sample dimension, the confidence intervals comprising the regional values are quite large, especially for small regions; therefore caution must be used when comparing regional values and yearly variations.

18   The standard deviation is equal to 9 in the Southern regions and 2,1 in the Centre-North ones.

19   The correlation with the monetary poverty is significant for the indicators of inadequacy of housing and difficulty in purchasing basic goods (equal 0,75 in both cases).

Figure 4: Percentage of families under the poverty line (left) and percentage of family with difficulties to access to health services (right)

(regions ranked by quartiles)

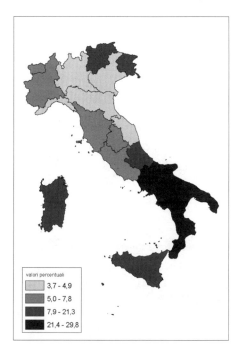 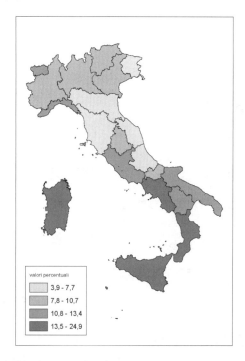

Table 2: Regional ranking within macro areas for monetary poverty and exclusion indicators in 2002

	RANKING (higher in the ranking = worse)	monetary poverty	housing problems	difficulty to access to health services	difficulty to access to child care	difficulty to buy basic goods
Center North	Piemonte	5	2	4	1	2
	Valle d'Aosta	4	12	3	4	12
	Lombardia	12	7	6	10	5
	Trentino Alto Adige	1	11	4	3	11
	Veneto	11	4	6	6	4
	Friuli Venezia Giulia	2	6	12	2	8
	Liguria	9	9	2	12	6
	Emilia Romagna	10	8	9	7	10
	Toscana	7	9	10	5	3
	Umbria	6	1	8	11	7
	Marche	8	5	11	8	9
	Lazio	3	3	1	9	1
South	Abruzzo	7	8	8	2	8
	Molise	3	5	7	4	7
	Campania	4	6	3	3	2
	Puglia	5	7	6	7	4
	Basilicata	2	1	5	5	6
	Calabria	1	4	2	6	3
	Sicilia	6	2	4	1	1
	Sardegna	8	2	1	8	4

Figure 5: Regional distribution of monetary poverty and difficulties to buy basic goods in 2002

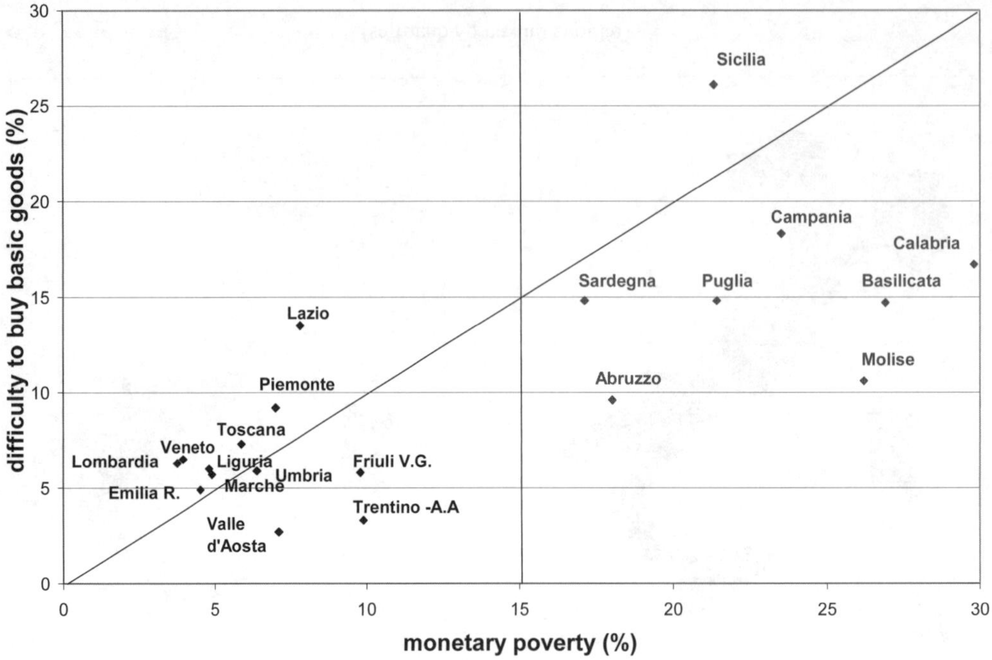

Targeting context indicators

Because of the difficulty to establish causality links among policy actions and objectives, context indicators are aimed at a "soft use". A limited use of targets has therefore been made.

The limitation concerns two aspects. First, only for a subset of context indicators, whose link to the policy actions was more direct, targets could be established. Second, since the achievement of targets is not fully under the control of policy-makers, sanctions and rewards were not attached to it.

The identification of benchmarks for the South to be reached by 2008[20] was carried out by experts coordinated by the Evaluation Unit of the Department of Development Policies (DPS). Moreover, in analogy with the choice of indicators, the final values for benchmarks were the result of interactions among DPS and regional administrations recipient of EU funds and responsible for selecting projects.

The identification of benchmarks was carried out by evaluating variables, trends and the comparative position of the area with more developed ones and by relating the expected results to objectives and strategies of the CSF[21]. Figures 1 and 2 show the targets, respectively for the South and for each Southern region, in the case of the context

---

20   Resources assigned for the CSF 2000-2006 can be spent until the end of 2008.

21   To obtain a balanced evaluation on how the sector strategies affect context indicators in different sectors, an iterative Delphi-like method has been used, through which the experts' opinions on the expected targets are assessed and then compared and revised in subsequent cycles.

indicator "irregularities in water distribution"[22]. In this case the expected reduction for the South was more than 10 percentage points within ten years.

In analogy to the CSF, regional programmes include the same set of context indicators with benchmarks referring to the regional situation. The setting of benchmarks for specific sectors and the use of the evaluation between national and regional objectives and actions represent an important innovation in regional programming and ex-ante evaluation. The purpose for introducing regional benchmarks is that conditions of regional competitiveness can be improved through interregional comparisons of competitive advantages, territorial policies and extensive use of evaluation and monitoring systems. Furthermore the monitoring of the competitive position of each region with regard to quantitative benchmarks should help policy makers to evaluate and, if necessary, readdress policy choices and projects' selection.

The "theory" for introducing regional benchmarking was that each Region should have known the target for the context indicators to be reached in the macro-area (South) as a whole at the end of the CSF programming period, as well as its own target, given the regional current situation, planned strategies, effort planned to achieve targets (assessed by the percentage of investment and the actions planned in that sector). In reality, regional decision makers have rarely used benchmarks for context indicators to improve and, if necessary, to re-address their actions. The top-down nature of the process through which choice indicators and benchmarks were chosen did not help rising regional awareness. Furthermore, when choice was made regional administrations did not have the support of internal evaluation units, which were subsequently established. On the other hand, context indicators with their targets have been commonly used in official documents of the Ministry of the Economy and Finance.

Insofar, we have considered cases were context indicators cannot be used, being measures of long-term objectives influenced by many variables, as hard targets, to which sanctions and rewards are linked. We now move to this different case.

Hard use of indicators: the case of measuring intermediate objectives

The task

A policy where institution building represents a pre-condition for policy effectiveness, as it is the case for Italian regional policy, calls for institution building to become an explicit target of policy. The case arises for institution building to be directly aimed at through a system of hard indicators, to which rewards and sanctions are linked. "Hard" indicators were indeed experienced in regional policies in a number of incentive schemes[23]; in what follows we focus on the experience of the "*6 per cent performance*

---

22 When the targets were set the last available year was 1998.

23 The Department for Development Policies has so far implemented nine incentive schemes; a few of them are on national funds (to accelerate financial commitments and spending of national resources for public investment (see Delibera CIPE n. 36/02), to get more timely and complete information from regional budget units to Territorial Public Accounts, etc..) and two on structural funds -4% plus a 6% national reserve-for a total of 10% total CFS commitments. The amount of structural funds reserve including national cofinancing equals to approximately 4,6 billion euros. The endowments of the 4% and 6% performance reserves on structural funds were approx. 2 and 2,6 billion respectively (including national cofinancing equal on average to 50%). For a survey of the existing mechanisms see DPS (2004).

reserve" where approximately 1.8 billion of EU Funds and national co-financing were distributed among the six Objective 1 Regions of the South of Italy[24].

The allocation of resources took place according to a competitive mechanism based on the performance achieved in a given period of time for ten indicators of "institutional enhancement" and two indicators related to the quality of programming (integration of projects and concentration of financial resources on a limited number of objectives), (see table 3). These are denominated "performance indicators". Six central administrations in charge of sector programmes included in the CSF were also competing on a similar mechanism based on a more limited number of indicators (four of institutional enhancement and one of integration of national with territorial strategies); their global endowment was around 0.8 billion[25].

In setting this policy the general problem of "incompleteness" raised in section 1 had first to be tackled. The appropriate institutions needed to implement regional policy are clear-cut but only in general terms : a rigorous evaluation unit; a good accountable control system; efficient and widespread one-stop-shops; well organized and competent Public Employment Services; well-functioning regional environmental agencies; good management of water and urban solid waste; (see table 3 with the complete definition of indicators and targets). However their effectiveness and efficiency can only be fully described with reference to a given context (location, time, etc.) and often only once the institution has been created and gears into action.

Setting up a "rigorous evaluation unit" can not by itself prevent the appointment of members through nepotism or isolating the unit in an "ivory tower" where it does not really play a role in the decision process; moreover, these and other negative features can not be prevented by fully describing the requirements, since verifiability can only be partial and, furthermore, they do change according to context. Some requirements of a good accountable system can be described as general standards, but many others depend on the specificity of organisations and local accounting systems: setting up regional environmental agencies does not by itself enable an improvement of Regions to deliver better policy, nor can many conditions for that to occur be stated in universal and verifiable terms.

In general some standards can be described, but they are often not enough to guarantee effectiveness. Two opposite risks then arise: that targets are too heavily specified with reference to a non-existing general standard; that they are left completely open-ended. In the first case, agents' behaviour might even be biased towards a formalistic satisfaction of targets; in the second case, targets end up not being binding. A mix of tools has then to be introduced, by setting requirements and accompanying it with a system of *interim monitoring* that allows completing possibly open-ended requirements along the process. This system is described in the following section.

---

24   European regulations for CSF 2000-2006 already required the implementation of a 4% performance reserve (for a total of 2 billion euros including national cofinancing) on a list of indicators (effectiveness of funds' management, quality of evaluation and monitoring activities, etc.) proposed by the European Commission. The 6% national performance reserve was introduced by Italy, thus enforcing the European proposal, on the basis of indicators and mechanisms chosen at national level. This paper therefore examines thoroughly the latter system which was an original initiative of Italy and where the degree of freedom in the overall design was very high. Results are presented in Table 4 also for the 4 per cent system.

25   The paper focuses on regional experience. Similar conclusions however apply also for the six central administrations in charge of sector programmes. Results presented in Table 4 also include the performance of central administrations.

Table 3: Performance indicators and their targets for Regions

OBJECTIVE	INDICATOR	TARGETS
A. INSTITUTIONAL ENHANCEMENT		
Implementation of national legislation fostering the process of public administration reform	• Delegation of managerial responsibilities to officials (legislative decree n. 29/93) • Set up and implementation of an internal control management unit (legislative decree n.286/99) • Implementation of one -stop shops • Implementation of Public Employment services	• Adoption of the decree 29/93 and managers' evaluation for the year 2002 • Set up and proof of activity of the internal control management unit • At least 80% of the regional population covered by the one-stop shops and at least 90% of papers processed on time • At least 50% of the regional population covered by employment offices
Design and implementation of innovation to accelerate and make effective structural funds spending	• Set up of regional and central administration evaluation units (L. 144/99) • Development of the information society in the P.A.	• Set up of the evaluation unit by April 2001, appointment of the director and experts by July 2001 • Transmission of data regarding at least 60% of total expenditure
Implementation of sector reforms	• Preparation and approval of territorial and landscape programming documents • Concession or management by a private-public operator of integrated water services (L.36/94) • Implementation for urban solid waste within optimal service areas • Set up and operational performance of regional environmental agencies	• Meet regional benchmarks of territorial landscape programming • Approval of the concession or management by a private-public operator of integrated water services • Choice of management mode and its implementation within optimal service areas • Appointment of the director of the agency and approval of management rules, allocation of resources and personnel to the agency
B. INTEGRATION Implementation of territorial integrated projects	• Incidence of commitments of integrated territorial projects on the total amount of resources budgeted for integrated territorial projects in the operational program	• Incidence of commitments and disbursements of integrated territorial projects on the total amount of resources budgeted for integrated territorial projects in the operational programme higher than the average over all the regions
C. CONCENTRATION Concentration of financial resources	• Concentration of financial resources within a limited amount of measures	• Concentration of financial resources within a lower amount of measures than the average over all the regions

Two further problems had to be taken into account in setting the system.

There is a first problem of true responsibility. In order to attach a financial reward to the achievement of a target, the assumptions need to be made that the administration which benefits from the conditional incentive is also fully responsible for the actions needed to achieve the result. Note that being fully responsible does not necessarily mean to be directly responsible but at least to have the means to create an incentive for the agents that are directly responsible to perform their actions.

The third problem concerns credibility and the risk of renegotiation. If agents were to think that renegotiation, possibly at political level, were to take place before rewards and sanctions were assigned, then the whole mechanism would collapse. In order to reduce the risk of renegotiation a strong and widespread consensus has to be established, and a cost for attempting to renegotiate must be somehow enclosed in the incentive scheme.

All these problems were tackled as described below.

Dealing with incompleteness: choice and definition of indicators and targets, measurability

Once the set of general goals was defined, indicators had to be chosen that could describe the institutional goal by limiting the scope for the administration to fulfill the target only in formal terms or reducing the risk for the administration to achieve the true goal but missing the formal target. Only under these circumstances can rewards and sanctions linked to the targets be efficient. Furthermore, indicators needed to be measurable and easy to monitor.

It became immediately clear that the choice of indicators featuring those characteristics required an intense technical partnership with the regional level of government who had access to better local information and possessed private knowledge on its own preferences and on what would make institutions truly effective. This partnership had to be set both before and after the establishment of targets.

Through meetings, discussions, and then working documents, the agents (local administrations taking part to the mechanism) slowly revealed their preferences as well as part of their private information. The way to deal with information incompleteness was then to work together with the regional level and in this way to enact a "knowledge revealing mechanism" with the aim of filling with specific content the generic target. It was a learning process for all the subjects involved through which priorities were better defined during time.

When at the end of this ex-ante process targets were left relatively open-ended, the "knowledge revealing mechanism" worked so as to allow a meaningful and agreed interpretation to emerge, administration by administration, of what exactly the requirement to be fulfilled was. Interim monitoring entrusted to a Technical Group made up by two members of the Central Evaluation Unit and two members appointed by Regions participating to the incentive scheme; targets were to be assessed administration by administration, and Report had to be prepared and made available to all parties every six months. Both an understanding and a consensus slowly emerged of what the relatively open-ended targets really implied for regions or central administrations. In other words: contracts (by which sanctions-rewards were attached to the accomplishment of targets) were slowly completed. Reputation of members of the Technical Group helped making this process feasible.

This process was (as we shall see) definitely successful; but setting the appropriate standards was not an easy task and not always fully satisfactorily. Let's consider a few examples.

First, reform in the sectors of water and urban solid waste management was deemed to be essential. The selection of indicators and targets required the identification of all reform steps (design of optimal territorial areas; choice of private partners for the management of the services; definition of a threshold of regional population that had to be interested by the reform in the given, short period of time) necessary as preconditions for better services to be offered to citizens.

Second, in the case of the implementation of Regional Environmental Agencies it was not possible to set a standard that could homogeneously describe the variety of monitoring activities that the Agencies could carry out, nor quality standards. The requirements had then the scope of describing, beside formal institution, the correct functioning of the agencies: to have a manager with an adequate staff; to have an internal regulation; to have a constant assignment of resources. In the case of one region the compliance resulted later to be only formal (the agency was instituted on the very last day to meet the target by using emergency decrees) and could not be accepted as the achievement of the indicator.

Third, to enhance the diffusion of territorial landscape programming, a strong pressure was put by the central administration in charge of the issue (Ministry of Culture) to set specific targets for each region describing in detail the administrative acts and the specific territorial areas involved. However, those targets resulted to be too ambitious for almost every administration involved. The Ministry then decided to offer an additional option to regions to approve administrative acts assessing the compliance of regional legislation with some national standards. This new definition was quite general and somehow open- ended. The results were mixed: in those cases where the regions had already shown a commitment by starting substantial steps to meet the target in its initial definition, the process continued and was easy to monitor and evaluate. In the other cases instead, where the new option was taken, there was often the suspect that compliance was only formal but there was no real way to take the analysis further.

On the whole, the choice of indicators and targets was the result of a partnership process that lasted for a significant period from the second half of 1999 to April 2001[26]. Cooperation in the design of mechanisms also enhanced the commitment of regional and central administrations; they often ended up treating the objectives to be achieved as their own priorities[27]. As for the Regions they had a chance to contribute to the choice of objectives and regard them as (feasible) goals for which they wanted to be considered accountable to their political market.

To be used in a "hard" way, *i.e.* to allocate public resources, indicators, besides being precisely defined and clearly linked to policy, must be fully measurable. Given that the assignment of public resources was made conditional on an evaluation of the performance of local administrations, the information used to express the judgment had to be reliable, replicable and complete. In some cases, information with those requisites was already available: this is the case of managers' responsibilities or activity of internal control units or activity of regional investment evaluation units, where the information was produced as the ordinary output of the action of the administrative offices involved.

In a few other cases, information was also of administrative nature, but had to be produced on purpose in a standard way so as to comply with the requirements of the performance reserve system. This is the case, for example, of the diffusion of information

---

26   When the document with indicators, targets and rules of assignment of resources was officially approved by CSF monitoring Committee.

27   See Brezzi M. *et al.* (2004)

society where Regions had to collect specific data on ICT connections between their offices in charge for managing structural funds and funds' recipients (provinces, municipalities, other local institutions, etc.) spread on the regional area. In the case of water and urban solid waste management, information on the percentage of population covered by different steps of the implementation of the ongoing reforms was not readily available and was the outcome of specific calculations.

In the case of implementation of Public Employment Services (PES) and one-stop-shops for enterprises, a formalised cooperation had to be established with other central administrations (the Ministry of Labour and the Ministry for Efficiency of Public Administration respectively) which had the specific knowledge to collect and to assess the quality of information. In the first case, the Ministry of Labour used its territorial network to collect data on the institutional setting of PES in each region on the basis of a specific list of items defined in partnership with DPS Evaluation Unit. In the second, a specific survey was launched to get information from each of the 1 870 municipalities of the southern Regions carried out also with the contribution of governmental offices at provincial level.

Enforcing the reward/sanction mechanism: responsibilities and risk of renegotiation

The second general problem that arises when using indicators in policy making – the problem of establishing a causality link between outcomes and policy actions – takes great relevance in the case of hard use of institutional indicators. In rewarding and sanctioning the achievement of given targets, it must be ensured that responsibility for the achievement of targets does actually fall onto the very agent that benefits for rewards and pays for sanctions.

This problem was addressed by identifying through partnership the true nature of responsibilities.

In a few cases, where clear identification of responsibility was lacking, specific devices had to be introduced. In particular, an incentive was introduced for other agents to cooperate towards the objective, thus "correcting" an inefficiency of the mechanism. One of those ways was precisely to put in place local incentive mechanisms rewarding agents at lower institutional levels. Another way, which was used for one-stop-shops, was to communicate very widely the importance of the indicator also signalling the initiative on websites, involving municipalities (with responsibilities for action) in specific workshops and events.

Some problems of mismatch between agents bearing sanctions and those bearing responsibilities remained. In the case of one region, the mechanism actually failed in correctly identifying the institution (the regional council-political level) that had to take steps to achieve the expected objective. For example in a number of cases the regional council had to produce legislation that could start reforms in specific sectors (regional environmental agencies, Public Employment Services, territorial and landscape programming, etc.) but did not have incentives to do so, thus affecting in the end overall regional performance.

A final problem was addressed by strongly relying on partnership and the intense role of interim monitoring: making sure that the mechanism was renegotiation-proof.

Even in presence of knowledge revealing strategies, precise definition, non controversial measurability of targets and indicators and clear identification of responsibilities, still the acceptance by administration of final evaluation results, according to rules that were put in place more than two years in advance, required some additional devices to enhance the robustness of the system. Regional policy makers could be tempted to collude to obtain the prize without achieving the targets *i.e.* without respecting the rules previously accepted. How could the mechanism deal with this drive to renegotiate?

First of all, the mechanism included a degree of competition on resources based on the fact that if some indicators were not achieved by some Regions the corresponding amount of resources was to be redistributed among them, according to their performance[28]. The presence of this mechanism enhanced peer control among institutions at a level that was not accessible by the central administration.

In addition, the role of the Technical Group (see the former section), composed of representatives of both the principal and the agents, in monitoring and finally evaluating results was crucial. During the years of implementation of the mechanism the Group "actively" monitored the progress of administrations, suggesting solutions for specific problematic issues, periodically meeting with the Regions to discuss the general progress. In a few cases, in presence of unpredictable unfavourable events affecting the possibility of achieving the targets, the group also implemented technical solutions to overcome the obstacles. (See for example the described case of one-stop-shops where the central level was actively involved in the diffusion of information given the inefficiency detected in the mechanism). At the end of the period, when the Group wrote the final Evaluation Report, it had acquired enough reputation of fairness and impartiality that no administration contested its judgment on the achievement of targets.

Furthermore, final evaluation was accepted since the process had always been very transparent and information was always available to the public. The document with indicators, targets, and rules of allocation was available on the web of the DPS. Each Region periodically wrote an assessment of its progresses on the basis of which the Technical Group prepared a general Monitoring Report that was publicly accessible every six months. A general assessment of the process was included in the most official documents of the DPS and the Ministry of Economy and Finance. Within this framework, the possibilities for Regions to put pressures on the evaluation were limited.

On the whole, the consensus- building process that accompanied the choice of indicators and targets was also extremely important in strengthening the commitment of regional administrators and politicians, making clear that attempts to renegotiate would have affected their image and credibility.

Regional performance and follow ups

Results must be assessed by the effectiveness of the hard use of indicators to actually enhance institution building in the targeted areas and by their capacity to effectively reward and sanction different behaviours. From both points of view, results are quite compelling.

---

28   This amount ended up to be consistent: the amount of money corresponding to the endowments of indicators that were not achieved that, according to this mechanism, was to be redistributed was higher than 20 per cent of overall initial budget. The amount was redistributed according to specific performance and increased the variance of performance among participants as measured in terms of final allocation on original budget.

On the basis of the rules of allocation of financial resources and the targets on specific indicators officially stated in April 2001, more than 2 billion euros[29] of performance reserve resources were assigned to administrations in March 2003. Each administration involved had a potential endowment equal to six per cent of its original budget. The full amount could be gained if all targets were reached; otherwise resources were only partially assigned, according to the number of targets achieved.

Results first show that on average the performance of administrations in achieving the targets was very satisfactory since more than 60 per cent were achieved, reflecting significant progresses in the implementation of reforms in various fields and innovations in administrations; variance in the performance of participants was high (fig.6).

Figure 6: Performance indicators achieved by Region, March 2003

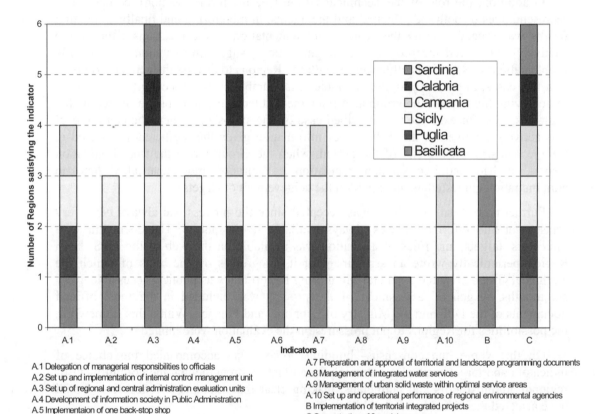

A.1 Delegation of managerial responsibilities to officials
A.2 Set up and implementation of internal control management unit
A.3 Set up of regional and central administration evaluation units
A.4 Development of information society in Public Administration
A.5 Implementaion of one back-stop shop
A.6 Implementation of Public Employment Services

A.7 Preparation and approval of territorial and landscape programming documents
A.8 Management of integrated water services
A.9 Management of urban solid waste within optimal service areas
A.10 Set up and operational performance of regional environmental agencies
B Implementation of territorial integrated projects
C Concentration of financial resouces

On the other hand, variability was very high. Regions participating to the mechanism received quite different rewards reflecting the number of targets achieved: one Region (Basilicata) got almost 135 per cent of its initial endowment[30], three Regions (Campania,

---

29   The remaining amount of approx. 0.6 billion euros, was assigned by the CSF Monitoring Committee in March 2004. For a detailed description see http://www.dps.tesoro.it/uval_linee_premialita.asp

30   Note that, because of the mechanism of indirect competition that redistributes to each administration according to its performance the resources that are not assigned in the first run (if some indicators are not achieved by some administration), the best performer gets more than its 100%. Basilicata also got a special performance premium for its excellent performance. In addition indicators have different weights that influence the final allocation. For a detailed description of results also for central administrations involved see Anselmo I. et al. (2003).

Sicily and Puglia) got from 98 to 79 per cent, while two Regions (Sardinia and Calabria) got around 40 per cent[31] (see Table 4).

Differences in performance are also clear from the point of view of the indicators achieved: one outlier (Basilicata) satisfies all the indicators (12); a group of three Regions (Campania, Puglia and Sicily) who have achieved 8 or more targets, and two regions (Sardinia and Calabria) have achieved 4 or less targets.

Table 4: Performance of Administrations as percentage of potential resources obtained [1]

Ranking	Resources assigned on the basis of the competitive mechanism /potential resources[2] (%)			
	6% Performance Reserve		**4% Performance Reserve**	
	Regions			
1	Basilicata	134,9	Puglia	108,6
2	Campania	98,2	Sicilia	107,6
3	Puglia	88,9	Campania	103,9
4	Sicilia	79,5	Basilicata	103,3
5	Sardegna	40,9	Sardegna	102,8
6	Calabria	38,6	Calabria	62,5
	Public Administrations [3]			
1	Econ. Competitiveness	129,8	Education	157,1
2	Education	77,0	Research and Dev.	130,0
3	Research and Dev.	70,6	Fishing	109,5
4	Law Enforcement	57,8	Econ. Competitiveness	109,5
5	Fishing	51,4	Technical Assistance	108,9
6	Transportation	49,2	Law Enforcement	107,9
7	—		Transportation	50,0

Source: Department for Development Policies, Ministry of Economy

[1] For the 6% mechanism allocation see March 2003 CSF 2000-06 Monitoring Committee; for the 4% see EC COM March 2004.

[2] Potential resources correspond to the original budget assigned to each Administration. Values can be greater than 100% since non-assigned resources are redistributed to Administrations that have shown good performance.

[3] Technical Assistance does not participate to the 6% mechanism.

But were sanctions and rewards always satisfactorily attributed? Do they represent a good picture of institutional advancement? On the whole the answer is positive, but there were problems.

In general, two possible mistakes can be made in evaluating the performance of administrations on the base of indicators that correspond to intermediate objectives. On the one hand, it is possible that because of non-compliance with formal accomplishments substantial results are not recognised. On the other hand, thanks to only formal

---

31   In March 2004 the European Commission officially assigned the 4 %performance reserve on the basis of the Italian proposal. The overall performance of administration also on this different mechanism turned out to be quite satisfactory, with only one region and one central administration getting partial amounts. See Table 4 for results.

compliance the reward can be given even if it does not correspond to real progress and improvement, for example, in the quality of services offered to citizens.

This second type of error is strictly connected to the intermediate nature of the indicators chosen who often only refer to the existence of the appropriate institutional setting for a service to be provided to citizens. This is the case for example of water and urban solid waste management where the mechanism was looking at the administrative implementation of the reforms and could not (since than the data would have not been available, reliable and complete to distribute public resources) look at if citizen were actually getting better services because of it. In addition, in some cases the administrative acts needed to achieve the indicators were produced in order to get the incentive but there were no follow ups in the reform process started and the indicator achieved, after the deadlines.

Actually, both in the case of one-stop-shops and PES some steps forward were already taken. In the case of one-stop-shops by looking not only at their diffusion on the regional area but also at the time length of the procedures; in the case of PES by looking not only at the institutional setting but also at the services that were available in each employment centre. A further improvement would be to understand if those services match the needs of citizen and are then effectively used by them.

To address the issue of whether institutional progress was indeed effective, and such as to truly enhance the quality of policy-making, the decision was taken to make, after the "game" was over, a soft use of hard indicators.

A new monitoring initiative is today in place where additional information is asked to regions in order to understand what is happening after the end of the performance reserve mechanism. The aim is precisely to understand in which cases the initiative was successful in starting reforms. Indeed, in a few cases innovations spurred by the mechanism are now part of the ordinary regional activity; this is the case for example of regional evaluation units that in almost each region have acquired a very relevant role, of internal control units that are generally fully operational, or for Regional Environmental Agencies who in most case are carrying out a lot of different monitoring activities across regions. On the opposite side the new monitoring initiative helps in identifying situations of only formal compliance where the reform process was abandoned just after the achievement of the indicator. (Very strong difficulties were experienced by regional administration in the implementation of urban solid waste reform. The only region that succeeded in getting the target at a very early stage seems not to have proceeded to further steps after September 2002, while other regions are now more advanced). In the field of water management instead further steps towards the full implementation of the reform were taken by five out of six regions.

Results and lessons: taking the process forward

The Italian experience in the development and use of territorial indicators to guide decision making offers an interesting ground for comparative analysis. This paper has reviewed the technical and political basis of the selection process of indicators - developed within the EU Community Support Framework and used to support the new strategies for regional development implemented since 1998 - and the implications for policy making.

A twofold approach has been adopted in the use of indicators – a soft and a hard use - in order to tackle the problems resulting both from the incompleteness of information, that prevents from turning desired outcomes into verifiable indicators, and from the fuzziness of causality link between policy actions and objectives.

A *soft use* of context indicators has been adopted for ultimate policy outcomes when both problems were very relevant and could not be overcome. Different aspects of the same phenomenon were captured by a variety of indicators that reflect the multi-dimensional aspects of regional development. Context indicators are aimed at three tasks: a) pinning down regional weaknesses and strengths; b) refining regional policy objectives; c) increasing the accountability of all the stakeholders involved in decision making.

The choice of territorial indicators involved all the relevant actors: central administrations coordinating and monitoring the implementation of the strategy, Regions with a fundamental role in the selection and promotion of projects, highly qualified public and private experts. This approach has contributed to identify regional needs and potential, to refine the objectives and coordinate policy actions, and to increase the responsibility of the administrations implementing the policies.

A *hard use* of indicators, to which rewards and sanctions are linked, has been adopted for intermediate policy objectives concerning institution building, - an essential precondition for the effectiveness of regional policies – when both problems could be more effectively addressed. While the causality link problem was addressed by matching outcomes with responsibilities, these process indicators were heavily affected by the problem of information incompleteness: it was often hard to describe ex-ante in a verifiable way, desired outcomes of institution building. This problem was then tackled by setting, both before and after the choice of targets, knowledge revealing mechanisms through effective partnership among principal and agents.

The use of partnership helped addressing an additional issue which arises when using indicators to assign rewards. A widespread consensus was created which strongly reduced attempts to renegotiate and indeed allowed no renegotiation and prevented legal disputes after rewards and sanctions were decided.

Though both experiences examined in the paper have been successful, the *hard use* of indicators has insofar proved to be more effective.

The *soft use* of indicators in the case of ultimate outcome for citizens and firms has certainly allowed a better focusing of some projects and of policy monitoring. But it must be underlined that the policy debate both at local and national level, is not yet influenced enough by the use of indicators. The strengthening of partnership with private actors is indeed required to make this method more effective.

As for the *hard use* of indicators, it has proved to be very effective both in terms of providing a strong politically-sensitive incentive to Ministers and, especially, to Region's Governors to care about institutional advancement, and of rewarding and sanctioning in a blunt way successful and unsuccessful behaviours: about 2.6 billion euros were allocated through this system and some administrations lost as much as 60 per cent of their potential resources.

Two main limits in using indicators for policy making have been pointed out in the paper. First, the risk exists for the hard use, and could not be fully eliminated through information-revealing mechanism, to interpret formal compliance as substantial achievement. Second, communication to the public and the mass media coverage was insufficient and therefore, the impact of the system of indicators on accountability was inadequate. In the case of institutional indicators, both these problems and the former have been addressed by launching a new initiative to monitor the implementation of the reform processes after the end of the performance reserve mechanism and by giving high visibility to these results through the DPS website.

This initiative stresses the strong role "political judgment" plays on the use of indicators. In a world where policy evaluation is important, there is room for a less ambitious, but fundamental role of indicators in terms of accountability: to enhance the general communication to the public of policy objectives, revealing policy makers' preferences and results in order to improve policy making.

References

Anselmo I., Brezzi M., Raimondo L., Utili F. (2003), Making administrations accountable: the experience of the Italian performance reserve system, paper presented at the fifth European Conference on evaluation of the Structural Funds, Budapest 26/27 June,

(http://europa.eu.int/comm/regional_policy/sources/docconf/budapeval/work/anselmo. doc)

Barca F. (2001), Rethinking partnership in development policies: lessons from a European policy experiment, paper presented at the Conference "Exploring Policy Options for a New Rural America". Kansas City 30 April – 1 May.

Barca F. (2003), Cooperation and Knowledge-pooling in Clusters: Designing Territorial Competitiveness Policies, in Cooperation, Networks and Institutions in Regional Innovation Systems, D. Fornahl and T. Brenner eds., Edward Elgar Publishing.

Brezzi M., Raimondo L., Utili F. (2004), Competition and accountability in the 6 per cent performance reserve system in Italy, paper presented at the 6th Conference of the European Evaluation Society, Berlin 30 September – 2 October.

Dipartimento per le Politiche di Sviluppo, Ministero dell'Economia e delle Finanze (2004), Premi e sanzioni per le politiche di sviluppo: analisi dei meccanismi di premialità, February, Rome, Italy (www.dps.tesoro.it).

Dipartimento per le Politiche di Sviluppo, Ministero dell'Economia e delle Finanze (2004), Rapporto Annuale del DPS 2003, Rome, Italy.

HM Treasury, Department for Trade and Industry, Office of the Deputy Prime Minister (2003), A modern regional policy for the United Kingdom, (www.dti.gov.uk/europe/consultation.pdf)

OECD (2003), Conclusions of High Level Meeting of the Territorial Development Policy Committee, Martigny, Switzerland, 25-26 June 2003, (www.oecd.org)

Measuring for Decision Making
Official Statistics for Decision Making and Evaluation: Territorial Indicators

Luigi Biggeri

President, National Institute of Statistics, Italy

Abstract

Mutual dealings and synergy are even more frequent among producers of official statistics and those expressing qualified and clearly outlined demand of statistical information to be used for planning, monitoring and evaluating the activities of the policy. It is even more intense with reference to the needs of technical and methodological support in analysing socio-economical phenomena which is necessary to affect.

The demand for information from those designed to plan and implement interventions at local levels is increasingly aimed at a "micro" knowledge of the territory and very often refers to parts of the territory that go beyond and/or overlap their administrative boundaries.

In this general framework, the urge coming from institutional bodies to greater and more detailed statistical information on the sectors in which they operate is a driving force for the strengthening of the virtuous circle: new demand-new supply.

The paper focus on the role of official statistics in the commitment to these topics, especially items related to actions for Structural Funds, is growing and seems to be heedful to the statistical information needs of public decision-makers towards indicators for assessing the effectiveness of the interventions and, especially, for an in-depth knowledge of the territory. In particular it describes the role of Istat, as the main provider of official information, thus meeting the requirements of reliability, transparency, impartiality, and furthermore being one of the National Statistical System (SISTAN) actors, has always positively met such stimuli, launching cooperation activities with national, regional and local administrations.

The attention to official statistics as a valid support to the actions of policy makers, through a more organic planning for production of statistics, indicators and adequate technical tools, has recently turned into a further concrete cooperation project between Istat and the Ministry of Economy, Finance, Department for Development and Cohesion Policies (DPS). The project title is "Territorial and sectorial statistical information for structural policy 2001-2008"

The increased request gave a strong impulse to the overall supply for statistics, starting up a time where available information are positively exploited and new production tools are used.

The effects of the increase in supply do not go only to the benefit of a *policy maker* or the subject that has demanded for information, but all the people take advantage from them, including scientific community.

Official statistics has to support assessment and monitoring of the actions, but above all has to maintain the culture of assessment that is still not developed very much in Italy. Official statistics can rely on many tools to improve the availability of statistical information: as an example, the use and exploitation of administrative archives (data mining, record linkage e statistical matching) or the use of statistical models (models for the estimates in small areas), the exploitation and the widening of current surveys.

Greater efforts need to be made in order to have policy-makers put forward the demand in a more organic way and, at the same time, to implement resources for the development of official statistics.

The experience made so far is the basis for the development of a dynamic communication system between those who express needs for statistical knowledge, mainly at the territorial level, and those who have to produce statistical information.

Introduction

Nobody has ever doubted that statistical information and statistical methods are indispensable for taking rational decisions. However for a long time even policy makers have rarely and badly used the statistical information available and, at the same time, producers of official statistics have not always supplied the necessary statistical data, often requested in a not well organized and articulated information demand.

Recently things have changed and governments at different levels are more and more interested in formalizing their decision processes and in evaluating their programmes, activities and especially intervention policies in economic and social areas. There are several reasons for such a renewed interest. One of them is the continuous process of decisional and institutional decentralisation, with a particular attention to territory. Obviously, this implies adequate information and, above all, specific *statistical information systems and indicator sets* that official statistics should implement, in the interest not only of public decision-makers but also of citizens, so that they can exercize a documented democratic control.

Istat, as the major expression of official statistics in Italy, is ever more often called on to play a considerable role in broadening statistical knowledge of social and economic phenomena for decision-making and evaluation purposes at national level. Special emphasis should be placed on deepening territorial dimension, which in Italy is characterized by highly articulated elements and significant gaps in development.

It should be noted that today, as never before, the synergies in progress have been so intense between those who, for institutional reasons, demand for qualified information to orient, direct, monitor and evaluate policy-making and those who provide statistical information, in particular official statistics. In this overall framework, the active push coming from institutional bodies interested in a greater and more detailed statistical information helps us better investigate the fields they operate in and, above all, acts as a driving force to strengthening the vicious circle "new demand–new supply". On the other hand, Istat has always positively reacted to such a push and has more and more often started significant experiences of institutional cooperation in the respect of the principles of reliability, transparency and impartiality required by public statistics.

In this report, a statistical theoretical approach as well as the current policy-makers demand for statistical information will be illustrated with particular focus on the production of sectoral and territorial statistics. In this context, the experience made in the construction of territorial indicators within the Operative Project will be presented. The title of the project is "Territorial and sectoral statistical information for 2001-2008 structural policies", and it is carried out by Istat in collaboration with the Department for development and cohesion policies (DPS) of the Ministry of Economy and Finance. The aim is to highlight how information demand arises, how it is defined and specified, which are the answers as regards the construction of a set of indicators, which are the advantages and which problems are met both in the construction of the indicator system and in their interpretation. To give a reference framework and a logic order to the presentation, we will start recalling the steps that must be implemented to define, carry out and evaluate intervention policies; whereas the development and the principal uses of indicators for the development of regional policies are illustrated by Fabrizio Barca, director of DPS.

Policy definition and evaluation: a statistical theoretical approach

For the reasons mentioned above, the design of policy interventions and their evaluation have become, as it is used to say, a strategic activity at any level since it is an irremissible means:

1. Of s*cientific support for decisional processes* to make more adequate choices and to rationalize interventions, programmes and actions.

2. Of *control* of the feasibility and *effective implementation of the programmed objectives* with interventions and activities, in terms of quantity, costs, efficiency, efficacy, process and product quality and *impact of implemented programmes;*

3. For ensuring a *guarantee function* with reference to users, to the investments made and to the society as a whole.

To specify how *policy intervention design and the ensuing impact evaluation* should be organized, we can refer to the simplified framework illustrated in Picture 1 (Biggeri, 2000):

Framework analysis highlights some important and specific aspects that must be taken into consideration to organize policy design and evaluation. As a matter of fact, it is necessary:

1. To analyze the context and real situation (a good knowledge is required of how the phenomenon works and how the involved units behave), and the problem that we have to face, to correctly plan the policy, the intervention and the connected information system;

2. To simulate the actions on which intervention is based with macro or micro models, in order to highlight and evaluate their possibile consequences, the possible need of modifing the intervention and, in any case, to choose among the various alternative actions;

3. To evaluate each phase of implementation of the actions and the obtained results;

4. To use result and evaluation analyses for learning aims (that within policy evaluation is a very important aspect) and, if necessary, to change the plan and the operative characteristics of the intervention and/or to plan or to improve the information system already available;

5. To disseminate evaluation results also as a means of social control by general public and by interested bodies.

Figure 1. Simplified framework of the design, the implementation and the evaluation of an intervention policy

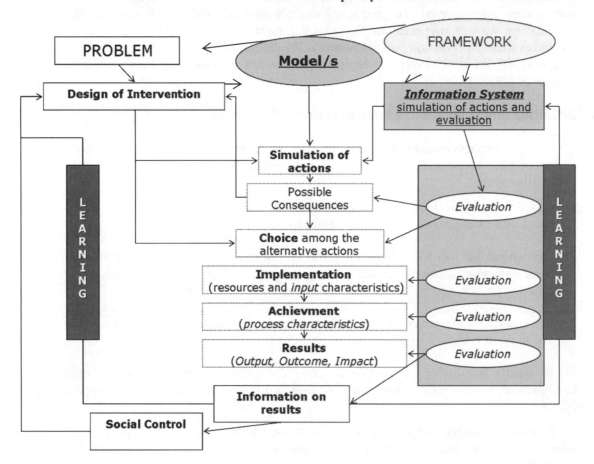

This kind of research is different from others both because of its aims, that are precise and definite, and because of its operative conditions (that involve decisions). Both these elements influence the theoretical design of the research and its practical implementation that, as usual, will have to find an appropriate "compromise" among the three criteria of representativeness, randomisation and realism (the latter in particular for explanatory variable choice).

Fundamentally for these reasons, even considering the experimental approach, the statistical design that better suits the evaluation process is the one called "controlled investigations" design that comprises the almost-experimental designs and the designs effective for observational studies or, in particular, to make comparisons; all these designs often represent ingenious adaptations of experimental designs (obviously releasing some of the criteria and of the hypotheses that are at their basis).

As everyone knows, to project these statistical designs it is essential to deeply know the nature and characteristics of the programme or of the process working model, etc that must be evaluated together with its objectives. For example, it is necessary to know which are the elements that influence programme results and how these elements presumably interact among themselves. Obviously the effects of the different characteristics of the programme and/or of the various elements must be measured using *response variables* strictly connected to the objectives. Undoubtedly, the analysis must be done considering the real operative conditions and consequently the characteristics of the decisional process (as highlighted in figure 1).

It is therefore strategic to define a reference framework of the situation which is the subject of the study and/or a working model, which can be more or less detailed depending on the evaluation aims, the field of interest of the programme and considering the existing economical and sociological theories. If these theories do not exist or are not convincing, it is necessary to use empirical evidence, through a sociological, economic, managerial, engineering study of the organisations and the processes involved in the programme or in the intervention (in this case, the importance of the interdisciplinary cooperation is evident).

Two further considerations derive from the framework.

Firstly, it is necessary to have adequate quantitative and qualitative information presented, if necessary, in an appropriate and pertinent statistical information system for definition and management (of the intervention, etc) and for evaluation; there is no doubt that to plan and evaluate in an objective way, it is necessary first "to measure", then to have adequate measures of the variables of interest and plan the opportune quantitative and qualitative indicators. It is therefore necessary to deeply know the characteristics of data and indicators and also their possible interpretative limitations (expecially if we use proxies of the theoretical indicator, without taking for granted that the supposed associative link between the proxy and the related indicator is unchangeable both in time and space); considering that generally many elements act interdependently to cause results, and it is therefore difficult to isolate the effects caused by each element; taking into account that often there is the need to"standardize" the indicators, to eliminate the effect of the structural characteristics of inputs and/or of the reference framework.

Secondly, for interpretation purposes, we always have to remember that evaluation aims at understanding if the policy (the intervention) implemented has reached its planned objective, modifing the phenomenon or, rather, the conditions and/or the behaviours of individuals belonging to the reference population observed in the real situation. As various authors underline, the fundamental methodological problem of an impact evaluation is that generally it cannot be reduced to measure only changes of a phenomenon or of behaviours between the previous situation and the situation after the intervention. Unless the *coeteribus paribus* condition is respected, this difference is not only attributable to the implemented policy or to the realized intervention, but it also depends on a variety of elements, among which the typical development of the phenomenon, apart from the intervention itself. What we have to measure is the *net contribution* of the intervention, in other words the difference between what happened after the implemented policy (*factual event*) and what would have happened without that policy (*counterfactual event*).

Policy-makers' demand for statistical information: Istat efforts to satisfy the requests

As already mentioned, after a long period characterized by a substantial lack of quantitative and in particular evaluation culture, in Italy a new approach is now being asserted, more oriented towards the measurement of phenomena and its use for correct policy-making.

Istat has tried and tries to meet this demand by fostering the overall growth of the National Statistical System (SISTAN) through the National Statistical Programme and the work of sectoral "quality groups". In addition, Istat[1] organises every year the National Statistical Conference, a significant moment where producers and users of official statistical information convene to discuss as well as to share methods, experiences and perspectives for a more effective meeting between demand and supply of public statistics. Moreover for over ten years Istat has drafted an Annual Report that is an occasion for an evidence-based reflection on Italy's economic and social situation and for a comparison with other countries' situations and trends.

The Report does not only deal with Italy's macroeconomic evolution but it also contains detailed analyses on business competitiveness, labour market effectiveness and productivity, features of the welfare system and so on. The Report preparation is also an opportunity to check the quality and consistency of different data on the same phenomenon as well as data on different phenomena arising from different statistical sources. In the end, the Report highlights the most important results obtained from statistical surveys (thus increasing the value added in the presentation of the results of each single survey) and provides possible solutions to problems of economic and social policy.

Today, however, to meet policy-makers' demand for statistical information Istat more and more often participates in ad-hoc conventions with Ministries, Regions etc, that envisage the implementation of statistical information systems for decision-making and for evaluating the impact that action policies have on specific fields.

However, the context shows the consequences of some important shortcomings. First of all, little importance is given to the planning of information needs that will have to be met subsequently. This is especially true when planning complex evaluation actions, which often suffer from an overlapping of various disciplinary approaches (economic, sociological, political, financial etc.). Secondly, there is a tendency to underestimate the financial resources and the technical-scientific competence necessary to carry out the planned process of measurement/evaluation; furthermore it is on territory that the most important - as well as specific – information needs are expressed even if financial investments and human resources are inadequate in this field.

However, there are also cases of conventions and cooperation relationship that are gaining excellent results, both in the production of regular analysis and evaluation reports and in benchmarking exercises. No doubt, one of them is the cooperation relationship with the DPS of the Ministry for Economy and Finance aimed at building up indicators that can be used for the development of Regional Policies.

---

1   The organisation of the National Statistical Conference is among ISTAT institutional duties as established by paragraph 15 of the Legislative Decree 6 September 1989, no. 322

This kind of activity was requested in 1989 when regional policies had become a community goal, thus emphasising the need for all the actors involved in the implementation and programming processes to be provided with a harmonised statistical information basis. Later, this activity widely developed in the context of the problems connected to measurement and evaluation in coincidence with the start of 2000-2006 cycle of structural funds[2], both to identify areas eligible for funding and to check the criteria for breaking down financial resources.

The main results are contained in the "Programme of Southern Italy Development" (PSM), where the European pushes to the programming of development policies have been implemented in Italy in an original way, through a marked theoretical and quantitative approach in relation to the past. In this document there is a macroeconomic model containing the main instrument-objective relations through which to develop a new policy of public investments based on:

- renunciation of past welfarism

- enhancement of the existing strengths

- a system of indicators for the measurement of the planned objectives

- the relation between the impact of priority actions and the overall objective

Moreover an attempt was made to clarify the link between the choices made in regional and national programmes (POR) and the overall objectives established for the entire economy of Southern Italy.

The first experiences have then enabled us to launch a new phase of activities and studies aimed at supporting official statistics for decision-making through a more organic programme for the production of statistics, indicators and adequate technical tools. This has led to the already mentioned project "Territorial and Sectoral Statistical Information for the 2001-2008 structural policies" whose basic characteristics will be presented below in this report.

Such a project, that develops in a wide time lag (September 2001-December 2008) long enough to fulfil the objectives set, represents only one of the numerous experiences that Istat has been carrying out in this field. But perhaps the most representative characteristics of this project are its being an in-depth study of statistical information on territory and its implementation according to the logical framework of Figure 1, as illustrated above.

The project "Territorial and sectorial indicators for structural policies"

The project mentioned above is co-financed by Istat (30%) and Structural Funds for Objective 1 areas (70%) and aims to contribute to the overall objective of increasing and improving statistical information, especially at territorial level, so that the effects of structural programmes can be better measured.

Although this project represents one of Istat's strategic activities in partnership, it is not the only one. During the last few years many other relevant and qualified activities have been settled such as designing the information system on Handicap and Child labour

2   In programming Structural Funds for 1994-99, Istat launched a project entitled "Information systems for local/territorial policies" aiming at producing detailed statistical information at local level. The project has not been developed much both for the reduced funds and the limited time horizon.

within the social policy. Furthermore it has to be mentioned how relevant the surveys on Health and Social Services supply at territorial level is, which will allow the development of other two information subsystems.

In the case of the project on Territorial and Sectoral Statistical Information, the overall objectives of action policies are set at the community level and then adjusted to more specific national objectives. Wider actions at territorial level have emphasised the need for enhancing information and cognitive bases. The increased demand for statistical information arises - above all - from the need to complete and implement the set of "key context" regional indicators and the "breach variables" indicated in the Community Framework of Support for Objective 1 Regions (QCS). These are the primary tools to measure the initial socio-economic situation and the existing structures as well as to monitor progress and results of public interventions towards local development. It is therefore obvious that the main focus of this activity was - and is - what statistical information and what set of indicators are adequate for this kind of measurement and analysis with the aim of continuously improving them. It was thus necessary to study in-depth the methodological design underlying regional indicators for decision-making and evaluation.

Moreover it should be noted that each action of the project focuses on territorial variables and indicators that have been defined in close cooperation with the Department for development and cohesion policies (DPS):

1. Elaboration - for the purpose of programming development policies - of a system of regional economic accounts concerning employment within specific territorial areas (territorial sections, regions, labour local systems), even through the design of estimation models and the connection between preliminary and final series;

2. Updating, control, improvement and implementation of "key context regional indicators" and of "breach variables" since they represent the system of indicators that are at the basis of a process of macro evaluation of the effects of the actions carried out through the Structural Funds;

3. New production of "key context regional indicators" and "breach variables" through the inception of activities linked to the production of basic statistical information in those specific areas that represent community and national priorities (such as poverty and social exclusion, water system, ICT equipment and use by enterprises, etc.);

4. Specific territorial elaborations and production of integrative indicators with a more detailed territorial articulation than that available at the moment (territorial sections, provinces, local labour systems);

The results of the activities implemented by the project until now are a lot. Without going into details[3], it can be said that the work begun at the end of 2001 resulted in the:

---

3   For a more detailed description of the project contents please visit the website http://www.istat.it/Banche-dat/index.htm or refer to the text presented at the VI National Statistical Conference that is available at http://www.istat.it/Eventi/sestaconf/interventi/cuciani.pdf . Moreover on February 2, 2004 a Seminar on the results of the project was held at Istat, Aula Magna. It was also an opportunity to deepen topics which will be dealt with in the next few years. The related documents can be found at http://www.istat.it/Eventi/seminarioterritorio.htm.

- **Production of regional statistical indicators**. This is probably the most relevant activity of the whole project, considering both available resources and the importance the indicators have for the effect evaluation on Objective 1 regions. There are 111 regional indicators (14 "breach variables" and 97 "key context indicators" articulated in six line of intervention provided for by QCS) organized following the Italian regional division and the deriving territorial aggregations; they are available in time series from 1995 until the most recent available datum. This data base is integrated with meta-information that explains the objectives, even to non institutional users. Considering the system of indicators, Istat has the duty of:

  - assuring transparent definitions, classifications, elaboration techniques and evaluation that are agreed at national and international level.

  - harmonizing the indicators considering the Italian context as regards availability and utility in providing information;

- **Estimate of socio-economic aggregates with a greater breakdown than the traditional one**. It is worth noting that big efforts were made to increase the information available for the 784 local employment systems in Italy. In this connection, it is possible to have accurate information about the value added produced and employment by macro sectors of activity, resident population employed, unemployment; these quantities are also available in time series.

- **Enhancement of the existing territorial statistical information**. The most relevant activities regard the production of two territorial data banks containing variables and indicators on infrastructures in Italian provinces (NUTS3) and on the most important socio-economic aggregates available for municipalities (level LAU2).

The potential of the indicators is enormous: they allow us to make temporal and spatial comparisons, more specific sectoral analyses as well as the analysis of regions' convergence towards common or optimum values. On the other hand, when evaluating the effects of intervention programmes, "key context indicators" do not allow us to distinguish the so-called exogenous factors; during a given time lag, changes in economy can be caused by factors that are not linked to the actions carried out through the programmes: the increase in active population may cause an increase in unemployment notwithstanding the employment policies implemented by the Structural Funds.

Other direct and indirect advantages linked to the implementation of the informative system for structural policies

The attention towards territory arises from a general need of phenomenon knowledge in the articulated Italian context still subject to north-south dualism and where often economic and social deviance coexists with situations of excellence. Moreover, territory has become even more important for the implementation of the programmes that are co-financed by Structural Indicators since it is just within territory, and in particular through Regions, that objectives (even though in coherence with national and communitarian levels), policies, actions and result evaluation are determined.

From the point of view of statistical information, territory represents an active variable since it is often correlated with many other phenomena; but also from the point of view of action evaluation it represents an active variable since it can influence success or failure of an action (for instance, the level of infrastructures, human and cultural resources of an area, etc).

Two important elements stem from this situation:

- In the phase of intervention planning, the information available with an adequate territorial detail must be generally wider than the information used for evaluation (for proper and further information about the contextual situation, see figure.1);

- Due to the implicit correlations between territory and social and economic phenomena, it is necessary to study the interrelations between base conditions, tools and the actions to be implemented.

It is therefore clear that official statistics has to supply more statistical information that must be compatible with action government levels. However policy areas do not often coincide with the usual administrative sections (regions, provinces and municipalities) that represent the territorial dominions usually utilized by statistical production. Negotiated programming instruments (territorial pacts, area contracts, programme contracts etc.) and territorial integrated Projects - instruments planned for by Operative Regional Programmes (POR) - focus on local realities sometimes at a sub-municipal level, often at a sub-provincial level and more often they represent sections of territory that overlap administrative divisions.

Therefore information demand that more and more often is required is addressed to "micro" knowledge of territory and on these dominions the possibility to carry out temporal comparisons is also called for, in order to estimate the effects of actions.

Since surveys at territorial level are not always available, this means that it is often necessary to improve and increase the availability of statistical information testing the use of administrative archives (data mining, record linkage and statistical matching), the use of statistical models (estimation models for small areas), the enhancement and the widening of current surveys are only some of the tools that official statistics has to widen knowledge on territory. It deals with the activity of learning and improvement highlighted in Figure 1.

An interesting example in this respect derives from Istat participation in a working group aimed at identifying territorial areas suffering from industrial crises. After a preliminary experimental phase based on the analysis of statistical provincial indicators, a more detailed territorial dimension (local labour systems) was examined. The strength that allowed us to apply an original methodology for the identification of critical areas has been the availability of new data and indicators based on local labour systems, a territorial entity more suitable to underline critical situations than the provincial dimension which often, due to its administrative nature, hides phenomena that occur in circumscribed areas.

From the point of view of learning and improvement, another result (output) which is not explicitly represented, but not less important, regards the possibility of systematizing the boost coming from the new demand expressed by the Institutional actors. As a matter of fact, it is clear that improvements in methodology and production (also in the improvement of production timeliness of territorial statistics) - both obtained and to be obtained - will become a part of the ordinary supply in order to enhance official statistics as a whole. In this context we have to remember that many of the activities provided for by the project are already an integral part of the National Statistical Programme (NSP).

It is clear that a new demand for territorial statistical information cannot be met only through its production and/or dissemination but goes together with an intense activity of organisation, analysis, elaboration in the kind of "what happens if" and therefore with the need to supply clear decision-making instruments. Therefore Istat has to manage technical assistance activities and accompanying measures, studies and enhancement of detailed territorial data bases (municipalities and local labour systems).

Finally, the publication of statistical information, reports and analyses has - and will have - considerable consequences for local actors and all the other actors involved in local development; in the future, through a wide dissemination of the obtained results, they will have a great availability of social and economic statistics at a regional or – in many cases - sub-regional levels and the citizens can have a social control over the interventions. Increased territorial information has both a direct and indirect impact. If it is true that those who have demanded for specific information are the first users of it, it is also true that the indirect effects on the whole population are far from being irrelevant, also for the scientific world or for their use in various contexts.

In particular, the demand for territorial statistics has generated at least three types of impacts:

1. A relational impact, meaning an intense cooperation activity and an exchange of territorial data and methodologies among the various competent sections of Istat; which has surely contributed to increase sensitiveness to the topics of territorial data and indicators.

2. An institutional impact, through the involvement and sensitisation of other administrations or bodies to the provision and production of territorial data; which has contributed to disseminate a "good practice" model of institutional relationships within Istat and Sistan for data production and information sharing.

3. An external impact to meet the demand for information on territorial indicators coming from other actors not directly involved in policy-making (local authorities, universities, students, enterprises, etc.). Moreover, a contribution to the achievement of this goal has been the improvement of data accessibility (internet, paper publishing) for a wider range of users.

The attention that Istat is giving to territory in the production of official statistics proves how urging the problem is. Much can - and will - be done in the next years to improve the information available for evaluators, policy makers as well as the academic and scientific world.

Open issues and final conclusions

The activities and products of this project testify the pivotal role that official statistics plays to support evaluation and policy. Besides, it confers an important appreciation to Istat professionalism. This experience represents a change of course in the relationship between official statistics and the subjects involved in policy choices: in the past these two worlds were nearly detached and the dialogue between them took place in the distance; nowadays the need for correct, transparent, impartial and public statistics represents a crucial element for a more conscious implementation of the activities whose aim is the development of our country.

Many are, however, the issues to be solved before fully reaching the goal of production and dissemination of territorial statistical indicators. First of all, it should be stressed that the functions of those who design indicators able to measure or to evaluate policy effects need to be better integrated with the functions of those who are (then) called on to implement them. Such an exchange of competence can prevent, on the one hand, the risk of a bad or distorted reading of the indicators; on the other hand, it is functional to identify the best result among the possible ones.

It is, therefore, necessary to point at a more systematic demand from institutional bodies not only through coordinating the needs of the subjects that express it (central administrations, regions, local authorities), but also through setting up common rules and schemes to be applied in the various contexts of evaluation and monitoring. All this aimed at optimising the limited resources available.

Another possibility is to improve basic surveys in general. Looking carefully at the territorial dimension, while programming, can affect future production costs as well as the enhancement of quality in basic information. Following this view, awareness in Sistan bodies needs to be increasingly raised, especially in the Regions which are often a not-yet explored information source, and it may also be obtained by strengthening the functions of the "quality groups" envisaged for the drawing up of the National Statistical Programme (NSP).

Last, but not least, the issue of the resources available needs to be mentioned. In Italy, considerably few resources are devoted to the production of official statistics and to research activity in general, which of course is a very critical point.

The prevailing idea is that information is a good and not a cost; it is rather something all the people have or need to have. Unfortunately, this is increasingly less true and it is even less true when information is required at a detailed territorial level. Efforts should be made to increase the resources available. It is therefore indispensable that those responsible for development actions, especially Regions, include in their budget the necessary means to increase the information basis that can be used for more correct and punctual evaluation and monitoring. This is even truer in view of the new programming cycle of the Structural Funds, a large share of which has currently been allocated to the Regions through the POR.

The growing complexity of development policies - in terms of variety of areas involved, interventions at detailed territorial levels, cognitive needs for programming, evaluation and monitoring – challenges official statistics and the National Statistical System in terms of efforts, projects, survey methodologies, coordination and resources to be used. In this changing context, we cannot ignore the implications that will arise from the reform process of EU structural policies after the enlargement to 25 Member States and the mounting request for subsidiarity coming from Regions in programming their structural policies.

The above mentioned project is considerably improving data and territorial statistical indicator availability while keeping a high-degree reliability, typical of official statistics. But to improve the culture of measurement, in particular about territory - as everyone is expecting - all the actors involved have to give their indispensable contribution.

If from one side we ask for systematic, well projected and adequately financed territorial statistical information, from the other side it is the duty of official statistics and of all the Sistan bodies to direct and to manage this demand, using the highest number of available resources. From the confluence of these two urges, we expect a better knowledge of territory and the availability of adequate indicators for implementation and control of development policies. In other words, a better service for society and our country in the next few years.

References

Biggeri L., Problemi riguardanti la misura statistica per le valutazioni delle politiche, in Rivista Italiana di Economia, Demografia e Statistica, Roma, Ottobre-Dicembre 2000.

Cipe, "Orientamenti per la programmazione degli investimenti nel periodo 2000-2006 per lo sviluppo del Mezzogiorno", Delibera n.71/99 del 14/5/99;

Cipe, "Programma Statistico Nazionale", Delibera n.97/2001 del 15/11/2001

ISTAT, I sistemi locali del lavoro 1991, Roma 1997;

ISTAT, Programma Statistico Nazionale, triennio 2002/2004, Roma 2001;

Ministero del Tesoro, del Bilancio e della Programmazione Economica , Programma di Sviluppo del Mezzogiorno (PSM), Roma, 30 settembre 1999;

Ministero dell'Economia e delle Finanze, "Quadro Comunitario di Sostegno per le regioni italiane Obiettivo 1 2000-2006";

Ministero dell'Economia e delle Finanze, Programma Operativo Nazionale "Assistenza tecnica e Azioni di sistema", Roma, gennaio 2001;

Ministero dell'Economia e delle Finanze, Programma Operativo Nazionale "Assistenza tecnica e Azioni di sistema" per le Regioni Obiettivo 1 2000-2006- Complemento di programmazione, Roma, 16 luglio 2002;

Pellegrini G., Fondi Strutturali 2000-2006: il contributo del gruppo di contatto, Giornale del Sistan n.13 2000, Roma.

Measures of Australia's Progress – A Case Study of a National Report Based on Key Economic, Social and Environment Indicators

Dennis Trewin, National Statistician, Australian Bureau of Statistics

Jon Hall, Australian Bureau of Statistics

Introduction

Measuring a nation's progress - providing information about whether life is getting better - is one of the most important tasks that a national statistical agency can take on. For almost 100 years, the Australian Bureau of Statistics has been measuring Australia's progress through the multitude of statistics we publish relating to Australia's economy, society and environment. However, for the most part, our statistical publications have tended to focus on each of these three broad areas in isolation.

To address this issue and to contribute factual information to the discussion on progress, the Australian Bureau of Statistics (ABS) has produced two volumes of Measures of Australia's Progress (MAP) the most recent in April 2004. It plans to update the publication on an annual basis. The United Kingdom Department of Environment publication "Quality of Life Counts" has provided something of a model.

It was an intentionally experimental publication. I noted in the Foreword that the project was ambitious, and one that would develop over time. We sought comments and received a lot of feedback, most of it favourable. This encouraged us to continue with the development.

In this paper, I will provide more information on the driving force that led to MAP, describe the publication; the underlying logic and the reasons we chose this logic; the indicators and the steps we undertook to agree on the indicators. I will also describe the public reaction, both positive and negative, and the influence the publication has had particularly on policy debate.

Of course, there are lessons learned from an experiment like this and they are summarised. Finally, I will outline our future plans with MAP and possible international links.

What Drove MAP?

Recent years have seen growing public interest in the interrelationships between economic, social and environmental aspects of life. There have been, for example, debates about the sustainability of economic growth and a recognition that the environment is neither an inexhaustible source of raw materials nor capable of absorbing an unlimited amount of waste. Similarly, progress relates to social concerns such as health, education and crime and whether and how economic growth benefits those areas. The 1992 Earth Summit in Rio de Janeiro was a catalyst for discussion, as were calls for better measures of social concerns to supplement the System of National Accounts. There is a great deal of interest as well in developing a broader set of economic statistics that give values to things hitherto left outside the traditional economic system. Around the world a consensus is growing that countries and governments need to develop a more comprehensive view of progress, rather than focusing mainly on economic indicators such as Gross Domestic Product (GDP).

Because of these interests we co-hosted a significant and well attended conference in 1997 on "Measuring Progress: Is Life Getting Better?" (Eckersley, 1998). The Conference was attended by many eminent Australians who agreed that we needed better measures of progress. It was generally agreed that there had been too much emphasis on GDP. Whilst it was seen as a very important element of progress, it was not sufficient to rely mostly on GDP as a measure of progress. However, there was not agreement on the best way of doing this. Some preferred a composite indicator such as the Genuine Progress Indicator but others rejected that approach because of the value judgments involved. I also presented an approach based around extensions to the national accounts such as the Statistics Netherlands SESAME approach (see Keuning, 1997). Whilst this was seen as a very useful analytical tool, it was both data and labour intensive and only likely to give information on progress in selected domains. The third approach was a "suite of indicators" approach and that is what was finally adopted. The suite contains economic, social and environmental indicators.

In our application of the suite of indicators approach, key aspects of progress are set out side-by-side and the discussed links between them discussed; readers make their own evaluations of whether the indicators together imply that Australia is on balance progressing and at what rate. The approach makes no overall assessment about whether the array of statistical indicators presented implies that life is getting better or worse. Instead, the suite of indicators leaves each individual reader to apply their own values and preferences to the evidence, and to arrive at their own overall assessment of national progress.

Although we adopted the suite of indicators approach, it is not without its problems. The choice of indicators could not be made using statistical criteria alone; it has required us to exercise judgment albeit based on the views of experts. Any of thousands of measures of progress could have been chosen, but we present just 13 headline dimensions, most of which use one headline indicator. Although we explain the criteria we have used to select indicators, there is a large element of judgment, both in choosing the dimensions of progress to include and in choosing the statistical measures for those dimensions of progress. These issues are discussed in more depth in Section 4.

What Does the Publication Look Like?

The best way of doing this is to describe the main contents. I will use the "health" dimension for illustration purposes. It comprises the following.

- An essay describing the ABS approach to describing progress and why it chose the suite of indicators rather than alternative approaches. The essay also describes the process for choosing the dimensions of progress and the criteria for selecting representative indicators of progress.

- An essay outlining a framework for measuring progress.

1. Environmental progress equates to a reduction of threats to the environment and improvements in the health of our ecosystems.

2. Economic progress equates to enhancing the nation's income (broadly Australians' real per capita levels of consumption) while at least maintaining (or possibly enhancing) the national wealth that will support future consumption.

3. Social progress equates to increases in the wellbeing of the population; a reduction of threats to, and increases in social cohesion; and protection and enhancement of democratic rights.

It then goes on to describe the most important dimensions of progress within each of these domains. These are outlined in Annex 1. It also discusses the most important aspect of each dimension as a prelude to choosing an indicator. Box 1 provides an example for health.

Box 1.

Health: An indicator describing how long Australians live while simultaneously taking into account the full burden of illness and disability, would be a desirable summary measure of progress. But although such indicators have been developed they are not available as a time series. Life expectancy at birth is one of the most widely used indicators of population health. It focuses on length of life rather than its quality, but it usefully summarises the health of the population.

- There is a chapter on Population to provide contextual information about population and its composition (e.g. age, sex, ethnicity) and its geographic distribution. Population has an important influence on many dimensions of progress and is used as a denominator in some indicators.

- The bulk of the publication is made up of discussion of each dimension and the indicators. On average, there are about seven pages per dimension which is a mixture of text, graphs, tables and boxes. There is an underlying structure of:

  - key points

  - progress and the headline indicator (includes discussion of other indicators)

  - some differences within Australia

  - factors influencing change

  - links to other dimensions of progress

    Boxes are used to highlight particular points of importance.

    Table 1 describes the chosen domains and headline indicators.

- Two essays on issues of particular interest

  - multiple disadvantage

  - comparisons of progress indicators with other (selected) countries.

  The full publication is available on the ABS web site (www.abs.gov.au).

Table 1: Dimensions and Indicators of Progress

DIMENSION	HEADLINE PROGRESS INDICATOR
Health	Life Expectancy at Birth
Education and Training	People aged 25-64 with a vocational or higher education qualification
Work	Unemployment rate
National Income	Real net disposable income per capita
Financial Hardship	Average real equalised average weekly disposable income of households in the second and third deciles of the income distribution
National Wealth	Real national net worth per capita
Housing	No headline indicator (but a data based discussion of housing)
Productivity	Multifactor productivity
The Natural Landscape	Threatened birds and animals; annual area of land cleared; salinity, assets at risk in areas affected by salinity; proportion of water management areas where use exceeded 70% of sustainable yield
The Human Environment	Fine particle concentrations, days health standards exceeded
Oceans and Estuaries	No headline indicator but several supplementary indicators are discussed
International Environmental Concerns	Net greenhouse gas emissions
Family, Community and Social Cohesion	No headline indicator but a range of supplementary indicators are discussed
Crime	Victims of personal and household crimes
Governance, Democracy and Citizenship	No headline indicator but a range of supplementary indicators are discussed

The Underlying Logic

Choosing the concept: progress, wellbeing, sustainability and the like

Different commentators in this field start from different primary concepts, which include the following.

- **Progress**, which considers whether aspects of life - environmental, social and economic - are improving.

- **Quality of life**, which is linked strongly to (sometimes synonymous with) wellbeing and can also be used in a collective sense to describe how well a society satisfies people's wants and needs.

- **Wellbeing or welfare**, which is generally used to mean the condition of being well, contented and satisfied with life. It typically includes material, physical, social and spiritual aspects of life.

- **Sustainability**, which considers whether an activity or condition can be maintained indefinitely. Although it has most commonly been used when considering the human impact on environmental systems (as in "sustainable fishing"), it can also be extended to economic and social systems.

There is, of course, a good deal of inter-relationship between these concepts.

Measuring Australia's Progress focused on progress. We chose progress for several reasons.

Measuring progress meant considering whether things were moving in the right direction or not. It did not require us to announce whether a certain level or pattern of activity is sustainable. This is a far more difficult question. The ABS did not feel confident about pronouncing on sustainable development when there is little consensus among experts about the term, other than in very general terms. Consider, for instance, greenhouse emissions. Most would agree that, other things equal, a reduction in greenhouse emissions represents progress. But, because of the uncertainties around global warming, it would be much harder to reach agreement about whether the reduced level of emissions was sustainable over the longer-term.

Second, a focus on progress allowed us to give more prominence to the health of the economy and environment than would usually be covered in a project focused on wellbeing or quality of life. It is unlikely that a discussion about wellbeing (used in its traditional sense) would cover economic indicators of productivity or competitiveness for example.

Choosing an audience

The target audience will help dictate the contents, and so a key decision early on must be: for whom are we measuring progress? Possible audiences include policy makers; academics and other experts; and the general public. Each group has rather different requirements and the ABS already serves them in different ways.

Policy makers want statistical information to help them formulate and evaluate policy. And the ABS has a clear role in informing government policy, although we are careful not to evaluate it.

Academics and experts want statistical information to assist their work and research. The ABS already releases very detailed information on many aspects of life that would feature in any discussion on progress: health, income, the environment say. We felt a measuring progress style project is not the place to repeat that level of detail.

The public want statistical information to enhance and inform discussion and decision-making. Many of the statistics the ABS release are of interest to the general public, and some of our publications are targeted at a very wide audience. *Whether life is getting better* is a question in which everyone is potentially interested. It is also a natural precursor to that most important national debate "Where is Australia heading, and do we like the direction?"

Measuring Australia's Progress was targeted at the general public. We were careful to ensure that the publication looked at the nation's, not the government's progress, and so avoided looking at indicators tied to certain policies. But there has been wide interest in the publication from both policy departments and academics.

Choosing the basic approach

We are aware of three main approaches used in this field.

The suite-of-indicators approach sets out key aspects of progress side-by-side and discusses the links between them; readers make their own evaluations of whether the indicators together imply that a country is on balance progressing and at what rate. There is an element of subjectivity in such an approach. The choice of indicators cannot be made using statistical criteria alone; it requires some judgment both in choosing the dimensions of progress to include and in choosing the statistical measures for those dimensions of progress.

The one-number approach combines information about progress across a number of fronts (such as health, wealth and the environment) into a single composite indicator. Such composite indicators can be set in contrast with narrower indicators such as GDP. A good deal of effort has been put into trying to develop a single measure of progress (most notably the Genuine Progress Indicator, Cobb and Halstead 1995), and the Human Development Index but not everyone is convinced of their merit or whether their compilation is an appropriate function for a national statistical office.

Composite indicators have their drawbacks. First, the choice of the components is subjective. Second, movements in composite indicators are difficult to interpret: when presented with an indicator moving in a certain direction, an obvious question to ask is "which components are driving the movement?" Answering that question requires stepping back towards a suite of indicators style analysis. And third, difficulties arise when one wishes to combine several indicators into one number. There is usually not a common measuring unit (e.g. dollars) used across the indicators.

The accounting framework approach presents social, economic and environmental data in one unified system of accounts, measured in various units. Potentially this is a powerful tool for analysts, and a detailed set of accounts will complement indicators. However, such a complex system may be too difficult to interpret for anyone wishing quickly to form an overall view of progress. Most importantly, such an approach requires a great deal of data and is difficult to construct. The Dutch System of Economic and Social Accounting Matrices and Extensions (SESAME) is the most advanced systems of integrated accounts that we are aware of (Keuning 1997).

Measuring Australia's Progress used the suite of indicators approach.

Choosing Dimensions of Progress

Whichever approach one uses, to understand progress one must examine many aspects of people's lives - their health, the quality of their environment, their incomes, their work and leisure, their security from crime, and so on. So progress is multidimensional. Moreover, the dimensions of progress are intertwined. To earn more income, people may need to work longer hours and so have less leisure time. Increased industrial activity may generate more money to spend on health care, but it might also lead to more air pollution and hence to poorer health. In order to measure progress one needs first to select the dimensions of progress that should be measured. Only then can one choose a statistical measure for each. It is important to recognise that any publication using a suite of indicators will necessarily be both partial and selective - partial because not every dimension of progress is included and selective because progress in each of the included dimensions is measured using just one or two indicators.

Selecting the dimensions of progress to be measured is arguably the most difficult part of a project. The statistician's job is to recognise and minimise the inherent subjectivity in choosing dimensions. Two approaches are key. First, it is important to recognise there are many ways of looking at the world and that the statistician's view is not the only one. Second, it is important to be open about how the dimensions of progress were chosen. It is perhaps inevitable that there will always be those who disagree with the choices you have made: what is important is they have some understanding of why those choices were made.

It is also important to recognise that society's views of progress, and of what is important, change over time, and that there are also some aspects of progress - governance and democracy, for example - that are seen as important now, but for which there are no agreed statistical measures yet.

Consultation

Whichever approach is taken, it is likely that anyone undertaking a project in this field will want to consult widely about aspects of the project, particularly the areas of progress that should be measured. There are at least three broad ways of taking on board the views of the world outside the statistical office, all of which should probably be used to greater or lesser degrees.

- referring to international standards or practice;

- referring to current policy issues and debates; or

- referring to the views of stakeholders and the general public.

Listening to the views of stakeholders was particularly important in MAP's development. Giving stakeholders some ownership in the publication was almost as valuable a determinant of the publication's success as the advice they gave. A Reference Group of experts was established to help us develop MAP but there was also extensive public consultation.

Choosing the progress dimensions in Measuring Australia's Progress

The progress dimensions presented in MAP were chosen in three key steps.

First, we defined three broad domains of progress (social, economic and environmental). Second, we compiled a list of potential dimensions of progress within each of the three domains. Third, we chose a subset of what were determined to be the most important dimensions for which we would try to find indicators. This was an iterative process and several steps were revisited after listening to the views of the many people we consulted during the publication's development.

From domains to dimensions

To identify the major dimensions, the three domains were considered in detail and partitioned into a number of dimensions of progress to ensure that the important aspects of economic, social and environmental progress were considered.

Economy. We began with the systems of economic accounting that guide the ABS program of economic statistics, and concentrated on the major stock and flow variables represented in those systems. Our aim was to find one primary flow variable (which would express changes in the volume of Australia's economic activity) and one primary stock variable (which would express changes in Australia's wealth). In the first release, other economic indicators are provided as supplements to these two key measures of economic progress. In the second release, productivity was also included as one of the dimensions given its key role in economic progress.

Society. We began by considering key dimensions of social concern, which are underlaid by a view of fundamental human needs and aspirations. The ABS program of social statistics is guided by a social concerns framework, the design of which has drawn on many other frameworks and initiatives, such as those developed by the UN, the OECD and the EU.

Environment. We began by considering major ecosystems and environmental resources that are recognised in international frameworks such as the System of Economic and Environmental Accounting.

Once a list of dimensions of progress that might be presented had been compiled, we selected the subset that would be presented. A balance had to be struck – if we showed too many indicators, readers would not be able to assimilate them; if we showed too few, important aspects of progress would be omitted, and the overall picture might be biased. Ten to twenty indicators seemed about right, and the choice of those 10–20 headline dimensions was guided by the expert group and ABS subject matter specialists as well as public consultations. We also selected some supplementary dimensions (dimensions that were judged less important but still necessary to investigate for those wanting a more comprehensive overview of progress).

Choosing the indicators of progress

The next step is to find indicators to express the dimensions of progress. Ideally, we were seeking to find just one headline indicator to measure progress in each dimension.

A useful first step is to take each dimension of progress in turn, and ask "Why is this dimension particularly important to the nation's progress? What are the key facets of progress in this dimension that any headline indicator should seek to express?" See Box 1 above for an illustration with the Health dimension.

There will be some subjectivity in this process but that subjectivity can be reduced by agreeing to a set of criteria on which indicator selection will be based. For Measuring Australia's Progress we used a number of criteria (see Annex 2), some of which are commonly used for selecting any good statistical indicator. Others were designed especially for MAP: two of these *ad hoc* criteria were particularly influential in deciding the final indicator set.

Indicators should focus on the **outcome**, rather than, say, the inputs or other influences that generated the outcome, or the government and other social responses to the outcome. For example, an outcome indicator in the health dimension should if possible reflect people's actual health status and not, their dietary or smoking habits or public and private expenditure on health treatment and education. Input and response variables are of course important to understanding why health outcomes change, but the outcome itself must be examined when one is assessing progress.

We also judged it was important that movements in any indicator could be **unambiguously associated with progress**. For instance, one might consider including the number of divorces as an indicator for family life. But an increase in that number is ambiguous - it might reflect, say, a greater prevalence of unhappy marriages, or greater acceptance of dissolving unhappy marriages. Applying this no-ambiguity criterion depends crucially on interpreting movements in one indicator, assuming that the other indicators of progress are unchanged. For example, some would argue that economic growth has, at times, brought environmental problems in its wake, or even that the problems were so severe that the growth was undesirable. Others would argue that strong environmental protection might be retrograde to overall progress because it hampers economic growth. However, few would argue against economic growth or strong environmental protection if every other measure of progress was unaffected: that is, if growth could be achieved without environmental harm, or if environmental protection could be achieved without impeding economic growth.

Presenting the work

There are, of course, many ways in which work might be presented. The progress indicators provide the building blocks to which readers can apply their own evaluations to assess whether a nation is on balance progressing and at what rate. Readers can use a publication in three ways to assess progress:

- first, by examining the data and reading comments about each indicator's historical movements;

- second, by reading the discussion of links between indicators; and

- third, by reading the comments about factors that influence change and the national assets that may support future progress.

Although data can be presented in a variety of ways and the comments made about the progress indicators can vary, some common features are important and should be discussed for each. These are described in Section 3.

Disaggregated national data

Although an aspect of life for a nation as a whole may be progressing or regressing, the rate of change - or even its direction - may not be mirrored in every region, or in every industry or every population subgroup. One cannot discuss every difference within a country for every indicator. But one can discuss some of the more significant differences and provide signposts to the more detailed and disaggregated data sets underlying the indicators.

Direction and rate of change

Both the direction and rate of change in a progress indicator are important. It is informative to see whether an indicator is increasing or decreasing, but the rate of increase is also informative, particularly when compared with historical rates.

Past, present and future

Each indicator might focus on progress during the recent past (typically the past ten years in MAP). Where possible, though, reference should be made to progress over the longer term. Some indicators move only slowly, and so a longer time horizon is needed to perceive any appreciable change. For other indicators, the longer lasting trends that are of greatest interest are overlaid by cyclical and other short term variation (e.g. the business cycle or regular climatic patterns such as El Niño).

How the indicators relate to one another

Each aspect of progress is related, either directly or indirectly, to most of the others. Change in one dimension of progress is typically accompanied by change elsewhere. Therefore it is important to consider the full array of indicators together.

Broadly, we may think of two types of relationship between different areas of progress - trade-offs and reinforcements.

- *Trade-offs* occur when one area of progress improves at the expense of another. In some cases, trade-offs arise after a change of preference: spending on education might be cut, for example, to give more money to health. But they also occur as flow-on effects: for example, economic activity rises and so might greenhouse gas emissions.

- *Reinforcements* occur when one aspect of progress improves and strengthens another. For example, as economic production rises, so might employment.

In reality, the overall effect of a change in any one dimension is much more complex. An intricate system of trade-offs and reinforcements come into play when any dimension of progress changes. Suppose, for example, that factory output increases. This generates more income, and so there is more money to pay for health care, for instance. But increased factory output might also increase air pollution, which is harmful to people's health or might be detrimental to other economic activity such as agriculture. Although within the indicator commentary one might mention some of the more obvious links, it is not practicable to mention every relationship. Rather, one should remind readers that there are many possible links between indicators.

Public Reaction to Measures of Australia' Progress

Projects such as MAP are still quite new, potentially politically sensitive, and require some subjectivity. One of the ABS's greatest assets is its political independence. Without this independence and trust in the way we exercise this independence, it would almost certainly have been very difficult to prepare a publication such as MAP without compromising our statistical integrity.

The public reaction to MAP was overwhelmingly positive. Nevertheless, during the development of Measuring Australia's Progress, three areas provided a particular challenge and not everyone was happy with what we did. They are:

- subjective indicators;

- poverty as a dimension of progress;

- the overall balance of numbers of economic, environmental and social indicators.

1. Subjective Indicators

During MAP's development, there was a good deal of discussion about whether the publication should include some subjective indicators, most notably a measure of happiness. Although the ABS of course agreed that the way people feel – be it about themselves, their country or society – is important in any assessment of progress, the measurement of these feelings presents a very real challenge to statisticians. It is particularly difficult to measure change over time in these areas: improvements in living standards (income say) might bring increased happiness for a short time. But after one gets used to life with a higher income, a subjective statistical indicator might suggest we feel no more or less happy than before. But that is not to say that if we moved back to the lower, original, income we wouldn't feel less happy.

MAP broke the world into dimensions of progress that, although linked to one another, are discrete: health is conceptually distinguishable from education which is distinguishable from biodiversity *etc*. But in this context, happiness is not a separate entity. On the one hand, happiness may be seen as a summation or integrating concept - it depends (to a degree at least) on all the other progress dimensions taken together. On the other hand, happiness may be seen as a super dominant concept - if we were able to judge that happiness had indeed increased then we might be tempted to assert that there had been progress almost regardless of what had happened in the other dimensions. Thus happiness appears to occupy a different part of the semantic space from our headline dimensions. (Happiness measures in Australia have shown little change over the last 50 years!)

2. Measuring Poverty

Although it is probably important that the distribution of income is discussed in any assessment of national progress, choosing a headline indicator for poverty is particularly difficult. The very word "poverty" is loaded and without an agreed definition. Moreover poverty is both an absolute and relative concept. It is absolute because there is arguably some absolute level of income below which one can be considered to be poor. And it is relative because that *poverty level* will depend - or so many people believe - on the income of others in society.

When assessing progress in this dimension a statistical agency might choose to use a progress indicator that focuses on the absolute income of the poorest members of society, rather than consider changes in the income gap between rich and poor. Although this measure meets our criteria for unambiguity (in that an increase in income among the poorest in society would be viewed by everyone as unambiguously good) it is also controversial: by using this measure the statistical agency could be accused of siding with those who view poverty as an absolute and not a relative concept. However, if the statistical agency decides to associate reductions in relative poverty with progress - perhaps measuring progress with the Gini coefficient - they run the risk of using an indicator that not everyone sees as an unambiguous measure of progress: some might argue that movement towards a more even distribution of income is not progress, because it removes some of the incentives to work harder.

In Measuring Australia's Progress we used an absolute measure of poverty as our headline indicator: we looked at the real income of the poorest Australians, and felt few would argue that a rise in this indicator did not represent progress. But the commentary for this dimension also discussed the concept of relative poverty (and the distributional aspects of other variables).

3. Balance

As MAP began to take shape we realised there were going to be rather more indicators that were primarily environmental and social than there were economic indicators. We wanted to ensure that the publication was seen to be balanced, and so we explained why the number of indicators associated with a domain was not a measure of the domain's relative importance to overall national progress. We explained that: "Just two headline indicators - national income and national wealth - were used to encapsulate economic progress. They consolidate major flows and stocks relevant to national progress." There was no similarly compact set of indicators to encapsulate progress in the social and environmental domains. Not everyone who read the publication understood this however.

The publication received a good deal of coverage in the Australian press. And so it went some way to achieving its main objective: to stimulate and inform debate. Nearly all of the coverage has been favourable but MAP attracted one quite prominent critic, who claimed that the ABS had fallen unwitting victim to a broadly green and left wing agenda and was not balanced. He was particularly concerned that "environment" was treated as a domain of the same status as "economic" and "social" when opinion polling showed the public regarded the environment as far less important than social and economic issues. The critic also cited as proof the imbalance between numbers of environmental and economic indicators and what he saw as lack of balance in the Reference Group.

He went on to claim that the ABS had no right to measure progress because it was inherently subjective, and therefore, not suitable territory for a national statistical agency. This allegation was of more concern. On balance, and after discussing the publication with a variety of key stakeholders, we still believe that the ABS is better placed than any organisation in Australia to produce a publication assessing progress. But it is an important question and reinforces the importance of maintaining objectivity.

In the second issue of MAP a number of changes were made. First, we adjusted the balance between the number of economic, social and environmental headline dimensions of progress. *Productivity* was elevated to headline status, while the dimensions of *land*, *water* and *biodiversity* were combined to give a new dimension entitled *the natural landscape*, which will stress the links between those three areas. This at least gave the perception of greater balance.

Second, we paid more attention to some areas of progress that were rather underdeveloped in the first issue. We included a more detailed discussion about the importance of governance. We also included material that sets out MAP's underlying framework more clearly as well as an essay showing MAP's place within the philosophical spectrum of approaches to measuring progress, sustainability, wellbeing and the like.

Influence on Policy Debate

This is difficult to assess. It is fair to say the report has had more influence on public debate rather than policy debate. MAP received widespread media coverage particularly at the time of release. It is often cited as a reference in Parliament and elsewhere. I am also often asked to give presentations based on MAP, both to public and private audiences. There seems to be a real interest in having a well thought through, holistic and facts based presentation on progress. GDP is no longer seen as the main indicator of growth although its role as a measure of progress remains fundamental.

There have been several comments from influential people that it is great to have an objective, trusted view of what is happening in their country, particularly after the second release. MAP clearly provides a valued point of reference. As clear evidence of its value,

I won the Society category in the "Smart Australian" prize for what the judges regarded as a very important initiative to informed debate in Australia.

Major Lessons Learned

Even with the benefit of hindsight, we were pleased with how we developed the project. Nevertheless, there were important lessons learned.

- Maintaining objectivity is critical as is presenting the report as an assessment of progress in Australia rather than as a review of government performance. (We had an early warning of the importance of this - when a journalist first heard of the publication, he referred to it as a report card on the Government. It reinforced that we must not design the publication in this way.)

- Widespread consultation is necessary - not just with government agencies. The community can have very different views on what is progress.

- Balance is essential. Also, it is important to do what can be done to avoid perceptions of lack of balance. Transparency is clearly important.

- It is best to treat the first publication as experimental and deliberately seek comments. Get it out rather quickly rather than trying to produce the perfect publication. It is much easier to obtain informed comment on an actual publication rather than a concept.

- Listen to your critics even though you may differ from their points of view. Try to react to the criticisms. I spent several hours having a one on one discussion with our main critic and made changes to some (but not all) of the criticisms. He did not criticise the second release of MAP.

- Develop a media strategy.

Future Plans with MAP

We plan to have annual releases with MAP. It will not be in hard copy form every year. For some years it will be web based only. Also, the amount of effort put into analysing the dimensions may vary depending on the availability of new data or the topicality of the issues.

The first issue was experimental and we received a lot of useful feedback. The second issue was revised taking account of this feedback. We are now in a period of continuous improvement for a few years. Some dimensions will attract more development work than others. Family and community, and government, democracy and citizenship are two such cases.

We will also include more analysis on "equity" or the distributional aspects. This is done rather extensively for financial hardship but not all the other indicators.

Subjects for essays will need to be considered. They should be on topical issues. One area of interest is regional differences within Australia. Others would like us to extend the work on international comparisons. We will also include more essays that link different dimensions of progress.

There is one dimension of progress that has grown in importance but is not in the current version of MAP. This is national security. We have not thought about this yet. No doubt it is an area of concern for other countries and international collaboration may be useful.

References

Cobb, C and Halstead, T (1995), "The Genuine Progress Indicator".

Eckersley, R (1998), "Measuring Progress: Is Life Getting Better?", CSIRO Publishing.

Keuning, S (1997), SESAME: An Integrated Economic and Accounting System, International Statistical Review 65(1).

Annex 1

Selected Dimensions of Progress

The Environment

Environmental progress equates to a reduction in threats to the environment and improvements in the health of our ecosystems.

In order to assess progress, what dimensions (aspects) of this domain should be considered? Dimensions chosen were:

- the quality of the natural landscape (land, water, biodiversity)
- the environmental quality of settlements
- the environmental quality of oceans and estuaries
- Australia's contribution to global environmental concerns.

The Economy

Economic progress equates to enhancing Australia's national income (broadly Australians' real per capita levels of consumption) while at least maintaining (or possibly enhancing) the national wealth that will support future consumption.

In order to assess progress, what dimensions (aspects) of this domain should be considered? Dimensions chosen were:

- National wealth
- National income
- Productivity

Social

Social progress involves increases in the wellbeing of the population; a reduction of threats to, and increases in social cohesion; and protection and enhancement of democratic rights.

In order to assess progress, what dimensions (aspects) of this domain should be considered? Dimensions chosen were:

The wellbeing of the population

- Health
- Education and training
- Work

- Housing

- Financial hardship

  Social cohesion

- Family and community

- Crime

  Democracy

- Governance, democracy and citizenship

Annex 2

Criteria for Choosing Progress Indicators

Measures of Australia's Progress is designed for the Australian public, and the commentaries are meant to be easily understood by readers who may not be expert in either the subject matter or statistical methods. In many cases, our choice of indicator has had to strike a balance between considerations of approachability, technical precision, and the availability and quality of data.

In the view of the ABS, a good headline indicator should:

- be relevant to the particular dimension of progress

- where possible, focus on outcomes for the dimension of progress (rather than on say, the inputs or processes used to produce outcomes)

- show a "good" direction of movement (signalling progress) and "bad" direction (signalling regress) - at least when the indicator is considered alone, with all other dimensions of progress kept equal

- be supported by timely data of good quality

- be available as a time series

- be sensitive to changes in the underlying phenomena captured by the dimension of progress

- be summary in nature

- preferably be capable of disaggregation by, say, geography or population group

- be intelligible and easily interpreted by the general reader.

Statistical Indicators for Broad Policy Purposes in Ireland: Developing the Consensus between Statistics and Politics

Donal Garvey

Director General, Central Statistics Office, Ireland

Abstract

In December 2003 the Central Statistics Office published "Measuring Ireland's Progress" - a Report containing 108 indicators covering 48 domain themes. The purpose was to present a manageable set of indicators which, taken together, would broadly summarise the progress being made in Ireland in achieving desirable outcomes for society. More than half of the indicators relate to social domains, reflecting the emphasis on societal outcomes as the ultimate aim of policy measures. The other indicators cover the economy, innovation and the environment.

This paper describes the institutional and political environment in which the need for a set of indicators was discussed and developed. The relevance of discussions at Social Partnership which, since 1987, has been a key basis for government policymaking is described. The proposals in reports of the Irish National Economic and Social Council (NESC) were influential. The links which were made between ideas being developed by the National Statistics Board (NSB) and the discussions at Social Partnership and the NESC were particularly important. These links between the NSB, the NESC and Social Partnership were the glue which positioned the CSO to progress the National Indicators project with confidence. The actual set of indicators was chosen independently by the CSO and the rationale behind the choices made is described. In conclusion, the paper reflects on the media, policy and political reaction to the publication and where the future might lie.

Introduction

The core business of National Statistical Institutes (NSIs) has always included the publication of key statistical indicators such as the Unemployment Rate or the Consumer Price Index. Measures such as these are often used in the disbursement of public resources and in contractual situations; they are also used for statistical benchmarking over time and across regions or countries; and are developed according to statistical principles and definitions which are discussed and agreed in international recommendations. Statisticians guard the definitions jealously and in the absence of these internationally agreed definitions, the measures would not be very useful for benchmarking purposes across countries.

Over the past few years, both at national and international (particularly EU) level, there has been a veritable explosion in the demand for statistical indicators. Very often the indicators were specified without seeking advice from the NSIs on whether the required data were even available; whether better and more robust indicators were feasible; and whether real comparability was possible either across countries or even within a country over time. I find it curious that some statisticians seem to be of the view that they should not be particularly pro-active in relation to the need for active NSI involvement in the work - all the more so since the proliferation of poorly defined indicators could result in the misallocation not only of statistical resources, but ultimately and more importantly significant programme resources.

While I will briefly refer at the outset to the EU context, the main purpose of this paper is to discuss issues around the need for statistical indicators at national level; and to describe the institutional and political environment in Ireland which led to the publication of "*Measuring Ireland's Progress*" by the CSO in December 2003. I will also reflect on where the future role of the CSO might lie in the context of the use of statistical indicators for deeper evidence based policy making.

EU Statistical Indicators

Over the past few years there has been a significant increase in the number of indicators (now running into the hundreds) required to support EU policy. This has been driven by the "open co-ordination" approach to benchmarking, whereby statistical indicators are selected to measure the extent to which member states are achieving certain key political objectives agreed in EU Councils. To even add to the challenge, the basic indicators were often accompanied by a long list of sub-indicators or disaggregations. The NSIs were not always consulted on the feasibility of the proposed indicators with the result that some might have been sub-optimal in relation to data availability, data quality and comparability.

I find it interesting to reflect on why statistical indicators were specified at EU level very often without the involvement of statisticians. Had the statistical system reached a point where it was "out of tune" with the needs of policy makers? In Europe, were the statistical systems so overstretched with the information needs to support the large political initiatives such as The Single European Act, EMU and Enlargement that it was recognised that the system was not resourced to respond quickly? In general, are statistical systems not sufficiently resourced to respond to the information demands of complex, modern democracies? Or was it something else entirely - perhaps it was considered "safer" from a political point of view to keep control of the statistical indicators away from statisticians.

Some Implications in Ireland

This strong focus on indicators at EU level coincided with the emergence of a similar pattern in Ireland - it seemed as if economic consultants could no longer submit a report without the inclusion of long lists of statistical indicators which suddenly were being advanced as essential to understanding everything. These were in addition to the hundreds of indicators required at EU level. Many of the indicators were similar to, but yet slightly different from, one another. In the CSO we were concerned to try and put some kind of structure around the expectations that all kinds of indicators could be easily developed and to reduce the risk that some proposals could be less than fully focussed (which could ultimately undermine strategies for linking statistics more actively to evidence based policy making), so the question was raised for discussion at the National Statistics Board (NSB).

Institutional Environment for Statistics in Ireland

Up to 1949 official statistics were produced by the Statistics Division within the Ministry for Industry and Commerce. The Statistics Act, 1926 provided the framework within which the tradition of good quality official statistics was developed in Ireland. In 1949 there was a debate in Parliament on the need for a professional and independent statistics office which would produce data free from the influence of any Minister - the debate encompassed many of the issues subsequently embodied in the UN Fundamental Principles of Official Statistics. The CSO was established as an independent office within the aegis of the Taoiseach (Prime Minister).

The Statistics Act, 1993 (which came into effect in 1994) replaced the older statistics legislation. It gave the CSO authority to co-ordinate official statistics compiled by public authorities, particularly in relation to statistical standards and classifications. It also gave the CSO authority to assess the statistical potential of administrative records and required public authorities to consult the Director General of the CSO if they proposed to introduce, revise or expand (a) a data collection; or (b) the way data holdings were structured or stored.

The legislation was very strong in relation to the independence of the Director General who was given sole responsibility for deciding on professional methodology and statistical standards; the content of CSO publications; and the timing and methods of dissemination of statistics. The legislation also formally constituted the National Statistics Board.

National Statistics Board (NSB)

The Statistics Act 1993 formally constituted the NSB which had been operating since the mid 1980s. The NSB is a small, very active, advisory Board which includes highly influential people in a number of facets of Irish life. There are 3 official members - an Assistant Secretary General (or equivalent or higher grade) in the Departments of (a) the Taoiseach and (b) Finance; and the Director General of the CSO ex officio. (The current Secretary General in the Department of the Taoiseach and his predecessor were both members of the NSB). Three members are nominated by organisations representative of the users and providers of official statistics - up to now the nominations have represented (a) the Irish Congress of Trade Unions (ICTU) (b) the Irish Business and Employers Confederation (IBEC) and (c) the Farming organisations. The final 2 members are nominated by the Taoiseach and tend to be very active users of statistics; one of these has always been an eminent and highly respected Professor of Economics who has chaired the Board.

What has been particularly useful in the context of statistics is that some of the official and other NSB members are also active and influential participants in the Social Partnership discussions and in the deliberations of the National Economic and Social Council (NESC). The formal (and indeed informal) discussions at the NSB can be used to tease out the statistical requirements of emerging policy. This has the advantage that the Director General of the CSO is made aware very quickly of the issues exercising the interests of key policy makers and other participants in important national discussions. But also the CSO can have some influence on the content of policy documents as they are being developed in so far as they relate to statistics.

When we raised CSO concerns about the proliferation of statistical indicators at the NSB, the Board was in the process of developing a new strategy for statistics, focussing on statistical needs to support better evidence based policy making. Some Board members were also involved in a NESC project aimed at benchmarking the progress on commitments made in the existing Social Partnership agreement; and were preparing the negotiations for the following agreement. These links between the NSB, the NESC and the Social Partnership discussions have facilitated the speedy flow and filtering of information and have been the "glue" which held together the coherence between the statistical requirements of key policy documents and what was feasible statistically.

The NSB was concerned that one of the consequences of the proliferation of demands for indicators could be that public resources were at risk of being diverted into sub-optimal, stand alone statistical collections by Ministries. Early in 2003, in the context of the publication of an NSB Report (*Developing Irish Social and Equality Statistics to meet Policy Needs*) the opportunity was taken to obtain Government agreement that the CSO should publish a National Progress Indicators report by the end of that year.

Social Partnership in Ireland

The Irish economy faced significant challenges during the 1980s and into the 1990s (see Annex 1). There was very little net job creation over a twelve-year period, with the numbers at work in the very early 1990s almost at the same level as in 1981. The unemployment rate increased from about 10 per cent in 1981 to over 17 per cent in 1986. Net outward migration, which had been a feature of Irish experience since the famines of the mid-19th century right up to the 1970s (when there was significant net inward migration), re-emerged very strongly in the second half of the 1980s. Industrial relations were fractious and adversarial with significant numbers of workdays lost through industrial disputes. Government debt appeared to be at risk of spiralling out of control.

The sense of national crisis generated by this very gloomy scenario caused some of the key interest groups in society to reassess whether their objectives could be better pursued on the basis of a negotiated social agreement within a context of greater consensus on broad policy issues. The discussions at the NESC and the publication of its *Strategy for Development 1986-1990* were very influential. This led to the emergence of a Social Partnership model in Ireland in 1987.

Since 1987 there have been six Social Partnership agreements (Annex 2) and this system of social participation has been an important basis for government planning and policy making. The agreements have determined pay increases in both the public and private sectors; but they also involve a negotiated approach to strategic issues in economic and social policy. The earlier agreements were driven by the parlous state of the economy and the labour market and the first three were negotiated by Government with ICTU, IBEC and the Farming organisations, and focussed mainly on ameliorating unemployment. The later agreements also involved groups with a particular focus on women's issues, and groups representing the disadvantaged in society who were working to counter social exclusion. More than previously, these later agreements were concerned additionally with distribution issues and the promotion of social inclusion.

Social Partnership and Statistics

Reference to statistics was fairly sparse in the earlier agreements (Annex 3). As the negotiated areas of public policy widened, participants in the Social Partnership process began to realise that they needed some way of tracking the outcomes for society. In 2002 the NESC published two reports dealing with statistical indicators - the first was set in the context of benchmarking the progress of the *Programme for Prosperity and Fairness* (the Social Partnership agreement from 2000 - 2002) and proposed 20 headline indicators and 60 background indicators; the second was set in the context of sustainable development and proposed 18 headline indicators and 12 background indicators.

The most recent national Social Partnership agreement (*Sustaining Progress, 2003*) has a number of specific references to the CSO, one of which is a request to the CSO to develop a set of national progress indicators. This, in conjunction with the Government agreement referred to in section 5 above, was the wide societal expression of interest, priority and support which the CSO relied on as its remit to push ahead with the work, which resulted in the publication of "*Measuring Ireland's Progress*" in December 2003.

CSO Approach

Many different alternatives are, of course, available for inclusion in an indicators publication. From the outset it was evident that great care was needed to ensure that, even though this was going to be a different kind of publication than the norm for the office, what was ultimately published would be widely welcomed and recognised as an independent, professional piece of work - the kind of publication that Irish society would expect of the CSO. It was also recognised that detailed consultations on the selection of indicators carried a risk that the whole process could become bogged down, since there was a possibility that only those indicators giving a largely positive picture would be supported. Finally, there was a need to educate users on the debate that had commenced both at home and abroad so that they could better understand the context of both the publication and our selection of indicators. It was therefore decided

1. to publish the report in two volumes. Volume 1 would contain the numbers and Volume 2 would constitute a separate "Background Report" which would try to develop a conceptual framework for the selection of indicators and which would include information on some known national and international developments in this area;

2. to independently select within the CSO a set of indicators according to this framework;

3. to describe the choices made as a "preliminary set of key national progress indicators for Ireland" and to invite feedback following (rather than before) publication in order to give users the opportunity to influence future publications; and

4. to keep the NSB well briefed on progress. The Board was supportive and encouraging; and the Department of the Taoiseach was a particularly strong ally.

Conceptual Framework - "Volume 2 Background Report"

This report described the purpose of a set of indicators as providing a synoptic, high level analysis of the economic, social and environmental situation in Ireland, intended to provide a context for broad discussions with the Social Partners and within society generally. The discussion also made it clear that the intention was to select a fairly manageable set of indicators rather than a large set which might just overwhelm users.

The report provided information on the domains of policy interest, the headline indicators and background indicators (disaggregations) in 4 national proposals (by the NESC, Competitiveness Council and the Combat Poverty Agency), for 5 sets of indicators used by international bodies (EU, UN and OECD) and for some work by the ONS, the CBS Netherlands and the Australian Bureau of Statistics. Users found this information very helpful as it put in context what the CSO was attempting and also illustrated fairly sharply the difficulties in trying to cope with an ever increasing number of indicators.

The domains of interest in some of the national and international indicators reports were compared and account was also taken of a social framework developed in an earlier NSB report. It was decided that, for an Irish context and user group, the selected indicators would represent ten domains:

- Economy

- Innovation and technology

- Employment and unemployment

- Social cohesion

- Education

- Health

- Population

- Housing

- Crime

- Environment

The 108 chosen indicators were grouped within 48 themes within these domains; for example, there are 10 indicators for "Social cohesion" grouped under the four themes - Voter turnout; Official development assistance; Risk of poverty; and Gender pay gap.

Criteria for selecting the Indicators

In the context of providing statistical information to show, where possible, the outcomes under a number of priority areas for Irish society, it was decided to present a small number of high quality indicators in each of the ten domains of interest. The European Commission had identified seven criteria to be considered in assessing the quality of indicators:

- Easy to read and understand

- Policy relevant

- Mutually consistent

- Timely availability

- Comparable across countries

- Selected from reliable sources

- Not too large a response burden

The NSB, in its *Strategy for Statistics 2003-2008*, reiterated the need for a national progress indicators report and requested that the selected indicators should be consistent with international statistical concepts and facilitate international benchmarking. It was decided, in so far as it was achievable, to present the indicators in both a national and international context. The national context could, for example, be a longer time span or a regional breakdown. The international context was chosen to be the existing (at the time) fifteen EU countries and also the ten countries who at the time of the work were hoping to join the EU.

Within this broad frame of guidance, experienced subject matter statisticians within the CSO signed off on the indicators to be included in the publication.

Launch of the Indicators Publication

As has been mentioned already, the NSB had been considering strategies which would involve statistics more in providing better support to the formulation of policy and the monitoring of outcomes. The Social Partnership agreement (2003-2005) *Sustaining Progress* also requested the CSO to support a move towards more evidence based policy making by developing a set of national progress indicators. We decided to devise a release strategy which would maximise buy-in across a broad sweep of society. In discussions with the Department of the Taoiseach, it was decided that the Taoiseach and the D-G of the CSO would launch the Report at a pre-Christmas Social Partnership function. This function was well attended both in terms of numbers, but more importantly in terms of people of influence in a vast array of stakeholder organisations in Ireland. The publication was seen to be "for them".

The press release which accompanied the report was prepared, without outside involvement, by the CSO and said that "the indicators presented in the report provide a mixed picture of Ireland's performance and current well-being relative to other EU countries". It went on to mention seven points "where Ireland is performing well" and nine points "where further progress is possible". Even though it is exactly what is expected of the CSO in Ireland, this balance reinforced the role of the publication as being an objective, professional piece of work geared to support evidence based policy making at a high level.

The way in which the launch was handled ensured a strong alignment with the work on the part of the political system as well as from policy makers and the various interest groups. It could only have worked in this particular way because of the strong links between the Department of the Taoiseach with the NSB, NESC and Social Partnership.

There was a very positive media (press, radio and TV) reaction to the publication although, as seems to be the norm, there were more stories around the indicators where further progress is possible. In the months following publication the Report was used in articles by economic and social commentators; and also in some parliamentary debates. Finally, the report was used by participants in the Social Partnership process, particularly those representing the disadvantaged or marginalised in society.

Feedback

At the time of publication feedback was invited. Since the publication was already in the public domain it was more difficult to propose that some of the more challenging indicators should be deleted - these suggestions might well have surfaced if there had been advance consultations. The three main aspects of the formal feedback were

- Evidence based policy making needs publications like this; continue to publish on an annual basis.

- Could a similar report be produced for Regions of the country?

- The easy access to comparable international data was very useful.

On the basis of the feedback it has been decided to continue annual publication, although the timing has been shifted to a March/April target in order to include an extra year of data for a number of the indicators.

The Future

The key point in the Irish example described in the paper is that the CSO, with the active assistance of an influential NSB, has been able to build a bridge to the policy makers; while at the same time reinforcing its professional reputation. Of course, the institutional arrangements differ from country to country.

At the level of individual countries there are challenging questions around issues linked to evidence based policy making, societal outcomes and statistical monitoring at a detailed programme level. In my opinion considerable effort should be made to define and measure key outcomes for society. Such measures should be independent and unbiased; and should not generate controversy around their objectivity whenever they are published. This line of thought suggests that NSIs (which generally command a high level of trust in society) should be actively involved in developing the indicators and responsible for their publication. Since many of the critical outcomes revolve around the efficiency of service delivery, it seems that many of the indictors required will be developed from administrative data - perhaps linked across different administrations and over time, involving longitudinal record linking. Some serious questions that arise are:

- How can the UN Fundamental Principles of Official Statistics be used to improve the quality and dissemination of administrative statistics?

- How can one overcome the particular difficulties and sensitivities that may arise when statistical indicators are used also as performance measures to monitor the efficiency of service delivery?

- Is there a risk that political concerns could come into play (and would have to be resisted) in relation to the selection of indicators, their measurement and the control of information?

- Might the very existence of statistical indicators generate unintended negative behaviours in certain areas of service delivery, where the quality of service might take second place to the focus on meeting targets? "*When a statistic becomes a target it is no longer a statistic*".

Clearly this is challenging territory for NSIs and the institutional position and independence of the NSI has to be very strong in order to minimise any risks to its credibility. Yet, in most of our countries, the statistical office would be accepted by the public as an "honest broker" in relation to the publication of information on the delivery of services and the apparent societal outcomes - so from the point of view of informing society, statisticians should not avoid being pro-actively involved.

Annex 1. Net Migration, Workdays Lost, Labour market (q2 of year), and Government Debt in Ireland

Year	Net Migration	Days Lost [2]	At Work	Unemployed	Unemploy. Rate	Gov't Debt [3]
		(000)			%	% of GDP
1981	2	434	1,146	126	9.9	89.1
1982	-1	434	1,146	147	11.4	86.5
1983	-14	319	1,144	181	13.6	96.5
1984	-9	386	1,122	204	15.4	101.6
1985	-20	418	1,097	220	16.7	103.0
1986	-28	309	1,095	226	17.1	109.7
1987	-23	264	1,111	226	16.9	112.4
1988	-42	143	1,111	217	16.3	108.3
1989	-44	50	1,111	197	15.0	97.7
1990	-23	223	1,160	172	12.9	94.1
1991	-2	86	1,156	199	14.7	95.5
1992	7	191	1,165	207	15.1	92.3
1993	0	61	1,183	220	15.7	95.1
1994	-5	26	1,221	211	14.7	89.7
1995	-2	130	1,282	177	12.2	82.0
1996	8	115	1,329	179	11.9	73.5
1997	19	75	1,380	159	10.3	64.7
1998	17	37	1,494	126	7.8	53.7
1999	17	216	1,589	97	5.7	48.7
2000	26	97	1,671	75	4.3	38.3
2001	33	115	1,722	65	3.6	35.9
2002	41	21	1,764	77	4.2	32.7
2003	30[1]	37	1,793	82	4.4	32.1
2004	32[1]		1,836	84	4.4	

[1]Preliminary.

[2]Days lost because of industrial disputes

[3]"National Exchequer Debt" up to 1989 and "General Government Debt" (EU Definition) from 1990 onwards.

Annex 2. Social Partnership Agreements in Ireland

1988: Programme for National Recovery

1991: Programme for Economic and Social Progress

1994: Programme for Competitiveness and Work

1997: Partnership 2000 for Inclusion, Employment and Competitiveness

2000: Programme for Prosperity and Fairness

2003: Sustaining Progress

Annex 3. Examples of References to Statistics in some of the Social Partnership Agreements

Programme for Competitiveness and Work (1994)

"1.66   Resources within the Central Statistics Office will be reallocated or increased, where appropriate, so as to allow for the improved collection and compilation of service statistics, which will be required for the services information base that it is proposed to establish."

Partnership 2000 for Inclusion, Employment and Competitiveness (1997)

"5.11   The development of statistical methods to evaluate the full extent of the contribution of unpaid work, mainly done by women and their contributions to the national economy, including their contribution in the unremunerated and domestic sectors, will be undertaken during the course of this Partnership. The CSO will undertake a pilot study based on a time-use survey during 1997 as the first stage of this process."

Programme for Prosperity and Fairness (2000)

"10.   NESC will be requested to consider the development of a framework by June 2001 to bring into operation national progress indicators to measure economic, social and environmental development. This will encompass the availability and use of new forms of data sources, including Time Use Surveys, National Household Accounts and National Satellite Accounts."

"12.   A co-ordinated strategy including the relevant Government Departments, the Equality Authority and the Central Statistics Office will develop a system for the collection and dissemination of disaggregated data for women and, in relation to health, education and training, for Travellers."

"21.   The Department of Justice, Equality and Law Reform will put arrangements in place to review and identify key statistical needs in relation to people with disabilities or categories of people with disabilities for the purposes of informing policy, planning and the delivery of services."

Sustaining Progress (2003)

"The key national economic and social development tasks to be accomplished relate to the following priorities, as agreed between the social partners, are as follows … Progress in this regard will be monitored having regard to National Progress Indicators proposed by the NESC and being further developed by the Central Statistics Office."

"1.14   The strengthening of information systems to enable services to be delivered on the basis of the best available evidence and knowledge, including financial management and evaluation systems, will command a high priority so that value for money and quality of outcomes can be better assessed across the public service and service planning can be further enhanced."

"5.1.2 put in place the data framework to support evidence based policy making, as well as the critical evaluation, monitoring and review of social inclusion programmes and initiatives;"

"The CSO will develop, under the guidance of the National Statistics Board (NSB) and the Cabinet Committee on Social Inclusion, a framework for social and equality statistics. The NSB will work with a range of interested parties, including the social partners, in developing this initiative."

"The CSO will take a lead role in the development of the potential of administrative data across Government Departments and Agencies in conjunction with the Senior Officials Group on Social Inclusion."

"A set of national progress indicators will be developed by the CSO building on Benchmarking the PPF (NESC 107) and National Progress Indicators (NESC 108) reports."

"17.6   The recent CSO Survey of Pension Coverage (Quarterly National Household Survey 1st Quarter, 2002) has provided statistics which will enable the Pensions Board and others to measure and track the trends in coverage. It will also enable the extent and effects of the introduction of PRSAs to be monitored. The full Survey should be repeated at regular four-year intervals, commencing in the first quarter of 2006; and the first two questions (providing overall coverage figures) should be asked every second year commencing in the first quarter of 2004. Having a full report in 2006 will also link in with the Minister's statutory obligations (as per the Pensions Act, 2002, Part X), to report on the development of occupational and other pensions three years after the introduction of PRSAs."

Improving Economic Indicators

Measurement of Government Output and Productivity for the National Accounts in the UK: "The Atkinson Review"

Joe Grice

Executive Director, Atkinson Review

Abstract

The UK began in 1998 to measure the output of Government services through direct output measures rather than by assuming output=input. These methods are now being reviewed by a team led by Sir Tony Atkinson, one of the UK's most eminent economists. An Interim Report, published in July 2004, recommends principles for the measurement of government output, inputs and productivity. It sets out a work programme for improving measures of output in Health, Education, Public Order and Safety and Social Protection. The paper explains the principles proposed in the Interim Report, in relation to international guidance, the improvements needed to current UK measures including measurement of quality of services, and some particular examples of new methods which may be recommended for the UK in the Final Report, in January 2005.

Public Services and the National Accounts

Public services are part of the wider economy. Their output is measured alongside the output of the tourist industry, manufacturing, car maintenance and all other areas of employment and production. When newspapers write about economic growth rates in different countries, the "economy" includes the public services as well as the market sector. We need consistent conventions on what to measure, and how to measure it, if those international comparisons are to be valid.

For the market sector, national accounts measure what has been bought and sold, at the prices people are willing to pay. For public services, there is no price, though there may be some charges or co-payment which do not reflect full costs to the producer, or the value to the individual who receives the services. So what should be measured?

Measuring Government Output

For a long time, national accounts measured the value of government outputs as being the same as what was spent. Output = input, by definition or by convention.

The problem is that this approach allows no potential for productivity change in public services. The market sector likes to be able to say "better quality than last year, and more of it, but half the price". Even if the public service makes the same improvement in delivering better services for less cost, the national accounts would not show the effect. Output would simply be recorded as what was spent.

The 1993 revision to the United Nations *System for the National Accounts*, the international gold standard in guidance for the national accounts, concluded that in future national accounts should use direct measures of output in public services, rather than just measuring inputs. In 2001, guidance consistent with the SNA was published by Eurostat in *the Handbook on Price and Volume Measures in National Accounts*. A European Commission Decision in December 2002 required, with the force of European law, all member states to implement these methods, including direct measurement of Government outputs, in national accounts from 2006 onwards. (Denmark has a derogation till 2012.) The Commission's aim was to harmonise measures of GDP growth.

UK Experience of Direct Measurement of Government Output

Table 1 shows the measures which were introduced progressively in the UK from 1998. For health, there was a cost weighted activity index based on numbers of hospital treatments and consultations with general practitioners. The more people went to hospital, the higher the output of the health service. Doctors and nurses are busier, seeing more people. But the measure has limitations. People may need to go to hospital several times because their first treatment did not succeed. This measures activity. It does not measure outcomes, in the ways that would be important to health economists, epidemiologists and indeed patients. We therefore think it was only an approximate measure of health output in the sense required by the SNA.

For education, the measure is mainly numbers of pupils in school. That is affected by birth rates. It also reflects the number of young people who stay on after 16, and that can be seen as a measure of success of schools. But there is no direct measure of whether children are doing well at schools – whether they learn to read, whether they are confident with numbers and grow up to be statisticians. If the Government spends money getting more teachers, or more books and computers, to improve the results from education, we might feel as parents that our children are getting better output. But actually the output measure would not change, because there is still the same number of pupils. In the UK, we currently add 0.25% a year to the education output measure to allow for examination successes, but this is not a very sophisticated measure.

The other measures are shown. Again, they cover activities – things that can be counted. They all have some problems, with some perverse incentives which I explain later. They do not capture everything that matters to people who receive services.

Basically, the United Kingdom had gone further and faster than other countries in implementing the 1993 SNA changes. In itself, that was to be applauded (and the Atkinson Review firmly believes this was the right direction to take). But pioneering the way forward has its own risks and it was with this background that Len Cook, the UK National Statistician decided in December 2003 to ask Sir Tony Atkinson to review the methods being used and to make recommendations to him about the way forward.

Measuring Productivity of Public Services from the National Accounts

If outputs are measured separately from inputs, it is possible to compare the rate of change in outputs and the rate of change in inputs. If there has been an increase in spending, has there also been an increase in output? Has output increased more than inputs, showing a productivity increase? It is of, course, necessary to use the volume of inputs rather than just cash spending, to take out the effect of changes in labour costs and prices.

The Office for National Statistics published several articles on the measurement of productivity in the public services from National Accounts data (see References below). The latest of these articles was published in May 2003. Figure 1 shows that measured productivity fell, particularly in the period after 1997 when there was a sustained increase in inputs. This analysis attracted considerable attention in the UK. On the one hand, the Government was committed to improving public services and was willing to spend more money on them. On the other, there did not seem to be a measured increase in outputs which matched the extra spending. Productivity of public services seemed to have fallen.

There were naturally questions about what was being measured, and whether the National Accounts really captured the actual output of public services. This was part of the context within which Sir Tony's review has had to operate. Official statisticians are, and need to be, immune to political pressure and bias. But it needs to be recognised that public services are inherently of high political sensitivity.

Public Services: management and measurement

In all democratic countries, the public pay for services through taxes and depend on them for vital areas of their lives. It is therefore natural for our politicians to be concerned to improve services, and to be able to measure improvements. This may take different forms in different countries and at different times.

Government Ministers may want to say "we are spending more money on this service". Or they may say "we employ more doctors and nurses than ever before". These clearly measure the inputs to the service, but are generally fairly easy to count – though open to interpretation.

Ministers, and managers of public services, may also talk about the volume of their activities – "a record number of hip replacement operations this year", or "more nursery school places for children under 5".

These measures match the way national accounts often identify inputs and outputs – what is spent, what activities are performed. However, there are many other ways in which the achievements of public services are measured. In many cases, measurements have been linked with targets and other ways of incentivising improvement in services. Some examples are:

- Achieving minimum standards – day nurseries and nursing homes must comply with standards which are monitored by independent inspectors;

- Population coverage – general practitioners were paid more money if a certain percentage of children under 5 were vaccinated against infectious diseases

- League tables – there are published tables showing the proportion of children in each school who reach a particular standard in tests and examinations;

- Maximum waiting times – targets that no patient should wait more than 12 months for hospital treatment;

- Success rates – death within 30 days of an operation; proportion of prisoners who reoffend within 2 years.

Measuring what Matters

So, in the UK, there are systems for measuring many aspects of public services, to support management systems and public accountability as set by the Government of the day. The measures may not be ideal, and there are issues about interpreting them.

Measurement systems may change quite frequently, to reflect developments in services, new legislation and changing public concerns.

This means there is information available about public services which is not currently used in the national accounts. Some of this information tells us about things which are important to people who use the service, where they might pay a higher price if this was a market. Patients who can afford it are willing to pay for quicker treatment; parents might pay money to help their children pass exams. These aspects of output are relevant to the requirements of the SNA and Eurostat guidance. But they are not yet reflected in the measures of "activities" which are used in the UK national accounts.

The Atkinson Review is therefore able to draw on some wider data sets, and considerable expertise in using and interpreting them. But we have not approached our work just by looking for new data. We believe that the indispensable first requirement is the formulation of a well-based and widely accepted set of principles to underlie the measurement of public service output. It is only on that basis that we can decide which sorts of information should be used, and how it should be used.

Our work is technical, and has to meet high professional standards of objectivity, and be in line with international guidance. But it also deals with issues about public services which are important to millions of people in the UK who use schools and hospitals, and are protected by the police and fire service. These issues, and the statistics which measure them, are therefore inherently and unavoidably of great political sensitivity.

The Atkinson review

How the Review Has Worked

The Review is led by Sir Tony Atkinson, Warden of Nuffield College, Oxford, and one of the UK's most distinguished economists. Tony began his career as a colleague of Sir Richard Stone, who developed the UK national accounts during the Second World War and chaired the first United Nations SNA. Tony is supported by a team of 12. The Review is independent of the Office for National Statistics though we work closely with them, and with other Government departments.

The Review began in January 2004. I lead the team, on loan from the Treasury, as Deputy Head of the UK Government Economic Service. Other team members are experts from Office for National Statistics, the Bank of England and other public service government departments.

Our terms of reference are:

To advance methodologies for the measurement of government output, productivity and associated price indices in the context of the National Accounts, recognising:

1. the full scope of government outputs;

2. differences in the nature and quality of these outputs over time;

3. the relationship between government outputs and social outcomes;

4. the need for comparability with measures of private sector services' output and costs;

5. the existing work of the Office for National Statistics; and

6.   the appropriate measurement of inputs, including quality and the distinction between resource and capital, so that, together with the measurement of output, light can be thrown on developments in government productivity."

Since we are concerned with measurement of government output, we have worked closely with officials from the Departments concerned. We chose to prioritise four areas of government output which cover about two-thirds of spending on government final consumption (2003 figures):

- Health 31%

- Education 17%

- Social Protection 11%

- Public Order and Safety 9%

For each of these areas, we agreed an action plan with the relevant Government department to review the issues and develop new measures, where they were needed. The action plans are specific, phased and timetabled. They run up to the spring of 2004; our Review itself finishes in January 2005 but the various agendas it is concerned with will naturally continue for some time into the future. In working with Departments, we are clear that their work informs, but only informs, our independent Review. Its report and recommendations are solely the responsibility of Sir Tony Atkinson. Ministers are involved in ensuring their Departments co-operate with the project but they have no role in shaping its work or the recommendations. Moreover, decisions as to whether to accept some or all of the recommendations of our report will be made, not by ministers, but by Len Cook, the National Statistician, as a professional matter.

What the Review Covers

The coverage of Health and Education is fairly clear. Public Order and Safety includes police, prison services, courts and also the fire service. Social protection covers social services, such as nursing homes for elderly people – where they are funded by the government – and also the administration of social security payments.

Broadly, we are looking at measures of services paid for by central or local government and provided to people individually, or to society collectively. Of course, much public spending goes on direct payments to people who are poor or in need – these transfer payments and are outside our remit. Such money can be spent by individuals as they wish and their spending is counted as household consumption in the national accounts; we must not double count.

Some of the areas we are reviewing are primarily about services to individuals – a medical treatment or education for a child. Some are provided collectively – we all benefit from knowing there is a fire engine standing by, whether or not our house is on fire. International guidance is that there should be output measures for both individual and collective services – but it is recognised to be harder to do this for collective services. One major collective service, Defence, has not so far been covered by our Review or by previous ONS work. How to measure defence output raises considerable conceptual issues. These issues are not necessarily intractable but they are of an order of magnitude more complex than for some other public services.

Most of our work is focused on better measurement of output. But a surprisingly large set of issues also emerged concerning the other half of the productivity ratio: inputs.

The data for inputs – spending – published in the National Accounts do not match precisely the figures which any one Government Department thinks it has spent. That is partly because most services are provided separately for England, Scotland, Wales and Northern Ireland. Four sets of spending figures have to be combined, and then turned from financial year (which ends in March) to calendar year. There are other adjustments, such as disregarding transfer payments. We have found there is a lack of transparency in this system, so spending Departments do not always have a clear understanding of the figures used in the National Accounts. Countervailing, ONS has not always been able to locate the detailed knowledge in Departments to help it understand what is happening to spending. Spending figures come by way of the Treasury, giving further complexity. Errors are possible, and they do happen.

Interim Report July 2004

When he set up the Review, Len Cook asked for an Interim Report in July and a Final Report in January 2005.

In publishing the July Interim Report, Tony Atkinson invited comments on the work so far. We have received many helpful comments. But the broad thrust has been largely welcomed, and with general approval of its thinking.

The report explains the purpose of the Review, the history of measuring Government output in the UK National Accounts, the international context, and the functions and limits of the national accounts. It then sets a methodological framework and an approach to implementation.

A key recommendation is that the measurement of government output and of inputs and productivity should be based on a set of principles, within the framework set by international guidelines. These principles have so far met general approval from those who have read the report. We will review them further, and refine them in the light of the comments, but expect the final report to take the same broad approach.

The principles are:

Principle A: the objective should be to measure output from government spending in terms of its incremental contribution to individual or collective welfare, in the same way as market output.

Principle B: the procedure of defining direct output indicators within a government function should start by seeking to identify the services provided by government to households and firms, and attempts made to find data to reflect these services as comprehensively as possible (rather than working back from available indicators). Where, initially, it is necessary to apply an indicator from another service, this should be explicit. The coverage of indicators within a function should be reassessed on a regular basis.

Principle C: formal criteria should be set in place for the further extension of direct output measures. Specifically, the conditions for introducing a new directly measured output indicator should be that (i) it covers adequately the full range of services for that functional area; (ii) it makes allowance for quality change; (iii) effects of its introduction have been tested service by service, and (iv) the context in which they will be published has been fully assessed, in particular the implied productivity estimate.

Principle D: measures should cover the whole of the United Kingdom; where systems for public service delivery and/or data collection differ across the different countries of the United Kingdom, it is necessary to reflect this variation in the choice of indicators.

Principle E: the measurement of inputs should be as comprehensive as possible and, in particular, should include capital services; consideration should be given to the split between current and capital spending.

Principle F: criteria should be established for the quality of price deflators to be applied to the input spending series; they should be sufficiently disaggregated to take account of changes in the mix of inputs and should reflect full and actual costs.

Principle G: independent corroborative evidence should be sought on government productivity as part of a process of "triangulation", taking account of the timing of inputs and outputs.

Principle H: value should be seen as adjusted for quality; for each service, explicit consideration should be given to the incorporation of quality change as an element of value added; for each spending function, consideration should be given to the extent to which quality change is captured by the changing activity mix, and to the way in which output measures for government should be adjusted for increased real value in an economy with rising real GDP.

The Interim Report also discussed the way output measures should be improved in Health, Education, Public Order and Safety and Social Protection.

Principles

Principle A says output from government spending should be measured in terms of its incremental contribution to individual or collective welfare. Note that we are not proposing that output is synonymous with outcome measures, used in other areas of public services performance measurement. We are proposing that output should measure **the direct contribution of the spending concerned to outcomes**. In accordance, *Principle H* says that value should be seen as adjusted for quality. Quality change should be measured as part of output. We should not just measure activities, without considering how much value they give to the user. For example, we may do the same number of operations for a rare condition now as we did 10 years ago. But if surgeons have improved their techniques, more patients survive after the operation now than they would have done. That is a change in quality, and an increase in the value of what the Health Service is providing, which is very important. But it would not be measured if we counted only the number of operations.

This is in line with international guidance. The SNA is explicit that output should be quality adjusted. In the UK, we have at present a quality adjustment to our education output figures, though the basis of that is not ideal. In other areas, it would be a significant change to introduce quality measures. There is much challenging work to be done to decide in each area which aspects of quality really matter in giving value added to the person who receives service. Then, we need to find information which robustly and validly measures quality change. This is not always easy. But our principles say we should go in this direction. As the SNA says, output has to be understood as including quality of service, not just a volume of activities.

The last few words in *Principle H* raise another issue. It says consideration should be given to adjusting output measures for government for increased real value in an economy with rising real GDP. The example discussed in the report is that the fire service gives value by preventing fires which would destroy our valuable homes, offices and other buildings, or putting fires out quickly with minimal damage. The more valuable our possessions, the more we have to lose, and so the greater the value of the fire service to us. This is but one example: similar considerations can be said to apply in the field of public order and safety, education or the Health Service. This opens up some very interesting ideas for future work.

Principles B, C and *D* are all concerned with the completeness of indicators used in output measures. We found that in some services, we were using measures which covered as little as 40% of spending as a proxy for the output of all spending. This has a risk of distortion. We also found that in most cases, we used output data only from England, then grossed up by UK spending. Scotland, Wales and Northern Ireland have devolved responsibility for health, education, social services and to some extent for public order, and have in some cases different legislation and different systems. Their spending priorities may differ from England. So there is a risk of error if we fail to use separate data from these countries. It is wrong in principle. Len Cook, who comes from New Zealand, calls this the "small country" issue. He rightly feels strongly about it, as does Tony Atkinson.

Principle E says the measure of inputs should include capital services. At present, the National Accounts include only a measure of capital depreciation. But if the Government is using an asset, such as a school, it also receives value from the building, and this is left out of the National Accounts at present. This is a point where our advice differs from the current international guidance in the 1993 SNA. But the SNA is under review at present. We understand that the proposal to move to capital services has already been made, and the Atkinson Review supports that change.

Principle G is about measurement of productivity. Any measure of productivity is only as good as the measures of outputs and inputs upon which it is based. They may be subject to error, for any or all of the reasons set out above. Moreover, we may also know something directly about the factors that are likely to affect productivity. So the suggestion is that we treat the three as a triangle and examine whether the three hang together and tell a consistent story. If, for example, outputs and inputs imply a sharp fall or rise in productivity, do we have independent corroborative evidence to support the proposition that there was such a sharp change? If so, we can be more confident that this is a description of the real world. If not, we might want to iterate back and question whether it is the outputs or input measures which are faulty.

The report also discusses the fact that some spending classified as "current", such as staff training, will have results over many future years and cannot be expected to improve output in the initial period. It has many of the attributes of capital spending, and we have termed it quasi-capital. If there is a big expansion in staff numbers and staff training, as has happened in some parts of the UK public services in recent years, there will be a dip in productivity as measured from the National Accounts. So there is need for caution in making these calculations, and interpreting them.

Finally, the national accounts are not the whole story. Nor should they be; they are designed principally to support aggregate economic management. They are not designed as a means of measuring public service performance against the wide range of desiderata that the population demands. Public services may have improved in ways which matter to people who receive them, but are not, nor should be, measured in the national accounts. We suggest a range of sources should be used to assess the way outputs and value for money have improved, not just a single measure.

Work in Progress in Different Spending Areas

The report then goes on to describe the current UK output measures in each of four areas, to comment on how far they meet the principles and what changes are desirable, and to summarise the development work which is under way.

Health

A cost weighted activity index for health output has been used in the National Accounts since 1998. A major problem with this index was that it treated all hospital inpatient episodes as being of equal weight. That would include both a day case operation to remove a cataract and a heart transplant operation, though their actual costs are very different. The Review team therefore worked with the Department of Health and colleagues in the Office for National Statistics to introduce an improved measure of health output. This was used in the National Accounts from June 2004.

The new measure is still a cost weighted activity index, i.e. it does not include quality measures. But it uses a much larger number of different categories of health activity, with a big expansion in the number of different types of hospital inpatient treatment. So the categories are now more homogenous, which makes the index more satisfactory. If the pattern is a bigger increase in more expensive hospital treatments, this would now show up in the aggregate index. Up to 2004, this would not have affected the index since all hospital treatments had equal weights. Similarly, the new index now uses many more categories of general practitioner prescription drugs, rather than just counting the total number of prescriptions.

The new measure is better in other ways, too. It is based on more reliable, audited, data sources. It covers new ways of providing health services: for example, NHS Direct (a telephone service) and Walk-in Centres, These rapidly expanding activities were not picked up by the previous measure at all. The new measure also captures much more timely information.

While the Atkinson Review has welcomed the new health output measure as a major improvement, there is more to be done. The measure of general practitioner consultations is not ideal, as it is based on a household survey and so sampling error affects the reliability of the time series. We are exploring alternatives which would give better long term measures of general practitioner outputs. We have not yet included measures of health output from Scotland, Wales and Northern Ireland, but this should be possible in a year or so.

Measuring quality also remains a major topic on the agenda. The Department of Health has commissioned the University of York Centre for Health Economics and the National Institute of Economic and Social Research to make proposals for measuring health output which incorporate quality measures. The researchers are keeping us informed of their work. Quality of health services has a number of dimensions, which WHO has grouped as outcomes and responsiveness (see References below). Health outcomes include for example mortality after operations; more widely, we should take account of research on which treatments have most value in quality adjusted life years and of data from standard measurement tools like SF36 on patients' abilities to lead a normal and comfortable life. On responsiveness, one issue of importance to the UK is the length of waiting times for investigations and treatments: it is clear that treatment given quickly is worth more to the patient than treatment given after a long wait.

Education

The UK currently measures schools output by pupil years, with an additional 0.25% a year for improving quality. This is the only explicit quality adjustment in the UK National Accounts at present, and was based on the fact that examination pass rates had been improving in the early 1990s, when the measurement was introduced. It has not been updated since then. Pupil years are weighted by the unit costs of different types of school. International guidance is that the measure should be pupil hours: we are considering whether it would be desirable to make a change in the UK, perhaps taking into account school absence rates. We would also like a clear basis for measurement of the quality of education. One avenue for exploration is the potential use of up to date examination and other test results. The Interim Report set out some suggestions for how this could be done. The Report also suggested that we might make some use of reports on the quality of schools from the independent schools inspectorate, Ofsted.

The question of the total value of education and training is wider than our review. For example, universities are classified as private sector bodies in the UK. They are therefore outside the scope of our Review, which looks solely at the public sector. There is also much investment in training by employers. We see scope for a satellite account for education and training which draws together information on these areas, and considers how to measure their economic value, given the way in which they affects earnings, and other aspects of life, in the future.

Public Order and Safety

The UK has some direct output measures for public order, such as number of arrests and the number of nights prisoners spend in prison. These do not fully match the all the objectives of the criminal justice system, which aims to prevent crime as well as dealing with offenders. For example, education and social support which enable a former prisoner to live without re-offending clearly add social value, but would not be measured by counting nights in an overcrowded prison which is not able to support rehabilitation.

Criminal justice is primarily a collective service. We are looking at ways of measuring the benefit to society as a whole from criminal justice services. There is much overlap of activity between the police, prosecutors, judges, prisons, probation service and so on in dealing with offenders, and some of the activity is actually unproductive – for example if someone accused of a crime is brought to court but the lawyers or the police are not ready to go ahead that day. So we do not want a cost weighted activity index which just adds up all these separate activities as though each one was good in itself. More generally, indicators have to be interpreted carefully. For example, if the number of crimes committed is going down, with a reduction therefore in the number of cases dealt with by the police, then the public order services have had some success. It would be a mistake to score this just as a reduction in the output of the police service. But criminal behaviour is also affected by other social and economic changes, so these have to be taken into account before deciding how much value to attribute to the public services. This is a complex area.

Our work is also dealing with fire services and with civil courts.

Social Protection

The final major area of our work, so far, is social services. For example, spending by local government on home help services to enable vulnerable elderly people to cope in their own homes, or on residential/nursing home care, where this is necessary and appropriate. There are also children's services, ranging from the work needed to place a child for adoption, though various ways of protecting children at risk, to intensive residential care for some very disturbed young people.

The UK national accounts already include some measures of activity, but they match only about 40% of the spending on social services. Working with the government departments concerned, we think we can improve the completeness of the cost weighted activity index by making more use of data already collected. This will not take account of the quality of services. This is a difficult area and it is likely that more research will be needed to decide what sort of quality indicators would be appropriate. They are likely to vary between different groups of people. There does not seem to be a single concept, like the "quality adjusted life year" for health, which could be applied in all cases.

Conclusion: what next?

Final Report

The Atkinson Review will produce a Final Report in January 2005. The themes will probably be similar to those in the Interim Report, but we will revise and refine the proposed general conceptual framework and the principles which embody it, in the light of discussion and comments received. We also hope to report further progress on health, education, public order and social protection, and make specific recommendations for change, or for further work if necessary.

Len Cook, the National Statistician, will decide whether or not to accept some or all of those recommendations. He has been strongly supportive of our work and we are working within the Office for National Statistics to be sure the work can be taken forward. This is not an area where there is any value in holding back information to produce unnecessary surprises. But the National Statistician's judgment is quite properly reserved till he has our Report.

International Context

Our work has been based on international guidance. The European Commission Decision means that all European Member States - Denmark apart - should be using direct output measures for government services in their national accounts from 2006 onwards. We hope we can move forward together in sharing experience of how best to do this. The Interim Report quotes examples from several countries that already have some direct output measures, and we can all learn from each other.

Tony Atkinson has had very constructive and helpful discussions with the OECD and Eurostat to discuss the Interim Report. Both of those bodies have a crucial role in the international governance of national accounting. But we also recognise that both those bodies have an equally important role in supporting individual countries in this area, and ensuring that formal guidance is clear, helpful and consistent.

In conclusion, I hope I have helped to explain why we believe the issues covered by the Atkinson Review are as practically important as they are intellectually interesting and challenging. If countries can make progress together on these agendas, the potential for making our economic measures more meaningful is substantial. At one level, that is of macroeconomic interest in ensuring well-based and consistent measures of GDP across our economies. At another level, it is of interest in the accurate and dispassionate appraisal of public services' performance. Finally, it is of interest to us individually, as tax payers and as users of government services.

Table 1. Direct Output Measures in the UK National Accounts

Function	Spending in 2000	When Introduced	Main Components
Health	30.3%	1998	Cost weighted activity index of hospital treatments, GP consultations, prescriptions
Education	17.1%	1998	Pupil numbers with 0.25% quality adjustment
Social protection – social security administration	2.7%	1998	Number of benefit claims for 12 largest benefits
Public order and safety – prisons, courts and probation	3.0%	2000	Number of prisoner nights, number of court cases and cost weighted activity index for probation
Public order and safety - fire	1.1%	2001	Number of fires attended of different types, other special services
Social protection – personal social services	7.4%	2001	Numbers of adults and children in residential care. Number of hours of home help

Figure 1. Government Productivity Estimates Implied by UK National Accounts (2000=100) (from Pritchard, 2003)

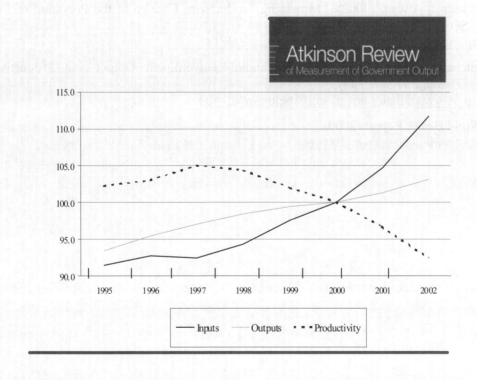

References:

Ashaye, Timi, (2001), "Recent Developments in the Measurement of General Government Output", *Economic Trends*, November.
http://www.statistics.gov.uk/CCI/article.asp?ID=110&Pos=&ColRank=1&Rank=374

Atkinson Review: Interim Report (2004), *Measurement of Government Output and Productivity for the National Accounts,* July, London.
http://www.statistics.gov.uk/about/methodology_by_theme/atkinson/

Baxter, Michael, (2000), "Developments in the Measurement of General Government Output", *Economic Trends*, September.

Caplan D., H. Neuburger (1998), "The Measurement of Real Public Sector Output in the National Accounts", *Economic Trends,* February.
http://www.statistics.gov.uk/about/methodology_by_theme/atkinson/downloads/ONS-NA.pdf

Caplan, David, (1998), "Measuring the Output of Non-Market Services", *Economic Trends*, October.
http://www.statistics.gov.uk/CCI/article.asp?ID=26&Pos=&ColRank=1&Rank=374

Pritchard, Alwyn, (2001), "Measuring Productivity in the Provision of Public Services", *Economic Trends*, May.

http://www.statistics.gov.uk/cci/article.asp?id=92

Pritchard, Alwyn, (2002), "Measuring Productivity Change in the Provision of Public Services", *Economic Trends*, May.
http://www.statistics.gov.uk/cci/article.asp?id=131

Pritchard, Alwyn, (2003), "Understanding Government Output and Productivity", *Economic Trends*, May.
http://www.statistics.gov.uk/cci/article.asp?id=400

World Health Report (2000).
http://www.who.int/whr/2000/en/

OECD'S Role in Global Governance: The Contribution of Structural Indicators and Benchmarking

Jean-Philippe Cotis
OECD Chief Economist

Introduction

This session is devoted to improving economic indicators. I would like to go beyond the "nuts and bolts" aspects of compiling quality economic indicators to illustrate the crucial role statistics play in shaping and defining the public policy advice that we give to member countries. I shall do this by way of example, using OECD structural indicators to enlighten the debate on Europe's economic long term performance. Is Europe really in decline? If so, by how much? And above all, for what reasons?

But first I want to outline a typology of the different types of world governance and to say something about where the OECD stands in this context. This is needed to explain why the "benchmarking" of structural indicators is central to the OECD's mission. Indeed, it shows clearly that the use of structural indicators derives quite logically from the type of governance in which the OECD is engaged.

A typology of world governances

There are I believe at present two main types of world governance. The first, which I shall call "direct governance", applies to international entities regulating global phenomena by means of instruments which are global in scope. The object of such regulation is to control phenomena which cannot be controlled at national level and to influence the actual nature of globalisation. An example of this type of governance is the Kyoto Protocol on greenhouse gases. Another example is the creation of a global system for the free movement of goods, with the WTO being the institution driving this governance.

The second type of world governance, I call "indirect governance". It is more discreet and more diffuse, but nevertheless essential. Indirect governance does not target collective inefficiency at world level, but seeks rather to reduce certain local inefficiencies. In other words, the object of indirect governance is to influence phenomena which are undoubtedly global in origin, but their proper management mainly involves effective domestic policies. The list of global phenomena which can only be managed nationally is long. It includes, to name a few, population ageing, financial pressures on health systems and adapting education systems to scientific and technical progress.

The idea that certain problems, typically viewed as national issues, actually derive from globalisation may seem paradoxical. Certainly the channels of impact are not always clear, yet they can be powerful. For example, global economic integration tends to result in levels of development converging and this, in turn, has an impact on social and demographic trends.

There are a large number of problems which are shared, but which do not require centralised decisions involving direct global governance. Each country has its own social and cultural characteristics and the requirements of democracy often call for locally approved solutions.

Substantial cultural and institutional diversity in approaches to public policy is also a potential source of progress. Of course, countries could feel their way alone and proceed by trial and error. But this would turn out to be a long and costly period of time. Instead, it may be time saving and enlightening to experiment by proxy, by observing others.

Mutual observation, however, may also be costly, as it requires considerable time and expertise and a detailed knowledge of other countries. But economies of scale are possible, through the establishment of international institutions specialising in comparative analysis and capable of drawing public policy conclusions. The drawback, however, for a country delegating these analyses to a third organisation is that it cannot be directly involved in the analytical process and may subsequently feel alienated from the findings.

The ideal solution is to invent an organisation where every country can be involved in selecting the issues, discussing results with the experts and, lastly, debating with their foreign counterparts what practical conclusions should be drawn. This latter point – discussions with foreign counterparts and peer pressure – is very important for promoting reforms. I can tell you from personal experience that when you go back to your capital after taking a barrage of questions of the "but why do you do it so badly?" variety, you have a big incentive to improve things.

Ideally, therefore, one would like to create a hybrid organisation which was both a centre for international expertise and a club where one could discuss what policies to pursue with foreign colleagues. If you subscribe to this reasoning, you have just invented the OECD – an institution which is an emblem of indirect governance. And I would congratulate you.

However, that is not the end of the matter. It is one thing to say that indirect governance is desirable, but for it to be politically and technically feasible is quite another. There are many obstacles that need to be overcome.

Countries find many arguments against extending indirect governance. While sometimes they are excessive they are not always completely unfounded. They are excessive when they amount to a chronic rejection of anything new and an opening up to the outside world. In contrast, it is reasonable to guard against the risks of ideological imperialism, resulting in the application everywhere of stereotyped solutions which do not respect legitimate societal choices.

Hence, if indirect governance is to be effective and accepted it has to respect everyone's cultural specificity while at the same time keeping a certain critical distance.

When gauging an economy's performance by means of international comparisons, it is thus important to be able to distinguish between what are "legitimate" societal choices and what denotes real public policy failings.

How then are allowances to be made? And how are national performances to be compared while at the same time taking account of legitimate local characteristics?

The use of structural indicators and benchmarking

This is where structural indicators and benchmarking come into play. The OECD has built an impressive array of analytical tools over the years, taking great care to apply rigorous methods and the latest expertise.

Benchmarking is used in many structural policy fields. Examples include the environment, international trade, pensions, health, education – with the famous PISA surveys, labour markets, financial markets, product markets, R&D and innovation and macroeconomic policies.

The OECD has developed indicators in all these areas. Describing each of them would be wearisome. Rather, I would like to stress that for indicators to be effective in shaping public policy they need to have one common characteristic. And that is they have to look beyond "apparent performances" and extract from them what really stems from the effectiveness of the policies involved and what stems from respectable societal choices.

Work of this sort does not depend on simple descriptive statistics, but has to be based on economic analysis and model-building. It has then to be scrutinised, criticised and debated by experts from national administrations and academia in an objective manner.

In order to give concrete form to these abstract points, I should now like to return to the questions I posed rhetorically at the beginning of my talk. The subject of economic decline is at present agitating European societies. I would like to show how a benchmarking-type approach can inform such debate and help to reshape economic policy.

You probably know the basic facts: the major continental European countries, whose living standards had been converging towards American levels since the end of World War II, have been experiencing a major reversal of their fortunes for the past 20 years. Convergence came to a halt in the early 1980s and the continental European countries went into a phase of relative decline vis-à-vis the United States during the 1990s

Initial analysis would suggest that it is not the level of productivity in Europe that is responsible for this divergence, but rather the utilisation of labour, i.e. the number of hours worked per capita (Figure 2).

That observation has prompted a rather lively debate, with:

- Some Anglo-Saxon commentators blaming continental Europeans for being lazy. For instance, a recent article in the British press was entitled: "Old Europe must change its lazy ways";

- While numerous Europeans and some sympathising English-speaking economists retort that increased leisure promotes well-being and, to simplify matters, say that "If the Americans work too much, that's their problem. Each to his own".

Approached in this way, the debate has every chance of being sterile. Why? Because the indicators underlying the debate concern apparent performance and do not go into depth on the issues.

Figure 1: Real per capita GDP has dropped relative to the United States

Trend indices, based on 2000 PPPs and 2000 prices [1]

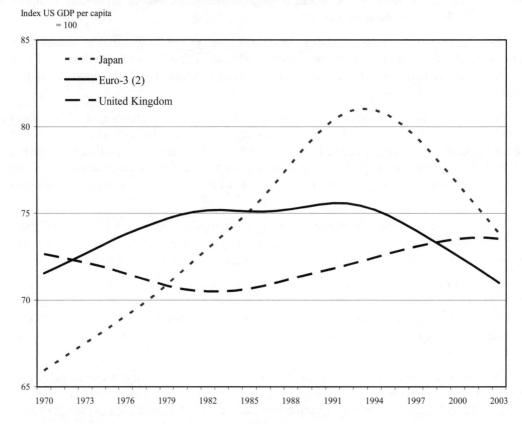

1. The trend is calculated using a Hodrick-Prescott filter (smoothing parameter set to 100) over a period
   which includes projections through 2010.
2. Euro-3 refers to Germany, France and Italy.
Source: OECD *Annual National Accounts*.

A more detailed analysis reveals, for example, that continental Europeans are indeed suffering from a productivity gap vis-à-vis the United States. Apparent labour productivity statistics only measure the productivity of those in work. Yet it is known in Europe that a lot of people with low-level skills are unable to find a job. Moreover, the small number of hours worked also tends to bias upwards calculations of hourly productivity.

So it is important to go beyond appearances. Doing so, one reaches the conclusion that productivity in the major countries of continental Europe is probably still lagging 10 to 15 per cent behind that of North America.

Figure 2: Differences in labour utilisation continue to be important in explaining differences in GDP per capita

Percentage point differences in PPP-based GDP per capita with respect to the United States, 2002

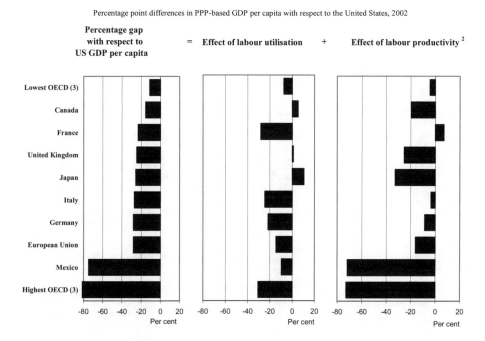

| Percentage gap with respect to US GDP per capita | = | Effect of labour utilisation | + | Effect of labour productivity [2] |

1. Labour resource utilisation is measured as total number of hours worked divided by population.
2. Labour productivity is measured as GDP per hour worked.
Source : OECD.

Figure 3: The interpretation of growth decompositions requires care

2002 figures

Productivity per hour worked [1]

Employment rate [2]

1. Real GDP in 2000 prices and PPPs per hour worked.
2. Total employment as a percentage of the population aged 15-64.
Source: OECD.

Figure 4: Labour utilisation and productivity gaps relative to the U.S

Percentage gap with respect to the United States level, 2002, 2000 PPP

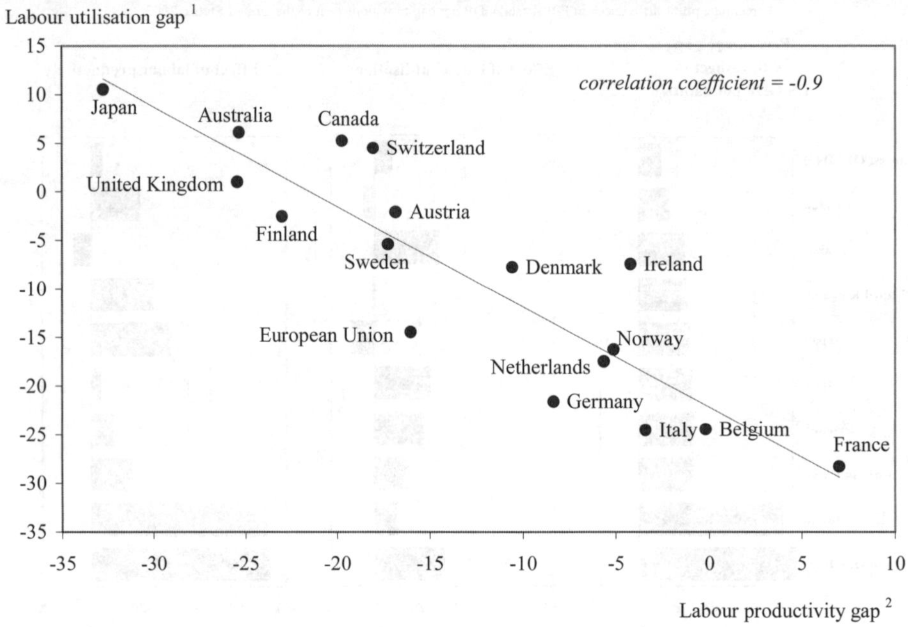

1. Labour resource utilisation is measured as total number of hours worked divided by population.
2. Labour productivity is measured as GDP per hour worked.
Source : OECD.

The next step is to understand why this is so and assess the responsibility of the various factors capable of influencing productivity. The potential factors include the quality of education systems, R&D intensity, the degree of openness and competition on product and financial markets, etc.

To be able to conduct the analysis, a battery of indicators needs to be established using the statistics available, or indeed by creating indicators on the basis of a detailed analysis of each country's regulatory system. Then an empirical examination of these indicators is needed to establish if there is a measurable relationship with countries' economic and social performances. This is done mainly by means of sophisticated econometric methods.

I should like by way of illustration to show you a few indicators that seek to capture on the one hand the strictness of the legislative and regulatory framework in the labour market and, on the other, the obstacles to entrepreneurship. These indicators go back some time and an updated version will be made public in a few months. They suggest that regulatory red tape in Europe is fairly cumbersome.

Figure 5: Employment protection legislation and barriers to entrepreneurship in selected OECD countries

Employment protection legislation

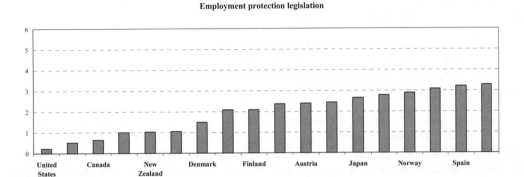

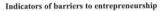

Indicators of barriers to entrepreneurship

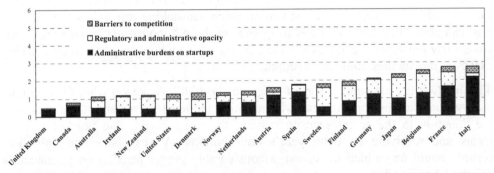

1. The scale of indicators is 0-6, from least to most restrictive.

Source: Nicoletti, *et al* (1999), "Summary indicators of product market regulation with an extension to employment protection legislation," OECD Economic Working Papers no. 226.

When these indicators are fed into econometric and statistical analyses, they help to explain in part why productivity in Europe lags behind the level in the U.S. It would appear that product markets which are less open to competition restrict the entry of new firms and, by the same token, an economy's capacity to catch-up.

According to our estimates, if those sectors that lag behind in terms of productivity were to modernise their regulatory framework and align it on best practice, their productivity could increase by as much as 10 per cent.

All in all, our recent work on growth suggests that structural policies and regulatory frameworks play an important role in the medium-term performances of the OECD economies.

Without any international comparisons, it would have been impossible for a decision-maker to determine whether his country's structural policies were appropriate or not. How can competition policy or product market regulations be judged in isolation?

Let's now turn to labour utilisation. In particular, does the low level of utilisation in Europe reflect only cultural factors – a reasonable preference for leisure according to some, a lack of enthusiasm for work according to others – or is it indicative of inappropriate public policies? And what is the relative importance of these different influences?

As you know, labour utilisation depends both on the employment rate, i.e. the number of people in work, and the length of the working week.

I do not want to get involved today in any impassioned debate about the number of working hours. I would prefer to concentrate instead on the employment rate in order to better identify the sources of Europe's weakness in this area.

What international comparisons immediately suggest is that the employment rate in the 25-55 year-old age group is very similar and high in every OECD economy. At the same time, what really sets the major continental European countries apart is the low employment rate in the over 55 year-old age group.

Are these early exits from the labour market the result of a spontaneous choice of lifestyle on the Europeans' part? Or are they largely influenced by what might be described as Malthusian public policies? That is, policies that are designed to use pension and early retirement schemes in a misguided attempt to reduce unemployment by giving older members of the labour force a strong incentive to retire.

To distinguish between what depends on public policies and what are individual choices, the OECD's economists embarked on some painstaking research which allowed them to calculate "implicit tax" rates weighing on those "good souls" who refused the generous early retirement packages available at age 55, or who wanted to go on working after 60 even though they could have retired.

This implicit tax measures a sort of "income shortfall". A person who, for example, wants to go on working for one year after reaching the legal retirement age is making a double donation to the social security system, the latter saving one year of pension payments and receiving an extra year's contributions. A year later, the individual concerned should be entitled to receive a considerably bigger pension on permanently leaving the labour market.

Usually, however, this is not the case and the pension remains the same. The atypical person concerned will have suffered a substantial and potentially very discouraging loss of income, or implicit tax.

As you can see from Figures 6 and 7, this implicit tax is high in a lot of European countries for those over 60, and higher still for 55-year-olds. In the latter case, the implicit tax is very high in Luxembourg, the Netherlands, Spain, Portugal, Belgium, Austria, Finland and France. And it is low in New Zealand, Italy, Iceland, Sweden, Norway, Japan, Korea, Canada and the United States.

Figure 6: Disincentives in old age pension systems discourage older persons from working

Implicit tax rates on continued work over next 5 years in current old age pension systems[1]

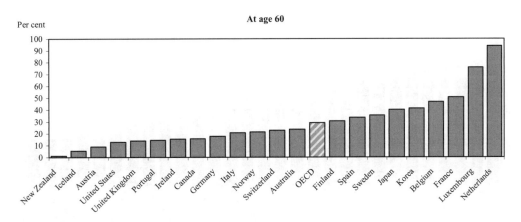

1. Single worker with average earnings.

Source: Duval, R (2003), *The retirement effects of old-age pension systems and other social transfer programmes in OECD countries*,
OECD Economics Department Working Paper No. 370.

Figure 7: Disincentives to older workers are also high in social transfer programmes

Implicit tax rates on continued work over next 5 years in current social transfer programmes[1]

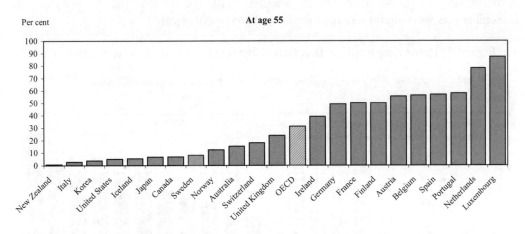

1. Single worker with average earnings.

Source: Duval, R (2003), *The retirement effects of old-age pension systems and other social transfer programmes in OECD countries*,
OECD Economics Department Working Paper No. 370.

Turning now to the employment rates of older workers, one typically finds, strangely enough, that countries where the implicit tax is low tend to have high employment rates among older workers, while those with a high implicit tax rate have extremely low employment rates.

Figure 8: Work disincentives bear on the older-worker employment rate

Employment of men and women in the age group 55-64 as a percentage of the population in the same age group, 2002

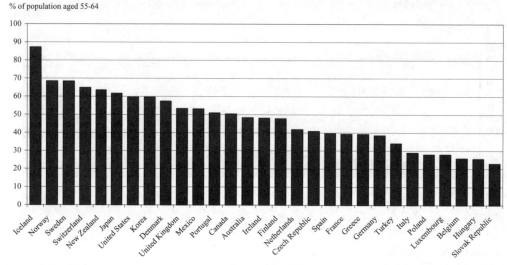

Source: OECD.

Astonishingly enough it seems that the laws of economics do explain a lot. Even where social issues are concerned. Given this state of affairs, is North America intrinsically more hard-working than Europe? Perhaps not.

When one simulates the way older workers might behave if pension scheme parameters with regard to work were neutral everywhere, the differences in labour force participation are found to be much smaller, with the Dutch, the French and the Luxemburgers working no less than the Canadians or Americans!

Figure 9: Removing implicit taxes on older workers would raise participation

Simulated level of labour force participation of older workers in 2025 under different pension reform scenarios

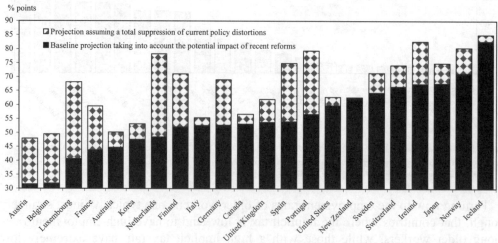

Source: OECD.

All in all, what this benchmarking exercise shows is that public policies count when it comes to labour utilisation rates. Also, policies which were simply neutral with regard to labour would do a lot to bring the material living standards of North American and continental Europeans closer together.

These findings have obviously prompted the OECD to plead strongly in favour of ambitious pension system reforms.

Having spent over 20 years in national and international economic administration, I have become firmly convinced that indirect governance and well-argued instruction are essential to nations' prosperity. They are discreet, but nevertheless vital forms of governance.

Perhaps, however, they do need more prominence in the public debate so that instruction extends beyond the inner sanctum of government.

This is why the OECD will in the coming months be launching a new publication designed to ensure that the results of its benchmarking work are widely circulated. The studies in the publication will also be discussed in our working parties which bring together members of the OECD Secretariat and representatives of national administrations. In this way, we will be able to gauge the progress made every year by the OECD as a whole and by each member country. The aim is to identify the main areas in each country where reforms are needed and, at our own modest level, to facilitate their implementation and acceptance by the public.

The Impact of Statistics on a Competitive and Knowledge-based Economy

Adelheid Bürgi-Schmelz

Director General, Swiss Federal Statistical Office

Abstract

Competition means to strive to outperform others, consciously or unconsciously, with respect to an objective such as profit, speed, quality, volume, position or prize. It means to be in a state of rivalry. Within the context of the global economy, success requires more than the conventional means, i.e. natural resources, labour and availability of capital.

Success in such an economic competition requires considerable know how in the respective areas. We will look at some of the most common success factors and the corresponding comprehensive indicators. Science and technology indicators as well as indicators for the human capital will be considered including some scoreboard results.

These indicators are the result of scientific methods applied in official statistics. This leads to the role of official statistics in a knowledge based economy. While official statistics cannot present a simple equation that explains everything, the direct and indirect success factors contributing to a competitive and knowledge based economy, it can help to identify key success factors, interdependencies and thus, hopefully, lead to adequate political decisions that enable economic growth.

In order to illustrate this role, several examples are presented. They show the close cooperation between politics and official statistics in important areas on the Swiss political agenda.

There is no silver bullet that allows for achieving a higher level of competitiveness in knowledge-based economies. But there is hope: Statistics, i.e. knowledge itself, is an excellent means to identify strengths and weaknesses of an economy. Based on the evidence gained, politicians can and should take measures to further develop the competitiveness of their respective countries.

Introduction

"I love the winning, I can take the losing, but most of all I love to play." (Boris Becker, 1967-)

Competition means to strive to outperform others, consciously or unconsciously, with respect to an objective such as profit, speed, quality, volume, position or prize. It means to be in a state of rivalry. A competition leads to a ranking of the participants. One example is the ranking of national economies published by the World Economic Forum:

Table 1:   Growth Competitiveness Index rankings and 2003 comparisons

Country	GCI 2004 rank	GCI 2004 score	GCI 2003 rank*
Finland	1	5.95	1
United States	2	5.82	2
Sweden	3	5.72	3
Taiwan	4	5.69	5
Denmark	5	5.66	4
Norway	6	5.56	9
Singapore	7	5.56	6
Switzerland	8	5.49	7
Japan	9	5.48	11
Iceland	10	5.44	8
United Kingdom	11	5.30	15
Netherlands	12	5.30	12
Germany	13	5.28	13
Australia	14	5.25	10
Canada	15	5.23	16
United Arab Emirates	16	5.21	—
Austria	17	5.20	17
New Zealand	18	5.18	14
Israel	19	5.09	20
Estonia	20	5.08	22

Source: World Economic Forum Global Competitiveness Report 2004-2005 October 13, 2004.

Within the context of the global economy, success requires more than the conventional means, i.e. natural resources, labour and availability of capital. In the last century, Switzerland became a highly competitive economy although natural resources are scarce and wages are high. Interestingly enough, the economic activities are spread over a broad range of industries and services and are by far not limited to the chemical industry and financial services.

Figure 1. Parts (in %) of economic activities in Swiss GDP 2002

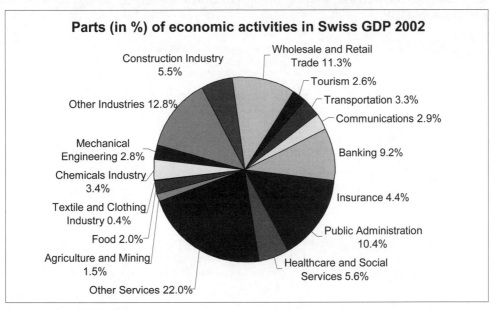

Source: Swiss Federal Statistical Office 2004.

From Figure 1, we can see that the Swiss Gross Domestic Product (GDP) depends on many sectors, e.g., chemicals industry, mechanical engineering, construction, textile industry, banking, insurances, tourism, wholesale and retail trade, transport etc. Very often, Swiss products and services are expensive and compete based on high quality, custom built solutions and high tech applications.

Success Factors

"We want to be first; not first if, not first but; but first!" (John F. Kennedy, 1917-1963)

Success in such an economic competition requires considerable know how in the respective areas. We will now look at some of the most common success factors and the corresponding comprehensive indicators. Science and technology indicators as well as indicators for the human capital will be considered including some scoreboard results.

The Impact of Science and Technology

One of the broadly accepted success factors in knowledge based economies is the progress of science and technology in a country. To determine this progress, science, technology and innovation indicators are calculated annually for all OECD and EU member countries.

One of the most common indicators is the number of patent applications. On Table 2, we see the number of patent applications to the European Patent Office (EPO) from 1998 to 2001. One can easily conclude that overall, there is a considerable increase in patent applications - and I am happy to report that Switzerland is at not bad a position.

The OECD Science, Technology and Industry STI Scoreboard provides a summary of trends in the knowledge based economy. The more than 200 indicators cover the creation and diffusion of knowledge, the information society, the global integration of economic activity and productivity and economic structure. Table 3 is part of the STI Scoreboard 2003. It shows that R&D expenditure has increased steadily over the years. Along with other countries, Switzerland holds a strong position with respect to the ratio of R&D expenditures to GDP.

Table 2: Patent applications to the EPO by country 1998-2001

Country	Total number				Per million inhabitants			
	1998	1999	2000	2001	1998	1999	2000	2001
EU-25	41 576	44 795	49 175	49 203	92	99	109	109 s
EU-15	41 365	44 584	48 890	48 929	111	119	130	129 s
EUR-12	34 076	36 666	40 258	40 347	113	122	133	133 s
BE	1 197	1 190	1 282	1 183	117	116	125	115
CZ	55	56	68	59	5	5	7	6
DK	646	790	826	832	122	149	155	155
DE	17 908	19 584	21 498	21 598	218	239	262	263
EE	6	5	7	6	4	4	5 p	4 p
EL	57	61	46	50	5	6	4	5
ES	609	674	735	723	15	17 e	19 e	18
FR	6 377	6 722	7 148	7 023	109	115 e	122	119 e
IE	137	175	238	178	37	47	63 ep	47 ep
IT	3 262	3 374	3 778	3 830	57	59	65	66 e
CY	2	4	4	5	3	6	5	7
LV	5	4	1	8	2	2	1	3
LT	1	1	3	3	0	0	1	1 bp
LU	53	70	63	76	126	164 e	144 e	173 be
HU	74	69	108	99	7	7	11	10
MT	2	3	7	4	5	8	18	9 e
NL	2 422	2 622	2 992	3 187	155	166	189	199
AT	994	975	1 071	1 156	123	121	132	142
PL	35	22	35	36	1	1	1	1
PT	21	38	31	38	2	4	3	4 e
SI	18	35	37	46	9	18	19	23
SK	12	11	16	10	2	2	3	2
FI	1 038	1 180	1 376	1 306	202	229	266	252
SE	2 032	2 055	2 220	2 157	230	232	251	243
UK	4 610	5 073	5 586	5 593	78	85	94	93 e
EEA-18	41 721	44 964	49 304	49 347	110	118	129	129 s
IS	19	22	33	35	69	82	119	122
LI	27	33	22	24	851	1 023	665	732 e
NO	311	325	359	360	70	73	80	80
CH	2 336	2 362	2 555	2 569	329	332	357	357
BG	9	8	9	5	1	1	1	1
RO	8	6	7	4	0	0	0	0
TR	15	32	24	32	0 i	0 i	0 i	0 i
CA	1 197	1 342	1 529	1 451	39	44 i	50 i	47 i
JP	14 589	15 514	18 066	20 114	116	123	142 i	158 i
RU	172	222	206	162	1 i	2 i	1 i	1 i
US	24 878	26 896	28 860	27178	92	99	102 i	95 i

i: Reference data on population come from OECD/MSTI.

Source: Eurostat. National Patent Indicators Statistics in focus. Science and Technology.
ISSN 1609-5995. 9/2004.

Table 3: Gross domestic expenditure on R&D as a percentage of GDP.

	1992		1996		2000		2001		2002		2003	
Australia	1.52		1.66		1.54		..		..		..	
Austria	1.45	c	1.60	c	1.86	c	1.92	c,p	1.93	c,p	1.94	c,p
Belgium	..		1.80		2.04		2.17		..		..	
Canada	1.64		1.68		1.92		2.03		1.91	p	1.87	b,p
Czech Republic	1.72	d,t	1.04		1.33		1.30		1.30		..	
Denmark	1.68		1.85	c	..		2.40		2.52		..	
Finland	2.13	c	2.54	c	3.40		3.41		3.46		..	
France	2.38		2.30		2.18	a	2.23		2.20	p	..	
Germany	2.40	c	2.25	c	2.49	c	2.51		2.52	c	2.50	c
Greece	..		..		..		0.65	c	..		..	
Hungary	1.04	d,t	0.65	d	0.80	d	0.95	d	1.02	d	..	
Iceland	1.35		..		2.75	c	3.06		3.09	c	..	
Ireland	1.04	c	1.32	c	1.15	c	1.15	c	..		..	
Italy	1.18		1.01		1.07		1.11		..		..	
Japan	2.89	l	2.78	a	2.99		3.07		3.12		..	
Korea	2.03	g	2.60	g	2.65	g	2.92	g	2.91	g	..	
Luxembourg	..		..		1.71		..		..		..	
Mexico	..		0.31		0.37		0.39		..		..	
Netherlands	1.90		2.01	a	1.90		1.89		..		..	
New Zealand	1.00	a	..		..		1.18	a	..		..	
Norway	..		..		..		1.60		1.67		..	
Poland	..		0.67		0.66		0.64		0.59	b	..	
Portugal	0.61		..		0.80	c	0.85		0.93	c	..	
Slovak Republic	1.78	a,d,t	0.92	d	0.65	m	0.64	m	0.58	m	..	
Spain	0.88	a	0.83	c	0.94		0.95		1.03		..	
Sweden	..		..		..		4.27	m	..		..	
Switzerland	2.59		2.67		2.57		..		..		..	
Turkey	0.49		0.45		0.64		..		..		..	
United Kingdom	2.02	a	1.88		1.84		1.86		1.88		..	
United States	2.65	j	2.55	j	2.72	j	2.74	j	2.67	j,p	2.62	b,j,p
Japan (adj.)	2.71	b,l	..		..		..		..		..	
EU-25	..		1.71	b	1.80	b	1.83	b	1.83	b,p	..	
EU-15	1.87	a,b	1.80	b	1.88	b	1.92	b	1.93	b,p	..	
Total OECD	2.18	b	2.12	b	2.24	b	2.28	b	2.26	b,p	..	

a Break in series with previous year for which data is available.
b Secretariat estimate or projection based on national sources.
c National estimate or projection adjusted, if necessary, by the Secretariat to meet OECD norms.
d Defence excluded (all or mostly)
g Excluding R&D in the social sciences and humanities.
h Federal or central government only.
j Excludes most or all capital expenditure.
l Overestimated or based on overestimated data.
m Underestimated or based on underestimated data.
p Provisional.
t Do not correspond exactly to the OECD recommendations.

Source : OECD, Main Science and Technology Indicators, May 2004.

The European Innovation Scoreboard (EIS) was developed at the request of the Lisbon European Council in 2000. The twelve most widely available indicators are used to calculate a compound measure, the summary innovation index which is shown in Figure 2. Countries above the horizontal dotted line have a current innovation performance above the EU average, while the trend[1] for countries to the right of the vertical line improved faster than the average EU trend.

Figure 2: Summary Innovation Index

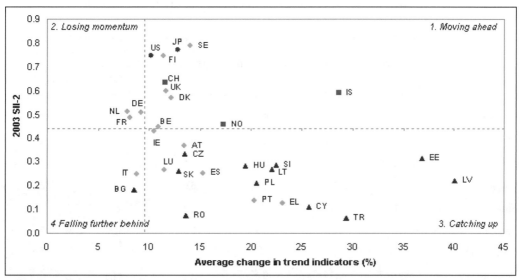

Source: European Innovation Scoreboard 2003. http://trendchart.cordis.lu/scoreboard2003/index.html

The Impact of Human Capital on the Economic Well-Being

Knowledge is dependent on a strong carrier – women and men educated to utilize knowledge acquired. Knowledge together with its carrier forms the human capital needed in a knowledge-based economy. Since education is a prerequisite for knowledge, we are interested in knowing what difference this makes in economic terms.

The 2004 edition of the OECD publication "Education at a Glance"[2] provides a rich, comparable and up-to-date array of indicators on the performance of education systems of OECD countries that represent the consensus of professional thinking on how to measure the current state of education internationally. One of the indicators, A11, is dedicated to the returns of education. The indicator is based on the level of education completed by the population with income from employment. On this basis, earnings relative to the earnings of people with upper secondary education can be computed. Even more advanced calculations consider the rate of return on educational investments. The rate of return (RoR) represents a measure of the returns obtained, over time, relative to the cost of the initial investment in education. Rates of return can be measured from the private individual's point of view or from society's point of view. Private rates of return measure

---

1   The trends are calculated as the percentage change between the last year for which data are available and the average over the preceding three years, after a one-year lag. E.g., when the most recent data are for 2002, the trend is based on the percentage change between 2002 and the average for 1998 to 2000 inclusive.

2   Education at a Glance: OECD Indicators – 2004 Edition. OECD Code 962004081P1. 9/2004. http://www.oecd.org/edu/eag2004

the future net economic payoff to an individual of increasing the amount of education undertaken. Social rates of return measure the benefits to society of additional education.

Table 4 shows social RoR calculations. One can see a positive influence between the educational level and the return of the educational effort for society.

Table 4:   Social internal RoR

A.11.7. Social internal rates of return (RoR) for individuals obtaining a tertiary-level degree or an advanced research qualification (ISCED 5(A, B)/6) from an upper secondary or post-secondary non-tertiary level of education (ISCED 3/4) (2001)

OECD countries	RoR when the individual immediately acquires the next higher level of education		RoR when the individual, at age 40, begins the next higher level of education in full-time studies		RoR when the individual returns, at age 40, to acquire next higher level of education in part-time studies (duration is doubled)	
	Males	Females	Males	Females	Males	Females
Australia	8.3	7.6	5.5	1.7	6.9	-0.1
Denmark	4.9	3.5	2.7	0.2	3.6	-0.5
Finland	10.5	8.7	8.6	5.4	8.9	4.3
Hungary	16.1	9.1	13.4	6.6	11.6	5.1
Spain	8.1	6.7	10.2	6.2	12.3	4.9
Sweden	8.2	6.5	6.5	3.9	12.7	7.6
Switzerland	6.7	4.9	--	--	4.6	1.8
United Kingdom	12.6	13.7	6.2	10.3	11.8	10.9
United States	11.1	7.9	8.0	3.2	7.3	0.8

Source: OECD. See Annex 3 for notes (www.oecd.org/edu/eag2004).

The OECD report "Education at a Glance 2004" then investigates the matter of macroeconomic returns to education. Box 1 summarizes some of the findings:

Box 1. Estimating the macroeconomic returns to education

A large body of empirical research has confirmed a positive link between education and productivity. Better educated employees are generally more productive, and may raise the productivity of coworkers.....

Studies of the macroeconomic returns to education are methodologically diverse and based on two broad theoretical approaches. The first, a neo-classical approach, models the relationship between the stock of education and the long-run level of GDP. Most studies follow this tradition. A second approach derives from "new-growth" theory and models the relationship between the stock of education and the rate of growth of GDP. Whether increases in the stock of education primarily affect the level of output, or its growth rate, is still unclear. Concerning the magnitude of the returns, the available studies indicate that in the neo-classical models a one-year increase in average education raises the level of output per capita by between 3 and 6%. Studies of the "new-growth" variety find that the same increase in average education raises the rate of growth of output by around 1%.

Source: Education at a Glance: OECD Indicators - 2004 Edition. OECD Code 962004081P1.9/2004. http://www.oecd.org/edu/eag2004, p.187

But it should be noted that human capital development is not only a tool for enhancing economic growth and productivity. Enhancing human capital is a means to achieve broader goals. "Sustainable development and social cohesion depend critically on the competencies of all of our population – with competencies understood to cover knowledge, skills, attitudes and values.[3]" The OECD Program DeSeCo[4], using a collaborative interdisciplinary approach, defined a set of key competencies that are critical for coping with the demands in a knowledge-based society and for enhancing sustainable socio-economic development.

The Role of Official Statistics

"If you have knowledge, let others light their candle with it." (Winston Churchill, 1874-1965)

In each competition, a procedure or a means is needed to determine the winner and the relative positions of the other participants or rivals. In the previous section, we have used indicators as if they were a natural resource. But they don't grow on trees! They are the result of scientific methods applied in official statistics. It is the role of official statistics to provide unbiased means to determine, in a competitive economic environment, who has reached what position and to help analyze the reasons for that.

While official statistics cannot deliver political solutions to economic issues, it contributes by measuring positions or results and by making this knowledge available to everybody. The political decision makers are responsible for using this knowledge. This leads to evidence based decision making.

In the previous discussion, we looked at the impact of human capital on economic well-being. The traditional contribution of official statistics consists of calculating indicators that describe the formal level of education of the population in the working age bracket and use this to measure the knowledge of this part of the population. These output related statistics are used as an approximation for the educational outcome, i.e., the knowledge acquired in the process.

During the nineties, the OECD International Adult Literacy Survey has focused on the adult reading skills as an outcome of the educational systems of 14 OECD countries. Recently, a Canadian study[5] has shown that the level of reading skills is a better measure of human capital than the traditional indicators based on formal education levels completed.

This example shows that the role of official statistics is not to calculate as many indicators as possible, but to develop models that are close enough to the reality observed that few, but pertinent, consistent, transparent and simple indicators can be derived to describe and quantify and the relevant dependencies and interdependencies.

---

3   Meeting of the OECD Education Ministers, Paris, 3-4 April 2001; Investing in Competencies for all (communiqué): http://www.oecd.org/dataoecd/48/24/1870589.pdf

4   The OECD DeSeCo (acronym of Definition and Selection of Competencies) program was carried out under the leadership of Switzerland (i.e. SFSO). Final Report: Rychen, D. S., & Salganik, L. H. (Eds.). Key competencies for a successful life and a well-functioning society. Göttingen, Germany: Hogrefe & Huber. 2003.

5   Coulombe, S., J-F Tremblay and S. Marchand Literacy Scores, Human Capital and Growth Across 14 OECD Countries, Statistics Canada and Human Resources and Skills Development Canada, Ottawa 2004.

In other words: While official statistics cannot present a simple equation that explains everything, the direct and indirect success factors, contributing to a competitive and knowledge based economy, it can help to identify key success factors, interdependencies and thus, hopefully, lead to adequate political decisions that enable economic growth. In this sense, official statistics provides a valuable means that is a necessary precondition for a competitive knowledge based economy.

In providing benchmarks and insights, official statistics must be both effective and efficient. Since budget cuts put a lot of pressure on national statistical offices, efficiency has become a matter of survival. Effectiveness however, depends on a lot of external factors. E.g., it is not effective to produce a huge amount of indicators if the user cannot digest the wealth of information. To avoid this pitfall, users and statisticians must sit together and discuss in advance the requirements both in terms of information and in terms of usability.

Three Examples Showing the Demand for Indicators in Swiss Politics

"Es ist nicht genug zu wissen, man muss es auch anwenden; es ist nicht genug zu wollen, man muss es auch tun." (Johann Wolfgang von Goethe, 1749-1832)

In order to illustrate the role of official statistics, several examples are presented. They show the close cooperation between politics and official statistics in important areas on the Swiss political agenda.

Carbon Dioxide Emissions[6]

The Swiss constitution requires a balance between nature and human requirements. This has led to a law on CO_2 emissions, put in force in 2000. The law is designed to reduce energy-related CO_2 emissions, i.e. emissions from the use of combustibles and motor fuels. The overall goal is to reduce the 1990 level of emissions by 10 per cent until 2010, combustible fuels by 15 per cent, motor fuels by 8 per cent. The CO_2 Law's goal is in line with the commitment taken under the Kyoto protocol on climate change, which requires a reduction of green house gas emissions of 8 per cent over the same time span. Among the six greenhouse gases covered by the Kyoto protocol, CO_2 accounts for more than 80 per cent of total emissions in Switzerland.

In a first phase, the CO_2 Law relies upon existing policy instruments (e.g. distance-related heavy vehicle fee HVF, Energy Law) and gives high priority to voluntary measures. In a second phase, not before 2004 and only if the reduction targets cannot be achieved through these measures alone, the government is to levy an incentive tax on fossil fuels (CO_2 tax). In order to follow the process, the law demands to regularly

---

6   Sources for this section include:
        Swiss Federal Law on the reduction of CO_2 emissions (CO_2 Law) of 8 October 1999, in force since 1 May 2000.
        Swiss Agency for the Environment, Forests and Landscapes: Emissionen nach CO_2-Gesetz und Kyoto-Protokoll, Bern 31.08.2004.
        Swiss Federal Chancellery, Swiss Federal Statistical Office: Indikatoren als strategische Führungsgrössen für die Politik, Neuchâtel 2004.
        Swiss Federal Statistical Office, Swiss Agency for the Environment, Forests and Landscapes, Swiss Federal Office for Spatial Development: Monitoring Sustainable Development MONET http://www.monet.admin.ch
        Swiss Federal Statistical Office: Environment Switzerland 2002 – Statistics and Analyses. Neuchâtel 2002.

evaluate the effects of implemented and planned measures on the basis of statistical surveys.

Phase one's voluntary measures include declarations whereby fuel consumers make a commitment to limit their emissions. Up to now more than 600 firms of 45 companies mostly involved in the chemical, paper and steel-making industries have formally pledged to cut their CO_2 emissions to 13.1 per cent below 1990 levels. Some other 30 groups of companies are involved in processes of target agreement or audit. They are expected to sign agreements in 2005.[7]

Figure 3:   Carbon Dioxide Emissions according to the CO_2 Law

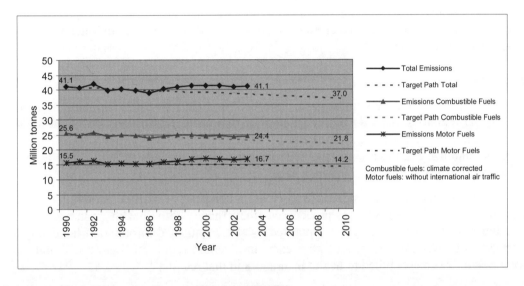

Source: Swiss Agency for the Environment, Forests and Landscape (SAEFL)

We're in 2004 now, i.e. in the first year, in which the introduction of a CO_2 tax would be possible – time to take a look at the course of events: After a moderate reduction during the economic slump in the beginning of the 1990ies, emissions have gone back up between 1997 and 1999. Since 1999 they remain stable – on the level of 1990. Combustibles' emissions show an overall slightly decreasing trend, while still lingering above the target path. Emissions of motor-fuel use are increasing and hence far away from the target of minus 8 per cent.

Due to this statistical information policy makers may assert that the measures already enacted fail to have the desired effect, and act on the basis of this statement. This is exactly what the Swiss Federal Council has done by recently submitting four proposals for a CO_2 tax to consultation. It will take a final decision after the evaluation of the consultation.

This case shows how a single indicator can be a crucial instrument for political decision making. It provides transparent and reliable information on the success or failure of reaching a political goal, in particular of course when the objective is quantified. On

---

7   Clearly, this requires innovative solutions developed in the respective industries producing the production equipment needed to manufacture chemicals or to produce energy itself. ABB Switzerland is a good example for this.

other occasions, the same indicator may be of relevance not as a single indicator but as part of a larger system. The CO_2 emissions indicator, to stick with this example, is included in a set of indicators, which has been compiled to serve as strategic management measure for politics. The set provides the government with a regular overview on key policy figures and an account on the degree of achievement of objectives. CO_2 emissions per GDP and per kilometers traveled report on the energy efficiency of the economy and of traffic. These are important figures for both economic competitiveness and environmental protection. On this account the two indicators figure in the Swiss monitoring system for sustainable development, called MONET. Embracing a long-term perspective, this indicator system is a precious knowledge source for decision makers in government, administration and economy, and also for the broader public. It furnishes facts and figures on the whole of social, economic and ecological developments and allows us to analyze both the current situation and overall trends in reference to a sustainable development.

Health Care

Swiss health care expenditures grew up to 11.2% of GDP in 2002, ranking 2nd among the OECD countries. This development implies that an increasing portion of the GDP must be paid for by the economic activities related to a decreasing portion of the GDP. In order to stabilize health care costs, a revision process is currently going on for the law governing health care services and insurances.

One of the measures considered is to create a competitive market among physicians by modifying the agreement procedures they have with health insurances for reimbursement. Such a strategy is supported by some statistical information indicating a correlation between the density of physicians in a certain region of Switzerland and the total cost of treatments billed to health insurances in that region.

The most used health cost database in Switzerland (Datenpool Santésuisse) relies on cost information for treatments paid for by the mandatory health insurance. It allows for analyzing both, cost and number of medical visits generated by the insured individual of a given canton, with respect to the number of physicians in the same canton. Figures 4 and 5 are the result of this analysis work done by obsan, the Swiss Health Observatory (obsan)[8] that is part of the Swiss Federal Statistical Office.

When the number of physicians increases, different underlying mechanisms are involved, to compensate for the decrease of patients: General practitioners will increase their activity during one visit which leads to an increase of the cost per visit. Specialists will increase the number of contacts they have per patient.

An important goal of the Swiss health law revision is to introduce more incentives for doctors to be efficient and cost conscious in their treatments[9]. To create optimal competitive conditions, both identified mechanisms need to be limited, with the introduction of various tools as, for example guidelines to limit unnecessary medical acts and a gatekeeper system to reduce the direct access to the specialist.

---

8   Reference documents are available in German and French only:
     http://www.obsan.ch/themen/versorgung/d/index.htm and
     http://www.obsan.ch/themen/versorgung/f/index.htm respectively.

9   At the same time, work is under way to standardize treatment quality. The idea is to ensure the quality level
     required for medical treatments to be effective.

Figure 4: Cost per medical visit and density of physicians – general practitioners, 2003

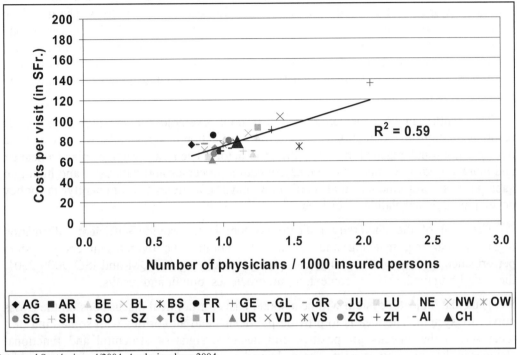

Source: Datenpool Santésuisse, 4/2004. Analysis: obsan 2004.

Figure 5: Number of medical visits and density of physicians – specialists, 2003

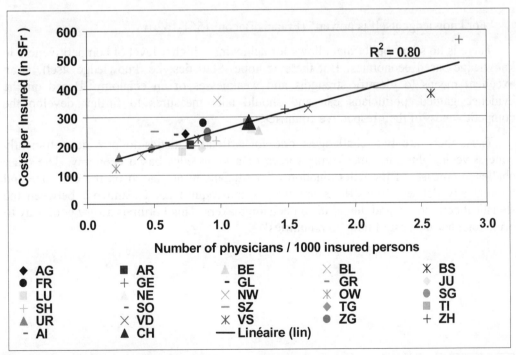

Source: Datenpool Santésuisse, 4/2004. Analysis: obsan 2004.

Swiss Universities

In Switzerland, the federal government and the governments of the cantons have started a major project to reorganize the Swiss university system by 2008. The goal is to have a competitive and coherent university system that covers both, education and research, for all types of Swiss universities. To support this process and to monitor the Swiss university system, the universities, their organisations, the governmental institutions and the Swiss Federal Statistical Office work together to develop a university indicator system.

This work can be considered as a text book example for satisfying the OECD recommendations made in 2003: "…the tertiary education reforms under way have raised new questions and engaged more and different actors. The new directions place a heavier and more varied set of burdens on data collection processes and data uses, and highlight gaps in basic information that until now have not figured prominently in policy development or stakeholder decisions."[10]

The goal of the university indicator system is to provide sufficient information regarding learning, teaching and research to monitor the overall university system performance. In line with the classical quality models e.g., EFQM and ISO 9000-2001, the underlying model covers context, input, processes, output and results.

Thus, the indicator system will be a sound basis for political discussions on the Swiss university system. The idea is to provide politicians and authorities with some kind of a radar screen that checks for positive and negative signs of structural and functional changes in the university system. These changes might be desired and therefore should be supported, or they might be undesirable and thus require immediate countermeasures.

Conclusion

"For knowledge itself is power." (Francis Bacon, 1561-1626)

There is no silver bullet that allows for achieving a higher level of competitiveness in knowledge-based economies. But there is hope: Statistics, i.e. knowledge itself, is an excellent means to identify strengths and weaknesses of an economy. Based on the evidence gained, politicians can and should take measures to further develop the competitiveness of their respective countries.

Thus, there are two challenges: one for official statistics to provide sufficiently conclusive insights into the driving forces of a knowledge-based economy. The other challenge consists of the determination of politicians to act based on the evidence and without any delays. Both efforts are related and require good teamwork between the statistical community and the political decision makers. This Forum is a very good way to bring together the best of both communities!

---

10   OECD Review of the Swiss Tertiary Education System. Examiners' Report. July 2003. http://www.gwf-gsr.ch/html/frameset-e.htm

Measuring the Environment

Composite Indicators of Environmental Sustainability

Bedřich Moldan[1], Tomáš Hák, Jan Kovanda, Miroslav Havránek, Petra Kušková

Charles University Environment Center, Prague

The use of environmental indicators at the international level was pioneered by the OECD, which published in 1974 its "Core Set of Indicators" (OECD, 1974) recommending use of them by the EU Member States. Since than, a large number of environmental indicators are regularly published by many intergovernmental, international and national institutions. In addition to the continuous work by OECD, the most outstanding ones are at the global level indicators produced by UNEP (the Global Environmental Outlook series, UNEP 2002), UNDP (annual Human Development Report, UNDP 2004), World Bank (World Development Report series, WB 2004), and World Resources Institute (World Development Report series, WRI 2003). At the European level, many indicator-based reports are produced by the European Environment Agency (e.g. the so-called Dobříš Assessment Series, EEA 2003, or Environmental Signal Series, EEA 2004).

The concept of the environment and its protection gradually evolved from the Stockholm UN Conference on the Human Environment in 1972 through the UN Conference on Environment and Development in Rio de Janeiro in 1992 to the World Summit on Sustainable Development in Johannesburg in 2002. According to the current understanding based on results of the Johannesburg Summit, the environment is seen as one of the three pillars of sustainable development. This broader view does not restrain the distinct role of the environment but points out its essential interconnection with the other two pillars, namely the economic and social pillar. Therefore, it is appropriate to use the term "environmental sustainability" that stresses both the specificity of the environment and its fundamental anchoring within the sustainability framework.

Accordingly, there is a need for indicators that could cover the linkages between the environmental and the other two dimensions of sustainability. The indicators that show the degree of decoupling between the environmental pressures (such as the emissions of harmful substances) and the economic performance (such as the GDP) are a good example of indicators capturing such linkages (OECD, 2002). Such indicators cover well some of the essential features of sustainable development but by no means cover the issue of environmental sustainability as such for which a growing demand is noticeable.

Decision-makers as well as the general public would like to know in one glance what the environmental situation in a given country (or region) is. There is a clear request for developing a single indicator that could serve as an overall measure of environmental sustainability. We may look for inspiration at the other two pillars of sustainable development. In the economic sphere a commonly accepted indicator is the **Gross Domestic Product (GDP)**. It represents the total value of goods and services produced by economy over a certain period of time (a month, a season, a year etc.). It is a model of a very robust indicator very widely used. In the social sphere no such indicator exists but

1   Corresponding author: U Krize 8, Prague 5, 158 00, Czech Republic; bedrich.moldan@czp.cuni.cz

the **Human Development Index (HDI)** is regularly compiled and published by the UN Development Program for more than ten years. It is a composite index that measures average achievements of a country in three basic aspects of human development: longevity, knowledge, and a decent standard of living. Longevity is measured by life expectancy at birth; knowledge is measured by a combination of the adult literacy rate and the combined primary, secondary, and tertiary gross enrollment ratio; and standard of living is measured by adjusted GDP per capita. It is gaining growing respect and is more and more used and quoted (UNDP 2004).

Both the Gross Domestic Product and the Human Development Index essentially satisfy the three essential criteria of salience, credibility and legitimacy (Cash et al., 2004; Parris and Kates, 2003). **Salience** means that the indicator is interesting, useful and relevant for the user. It must show something "that really matters" for him. As the user is mostly a decision-maker, there is a request for policy relevance. However, policy implications should be obvious and unambiguous. Moreover, the indicator should be able to serve as a benchmarking instrument, to show trends in time and set targets. **Credibility** deals with the scientific validity of the indicator i.e. quality of data used for its construction, the methodology of aggregation, and other transformations, adequacy of presentation and similar issues. The third aspect is **legitimacy**. It touches the perception of the indicator, its methods of construction and the competence of the producer as seen from the point of view of a wide range of potential users and stakeholders whose interests, values, or beliefs might be affected by the indicator. For OECD, legitimacy flows directly from the process of seeking a consensus among the member countries. Other stakeholders like the representatives of business, trade unions, and environmental non-governmental organisations routinely take part in the OECD expert-level discussions.

Regarding the Gross Domestic Product the criterion of credibility and legitimacy is satisfied by a general consensus that the national statistical offices or similar institutions of that type are fully competent institutions to produce impartial and reliable information. In addition, the intergovernmental institutions namely UN, Bretton Woods institutions, OECD, and Eurostat are supervising the national bodies. As for salience, one objection points out that a "flow" indicator does not capture the "real wealth of nations" (Serageldin, 1995), another to the fact that the "grey" economy is not covered. A lot of criticism is raised by environmentalists, e.g. that the GDP does not capture the depletion of natural resources or that evidently harmful activities or events are counted as assets (Hamilton, 1994; Cobb, Halstead and Rowe, 1995; Meadows, 1998). However, any proposed corrections do not result in a truly substantial change of the original approach. The important feature is that the resulting numbers are obtained in a clear and transparent way. According to our opinion the most important feature of the GDP, which adds both to its salience and credibility, is that the level of arbitrariness in constructing the indicator is minimal and, in addition, is legitimized by a very broad international consensus and a standardized methodology used for a long period of time with no substantial changes. Despite all the criticism the GDP is universally accepted as a reliable measure of the overall economic development of a given country or other well-defined, sub-national or supranational unit. Indeed, the Gross Domestic Product is such a powerful indicator that it more or less directly defines the level of economic achievement.

The Human Development Index, on the other hand, is far less robust indicator regarding all three criteria of salience, credibility, and legitimacy. All of them could be questioned. Its three components certainly do not cover all the aspects of human development even if they arguably capture the very important if not the most important ones. Nevertheless, the selection of the factors (and their sub-factors) is essentially arbitrary as well as the method of calculation of the index. The UN Development Program, despite UN being a large and respected organisation, is not universally accepted as an "arbiter" on what is and what is not human development. Despite that the HDI serves as an acceptable benchmark for assessing human development particularly in countries within the "middle part" of the scorecard of the world. To some extent the history of the Human Development Index may serve as a witness that a highly aggregated indicator, if properly designed, may serve as an overall measure of such a complex and difficult phenomenon called "human development". It is simple, understandable, and transparent and focuses on the very basic but quantifiable prerequisites of any decent human life.

In the field of environmental sustainability several composite indicators have been proposed. We selected six of them.

Environmental Sustainability Index (ESI) is published by the World Economic Forum (World Economic Forum, 2002). It is a measure of the overall progress towards environmental sustainability, developed for 142 countries. The ESI scores are based upon a set of 20 core indicators each of which combines two to eight variables for a total of 68 underlying variables. The ESI permits cross-national comparisons of environmental progress in a systematic and quantitative fashion. It represents a first step towards a more analytically driven approach to environmental decision making.

The European Union's Joint Research Center in Ispra developed the **Dashboard of Sustainability (DS)** as a software which allows presenting complex relationships between economic, social and environmental issues in a highly communicative format aimed at decision-makers and citizens interested in sustainable development (JRC, 2004). For the WSSD, the CGSDI (Consultative Group on Sustainable Development Indicators) published the "From Rio to Jo'burg" Dashboard, with over 60 indicators for more than 200 countries – a tool for elaborating assessment of 10 years since the Rio Summit (http://www.iisd.org/cgsdi/dashboard.htm).

Wellbeing index (WI) combines 36 indicators of health, population, wealth, education, communication, freedom, peace, crime, and equity into the Human Wellbeing index, and 51 indicators of land, biodiversity, water quality and supply, air quality and global atmosphere, and energy and resource use pressures into an Ecosystem Wellbeing index. The two indexes are then combined into the Wellbeing/Stress Index (Prescott-Allen, 2001).

Ecological footprint (EF) was firstly published in 1996 by Wackernagel and Rees. The EF of a specified population can be defined as the area of ecologically productive land needed to maintain its current consumption patterns and absorb its wastes with the prevailing technology. People consume resources from all over the world, so their footprint can be thought of as a sum of these areas, wherever on the planet they are located (Wackernagel and Rees, 1996).

Living planet index (LPI) is an indicator promoted by the World Wildlife Fund. It tries to assess the overall state of the Earth's natural ecosystems, which includes national and global data on human pressures on natural ecosystems arising from the consumption of natural resources and the effects of pollution (Loh, 2002):

The Eurostat's material flow indicators are based on economy-wide material flow analysis, which quantifies physical exchange between the national economy, the environment and foreign economies on the basis of total material mass flowing across the boundaries of the national economy. Material inputs into the economy consist primarily of extracted raw materials and produced biomass that has entered the economic system (this biomass is composed of, for example, harvested crops and wood). Material outputs consist primarily of emissions to air and water, landfilled wastes and dissipative uses of materials (e.g. fertilizers, pesticides and solvents). As an example could serve the indicator of **Direct Material Consumption (DMC)** defined as a sum of all domestic extraction flows (extracted raw material, harvested biomass, etc.) including imported and excluding exported material flows (both raw materials, biomass and semi-manufactured/manufactured products) (Eurostat, 2001).

To illustrate these indicators and indices we present performance of the G-7 countries regarding these indicators expressed as a rank (Tab. 1). To enable a simple comparison between the countries we have constructed radial graphs for each country in a similar way (Fig. 1). We have drawn the ranking charts for the Gross Domestic Product, Human Development Index, Environmental Sustainability Index, Wellbeing Index, Ecological Footprint and Domestic Material Consumption. The rank in the Dashboard of Sustainability is presented as the Sustainable Development Index, i.e. average of all four components representing the four pillars (environmental, economic, social and institutional) as well as the rank only for the environmental pillar. The Living Planet Index does not calculate the overall score for individual countries but presents scores of its elements. We have selected the "CO_2 footprint" that is in fact the amount of CO_2 emissions per capita.

Table 1. Ranks of the G-7 countries by the selected indices

	Canada	France	Germany	Italy	Japan	UK	USA
DMC[1]	7.	4.	5.	2.	3.	1.	6.
WB[2]	1.	6.	2.	5.	3.	7.	4.
EWB[3]	1.	6.	2.	4.	7.	5.	3.
ESI[4]	1.	2.	4.	6.	5.	7.	3.
EF[5]	6.	4.	2.	1.	3.	5.	7.
EF-CO_2[6]	6.	1.	5.	2.	4.	3.	7.
HDI[7]	1.	5.	6.	7.	3.	4.	2.
DS-SDI[8]	3.	4.	1.	7.	5.	6.	2.
DS-SDIenv[9]	2.	3.	1.	6.	5.	7.	4.
GBL[10]	1.	3.	6.	4.	7.	5.	2.
GDP[11]	2.	7.	3.	5.	4.	6.	1.

Note: The lower score, the better result

[1] DMC – Direct Material Consumption Indicator, 2000; Data source: Eurostat, 2002; Canada, USA, Japan – estimation EC EVG1-CT-2002-00083 (MOSUS)

[2] WB – Wellbeing Index, end of 90'ies; Data source: Prescott-Allen, 2001

[3] EWB – Ecological Wellbeing Index, end of 90'ies; Data source: Prescott-Allen, 2001

[4] ESI – Environmental Sustainability Index, 2002; Data source: World Economic Forum, 2002

[5] EF – Ecological Footprint, 1999; Data source: Living planet report, 2002

[6] EF-CO2 – CO2 Ecological Footprint, 1999; Data source: Living planet report, 2002

[7] HDI – Human Development Index, 2002; Data source: Human Development Report, 2004

[8] Ds-SDI – Dashboard of Sustainability, 2000; Data source: Dashboard of sustainability; UNCSD set

[9] Ds-SDIenv - Dashboard of Sustainability, 2000; Data source: Dashboard of sustainability; environmental part of UNCSD set

[10] GBL – GeoBiosphere Load, end of 90'ies; own calculation by the authors

[11] GDP – Gross Domestic Product, 2001; Data source: Human Development Report, 2004

If we look at the selected indicators from the point of view of the Driving Force-Pressure-State-Impact-Response framework we may observe that the indicators ESI, DS, and WI contain some elements of all five parameters of the framework including certain aspects of the responses. In contrast, the environmental part of the Dashboard, EF, LPI, and DMC does not contain any elements of response. Comparison between the first of the indicators and GDP/HDI shows a relatively high level of correlation between them. On the other hand, the second group documents a quite different picture.

The assessment of the selected indicators is based on the three important criteria of salience, credibility and legitimacy. Let's start with the salience. We have stated that indicators of environmental sustainability should deal with some important links between the environmental and the other two pillars of sustainable development. From this point of view the responses may be seen as such links. However, in our opinion, this is not the case. The proper links to be captured are those between the physical anthropogenic activity affecting directly or indirectly the environment and the environmental parameters. The four indicators, namely environmental part of the Dashboard, the Ecological Footprint, the Living Planet Index, and the Direct Material Consumption are, from this point of view, better suited for being accepted as the indicators of environmental sustainability. However, all of them are capturing only some partial elements of the environmental parameters.

All the presented indicators have serious problems regarding the other two criteria, namely credibility and legitimacy. Probably the most important comment is that basically in all cases the selection of the sub-parameters of the indicators is arbitrary. The elements of all the indicators are certainly important ones designated by excellent experts but still the selection lacks clear scientifically objective base. This objection is particularly valid regarding the Ecological Footprint. The resulting value of the indicator is dominated by the concept of the CO_2 absorption that is questionable. In addition, the method of aggregation is in all cases not without problems (JRC, 2002). The legitimacy of all presented indicators is probably the main problem. However, as we have seen from the example of the Human Development Index, the legitimacy is something that may not be obtained easily and instantly but still it is possible to achieve gradually. We may hope that if the scientific community brings some truly salient and credible indicator of environmental sustainability, the legitimacy may be finally earned. An encouraging example of such process is the ongoing effort to develop an "agreed set of sustainable development indicators" by OECD (OECD 2004) or the structural indicators used by the European Union (European Commission, 2003).

As a contribution to the international effort to develop a suitable indicator of environmental sustainability we propose a composite indicator that we call the **Geobiosphere Load Index (GBL)** (Moldan et al., 2004, under review). As our basic approach – keeping in mind the D-P-S-I-R framework – we have chosen to focus on the pressures. We fully acknowledge the fact that it is the impact what really matters. And there is already convincing evidence that, e.g., there is a direct relation between air pollution in European cities and number of cardiorespiratory diseases and deaths (Clancy, L. at al., 2002). However in general, exploring such causality requires long term series of data, epidemiological studies, application of economic valuation techniques, risk analysis, etc. And finally, unambiguous results are hard to achieve. The pressure indicators best comprehend the fundamental stresses that human activities put on environment. The GBL index is calculated in a transparent way according to a straightforward formula. By proposing a single index based on only three clearly defined indicators (sub-indices) we fulfill the first of the fundamental prerequisites: A small number of individual indicators situated at the same step in the cause-effect chain (OECD, 2001). Formally, our proposed GBL resembles the UNDP's Human Development Index based on three fundamental components of a dignified human life: These three components are characterized by comprehensible indicators that are then put together by a simple and transparent mathematical formula. The small number of sub-indices adds to the transparency of the resulting index.

Our index is constructed in a similar way based on three indicators capturing – in our opinion – the most important factors of environmental sustainability. Energy, materials and land can be regarded as the essential components and prerequisites of nature's services (Daily, 1997). The idea of ecosystem services is well established and is currently developed as a fundamental concept by the ongoing Millennium Ecosystem Assessment Program (Alcamo et al., 2003). The provision of energy and materials basically equals the provision of ecosystem services (such as food, fiber, energy resources, biochemicals or freshwater). Land – in relation with other environmental media – is a prerequisite for all kinds of ecosystem services (besides mentioned provisions services further supporting services as e.g. primary production, regulating services as e.g. climate regulation, and cultural services as e.g. recreation).

Calculating the index (i.e. the aggregation) requires "translating" the values of the constituent variables into physical measures – tonnes, joules and hectares. The data/variables for the indicators are based on more or less accepted accounting frameworks. The material component of the GeoBiosphere Load index is based on data and indicators of the economy-wide material flow analysis (MFA). From the menu of the MFA-based indicators, we have chosen the Domestic Material Consumption (DMC). As shown in a recent study based on LCA analysis the DMC indicator does not only capture the pressures, but corresponds well also with the impacts on the environment such as climate change, acidification, loss of biodiversity, toxic effects, etc. (van der Voet et al., 2004), Energy flow analysis (EFA) is a methodological framework that provides pressure indicators analogical to MFA indicators. Consumption of energy relates closely to the amount of most harmful emitted pollutants (SO_2, NOx, SPM, CO_2) and in most cases also shows the issues of the source scarcity and/or source depletion. Since the EFA-based indicators are not available we have used the Total Primary Energy Supply (TPES) indicator for our pilot GBL calculation. Besides the energy and material flows, land and land (area) requirements are the third important category of resource inputs for any economic activities. The land requirement indicator can stand – among others – a proxy for the pressures on biodiversity. The loss of biodiversity resulting from human activities is thought to be one of the most pressing problems of global environmental change (Haberl, in print). There are several types of mechanisms of human impacts on biodiversity (McNeely et al. 1995) but in this case we may assume that there is a relation between land use and biodiversity (effects of habitat loss and fragmentation). An appropriate proxy for the land requirement indicator is a subject of further research (several potential directions as an adjusted ecological footprint measure, Human appropriation of net primary production (HANPP) or adjusted land use indicator are considered). Ecological footprint data have been used for the presented application.

The resulting index is constructed as an "average" of the individual indicators (sub-indexes). The result – in the format of a rank – of our calculation of the GBL index is in Tab. 1 and Fig. 1.

The GBL certainly does not capture all environmental problems caused by human activity, e.g. all the harmful effects of transport, dispersal of chemicals, direct influence on climate and/or on biodiversity. However, given the high correlation between selected indicators and such phenomena like production and consumption of chemicals (correlated with material indicators), emissions of greenhouse gases and some "classic" pollutants (correlation with energy indicators) or loss of habitats (correlation with land indicators) even these factors are captured to some extent.

Figure 1. Performance of the G-7 countries regarding the selected indicators expressed as a rank

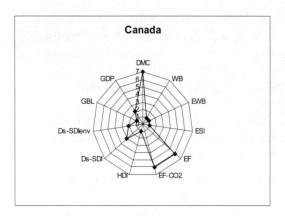

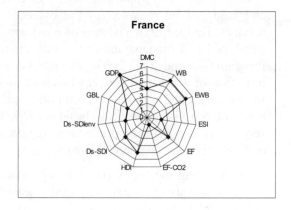

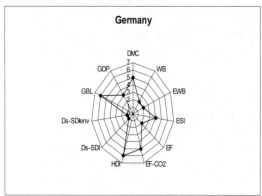

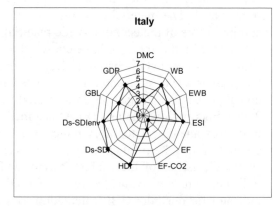

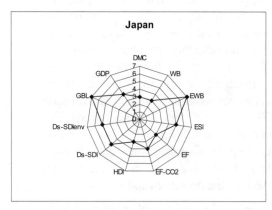

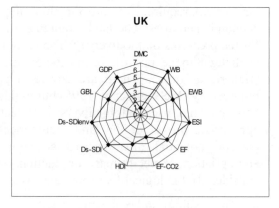

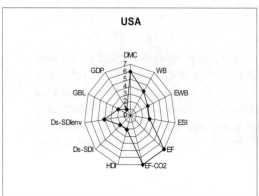

References:

Alcamo, J. et al. (2003): Ecosystems and Human Well-being. A framework for Assessment. Millennium Ecosystem Assessment. Island Press. 245 pp.

Cash, D.W., Clark, W., Alcock, F., Dickson, N.M., Eckley, N., and Jaeger, J. (2004): Salience, Credibility, Legitimacy and Boundaries: Linking Research, Assessment and Decision Making. Global Environmental Assessment Project, Harvard University (under review) (http://www.ksg.harvard.edu/gea). 24 pp.

Clancy, L. at al. (2002): Effect of air-pollution control on death rates in Dublin, Ireland: an intervention study. Lancet, 2002, 360:1210-1214.

Cobb, C., Halstead, T. and Rowe, J. (1995): Redefining Progress - The Genuine Progress Indicator: Summary of Data and Methodology. Redefining Progress. San Francisco.

Daily, G.C. (ed.) (1997): Nature's Services. Societal Dependence on Natural Systems. Island Press, Washington, DC. 392 pp.

EEA (2003): Europe's environment: the third assessment. Environmental assessment report No 10. 343 pp.

EEA (2004): EEA Signals 2004. 36 pp.

European Commission (2003): Communication from the Commission: Structural Indicators. Brussels, 16.10.2002; COM(2002) 551.

Eurostat (2001): Economy-wide Material Flow Accounts and Derived Indicators. A Methodological Guide. 92 pp.

Global Leaders of Tomorrow Environment Task Force, World Economic Forum in collaboration with Yale Center for Environmental Law and Policy Center for International Earth Science Information Network at Columbia University. 301 pp.

Haberl, H., Erb, K.H., Plutzar, CH., Fischer-Kowalski, M., Krausmann, F. (2004): Human appropriation of net primary production (HANPP) as indicator for pressures on biodiversity. In Moldan, B., Hak, T. and Bourdeau, P. (eds.): SUSTAINABLE DEVELOPMENT: HOW TO MEASURE PROGRESS THROUGH INDICATORS. In preparation for print by Island Press.

Hamilton, K. (1994): Green Adjustments to GDP. Resource Policy, 20 (3), 155-168.

JRC (2002): State-of-the-art Report on Current Methodologies and Practices for Composite Indicator Development. Institute for the Protection and Security of the Citizen Technological and Economic Risk Management, report by the Applied Statistics Group. 72 pp.

JRC (2004): Dashboard of Sustainability (http://esl.jrc.it/envind/dashbrds.htm).

Loh, J. (ed.) (2002): Living Planet Report 2002. World Wildlife Fund. 39 pp.

Meadows, D. (1998): Indicators and Information Systems for Sustainable Development. A Report to the Balaton Group, published by The Sustainability Institute. 95 pp.

Moldan, B. et al. (2004): GeoBiosphere Load: Proposal for an Index. A paper for the Assessment of Sustainability Indicators Project undertaken by SCOPE, Paris (under review). 11 pp.

OECD (1998): Towards sustainable development. Environmental Indicators. OECD publications. 129 pp.

OECD (2001): Environmental indices: Review of aggregation methodologies in use. ENV/EPOC/SE (2001)2. 34 pp.

OECD (2002): Indicators to Measure Decoupling of Environmental Pressure from Economic Growth. SG/SD(2002) 1/FINAL. 108 pp.

Parris, T.M. and Kates, R.W. (2003): Characterizing and Measuring Sustainable Development. Annu. Rev. Environ. Resour. 2003. 28:13.1–13.28

Prescott-Allen, R. (2001): The Wellbeing of Nations. A country-by-Country Index of Quality of Life and the Environment. Island Press. 341 pp.

Serageldin, I. (1995): Sustainability and the wealth of nations: preliminary draft. World Bank, Washington, DC. 19 pp.

UNDP (2004): Human Development Report 2004. 283 pp.

UNEP (2002): Global Environment Outlook 3. 416 pp.

van der Voet, E., van Oers, L., Nikolic, I. (2004): Dematerialisation: not just a matter of weight. Development and application of a methodology to rank materials based on their environmental impacts. CML rapport 160 - Section Substances & Products, Centre of Environmental Science, Leiden.

Wackernagel, M. and Rees, W., (1996): Our Ecological Footprint. Reducing Human Impact on the Earth. Gabriola Island, BC, New Society Publishers.

WB (2004): World Development Report 2005: A Better Investment Climate for Everyone. 288 pp.

World Economic Forum (2002): Environmental Sustainability Index. An Initiative of the

WRI (2003): World Resources 2002-2004. Decisions for the Earth. 315 pp.

The Reduction of Complexity by Means of Indicators – Case Studies in the Environmental Domain

Walter Radermacher

Federal Statistical Office, Germany

Abstract

This paper sheds light on the process of constructing statistical indicators and on the actors involved. It is shown that the model of indicator-building presented is based on co-operation between the actors of politics, science, and statistics and that it enhances discussion with the general public - provided that the information is successfully transmitted. By using case studies from the environmental domain - showing the problem of short-lived indicators and of disregarding an actor involved - an optimistic construction process for indicator-building is developed. The model takes account of all relevant actors (statistics, science, and politics) and of the complexity of their work systems. Analysing the case examples also shows that indicator-building cannot be a linear process but is rather an iterative decision-making process where satisfactory sub-solutions are found and sub-targets are met. Aggregating the indicators is done as a rational process in that procedure of indicator-building.

Indicators and the conflicting goals of statistics, science, and politics

Generally, what is meant by statistical indicators is quantitative variables measured or calculated which, individually or as part of a set, allow to obtain as much valid empirical information as possible on a specific matter (indicandum). Consequently, the purpose of indicator-building is to represent the complex reality - the state of a society, its social, economic and ecological connections, and their development - by means of an informative indicator (Schäfer et al. 2004, pp. 167 et seqq.). The main structures and developments of reality are to be represented by statistical information. Reality itself is complex. Extracting from it the essential requires a process of knowledge-finding where the essential is separated from the non-essential and where small descriptive "information atoms" are aggregated in a stepwise process to form larger artefacts, which then can represent more comprehensive sub-systems of reality. The most prominent and most successful approach of that type is national accounts. Using a wealth of individual specialised information, a theory-based, consistent empirical overall picture of the business cycle is developed there, leading to macro indicators such as growth, income, etc. This example illustrates how larger and smaller sections of reality correspond with larger and smaller pieces of statistical information and what the (hierarchical) relations between the latter are like.

For quite some time already, indicators have been in the focus of the general public. At the theoretical and political levels, a multitude of indicators are discussed and increasing attention is paid to their empirical implementation. Compared with many project-oriented measurements of other providers, official statistics not only meets the criteria of objectivity and neutrality but also offers the advantage of having regular publications and long-time statistical series.

Empirical implementation involves not only mere statistical measurability. A fundamental task of statistics is to provide information (as opposed to data). Statistical data will become relevant information only if they meet the requirements of the users (for example, politics). Therefore, relevance is the comprehensive quality measure from the users' point of view and, consequently, is observed at the national and European levels. At the European level, for instance, the relevance of statistical surveys is laid down in the basic Article 10 of the European statistics law (Council Regulation (EC) No 322/97 on Community Statistics. To meet the quality requirement (relevance) at the national level, the survey programme of official statistics in Germany is developed in a dialogue with data users and is largely laid down in legal provisions. The trade-off between statistical measurability and relevance should be found in that dialogue.

What is decisive for information provision, apart from relevance, is methodology. In Germany, it is laid down in Article 1 of the Federal Statistics Law that data acquisition must be based on using scientific findings and on applying appropriate methods. However, methodology reaches far beyond official statistics and has general importance for empirical work. Disregarding the methodological frame may cause serious errors. This means that indicator construction has to cope with the conflicting goals of statistical measurability, scientific consistency, and political relevance. When applying this to indicator construction, three major "actors" will emerge: statistics, science, and politics. Every individual actor has a complex work system of his own. To illustrate those work systems, a pyramid picture is helpful (chart 1). The pyramid base describes the highly detailed work system, whereas the top part describes the very general work system - in between there is a middle level. Applying this to the work systems of the three actors provides the following picture:

Figure 1. Work systems of the actors

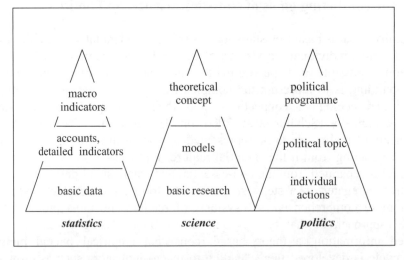

The base of the political pyramid comprises a broad block of individual actions that are taken to arrange the living together in the society (to keep up or set up order). Individual actions may be structured or grouped by their content to form goals of political topics. To achieve such goals, action packages are adopted. At the general level shown at the top, there is the political programme, characterised by the vision and goals of the policy concerned. At all levels (especially the middle level), decision-making is influenced by various interest groups (lobbyists) and markets.

What is closely connected with the political discussion on goals is the contribution that can be made by statistical reporting systems to measure progress made on the way towards those goals. An item may be represented by different tools and in different detail. In the base of the data pyramid, there are the basic data on selected specific topics, which are collected by subject-related surveys. The basic data are applied in many ways for specialised planning and research. Above them (middle level), there are indicators that are already more aggregated or more selective in terms of subject matter and that are integrated in a set of indicators, e.g. as sub-indicators. At the same level, there are the accounting approaches, where basic data from various sources are integrated in consistent methodical frames, thus allowing a systematic and more analytical view of the matter in question. As mentioned before, the most prominent example of such accounting approaches is national accounts, while another example is environmental-economic accounting which describes the interaction between the economy and the environment. The top level of the pyramid represents a very specific section of statistical information through a very small number of indicators. At the top of the pyramid, there may be a complex figure, a macro indicator such as the gross domestic product. Indicators at that top level may be less demanding in terms of consistency, but they provide early information that is relevant for decision-making. The purpose here is not to represent a matter in every detail and with all aspects and processes; instead, the complexity is to be reduced to relatively few simple measures (Radermacher 1998, p. 240). Macro indicators address especially politics and the general public, and they provide a more compact picture. However, the use of indicators always depends on whether, and to what extent, they are underpinned by, and combined with informative data and indicators (from the lower levels).

To provide a consistent overall picture, the above pyramid picture must also include the sphere of science. The most detailed manifestation of the scientific work system is basic research. The results of basic research are integrated into the level above, where models are developed. The top is formed by the theoretical concept used to present a matter, which again is influenced by the relevant paradigms of a science.

In the following chapter, examples will show what happens when actors or pyramid levels are disregarded in indicator-building.

The science-based, the political and the statistical approach to indicator construction

Dominance of science (with the example of the green national product)

In the 1980s, criticism of the national product (or the domestic product) as an indicator increased because it dominates the economic discussion, while disregarding environmental aspects. Critics demanded an indicator that both represents economic development and takes account of the utilisation of nature involved (external effects such as depletion of raw materials, deterioration of air and water quality, reduction of plant and animal species, etc.). The vision was to have an indicator covering economic development as a function of nature utilisation: The idea of the "green national product" was born. The intention was to calculate "only" a kind of consumption of natural assets, which could be used to indicate a genuine, "pure" growth figure (see Brouwer et al. 1999, pp. 13 et seqq.). To determine such consumption of nature, it was attempted to perform a valuation using a neo-classical economic concept. To put it in simplified terms, that concept was based on two theses:

- Thesis 1: We live in a deterministic-linear world of mechanical functions, which can exactly be represented by economic theory (through a mathematical equation). A balance will be reached with marginal movements and changes.

- Thesis 2: Individual preferences reflect the standards of the society, i.e. values and valuations do not have to be (newly) generated. If there is no relevant market (e.g. a market for the climate), the procedure will not change because a market value is (technically) simulated or shadow prices are determined through a survey.

Consequently, a green national product based on that approach will lead to a fictitious balance of the overall economy, with nature integrated. The neo-classical approach is impressive because of its purely theoretically developed model solutions, its methodical consistency, and its formal elegance in valuing environmental aspects (Radermacher 1998, p. 238); however, it was not possible to implement it in practice. The reasons for the failure of that approach are contained in the above theses: Integrating nature into the green national product is not a marginal movement but rather a massive structural change, modifying all values (even the actual market values). Consequently, there are massive problems of valuation when determining the consumption of natural assets.

If we apply this to the pyramid pictures, we get three statements (chart 2):

- The construction process of indicator-building runs once: Based on the theoretical concept (of theses 1 and 2), basic research has to define what elements of natural assets and what services provided by nature should be valued by what methods. Then, statistics has to collect the basic data required for the equation. Subsequently, the basic data are "summed up" to form the macro indicator (the green national product) weighted by prices.

- With that approach, the middle level of the pyramid is irrelevant: There is always a direct top-down (or bottom-up) movement. The interpretation of the results is overburdened with theoretical assumptions and the indicator is attached with a degree of importance that it just does not have.

- Altogether, the approach of the green national product ignores the political pyramid; there is no assessment by politics.

Figure 2. Neo-classical approach to the green national product

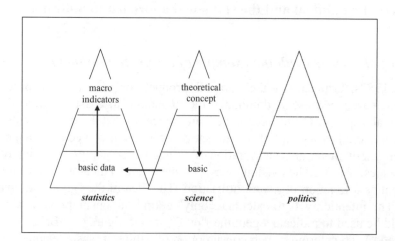

Goals set by politics (e.g. increasing the share of renewable energy sources) must be achieved by structural intervention influencing both the economy (e.g. production of wind power stations) and the quality of landscape, ecosystems, and biodiversity. Assessing environmental aspects cannot be a matter constructed and measured by experts alone, as is stated by thesis 2. Basically, what is needed is a decision to be taken by the society or by politics - a decision which, on the one hand, reflects the public opinion and is in accordance with the preferences of the electorate and, on the other hand, integrates long-term and global aspects (sustainable development). In this context, individual preferences cannot always be determined synthetically (e.g. by analysing the willingness to pay) and if it can be done statistically, the information value of the measurement is doubtful. For instance, a target for reducing gases affecting the climate, which among other things takes account of future generations' interests and of international aspects, cannot be set by market and opinion analyses. Therefore, politics has to take over the task of assessment. Consequently, individual preferences in turn depend both on processes of opinion-forming in the political sphere and on the indicators examined here.

Therefore, the attempt to develop and establish a green national product as an aggregate in official statistics has failed - at least in Germany - and there will be no such figure in future either, because the valuations that would be required are just too complex.

Dominance of politics (development of topic-specific indicators)

As another example of a current form of indicator-building that cannot be reconciled with the pyramid model of chart 1, a frequent pattern in the development of topic-specific indicators in the environmental sphere will briefly be examined in the following: Departing from the middle level of politics, a political goal is set, for example the improvement of water quality. To achieve that goal, relevant individual actions and regulatory steps are initiated. Then, the effects on water quality have to be covered by basic statistics and represented by a topic-specific indicator. That approach to indicators leads to a dominant position of politics at the expense of theory and empiricism. Where such purely topic-based politics is dominant, there is a great risk that goals and political issues will change ("pollutant of the day"). Topic-specific indicators derived from the basic data are not necessarily embedded in an overall statistical system and frequently there are many sets of indicators existing in parallel that are hardly aggregated, or not at all. Summary and aggregative topic-specific indicators can hardly be operationalised. Consequently, the indicators are short-lived - outside the expert world - and cannot develop into relevant factors.

Again, for the same three reasons, the approach does not correspond to the pyramid model shown in chart 1:

- Again, one of the three actors is disregarded, this time it is science. (That exclusion is not entirely correct, but it is assumed in order to present the basic principle in a comprehensible manner.)

- As in the first example, the indicator construction process runs once.

- There is again a pyramid level not taken into account, in this case it is the top level.

Figure 3. Topic-specific indicators

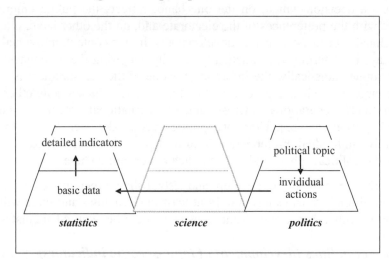

Dominance of statistics

With a purely statistical approach - putting it in extreme terms - there would be just one pyramid, which is the pyramid of statistics. Departing from a variety of basic data, statistics alone could develop more or less detailed indicators. However, that approach ignores relevance as an important quality requirement to be met by statistics. The demand for information by users (politics) would not be satisfied. Political decision-makers would have to use other sources to satisfy their need for information. In this context, one may well refer to the different possibilities and skills of different users in perceiving and processing the information offered (keyword: Water-Mondriaan, cf. Maasdam 2000). An environmental minister takes strategic decisions and needs information fitting the purpose. Too many and too detailed pieces of information are not adequate here. However, consistency should be achieved between the macro indicators and the details, so that - as if using a lift - one may change between the levels of presentation and the "granulation" of indicators.

The ideal-type construction process

Having given some examples of the typical problems in indicator-building, it will be examined in this chapter what a better construction process should be like. As has been shown by the above examples, all three actors must be involved and all three pyramid levels must be taken into account. Also, indicator construction cannot be linear but has to be an iterative decision-making process where satisfactory sub-solutions are found and sub-targets are met. In addition to the horizontal adequation problem caused by competing theories at the same level (between the three pyramids), the vertical aspect must be taken into account, too (Heine, Oltmanns (2002) pp. 4 et seq.). The vertical aspect of adequation examines the aggregation towards higher levels. A precondition here is that hierarchical structuring is possible. Consequently, crucial importance is attached to the discussion between the three actors at the same pyramid level (horizontal adequation) and the discussion within the individual work systems (vertical adequation).

A crucial step towards an optimised decision-making process is the attempt to find a reasonable balance between theory and practice. Pure pragmatism will not lead to solutions that are stable in the long term. Pure theory is not useful for practice. Therefore, decision-making processes will always consist of some "laboratory" (theory) and some "bazaar" (negotiations). What is going on in the laboratory is empirical science; in the bazaar, actual decisions on indicators are negotiated - ideally as a discussion between statistics, science, and politics, taking account of the work systems applied. It may actually be useful here to have different types of indicators at the same time (e.g. system-oriented indicators rather at the micro indicator level, problem-oriented indicators rather at the middle level). Considering the conditions of relevance and quality of statistics, it follows that building indicators must continuously be adjusted to changing user requirements. For such adjustment, framework conditions in terms of time, institution, technology, staff, and finance must be taken into account (Schäfer et al. 2004, p. 165).

A condensed and easily structured system of a small number of informative indicators is highly important, for example, for using the results within the political process as part of environmental monitoring. It allows one to quantify the impact of national economic developments and relevant political actions (e.g. fiscal policy, agricultural policy) on the environment. The goal should be to use macro indicators in order to develop an important information concept to include environmental aspects in other political areas (e.g. transport policy). Aggregating existing information to form key aggregates requires taking political goals as an orientation and taking account of social preferences. In turn, macro indicators should help to clearly define the limits of scope for action, thus to contribute to rendering the political discussion more rational and, where required, to contribute to correcting political goals. Aggregating the information strata towards the next higher (more general) pyramid level will thus become an interaction between classic information producers from science and statistics on the one hand and social and political decision makers on the other. The process character is expressed by the term "procedural rationality" (Radermacher 1998, pp. 238 et seqq. and chart 4). It is accompanied by an increase in the number of judging elements in the indicators constructed. As regards the rational discussion, science (in particular the social and communication sciences) is not only a participant in bazaar discussions but has also the function of process shaping and moderating.

Figure 4. Procedural rationality

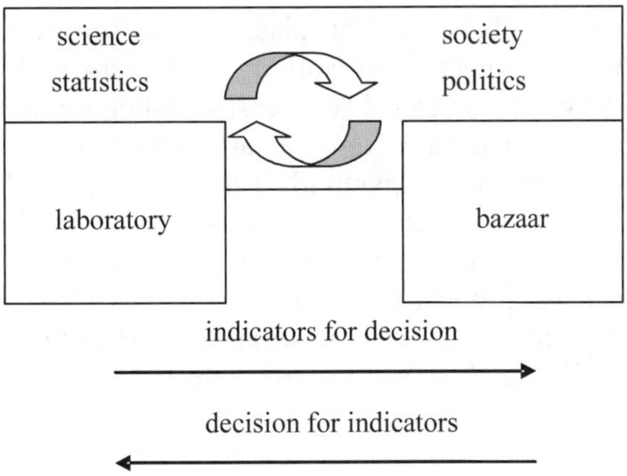

Case studies

Macro indicators of the state of the environment

When macro indicators were developed between 1998 and 2000 to describe the state of the environment, it was attempted in Germany to follow the ideal-type construction process described in chapter 3. The main goal was to develop macro indicators of the state of the environment by taking the example of the environmental section of "agricultural landscape and agricultural ecosystems". An earlier project had made a major contribution, developing a variety of indicators (about 100 individual indicators) to describe the state of the environment in that environmental section. An interdisciplinary project group was then set up, consisting of staff of the Federal Statistical Office, the ecological centre of the Christian Albrechts University of Kiel and the environmental policy research unit of the Free University of Berlin. Its task within the scope of a research project of the Federal Ministry of Education, Science, Research and Technology was to aggregate the wealth of information on the state of the environment of the agricultural landscape and agricultural ecosystems to form a small number of key indicators, without selecting only "important" indicators on the basis of more or less explicit criteria. A major goal of the project was to provide the findings, methods and approaches for the macro indicator construction of other ecosystems and environmental areas.

What entered into the proposals of the project group was not only the indicators existing already for the middle pyramid level but also various basic data (from the Federal Statistical Office, from environmental measuring networks, and from ecosystem research) as well as methods and approaches of statistical aggregation. From conceptual and methodological aspects, an ecosystem-oriented basic philosophy was chosen as a theoretical concept, i.e. a holistic system-based concept of the environment. Studies thus focus on the ecosystem, in addition to human health as a good that requires protection. The sectoral concept of the environment was abandoned. Consequently, ecosystem-based models and results of ecosystem-based basic research were included, too. As, finally, political guidelines and quantified political targets were taken into account, too, all levels of the three pyramids were represented.

The iterative process of dialogue took place in two forms: First, as a permanent dialogue accompanying the project at the working level in the project group (laboratory) and, second, in the form of two so-called "consensus-finding roundtables". As mentioned before, the project group consisted of representatives from science and statistics, thus covering already two of the three pyramids (in chart 1). In the consensus-finding roundtables, the dialogue with social user groups - which is indispensable in terms of methodology (keyword: procedural rationality) - was performed as follows: The project group (laboratory) put its proposed indicators, or their possible construction, for discussion to a group of representatives of social interest groups (middle level of the politics pyramid) at the bazaar. For that purpose, selected social user groups received in advance comprehensive information material on the project and the current state of research, connected with concrete questions that were discussed on the initiative of the project group (in order to get to the next higher pyramid level). The dialogue was moderated by a mediation expert (double function of science). As a result, shortcomings were detected, which were returned to the working group to be remedied, which dealt with them before the second round of discussions was held. The participants in the dialogue also succeeded, as had been hoped before, in finding answers to questions raised by the laboratory regarding the comprehensibility and acceptance of indicators and regarding various approaches to aggregation. The environmental policy research unit, supported by the Scientific Centre of Berlin, had a special function as it shaped, organised and monitored the project in that phase.

Altogether, that form of dialogue is considered very positive because a discussion has successfully been initiated both between the scientists and statisticians of the project and with representatives of social interest groups.

All in all, some 20 indicators were developed on the structural, material, and functional aspects of the environmental section of agricultural landscape and agricultural ecosystems that was taken as an example. Although the number of indicators may seem large, it should be noted that the methods applied in the project do allow further aggregation if required. The concepts and methods applied have proved suitable and have the potential to be applied to other environmental sections and to the general process of indicator construction.

For the sake of completeness, it should be noted that the indicators developed in that process have remained theoretical and that there has not been any regular empirical coverage of the macro indicators. Although politics was involved in indicator construction, the subsequent implementation was not supported because the financial burden of collecting the required basic data was too large. It may be concluded that, actually, the necessity of having macro indicators was not conveyed in a sufficiently plausible manner to politics and the general public. This shows how important it is to have an active information transfer between statistics, politics, and the public.

Further developing the indicator approach of the German sustainability strategy

A second and more recent example to be examined now is the current discussion in Germany on further developing the indicator approach of the sustainability strategy.

In 2002, the Federal Government defined 21 indicators for the 21st century as part of its sustainability policy and set quantitative targets for most of them. By choosing the indicators and defining the targets, the political sphere has focused on the priority problem areas where improvements are to be achieved by political actions. The leading indicators used within the scope of sustainability policy are to serve primarily as a communication tool for the general public, to represent problems and to measure the success of political actions.

Considering that goal, it is not sufficient to focus only on the leading indicators in the upper part of the pyramid. Instead, the level below must be examined, both for indicator construction itself and for the scientific and political analysis of the mechanisms influencing the development of the selected topics. Thus it can be checked whether the political actions have the desired effect. In other words, in order to be able to assess the effect of the actions and, above all, to be able to derive further actions from those findings, the detailed data basis of the middle and lower pyramid levels underlying the indicators must be examined. This refers not only to the direct effect on the relevant target - what is needed is a holistic approach. This is important because the core element of sustainability is integration, i.e. achieving goals simultaneously in the spheres of the economy, the environment, and social matters. Sustainability policy means co-ordinating various sectoral policies and balancing conflicting goals.

Therefore, the disaggregated data should be linked to each other through a consistent data structure, so that integrated analysis can be performed, including interrelationships between individual indicators (Schoer 2003, pp. 10 et seqq.). The integration requirement is easiest to meet at the middle pyramid level because what is generally dominant at the lower level is (more or less) selective data collection oriented towards individual specialised aspects. Therefore, the requirement of integrability for the sustainability indicator approach is best met by the accounting systems of statistical reporting, consisting of three major elements: "core system of national accounts", "satellite system of environmental-economic accounting" and "satellite system of socio-economic accounting". Such accounting can be supported and supplemented by model calculations or simulations to better assess the information content of the data and especially conflicting goals between the dimensions.

Developing an indicator approach for sustainability that is embedded in a data basis (middle or lower pyramid level) is necessarily designed as a long-term process. The strategy for an integrated sustainability policy should always include jointly co-ordinated (i.e. rational) further development of the indicator approach (in the laboratory and at the bazaar) and of its data basis. By way of aggregation, the leading indicators should be derived from the accounting approach or, at least, consistently be linked to it. In turn, this means that the further development of the accounting system (statistics pyramid) has to be oriented towards the sustainability policy (politics pyramid). Also, investments should be made in setting up analysis tools (science pyramid) for integrated sustainability reporting. The process of indicator setting by politics, which so far has been linear and running once, and the quantification by statistics would then be replaced by an iterative improvement process where science provides the appropriate model tools for integrated sustainability analysis.

An important step towards an integrated sustainability policy in Germany is the setting up of an interministerial committee in which not only politics but also statistics is represented. One of the future tasks of that committee will be to prepare proposals for the further development of the sustainability indicator approach. In any case, this year's press conference on environmental-economic accounting, which for the first time has been held jointly by the Federal Environmental Agency and the Federal Statistical Office, can be considered as an example of successful dialogue between statistics, science, and politics.

Conclusion

The case studies and explanations given above have shown that the construction of macro indicators must involve three actors – statistics, science, and politics – with their relevant work systems, from the detailed to the general level. To get to the next higher level in indicator construction, politics has to provide the assessment of social preferences. Only politics can perform the assessments required for that change of levels because it reflects the societal discussion. Applying that methodology, statistics and science have reached their limits in setting up the models and procuring data and facts.

To avoid macro or leading indicators being short-lived and to ensure their being accepted and demanded by the society, information transmission is of major importance. A central aspect of implementation is that as many potential users as possible should feel addressed by the information transfer. The message delivered by the indicators must be comprehensible; "plain" data will become a comprehensive source of information only when processed to meet user needs. Indicators are addressed first to politics, where they are an important basis for decision-making, and second to the general public. Successfully implementing macro indicators thus requires that they can be conveyed by the mass media. Taking account of the general public when presenting the results may have positive effects on politics: Good and sufficiently substantiated information provides not only insight into the societal situation - which for example involves the demand for a sustainable policy - but can also make social interest groups abandon their resistance to planned action packages (e.g. emission reduction requirements). Thus the information may actually have an enlightening effect and contribute to politics and its actions being supported by the population. For data interpretation and their representation (visualisation), the media play an important role.

References

Brouwer R., O'Conner M., Radermacher W. (1999): GREEned National STAtistical and Modelling Procedures: The GREENSTAMP approach to the calculation of environmentally adjusted national income figures. In: International Journal of Sustainable Development 1999, Vol. 2, No. 1, p. 7-31.

Heine K., Oltmanns E. (2001): Zur politischen Ökonomie der Statistik. Volkswirtschaftliche Beiträge No. 4/2001. Universität Marburg.

Maasdam R. (2000): Exploratory Data Analysis in Water Quality Monitoring Systems. Dissertation. University of Salford.

Projektverbund Forschungsstelle für Umweltpolitik, Ökologiezentrum Kiel, Statistisches Bundesamt (2002): Makroindikatoren des Umweltzustands. Vol.10 of the publication series Beiträge zu den Umweltökonomischen Gesamtrechnungen, Wiesbaden.

Radermacher W. (1994): Sustainable income: Reflections on the valuation of nature in environmental-economic accounting. In: Statistical Journal of the United Nations ECE, Volume 11, p. 35-51.

Radermacher W. (1998): Makroökonomische Kosten der Umweltinanspruchnahme. In: Zeitschrift für angewandte Umweltforschung. Vol. 11, Issue 2, pp. 234-251.

Radermacher W., Zieschank R., Hoffmann-Kroll R., Nouhuys J. v., Schäfer D., Seibel S. (1998): Entwicklung eines Indikatorensystems für den Zustand der Umwelt in der Bundesrepublik Deutschland mit Praxistest für ausgewählte Indikatoren und Bezugsräume. Vol.5 of the publication series Beiträge zu den Umweltökonomischen Gesamtrechnungen, Wiesbaden.

Radermacher W. (1999): Indicators, Green Accounting and Environment Statistics – Information Requirements for Sustainable Development. In: International Statistical Review, 67, 3, pp. 339-354.

Schäfer D., Seibel S., Radermacher W. (2004): Umweltindikatoren und Umweltziele. Anforderungen aus statistischer Sicht. In: Wiggering H., Müller F. (ed.): Umweltziele und Umweltindikatoren. Geowissenschaften + Umwelt, Springerverlag Berlin Heidelberg, pp. 163-182.

Schoer K. (2003): Die Rolle des Gesamtrechnungssystems für eine integrierte Nachhaltigkeitsberichterstattung. Umweltökonomische Gesamtrechnungen, Statistisches Bundesamt, Online Paper.

Statistics for Society

Indicators and Social Accounting for 21st Century Social Policy

Gøsta Esping-Andersen

Professor, Pompeu Fabra University

Introduction

The way we measure social welfare has changed very little over the past century. First, we still rely primarily on cross-sectional headcounts - snapshots of, say, the number poor, unemployed, or lone mothers in any given year. These may signal the magnitude of a problem but for policy-making they are of limited value. We need indicators that better identify the mechanisms that trigger an entry into and exit out of poverty or unemployment. We need information that tells us the reasons why some are more persistently poor or unemployed than others. Hence, we need to capture the dynamics that define life chances.

Secondly, the social accounts we use to measure government inputs easily yield a distorted picture of real social spending (and financing). The challenge is to construct a system of global, consolidated accounts, including not just *public* but also *private* welfare inputs and consumption. And thirdly, our social protection systems are in rapid transformation, above all moving from conventional "passive" income maintenance towards an increasingly service intensive and "activating" approach. A growing share of social outlays will inevitably have an investment character in the sense that an intervention now can yield long run dividends for both the individual and for society as a whole. The challenge is to distinguish social investments from social consumption.

This paper addresses these three questions.

Life Course Dynamics

The statistics available to diagnose social problems and define policy solutions are overwhelmingly of the snapshot type -- headcount data of the number of poor, unemployed, or low wage employed in any given year. To exemplify, the 1990 UN *Convention on the Rights of the Child* defined as a main aim that signature governments lower the rate of child poverty progressively. EU presidencies in recent years have embraced social targets for member countries, again pursuing goals related to the levels of employment, retirement, and poverty.

It is, however, not always evident that *levels* of a social ill capture the true challenge. To paraphrase Joseph Schumpeter's famous critique of Marxian class theory: "Classes are like an omnibus: always full, but always full of different people". The implications of unemployment, poverty, or low pay depend on whether the experience is chronic or just fleeting. Most of us have held any number of lousy jobs in our youth and, yet, here we are: all well-paid and well-fed.

Headcount measures, like the percentage poor, are certainly not irrelevant. They help capture the magnitude of a problem and may motivate policy makers to act. Annual poverty counts can help us separate cyclical changes from core structural poverty. And comparative poverty data across countries may alert us to differences in welfare state effectiveness.

But headcounts yield problematic and second-best information for two reasons. One, they may provoke erroneous interpretations. Two, they do not provide the information that is really needed for effective policy-making. I shall illustrate the problem by focusing on poverty, but the argumentation should be equally valid for most other social policy issues, be it low pay, precarious employment, homelessness, or unemployment.

Most OECD countries provide, if not annual then at least regularly updated statistics on the level of poverty. The overall national poverty count is not a very informative statistic because it bundles people at very different stages in their life course, from students to the old-old. Let me exemplify with some findings from recent Danish research. In international rankings Denmark is a low-poverty country. Measured as less than 50 percent of equivalent household income, the Danish poverty rate is about 7 percent (compared to 8 percent in Germany, 12.5 percent in the U.K. and 17 percent in the U.S.). But using a different accounting procedure, namely lifetime income, then we discover that a whopping 93 percent (!) of Danes have at one point in their adult lives been poor. So, is Denmark an exemplary case of low poverty or of universal poverty? In fact, yes, of both. Most Danes have experienced poverty because most Danes leave the parental home early and pass some years as students and youth with little income. For the vast majority this is voluntary, fleeting, and basically trivial poverty. One country may appear more poverty-ridden than another simply because there are more students and youth living in independent households. Other countries (like Spain and Italy) would exhibit substantially higher poverty rates were it not for the fact that young adults remain in the parental home until they marry. The utility of headcounts is vastly improved when disaggregated into key groups, such as the elderly, families with children, or lone parents. But how do we cleanse the headcounts of trivial poverty?

Armed with group-specific poverty rates, policy makers are on somewhat firmer terrain. Much research has documented that financial distress in childhood has long-term adverse effects for the child's school performance and later life chances. Hence, simply lowering child poverty *rates* will arguably produce social betterment. Still, the shortcomings of such a headcount measure are that it lumps together families for whom the poverty experience is momentary and transitory with families for whom it is persistent and possibly chronic. The long-term consequences of poverty in childhood are bound to differ in the former and latter case, and it is a safe bet that also the causes of the poverty spell differ. Failure to distinguish the two can produce inefficient and even counterproductive policy. A simple cash assistance approach might very well be the correct remedy for transitory poverty (due, say, to momentary illness of the breadwinner), but this will not address in any meaningful way the causes of persistent poverty – thus potentially reinforcing the persistency. Similarly old-age poverty statistics, routinely calculated for the population 65+, may misrepresent the real situation. There is typically a marked fall in pensioner incomes as the elderly age. A summary statistic, therefore, is the mean of recent pensioners who normally do very well and very old retirees, who often do quite poorly. Clearly, the policy problem is not the "elderly", but the progressive decline in income in the process of aging.

Headcount measures can mislead. Take low-wage employment, a hotly debated issue in contemporary advanced economies. Recent comparative data suggest that low-wage work is on the rise, fuelling fears of social exclusion and of impending polarisation. But is a rise in the rate of low-pay necessarily alarming? It depends very much on *who* they are, and at what *phase of the life cycle* they find themselves. The numbers of low paid may be swelling simply because more youth are seeking easy-entry stopgap jobs. If they subsequently move into good jobs, why worry? Alternatively, if many low-paid workers are sporadic second earners and household incomes are adequate, then again, why worry about polarisation and social exclusion? If most social ills are transitory and brief, their effect on citizens' life chances may be miniscule.

This brings me to a core problem with cross-sectional headcount indicators: the problem of *selection bias*. A poverty or unemployment headcount will invariably lump together a very diverse clientele, in particular in terms of the mechanisms that drove people into poverty or unemployment. A one-for-all policy, be it cash assistance or "activation", may be well-tailored for some but simply wrongheaded for others. How would a policy maker know? The ideal way to assess the effectiveness of a policy would be to conduct a scientific experiment, randomly assigning individuals to an experimental and a control group. This is not possible in the real world. Hence, we are forced to base our evaluations on *post hoc* information: an "activation" measure may be deemed a success by the percent people who exit unemployment or assistance dependency. But do we really know whether they exited unemployment because of activation? No we do not, because we will never know whether the success cases would have exited even in the absence of an activation programme.

The point is that success and failure in life is very much a function of selection mechanisms that, in great part, occur at a very early stage in peoples' lives. Almost always, they occur far earlier than when we observe the people. Activation of the unemployed works quite effectively for adults who from childhood managed to develop strong cognitive and motivational skills; it is unlikely to work for people who were under-stimulated during childhood. As so much evaluation research has shown, the trigger mechanisms of social problems in adulthood often originate in (early) childhood. Those who began well are far more likely to end up well. For those who begin poorly, say because they grew up in poverty, in broken homes, or with multiple social pathologies, remedial policies later in life are far less likely to work. Unless we have information on the relevant selection mechanisms at work, we are unable to define which policy intervention is the most effective.

From a policy-making point of view, the vital information lies in the flows and in the triggers of transitions. To give an idea of how different our view of poverty appears when we include dynamics, Table 1 compares cross-section poverty headcounts with data on persistency.

Poverty in Child Families. Cross-sectional Headcounts and Dynamics

Kaplan-Mayer Survival Functions, 1994-2001

| | Poverty (2000) | Rate of Poverty Persistency | | |
		Year One	Year Two	Three + years
Denmark	2.4	.410	.282	.026
France	7.3	.590	.418	.128
Germany	9.0	.490	.303	.091
Italy	16.6	.635	.411	.161
Spain	13.3	.597	.369	.120
U.K.	15.4	.494	.287	.110
U.S	21.9	.814	.704	.576

Wilcoxson test for equality Pr>Chi2 = .0001 (Chi2=26.53)
Source: ECHP, waves 1994-2001, and for the U.S., the PSID, 1993-1997. Poverty rates are from LIS.
Note: Income poverty is <50 percent of median, and moving out of poverty is >60 percent of median.

These data suggest there is no simple relationship between poverty levels and persistency. Germany has a higher rate of poverty than France, but the poor are more mobile. In Germany more than half exited poverty within one year, compared to only 40 percent in France. Similarly, the U.K. poverty level is twice the French, but in the U.K. there is far less persistent poverty. Italy and especially the U.S. combine high levels of poverty with exceptionally low mobility.

If, like in Denmark, the majority of poor families in one year are no longer poor in the next, the character of that nation's poverty problem is clearly very different than in, say, the U.S., producing very different types of risk and requiring arguably very different policy remedies. If the only information we had were the poverty rates in column one, we would remain basically blind from a policy making point of view.

The dynamic data on persistency and transitions is more informative because it helps us differentiate the "soft" from the "hard" core poor. Most would agree that the latter constitute the really urgent objective of policy. Still, we need to know what factors distinguish the transient from the persistently poor. What are the immediate triggers– or perhaps deeper embedded selection mechanisms—that produce poverty in the first place? And what are the factors that differentiate the long-term poor from the rest?

To answer such questions we need micro-level panel data that follow individuals over time, preferably with as much information as possible regarding their social origins and the circumstances that guided their early life. Equally importantly, such data help us identify the correlates of a social problem. A simple headcount measure of poverty does not tell us very much about the true experience of being poor. Does it entail true hardship? Will it have lasting adverse effects for a person? Is poverty (or unemployment) associated with genuine social exclusion?

It is well known that year-to-year changes in income are uncorrelated with year-to-year changes in consumption. People smooth their consumption over longer periods, they can draw upon familial support in periods of hardship and, hence, limited periods of low income or poverty may not at all translate into any material hardship. Again, it all depends on dynamics. Protracted income poverty will affect medium and long-term consumption; transitory low income will most likely not. The same goes for measures of multi-dimensional deprivation. To exemplify, if we monitor year-to-year poverty rates in the EU member states during the 1990s, most countries exhibit a rise (if in most cases, a modest one). But if we follow the ECHP's 9-item social deprivation index over the same years, the situation is improving in just about all cases. In other words, we register rising income poverty but declining deprivation.

Research that follows this kind of approach has enjoyed a boom in the past decade, mainly thanks to the growing availability of panel data, such as the American PSID, the Swedish Level of Living panels, the German Socioeconomic panel, the ECHP, and so forth. [1]As a result we have made giant leaps in understanding the true nature and causes of social ills. We now have, for example, a vast accumulation of research on the long-term impact of child poverty. To exemplify, US research suggests that a child from a poor family will have two years less schooling than a non-poor child. Later, that child will earn substantially less and, worse, will much more likely become a poor parent – thus reproducing the syndrome from generation to generation. Similarly, we also have growing evidence that cognitive stimulation in early childhood is key, not only for educational attainment but also, further ahead, for career prospects. There is very strong evidence that early intervention programmes, like Head Start in the U.S. or universal high-quality day care attendance (like in Scandinavia) effectively diminish adverse effects of social origin. Here, then, is one telling example of how dynamic life course data

---

1   Some countries, like Denmark and Sweden, also utilize integrated population registry data – a truly potent data source.

help us identify the root causes of social ills and subsequently how best to design effective policy.

Contemporary research routinely distinguishes between three types of immediate triggers of poverty entries and exits: demographic events (like divorce, lone motherhood, additional family members), labour market events (like unemployment, changes in earnings and labour supply), and public income support (the termination of unemployment benefits, for example). It is interesting to note that the relative importance of such triggers differs markedly between countries. In the U.S. (and the U.K.), demographic variables tend to be more important than in Europe – especially with regard to lone motherhood -- while in most of Europe it seems that labour market triggers predominate. One trigger that is of universal importance is the employment of mothers: when mothers work, the risk of child poverty declines by a factor of 3 or 4.

This known, we are clearly much better placed to design a policy menu that more effectively addresses both the deeper and the more immediate causes of, say, poverty. The importance of early childhood intervention programmes to correct for a poor start is evident. And if we aim to minimize poverty in child families, perhaps it would be far more effective to help reconcile motherhood and employment (say via day care) than to provide cash assistance to poor parents.

Micro-level panel data, then, furnish the kind of information we really need in order to tailor policies to the specific causes of a social problem. It is important to add that these very same data are the best from the point of view of subsequently monitoring the effectiveness of a welfare state's income support and service provision system. We need to follow individuals for a long time in order to know whether, say, "activation" was truly effective in moving people into employment. It is very possible that an exit in one year is followed by recidivism the next year.

The real point is that our statistics need to better reflect the way that citizens' lives unfold in the real world. Social risks, needs, and well-being are interconnected across the life course. Starting poorly increases the probability of more unemployment, precarious jobs, and low incomes in adulthood. This will, in turn, increase the likelihood of poverty in old age. The kinds of social indicators that will be most relevant for the kind of society and economy that is evolving are those that adequately capture such life course linkages.

The need to develop dynamic indicators is also urgent considering the rapid ongoing changes in the distribution of social risks. In the post-war welfare state it could be pretty safely assumed that most social risks were concentrated in the inactive phase of peoples' life course, old age in particular. Full employment and strong wage growth ensured that the standard male breadwinner family was adequately provided for via his wage income. The new society has changed all this and what, in particular, we see is a new concentration of risks among young adults who, we should not forget, are also the parents of today's children, tomorrow's working age population and, at mid-Century, of the cohorts that will be entering into retirement.

Social Accounts

The social accounting that currently prevails is in a double sense problematic. Firstly, social expenditure statistics are myopically limited to public spending levels and this finds its echo in the policy debate which is myopically concerned with issues of public finance. What matters is the overall resource allocation that goes to social protection. Put simply, our total welfare package derives from three inputs: government, markets, and family. A rise (or fall) in the welfare input from any of these three pillars will have immediate repercussions on the others. Cutbacks in public pensions will fuel private pension plans and/or necessitate more economic support from kin. There are very important second-order consequences that arise as a result, and these must be explicitly factored in when we debate social spending policy. The total welfare outlays may look the same when comparing countries with different welfare mixes, but welfare distributions may end up being very different.

Secondly, our social accounts are unable to distinguish between outlays that yield identifiable economic returns (and, hence, are investments with a future payoff) and outlays that are not. Of course, we have for many decades recognized that education and health spending are investments in a healthier and more productive workforce. Yet, we still do not possess any method that helps us to adequately identify the returns. By and large, the post-war welfare state was built around income transfer programs, in particular old age pensions. The changing role of women and the evolving needs structure all imply that the welfare state must shift its bias from traditional "passive" income maintenance towards servicing families. As welfare states become more service intensive, the direct and indirect effects of social outlays will unavoidably change. Like education and health, we need to know the net returns from spending on active labour market policies, day care, pre-school education, old age services, and so forth.

Consolidated accounts

These are necessary because we need to measure *total* welfare inputs and outputs. The real unit of analysis is not the welfare state, but welfare regime, which is the joint contribution of state, markets and family. Social policies are too often defined by narrow actuarial thinking, namely what can we afford to spend in the public sector. Beginning with actuarial limitations is like putting the cart before the horse. The first question in any policy debate must concern the objective. The second is about equity: how to allocate the burdens and benefits in the pursuit of the objective. Once these are decided, then we can call upon the accountants.

Allocating welfare responsibilities to any of the three welfare pillars has consequences for the other two. Take elderly care: the absence of public provision will compel citizens towards intra-familial care and/or towards market provision. The overall societal resource use will probably change little however we allocate care provision. But, any given allocation will engender second-order effects. The market option is, for the majority of households, usually inaccessible. Quality elderly care will typically be affordable to the top 3rd of the income distribution, at best. Private for-profit providers may offer more choice, but they are rarely cost effective due to high transaction costs and potential over-provision (and will therefore push up GDP use beyond what is necessary).[2] If both state and markets "fail", the result is either that we abandon the frail elderly altogether, or that the family must internalise care giving. This, in turn, implies reduced female labour supply, lower tax revenues to the exchequer, and less household income. This is but an example. Nevertheless, it should illustrate the basic point that our accounting practice must reflect welfare *regimes* and not solely welfare states.

The OECD has taken a first important step with its "net social expenditure" calculations. Albeit still in its infancy this approach, firstly, allows us to estimate *real* public social expenditure. Published public spending data are fictitious because a) they

---

2   Total US health spending is now around 14 percent of GDP and it has been estimated that 3-4 percent are administrative and transaction costs, like billing, most of which would disappear in a fully public health care regime.

omit tax-claw-backs (which can reduce real spending considerably); and b) they ignore tax subsidies to families and/or private providers (which can raise spending considerably). Secondly, total expenditures must include mandatory and voluntary private spending programs, be they employer occupational benefits, non-profit programmes, or individual plans. Most of these are, in the first place, supported by tax write-offs. Thirdly, they should (but usually do not) include also client co-payments. These can be quite significant. Returning to the elderly care example, Denmark's and Sweden's outlays for care to the frail elderly amount to ca. 3 percent of GDP. In reality, perhaps 20 percent of care/nursing home spending is covered by patient co-payments (levied from the pension). Fourthly, no real attempts have yet been made to monitor non-monetarized familial care. All in all, *net* social accounting of the OECD type shows that conventional social spending comparisons are unreliable, if not outright meaningless. At the level of gross public outlays the gap between Sweden (the prototypical generous welfare state) and the US (the prototypical lean one) seems enormous. At the level of net consolidated expenditure, the gap closes. [3] This is illustrated in Table 2.

Table 1.   Total GDP Use for Social Protection

	Sweden	Germany	USA	Sweden/USA Ratio
Gross public expenditure	35.7	29.2	15.8	2.26
Net public Expenditure 1)	28.5	27.3	17.5	1.63
Net private Expenditure 2)	2.2	1.6	8.1	
Net total social Expenditure	30.6	28.9	25.6	1.20

1) after tax claw-backs and other indirect taxes, plus tax subsidies
2) includes mandatory and voluntary plans, but excludes out-of-pocket payments

Source: W. Adema, Net social expenditure. Labour Market and Social Policy-Occasional Papers, no.52. OECD (August, 2001).

From a policy-making perspective what is important is the total level of resource use being dedicated to a given social objective. At the end of the day it will, in any case, all come out of households' aggregate income, call it taxes, withheld earnings, private insurance premiums, or out-of-pocket spending. The average US family is saddled with a total social protection burden that compares with that of the average Swedish family. The policy-making issue reduces to two questions: one, would we obtain efficiency dividends with one type of allocation compared to the other? Two, which allocation ensures most welfare for most citizens?

Investment Accounts

It would be helpful to distinguish what is of an investment character from what is current consumption. This is no mean challenge, considering that existing social accounts (dating basically to mid-20th Century) consider most public and almost all social expenditures as purely consumption expenditure. Granted, economists have for decades argued that some outlays, like education, are investments in human capital. Yet, we have no operable framework for estimating their return. In the post-war welfare state, being exceedingly income-transfer (and especially pension) biased, the need to distinguish social investments from consumption was minor. It becomes an urgent question when

---

3   Were we to adjust these figures for national differences in population age composition, the discrepancies
       would become even smaller.

spending must be redirected in favour of pro-active policies, servicing families, building life-long learning opportunities, or activation programs.

It is not easy to distinguish social investment from consumption. Contemporary thinking has made only modest progress with its attempt to separate "passive" from "active" policies. Social assistance benefits are probably easily classified as passive "consumption", meaning that they yield few economic returns. Yet, things get complicated when we consider that income support to families with children may enhance children's school performance. Or, take programs in support of working mothers: once again, simply the fact that mothers work means sharply reduced child poverty, an implicit job-multiplier, and additional tax revenue to governments. Care for the elderly is likewise Janus-headed: taking care of disabled aged may not constitute an investment in our future productive potential and, yet, failure to do so implies that many women will be forced to reduce their labour supply.

Besides education and training programmes, there are a number of social policies that are easy to identify as representing investments in individual productivity and collective wealth creation.

- Most generically, all spending towards child welfare has a potential pay-off. Cash benefits to families with children create financial security and prevent child poverty, two factors that are crucial for children's school success and later earnings potential. Early pre-school programmes, and most of all universal, quality child care, have a powerful equalizing effect on children's cognitive and motivational development. [4]

- Likewise, programs that facilitate mothers' attachment to paid employment harbour a strong investment component on two dimensions at once. Firstly, the lack of such may produce Southern European type fertility collapse. In today's world we need to recognize that the cost-calculus of having children has changed dramatically. A child-less future is unquestionably problematic macro-economically. Secondly, if women do have children and if this implies major career interruptions, this has substantial consequences for their cumulative life-time earnings potential, meaning diminished household income, higher risks of old age poverty, foregone tax revenues, and a lower contributor/retiree ratio. Subsidized child care requires large public outlays, but these are more or less recuperated via mothers' superior life time earnings and tax payments (see below).

- It is more complicated to pinpoint precisely the investment component of many income maintenance programs for working-age households – such as unemployment benefits. The reasoning is more circumscribed, but it has for long been recognized that strong welfare guarantees stimulate greater risk-taking during work life. Also, workers will arguably be less resistant to change if their welfare is assured in the event of redundancies. Generally speaking, flexible and dynamic labour markets require off-setting social security.

This is not meant to be an exhaustive overview of how to set up a system of social investment accounts. The idea is simply to pinpoint the need to revise existing practice so as to construct a more realistic and workable accounting practice. To provide one empirical illustration of how an (expensive) social programme may yield long-term

---

4   Head Start and Sure Start type programs have been shown to yield huge returns in terms of disadvantaged children's later performance. One might surmise that if the US Head Start programme were extended to, say, 30 or 40 percent of American children, the US would be able to reduce the size of its school-drop out and functionally illiterate population to European levels (the percent young Americans falling into the lowest cognitive level is 20+, compared to roughly 5 percent in Scandinavia and Germany).

dividends, I have attempted to estimate the relationship between initial cost and subsequent returns of providing subsidized day care for pre-school age children.[5]

I use Denmark as the base for my calculations. Firstly, Denmark is the world leader in terms of providing basically universal, high quality coverage for the 0-6 year olds. Secondly, Danish financing (on average, 2/3rds public subsidy, 1/3rd parental co-payment) is demonstrably of a level sufficient to ensure affordability to all. Thirdly, the system is also broadly applauded for its high quality in terms of pedagogical standards. Hence, Denmark would appear to offer a good benchmark.

My calculations, presented in Table 3, must be regarded as approximations. We first need to establish the costs to the public purse connected with the provision. Secondly, since day care permits mothers to remain employed, there are both individual and social returns. The mother will receive continuous wage income instead of no earnings during her period of interruption, and she will also experience less human capital depreciation and, thus, a far higher level of lifetime earnings. To identify the depreciation effect, I apply an estimate derived from the standard Mincer approach to cumulative lifetime earnings estimations. The social returns derive from the additional tax revenues that the mother will pay to the exchequer and, again, this is the composite of the tax on earnings for the period she does not interrupt employment plus the added level of taxes she will pay due to higher lifetime earnings. I use a stylized case of a 30-35 year old mother who has two children, returns to employment immediately after maternity leave, and continues to work until age 60. I conservatively assume that her wage is 2/3rds of average worker wage. If, more realistically, her earnings hover around the mean, the effect would be far greater.

This illustration suggests that the returns to social policies, in this case day care, can be considerable. Indeed, the mother who originally benefited from the service has, over the space of her career, not only fully reimbursed the original outlay but has actually paid the government a "dividend" of D.Kr. 260.000. This is just about equal to a 50 percent net return on the original investment, not a bad deal at all.

---

5   On behalf of the British Labour government, Price-Waterhouse has conducted an analogous costing-out study for Britain, producing very similar results to the ones I present here.

Table 2. Dynamic Accounting of the Costs and Returns from Day Care Provisions

Assumptions

- Mother, at age 30-35, has two kids

- She does not want to interrupt employment (except for one year maternity).

- Her wage is 67% of APW and

- She will continue working until age 60

- We apply 1.5%p.a. "Mincer estimate" of cumulative loss for a 5 year interruption

	D.Kr.
Cost to government:	
2 years in creche (x2)	= 168 000
and	
3 years in pre-school (x2)	=342 000
Total	510 000
Gains to mother:	
5 years with full earnings and	=800 000
life-time wage gain from no interruption	=1 400 600
Total	2 200 600
Gains to Exchequer:	
Additional revenue from 1. and	=280 000
additional revenue from 2.	=490 000
Total	770 000
Net return to Exchequer	
On original outlay (770 000 – 510 000)	**260 000**

Some expenditures have a long pay-off span. Take the day care example above. Any government dedicated to building up a substantial supply of pre-school places will face the immediate challenge of raising sufficient tax revenue over few years. Accounting-wise, the objective may appear financially prohibitive. But, it is easy to show that a large investment now will yield possibly huge additional tax revenues in the future. And it may simultaneously lower government expenditure on other social programmes. To illustrate, child poverty almost ceases to exist when both parents work. Hence, a programme that helps reconcile motherhood and careers will also diminish the costs of income support to poor child families. Here, as in a host of similar social policy situations, the most meaningful accounting practice is one akin to company accounts: the initial outlay in capital equipment is amortised over many years.

Social Inclusion – Do We Have the Right Indicators?

Bjørn Hvinden

Professor, University of Science and Technology, Norway

Introduction

Currently many national governments and transnational organisations adopt indicators to depict states of and changes in social inclusion. To an increasing extent such indicators are interpreted – by governments or organisations themselves, by the media and by the general public – as signs of the success or failure of policy efforts. Indicators are used to argue that one should stick to a given course of policy, or alternatively, to call for the replacement of established policy instruments with something else. From this perspective it is essential that the picture drawn by indicators on social inclusion is a valid and convincing one. My main points are as follows:

- Many indicators in use are the result of unhappy compromises between the ideally desirable and the economically or technically most feasible. Partly for this reason indicators in use tend to focus on access to material resources or purchasing power and neglect people's scope for using these to improve their situation in a somewhat longer time perspective.

- The total menu of indicators related to inclusion or exclusion is biased towards characteristics of individuals or households, e.g. what they have in the way of incomes and paid work, knowledge, health or social contacts. Usually we learn much less about what characterise the social contexts or environments where these individuals or families operate, e.g. whether poor and unemployed people live in neighbourhoods or communities where most others are also poor and unemployed, or whether these environments are more mixed and heterogeneous.

These points are related to more general issues of what social inclusion and exclusion mean, and what we assume to be the most important factors leading to social inclusion or exclusion. A rapidly growing literature deals with these issues (Room 1995, Jordan 1996, Stewart 2000, Woodward & Kohli 2001, Atkinson *et al.* 2002). In my view persistent poverty or multiple deprivations can both be a cause and a result of social exclusion. Yet, poverty or multiple deprivations are not the same as social exclusion, for instance because there are also forms of exclusion where poverty plays a minor or no role. The paper touches upon the issues of definitions and causal mechanisms but concentrates on the pictures of inclusion and exclusion given by indicators in use, and discuss some possible improvements of these.

What do we mean by a social indicator?

Statistical agencies and other organisations produce a large amount of data about social conditions that potentially may be elevated to the status of "social indicators". Similarly, the boundaries between a growing body of results from social research and social indicators are also fairly blurred or soft. As a researcher I would argue that we need both; research going more in-depth into causal relations and dynamics, as well as social indicators of a more standardised format and produced on a routine basis. By and large, the purposes of the two are different.

The point with calling some piece of statistical information a social indicator must be that it highlights an important social phenomenon in a simple and compact way. Obviously it is a question of judgment which social phenomena are important but with some reservations there seems to be a broad consensus about this. A social indicator must give the possibility to quickly get an idea about the state or change of the phenomenon in question and allow for comparison with information about the corresponding states or changes in other settings, e.g. in other countries or regions ("benchmarking"). Social indicators should be readily available, updated regularly, and fairly easy to understand for others than the technical specialists.

As representatives of statistical agencies often remind us; social indicators are not for free. Especially if many different countries are to collect and present similar indicators in a coordinated way, the costs grow proportionally, if not exponentially due to transaction costs, translations, etc. This may lead to a preference for indicators that can be extracted or produced on the basis of existing registers, often based on statistics that is collected as matter of routine through administrative systems, for instance related to employer's reports about salaries paid to employees, taxes, charges and cash transfers, residence and housing registers, and other existing data bases. This may for instance be used to produce indicators about income distribution before and after taxes, and the proportion of individuals and households with low incomes or below 50 or 60 % of the median disposable income (e.g. Eurostat 2002, 2004; EC 2003, 2004, Atkinson *et al.* 2004, OECD 2002).

To the extent that decision-makers and the media require many updated indicators, the greater the likelihood is that these will be produced on the basis of administrative registers. Although these indicators may be of value as far as they go, there is a danger that considerations of costs and availability will determine what social indicators will tell us about; that is, what aspects of society's functioning we hear and read about on a regular basis. There are often other and less available pieces of information that are equally or even more important to obtain, but where special steps to collect this information, e.g. through population or subpopulation surveys, are required.

There could be other arguments for "fewer and more relevant" indicators: If too many indicators of the same or related phenomena are produced regularly this will easily create information overload and diminish the usability and value of the set of indicators. From this perspective the ideal appears to be as few indicators as possible. This will, however, have to be weighted against the fact that a range of important social phenomena are complex or ambiguous. We may lose essential information if we only use one indicator. One could give many examples of this but let me mention two:

- *Gender equality in labour market participation*: Often one can see used the difference or gap between the employment rates of men and women as an indicator of the degree of equality. But unless we also have some indicator of differences in volume of work, e.g. hours per week, we will get a misleading picture of the actual degree of gender quality. Women in many countries work fewer hours per week than the standard weekly hours of employed men, while men work more overtime than women. Obviously these patterns reflect a strongly gendered division of unpaid care and housework. Therefore, changes over time in the direction of full equality tend to be less impressive if we use a time series of hours worked and not only of a time series of employment rates of men and women (Statistics Norway 2003). The rates of men and women working part-time are poor substitutes for figures for actual hours worked by men and women.

- *Economic exclusion of disadvantaged groups*: Recently there has been a tendency to use the rate of receipt of particular income maintenance benefits (e.g. disability-related benefits like invalidity pension) as an indicator of the extent of exclusion from the labour market of a particular population group (e.g. adults with impairments). We know, however, that people with a limited or no record of past employment or earnings may not qualify for income replacement insurance benefits, and consequently be dependent on family maintenance or general means-tested assistance. To the extent that people out for work do qualify for income maintenance benefits, there is often a scope for substitution, in the sense that more than one benefit may be payable to persons in fairly similar circumstances (if not at the same time). Therefore we will usually be more enlightened if we also have figures for the overall inactivity rate (and preferably also for the activity rate and hours worked) for the group in question. Alternatively, it is informative to know what proportion of the overall inactivity of an age and gender group that is related to having some sort of impairment. Eurostat's Van Bastelar & Blöndal (2003) have provided interesting figures on the latter. An otherwise impressive OECD (2003) study of disability policy, *Transforming disability to ability*, fails to link its figures on benefit recipiency and inactivity among people with impairments to OECD's overall figures for benefit recipiency and inactivity in the population of working age in different countries (OECD 2004).

The general point here is that it is often necessary to have a couple of different but complementary indicators of the same social phenomenon, to fully appreciate current states or changes in this phenomenon.

What aspects of social inclusion should indicators capture?

As suggested by Room (1995: 3-5), Woodward & Kohli 2001: 2) and others, to be socially included means that one participates in important social arenas and is part of significant social relationships, and that one through this participation is enabled to live a full human life. In this understanding social inclusion is primarily a *relational* concept, not only a *distributive* one (Hvinden 1995). Conversely, social exclusion refers to situations where one is prevented from or denied full participation in such arenas and relationships, and consequently is unable to live a full human life. When we talk about exclusion we usually think of a situation of some duration or permanence.

Moreover, we tend to assume that there is a broad consensus about what social arenas and relationships which are important, and that most people would value participation in these. Obviously there are exceptions, for instance people who prefer to live outside these arenas and relationship, and therefore do not participate. At the same time one should be careful not to infer that people who appear to have rejected to participate or to have withdrawn from the arenas and relationships valued by most others, have done so solely on the basis of volition or free choice. There are many examples of minorities, e.g. ethnic groups, who have used withdrawal and partial encapsulation as a survival strategy in relation to an adverse environment or oppressive majority society (Hvinden 2001). In other cases there may be more or less hidden barriers, e.g. institutional discrimination, that operate to prevent or discourage the participation of individuals and groups with particular characteristics or backgrounds.

Social exclusion and family life

What are the important social arenas and relationships that people may be included in or excluded from? Arguably, the most fundamental and universal of them are family relationships, something that most of us take for granted and do not reflect very much about. Yet, when we move towards the margins of society, where we arguably find those of us who are most completely excluded, and the possibility to have or be part of ordinary family relations is not a matter of course. Let me mention some examples: In many countries have had far-reaching policies of eugenics, where some parts of population have been seen as bearers of undesirable genetic material and therefore exposed to forced sterilisation or abortion (e.g. Broberg & Roll-Hansen 1996, Roll-Hansen 1999). These policies have for instance been targeted at people with intellectual or learning disabilities or physical diseases with a strong heredity component. But also people belonging to particular ethnic minorities have been overrepresented among those exposed to forced sterilisation, e.g. because their life styles have made them vulnerable in relation to the diffuse and discretionary criteria set down in sterilisation laws (e.g. Haave 2000).

Even if people have not been denied the possibility to have children, they may have been prevented from having ordinary family lives because their children were taken into care and put in orphanages or foster homes. Although these interventions tend to been justified in terms of protecting the interest of the child it is striking that people from ethnic minorities or indigenous populations have been strongly overrepresented among those who have had their children taken into care (e.g. Hvinden 2001). Moreover, the small but significant proportion of adults living in total institutions for substantial periods, e.g. from separate care institutions for people with severe impairments to prisons, are de facto prevented from having an ordinary family life. Some research also indicate that even women with physical impairments who are not living in institutions meet many hindrances in their efforts to have children and an ordinary family life (Grue & Lærum 2002). In most countries the possibilities for lesbian and gay couples to have their relationships recognised formally, for lesbian couples to have children and for both lesbians and gays to adopt children, are strongly constrained, legally and otherwise. Finally, let it be mentioned that recent family statistics from some Western countries suggest that as consequence of more frequent break-ups of marriages and consensual unions a growing proportion of fathers in younger cohorts are not living together with their children (Skrede 2002, 2003).

What are the broader implications of these examples? First, situations which both subjectively and objectively may be seen as expressions of social exclusion may reflect strongly conflicting values and considerations. But who have said that social indicators should only deal with uncontroversial issues? Second, some forms of social exclusion may be the consequences of past or current public policies and interventions in the lives of citizens. Third, that there may be good reasons to include indicators of family relations, partnering and parenting, in the standard batteries of social indicators, although these as other indicators have to be interpreted with some caution.

Social inclusion and employment

Another key area for inclusion and exclusion is economic activity, and in most countries; paid work, family maintenance or public income maintenance. Participation in economic activity, as wage earner or self-employed, is basic and most directly so for adults, both for the material rewards it gives as well as the scope for using knowledge and skills, the social relations it involves, and the dignity and self-respect that paid occupation often (if not always) brings. Some paid work is boring routine with no learning content or career prospects, involving exposure to health hazards and injuries, or perceived as social demeaning and stigmatising. We do not only need information about whether people are in paid work or not but if they are, indicators of the qualities of this work, even it this aspect in some contexts may seem a luxury. Moreover, an important aspect of participation in paid work is obviously to what extent one is able to be economically self-sufficient and provide for oneself and a family. Indicators about whether incomes from work enable people to be self-sufficient and to provide for a family are important.

As I already touched upon, there is huge variation between countries in the extent to which both women and men are family providers. Again conflicting values are involved, especially on whether both parents of small children ought to be in paid work. The trend in most countries in Europe is clearly that adult women, both in general and as mothers of small children, have increased their participation in paid work, while the level of participation differs strongly. One of several important implications of the trend towards increased female labour market participation is an equalisation of incomes between partners or spouses in the short term, and that more women are building up entitlements to their own income transfers, e.g. pensions, that is, become less exposed to poverty in old age or if they get an impairment.

When we consider exclusion from paid work there is strong evidence that people with impairments are the group at greatest risk. For instance, in Norway where the overall rate of employment is among the highest in Europe, the rate of employment for people with employment is 62 per cent of that of the total adult population (Statistics Norway 2004). As can be seen from Table 1 this relative employment rate decreases with age, and we find broadly the same pattern for women and men.

Table 1. Relative employment rates for people with impairments in Norway by gender and age

Age	All	Women	Men
All (16-66)	.62	.62	.63
16-24	1.01	1.10	.88
25-39	.68	.70	.66
40-54	.61	.61	.62
55-59	.57	.53	.64
60-66	.55	.58	.52

Source: Statistics Norway (2004)

Estimates of the size of adult population with impairments vary cross-nationally, partly as a result of the ways in which disability or impairment has been defined and operationalised in survey instruments, and how jointly agreed definitions have been translated and understood in individual countries, for instance:

- Data from the European Community Household Panel (ECHP) from the late 1990s suggested that about 15 per cent of the population 16-64 had a severe or moderate disability hampering them in daily activities (Eurostat 2001).

- An ad hoc module on disability and labour market experience was attached to the European Labour Force Survey in 2002, but the results have not been fully reported (Dupre & Karjalainen 2003). Provisional findings indicate, however, that about 16 per cent of persons aged 16-64 living in private households in 25 countries had a long-standing health problem or disability.

- According to the findings from the Norwegian national survey about 15 per cent of the adult population 16-66 years old reported that they were restricted in their daily activities related to impairments (Bø 2003).

- Furthermore, the ECHP survey indicated that for the fourteen EU countries taking part, 68 per cent of those with severe disabilities were economically inactive, 46 per cent of those with moderate disabilities, and 30 per cent of those with no disabilities (Eurostat 2001).

- In the 2002 ad hoc module to the European Labour Force Survey it was found that the rate of inactivity ranged from 78 per cent for those with very severe impairments, 47 per cent of those with severe impairments, to about 26 per cent for those with moderate to no impairment (Dupre & Karjalainen 2003).

Even if one takes into account methodological limitations of these kinds of survey-based estimates the findings are so striking that figures for the activity rates of people with and without impairments should be a part of the standard repertoire of social indicators. As indicated before, one cannot rely exclusively on statistics that are collected on a routine basis as part of administrative registrations, e.g. the number of people claiming or receiving particular public benefits. But as a number of social indicators are based on population surveys anyway, e.g. labour force surveys, it is important that they include questions about whether people are exposed to activity restrictions related to impairments, as a regular and not just ad hoc or occasional module.

Why are people with impairments so strongly overrepresented among the economically excluded? In a small but significant number of cases the impairments are so severe and capacity-limiting that the person can hardly perform any work at all. But the large majority of people with impairments could be in work; full- or part-time, if the conditions of work were adjusted or accommodated for this purpose. This is ample evidence that the most important factor in the exclusion of people with impairments from economic activity is social and environmental barriers, such as lack of physical access to transport, buildings and workplaces, lack of usability of work equipment, computers, etc., and lack of organisational flexibility regarding work tasks and working time (e.g. Grammenos 2003, Hvinden 2004a, 2004b). Strongly related to this are attitudinal barriers, ignorance and lack of awareness, stereotypes and prejudices in the social environment, both from managers and co-workers.

The case for a stronger focus on contexts in social indicators (i): factors facilitating and preventing participation

Obviously "individual" factors do play some role in generating the low level of inclusion in economic activity for people with impairments. Many people with impairments do lack the vocational qualifications and work experience required in most jobs. But this is to a great extent the results of the ways in which educational institutions function, and especially the lack of access and accommodation to the needs of pupils and students with impairments (NOU 2001: 22). In many countries a dominating element in vocational rehabilitation schemes and "from welfare to work" schemes is attempts to improve the individual qualifications or human capital of people with impairments through re-education, training or special work placements. But this focus on individual resources is only relevant to certain point.

If social indicators are to help decision-makers, the media and the general public to understand why people with impairments are at so higher risk of economic exclusion, these indicators need to a greater extent to highlight the characteristics of the social environments or arenas that affect people's likelihood of finding and keeping a job. More attention should be given to the extent to which people with impairments experience that they have access to workplaces and what scope there is for adjustments and flexibility in work assignments and working hours. A number of important innovations have recently been made in this respect (see also Furrie 2003), for instance:

- Statistics Canada (2001) Participation and Activity Limitation Survey

- Study by SINTEF Norway and the University of Namibia (2003) on the Living conditions among people with disabilities in Namibia

- The ad hoc module on the employment situation of people with impairments in the quarterly labour force surveys repeated four times since 2000 in Norway (Bø 2003, Statistics Norway 2004).

With some variations the core idea behind the methodology of these studies is to design survey interview instruments to highlight how social contexts and environments function as facilitators and barriers for participation:

- A set of screening or filter questions is used to identify respondents with impairments.

- These respondents are asked a module of questions of specific aspects of environments, e.g. issues of access, usability & requirements for adjustments, in the contexts of education, employment, social participation, transport, goods and services, etc.

- Here facilitators are operationalised as "what makes it easier to participate", while barriers are specified as "what makes it harder to participate" (including products, technology, person support, attitudes, natural environment, services, systems and policies).

The questionnaire used by Statistics Norway has for instance produced these indicators of economic inclusion and environmental factors affecting inclusion in Norway (Statistics Norway 2003):

- The proportion of people with impairments in employment who had had adjustments made in their work arrangements (49 per cent) and of these; work tasks (29 per cent), working hours (23 per cent), physical arrangements (19 per cent).

- The proportion of people with impairments in employment with adjustments undertaken who required additional adjustments in work arrangements (19 per cent).

- The proportion of people with impairments in employment without adjustments who required adjustments in work arrangements (20 per cent).

- The proportion of people with impairments outside employment who wished to work and would require adjustments in work arrangements in order to be able to do so (23 per cent).

These indicators have immediate policy relevance, as they point to practical steps that employers can be encouraged to take and where public authorities can provide financial support in order to avoid that the costs of making these adjustments will be an excessive burden for the employer.

Similarly, we need more regular indicators on the "human resource management" of enterprises, that is, employers' strategies and actual practices regarding recruitment, hiring, retention and career development of people with impairments and other groups at risk of exclusion. In this respect even surveys of the espoused values and attitudes of managers may be helpful, even if they may to some extent encourage socially desirable responses. For instance, the international and comparative Cranfield surveys of management indicate that enterprises to a very limited extent have developed special strategies regarding the recruitment of job applicants with impairments, although there are also cross-national differences in this respect (Brandi *et al.* 2003: 18-20).

The evidence that people with impairments are at so much greater risk of economic exclusion than people without impairments is to a growing extent interpreted as a indication of institutional discrimination, that is, a sign that there are exclusionary mechanisms inherent in the way late modern or "post-industrial" economies operate.

What appears to be rational choices on the part of individual actors, e.g. on the part of private enterprises or public corporations and their managers, in a context of greater economic openness and market competition, produce outcomes that are deeply irrational on a societal level and that also have adverse effects for many individuals (Hvinden 2004a). Moreover, many of the micro-level choices appear to be determined by short-term considerations, while neglecting the longer term consequences (e.g. the coming labour shortage related to demographic ageing). Of course one should not rule out the possibility that extensive, more or less generous, public income maintenance schemes create work disincentives for some sections of the adult population. But most countries have in recent year tightened up their income maintenance schemes, made eligibility criteria more stringent, reduced replacement rates and duration of benefits, and increased activity requirements for recipients. This suggests that work disincentives are largely balanced by stronger control of access to these schemes.

Several transnational organisations, and in particular the European Union, have in recent year put the fight against discrimination on a variety of grounds, among them disability, on the agenda (cf. Article 13 of the 1997 Luxembourg Treaty, two directives from 2000, and a wider anti-discrimination action programme for mainstreaming these concerns through standard setting to promote universal design, etc). These steps are important in themselves, but also as means to correcting imperfections in the operation of a single European market (Hvinden 2004a): The social regulation instruments mentioned above may counterbalance some of the exclusionary mechanisms in a more open and competitive market, given that all member states commit themselves to enforce compliance with the new regulations and directives, and the European Court of Justice will follow up with the development of case law. In this context it is of great importance that both the EU Commission and national governments in the years to come regularly produce valid indicators about to what extent people with impairments and other groups at risk meet equal treatment or discrimination, to what extent complaints are filed and cases are taken to court, and more positively, what practical steps that are taken nationally to promote equal opportunities for all citizens, for instance through accommodation to the diversity of people's needs and requirements

The case for a stronger focus on contexts in social indicators (ii): social capital as a collective resource

Also in the context of social inclusion there are good reasons to seek inspiration in the growing area of research on social capital (OECD 2001, Putnam 2000). Here several multilevel studies have suggested that the existence of strong networks, norms of reciprocity and trust in a community or social environment may diminish significantly young people's risk of drop-out from school and the associated risk of becoming socially and economically excluded consequently (Coleman 1988, Field 2003). Individuals' access to the appropriate forms for social networks may strongly influence their prospects of finding work. By contrast, it may effectively diminish a person's prospects of getting a job and income from employment if he or she is living in a locality characterised by social erosion, with weak social networks and weakly developed collective social capital. But paradoxically, even living in a tightly integrated community may work to your disadvantage if you are a person with limited individual human capital and contacts outside your close circle of family and friends, and this is also the case for most other people in this community. In this sense living in a more mixed community that provides links to people in situations dissimilar from your own may be beneficial. Inspired by this approach, social indicators may to a greater extent than today provide information both about individual characteristics and the qualities of the social environments of these individuals. For instance, one should count the number of individuals who have low incomes or who are out of work, but also ask whether these individuals are living in communities where this is also the case for most other people.

Some concluding remarks

In recent years it has more often been argued that social indicators should not only deal with what people have access to of material resources, e.g. their purchasing power, or "primary goods" but that it is even more important to address people's scope for using these and other resources to improve their own well-being and gain more control over their own life in a longer time perspective. Amartya Sen and others (Nussbaum 2000, Raveaud & Salais 2001) have argued that we should focus on people's effective freedom, their functioning and capability. This capability perspective has with some success been adopted by the United Nation Development Program (UNDP 2004) in the form of several new social indicators, for instance the Human Development Index (HDI) based on three elements; information about health, knowledge and economic resources. There may be some limitations here, partly related to the ways in which knowledge and economic resources have been operationalised, partly related to the availability of data. Some may also raise doubts about the usefulness of this kind of composite measure. Yet, in my opinion the HDI represents an important innovation that other agencies, both national and transnational, may well be find inspiration in and seek to develop further.

More specifically, Sen (2000) has argued that social exclusion may be conceptualised as *capability deprivation*, and this may also be source of further development of social indicator. As shown by Salais (2003) one may also argue that a stronger focus on barriers and hindrances to access in the environments where people operate or want to participate is compatible with a capability perspective. In other words, a capability perspective on inclusion and exclusion does not necessarily imply a focus on individual characteristics.

Recently the European Union appears in some contexts to have embraced a broader capability-oriented understanding of social inclusion (CEU 2004: 8):

"Social inclusion is a process which ensures that those at risk of poverty and social exclusion gain the opportunities and resources necessary to participate in economic, social and cultural life and to enjoy a standard of living and well-being that is considered normal in the society in which they live. It ensures that they have greater participation in decision making which affects their lives and access to their fundamental rights".

From this perspective, it is unfortunate that in practice indicators on financial resources and especially persistent poverty still tend to dominate when the EU bodies summarise and compared the situation regarding inclusion and exclusion in its member states. It is to be hoped that the EU and other supra-national bodies will give greater emphasis to capability-oriented indicators of social inclusion in the years to come.

References

Atkinson, T., Cantillon, B., Marlier, E. & Nolan, B. (2002) *Social indicators: The EU and social inclusion*, Oxford: Oxford University Press.

Atkinson, T., Marlier, E., & Nolan, B. (2004) Indicators and targets for social inclusion in the European Union, *Journal of Common Market Studies*, 42, 1, 47-75.

Brandi, S., Hildebrandt, S., Nordhaug, I.W. & Nordhaug, O. (2004) Inkluderingsledelse: Utnyttelse av mangfold i arbeidslivet (Inclusion management: exploiting diversity in working life), Oslo: Universitetsforlaget.

Broberg, G. & Roll-Hansen, N. (1996) Eugenics and the welfare state: Sterilisation policy in Denmark, Sweden, Norway, and Finland, East Lansing: Michigan State University Press.

Bø, T.P. (2003a) Funksjonshemmede på arbeidsmarkedet – rapport fra tilleggsundersøkelse til Arbeidskraftundersøkelsen (AKU) 2.kvartal 2002 (Disabled people in the labour market – results from an ad hoc module in the Labour Force Survey (LFS) 2nd Quarter 2002), Report 2003/4, Oslo: Statistics Norway.

Bø, T. B. (2003b) Funksjonshemmede på arbeidsmarkedet – rapport fra tilleggsundersøkelse til Arbeidskraftundersøkelsen (AKU) 2.kvartal 2003 (Disabled people in the labour market – results from an ad hoc module in the Labour Force Survey (LFS) 2nd Quarter 2003), Report 2003/25, Oslo: Statistics Norway.

CEU (2004) *Joint report by the Commission and the Council on social inclusion*, 7104/04, SOC 114, ECOFIN 80, EDUC 46, SAN 49, 5 March 2004.

Coleman, J. S. (1988) Social capital in the creation of human capital, *American Journal of Sociology*, Supplement, 94, S-95-120.

Dupre, D. & Karjalainen, A. (2002) Employment of disabled people in Europe in 2002, *Statistics in focus*, Theme 3, 26/2003, Luxembourg: Eurostat.

EC (2002) *Joint report on social inclusion*, Luxembourg: Office for Official Publications of the European Communities.

EC (2004) *Joint report on social inclusion*, Luxembourg: Office for Official Publications of the European Communities.

EC (2003) Annex I: Key indicators per member state, in *The social situation in the European Union*, Luxembourg: Office for Official Publications of the European Communities.

Eurostat (2001) *Disability and social participation in Europe*, Luxembourg: Office for Official Publications of the European Communities.

Eurostat (2002) *European social statistics: Income, poverty and social exclusion, 2nd report*, Luxembourg: Office for Official Publications of the European Communities.

Eurostat (2004) *Eurostat yearbook 2004: The statistical guide to Europe*, Luxembourg: Office for Official Publications of the European Communities.

Field, J. (2003) *Social capital*, London: Routledge.

Furrie, A. D. (2003) Measuring disability and measuring the impact of living with a disability, Ottawa Canada: Adele Furrie Consulting Inc.

Grammenos, S. (2003) *Illness, disability, and social inclusion*, Louglinstown, Dublin: European Foundation for the Improvement of Living and Working Conditions.

Jordan, B. (1996) *A theory of poverty and social exclusion*, Cambridge: Polity Press.

Hvinden, B. (1995) Poverty, exclusion, and agency, *Research in Community Sociology*, 5, 15-33.

Hvinden, B. (2001) Storsamfunn og minoritet. Sammendrag av resultatene av delprogram om romanifolket (taterne) og det norske samfunnet (Society at large and minority. Summary of the results of research programme about romani people (travellers) and the Norwegian society), Oslo: The Research Council of Norway.

Hvinden, B. (2004a) How to get employers to take on greater responsibility for the inclusion of disabled people in working life, in Marin, B., Prinz, C. & Queisser (eds.)

Transforming disability welfare policies: towards work and equal opportunities, European Centre Vienna, Aldershot: Ashgate.

Hvinden, B. (2004b) Nordic disability policies in a changing Europe: is there still a distinct Nordic model? *Social Policy and Administration*, 38, 2, 170-189.

Haave, P. (2000) Sterilisering av tatere (Sterilisation of travellers), in Hvinden, B. (ed.) *Romanifolket og det norske samfunnet (The romani people and the Norwegian society)*, Bergen: Fagbokforlaget.

NOU 2001: 22 From user to citizen: a strategy for the dismantling of disabling barriers, Oslo: Ministry of Social Affairs.

Nussbaum, M. C. (2000) *Women and human development*, Cambridge: Cambridge University Press.

OECD (2001) *The well-being of nations: the role of human and social capital*, Paris: Organisation for economic co-operation and development.

OECD (2002) *Society at a glance: OECD social indicators*, Paris: Organisation for economic co-operation and development.

OECD (2003) *Transforming disability into ability*, Paris: Organisation for economic co-operation and development.

OECD (2004) *Labour force statistics 1983-2003*, Paris: Organisation for economic co-operation and development

Putnam, R. D. (2000) *Bowling alone*, New York: Simon & Schuster.

Raveaud, G. & Salais, R. (2001) Fighting against social exclusion in a European knowledge-based society: what principles of action? In Mayers, D., Berghman. J. & Salais, R. (eds.) *Social exclusion and European policy*, Cheltenham: Edward Elgar,

Roll-Hansen, N. (1999) Eugenics in Scandinavia after 1945: change of values and growth in knowledge, *Scandinavian Journal of History*, 24, 199-213.

Room, G. (1995) Poverty and social exclusion: the new European agenda for policy and research, in Room, G. (ed.) *Beyond the threshold: the measurement and analysis of social exclusion*, Bristol: The Policy Press.

Sen, A. (2000) *Social exclusion: concept, application, and scrutiny*, Social Development Paper, Office of Environment and Social Development, Asian Development Bank.

Salais, R. (2003a) Social exclusion and capability, manuscript, International Research Conference on Marginalisation and Social Exclusion, Ålesund Norway, May 21-23.

SINTEF Norway / University of Nambia (2003) *Living conditions among people with disabilities in Nambia*, Oslo: SINTEF Unimed.

Skrede, K (2002): Towards gender equality in Norway's young generations? I Carling, J., (ed.) (2002): *Nordic demography: Trends and differentials*. Scandinavian Population Studies, Volume 13, Oslo: Unipub/Nordic Demographic Society: 191-218

Skrede, K. (2003) Gender, Generations and Life Courses in the Melting Pot, i Eriksen, J. og L. Gulbrandsen (red): *Natalie Rogoff Ramsøy (1924 - 2002): En pionér i norsk og internasjonal sosiologi - et minneskrift*, NOVA-rapport 10/03, NOVA, Oslo: 58 - 85

Statistics Canada (2001) Participation and Activity Limitation Survey

Statistics Norway (2003) *This is Norway: what the figures tell*, Oslo: Statistics Norway.

Statistics Norway (2004) *Labour force survey. Ad hoc module on disabled people, 2nd quarter 2004: More disabled people employed* (http://www.ssb.no/vis/emner/06/01/akutu/art-2004-08-25-01.html accessed 26 Nov 2004)

Stewart, A. (2000) Social inclusion: an introduction, in Askonas, P. & Steward, A. (eds.) *Social inclusion: Possibilities and tensions*, Basingstoke: Macmillan.

UNDP (2004) *Human development report 2004*, New York: United Nations Development Programme.

Van Bastelaer, A. & Blöndal, L. (2003) Labour reserve: people outside the labour force, *Statistics in focus*, Theme 3, 14/2003, Luxembourg: Eurostat.

Woodward, A. & Kohli, M. (2001) European societies: inclusions/exclusions? In Woodward, A. & Kohli, M. (eds.) *Inclusions and exclusions in European societies*, London: Routledge.

Social Indicator Systems – Foundations for Policy Design and Evaluation?

Ken Tallis[1]

Australian Institute of Health and Welfare

Introduction – Scope and Argument

My departure point is the following version of a key question being addressed at this Forum–

What is required to create a suite of social indicators that will guide decision making, especially the design and evaluation of social policy?

To be confident that a suite of indicators can truly guide policy (rather than just providing general contextual information for community discussion of social issues), one must have established both:

- the institutional/political basis; and

- the scientific/statistical basis

for initiating, creating and applying a suite of policy-relevant indicators.

Institutional/political considerations give rise to both pre-conditions and post-conditions for the success of a social indicator project. The pre-conditions include engaging with policy designers and evaluators at the outset of the project, and building policy-related elements into the conceptual framework. The post-conditions include engaging with policy designers and evaluators after the suite of indicators has been generated, and analysing and interpreting the indicators in such as way as to encourage their application to policy design and evaluation.

The sci*entific/statistical* requirements for creating **social-indicators-for-policy** are more stringent than those for creating **social-indicators-as-context**. For example, social-indicators-for-policy must help to make visible the key places where the instruments of policy (the inputs and other resources that have been supplied through policy, the processes that have been engineered, or the outputs that have been produced) connect with social outcomes. Traditional suites of social indicators, which sometimes focus on just measuring the outcomes, may be unhelpful in this regard.

The need to translate indicators into policy and practice can draw social statisticians into a closer engagement with those who design and evaluate policy than has traditionally been the case in most countries. For example, those who develop suites of social indicators sometimes act in the belief that their responsibility ceases (indeed, for the sake of their independence, must cease) when the body of information has been created – and they commonly act in the faith that the translation into policy-relevant knowledge and policy action *will flow* thereafter (but flow from the efforts of others).

---

1   The views expressed in this paper are those of the author, not of the Australian Institute of Health and Welfare, the National Health Performance Committee or any other agency or body mentioned herein.

In this paper, I devote relatively little space to methodological matters (such as the technical requirements for defining social indicators that are comparable across time, geography and subpopulations; are sensitive to changes and differences in patterns; encapsulate an appreciable part of the total variation in some dimension of social experience; and collectively span the major dimensions of social experience). There is an abundant and long-standing literature that provides neat formulations of the methodological principles.[2] Instead, I concentrate on distilling the experience gained during some Australian work-in-progress (namely, the suite of National Health Performance Indicators) that is developing social-indicators-for-policy. So far, that experience has been promising. But the policy dividends cannot yet be declared. Moreover, although we have drawn some early lessons from the NHPI experience, the principles for developing a suite of social-indicators-for-policy are still inchoate, and the draft formulations of those principles are far from neat.

It is timely to discuss the question of what conditions (institutional/political conditions and scientific/statistical conditions) must be established to ensure that an investment in social indicators will be fruitful. Interest in creating large-scale indicator systems –at both the national and the international levels– has waxed and waned in recent decades. And the waxing or waning has, in part, reflected *growing or diminishing confidence that suites of indicators can truly guide policy and other decision making.*[3]

Social Indicators within the Universe of Social Statistics

I take it as an axiom that a good system of **social statistics** is an essential foundation for decision making.

But the term "social statistics" covers a very broad spectrum of products and activities. It encompasses, among other things:

- comprehensive social information systems,
- integrated social accounts (social accounting matrices) or social modelling, and
- suites of social indicators.

If an investment is to be made in a suite of **social indicators** on the grounds that it will guide policy, then one must be confident that developing indicators would be a better investment for that purpose than would some other statistical activity. Better than, say, just delivering well-constructed databases to the modellers.

Suites of Social Indicators and the Phases of Policy

Social statistics (broadly construed) can support several different phases of policy, such as the following:

- **Policy focus** – drawing attention to aspects of society that merit attention or intervention.
- **Policy design** – developing a detailed strategy for a social intervention or for encouraging an environment in which social improvement can occur.

---

2   For some principles for specifying social indicators, see AIHW (2001a) pp.386-388 and ABS (2001a) pp.11-12.

3   See, for example, 'Demise of the Social Indicators Movement' in Ekos Research Associates (1998a), p.43.

- **Policy evaluation** – assessing the effectiveness of interventions in achieving desired social outcomes.

I shall argue that a suite of social indicators should certainly be an effective aid to the first phase, is possibly an inferior aid to the second, and may or may not aid the third. In all phases, the institutional bases for successful influence are at least as important as the statistical bases.

A Case Study

To flesh out the arguments, I draw on a case study, namely, Australian experience in creating and applying a suite of indicators that measure the performance of the health system – the National Health Performance Indicators (NHPI), which encompass indicators of health status and outcomes, the determinants of health and, importantly for the present topic, the performance of health services.

At first glance, the NHPI is a somewhat constrained illustration of the Forum's theme – it covers only one dimension of society; and it relates mainly to national or sub-national indicators, rather than to international indicators. Nevertheless, the experience is relevant because the NHPI (unlike many suites of social indicators) was explicitly developed with the aspiration that it would be used to guide policy action, by making visible:

- **Position** – where the eight Australian states and territories are positioned relative to one another in matters of health, and where Australia is positioned relative to other developed countries.

- **Progress** – what progress in matters of health has been achieved by Australia as a whole and by its states and territories.

This paper summarises lessons from the NHPI regarding the institutional and statistical bases for creating and applying a suite of policy-relevant indicators.

Discussion Points

This paper concludes by exploring the extent to which lessons drawn from the Australian National Health Performance Indicators may be generalisable to other dimensions of society, other institutional settings or other countries.

Case Study – Creating and Applying Australia's Suite of National Health Performance Indicators

Institutional Background to the Project

The Australian health system is highly effective but very complex.[4] Australia consistently ranks among the best-performing group of countries against such measures as healthy life expectancy, for example. Health services are delivered by many providers in both the public and the private sectors, and the health industry is subject to a range of funding and regulatory mechanisms. Within the public sector, responsibilities for both service provision and funding are split between multiple levels of government – chiefly between the Australian government and the eight state and territory governments.

Overall co-ordination of major components of the health system is provided by the Australian Health Ministers' Advisory Council (AHMAC) – the heads of federal, state

---

4   For a more extensive description of the Australian health system, see AIHW (2004b) pp.5-8.

and territory agencies responsible for health. AHMAC has established an interlocking system of committees to superintend such matters as: the priority areas for health activity and reform; safety and quality in health care; and health information.

As part of its governance arrangements for health information, AHMAC established the National Health Performance Committee (NHPC), a multi-jurisdictional body with responsibility for developing and reporting statistics on the performance of the Australian health system, with a view to improving both service performance and health outcomes. Major activities of the NHPC in recent years have included developing a National Health Performance Framework (NHPF) –see Annex 1– and delivering a biennial report on about fifty National Health Performance Indicators (the NHPI report) – see Annex 3.

Motivations for the Project

A key aspiration of the suite of National Health Performance Indicators was that it should galvanise and guide action to improve health system performance and health outcomes in Australia.

To inform analyses of *position,* the NHPI was designed to support better understanding of health outcomes and health system performance at multiple levels of the system, although the data presented in the NHPC's biennial reports relate chiefly to the Australian, state and territory levels. And to support analyses of *progress,* the NHPI includes, wherever possible, consistent time series (although, for many indicators, the series are still rather short and subject to statistical breaks).

Institutional and Statistical Setup of the Project

The NHPF and NHPI were developed through a multi-jurisdictional technical and consultative process over a period of several years.

Lying underneath the three-tiered NHPF is a conceptual model for health – see Figure 1. Tier 1 corresponds with the "Health and wellbeing" block of the model; Tier 2 with the "Determinants" block; and Tier 3 with the "Interventions" and "Resources and systems" blocks.

The higher-level conceptual structure of the NHPI shows some clear resemblances to frameworks for indicators developed by other national and international projects – although the suite of fifty NHPI indicators is tailored to Australian health concerns, to our own institutional environment and to the data that are available through our national health information system.

In conducting its statistical work, the NHPC has faced the same problems that arise whenever one tries to develop suites of social indicators, such as – *selection problems* (how to choose a compact set of indicators from the vast array potentially derivable from the national health information system); and *problems of inconsistency, noise and proxying* (how to make the indicators robust to differences between data that flow from different jurisdictional health systems; how to handle errors and noise in the data; how to deal with the fact that some of the available measures are only approximations to one's preferred measures; and so on).

In addition –because the suite of indicators was intended to inform policy– the NHPC was conscious from the outset that it would have to deal with the problem of confounding, non-policy influences:

"Given that overall health outcome is a product of social, environmental and health system factors, **there are difficulties in linking the efforts of the health sector with**

observable health outcomes. There is a continuum of outcomes from those that are directly influenced by the health system to those that are not and are affected by a range of external factors. A distinction can be made between 'intermediate' outcomes attributable to the actions of the health sector and higher level outcomes that cannot be attributed to the efforts of the health sector alone. The outcomes selected to measure performance of the health sector should be based on such intermediate outcomes, e.g. survival rates after transplant, functionality after hip replacement and absence of preventable disease in the community."

"In the short term, as appropriate health system performance indicators are being refined and developed, it may be necessary to use process measures…to represent the performance of the system. Once appropriate measures (and information sources) are developed over the long term, it will be possible to build up meaningful measures of the efficiency and effectiveness of health outputs and the impact on health outcomes."[5]

Figure 1. Conceptual Framework for Australia's Health

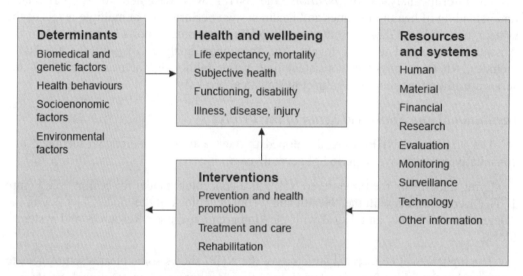

Source : AIHW (2004b) p.3.

Further Activity Flowing from the Project

Since compiling its most recent biennial report, the NHPC has turned its attention to three further stands of work, all relevant to the themes of this Forum–

- creating spin-off, thematic bulletins that distil the key policy-relevant messages from the NHPI report,

- providing information and methodological advice that will encourage the "benchmarking" (broadly construed) of health systems, regional health services and health service establishments, with a view to spreading good practice, and

- enriching the comparison of Australian health (risk and protective factors, health service performance, and health status and outcomes) with health in other countries.

---

5   See AIHW (2004a) pp.3-4. [Emphasis added.]

Experiences and Lessons – Institutional/Political Basis for a Suite of Policy-Relevant Social Indicators – Some Pre-Conditions

The following three sections of the paper draw on the NHPI experience to suggest some "lessons" about:

- institutional pre-conditions that will improve the chances of success for a social indicators project,

- the statistical basis for generating a suite of policy-relevant social indicators, and

- institutional post-conditions that will reduce the chances of the social indicators project being still-born (that is, scientifically successful but never finding its intended policy applications).

This list of lessons makes no claim to be comprehensive – it is drawn specifically from experience in the Australian NHPI project, which has not traversed all the territory that might be covered by other indicator projects in other fields, other institutional settings or other countries. Moreover, this formulation of the lessons must be regarded as draft rather than definitive (notwithstanding my frequent use of the word "must") – the NHPI project has been running now for several years, but it is still work-in-progress.

Lesson 1 – Policy applications must inform all stages of the indicators project, not be grafted onto it after the event.

Throughout the Australian national health information system, there is strong emphasis on making statistics useful to policy makers and others who must address such questions as the following:[6]

- What are the most important gradients of mortality and morbidity (such as age, sex, ethnicity, geography and socio-economic status)?

- What are the other key epidemiological differentials and trends?

- What is the optimal balance for resourcing, say, primary health care (both preventive and curative) vis-à-vis other health services (such as acute care)?

- How can health and allied care be co-ordinated across the patient lifecycle, across acute-chronic phases of illness and across service providers?

- What are the key contrasts in health outcomes and health system performance – contrasts between Australia and other countries, or between one Australian state and another, or between one service provider and another– and what intelligence can one distil therefrom regarding good policy and practice?

- What are the key contrasts regarding progress in health outcomes and health system performance – and what intelligence can one distil therefrom?

And when the NHPI project (which sprang from our national health information system) was initiated, a year-long consultation process was undertaken to ensure that the project would not just deliver answers to key questions about national health performance, but that those answers would be articulated in such as way as to *point to policy actions,* such as – rebalancing resources across the phases of health care; or

---

6   This is neither an exhaustive nor a systematic list of questions about the Australian health system and health outcomes, and it has no particular status; it is based on discussions during the NHPI project and at a recent national conference – see AIHW (2004c).

redirecting effort to address the health needs of, say, certain disease groups, subpopulations or regions; or transplanting successful ways of organising health services from well-performing units to less-well-performing units (through benchmarking or other processes); and so on.

Lesson 2 – The conceptual framework for the indicators project must embrace not just outcomes, but also interventions and the links between interventions and outcomes.

Outcomes in health, like those in other dimensions of society, are the joint result of multiple influences, such as:

- endowments (including genetic factors, in the case of health);

- individual and collective behaviours (including behavioural risk and protective factors);

- socioeconomic and environmental influences (including income, occupation, ambient risk and protective factors); and

- interventions (including health promotion and prevention, treatment and care).[7]

A comprehensive *national health information system* should encompass measures of outcomes and measures of all the influences on outcomes. And if a *suite of health indicators* aspires to guide policy, it must extend beyond outcome measurement, and link to the concepts that are the policy-makers' stock-in-trade.

The National Health Performance Framework extends well beyond the measurement of differentials and trends in outcomes. The frameworks for some traditional suites of social-indicators-as-context may centre on the measurement of outcomes (say, health status) – and they may resort to other measures (such as input, process or output measures) as a second-best, when such measures are needed to address shortcomings in the available data on outcomes (to compensate for, say, missing, partial or slow moving data). But the NHPF has *deliberately* taken account of policy instruments, such as – the inputs or other resources supplied through policy, the processes engineered, or the outputs produced. A whole tier (Tier 3) of the NHPI framework is devoted to concepts and measures that can help assess the performance of the health system and the efficacy of policy.[8]

Lessons 1 and 2 bear upon the "intellectual" aspects of institutional pre-conditions for the success of a social indicators project that aspires to be policy-relevant. But the heart of the institutional/political pre-conditions for success is expressed in Lesson 3.

Lesson 3 – Policy designers and evaluators must be engaged in the indicators project from the outset.

The consultation process that led to the National Health Performance Framework (and to the initial specification of the aspects of the health system for which it would be desirable to develop indicators) engaged policy makers across the entire Australian health system – top-level administrators who are responsible for overall health policy design for whole political units (the Australian government or a state or territory government); those

---

7   For a more systematic exposition, see, for example, the conceptual framework for Australia's Health (AIHW (2004b) pp.2-3).

8   For the structure of the NHPI's Tier 3, see Annex 1.

who design or evaluate service delivery programs (such as primary or acute care, or care for particular sub-populations); and those who are responsible for health service delivery.

Without this consultation process, some key policy needs would, in all likelihood, has been omitted from the NHPF or, just as fatally, have been represented in naïve ways.

Experiences and Lessons – Statistical/Scientific Basis for a Suite of Policy-Relevant Social Indicators

The NHPI experience has also provided some suggestions (but not yet any definitive principles) about how to create a suite of indicators that has the potential to guide decision making.

Lesson 4 – The indicators chosen must go beyond outcome measurement, to connect with (feasible) policy action.

As I have already outlined under Lesson 2, the framework for the NHPI goes beyond health outcomes. And this conceptual thinking has been realised during the statistical process in several ways.

First, the needs of policy have been embedded in the NHPI **criteria for selecting indicators**.[9] Those criteria go beyond the traditional technical design principles for social-indicators-as-context, and include such requirements as the following:

- The indicators should be relevant to policy and practice (i.e., the indicators should point to feasible actions that can lead to health improvement). (Criterion 5)

- The indicators should galvanise multilevel action (i.e., the indicators should point to policy and practice that could be undertaken at the national, state, local or community level by individuals, organised groups and public and private agencies). (Criterion 4)

- The indicators should reflect results of previous actions when measured over time (i.e., if a change in policy or practice has been undertaken, tangible results should become visible in the indicators, revealing improvements in health). (Criterion 6)

Second, key performance ratios (such as output/input, outcome/output and outcome/input ratios) that are meaningful to policy designers and, especially, to policy evaluators have been included in the NHPI suite.

Lesson 5 – The suite of indicators must make visible those variations in position and progress that relate to differences in policy and practice.

One of the major aspirations of the NHPC is that its indicators should not merely provide a biennial "report card" on the performance of the Australian health system, but that it should allow people or organisations in charge of the system (or particular segments of it) to perceive where other systems (or other segments) are doing better – and thereby be guided to action for improvement. In the language adopted for this Forum, the NHPI is intended to make visible the variations in both position and progress.

So far, the NHPI has done well at making visible some key intra-national variations:

- **Intra-national position**. How does the performance of each Australian state and territory health care system compare with that of other states' and territories'

---

9   For the complete list of criteria that guided the selection of NHPI indicators, see Annex 2.

systems? What are the key intra-national variations in health outcomes? What clues are provided regarding the systemic foundations of the best outcomes – foundations such as the comparative volumes of resources marshalled in different states and territories, where those resources are concentrated, or how they are organised?

- **Intra-national progress.** How has performance improvement in each Australian state and territory health care system compared with improvement in other states and territories? What are the key variations in rates of outcome improvement? What clues are provided regarding the systemic foundations of the greatest improvements?

The biennial NHPI report itself disaggregates the indicators only down as far as state/territory level. But the NHPI suite has been designed so that many of the indicators can also be derived at the level of, say, individual management units (such as regional health authorities) or individual health service establishments (such as hospitals). Derivations of those kinds would support benchmarking between units at those lower levels of aggregation, and would provide a guide to policy design and performance improvement.

The NHPC aspires to deliver indicators that also support a better understanding of Australia's position and progress in health vis-à-vis other developed countries. But the latest NHPI report contains internationally comparable data for only a few indicators. The availability of such data is the problem. For example, an examination of one of the richer sources (OECD Health Data 2004)[10] suggests that:

- For **Tier 1 (Health status and outcomes)** of the NHPI framework, there is a reasonably large range of internationally comparable indicators.

- The set of internationally comparable indicators is thinner for **Tier 2 (Determinants of health),** and is confined chiefly to a few key risk factors (such as rates of smoking and obesity).

- There are rather few internationally comparably indicators for **Tier 3 (Health system performance)**, and those that are available relate chiefly to the size and composition of the health workforce and health expenditures.

In the main, the internationally comparable indicators are richest for the tiers relating to outcome measurement (a traditional focus of social-indicators-as-context), and are poorest for the tiers that draw connections to policy instruments and service performance (needed for social-indicators-for-policy).

Lessons 4 and 5 suggest some properties that a suite of policy-relevant indicators should exhibit. But equally important is the statistical environment that gives rise to and supports the indicators.

Lesson 6 – The suite of indicators should spring from comprehensive national information systems.

Australia has an excellent national system of health information, and development of the NHPI would scarcely have been possible without it. Indeed, among the dimensions of Australian society, health is possibly the one most richly supplied with information:

- The Australian Bureau of Statistics (ABS) conducts regular large-scale sample surveys of population health and disability, including self-assessed health status, risk factors and contact with services; other surveys (such as a survey of patient

---

10   See OECD (2004a). For a list of the NHPI's Tier 1, 2 and 3 indicators, see Annex 3.

encounters with general practitioners) are conducted by the Australian Institute of Health and Welfare (AIHW).

- The AIHW and the ABS both assemble large databases from administrative by-product data – these encompass health service records (hospital and mental health establishments and episodes), disease registers, workforce and finances (the supply and use of funds).

As a perusal of Annex 3 will suggest, both directly collected and administrative by-product data are needed to populate all three tiers of the NHPI framework with indicators. And it has been possible to construct preferred or proxy measures for many NHPI concepts – although there are some gaps and shortcomings that might be addressed, for example, by regular surveys that would make objective measures of health (such as body mass index or blood chemistry).

Administrative data have been crucial to populating NHPI Tier 3 (Health system performance), which is of great interest for policy. Over decades, multi-jurisdictional committees and working parties in Australia have laboured to:

- define common concepts of key measures for the health system – these are embodied in the National Health Data Dictionary and other repositories of metadata

- arrive at agreed commensurable datasets – these constitute the "National Minimum Data Sets" that all states and territories have agreed to deliver to the AIHW or other statistical co-ordination agencies, so that nationally consistent databases and analytical publications can be compiled.

This foundational work has meant that for many (but by no means all) indicators, the NHPC was able to draw on nationally agreed definitions and nationally consistent data when assembling the NHPI suite.

Experiences and Lessons – Institutional/Political Basis for a Suite of Policy-Relevant Social Indicators – Some Post-Conditions

I suggested earlier that suites of social indicators (as distinct from other statistical activities and products) are potentially most helpful to the first phase of policy (policy focus) and to the third phase (policy evaluation). But whether that potential is realised depends at least as much on the institutional setup for promulgating the indicators as on their statistical basis. The NHPI experience has provided some suggestions about what is required.

Lesson 7 – *The institutional processes must cement ownership of the indicators among the policy agencies.*

A major hazard threatening the effectiveness of a suite of social-indicators-for-policy is that it might be ignored or disavowed by those who are responsible for policy action. This hazard is particularly strong, of course, when the indicators make visible key inter-jurisdictional differences in "position" and "progress".

As discussed earlier, the prospects of achieving a suite of indicators over which the policy makers will have a sense of ownership is considerably enhanced *(even before indicator development begins)* if there is a well-established national system of data and metadata relating to the dimension of society to which the indicator suite will refer. Some important debates about concepts and statistical implementation will already have been resolved.

The setup and processes for the indicator development project itself are also important. The NHPI was developed by a committee that included representatives from every Australian state and territory, the federal government, statistical agencies and other industry and consumer councils. That committee oversaw and signed off every step of the NHPI development project, including – the National Health Performance Framework, the selection and compilation of indicators, and the analysis and interpretation of the data.

Lesson 8 – The indicators must be accompanied by persuasive accounts of key differences in position and progress.

Another hazard to the effectiveness of a suite-of-indicators-for-policy is that the findings about key differences in position and progress will be diluted by qualifications or disclaimers.[11] It is, of course, the case that qualifications *must* attach to almost every set of figures that points to a contrast between, say, the health outcomes in two jurisdictions. All such contrasts are subject to:

- noise in the data – raising doubts that the observed difference might be largely (or even wholly) an artefact of flaws in the processes of observation, and

- confounding influences – raising doubts that the observed difference might not be appreciably (or even at all) the result of a difference in policy or practice.

It may be quite unpersuasive to present just the indicators, accompanied only by footnotes about the qualifications on their interpretation. More persuasive are analyses that show (if it is true) that much of the inter-jurisdictional contrast persist even when data flaws and non-policy confounding influences are taken into account. Analyses of this kind can be difficult, and can demand styles of work that statisticians who construct social-indicators-as-context undertake rather infrequently. Of course, if the noise or confounding influences *dominate* the observed contrasts in jurisdictions' positions and progress against some indicator, then it may be questioned whether that indicator has earned its place in the suite.

Lesson 9 – Engagement with policy cannot cease when the suite of indicators has been delivered.

Statisticians who develop suites of social indicators sometimes act in the belief that their responsibility ceases when the body of information has been delivered. There are good reasons for this, of course. For example, the integrity and independence of statistical reporting are better preserved (and demonstrated) when the reporting is conducted at arm's length from policy debate, design and evaluation. But the effectiveness of social-statistics-for-policy then hangs on the faith that the translation into policy-relevant knowledge and policy action *will flow* once the body of information has been delivered. Such faith may not be warranted. After the latest NHPI report was compiled, the committee devoted considerable thought to ways of making its findings accessible; these included writing fact sheets that explain how to read the report and thematic bulletins that distil key policy-relevant messages.

---

11   …and hence would suffer the death of a thousand footnotes.

Discussion Points – Generalising to Other Dimensions of Society?

Health is only one area of social concern. A comprehensive system of social indicators should support the needs of policy in a wider range of areas, such as those depicted in Figure 2.[12]

Figure 2: Conceptual Framework for Australia's Welfare

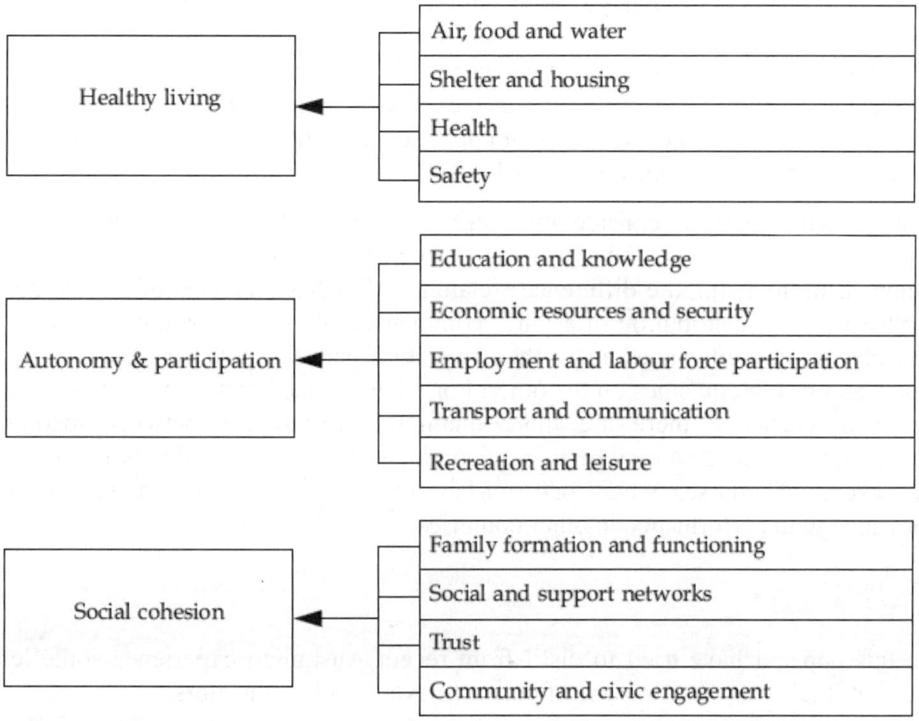

Source : AIHW (2003a) p.13.

To what extent are the lessons from the NHPI experience generalisable?

At the broadest level, the lessons about institutional and statistical requirements for indicator development and use should carry over from health to other dimensions of social concern. But replicating the NHPI experience for those dimensions may present difficulties.

First, the **conceptual frameworks** for other dimensions of society are at different levels of maturity and acceptance. In Australia, for example, there are well-worked-out frameworks for such dimensions as education and employment. Frameworks for other dimensions, such as recreation and leisure, have only recently been drafted or are works-in-progress.

Second, the **national information systems** for other dimensions may be embryonic or absent. In Australia, there are mature information systems for community services and housing. For dimensions such as transport and communication, there is a wide array of

---

12   For an extensive treatment of the thinking that underlies the conceptual framework in Figure 2 and of the principles and processes for populating that framework with indicators, see AIHW (2001a) ch.9 "Needs, Interventions, Outcomes: Measurement Frameworks".

information, but it has not yet been pulled together into a national system. Work on developing an information system for community and civic engagement has barely begun. These differences between the various dimensions of social concern stem in large part from the fact that long-standing **national information governance structures** (associated with multi-jurisdictional ministerial councils) have been established for health, community services and housing but for few other dimensions.

Third, for health, there is a well-worked out information model that (in the words of the NHPI) "links the efforts of the health sector with observable health outcomes". This model is underpinned by a large, long-standing body of clinical and epidemiological research; and the model has in turn underpinned the creation of a suite of health indicators that **connects with policy action** and makes visible the variations in outcomes that relate to differences in policy and practice. But the same apparatus is available for few other dimensions of society – and, without that apparatus, it is difficult to move beyond social-indicators-as-context to social-indicators-for-policy.

Fourth, while there is considerable variety in the health services and institutional arrangements from one Australian state to another, the **range of variation** is somewhat constrained. In the main, the differences relate to a few basic models of service delivery and to the mix and distribution of a fairly commensurable set of resources. Thus, it may be feasible to draw inferences about the connection between policy and practice on the one hand and health outcomes on the other. For other areas of social concern, the range of variation is greater – there are more qualitative differences between institutional arrangements, and the data may be more incommensurable. This difficulty becomes even more vexed, of course, when one wishes to compare Australian health system performance with performance in other countries.

Envoi

In this paper, I have tried to distil from recent Australian experience some lessons about what it takes to create a suite of policy-relevant social indicators.

Institutional Basis – Pre-Conditions	Statistical Basis	Institutional Basis – Post-Conditions
Policy applications must inform all stages of the social indicators project	Choose indicators that connect best with action and evaluation	Cement ownership of the indicator suite among policy agencies
Conceptual framework must go beyond outcomes	Make visible the variations in position and progress that spring from policy and practice	Provide persuasive accounts of key differences in position and progress
Engage with policy-designers and evaluators from the outset	Indicators should spring from the national information system	Continue engagement after delivering the suite of indicators

My coverage here of our Australian experience has necessarily been selective. More full-blooded accounts of the experience (as it relates to health indicators) can be found in AIHW (2001b) and (2004a) and (as it relates to welfare indicators) in AIHW (2001a).

Abbreviations

ABS   Australian Bureau of Statistics

AHMAC   Australian Health Ministers' Conference

AIHW   Australian Institute of Health and Welfare

NHPA (Australian) National Health Priority Areas

NHPC (Australian) National Health Performance Committee

NHPF (Australian) National Health Performance Framework

NHPI   (Australian) National Health Performance Indicators

OECD Organisation for Economic Co-operation and Development

WHO   World Health Organisation

References

ABS (2001a). *Measuring Wellbeing* (Cat. No. 4160.0). Canberra; Australian Bureau of Statistics.

ABS (2004a). *Australian Social Trends 2004* (Cat. No. 4102.0). Canberra; Australian Bureau of Statistics.

AIHW (2001a). *Australia's Welfare 2001.* Canberra; Australian Institute of Health and Welfare.

AIHW (2001b). *National Health Performance Framework Report.* Canberra; Australian Institute of Health and Welfare.

AIHW (2003a). *Australia's Welfare 2003.* Canberra; Australian Institute of Health and Welfare.

AIHW (2004a). Second National Report on Health Sector Performance Indicators 2003 – A Report by the National Health Performance Committee to the Australian Health Ministers' Conference. Canberra; Australian Institute of Health and Welfare.

AIHW (2004b). *Australia's Health 2004.* Canberra; Australian Institute of Health and Welfare.

AIHW (2004c). Access No.17 – Special Issue on the AIHW Conference "Vital Statistics, Vital Signs" 22-23 June 2004. Canberra; Australian Institute of Health and Welfare.

NOTE – All Australian Institute of Health and Welfare publications can be accessed free of charge at the website www.aihw.gov.au

Ekos Research Associates (1998a). *The Use of Social Indicators as Evaluation Instruments.* Ottawa. Report to Strategic Evaluation and Monitoring, Human Resources Development Canada.

OECD (2004a). OECD Health Data. <www.oecd.org – viewed 25 September 2004>

Annex 1. Australian National Health Performance Framework

Health status and outcomes (Tier 1) How healthy are Australians? Is it the same for everyone? Where is the most opportunity for improvement?			
Health conditions	**Human function**	**Life expectancy and wellbeing**	**Deaths**
Prevalence of disease, disorder, injury or trauma or other health-related states	Alterations to body structure or function (impairment), activities (activity limitation) and participation (restrictions in participation)	Broad measures of physical, mental and social wellbeing of individuals and other derived indicators such as disability adjusted life expectancy (DALE)	Age and/or condition specific mortality rates

Determinants of health (Tier 2) Are the factors determining health changing for the better? Is it the same for everyone? Where and for whom are they changing?				
Environmental factors	**Socioeconomic factors**	**Community capacity**	**Health behaviours**	**Person-related factors**
Physical, chemical and biological factors such as air, water, food and soil quality resulting from chemical pollution and waste disposal	Socioeconomic factors such as education, employment, per capita expenditure on health and average weekly earnings	Characteristics of communities and families such as population density, age distribution, health literacy, housing, community support services and transport	Attitudes, beliefs, knowledge and behaviours, e.g. patterns of eating, physical activity, excess alcohol consumption and smoking	Genetic-related susceptibility to disease and other factors such as blood pressure, cholesterol levels and body weight

Health system performance (Tier 3) How well is the health system performing in delivering quality health actions to improve the health of all Australians? Is it the same for everyone?		
Effective	Appropriate	Efficient
Care, intervention or action achieves desired outcome	Care, intervention or action provided is relevant to the client's needs and based on established standards	Achieves desired results with most cost-effective use of resources
Responsive	Accessible	Safe
Service provides respect for persons and is client orientated, including respect for dignity, confidentiality, participation in choices, promptness, quality of amenities, access to social support networks and choice of provider	Ability of people to obtain health care at the right place and right time irrespective of income, physical location and cultural background	The avoidance or reduction to acceptable limits of actual or potential harm from health care management or the environment in which health care is delivered
Continuous	Capable	Sustainable
Ability to provide uninterrupted, coordinated care or service across programs, practitioners, organisations and levels over time	An individual's or service's capacity to provide a health service based on skills and knowledge	System's or organisation's capacity to provide infrastructure such as workforce, facilities and equipment, and to be innovative and respond to emerging needs (research, monitoring)

Source: AIHW (2004) p.5

Annex 2. Australian National Health Performance Framework – The Criteria for Selecting Indicators

The indicators in this framework should (when used from program level through to whole-of-system level) have all or some of the following qualities.

Indicators should:

1. Be worth measuring.

    The indicators represent an important and salient aspect of the public's health or the performance of the health system.

2. Be measurable for diverse populations.

    The indicators are valid and reliable for the general population and diverse populations (Aboriginal and Torres Strait Islander populations, sex, rural/urban, socioeconomic etc.).

3. Be understood by people who need to act.

    People who need to act on their own behalf or that of others should be able to readily comprehend the indicators and what can be done to improve health.

4. Galvanise action.

    The indicators are of such a nature that action can be taken at the national, state, local or community level by individuals, organised groups and public and private agencies.

5. Be relevant to policy and practice.

    Actions that can lead to improvement are anticipated and feasible—they are plausible actions that can alter the course of an indicator when widely applied.

6. Reflect results of actions when measured over time.

    If action is taken, tangible results will be seen indicating improvements in various aspects of the nation's health.

7. Be feasible to collect and report.

    The information required for the indicator can be obtained at reasonable cost in relation to its value and can be collected, analysed and reported on in an appropriate time frame.

8. Comply with national processes of data definitions.

9. Facilitate the use of data at the health industry service unit level for benchmarking purposes.

10. Be consistent and use established and existing indicators where possible.

    "In considering the selection or development of relevant health system performance indicators it is important to keep in mind that indicators are just that: an indication of organisational achievement. They are not an exact measure and individual indicators should not be taken to provide a conclusive picture on an agency's or system's achievements. A suite of relevant indicators is usually required and then an interpretation of their results is needed to make sense of the indicators. Performance information does not exist in isolation and is not an end in itself; rather it provides a tool that allows opinions to be formed and decisions made."

"Some indicators should be ratios of output/input, outcome/output and outcome/input. There should also be a focus on measures of outcomes where there is a link between health system actions and health outcomes."

Source: AIHW (2004a) pp.3-4

Annex 3. Australian National Health Performance Framework – The Suite of Indicators

No.	Indicator	Description
	**Tier 1 — Health status and outcomes**	
1.01	Incidence of heart attacks	Incidence of acute coronary heart disease events ("heart attacks")
1.02	Incidence of cancer	Incidence rates for cancer
1.03	Severe or profound core activity limitation	Severe or profound core activity limitation by age and sex
1.04	Life expectancy	Life expectancy at birth
1.05	Psychological distress	Level of psychological distress as measured by the Kessler 10
1.06	Potentially avoidable deaths	Number of potentially avoidable deaths
1.07	Infant mortality	Infant mortality rates
1.08	Mortality for National Health Priority Area diseases and conditions	Death rates for NHPA diseases and conditions
	Tier 2 — Determinants of health	
2.01	Children exposed to tobacco smoke in the home	The proportion of households with dependent children (0–14 years) where adults report smoking inside
2.02	Availability of fluoridated water	Proportion of the population served by a reticulated water supply that provides satisfactory fluoride levels (whether artificial or natural)
2.03	Income inequality	Ratio of equalised weekly incomes at the 80th percentile to the 20th percentile income
2.04	Informal care	Number engaged in informal care
2.05	Adult smoking	Proportion of adults who are daily smokers
2.06	Risky alcohol consumption	Proportion of the population aged 18 years and over at risk of long term harm from alcohol
2.07	Fruit and vegetable intake	Proportion of people eating sufficient daily serves of fruit or vegetables
2.08	Physical inactivity	Proportion of adults insufficiently physically active to obtain a health benefit
2.09	Overweight and obesity	Proportion of persons overweight or obese
2.10	Low birthweight babies	Proportion of babies who are low birthweight
2.11	High blood pressure	Proportion of persons with high blood pressure
	Tier 3 — Health system performance	
3.01	Unsafe sharing of needles	Percentage of injecting drug users, participating in surveys carried out at needle and syringe programs, who report recent sharing of needles and syringes
3.02	Teenage purchase of cigarettes	Percentage of teenagers smokers who personally purchased their most recent cigarette
3.03	Cervical screening	Cervical screening rates for women within national target groups.

3.04	Breast cancer screening	Breast cancer screening rates for women within the national target groups
3.05	Childhood immunisation	Number of children fully immunised at 12 months and at 24 months of age
3.06	Influenza vaccination	Percentage of adults over 64 years who received an influenza vaccination for the previous winter
3.07	Potentially preventable hospitalisations	Admissions to hospital that could have been prevented through the provision of appropriate non-hospital health services
3.08	Survival following acute coronary heart disease event	Deaths occurring after acute coronary heart disease events ("heart attacks")
3.09	Cancer survival	Five-year relative survival proportions for persons diagnosed with cancer
3.10	Appropriate use of antibiotics	Number of prescriptions for oral antibiotics ordered by general practitioners (GPs) for the treatment of upper respiratory tract infections
3.11	Management of diabetes	Proportion of persons with diabetes mellitus who have received an annual cycle of care within general practice
3.12	Delivery by caesarean section	Caesarean sections as a proportion of all confinements by hospital status
3.13	Hysterectomy rate	Separation rates for hysterectomies
3.14	Hospital costs	Average cost per casemix-adjusted separation for public acute care hospitals
3.15	Length of stay in hospital	Relative stay index by medical surgical and other DRGs
3.16	Waiting times in emergency departments	Percentage of patients who are treated within national benchmarks for waiting in public hospital emergency departments for each triage category
3.17	Bulk billing for non-referred (GP) attendances	Proportion of non-referred (GP)attendances that are bulk-billed (or direct billed) under the Medicare program
3.18	Availability of GP services	Availability of GP services on Full-time Workload Equivalent (FWE) basis
3.19	Access to elective surgery	Median waiting time for access to elective surgery –from the date they were added to the waiting list to the date they were admitted
3.20	Electronic prescribing and clinical data in general practice	Percentage of general practices in the Practice Incentives Program (PIP) who transfer clinical data electronically or use electronic prescribing software
3.21	Adverse events treated in hospitals	Proportion of hospital separations where an adverse event treated and/or occurred
3.22	Enhanced Primary Care services	Percentage of General Practitioners using Enhanced Primary Care (EPC) items
3.23	Health assessments by GPs	Percentage of eligible older people who have received an Enhanced Primary Care annual voluntary health assessment
3.24	Accreditation in general practice	Number of accredited practices participating in the Practice Incentives Program (PIP) and the proportion of general practice services provided by these practices
3.25	Health workforce	Graduates in pharmacy, medicine and nursing as a percentage of the total pharmacy, medical and nursing workforce
		Percentage of health practitioners aged 55 years and over

Source: AIHW (2004a) pp.xviii-xix

The Information Society: Measurement Issues and the Impact on Policy Making

Information Society: From Statistical Measurement to Policy Assessment

Tony Clayton

UK Office for National Statistics

Abstract

Almost a decade on from the start of widespread official statistical interest in information society measurement, our understanding of social and economic changes associated with the field is still developing. In some areas technology development is still outstripping our ability to change organisational and legal frameworks to use the information it provides. In most, its effects on behaviour and economic performance are still working themselves out.

The range of statistical measurement issues posed by the Information Society range from the macro economic challenge of the "new economy", through understanding sector and firm level effects on behaviour and economic performance, to the results for lifestyle and income of households. In each area, the impact of information and knowledge has continued to grow. However, for many countries the most difficult area to enumerate and analyse has been the one closest to policymakers and managers - the world of electronic government.

UK attempts to measure the effectiveness of policy in this changing environment have set out to combine hard statistics on outcomes at micro and macro levels with case based evidence on the impact of policy. ONS has worked with other areas of government, with international bodies and with the private sector, to develop frameworks for benchmarking UK progress comparing best practice for citizens, for enterprise and in government, and using the results to redefine policy priorities.

Background to Indicators on the Information Society

International Development

Worldwide policy interest in the economic effects of Information and Communication Technology (ICT) was overshadowed throughout the 1990s by the inability of statisticians and economists to identify clear economic gains from the major investment in it. While it was clear that computers enabled process change in a range of industries, particularly in information based sectors such as financial services, the overall macro economic evidence justified Robert Solow's comment in 1989 "we can see computers everywhere except in the productivity statistics".

Macro-economic work, and even firm level consulting analyses, carried out during the 1980s and early 1990s failed to show conclusive benefits in performance resulting from ICT expenditure. Paul Strassman's[1] work on ICT spending and deployment by companies in 1985 indicated that technology investment could not be correlated with any

---

1   Paul Strassman, 1985, The Business Value of Computers

useful measure of business performance. A decade later, industry studies sponsored on both sides of the Atlantic, by one of the worlds largest consulting firms for enterprise ICT, showed that performance benefits could be identified. Effects were indirect, operating on intermediate factors such as customer satisfaction or process efficiency, and which then require good management to achieve better profits or higher firm productivity. Available gains were also shown to be highly contingent on complementary investments, mainly in changing business processes and methods of working[2]. However, throughout this period public and private investment in ICT, as a proportion of GDP and of total investment, continued to rise in most OECD countries

Government interest in improving coverage and quality of statistics on ICT quickly developed, particularly in countries which were major producers and users. By the time the framework for national accounts was reshaped in 1992 - 1995 there was consensus that not only computer equipment, but also the software systems and databases required to benefit from it should be counted in GDP as investment. Detailed work, defining products and services to count as ICT, and methods to calculate software investment, continued through OECD, the UN and the EU for a further five years, and have now been implemented in most OECD member states. In the US pressure from policymakers meant that ICT measures were identifiable in national accounting aggregates before most other countries. Assessments of ICT effects by 1999 led policy leaders, including Alan Greenspan, and economists to contest the existence (or not) of changes in the relationships between inputs and outputs, and of step changes in productivity. This marked the start of debate on the possibility of a "new economy", and propelled the search for indicators which would guide policymakers in a rapidly changing environment

Interest in the use of electronic networks followed soon after 1995, with surveys on the use of e-commerce in Scandinavian countries in 1998, and a very broad survey of "computer network use" in manufacturing by the US in 1999. OECD's Working Party on Information Society Statistics began the task of defining e-commerce, and producing standard questionnaires for both business and household use of computers and the internet, led by Statistics Canada, Scandinavian statisticians, and a number of other national statistical offices (NSOs). This produced a core of international agreement. By 1999 / 2000 draft surveys were taken up by Eurostat, then developed and implemented in a number of EU countries, including the UK.

A major focus of attention in the period of the internet bubble was e-commerce transactions, for which very large estimates had been made by private data providers, and which the first official statistics showed to be overstated. As ICT use surveys have developed it has become clear that "old" systems for electronic links between firms still play a vital role, and are larger overall than the internet. Productivity effects, it is believed, are as likely to flow from effective use of "closed" network systems as from internet use. One lesson learned from the initial round of international experience is that it may be more important to measure behaviour change by firms and individuals as result of technology than to measure precise details of the technology itself. Policy interest also seems to be placing greater emphasis now on the wider use of electronic information exchanges and links in business (not just transaction based e-commerce), and also on issues such as security and trust in the internet, both for firms and for citizens.

---

2   Andersen Consulting / PIMS, 1995, The IT Value Initiative

UK Policy Context

The 1980s and the first half of the 1990s saw in the UK, for the most part, reliance on market forces and competition to guide firms' investment in ICT, and only limited central government pressure to encourage wider use of network technologies in the public sector. It became evident however, that these policies were resulting in lower ICT investment in the UK than were being achieved either by similar market based policies in the US, or than more interventionist approaches in Nordic countries, Canada, Australia and some others. This realisation coincided with increasing evidence across Europe that enterprise competitiveness and growth was dependent on "intangibles", rather than traditional investments in established industries[3].

UK policy shifts were set out in the government's strategy for competitiveness[4] published in 1998, which included strong recognition both of the role of innovation in promoting productivity and growth, and of the role of ICT as an enabler. This paid specific attention to the role of electronic networks in creating new business models and routes to market, as well as the importance of the internet in improving links between firms, universities and other sources of knowledge and information in support of the innovation process. The white paper, and a subsequent strategy document setting out foundations for the policy in more detail[5], set an ambitious target to make the UK "the best environment for e-commerce" among the world leading nations.

This objective would require proactive policies in legal and administrative frameworks, in education, infrastructure, incentives, government practices and provision of services, to make up for earlier lost ground. It would also require support from industry, especially from major IT producers and users, and an "Information Age Partnership" (IAP) between industry leaders and government was created to provide strategic oversight. The strategy recognised that the UK had a number of inherent advantages, including language and historically strong performance in IT software and telecommunications, as well as strength in creative industries, which could help underpin improvement in its performance, certainly relative to other large EU economies.

However, the strategy could not at that time be based on a strong base of comparative performance and policy information. Given the increasing commitment across UK government and civil society to "evidence based policy" from the mid 1990s onwards, the IAP requested that a measurement programme be undertaken to monitor outcomes, identify progress, and to serve as a policy management framework. Policy departments involved in delivery led parts of the measurement programme, often using private sector sources; the Department of Trade and Industry's e-Commerce Benchmarking survey is a good example of this.[6] A significant part of provision of new statistics and indicators was undertaken by the Office for National Statistics (ONS).

---

3   Building Business for Europe, Clayton and Carrol, 1996, EU Panorama of Industry

4   Competitiveness White Paper, 1998, HMSO

5   e-commerce @ its best, 1998, UK Cabinet Office

6   International e-commerce Benchmarking Survey, annual from 2000, Department of Trade and Industry

Elements in ONS' statistical development for the Information Society

Work based on International Initiatives

Development and use of information society and economy statistics by ONS has covered four main stages. The first, referred to above, includes the initial steps to reflect IT software as capital formation in GDP, so that output and productivity effects are recognised, and to permit macro-economic analysis of the effects of ICT along similar lines to that in the US. It also included the adoption of OECD definitions for ICT as identified in national accounts, and for e-commerce and internet use in the first national surveys of business and household ownership and use of ICT in 1999 - 2000. These surveys gave an accurate base line for the assessment of policy to promote growth of internet use, and also good international comparisons not just in overall use levels, but in structure of use so that policy managers could see where adoption strategies were working, and where not.

The second stage, undertaken during 2002-3, involved adjusting measures of output in economic statistics to take better account of changes in the composition of products and services. Much of the need for this was driven by the need to reflect changes driven by technology, in the quality and capability of ICT equipment, and changes due to the increased output of ICT services. The use of hedonic prices for computers, which take specific account of the value of product performance features and the way in which they change over time in rapidly innovating sectors, began in 2002. Chain linking of output measures reflecting annual changes in the composition of output, rather than rebasing every five years, began in 2003. These methodological improvements, taken together, improve the assessment of real productivity changes and welfare gains, and reflect good practice elsewhere.

Local Initiatives

Stage 3 consisted of a benchmarking exercise, aimed specifically at IAP and Cabinet Office requirements to identify progress in development of e-commerce and electronic processes across the economy, society and government. The work was designed to compare outcomes in leading countries, the policies behind them, and comparative success in implementation. Benchmarking was designed to be more than a ranking of relative success and to support a framework that would allow participant countries to learn from good practice by others

The current, fourth, stage is designed to provide tools to evaluate the effectiveness of ICT and electronic networks in achieving the main economic policy objective, productivity and output growth. It is built round analytical techniques using firm level data, and its purpose is to show the impact of ICT deployment in different ways, in different types of firms. Understanding enterprise dynamics, and how behaviour and performance is affected by ICT, is seen as a prerequisite both to policy formation, and to developing appropriate indicators of progress.

The rest of this paper outlines these local initiatives, the third and fourth stages of UK statistical work on the Information Society, the contribution they have made to policy management, and a view of priorities for the future emerging from the work.

International e-Commerce Benchmarking

Benchmarking Principles

Partly thanks to a significant input from industry leaders[7], the structure of the UK's benchmarking exercise drew on approaches to measurement and learning that are often applied in commercial practice. The first phase of the work was to develop a framework for describing contributory factors and outcomes in the process of building an information economy, making effective use of electronic networks, and this work was undertaken jointly between academic experts, industry leaders and ONS. It then continued, largely driven by ONS, to seek existing measures to describe and compare both inputs and results across G7 economies plus Australia (where measurement work was well advanced) and Sweden (taken to be representative of well developed policy and statistical practice in Scandinavia).

This phase looked at the possibility of creating an overall index of success, and the issues involved in selecting and weighting appropriate metrics[8]. In the event, however, construction of a composite index turned out to be less important than selecting individual indicators that are meaningful to policy managers, and presenting them as part of an overall picture that enables comparisons to be made. In making judgments about differences between policy and outcomes across our nine countries, understanding and presenting the detail was more important to the process of learning than summary aggregates. In part this was because it became clear early on that most of the countries in the benchmark set had significant strengths which were of interest to others.

The second part of the exercise took a database of public indicators - judged so far as possible to be comparable across nine countries - with gaps identified. Work by consultants Booz Allan and Hamilton set out to fill gaps with original survey work or private sources where possible, further elaborating the conclusions on successful outcomes. Alongside this, in-depth contacts and structured interviews with policy-makers in each of the nine countries were used to identify the policy differences between them, and the factors which had led to different outcomes.

A considerable amount of judgment was required in this second area, illustrated in the project's final report by case studies. To test and communicate the lessons, policy leaders and their teams from all nine countries (UK, US, Canada, Sweden, Germany, France, Italy, Japan and Australia) met in a series of workshops to review conclusions of the exercise. This direct exchange of good practice between practitioners (both in policy management and statistical measurement) was one of the most valuable aspects of the process.

Approach to Measurement

In constructing a framework to compare inputs and outcomes between countries, IAP adopted an approach based on the "readiness - intensity – impact" model developed by OECD in the late 1990s (Fig 1). This represents the process of technology diffusion, and

---

7   Industry participation in this exercise was led by European directors of Sun, IBM, Philips, Oracle, Microsoft, and by the Confederation of British Industry

8   International e-Commerce Benchmarking; Methodology Report, 2002, ONS, available at http://www.statistics.gov.uk/StatBase/Product.asp?vlnk=9565&Pos=&ColRank=1&Rank=272

categorises types of indicators. The framework distinguishes between the three main stages of technology adoption:

- readiness, incorporating measures of infrastructure, skills and attitudes
- intensity, including measures of degree and type of technology use
- impact, representing changes in behaviour or performance in the economy or society

Figure 1: OECD's "S curve" model for technology adoption

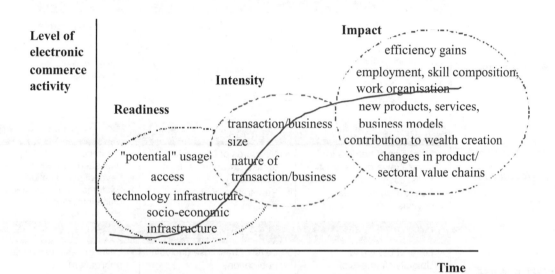

In applying this model, and attempting to elaborate it over the three main sectors - citizens/households, enterprises and government, we quickly found that some measures were common to all three. For example, the basic level of skills in the population and labour force, and the availability of broadband connections in public infrastructure, are similar for government users, for most citizens and for the majority of businesses. Also shared are the legal framework for electronic contracts and exchanges, and measures for security and trust.

However, some of the "readiness" factors such as attitudes to risk and innovation, and the ownership of ICT access devices, are dependent on sector. It therefore makes sense to split the "readiness" group of indicators into those that are sector specific, and the underlying environment covering market and political factors, and physical infrastructure for each country. In developing the framework, with independent consultants, indicators were grouped, by sector and by phase of development, into contributing factors affecting policy. For example, citizen and business sectors metrics for "digital divide" were included under use measures, to represent the problems in including "hard to reach" individuals.

Figure 2: Framework for Comparing National e-Economies

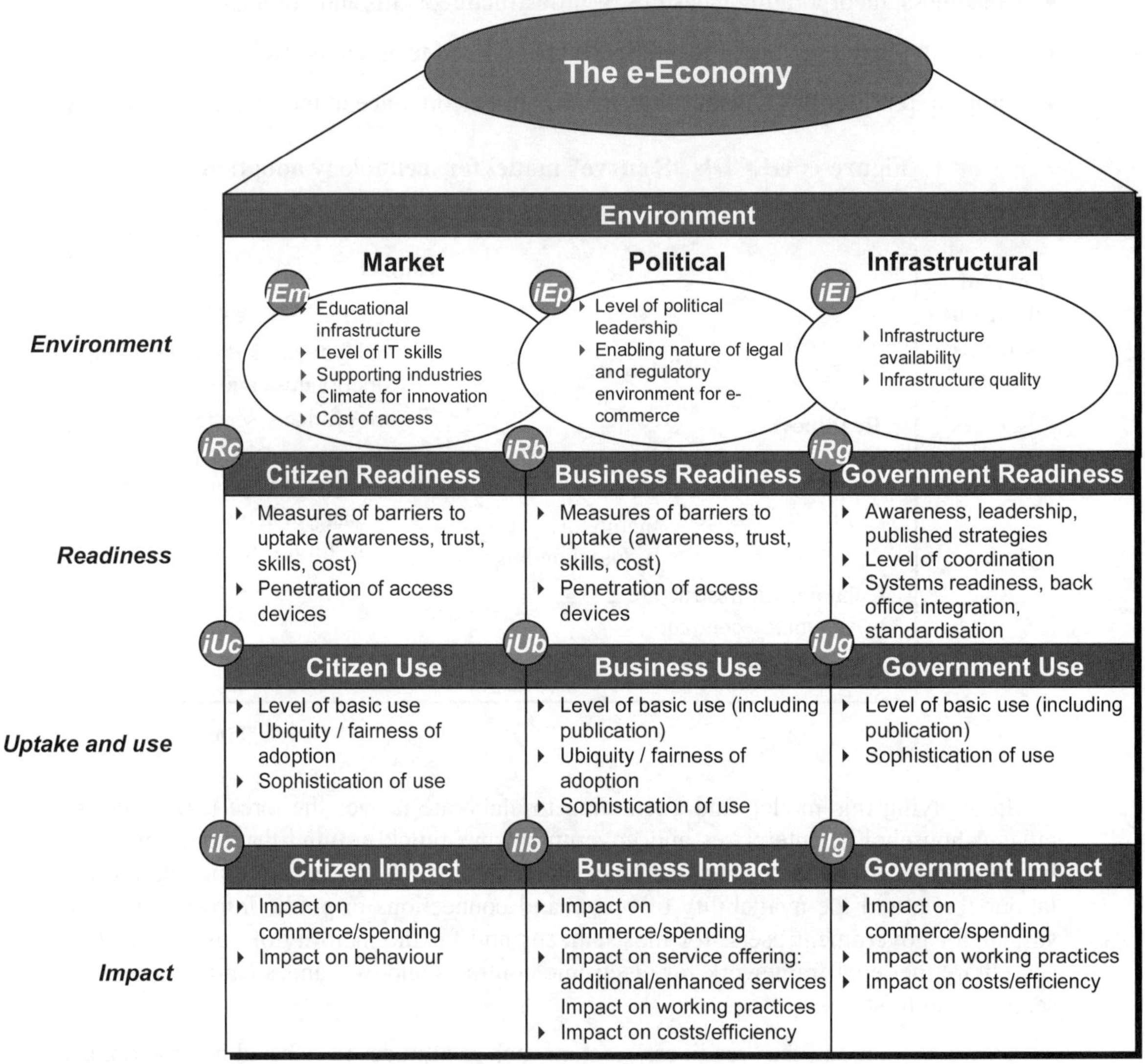

To measure the e-economy profile of each country, the framework tracks progress on over 100 indicators, grouped in twelve subsets defined by sector and/or stage of diffusion. Within each cell are two to five groups of contributing factors, which contain individual indicators. The majority of these indicators are taken from recognised official statistics, but a significant proportion come from surveys commissioned by UK government (particularly the DTI's business survey), from private sources, and from interviews conducted by Booz Allen.

The process of selecting and populating indicator sets showed two main areas of weakness in the data. Very little consistent data was then available on e-government at any of the adoption phases. The exercise therefore depended on assessments by the consultants of the state of development within each contributing factor. These measures - constructed as level charts - were based on structured interviews, and assessments of capability against fixed criteria. The other main area of weakness was in "impact" measures where very little hard evidence was available. We return to this area in section 4 below.

Learning from Measurement

Benchmarking is not - as such - a statistical technique. It requires a process of data gathering and comparison, but its objective is to enable learning through appropriate comparisons. The role of analysts and statisticians in the process is to ensure that the comparisons are appropriate, and that they are sufficiently precise to enable management or policy conclusions to be drawn.

As we worked through the project it became clear both to us and to policy colleagues that overall composite indicators were of much less value to understand effects of policy differences than the more focused indicators relating to specific groups and adoption processes. In particular we concluded that:

- in trying to understand why one country had succeeded in a particular area it was always necessary to look at original headline indicators, and that the composites tended to hide important differences under apparently similar overall results

- overall ranking of countries was not a helpful presentation format for best practice exchange, because it tends to induce defensive reactions; in practice we found that most of the countries included in our exercise had some area covered by the measurement set where it had either performed well in terms of level of achievement, or had made rapid improvements, which prompted further analysis of policy behind the results

- complex weighting of indicators is not worthwhile, even using expert input, for two reasons; first factors which are important for the adoption process change over time, so expert views in year 1 are unlikely to be robust over time, and second policy issues in countries which are well advanced on the adoption process are very different from those at an early stage. More useful is a simple transparent presentation of the data which leaves users free to make their own decisions on what is important.

In presenting the data it was much more important to show what the range of outcomes was, where good practice could be found, and how far a particular country was from it, than to show overall rankings. The reports to countries therefore used the presentation format shown in Fig 3 below, which:

- lists a range of indicators (in this case composites of a small number of closely related indicators)

- shows the range of performance achieved by the three leading countries in our dataset on each indicators (the shaded band)

- shows how a specific country compares with the performance of the top three on each indicator (the black dots)

This approach - effectively a graphical indicator - shows "good" performance. It also shows:

- where there are a number of "good performers" to learn from (e.g. "market" or "political/regulatory" in this example where three strong performers are tightly bunched) or

- where the range is wider (e.g. infrastructure) and

- the key areas of weakness (in this example, government use).

This type of approach can be applied to the individual indicators in the benchmarking indicator set or to composites if they are appropriately grouped.

Figure 3: Profile approach to Benchmarking

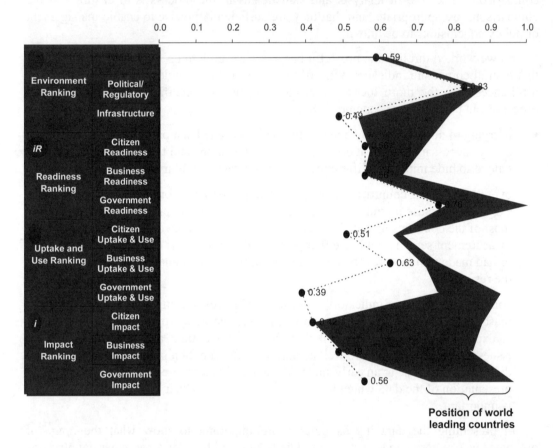

From this type of presentation, compiled separately for each country, policy managers can identify

- which areas the country is performing well in

- where it has something to learn from others - and if so from whom.

For the UK, this exercise showed that performance in most areas of "environment" was relatively strong, and that citizen and business readiness was close to world leading countries. Where there was cause for concern was in the areas of citizen and business use, and most of all in government use and impact. These conclusions helped to redirect UK policy on promoting e-commerce and e-business, and focus effort on necessary changes for the public sector. To facilitate this, the Office of the e-Envoy, which had handled e-commerce promotion across the economy, evolved into the Office of e-Government, with a central role in improving electronic service delivery.

The learning process between the nine countries centred on "good policy" lessons from countries in the "shaded band" above. In the event all nine featured as a good practice case in at least one performance group, although the US, Sweden, and Canada scored well in the majority. Examples of the cases used can be found in the final report from the study[9]. Individual reports from the study to each country drew attention to relevant case studies, attempting to focus attention on transferable lessons.

Lessons from the Benchmarking Exercise

Apart from the policy lessons for the UK quoted above, the benchmarking exercise made it clear that relevant and comparable data was still hard to come by. In order to quantify this, an attempt was made to "quality mark" the indicators used to show up the areas where information was least likely to be reliable, comparable, relevant or complete. The big gap areas are undoubtedly measures of impact, across the economy, and of government use and effectiveness.

Since 2002 there have been some improvements in data availability, and this should improve further across the EU as the legal framework for Information Society statistics takes effect, making large parts of the OECD framework mandatory for member states from 2005. This should help to improve the overall coverage as ONS sets out to update the framework during late 2004/early 2005, in collaboration with other UK government departments. However it will still leave gaps in impact and e-government measurement.

EU development of e-government metrics has so far been centred on "service availability and use" surveys, with availability surveyed on an EU wide basis by consultants, and use included now in household and enterprise surveys at national level. These new sources will be included in our update of the framework.

ICT Impact in the Economy

Macro-economic Studies

Much of the initial work to analyse effects of ICT on growth and productivity used national or sector data on capital, labour and ICT inputs, and output measures from national accounts. The methodology of growth accounting developed to do this is an extension of neo-classical approaches, and at first proved difficult because of deficiencies in measurement of rapidly changing technology within macroeconomic aggregates. Much of the 1990s has been spent ironing these out, through better price and output measures that take account of major improvements in product or service quality, and in the composition of economic output. An increasing amount of work has also been undertaken on complementary intangible inputs, such as skills or R&D.[10]

These improvements are far from complete, but do seem to have progressed to a point where economic analysts can be reasonably sure that:

- measured ICT investment and use explains an increasing proportion of output and productivity growth in most OECD economies, and does so in a consistent way

---

9   The World's Most Effective Policies for the e-Economy, November 2002, Booz Allen and Hamilton, available at http://e-government.cabinetoffice.gov.uk/assetRoot/04/00/08/19/04000819.pdf

10   What Drives Productivity Growth? K.J.Stiroh, 2001, FRBNY Economic Policy Review

- ICT impacts on productivity are significantly greater in the USA than in most other economies[11]

However, while such conclusions may help policy managers at the macro or national level, improving evidence for fiscal or monetary policy, they are less helpful for structural intervention, or for shaping incentives that operate at firm level. To do this requires greater understanding of enterprise dynamics, and how firms are affected by ICT investment and use.

Firm Level Impact Studies

Since the late 1990s ONS has recognised the potential value of firm level survey data to tell a more interesting and valuable story than by adding it up to create economic aggregates. The firm level information gathered has the potential to support analysis of patterns of growth, competition and change in the economy, to inform policy on how competitive processes actually work, and to relate processes to statistically significant outcomes. Over the last three years this capability has developed in a co-ordinated programme, to study drivers of productivity including innovation, ICT use and activities on multinational enterprises.

OECD has greatly assisted in this work through elements of its "growth project" including a very useful exchange and co-ordination programme of ICT impact work during 2002 - 2003. This encouraged firm level work on ICT effects across at least twelve member countries, where possible testing the same ideas about ICT effects on business in two or three countries. In this way it was possible to exchange good practice in analysis, and to test hypotheses on a wider selection of data. It produces a very helpful publication[12], on which a number of countries have gone on to build.

Current UK work is focused on firm level analysis both of investment in ICT, and of its use in different ways. Later in 2004 we expect to publish results of econometric analysis based on firm level ICT stocks in UK enterprises, brought together with structural business survey results which capture firm output and employment, showing significant positive productivity effects. However, these effects are not uniform across sectors, and they are conditional on other inputs. We expect that this work will throw new light on earlier macro-economic conclusions.

Work already published, using similar approaches, has focused on ICT use. Two projects have so far been completed, one focusing on trading via electronic commerce[13], the other on use of electronic business processes in areas other than buying and selling transactions[14]. Conclusions published on both these projects are provisional, but in both cases results have been proved over two or three year's data, and appear to be consistent

The exercise to test for productivity effects associated with use of electronic buying or selling by firms used data from the UK's annual business inquiry. After allowing for

---

11   The Case of the Missing Productivity Growth, 2003, S. Basu, J. Fernald, N. Oulton, S.Srivasan, NBER Macro National Conference.

12   The Economic Impact of ICT; Measurement, Evidence and Implications, 2004, OECD

13   e-Commerce and Firm Performance, 2003, Clayton, Criscuolo and Goodridge, http://epp.eurostat.cec.eu.int/portal/page?_pageid=1073,1135281,1073_1135295&_dad=portal&_schema=PORTAL&p_product_code=KS-04-001

14   e-Business and Labour Productivity in Manufacturing and services, 2004, Clayton and Goodridge, http://www.statistics.gov.uk/articles/economic_trends/ET609Good.pdf

labour and capital inputs, regional and sector effects, the impact of unit size and of any multinational firm connections, analysis showed that:

- productivity effects of e-commerce in manufacturing firms are positive, but show effects which are more complex than "production function" models used in much macro and micro work

- in addition to "efficiency effects" from e-commerce use which are significant in the manufacturing sector, there are pronounced price effects which give value added gains to buyers and losses to sellers

- in manufacturing sectors examined by linking firm level e-commerce use to price evolution in price surveys, it appears that increased competition due to electronic trading exerts a restraining influence on prices, probably due to increased competition as it becomes easier to search for alternative suppliers

This analysis showed that, in addition to influencing overall productivity in firms, electronic networks can alter the working of markets in which firms operate. Descriptive data (Fig 4) shows that use of electronic networks for procurement is associated with significant productivity gains, part of which is due to efficiency gains, but part due to competitive price effects.

Figure 4: Productivity in UK Manufacturing Firms, by type of e-commerce use

Value added per employee (£000's)

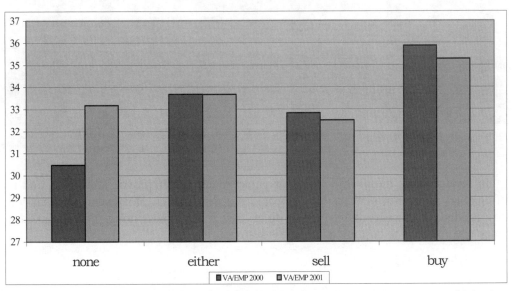

The second exercise used data from the enterprise e-commerce surveys, which since 2001 for the UK have included questions on the use of electronic business processes. In addition to asking about use of computers, the internet and other types of networks, the survey asks whether firms have linked other operational process to electronic buying or selling. The answers show that electronic integration of business operations is still relatively uncommon, especially among small firms.

The survey asks about electronic links between processes within each business, and also links to customers and suppliers. It is possible to classify firms in terms of the degree integration or linking they have, and also in terms of the external links. Responses have subsequently been linked to productivity data by firm from the UK annual business inquiry. The results show interesting differences in performance between manufacturing and service businesses.

Among manufacturing firms, those which have multiple electronic links show higher value added per employee that those with no links, which suggests an overall benefit from ICT use. But the best performing group, with value added/employee over 30% better than "unlinked" firms, contains firms which have at least five main operational process areas linked, including a direct link to suppliers' business systems. This is consistent with the "e-buying" conclusion above, in which firms use electronic networks to deal with suppliers.

Figure 5: Average labour productivity in manufacturing, by type of e-business link

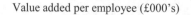

Value added per employee (£000's)

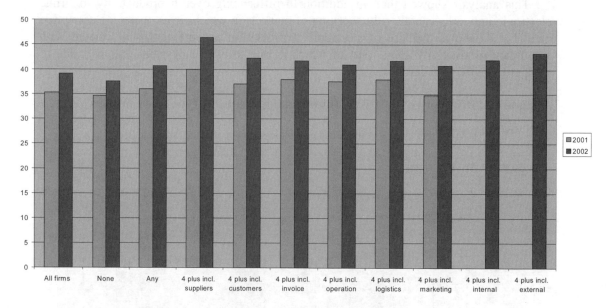

In service firms the overall levels of value added per employee are lower, and the differentials associated with using electronic process smaller. However, the firms with most productive employees are those with at least five business process areas linked, of which one connects to customers' business systems.

Figure 6: Average labour productivity in services, by type of e-business link

Value added per employee (£000's)

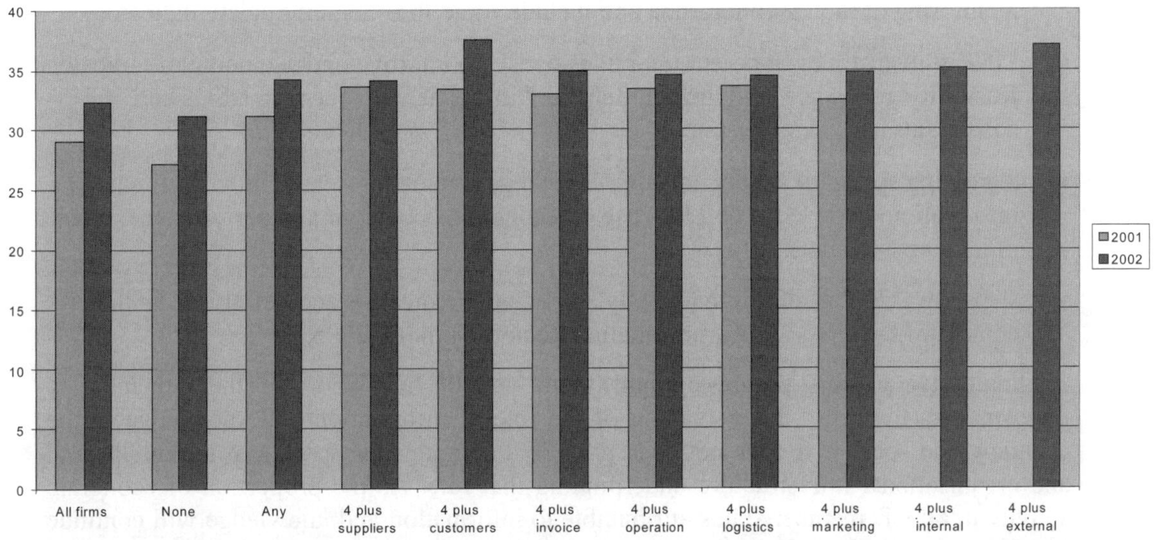

These initial results suggest that enterprise dynamics associated with ICT use differ significantly between manufacturing and services, and that policy incentives appropriate for one sector might not be appropriate for the other. There are policy conclusions here that can be fed into the public sector - on the benefits of electronic procurement, and on the possible gains from integration with service users.

Work is continuing to integrate this research with ICT investment evidence, as well as measures of employee skills and other inputs. Its aim is to secure evidence on how ICT assets, ICT use and complementary investments change behaviour and performance. From this evidence we will propose indicators that can be used to measure progress, and used as the most appropriate metrics for "impact" in our next round of benchmark comparisons.

Priorities for Measurement Development

Progress 2000 - 2005

The last four years have seen major advances in Information Society statistics, with more in the pipeline. Major milestones include:

- progressive, but still incomplete, implementation by NSO's of the methodology developed by OECD in the 1990s to treat computer software and databases as investment

- development of outline satellite accounts for the "information economy" in US, and of similar concepts in Netherlands

- agreement on OECD frameworks for measurement of ICT use in households and enterprises, and e-commerce metrics, and adoption by most EU member states

- adoption by the EU of a "second wave" of benchmarking metrics to monitor the progress of eEurope 2005 policy implementation

- adoption of a legal framework for Information Society statistics across the EU, making large parts of the OECD framework mandatory for member states from 2005

- development of Structural Indicators for the EU Council of Ministers, to improve monitoring of the Lisbon agenda and include some Information Society indicators

- SINE statistical development initiatives by EU to improve understanding of indicator feasibility, relevance, and impact, delivered in partnership between NSOs and consultants and / or academics

- a growing spread of academic, business and government research into the impact of information, knowledge and ICT use on economic behaviour and performance, much of it using NSO data

- steps towards a set of internationally agreed core indicators and definitions in the context of the UN's World Information Society Summit, 2005.

Impressive as this progress might seem, it still falls short of the demands by policymakers for better understanding of the role of information and knowledge in the economy and society. It does not even provide a comprehensive view of the intellectual and organisational infrastructure underpinning that role. As the proportion of economic activity in OECD member states attributable to information and knowledge will continue to grow over the next decade, this is a shortfall that must be met.

Priorities for future Information Society statistics development

The main challenge for statistical measurement is the speed of change. We are continually faced with requests for evidence on the role of information and knowledge which current statistics cannot answer. Policy makers complain, with some justice, that the statistical system takes too long to answer new questions. Among the demands currently aimed at us are:

- the need for greater international convergence in treatment of ICT and intangibles in national accounts, to further improve macro-economic analysis of the effects of ICT, information and knowledge

- requirements for data on the use (including intensity and type of use) of electronic processes by firms, as opposed to electronic transactions, and the need to provide estimates of even electronic commerce in the financial sector

- policy users' need to understand technology effects (for firms, individuals and households) on behaviour, while the focus of many survey approaches is on technology itself

- the need for a common approach to develop internationally agreed measures of effects and benefits from ICT in firms and households, integrating work at firm, sector and whole economy levels

- the inability of most statistics offices except the US to describe activities of multinational enterprises (MNEs) beyond their shores, despite the fact that MNEs dominate the knowledge economy, in that they make much of the ICT investment and undertake most R&D and innovation

The "black hole" in international Information Society measurement, government, is starting to be filled. There are initial surveys of ICT inputs to government, service outputs and user benefit, but no internationally agreed methodology. This is in part because of a broader problem - lack of international consistency in measuring government output across countries.

OECD role

OECD's role in developing Information Society statistics has been central, and must remain so. As a forum for developing measurement, disseminating best practice but with "feet on the ground" participation by statistics offices, it has a unique position. Among the areas which we see as particularly important are:

- leading co-ordination on macro-economic measures related to information and knowledge, particularly national accounts treatment of intangibles such as R&D

- developing common approaches for innovation and technology work, sharing good practice and building international frameworks for measurement and analysis of innovation creation and diffusion

- bringing metrics for skills and human knowledge more fully into Information Society measurement; this requires better co-ordination in classification of new skills / occupations, and developing comparable accounting approaches to labour markets

- building on the work on enterprise dynamics which has been very successful in analysis of ICT impacts and entry / exit of firms; a particular role OECD could undertake is to co-ordinate international micro-data projects which reflect international impact of ICT and innovation?

- improving understanding of the global integration of economic value chains, labour markets, information networks and knowledge exchange, to reflect the growing effects of the world's "single market" for knowledge and information; this has implications for regional measures within countries, as well as international statistics.

For OECD to be successful in tackling these issues it will need the support of NSO's. To build knowledge that policy makers need in these rapidly changing areas it will need them to work together and also to take some risks. Without a willingness to do this, the greatest risk is that policymakers will turn elsewhere for the knowledge they need.

Measurements in Support of Policy Decisions

Kaija Hovi

Director of Business Structures, Statistics Finland

Abstract

In Finland, the information society is seen as a central issue in the reforming of the economy and public administration. Keen to monitor progress, in its first national information society strategy, given as far back as in 1995, the Government charged Statistics Finland with the responsibility to provide reports at regular intervals and conduct occasional studies on the programme's impacts on society. There must be a link between policy and the measurement of its efficiency – in other words, statistics. Giving out a strategy means that we should also be able to measure the development towards the targets set in it.

The aim of the current Government Information Society Programme, launched in 2003, is to improve competitiveness and productivity, promote social and regional equality, and improve citizens' well-being and quality of life through effective use of information and communications technologies. The impact indicators are clearly expressed and include several statistical indicators for the measurement of the development. Statistics Finland has been able to provide policy makers with a considerable volume of statistics on the realisation of the development of the information society.

Introduction

Finland is generally considered a country that already has many of the elements of the information society. The concept of the information society is in itself complex, although commonly used. The concept knowledge-based society and other corresponding expressions, such as network society, have also been used in different contexts when emphasising certain specific features of information society development. The Committee for the Future of the Finnish Parliament uses the following definition: Information society is a creative society that is based on interaction. The information society is not just about new technology; it is more about a new way of doing things. From a theoretical perspective, the key concepts include networked form of organisation and growth based on innovations.

Finland has so far fared well in international comparisons regarding information society development and competitiveness. Citizens, enterprises and the public administration have extensively adopted the new information and communications technology. Use of the computer and the Internet is common in nearly all age groups. The mobile phone has become commonplace in nearly all population groups. The information and communications (ICT) sector as a field is undergoing strong growth.

Table 1. Households with an Internet connection, per cent by household size in autumn 1996, 1999 and in spring 2002 and 2004 (at least one appliance)

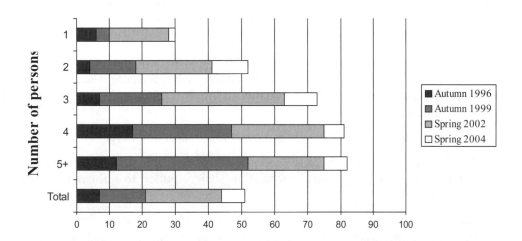

Sources: Finns and the future information society -surveys 1996 and 1999, Net commerce surveys 2002 and 2004, Statistics Finland.

A relatively homogenous social structure has clearly assisted Finland and the other Nordic Countries to progress in the building of the information society. Social equality has also made it possible for everyone regardless of background to receive good education. In addition, it has provided the prerequisites for a rapid diffusion of different ICT equipment and applications throughout the society. At the same time, the stability of the society has provided a basis for a feeling of solidarity, which has made it possible to unify resources effectively for the building of the information society. In a welfare state, nobody should feel that his or her basic security is threatened.

National strategies towards the information society

In Finland, the information society was seen as a central issue in the reforming of the economy and public administration in the early 1990s. In 1995, the Government made a decision in principle about the measures that should be implemented to develop Finland into an information society.

Keen to monitor progress, in its first national information society strategy the Government charged Statistics Finland with the responsibility to provide reports at regular intervals and conduct occasional studies on the programme's impacts on society. Giving out a strategy means that we should be able to measure the development towards the given targets. Systematic work to monitor the penetration of information technology, its potential applications, employment in the ICT sector and its impacts on the economy was started at Statistics Finland in the mid-1990s. The first compilation of the results of this work: *On the Road to the Finnish Information Society* was published in 1997 and the first survey on the topic: *Finns and the future Information Society* was conducted in 1996.

The first strategy was criticised for putting too much emphasis on technology. The national information society strategy reform in 1998 emphasised that Finnish society should be developed from the needs of ordinary people.

In 1999, the Finnish Government included in its portfolio many key objectives for developing the information society. They highlighted the role of the information society in reforming the economy, strengthening the content industry and improving the efficiency of public services. The objectives related to the development of people's skills, research and education, and the evolution of information networks and the services provided by them.

The aim of the current Government Information Society Programme, launched in 2003, is to improve competitiveness and productivity, promote social and regional equality, and citizens' well-being and quality of life through effective use of information and communications technologies.

The Information Society Programme has two impact objectives:

1. The Finnish information society scores high marks in international comparisons and Finland can also use its own information society policy to influence international developments.

2. Information and communications technology will be used in all organisations with the aim of improving service standards, making operations and processes more efficient and maintaining and improving competitiveness.

Both objectives will be measured with indicators, the first one with international comparisons on:

*   Share of investment in ICT of total GDP (OECD)

*   Contribution of investment in ICT capital to GDP growth (OECD)

*   ITU (International Telecommunications Union) Digital Access index

*   Impact of information and communications technology on the value added to market production (Statistics Finland, National Accounts)

*   Use of the Internet at work (Statistics Finland, Household Budget Survey)

*   Contribution of investment in ICT capital to GDP growth (OECD)

The role of the OECD is very important; three out of four of the international indicators come from the OECD.

The plan for implementing the Information Society Programme

The information society is a broad concept that in practice covers all areas of the Government Programme. The implementation of the policy programme will be monitored and promoted by several bodies, such as the Ministerial group on the Information Society Programme chaired by the Prime Minister, Information Society Council and its Sections, Information Society Programme steering and monitoring group, etc., etc.

The implementation of the Information Society Programme is divided into eight sections. The sections cover almost a hundred projects and measures that are managed by different ministries. At the same time, the objective is to co-ordinate the measures taken by state administration at the horizontal level in order to ensure, for example, that the measures to be implemented are neither overlapping nor inconsistent in nature. The sections of the Programme are as follows:

*   Telecommunications infrastructure and digital television

- Citizens' ability to utilise the information society

- Training, working life, research and development

- Electronic services in public administration

- Social welfare and health

- Electronic commerce and digital contents and services

- Government IT services

- Legislative measures

The competition for the Prime Minister's Best Practices Award seeks practices that promote the information society and presents prizes for the best ones it finds. A good information society practice is a project, action, device or service that improves human well-being and quality of life through effective use of information and communications technologies. A best practice can also be an endeavour to promote a process or service within an organisation.

The idea of giving prizes for best practices is to increase public awareness of the good practices that already exist, promote the spread of good practices associated with the information society throughout the entire community, and encourage innovation and further development of current practices.

A total of 266 entries have been registered for the Prime Minister's Best Practices Award for 2004, and for the competition for high-quality Internet services in public administration.

The impact objectives for each sub-sector are clearly written and they include several indicators for the measurement of the development.

List of indicators and examples:

- Increase in the number of digital adapters and broadband connections (estimate of the Ministry of Transport and Communications)

- A study on the various places where citizens use the Internet

- Number of household computers and Internet connections (Statistics Finland, Consumer Survey)

- Number of computers and Internet connections in different households (Consumer Survey of Statistics Finland) and the use of Internet by different age groups and sexes (Statistics Finland, Household Budget Survey)

- Use of the Internet for different purposes (Statistics Finland, Household Budget Survey)

Table 2. Penetration of broadband connection, other Internet connection and PC according to the size of a household in April-May 2004 as a percentage of all households

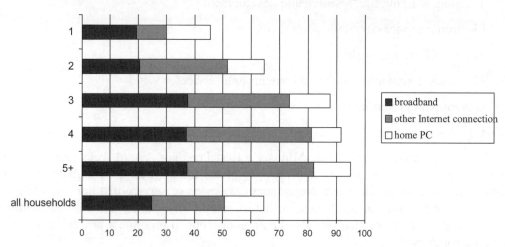

Source: Net Commerce Survey, Statistics Finland.

Table 3. The use of Internet for different purposes in spring 2004, as a percentage of 15-74 years old Internet users

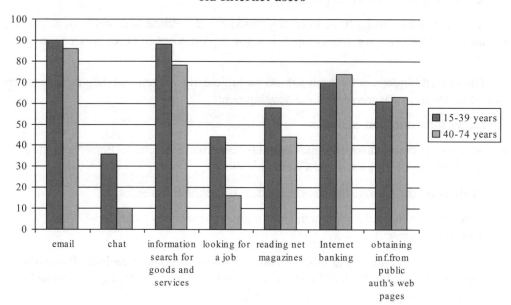

Source: Net Commerce Survey 2004, Statistics Finland.

- Share of citizens who feel that they have been pushed aside by the rapidly developing information technology (Statistics Finland)

- Losses caused by computer viruses to enterprises and citizens and amount of junk mail received at workplaces (Statistics Finland)

- Study on citizens' trust in electronic services

- Number of people who buy or have bought via the Internet and obstacles to buying via the Internet (Statistics Finland, Household Budget Survey)

- Management level assessment regarding the adequacy of recruits' and employees' information and communications skills (Ministry of Labour/Statistics Finland)

- Number of IT and media sector graduates and their share of the employed (Statistics Finland, Education Statistics)

- R&D expenditure (Statistics Finland)

- Number of new patents (National Board of Patents and Registration/ Statistics Finland)

- Involvement of information society sectors in innovations (Statistics Finland, Innovation Survey)

- Basic public services available on the Internet (Study of the European Commission)

- Study on the use of public Internet services and user satisfaction

- Number of general practitioners using electronic patient records (eEurope 2005)

- (For further details, see: http://www.tietoyhteiskuntaohjelma.fi/esittely/en_GB/introduction/)

The role of Statistics Finland

Statistics Finland has been able to provide policy makers with a considerable volume of statistics on the realisation of the development of the information society. However, policy makers are not the only customers interested in following progress towards the information society. The private sector, and its associations and research institutes also ask for public, impartial and reliable information, preferably with international comparisons. The OECD has provided a good forum for discussing guidelines for the production of such statistics.

Information society development may be evaluated from several different viewpoints. The stage of the development can be examined by evaluating how and to what extent various business sectors, government authorities and citizens have adopted modern information technology in their daily routines. The level and state of education, knowledge and research are central to information society development. Knowledge of and skills relating to information and communications technology are needed in all sectors in the information society.

Statistical monitoring of the information society must be interrelated with statistical offices' other work and operating framework. The current situation of the information society must be described, as well as its projected future development over a period of years.

The scarce resources of statistical offices can be used most effectively by exploiting existing statistical systems and inquiries, re-classifying or by attaching additional questions to surveys, and so on, for producing new information. A completely new enterprise survey is initiated very rarely in Finland.

Statistics Finland has studied use of the Internet and electronic commerce jointly with the other Nordic Countries since 1999. To ensure comparability of the results all the countries have developed and used a so-called "model" questionnaire. This model has been further elaborated on and approved by the OECD, and Eurostat has been using the same model since 2001. Normally, questionnaires for statistical data collections are supposed to remain unchanged for long periods, but this cannot be expected in the area of collecting data on the usage ICT and electronic commerce. This is a methodological challenge to statistical offices. On the one hand, the questionnaire must be updated with relevant questions according to user needs and, on the other hand, indicators must be provided that allow time series analyses.

Conclusion

Official statistics are expected, first and foremost, to give an accurate account of what is going on in society. Statistical offices must be able to provide relevant, reliable and up-to-date numerical information and support to decision-makers. Fulfilling this task is a major challenge to statistical offices at a time when society keeps changing fast and their resources are quite limited.

Information concerning the development of a phenomenon or on a given status quo can only be obtained through measurements, which may be based on research, statistics or administrative data. Statistics Finland produces continuously statistical data on the development of diverse topics with surveys on, for instance, time use, consumption, labour force, enterprises, education, culture, mass media, and so on. Information concerning important and essential issues pertaining to the development of the information society can also be obtained from these statistics.

It is no longer enough to view change from the national perspective; the effects of globalisation extend to the public sector, enterprises, non-governmental organisations and ordinary citizens in every country. Countries want to compare their own development with that of others and seek for best practices. In this work, official statistics play an important role and international co-operation is crucial.

References:

On the Road to the Finnish Information Society III. Statistics Finland, 2001.

On the Road to the Finnish Information Society IV. Statistics Finland, 2004.

Report of the Information Society Advisory Board to the Finnish Government on 14 June 2000.

Report of the Information Society Advisory Board to the Finnish Government on 20 June 2001.

Report of the Information Society Advisory Board to the Finnish Government on 11 December 2002.

Manuel Castells & Pekka Himanen: The Information Society and the Welfare State. The Finnish Model. Oxford University Press, 2002.

Internet use and e-commerce in enterprises, 2001 and 2002. Statistics Finland.

The Future of the Finnish Information Society: "A caring, encouraging and creative Finland – a review of the challenges of our information society" Discussion Proposal 10. Committee for the Future. Parliament of Finland, 2004.

Government Policy Programmes 2003, Information Society. In pages: http://www.tietoyhteiskuntaohjelma.fi/esittely/en_GB/introduction/

The Use and Abuse of Real-Time and Anecdotal Information in Monetary Policy Making[*]

Evan F. Koenig

Senior Economist and Vice President, Federal Reserve Bank of Dallas

Abstract

The main message of this paper is that policymakers should not necessarily take official government statistics at face value and should be open to alternative sources of information, including anecdotal reports and surveys. Specific instances are cited where official statistics have been misleading and where anecdotal or survey information has provided early warning of important changes in the economy. Important examples relate to the emergence of new information technologies during the 1990s and the collapse of the high-tech manufacturing sector in 2001.

Policymakers know not to put their faith in data series that are subject to large revisions. However, they often fail to recognize the extent to which the forecasts and policy advice they receive come from models that are estimated and evaluated ignoring revisions, and whose performance, therefore, is at once sub-optimal and overstated. In much the same vein, policy rules that seem to perform well in after-the-fact evaluations often perform poorly in real time.

Recent research has shed light on how forecasting relationships are properly estimated when data are subject to revision and has demonstrated that the payoff to correct estimation is often substantial. Archival requirements are not as onerous as might be expected, and historical vintage data sets have become more readily available.

The extent to which anecdotal reports and qualitative surveys are useful supplements to official statistical releases is underappreciated. Such reports and surveys are often more timely than official statistics. Moreover, respondents seem to filter out some of the short-term noise that makes economic turning points difficult to recognize in real time. Of course, skill and care are required when interpreting qualitative information just as much as when interpreting quantitative data. It helps if the qualitative information is collected from a large number and variety of sources and if continuity of sources is maintained over an extended period. A geographically decentralized institutional structure, like that of the Federal Reserve, facilitates the flow of anecdotal information to policymakers.

Financial asset markets are forward-looking. Financial asset prices are available almost continuously and are not subject to revision. Consequently, these prices might seem to be ideal forecasting tools. Unfortunately, however, the links between asset prices

---

[*]   The views expressed are those of the author, and may not reflect the views of the Federal Reserve Bank of Dallas or the Federal Reserve System.

and the real economy are not always straightforward, and the policy expectations implicit in asset prices are sometimes unrealistic.

The Importance of Revisions: The "New Economy" Challenge of the 1990s

The mid 1990s—from 1991 through 1998—were a period when economic forecasters over-predicted U.S. inflation year after year despite generally stronger-than-expected real GDP growth (Figure 1).[1] The unemployment rate consistent with stable inflation–the "non-accelerating inflation rate of unemployment" or "NAIRU"—was thought to exceed 6 percent at the beginning of the period, but NAIRU estimates were gradually revised downward as evidence that the economy could sustain a lower rate of unemployment accumulated (Gordon 1993, 1997, 2000, 2003). Today's estimates show a NAIRU path that declines from 6.2 to 5.0 percent over the decade of the 1990s, and which is below real-time estimates by anywhere from 0.2 to 0.4 percentage points. Revisions of this magnitude can be important. As of September, the U.S. unemployment rate was 5.4 percent. Consequently, if the current 5.0-percent NAIRU estimate understates the true value by 0.4 percentage points, then there is no slack remaining in the U.S. labor market. On the other hand, if the current estimate *over*states the true value by 0.4 percentage points, we have room for quite rapid growth in coming quarters without triggering upward inflation pressure. Revisions in the estimated NAIRU appear to translate into immediate, 1-for-1 movements in the Federal Reserve's target short-term interest rate (Koenig 2004). Thus, a NAIRU re-evaluation of the magnitude we saw in the late 1990s would mean a roughly 50-basis-point immediate change in the federal funds rate in the same direction.

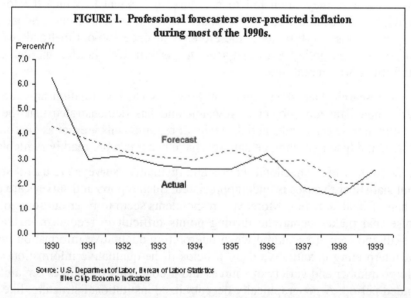

FIGURE 1. Professional forecasters over-predicted inflation during most of the 1990s.

Source: U.S. Department of Labor, Bureau of Labor Statistics
Blue Chip Economic Indicators

The importance of obtaining accurate real-time NAIRU estimates is brought home by Orphanides in a series of influential papers that examine the U.S. "Great Inflation" of the 1970s (Orphanides 2002, 2003). Orphanides argues that the main problem with U.S. monetary policy during the Great Inflation period was that it took at face value estimates of economic slack that proved, subsequently, to be far off base.

---

1   Over this eight-year period, actual Q4 over Q4 GDP growth exceeded the Blue Chip consensus forecast by an average of 1.4 percentage points.

Not surprisingly, in view of their importance for economic performance and policy, considerable effort has been devoted to trying to understand the causes of NAIRU movements. Recent research suggests that changes in profitability—influenced, in turn, by changes in the trend rate of labor productivity growth—are one important source of NAIRU variation (Brayton, Roberts and Williams 1999; Koenig 2001). Economic theory and common sense tell us that firms will want to expand production and employment whenever worker productivity (output per hour) is high relative to labor's real cost (the real wage rate), and to contract production and employment whenever productivity is low relative to labor's cost (Greenspan 2004). When productivity accelerates—as it did during the 1990s, with the spread of new information technologies—wages may lag productivity initially, raising profitability and encouraging non-inflationary output and employment growth. When productivity *de*celerates, productivity may lag wages for a time, lowering profitability and creating a 1970s-style tendency toward stagflation. More generally, movements in the NAIRU appear to be heavily influenced by movements in profitability, as measured by the ratio of labor productivity to the real wage.

Figure 2, adapted from Koenig (2001), presents evidence consistent with a NAIRU—profitability link. It shows movements in the NAIRU during the 1970s, 1980s and 1990s, inferred after the fact from the behavior of inflation, and also shows the ratio of productivity to the real wage in the non-farm business sector.[2] A strong positive correlation is evident. In particular, the estimated NAIRU rose markedly around 1970, at roughly the same time that profitability fell. Similarly, the estimated NAIRU fell markedly in the early 1990s, coincident with a rise in profitability.

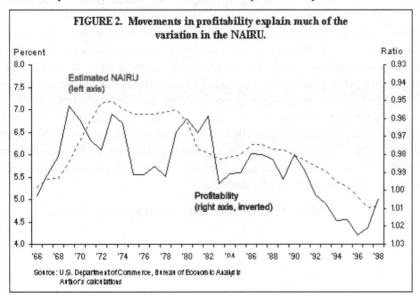

FIGURE 2. Movements in profitability explain much of the variation in the NAIRU.

Alternatively, Figure 3 shows a strong inverse, leading relationship between profitability and the realized unemployment rate. The intuition behind the figure is as follows: As policymakers gradually become aware of profitability-driven changes in the NAIRU, they adjust interest rates to stabilize inflation and achieve maximum non-inflationary employment, driving the realized unemployment rate toward the NAIRU. The unemployment rate falls with a lag in response to high profitability (a low NAIRU),

---

2   To obtain the estimated NAIRU, the Kalman filter is applied to a Phillips-curve inflation equation for the non-farm business price deflator. See Koenig (2001) for details.

and rises with a lag in response to low profitability (a high NAIRU). The lag between movements in profitability and movements in the unemployment rate is about three years.

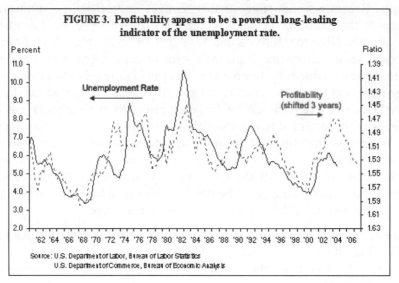

FIGURE 3. Profitability appears to be a powerful long-leading indicator of the unemployment rate.

Why the slow policy response? Part of the explanation is that the link between profitability and the NAIRU has only recently been recognized, so policymakers historically have not monitored profitability very closely. Another important part of the explanation, however, is displayed in Figure 4, which shows the ratio of labor productivity to the real wage as it appears in today's data, and as initially estimated. Clearly, the profitability data have been subject to large revisions: over the period from 1981:Q4 through 2002:Q4, the correlation between the two series is only 0.22. Post 1990—the period during which the NAIRU fell so markedly—it drops to 0.08. When today's data are used, profitability appears to have strong predictive power for inflation, as one would expect if movements in profitability are closely related to changes in the NAIRU. But when first-release data are used—the data actually available to policymakers in real time—then profitability's predictive power disappears (Koenig 2003). Profitability may, in other words, be quite useful for explaining shifts in the inflation–unemployment trade-off after the fact, but—at least as captured in the official statistics—it is of no help in recognizing NAIRU shifts in real time.

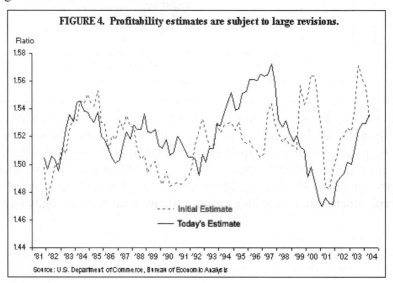

FIGURE 4. Profitability estimates are subject to large revisions.

In summary, good policy depends on information that is both accurate and timely. Variables that appear helpful for policy in analyses that rely on data as they appear today may be of little use in real time. History teaches that big policy mistakes are possible if decision makers take the results of such analyses at face value.

Different Types of Revisions

Not all official data series are subject to significant *ex post* revision. In the United States, the consumer price index (CPI) and the unemployment rate are prominent examples of series whose historical values are revised only to reflect new estimates of seasonal patterns. These revisions are trivial compared with the series' month-to-month variation, and can usually be ignored.

At the other extreme, major conceptual and methodological changes are potentially quite problematic. Pre-revision and post-revision data may be non-comparable, and due allowance must be made for possible structural breaks in estimated relationships. Examples of important conceptual and methodological changes include the recent switch from the Standard Industrial Classification system to the North American Industry Classification System for purposes of tracking sectoral movements in sales, production, and employment; the 1983 change in the Labor Department's treatment of housing prices in the consumer price index; the Commerce Department's 1999 decision to reclassify business software purchases as investment for purposes of calculating GDP; and the Labor Department's 1994 redefinition of "discouraged workers."

More routinely, revisions occur as new, more complete source data become available. The "advance" U.S. GDP report, for example, is released one month after the close of the quarter, before all data on investment, international trade and government purchases are available. The Bureau of Economic Analysis substitutes educated guesses for the missing data. A "preliminary" GDP report is released two months after the close of the quarter— at which point some of the missing data have been filled in. The so-called "final" report is released a month after that, and an additional revision is released annually. (The annual revision covers the three prior calendar years plus the quarters already released for the current year.) Revisions to important monthly series like payroll employment and industrial production follow a basically similar pattern. An advance estimate for each given month, based on incomplete data, is released during the following month. This estimate is revised in each of the subsequent two or three months, as missing data are filled in. There are also annual revisions to each series.

The extent to which movements in early statistical releases for a variable are a reliable guide to the *true* movements in that variable depends very much on how the relevant statistical agency fills in for missing source data (Sargent 1989). Most commonly, it is assumed that the agency simply extrapolates from the limited data initially available, so that early releases equal the truth plus statistical noise. According to this "noise" model, early statistical releases are more variable than later releases (which are based on larger samples). Moreover, if, say, GDP shows an out-size increase in the initial report, one can properly take the view that the increase is likely partly noise that will subsequently be revised away, as more complete source data become available. If GDP shows an out-size decline, similarly, then probably it will be revised upward in the future. Thus, future data revisions are negatively correlated with the statistical agency's early estimates. They are *un*correlated with the truth.

The "news" model of early statistical releases, in contrast, assumes that the statistical agency is sophisticated enough to look not just at currently available source data, but also at the past behavior of the variable in question and at other indicators as it tries to anticipate late-arriving source data. The agency announces its best estimates of the truth, given all of the information at its disposal. In this case, the truth equals the early release plus statistical noise, rather than the other way around. Early releases are *less* variable than later releases. Moreover, future data revisions are completely uncorrelated with the statistical agency's early estimates. Indeed, they are uncorrelated with any and all information available to the statistical agency at the time of the early estimates' release. They are positively correlated with the truth.

From the policymaker's perspective, whether a particular statistical report includes noise or is pure news is vital, because it determines whether that report ought to be second-guessed or ought to be accepted as the best estimate currently available. As noted above, an easy first-pass test is to determine whether early releases are more or less variable than revised releases. If more variable, it's likely the early releases can be second-guessed. Alternatively, one can look at the correlation between data revisions and early releases. Second-guessing is possible if this correlation is non-zero. (The noise model suggests that it ought to be negative.) Results of these simple tests are displayed in Table 1 for GDP, payroll employment, and industrial production. In each case, the test results fit the news model better than they fit the noise model.

Table 1. First-Release GDP, Jobs, and Industrial Production Don't Fit the Noise Model.

	Standard Deviation			Correlation		
	1st Release	Revised	Noise or News?	Revisions & 1st Release	Revisions & Revised	Noise or News?
GDP*	2.28	2.41	news	0.13	0.35	news
Payroll Employment**	1.80	1.96	news	0.29	0.48	news
Industrial Production†	4.02	4.35	news	0.13	0.40	news

Comments:

The "noise" model of first-release data predicts that they will be more variable than revised data, that the first-release data will be negatively correlated with subsequent revisions (the difference between revised and first-release data), and that revisions will be uncorrelated with revised data. The "news" model predicts that first-release data will be less variable than revised data, that the first-release data will be uncorrelated with subsequent revisions, and that revisions will be positively correlated with revised data. Noise first-release data can be second-guessed, whereas news first-release data should be taken at face value.

Notes:

* Q2/Q2 real GDP growth as first released and as it appeared after the first annual revision. (Annual revisions are coincident with release of Q2 data.) Data run from 1966 through 2001, excluding 1975, which is a statistical outlier.
** March/March non-farm payroll employment growth as first released and as it appears today. (March is the benchmark month for payroll employment.) Data run from 1965 through 2003.
† December/December growth in industrial production as first released and as it appears today. Data run from 1965 through 2003, excluding 1983, which is a statistical outlier.

Forecasting When Data Are Subject to Revision

Policymakers often fail to realize the extent to which the forecasts and policy advice they receive are based on models that are estimated either ignoring or mishandling data reliability issues. In particular, forecasting models are nearly always estimated using end-of-sample-vintage data—the latest data available at the time the estimation is performed. Similarly, when two or more variables are plotted together with a view towards displaying a lead/lag relationship between them, it is usually end-of-sample-vintage data that are shown. (Figure 3, discussed above, is an example.) The first problem with the conventional approach is that end-of-sample data are a mix of statistics that have been heavily revised and statistics that are only lightly revised—a mix of apples and oranges—and there is no reason to believe that the apples are related to one another in the same way as the oranges. In practice, for reasonably sized samples, heavily revised data—the apples—will dominate coefficient estimates. But this dominance creates a serious second problem when it comes time to use the model for forecasting, because the data that will be plugged into the estimated equations to produce a forecast are, inevitably, first release or lightly revised—oranges. Conventional practice constructs a cider press and then feeds oranges into it, expecting to get cider.

Looking at charts, the eye does much the same thing as a regression. There is a natural tendency to extrapolate the relationship between heavily revised data and heavily revised data (apples and apples) that applies to the greatest portion of the chart and assume that it holds for the most recent data, too, which are first release or lightly revised (oranges). In Figure 3, there's a tendency to think that because increases in profitability have, in the past, led declines in the unemployment rate, the most recent rise in profitability also portends an unemployment-rate decline. The past profitability increases plotted in the chart, however, incorporate the effects of many rounds of data revisions. The most recent rise in profitability could easily be revised away as additional source data become available.

The *correct* way to try to make a case that profitability is useful for predicting unemployment is to plot the unemployment rate with the early release profitability data that would actually have been available to a forecaster in real time. More generally, regression equations should relate whatever quantity is being forecast to the first-release and lightly revised data that would have been available at the time the forecast was prepared (Koenig, Dolmas and Piger 2003). It's oranges that belong on the right-hand side of forecast-equation regressions.

What vintage data ought to be on the *left*-hand side of a forecasting equation for estimation purposes? Presumably we are ultimately interested in forecasting the "truth"—what the left-hand-side variable will look like after it is thoroughly revised: We want to forecast apples. Even so, surprisingly, it may be oranges that belong on the left-hand side of the forecast-equation regression. Oranges do better than apples as a left-hand-side variable whenever the government statistical agency's early estimates of that variable are pure "news." Recall that an early estimate is "news" if it makes full use of the information that's available at the time that the estimate is prepared. Revisions to such estimates are completely unpredictable. From the perspective of the forecaster, then, the truth is the early estimate plus unpredictable noise. By using the early estimate on its left-hand side, the analyst eliminates unpredictable noise from the regression equation. Bottom line: apples are always safe for the left-hand side of the regression equation (because it is apples we ultimately wish to predict), but oranges will work better if oranges are the best-available estimates of the apples (Koenig *et. al.* 2003).

Based on the results in Table 1, there is little evidence of predictability in GDP, payroll employment and industrial production revisions. Hence, forecasting equations for these variables arguably ought to be estimated with early-release data (oranges) on the left-hand side.

In real-world settings, the payoff to proper estimation of forecasting equations can be substantial. In joint work forecasting current-quarter GDP growth, Jeremy Piger, Sheila Dolmas and I were able to cut root-mean-square forecast errors by 20 percent using the approach outlined here, compared with conventional estimation (Koenig *et. al.* 2003).

Data Requirements

As noted above, conventional practice is to estimate forecasting equations using latest-available data. Each period, as new government statistical estimates are released, the previous period's data are thrown out and replaced with data of the newer vintage. Forecasting equations are re-estimated using the new data, which extends out one period beyond the old data, and a new forecast is prepared. In common parlance, a "real-time" forecasting exercise is just an after-the-fact reproduction of this data, estimation, and forecast updating routine. For example, data from 2000, and extending back 50 years, might be used to estimate a model and produce a forecast of 2001 GDP growth. Then, data from 2001, extending back 51 years, would be used to re-estimate the model and produce a 2002 forecast. Etc. At each iteration, the entire data set is updated and used to obtain new coefficient estimates and a new forecast.

Carrying out this type of real-time recursive forecasting exercise requires a sequence of long data sets of different vintages. In my example, one would need a 50-year history of year 2000-vintage data, a 51-year history of 2001-vintage data, and so forth. Long time series of different-vintage data are difficult to assemble, and the prospect of collecting the required data has proven sufficiently daunting that real-time forecasting exercises of this type are rare.[3] The task has been made much easier recently, courtesy of Dean Croushore (currently at the University of Richmond) and the Federal Reserve Bank of Philadelphia, who have posted a collection of different-vintage data on the Internet (www.philadelphiafed.org).

An after-the-fact reproduction of conventional forecasting practice is of only limited interest if conventional practice is misguided, as was argued above. The *correct* way to estimate forecasting equations is to use, at each point *within* the sample period, only right-hand-side data that would have been available at that point. As time passes and the sample period is extended, old data are not thrown out and replaced with data of the latest vintage. Instead, old data are retained and latest-vintage data are added at the end of the sample. Estimation using this method requires short time series of many different vintages (one vintage for each date in the sample, regardless of the number of estimations), rather than long time series of several different vintages (one vintage for each estimation, regardless of the number of dates in each sample).[4]

---

3   Diebold and Rudebusch (1991) is a well known, early example.

4   A photo-album analogy may help clarify the differences in data requirements. Conventional procedure is to keep a single photo album that has, say, one photo per family member for each year since the family's inception. When a year passes, a new album is purchased and the old album is thrown away. The latest year's photos appear at the very back of the new album, on their own page. Photos from earlier years are mostly duplicates of those that were in the old album. But if Aunt Mildred has sent a picture of little Jimmy at age 10, and Aunt Mildred's photo is an improvement over the photo of 10-year-old Jimmy currently in the album, then the existing photograph is culled in favour of Aunt Mildred's contribution. Conventional recursive "real-time" analysis requires that one retain albums from earlier years, instead of throwing them out. Aside from those on the back pages, photos in successive albums are mostly duplicates. The Philadelphia Fed web site cited above has an album collection of this sort. For the real-time estimation approach proposed here, one needs to maintain a rather different photo collection. Old photographs are never thrown out or replaced. However, each year you add two new pages to your album. The first new page contains photos taken during the year just ended. The second contains photos taken by Aunt Mildred a year earlier, but which have only just arrived, and which are improvements over existing photos. There is only one album, but it has twice as many pages as a conventional album. (Just how much thicker the single album is depends on how many lags of each right-hand-side variable appear in the forecasting equation. In this example, I assume two lags. If three lagged values appear in the forecasting equation, the single album would have three pages for each one page of the conventional album. Etc.)

At present, the short series of many vintages required for proper real-time estimation and forecasting are easily extracted from hard copies of government publications. However, insofar as statistical agencies move away from print and toward purely electronic publication, after-the-fact assembly of real-time data sets will become more difficult. A conscious effort will be required to archive data as it appears at the time of each statistical release.

Anecdotal and Qualitative Alternatives to Conventional Statistical Reports

Oftentimes, the first indication of an important shift in the economy comes not from official government statistics, but from anecdotal reports and other sources of qualitative information. During the mid 1990s, for example, business executives began talking about a lack of pricing power and a relentless pressure to cut costs. Only later did surging productivity growth and the resultant high profitability become apparent in official statistics. Similarly, the first warning of the 2001 high technology downturn came from business contacts in the 11th Federal Reserve District—home to Texas Instruments and the Compaq and Dell computer companies.

One vital source of qualitative information relevant to U.S. monetary policy is the directors of the twelve regional Federal Reserve Banks and their branches. These directors—who include commercial bankers, business people, and community leaders—have an opportunity to communicate their economic knowledge and concerns directly to the regional Federal Reserve Bank presidents during bi-weekly conference calls and monthly board meetings. In addition, each regional Reserve Bank surveys a cross section of area business contacts about recent economic developments in advance of Federal Open Market Committee policy meetings. Summaries are prepared by the Banks, and the summaries are assembled into a document called the "Beige Book," which is available to both policymakers and the public.

Evidence of the value of the qualitative information obtained from business contacts takes several forms. There is, first, the attention that the Beige Book receives when it is released to the public. Press coverage is often extensive, especially when there is concern that the economy may be changing course. Just as one example, the *Wall Street Journal* often prominently displays a Beige Book analysis on the day following the report's release. Other evidence comes from scholarly articles. Researchers have read through old Beige Books, assigning them numerical scores based on the language used to describe unfolding developments. These numerical scores have been shown to have statistically significant predictive power for the national and regional economies—predictive power beyond that of conventional economic indicators available at the time of the Beige Book's release (Balke and Yucel 2000; Balke and Petersen 2002).

The Institute for Supply Management (ISM) is an important source of qualitative information external to the Federal Reserve System. Each month, the Institute surveys purchasing managers from over 400 industrial companies, asking whether orders, production, employment and other important indicators of business conditions are increasing, the same, or decreasing at their respective firms.[5] Diffusion indexes are constructed from the responses. Each diffusion index measures the percentage of respondents reporting that a particular indicator is rising, plus one half the percentage of respondents reporting that the indicator is unchanged. So, any reading above 50 signals

---

5   The ISM began a similar survey for the non-manufacturing sector in 1997 (versus 1948 for manufacturing).

that more firms are reporting increases than are reporting decreases. A large firm is given no greater weight than a small firm, and a firm experiencing rapid increases (or decreases) is given no greater weight than a firm experiencing modest increases (decreases). A summary diffusion index, the Purchasing Managers' Index (PMI), provides an overall assessment of whether the manufacturing sector is expanding or contracting.[6]

Compelling evidence of the information content of the PMI comes from financial markets. A recent Goldman Sachs study documents that medium-term interest rates respond more strongly to PMI surprises than to surprises in any other economic report, including the GDP, employment, retail sales, and industrial production reports.[7] The PMI has also been shown to have information for GDP growth beyond what can be inferred from growth in employment, industrial production, and retail sales (Koenig 2002).

Why are the Federal Reserve's Beige Book and the ISM's Purchasing Managers' Index so valuable? After all, given the qualitative nature of the surveys and their unscientific sampling, disputes about interpretation are inevitable. One advantage is timeliness. The PMI for each month is released on the first business day of the following month and is the earliest available economic indicator with broad coverage. The Beige Book survey schedule is closely coordinated with that of the Federal Open Market Committee, which sets short-term interest rates. In contrast, most government statistical reports are released with a lag of two weeks or more, are based on incomplete source data, and may be as much as a month out of date by the time that the FOMC gathers. Second, as discussed above, supposedly "hard" government statistical reports are subject to substantial after-the-fact revision—which means that their proper interpretation is not necessarily any more straightforward than the interpretation of "soft," qualitative survey results.[8] Finally, often policymakers are less concerned with the precise "truth" of what happened to output, employment, or sales in a particular month than they are about emerging trends in the data. Business executives appear to have a knack for recognizing these trends, and filtering out transitory fluctuations. For an example, see Figure 5, which plots 3-month annualized growth in manufacturing output along with a 3-month moving average of the PMI. The PMI picks up the persistent movements in factory output growth, and eliminates sharp month-to-month swings.

In practice, although anecdotal information may alert Federal Reserve policymakers to emerging trends and important shifts in the economy, action usually is deferred until there is some hard-data confirmation of the new trend or shift. Occasionally, however, waiting a month or more for government statistical reports to arrive is not an option. Such was the case in the wake of the 9-11 terrorist attacks. Fortunately, because of its Beige Book efforts, the Federal Reserve had an established network of business contacts to draw on—a network covering a wide range of industries and extending across the entire country. Based on long experience, the contacts were confident that they could speak

---

6   Six of the regional Federal Reserve Banks now conduct ISM-style surveys and compute ISM-style diffusion indexes for their districts, as a supplement to their Beige Book reports. The oldest such survey (Philadelphia) goes back to 1968.

7   See Hatzius and Crump (2003). A "surprise" is a one-standard-deviation difference between the realisation of an indicator and the Wall Street consensus forecast for that indicator. The financial-market impact is measured by the change in the two-year Treasury Note yield.

8   Beige Books are, of course, never revised, and the PMI is revised only when seasonal factors are re-estimated.

freely, without fear that firm-specific information would leak. Because they had spoken with these same executives on many previous occasions, in a variety of circumstances, Federal Reserve analysts and officials were able to put the information they received in proper perspective.

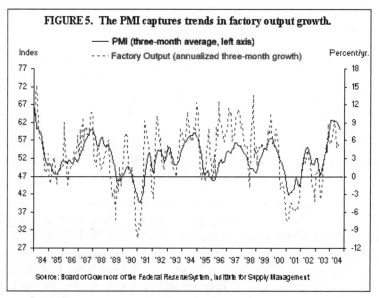

FIGURE 5. The PMI captures trends in factory output growth.

— PMI (three-month average, left axis)
---- Factory Output (annualized three-month growth)

Source: Board of Governors of the Federal Reserve System, Institute for Supply Management

Private-Sector Expectations and Financial Asset Prices

Fourth on Goldman Sachs' list of market-moving releases—after the PMI and the GDP and payroll-employment reports—is the Conference Board's Consumer Confidence index. The Consumer Confidence index is based partly on household expectations of future economic conditions. Private-sector expectations are a main ingredient in financial asset prices, as well, and obviously completely drive survey measures of household inflation expectations and professional forecasters' inflation, output, and employment predictions. An economic indicator that reflects expectations, which is not subject to revision, and which–in the case of asset prices–is available daily or even minute-to-minute, would seem to be ideal.

In practice, sorting out the policy implications of movements in asset prices and private-sector forecasts is problematic. Movements in asset prices due to changes in expectations are difficult to distinguish from those due to changes in liquidity and risk premia. Private-sector forecasts show the outcomes that people feel are most likely, but say little about the confidence with which these beliefs are held. Finally, policymakers may have information relevant to the economic outlook that is superior to that possessed by the private sector. Most obviously, policymakers likely have better information about how policy will react to various contingencies. There is always a question, then, about whether a shift in private-sector expectations signals new private-sector information that is deserving of the monetary authority's attention or, instead, reflects a possibly unwarranted change in beliefs about the future conduct of policy. Chances for misinterpretation are minimized if the monetary authority effectively communicates its objectives and its plans for attaining them (Bernanke 2004).

Summary and Conclusions

Statistical reports prepared by government agencies are both better and worse than we give them credit for being. Even the earliest government reports are surprisingly difficult to second-guess. Apparently, government statisticians rarely simply extrapolate from available source data to arrive at their estimates. Difficulties arise, however, when government data are used to estimate forecasting models. Contrary to conventional econometric practice, it is *not* safe to mix the lightly revised data that are typical toward the end of most sample periods with the heavily revised data that are typical toward the beginning. Achieving optimal forecasting performance requires that lightly revised data be used throughout the sample, since it is lightly revised data that inevitably will be substituted into the estimated equation when it comes time to prepare an actual forecast. Similarly, if you believe that one series is a good leading indicator of another, you should plot the second variable along with the government's *initial* estimate of the first, rather than estimates that may incorporate many after-the-fact revisions.

While using conventional government statistical reports for forecasting is, perhaps, less straightforward than is commonly believed, the advantages to using anecdotal and qualitative information are often neglected. Anecdotal and qualitative information is frequently more timely than conventional data, is less subject to revision, and better captures emerging trends. The Federal Reserve System places high value on anecdotal and qualitative information, and its institutional structure facilitates the flow of this type of information to policymakers from a wide range of sectors and regions of the country. These information channels have proven invaluable in times of crisis.

Asset prices and consensus forecasts or expectations surveys might seem to be ideal economic indicators, but policymakers need to know what is driving changes in private-sector expectations in order to determine the appropriate response. It may well be that the best response is simply to more effectively communicate policymakers' own objectives and plans.

References

Balke, Nathan S. and D'Ann Petersen (2002) "How Well Does the Beige Book Reflect Economic Activity? Evaluating Qualitative Information Quantitatively," *Journal of Money, Credit and Banking* 34, 114-136.

Balke, Nathan S. and Mine K. Yucel (2000) "Evaluating the Eleventh District's Beige Book," Federal Reserve Bank of Dallas *Economic and Financial Review*, 4th Quarter, 2-10.

Bernanke, Ben S. (2004) "What Policymakers Can Learn from Asset Prices," speech before the Investment Analysts Society of Chicago; Chicago, Illinois; April 15.

Brayton, Flint, John M. Roberts and John C. Williams (1999) "What's Happened to the Phillips Curve?" Board of Governors of the Federal Reserve System, Finance and Economics Discussion Paper 1999-49.

Diebold, Francis X. and Glenn D. Rudebusch (1991) "Forecasting Output with the Composite Leading Index: A Real-Time Analysis," *Journal of the American Statistical Association* 86, 603-610.

Gordon, Robert J. (1993) *Macroeconomics*, 6th ed. (New York: HarperCollins College Publishers).

Gordon, Robert J. (1997) *Macroeconomics*, 7th ed. (Reading, Mass.: Addison Wesley Longman Inc.).

Gordon, Robert J. (2000) *Macroeconomics*, 8th ed. (Reading, Mass.: Addison Wesley Longman Inc.).

Gordon, Robert J. (2003) *Macroeconomics*, 9th ed. (Boston: Addison Wesley).

Greenspan, Alan (2004) "Federal Reserve Board's Semiannual Monetary Policy Report to the Congress," testimony before the Senate Committee on Banking, Housing, and Urban Affairs, July 20.

Hatzius, Jan and Richard Crump (2003) "The GS Surprise Index: Strength Likely to Fade," Goldman Sachs *U.S. Economics Analyst*, No. 03/08, February 21.

Koenig, Evan F. (2001) "What Goes Down Must Come Up: Understanding Time-Variation in the NAIRU," Federal Reserve Bank of Dallas Working Paper No. 0101.

Koenig, Evan F. (2002) "Using the Purchasing Managers' Index to Assess the Economy's Strength and the Likely Direction of Monetary Policy," FRB Dallas *Economic and Financial Policy Review* 1, No. 6.

Koenig, Evan F. (2003) "Is the Markup a Useful Real-Time Predictor of Inflation?" *Economics Letters* 80, 261-267.

Koenig, Evan F. (2004) "Monetary Policy Prospects," FRB Dallas *Economic and Financial Policy Review* 3, No. 2.

Koenig, Evan F., Sheila Dolmas and Jeremy Piger (2003) "The Use and Abuse of Real-Time Data in Economic Forecasting," *Review of Economics and Statistics* 85, 618-628.

Orphanides, Athanasios (2002) "Monetary Policy Rules and the Great Inflation," Board of Governors of the Federal Reserve System, Finance and Economics Discussion Paper 2002-8.

Orphanides, Athanasios (2003) "Historical Monetary Policy Analysis and the Taylor Rule," Board of Governors of the Federal Reserve, Finance and Economics Discussion Paper 2003-36.

Sargent, Thomas (1989) "Two Models of Measurements and the Investment Accelerator," *Journal of Political Economy* 97, 251-287.

Measuring the Effectiveness of Public Services

Indicators on Public Administration:
Democracy, Efficiency, Due Process of Law

Richard Murray

Chief Economist, Swedish Agency for Public Management

Indicators may be had for many different purposes: for that of steering or control, for that of rewarding and mobilising. I take it that it is none of those purposes that the OECD under the heading of this session is asking for. I take it that it is for purposes of understanding that the OECD wants me and others to reflect on the needs and possibilities of indicators. In fact, what the OECD asks from us is advice on what facts we need in order to understand better what is going on in different policy fields. In this session the policy field is public administration.

Firstly, how to delimit public administration. Other sessions deal specifically with policy areas such as education, health, energy, crime. If that is the *meso* level of the public sector, that is not what I should talk about. Neither is the *micro* level. By that I refer to the agency or individual organisational level. Indicators on that level are mostly for steering, control, rewarding etc. The level I think is appropriate to address is the *macro* level.

What do I mean by macro level in this connection? Governance is a catch-word that catches what I suggest. By governance we mean the organisational setup of government, its systems of steering and control – in general, not the particular systems in various policy fields. And good governance means the well-functioning government.

In democratic states government is the vehicle for collective action, the instrument by which the popular will be realised. Therefore, for whatever purpose that democratically elected representatives decide to use that machinery for – whether it is to provide adequate housing for citizens, good education for all children or to defend their country – it should function well.

What is a well-functioning government? Can it be determined without reference to policies? Hardly, but those policies may be very general.

Let me start by giving an example of a rather narrowly conceived concept of a well-functioning government. The example has to do with attracting foreign direct investment (FDI). According to well founded theories of economics, economic growth depends crucially on institutions. As is well-known in this part of Italy Robert Putnam claimed that the civic institutions of the Italian cities in the north were lacking in the south and that that explained the whole difference of economic growth and well-being between north and south up to this very day. If therefore, good governance is conceived of as that institutional setup which stimulates FDI and economic growth, we should look for those characteristics of governance that has this effect.

Recently a study appeared which could pinpoint a fair amount of those institutions that promote FDI. The characteristics have to do with corruption, efficiency of the judicial system, rule of law, stability of the financial system etc. An index based on indicators for these characteristics is correlated with FDI, explaining why China is at the top and Russia at the bottom.

However, I do think most governments have a broader view on good governance. The EU-15 formulated in 1990 the Lisbon agenda for what governments can do to raise competitiveness and social welfare for the EU to become the world's most advanced region. In a recent report the Dutch Social and Planning Bureau has analysed and compared the success of the EU member states and their main competitors (the USA, Australia, Canada and New Zealand) in relation to this agenda.

The report distinguishes four areas: 1) macroeconomic policy, 2) distributional policy, 3) allocative efficiency and 4) quality of public administration. All four have to do, I think you will agree, with good governance, although some of these areas deal with policies in specific areas and therefore should be ruled out as part of the general good governance area. However, maybe it is necessary to take some general characteristics of specific policies into account when defining good governance in general.

There are indicators for performance in all four areas, drawn mainly from the Lisbon agenda. In the macroeconomic area it is economic growth, unemployment, labour market participation, inflation and budget deficit. Indicators for distributional policy are income inequality and poverty rate. Are these areas aspects of good governance or not? I leave the question open.

I think there will be more agreement on the latter two areas. Allocative efficiency is measured by indicators on cost-effectiveness (expenditures in relation to social situation) in areas such as health, education and crime. If a country achieves a high level of educational attainment with a moderate amount of expenditures or a low crime rate with reasonable expenditures that would be taken as an indicator for allocative efficiency. This, to my mind, has to do with good governance.

Quality of public administration, the fourth area, is measured by indicators on the size of bureaucracy, citizens' surveys on transparency, effectiveness of government interventions (implementation) and corruption. Unquestionably, this has to do with good governance.

The Swedish Government in the year 2000 launched a public administration action program. It was based explicitly on three main values: efficiency and effectiveness, rule of law and democracy. Whatever policies the Government of Sweden wanted to pursue it deemed it desirable that the government machinery should realise these values. They could therefore be taken as the base line for building indicators on good governance.

Anyone familiar with trying to measure elusive concepts such as these knows that one has to work with a bunch of indicators, not just one. The clue to selecting candidates for that bunch is to decompose the concepts.

I give you examples of how to decompose or break down the concepts of efficiency, rule of law and democracy. Efficiency could be measured straight on by productivity. Then there are many aspects of quality that may not be captured, such as adequacy, correctness, speed etc. Impact is not quality, but may sometimes be used as an indicator of quality. Rule of law is even more evasive. Some – but not all – lawyers would make distinctions between correctness of court decisions, due process and possibilities of appeal. And those concepts could be divided up even further. Due process is built up of correct handling, transparency and competence of staff. The concept of democracy should in this context be confined to those aspects that have to do with public administration and leave those aspects aside that have to do with voting and party system etc. Public administration is of importance for democracy to function in at least two respects: that of politicians' control of and possibilities to steer bureaucracy and that of citizens' possibilities to have a say on the administrative handling of their cases. The first aspect has to do with whether the civil service is a corps loyal to Government, whatever party it represents, whether they serve decision-makers with objective and relevant information etc. The second aspect has to do with transparency, processes for hearing citizens, efforts to understand citizens' preferences etc. I do not think I have exhausted the list, you may wish to add to it.

The point is that over-arching values like these may be assessed by being broken down into finer categories. However, ultimately they must be tested against the perception of citizens and elected representatives, in the same way that the indicators for good governance to promote FDI had been.

Means are often just as interesting as aims. In order to understand what promotes progress in relation to efficiency, rule of law, democracy and maybe some other over-arching value of public administration we have to relate means to values. There is a set of means that make up what is commonly referred to as public administration policy. They have to do with general ways and means to organise, steer and control public administration. In order to generalise on these general ways and means we have to categorise them: My suggestion is something like this:

- Organisation
- Internal regulation of agency work
- External regulation of agency work
- Resources: staff, technology
- Research & development
- Steering
- Control
- Other

By then constructing a matrix made of values (aims) and means we can start to analyse the relationship between what we do (public administration policies) and what we get (good governance).

The action plan of the Swedish Government in year 2000 could be analysed in this way. Although there was as much talk of the rule of law and of democracy as of efficiency a categorisation of the means showed that most of them aimed at efficiency and economic growth and were concentrated in the categories of resources (training of managers, monitoring personnel developments, use of information technology) and steering (quality award, benchmarking, performance indicators). Such matrices may prove to be a basis to build a firmer understanding about good governance and the policies aiming for it.

Healthy People: Three Decades of National Health

Edward J. Sondik, Director

Richard J. Klein, Chief, Health Promotion Statistics Branch, Office of Analysis and Epidemiology

National Center for Health Statistics
Centers for Disease Control and Prevention

Abstract

Healthy People 2010 is a program to improve America's health through disease prevention and health promotion. At its core, Healthy People is a system of health indicators initiated by the United States government to help guide actions to improve disease prevention and health promotion. In this paper we discuss the history of the initiative, the framework and scope of the indicators, the program's management and impact, and some of the key lessons we believe Healthy People gives us regarding national indicators.

Introduction

Healthy People 2010 is a program to improve America's health through disease prevention and health promotion. At its core Healthy People a set of disease prevention and health promotion health goals established by the United States government. The goals were established to guide its efforts and the efforts of everyone to improve prevention of disease and the promotion of health in general. The principal target audiences are many, ranging from the public to the medical profession to elected officials. As stated by the Secretary of Health and Human Services in the preface to Healthy People 2010 "It (Healthy People 2010) is a tremendously valuable asset to health planners, medical practitioners, educators, elected officials and all of us who work to improve health." The program is now in its third decade, having produced three sets of goals, a set each for 1990, 2000, and now the third set for the year 2010.

In effect Healthy People is a set of health-related indicators. Associated with the indicators are:

- Targets to be achieved by the year 2010; data sources – one for each indicator, identified for each indicator, each source providing data representative of the country as a whole (although subpopulations are very important was we discuss below);

- Each of the indicators together with its target is termed an objective;

- For the current edition, Healthy People 2010, there are two over-arching goals [to increase the number of years of healthy life and to eliminate disparities in health status in the United States population (a disparity refers to, for example, the higher mortality from cancer in the black population compared to the white population)].

- A science-based discussion of the importance and role of each indicator including a basis for understanding the relationship between the indicators and health outcomes; and a management process for the entire effort.

- Additional critical parts of the program are dissemination activities and a variety of groups who use and contribute to the overall program.

- Also critical are various avenues for the public and health professionals to help guide the program and share information and program initiatives aimed at enabling the US population to achieve the goals.

In this paper we discuss Healthy People's development and these essential program elements, along with the program's management and its impact. We stress the key elements of the program which include a reliance on an extensive public process of establishing the goals and objectives each decade; a fundamental reliance on health science to test the feasibility of the goals and drive the processes to achieve the goals; and the role of data in tracking progress toward meeting the goals.

Examples of Healthy People Objectives

Figure1 gives four examples of current Healthy People 2010 objectives, for tobacco use, overweight and obesity, mental health, and three measures of access to health care. In the Healthy People document these graphs are accompanied by text explaining the relationship between these risk factors (tobacco use and overweight) and the feasibility of, as well as strategies for, changing them. The mental health objective addresses the extent to which persons with depression are receiving treatment, and is an example of an objective related to intervention to address a specific health problem.

Figure 1: Examples of Healthy People 2010 Objectives
Overweight and Obesity

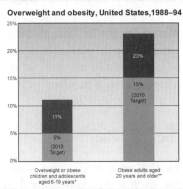

Overweight and obesity, United States,1988–94

*In those aged 6 to 19 years, overweight or obesity is defined as at or above the sex- and age-specific 95th percentile of Body Mass Index (BMI) based on CDC Growth Charts: United States.
**In adults, obesity is defined as a BMI of 30 kg/m² or more; overweight is a BMI of 25 kg/m² or more.
Source: Centers for Disease Control and Prevention, National Center for Health Statistics. National Health and Nutrition Examination Survey. 1988–94.

Tobacco Use

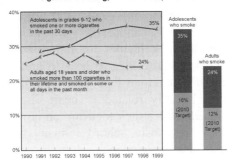

Cigarette smoking, United States, 1990–99

Figure 1: Examples of Healthy People 2010 Objectives, continued
Mental Health

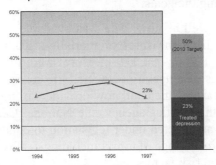

Adults with depression* who received treatment,** United States, 1994–97

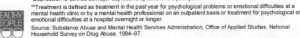

*Depression is defined as major depressive episode in the past year.

**Treatment is defined as treatment in the past year for psychological problems or emotional difficulties at a mental health clinic or by a mental health professional on an outpatient basis or treatment for psychological or emotional difficulties at a hospital overnight or longer.

Access to Health Care

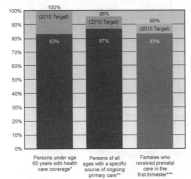

Access to health care, United States, 1997 and 1998

History

In 1979 the Surgeon General of the United States issued a report on the importance of Health Promotion and Disease Prevention. That report argued that health status in the United States could be measurably improved with more aggressive attention to prevention, that is, reducing the risk factors for injury and disease. The report was prompted by then recent gains in knowledge of how to prevent both acute and chronic disease. In particular, research had shown that significant improvements were possible from reducing risk factors especially related to heart disease and stroke, and some cancers. In addition, other research was then focusing on how these risk factors could be changed. The report struck a responsive chord – many believed it was time for a nationwide effort to apply this new knowledge.

In fact, the notion that it was time for a major effort to improve disease prevention led to the development and publication by the Department of Health, Education and Welfare of the first edition of Healthy People with goals for the year 1990.

Others were stimulated by the idea of nationwide health related goals. For example, in 1987 The National Cancer Institute of the National Institutes of Health published a report that set cancer control objectives for the year 2000. The report included a variety of indicators and goals for each. It also included an analytic model estimating the impact on various cancers from meeting the goals.

Of course, in 1979, as well as now, data was available to construct any number of health indicators, ranging from measures of mortality, death rates, to prevalence and incidence rates for disease. Perhaps the key measures were the overall death rate (deaths per 1,000 people), estimates of longevity (expected life span), the birth rate, and disease prevalence rates. These measures then and now provide the framework for public health. The principal federal health statistics agency, the National Center for Health Statistics, was formed in 1960 and was directed under legislation to conduct a variety of studies to provide information on a broad range of topics including deaths, births, health manpower, health facilities, health costs, risk factors, etc.

However, neither in 1960, nor in 1979 was there a designation of a single set of indicators to be used to guide health policy and health interventions, but with the 1979 publication of the Surgeon General's Report, however, many in the public health community felt that a critical set of indicators was important. However, since the focus of the report was on factors that could be modified, it was important to include with each indicator a target that was feasible to reach (with new efforts) by the year 1990. These indicators and targets – termed goals – were the basis for a report in 1980 that established what was to be the first phase of Healthy People.

The 1979 Surgeon General's Report was based on five topic areas each with an overall goal and two subgoals as follows:

Table 1. Healthy People 1979: Structure

Healthy Infants	*To continue to improve infant health, and, by 1990, to reduce infant mortality by at least 35 percent, to fewer than nine deaths per 1,000 live births.*
	Subgoal: Reducing the Number Of Low Birth Weight Infants
	Subgoal: Reducing The Number of Birth Defects

Healthy Children	*To improve child health, foster optimal childhood development, and, by 1990, reduce deaths among children ages one to 14 years by at least 20 percent, to fewer than 34 per 100,000.*
	Subgoal: Enhancing Childhood Growth and Development
	Subgoal: Reducing Childhood Accidents and Injuries
Adolescents and Young Adults	*To improve the health and health habits of adolescents and young adults, and, by 1990, to reduce deaths among people ages 15 to 24 by at least 20 percent, to fewer than 93 per 100,000.*
	Subgoal: Reducing Fatal Motor Vehicle Accidents
	Subgoal: Reducing Alcohol and Drug Misuse
Adults	*To improve the health of adults, and, by 1990, to reduce death among people ages 25 to 64 by at least 25 percent, to fewer than 400 per 100,000.*
	Subgoal: Reducing Heart Attacks and Strokes
	Subgoal: Reducing Death from Cancer
Older Adults	*To improve the health and quality of life for older adults and, by 1990, to reduce the average annual number of days of restricted activity due to acute and chronic conditions by 20 percent, to fewer than 30 days per year for people aged 65 and older.*
	Subgoal: Increasing the Number of Older Adults Who Can Function Independently
	Subgoal: Reducing Premature Death from Influenza and Pneumonia

As noted, Healthy People 2010 includes 467 objectives divided into the following 28 focus areas:

Table 1 cont. Healthy People 2010: Focus Areas (467 Objectives)

Access to Quality Health Services	Injury and Violence Prevention
Arthritis, Osteoporosis, and Chronic Back Conditions	Maternal, Infant, and Child Health
Cancer	Medical Product Safety
Chronic Kidney Diseases	Mental Health and Mental Disorders
Diabetes	Nutrition and Overweight
Disability and Secondary Conditions	Occupational Safety and Health
Educational and Community-Based Programs	Oral Health
Environmental Health	Physical Activity and Fitness
Family Planning	Public Health Infrastructure
Food Safety	Respiratory Diseases
Health Communication	Sexually Transmitted Diseases
Heart Disease and Stroke	Substance Abuse
HIV	Tobacco Use
Immunisation and Infectious Diseases	Vision and Hearing

Key Aspects of Healthy People

The following sections discuss (in some cases, very briefly because of space limitations) various aspects of Healthy People we believe have significance for national indicator programs in general:

Developing and managing Healthy People

Healthy People is managed by the United States government with extensive participation by the non-federal public and private health communities. In a sense this participatory process has been a hallmark of the program from its beginnings. It is this process that brings interests of these groups to the table and places before those leading the program in Washington advocacy for various points of view. In order to identify and set of the goals for 2010, the Office of Disease Prevention and Health Promotion (OPDPHP) under the Secretary for Health and Human Services, held a series of public hearings across the country, asking for testimony on the health problems, indicators and health interventions that should be included in the program. Suggestions included a wide range of topics and included some indicators that at the time had no nationwide data sources. Such indicators (and targets) were possible to include, designating them as "developmental objectives." Perhaps the key factor those testifying were asked to address regarding their proposals had to do with the feasibility of achieving change in the indicators. This is a key difference between a set of indicators and Healthy People, which is a set of goals (indicators and targets).

Government agency involvement

Despite its publication and management by the US federal government, the content of Healthy People is very much determined by the public health community. In creating each edition of Healthy People the opinions of the public and health professionals have been sought. The process by which public and professional opinion are brought to the program include public hearings held at several locations around the country, production of draft editions that allow public comment and the use of the internet—extensively—for the most recent edition, Healthy People 2010.

Public and professional guidance of Healthy People is also afforded through a Steering Committee and other committees drawn from health professionals and the public. Former Assistant Secretaries of Health, regardless of political party, serve as guides. Links to non- federal government professionals and the public are also achieved through the management of the individual Healthy People sections. For example, the section on diabetes is coordinated by staff of the Centers for Disease Control and Prevention and the National Institutes of Health, two agencies with strong links to the public health and biomedical research communities. In addition, Department of Health and Human Services holds periodic "progress reviews" on the extent to which goals are being met. The first set of reviews (one review for each of the 28 chapters) has just ended. There will be one or two more rounds of review during the decade. This first set of reviews was held with staff members of the Department.

The Healthy People conceptual framework

Healthy People is built on the conceptual framework with causality at its core—actions aimed at achieving positive changes in health status. The 2010 edition includes two overarching health goals, objectives, determinants of health, and indicators (and targets for) health status. Each phase of Healthy People has had a limited set of overarching goals that provide a framework for the entire effort. For 2010 the overarching goals are first, to help individuals of all ages increase life expectancy *and* improve their quality of life, and secondly, to eliminate health disparities among segments of the population, including differences that occur by gender, race or ethnicity, education or income, disability, geographic location, or sexual orientation. Under these goals are objectives divided into focus groups – for 2010 there are 28 such focus groups. The components fit together as follows:

> "Whether this systematic approach is used to improve health on a national level, as in Healthy People 2010, or to organize community action on a particular health issue, such as promoting smoking cessation, the components remain the same. The goals provide a general focus and direction. The goals, in turn, serve as a guide for developing a set of objectives that will measure actual progress within a specified amount of time. The objectives focus on the determinants of health, which encompass the combined effects of individual and community physical and social environments and the policies and interventions used to promote health, prevent disease, and ensure access to quality health care. The ultimate measure of success in any health improvement effort is the health status of the target population." --- From the background material for Healthy People 2010.

Population groups and minority populations

As indicated by the second overarching goal, the elimination of disparities in health status is of critical importance. This priority has led to the development of a template to guide the principal race, ethnicity and demographic factors in data collection. Table 2 shows the template; its importance cannot be overstated. Reducing health disparities between races or economic groups is one of very important and guides a significant portion of the data collection parameters associated with Healthy People. Of course, reducing disparities should be accomplished in a way that improves the average, so to speak. There are a variety of ways to measure differences between groups (disparities) but in general the sense is to improve those faring the worst, while improving the entire population.

Table 2: Healthy People Population Template

Race:
American Indian or Alaska Native
Asian
Native Hawaiian or Other Pacific Islander
Black or African American
White

Ethnicity:
Hispanic or Latino
Not Hispanic or Latino

Gender:
Female
Male

Socioeconomic status:	
Family income	**Education Level**
Poor	Less than high school
Near poor	High school
Middle/high income	At least some college

How the goals were developed

The process by which Healthy People goals are developed is designed to encourage advice from as many who are interested and have a stake in public health: the public, health professionals, the private sector and all levels of government. Prior to developing Healthy People 2010 goals, the federal government leadership asked the National Center for Health Statistics to assess progress toward the 2000 goals. As I've noted, the NCHS is one of the US agencies in the Federal Statistical System, and therefore is independent in its data collection and reporting activities. The evaluation served as the basis for assessing whether public health efforts were impacting critical health problems and, as well, whether there were critical problems not being assessed. Public hearings were held across the country, and the results collated by the Federal Government's Office of Disease Prevention and Health Promotion.

The results were then used by the principal federal health agencies and a blue ribbon non-federal advisory committee to create a draft of a new set of healthy people goals. This draft containing over 700 goals was published on the internet and widely distributed for comment.

In turn the federal agencies and the advisory committee produced a final volume with some 28 separate topic areas and 467 goals.

On data sources:

Healthy People emphasizes the necessary condition that quality data play in setting and monitoring progress toward goals. The same is true, of course of a set of indicators, regardless of whether specific goals have been set. In effect with indicators, each observer is setting goals of some sort, perhaps unspoken and unwritten, but still with some expectations of direction and value of moving in each direction.

On State health programs

Certainly one of the major benefits of the Healthy People Program is enabling State-based health promotion and disease prevention programs (and those of other organisations) to develop an agenda from a national menu of science-based goals. We have found that for Healthy People 2000 nearly all states had such programs, all derived from the national Healthy People goals. States draw liberally from the national program because, in effect, they helped to author this program in the first place. The rigorous descriptions of the topic areas, the measures and the goals are all developed in a scientifically rigorous manner way and with specifications that will allow the topic to be addressed at a state or local level if data is available.

One of the goals for the Healthy People program is to develop improved data sources. Toward that end some of the measures in Healthy People 2010 are termed "developmental". The importance of the indicator is outlined along with specifications for data sources, even though such data sources do not now exist. Healthy People management is encouraging, in this manner, the development of such data sources, which may exist at the state, but not at the national level.

Derivatives

Healthy People has spawned or at a minimum helped guide many State-based programs. A derivative program at the national level led by the Department of Health and

Human Services is Steps to a Healthier US. The program includes grants on reducing the burden of diabetes, overweight, obesity and asthma and addressing risk factors such as physical inactivity, poor nutrition and tobacco use in 40 communities. Diabetes, asthma, overweight and obesity were chosen as targets because of their rapidly increasing prevalence in the United States and the ability for individuals to control and even prevent these diseases through exercise, diet and other strategies.

Impact of Healthy People

It is difficult to determine the impact of this set of goals and objectives at least in terms of its causal role in changing health status. Perhaps the best testimony to its impact is that Healthy People is now in its third decade. The program has become an integral part of United States public health. Almost all state-based public health programs have borrowed liberally from the national program. And as we note below, the federal government has used Healthy People as the base for derivative programs designed to focus effort on the most critically needed changes in health behavior. The US Centers for Disease Control and Prevention, now undergoing a major transformation in program and structure, is using the goals-based structure, and the steps needed to achieve goals, as a major tool in setting the agency's direction.

Because Healthy People is science-based in the sense that the most recent scientific results are used in identifying critical indicators and understanding the import of their change over time, states have borrowed liberally from the program. The fact that the processes used in developing the program are fully in the spirit of "government in the sunshine," structured to support an open, inclusive discussion of the rationale for the goals and objectives may well be a principal reason for its widespread application. Another integrity-related aspect of Healthy People may be the frequent review of progress and the publication of both mid- and final decade reviews of the entire program. Data plays a key role, of course, in the evaluation and great care is taken in designating the data sources for Healthy People.

It is fair to ask whether Healthy People has had a role in the improving trends in heart disease and cancer, in reducing youth violence, in teen births, in reducing smoking, in reducing sexually transmitted diseases, and reducing infant mortality? While fair to ask, the answer must be based more on judgment than experimental science. While the rigorous evaluation is yet to be done, the public health community believes the program is very important witnessed by its widespread use in state programs.

The role of data in Healthy People

A data source is integral to any indicator, and data is all important to Healthy People. The National Center for Health Statistics (NCHS), one of the designated federal statistical agencies, is responsible for defining the data requirements for each objective as well as maintaining a data warehouse on the Internet of the latest data to date for each of the objectives. Some 50 per cent of the data in Healthy People is derived from surveys conducted by NCHS and the Vital Statistics System it coordinates.

For Healthy People 2010 NCHS authored a separate volume detailing the data requirements for each of the objectives. The purpose was to enable states and localities who wish to develop their own data sources, more specific to their own areas, to have the requisite specifications. The volume is also useful to those who wish to analyze the data. Healthy People 2010 includes some objectives, new to the program for which data sources have not been developed. The "developmental objectives" are designed to introduce important new dimension to the program that have not yet the requisite data sources. The goal is to encourage the development of such data sources at the national as well as state and local levels.

Leveraging the national Healthy People program

The impact of Healthy People is facilitated and leveraged through a network of health professionals who draw from Healthy People to create disease prevention and health promotion agendas for their regions or groups. A "toolkit" has been developed and is available through the internet to help the public health community draw from Healthy People, implement interventions to improve health, and in general, develop programs that support and complement the national effort. The toolkit consists of a variety of information drawn from sources across the country relating to how the Healthy People materials were used including for example, how they were expanded and extended, promoted, and used as teaching tools.

Conclusions

It is hard to imagine health promotion and disease prevention without the analytic and goal-directed base of Healthy People. If it didn't exist it would seem we would have to invent it. The key characteristics of its critical dependence on science to provide the necessary perspective on what factors are important in health and extensive national data courses to track progress are perhaps the critical components of Healthy People. The role of government is important to provide the resources to maintain and manage the program, but it is conceivable that another form of support could be possible. We see for example, non-federal support in many of the areas associated with informatics—standards come to mind—that are industry-based and supported, and are part of a public private partnership. The importance of reducing disparities is one of the key elements in the program, and the continued display of data that outlines disparities is important in making progress in improving health for all groups of the US population.

Healthy People is in its third decade and seems to be an integral part of public health. We expect it to be around for a fourth decade. Even as progress is made, new challenges, no doubt, will arise.

References

Healthy People: The Surgeon General's Report on Health Promotion and Disease Prevention, U.S. Dept. of Health, Education, and Welfare, Public Health Service, Office of the Assistant Secretary for Health and Surgeon General, U.S. Govt. Print. Off., 1979.

Healthy People 2010, Office of Disease Prevention and Health Promotion, Department of Health and Human Services, Washington, DC, available through the internet at http://www.healthypeople.gov/.

Regional Indicators and Fund Allocation

International Benchmarking as a Tool for Regional Policy Making: Experiences and Challenges

Christoph Koellreuter

Managing Director and Chief Economist, BAK Basel Economics, Switzerland

Abstract

Globalisation of markets and economic activities represent challenges that companies and governments can meet only through continuous adaptation and innovation. When it comes to the latter, the regional level is particularly important, because it is there where new knowledge is primarily commercialised into innovative products and production processes. Thus the creation and maintenance of innovation friendly framework conditions have become an important policy issue at the regional level.

This paper shows the principles of regional benchmarking and its role in regional policy making. First, the origins of benchmarking are discussed and how it finally arrived in the sphere of regions. Second, the specific requirements international regional benchmarking has to meet are elaborated before an example of international regional benchmarking – the IBC BAK International Benchmark Club[1] – is presented. The paper concludes with a discussion of the main uses of international benchmarking by regional policy makers and members of the regional civil society.

International regional benchmarking is an attractive tool for dealing with the effects of political fragmentation and/or over-centralisation, in developing a coherent vision for the region, for regional consensus building and last but not least for the development, implementation and controlling of policies having an impact at the regional level. Prime policy areas for international regional benchmarking are education, research and development, regulation of markets, taxation, social policies and infrastructure.

Meeting globalisation challenges: Regional level particularly important

Rapid technological progress, changing values, and new competitors represent challenges that companies and governments can meet only through continuous adaptation and innovation. When it comes to the latter, the regional level[2] is particularly important, because it is there where new knowledge is commercialised above all into innovative products and production processes. Why? Because innovative activity thrives where there is a spatial concentration of companies of the same and related industries or sectors, and these are clearly a regional rather than a national phenomenon. They are supported by the stimulation of domestic demand and a pool of specialised manpower, suppliers, and educational and research institutions.

---

1   Launched by BAK Basel Economics, founded and headed by the author.

2   Unless noted otherwise, this paper uses the word region to denote an economic region in the sense of an innovation, labour market or functional urban region.

Individuals and companies are able to benefit from the positive external effects (i.e. higher private productivities) that go hand-in-hand with regional industry clusters only if they work or are based in the region in question. The existence of regional externalities means for one thing that the market does not of itself guarantee the formation and continued development of innovative industry clusters, and for another that the decision-makers of the entire region that benefit from the cluster's externalities have to commit themselves to providing framework conditions of the right quality to ensure successful regional innovative activity. This includes – tailored as closely as possible to the specific needs of the regional industry cluster – investment in infrastructure, in specialised human capital and in application-oriented research and development, as well as first-class offerings in the areas of education, healthcare, culture, and leisure activities. Important, too, is a regulatory structure that characterizes the kind of open and flexible markets – for products, capital and labour – that are crucial to fast-paced renewal.

Innovation-friendly regional framework conditions have become even more important in a phase of fiercer competition between regions, because the increasingly mobile production factors capital, management and highly qualified manpower punish bad economic policies more quickly than ever. In this age of globalisation, therefore, policymaking has become more crucial to successful regional development than it used to be.

Today successful economic policies of a region rest on four central pillars:

1. A vision that is shared by the majority concerning the region's role in a world economy marked by an increasing division of labour. This includes a realistic assessment in which "league" the region is competing in, which industry clusters have a promising future in comparison with competing regions, and where restructuring is indicated.

2. A strongly supported conception of the type and quality of the location factors on which to base the region's future development. However, policymaking must concentrate on getting the framework conditions right. Policies can favour the formation of clusters, but they cannot create them. The formation and growth of regional industry clusters must ultimately be left to the market.

3. A collective willingness to learn. In particular, this means: rapid recognition of changes in the relevant environment of the region – especially changes in competing regions – the ability to pursue the regional vision and the framework conditions essential to its realisation with the necessary speed, and finally close monitoring of the effects of the decisions taken. The most important thing here is the readiness to learn from any mistakes made – by oneself and by others.

4. Closest possible geographical coherence between the functional region's territory and the authority for establishing the framework conditions affecting innovation. The more the two diverge, the less keen the potential beneficiaries of cluster-specific externalities will be to exert themselves to achieve the necessary framework conditions. One reason for this may be that too much authority resides with higher levels of government, another that the economic region in question is too fragmented politically. Or both of these conditions may exist in combination. In either case, other things being equal, lower regional economic growth can be expected. For these reasons, it is not surprising that many small countries in Europe that often make up just one economic region exhibit higher growth than many regions of similar size in large countries. Moreover, research in North America and Europe has shown that the

economies of regions where political entities have been succeeding in achieving good mutual coordination or have even joined forces politically have developed more dynamically than have politically fragmented regions.[3]

International regional benchmarking, i.e. the systematic and continuous comparison of economic (as well as ecological and societal) performance and of the relevant framework conditions of one's own region with the corresponding indicators of competing regions, is an integral part of the four central pillars of a successful region's economic policy, as this paper is intended to show. But first let us take a closer look at the concepts and applications of benchmarking in general and of international regional benchmarking in particular, and at a practical international regional benchmarking project, namely that launched by BAK Basel Economics under the auspices of the IBC BAK International Benchmark Club®

Benchmarking: Concepts and Applications

Benchmarking is a concept borrowed from land surveying. Literally, it means "...a marked point of known or assumed elevation from which other elevations may be established" (Webster's Encyclopedia – Unabridged Dictionary of the English Language, Portland House, New York, 1989).

This definition of benchmarking implies that benchmarking takes place in space and is nothing more than a comparison or positioning in relation to a specific or assumed reference point. Moreover, benchmarking is not necessarily a comparison with the highest (or "best") point, but with the point selected by the person or entity doing the benchmarking.

In the world of business and politics, benchmarking is dynamic rather than static. The position of the determined or assumed reference point will change with time, as will the positions of the points being compared with it. In a socio-economic context, therefore, benchmarking amounts essentially to social learning.

Learning processes are usually triggered when decision makers are put under pressure. It is not surprising, therefore, that benchmarking moved from its original field of land surveying first to the world of business subjected to strong competitive pressures in a functioning market economy.

For example, stock markets evaluate the worth and therefore the performance of listed companies continuously. Benchmarking, i.e. comparing the price of a company's share with its benchmark, e.g. a share price index, is a longstanding practice. Whenever a share's price underperforms in relation to the benchmark, the company's management feels increasing pressure to improve performance. Management then does whatever it can to improve things throughout the organisation – from research and development on through production, procurement, marketing and sales, etc. In doing so, it normally compares all these fields of activity with competitors, i.e. it evaluates specific benchmarks to learn something from them. Thus in business you hear about comparisons with "best in class" and about learning from "best practices".

---

3   Andrew Haughwout & Robert Inman (2002). "Should the Suburbs Help Finance Central City Public Services?", Brookings-Wharton Papers on Urban Affairs, third issue

Paul Cheshire, London School of Economics, & Stefano Magrini, University of Venice(2002): "The Distinctive Determinants of European Urban Growth: does one size fit all?"

The globalisation of markets and business activities has been gaining speed since the beginning of the nineties. The rapid spread of the free-market model since 1989 and the faster pace of progress in information and communication technologies have intensified competition between countries and regions. Regions at all levels have felt rising pressure to offer first-class framework conditions to internationally mobile factors of production such as capital, management and highly qualified manpower. Not only companies, but also the different tiers of government are now operating in an environment marked by stiff competition. So it was only natural for politicians to start using benchmarking, too. Pioneers in this area were the Australian and Netherlands governments[4]. While Australia's benchmarking was restricted to comparing the performance of different national infrastructures, the Dutch also applied benchmarking to labour and capital markets, taxation and education. The main conclusion drawn from this initial use of benchmarking in politics was that world-class positions can be lost when other countries and regions catch up or even pass them even though national performance in the tracked areas may not have declined in absolute terms. This made it clear, among other things, that benchmarking must be applied on a continuous rather than a one-shot basis. This ongoing confrontation with competitors awakens politicians to the fact that self-developed policies are not always the best.

In the latter half of the nineties, the institutions of the European Union also began to take a closer look at benchmarking methods. In particular, the European Union's "Lisbon Strategy" was strongly influenced by the benchmarking approach. Under this strategy, the European Union staked out the goal of becoming, by the year 2010, "the world's most competitive and dynamic economy and one capable of combining sustainable economic growth with more and better jobs as well as greater social cohesion". The implication here is that the European Union is aiming to overtake the current benchmark, the USA, in six years. The Lisbon Strategy is based explicitly on "open methods of coordination and benchmarking".

The methods of benchmarking encompassing information and analyses as an input to develop economic policy strategies have finally reached the regional level as well. Let us take a look at the way this application differs from the national and supranational levels and at the particular areas regional benchmarking is intended to cover.

Specific Aspects of International Regional Benchmarking

Compared with benchmarking at the national level, international regional benchmarking has to bear two specific aspects in mind:

1. As discussed above, regions are much more highly specialised with regard to industries, business sectors and spatially concentrated business functions than are countries, i.e. (larger) nation states. Specialisation can be advantageous for regions. On the other hand, industries and business sectors, or those centred at certain locations, can become technologically and/or economically obsolete. This implies that regions are faced with the challenge of attracting new industries or sectors in timely fashion as old ones show signs of dying out.

2. In contrast to the national level – as noted briefly in the introduction – the territorial borders of regional business activity and governmental authority often do not coincide. Compared with the national level, therefore, there is need for additional

---

4   European Round Table of Industrialists (ERT), Benchmarking for Policy Makers, Brussels 1996

information when it comes to regional comparisons of economic performance and of the politically determined framework conditions if economic and political borders do not coincide.

International regional benchmarking aimed at improving one's own economic growth is characterised by several elements: the selection of competing regions, the two levels of regional benchmarking, namely the comparison of performance on the one hand and the quality of the primarily politically influenced framework conditions affecting it on the other hand, and finally the requirements the regional benchmarking data are expected to meet.

Selection of Competing Regions

There would be little point in trying to compare the region in question with all other possible regions. It makes more sense to restrict comparisons to a specific "league" of regions, i.e. ones that have specialised in the same industries, business sectors and spatial economic functions. Based on the experience gathered by BAK Basel Economics, it is advisable to differentiate between the following groups of regions:

- Metropolitan regions: e.g. Amsterdam, FrankfurtRheinMain, Munich, Vienna, Milano, Lyon, Zürich, etc.

- High-tech regions: e.g. Basel, Karlsruhe, Grenoble, Oxford, etc.

- Regions with strong traditional industries: e.g. Veneto, eastern Austria, Lorraine, Saxony, etc.

- Alpine holiday regions: e.g. Savoie, Haute-Savoie, Valle d'Aosta, Sondrio, Belluno, Grisons, Valais, Tyrol, etc.

- Diversified, less specialised regions with elements of all of the above types of regions: e.g. Bassin Lémanique, south Baden, Franche-Comté, Salzburg, etc.

Other classifications might be possible, i.e. the OECD classification which also includes rural regions.

High-tech regions, in particular, have to compare themselves with regions lying outside Europe. For example, the Basel area, with its specialisation in life sciences, needs to measure up against regions like Massachusetts and New Jersey in the USA.

But the benchmarking interest should not focus only on competing regions in the narrow sense. Comparisons with neighbouring regions are often of interest, too – whether in the region's own country or across national borders.

Data Requirements

In contrast to the benchmarking of national economies, international regional benchmarking calls for more detailed data in terms of industries and business sectors as well as regional differentiation. The following indicators are of paramount importance when it comes to gauging the economic performance of regions: population, gross domestic product, number of employees, man-hours worked, and gross wage costs5 broken down by as many industries and business sectors as possible (40 – 60).

---

5   Also opening the way to the calculation of very important variables such as gross domestic product per capita, labour productivity and unit labour costs.

Unfortunately the official statistics in the EU member countries offer this data for only 8 – 20 industries and sectors, and the individual countries take anywhere from one to three years to publish the data6. To make matters worse, the official data offered at the NUTS3 level (e.g. German Kreise, French Départements, Italian Provinces and Swiss Cantons), which are essential to regional benchmarking especially in the countries of Germany, France and Italy, are even thinner yet. When it comes to elaborating meaningful and comparable indicators of ecological and societal performance at the level of Europe's regions (especially at the NUTS2 and NUTS3 levels), the data situation is not much better. The determination of comparable quantitative indicators of the quality of important location factors for regions in Europe at the NUTS2 and NUTS3 levels also leaves a great deal to be desired.

Regional Benchmarking of Performance and the Quality of Framework Conditions

A region wishing to compare itself with competing regions in order to achieve better regional growth will first of all be interested in a comparison of performance, both in terms of level and growth. Besides economic performance, the comparison should also embrace ecological and societal performance (sustainability benchmarking). But if the performance comparison is to yield conclusions that are useful for policymaking, one also has to gain knowledge about the quality of the factors underlying the region's performance and how it affects growth, productivity, employment, the environment and society at large. Since the early Nineties Europe's regions felt the competition for new businesses intensifying markedly as a result of globalisation. Individual regions needed to keep an eye on what their competitors were doing, so it was not surprising that a number of Swiss cantons and the Swiss Confederation asked BAK Basel Economics, which had had long experience in both dealing with the shortcomings of official statistics and producing international industry analyses and forecasts to establish an international regional benchmarking system. The buildup and current status of this system will be discussed in the following.

An Example of International Regional Benchmarking: The IBC BAK International Benchmark Club®

From 1994 – 1999 BAK focused mainly on the benchmarking needs of the Swiss regions. Because monitoring of the competing regions made it necessary to cover over half of the European Alpine Space (EAS: Baden-Württemberg, Bavaria, Austria, northern Italy, eastern and southeastern France, and Switzerland), BAK Basel Economics decided in 1999 to extend the coverage of the database of the IBC BAK International Benchmark Club® to include all of the EAS's regions at the NUTS2 level and also some of those at the NUTS3 level. This made the benchmarking offering attractive as well for regions outside Switzerland and opened the way for the IBC's first International Forum, which was held in June 2000. The resulting interchange of experience between delegates from regions at the European level substantially strengthened the foundation on which the benchmarking data and analyses rest.

---

6   Because Switzerland does not produce any official regional or cantonal GDP data, BAK Basel Economics has been estimating these figures for a number of years with the methods normally applied in the EU. A majority of the Swiss cantons and the Swiss Confederation make use of this data.

The lifeblood of the IBC's information offering is the database on the economic performance of regions. In autumn 2004 it embraces 46 industries and sectors and 14 sector aggregates in around 300 regions at the NUTS1, NUTS2, and in some cases even the NUTS3 levels. For the following countries it covers all regions at the NUTS1 level and most of the NUTS2 regions (as well as the NUTS3 regions in the European Alpine Space): Belgium, Germany, Luxembourg, Netherlands, Austria and Switzerland. In the cases of Italy and France, the database is restricted so far to northern Italy and to southeastern and eastern France.[7] As noted above, the data for all 46 industries and sectors in the 300 regions include the gross value added at current prices, at constant prices, and on a purchasing power parity basis, the number of people employed, the number of man hours worked, and the gross cost of wages and salaries. Compared with the data available elsewhere, this database is much more detailed in terms of both regions and business sectors, much more comparable both internationally and interregionally, and from one to three years fresher than the official statistics. This makes it possible to pinpoint and analyse the current position of a given region and the way it is changing in relation to competing regions and partner regions, and to do so in great detail in terms of industries and business sectors as well as geographically.

BAK estimates missing data on the basis of the methods used successfully by the EU member countries, at the same time making use of a great deal of data – most of it unpublished – from national statistical offices relating to their respective regions.

Already at the beginning of the nineties, BAK Basel Economics initiated efforts to supplement regional data on economic performance with data on ecological and societal performance in light of the challenge of achieving sustainable development. This groundwork has made it possible to launch the "MARS" project (Monitoring the Alpine Region's Sustainability) under the INTERREG IIIB Alpine Space Programme with 22 project partners from Switzerland, Austria, Germany, France, Italy and Slovenia, which is expected to be completed in 2005. BAK Basel Economics is supported in this project by an alliance of seven other European research institutes, which will contribute mainly to the ecological section.

As already indicated, the benchmarking of regional economic performance in all of its dimensions as well as its effects on the environment and society is only the first step. Regional decision-makers also want to know which determinants underlie regional economic development and which factors attract internationally mobile firms. They would also like to know more about the relative importance as well as the quality of the various location factors at competing locations.

For these reasons, BAK undertook representative company surveys in 1994, 1997 and 1999 on the importance and quality of individual location factors. It surveyed multinational companies headquartered in Switzerland (and in 1997 also ones based in Germany, France and the Netherlands) as well as heavily export-oriented SME's (small and medium-size enterprises) on the assumption that these firms have gathered experience of their own regarding the quality of different location factors at various places. In the first quarter of 2000 another survey was conducted among "location-sensitive" companies that had moved to new regions or had been founded since 1995. This last survey was carried out on a representative basis throughout the entire European Alpine Space. The surveys are of great interest to the representatives of regions,

---

7   The IBC performance Database is expanding further and will cover around 350 regions in 20 European OECD countries and in the United States of America (USA) by the end of 2004.

particularly with regard to the information they reveal about the relative importance highly mobile firms attach to the different location factors.

While the results of these company surveys on the importance of location factors generally seemed quite reasonable, the replies regarding the quality of location factors were apparently influenced more or less heavily by the cultural and psychological background of the people queried. Because this seriously reduced the ability of the company surveys to provide comparable data on the quality of location factors in various regions, BAK Basel Economics decided to start the job of producing hard data on the quality of important location factors within the framework of the IBC.

In the selection of the quantitative indicators of the quality of location factors, BAK was guided by the company surveys on the one hand and on the current status of empirical research in the fields of economic growth and regional economics on the other hand. For development of the concepts and for the acquisition, elaboration and updating of the indicators, BAK sought to enter into cooperation agreements with research institutes with a strong track record in the different technical fields. It proved relatively difficult, in fact, to motivate institutes in Europe to engage in research at the European regional level in their special fields. Many institutes are still oriented entirely to the national level or, when working internationally, do so at the national level only.

The available indicators of economic performance and of the quality of important location factors make it possible for regions to determine readily just where they stand in the current international competition among the regions. The view from the outside which the international regional benchmarking programme enables yields genuine added value. The international and interregional comparisons of the quality of important location factors, in particular, often prompt reevaluation of policy priorities that may have may have evolved on the basis of an inward looking political logic.

The international regional benchmarking offering can be accessed in various forms: Every July, the IBC BAK International Benchmark Club® publishes its yearly report for IBC members. The entire database on economic performance and on the quality of important location factors can be utilised in a variety of electronic forms. The latest results are discussed intensively every year in June at the IBC Forum of delegates from Europe's regions. Of course this Forum also serves as platform for a lively interchange of experience among the regions.

Probably the most important role is played by the IBC at regional benchmark forums, however: here the interested people from the member region take part in the discussion themselves. For these regional benchmark forums, the results are evaluated, presented and discussed with the focus entirely on the specific needs of the region in question.

In autumn 2004, the full and associated members of the IBC BAK International Benchmark Club® include, in addition to the Swiss Confederation and the Republic of Austria, the majority of the Swiss cantons and Austrian Länder as well as a few British, French, German, Italian and Spanish regions.

Table 1.   In 2004, the IBC database includes quantitative indicators of the quality of location factors for the following policy areas

Policy area	IBC location factor module	Indicators	Coverage end of 2004	Partner institutes
Education, science and technology policy	Innovation	Innovation resources: - Expenditure on research and development as percent of regional GDP - Sum of scores of Shang-hai Index of the research quality of the 500 best universities in the World - Part of employment with a tertiary education - Part of employment with secondary education Innovation processes: - Patents - Bibliometric indicators - Company start-ups	140 regions in 21 countries	- isi Fraunhofer Institut, Karlsruhe - Dun & Bradstreet
Fiscal and social policy	Taxation	Tax burden of companies and highly qualified man-power	65 regions in 21 countries	ZEW Zentrum für euro-päische Wirtschaftsfor-schung, Mannheim
Regulatory policies	Regulations	OECD Regulation Indices for product and labour markets; backward and forward extrapolation with the CATO Indices for Economic Freedom	21 countries	
Transport and infrastructure policy	Accessibility	Indicators of interconti-nental and interregional (European) accessibility	250 regions in 21 countries	Institut für Verkehrs-planung und Transport-systeme IVT of ETH Zürich

By mid 2005, the offering of the IBC BAK International Benchmark Club® is to be expanded as follows:

- In the "Regional Growth Factors Project", the methods of quantitative economic research will be used to test the hypotheses postulated by recent empirical research in the fields of economic growth and regional economics against the IBC data. The quantitative analysis of policy-sensitive growth determinants should help regions to better exploit their growth potential.

- As a consequence of increased division of labour between regions, the adequate positioning of a region in its industrial specialty has become much more important. BAK Basel Economics has therefore started to direct some of its benchmarking efforts to these specific needs: the "Tourism Module", launched in 1998, at present covers 25 Alpine holiday regions and 20 European metropolitan areas and will be extended to include regionally more specific destination levels by mid 2005. "Monitoring Life Sciences Locations" has been started in summer 2004 and will meet the specific benchmarking needs of regions specialised in pharmaceuticals, agrochemicals, gene- and biotechnology as well as medical engineering. First results will be presented by summer 2005. Further industry specific benchmarking modules are envisioned in the fields of investment goods industries and financial services.

At this point, not all the areas that affect regional development are covered adequately in the IBC database. Thus the IBC database is planned to be supplemented in coming development periods with indicators relating to subjects such as political fragmentation and overcentralisation, quality of life, culture and social capital. At the same time, the performance database (economy, environment and society) and the already existing location factor modules will be continuously broadened, deepened and updated, depending on demand by regions. Especially updating is absolutely essential in view of the accelerated pace of reform in various policy areas in different countries and regions. Geographic expansion of the IBC will continue also, depending on demand by regions.

Using International Regional Benchmarking in Regional Policy Making

Finally, let us turn to the contribution international regional benchmarking can make to the central policy elements of a successful region mentioned in the introduction:

1. International regional benchmarking facilitates the development and ongoing review of a vision defining the region's role in a world economy characterised by steadily increasing division of labour. It helps pinpoint those industries and sectors in which the region is clearly successful and which should be built up. Conversely, industries and sectors that are found to be declining in comparison with competing regions confront regional policymakers with a choice: should the decline be accepted as logical structural change within the region's strategic vision, or are the activities in question of sufficient strategic importance to justify furthering them by selectively improving the framework conditions.

2. International regional benchmarking should make it easier to reach a relatively strong consensus on the type and quality of the location factors that will pave the way for dynamic growth in the region. The external view that enables the region to make comparisons with competing regions can help reduce or even eliminate internal differences of opinion on the policies to be pursued.

3. International regional benchmarking and continuous comparison with the competition require a collective readiness to keep on learning at all levels. It helps if changes in the relevant environment of the region, and particularly those in competing regions, are perceived. This improves the region's ability to develop a vision of its own and to put the framework conditions called for by that vision in place with the necessary speed. Finally, it makes monitoring of the effects of the decisions taken that much easier.

4. International regional benchmarking is very suitable for highlighting the deficits that occur when the regional economic space is not matched by adequate political authority for defining the framework conditions of the regional economy. This is done by means of comparisons with regions that are not saddled with this sort of mismatching. Thus regional benchmarking supports the regions in question

   – in the articulation and organisation of the interests of the civil society, which play an important role in economic regions that possess inadequate policymaking authority

   – in the region's lobbying efforts to obtain a larger slice of the resource "pie", either from the central government and/or from the various decision-makers in politically fragmented economic regions

   – and finally in providing arguments in favour of transferring authority from the central government or, in the case of fragmented economic regions, from the smaller political units.

The Spatial Monitoring System of the German Federal Office for Building and Regional Planning (BBR) as a Tool for Political Counselling – From the Measurement of the Equality of Living Conditions to the Measurement of Sustainable Development

Wendelin Strubelt

Vice President and Professor, Federal Office for Building and Regional Planning, Germany

Introductory remarks[1]

According to the federal system of Germany, the Federal level is not in charge of the current planning and running of urban and regional affairs. However, according to the fundamental law (the German constitution), the federal level has a duty to observe the spatial development of Germany in regard to the fulfilment of the overall aim of the equality of living conditions. In order to deliver information and judgment about the fulfilment of this requirement, the Federal Government uses the tool of a spatial monitoring system, which is the basis of Federal reports about the spatial situation of Germany as well. In the beginning of the Federal Republic, the measurement of the equality of living conditions was mostly focussed on a difference in urban and rural areas. This changed considerably when it became apparent that the differences between urban and rural regions were overruled by growing differences and disparities between the urban regions in old industrialised regions and those in still booming areas.[2] Normally, the measurement of these disparities was done by judging if one region was below or above the national average. In addition, it was used as a tool to set limits for the subsidies which were supplied by programmes of regional development - a procedure comparable to the proceedings of the European Union and their regional Structural Funds. Beyond the internal discussion of such programmes and their effects on regional and urban development in the public, the considerations about the measurement of the equality of living conditions were more internal than public. This changed considerably when after the unification of Germany, the "normal" regional differences, which could be observed between urban areas and very peripheral rural areas on the hand (the traditional regional cleavages) and between old industrialised areas and booming urban areas on the other hand (the so-called south-north decline) was overruled by the differences between the East and the West of Germany. While the differences within the old Federal Republic were mostly due to different dynamics of regional development, to some part due to structural changes caused by the effects of globalisation, East Germany after unification

---

1   All maps and charts included in this paper are protected by copyright. All rights reserved. They belong to the Bundesamt für Bauwesen und Raumordnung, Bonn Germany.

2   Cf. Strubelt, Wendelin, Gleichwertigkeit der Lebensverhältnisse als Element der sozialen Integration. In: Kecskes, Robert et al.(eds.), Angewandte Soziologie. Wiesbaden 2004, p.247-285.

was heavily affected by transformation processes on account of the complete collapse of the centrally directed economy and the difficulties connected with the creation of a market economy, that means the abrupt adjustment of the regions of the former GDR caused by a process of deindustrialisation and a complete structural change in the rural areas. This resulted in a new wave of thoughts about regional disparities. Under the promise of the Federal Government that these differences soon would disappear and the recovery of these regions would form flourishing landscapes while the effects of these processes still were being desperately awaited, they were suddenly intensively discussed when at the end of 2004 the president of the Republic, the economist Köhler, stressed the point that those regional differences will continue and that these differences cannot be balanced by subsidies. This remark raised public discussions because it was misunderstood as a statement against the so-called equality of living conditions as an overall policy orientation. In the public discussion, this was in some areas and by some people understood as a statement of continuing and future benign neglect for regions in the East which fell behind others and as the open conviction of the politicians that nothing really can be done. Nobody really looked carefully at the figures and their regional distribution. Nobody asked in detail how the quality of living conditions could be measured and judged. This highlighted the fact that there is a big gap between the consideration of such overall targets and current documents about disparities or equalities. The problem is that for experts and those who are in charge of regional policies and regional development the facts are quite well known but that there is no general public discussion about the consequences of such constellations (disparities or cohesion), just some sort of public amalgam consisting of aspirations and convictions – some strange mixed constellation of frustration, helplessness and public complaining (in German: Jammern). In the context of the former GDR, this is more complicated because a lot of people living there have the orientation that the state, not them, has to offer solutions. If these solutions offered do not meet their aims then the state or the government will be blamed, sometimes even accompanied by very negative voting results favouring the protest parties on the left and/or on the right side of the political spectrum. One possibility to solve this problem is to publish and to inform about the living conditions more openly. And the fact that some publication by a private agency, which pinpointed quite frankly at the differences of living conditions in Germany and which dared to rank these living conditions made quite clear what important impact on the public discussion this can have as well. However, in this context public discussion only means a discussion of about a week in the newspapers, some radio and TV stations but then it disappears and as far as I know does not have any permanent impact. Taking this into consideration we have to take for granted that we need more of such public discussions on the one hand. On the other hand, in relation to the incompletion of empirical data and information we have to think about how the information about regional and urban living conditions can be concentrated in a way that this information is more open to and in the public than we can find it now in documents of different governmental levels.

Taking into consideration what a deep impact the evaluation of the educational system of the Federal Republic of Germany by the OECD had on the public discussion and on the discussions of many people with kids in Germany, the question will arise if there is a possibility of the OECD to compare living conditions not only in regard to education but also in regard to other important sectors in an international context. In my opinion, this comparison could deliver more detailed information based on common insights and professional advice in order to raise the question if the solutions of the regional, state or Federal Government for the development of the spatial conditions in order to raise the equality of living conditions have improved or worsened. Within the context of regions, states or nations, there should be conditions to measure such living conditions. In the following, I would like to present some facts and figures about the way how my institute has developed a spatial monitoring system since the beginning of the seventies to the status of now, at the beginning of a new century.

This system is based on data which have for a long time been regionally collected by the different official statistical offices. Due to the fact that the Federal level does not have any direct influence on urban and regional affairs, there was a lack of standard indicators to compare urban and regional development. The Federal Research Institute for Regional Geography and Regional Planning (a predecessor of our office) started the process of development of such an indicator system by systematically collecting data acquired from the different statistical offices of the German Federal states (Länder) and by persuading these agencies to develop a common system of regional indicators. Little by little, this led to the development of a system of statistical data leading to the idea and existence of an urban and regional monitoring system. The idea behind the construction of this system was not to develop a system of all the indicators which could be thought and wished for. We rather started the other way around by using the existent statistical data in order to develop a system of indicators to be collected and to be enlarged overtime and which should cover the whole country. In this way, a lot of data had to be excluded because they were not annually collected or only covering parts of the country. Therefore, the system is not yet complete as we have thought of. However, we have observed a lot of systems following brilliant theoretical constructions which clashed or failed because their aspirations did not meet the statistical reality. In this way, I would like to present you now some ideas about the system we have developed and some products of the system which will allow you to judge if it is also worth to be discussed in an international context.[3]

Remarks concerning the East-West differences in Germany

Let me start with some facts and figures about the greatest disparities in regard to the equality of living conditions we can observe now in the context of Germany. If we look at the **map** of the distribution of **unemployment** all over Germany, it is more than evident that the general structure of these disparities is characterised by the East-West differentiation. Not only this differentiation can be observed but, as I said before, the differentiation between the north and the south of West Germany as well. This is not the only possibility to measure such disparities. There are others as well. Some are concerned with the measurement of **purchasing power** and some are more generally concerned with the **migration** of people. In this way, we can also see that in West Germany the population is still continuously growing while the East is typified by areas which people tend to leave. This does not only go in regard to the actual migration by now but also in regard to **the prognosis** we have done about the future population development. In some way all these figures typify the growing disparities within Germany on the one hand. On the other hand, if we look more closely at the **population development of different towns** for instance, we can see that, beyond the overall picture of growth and shrinking showing the differences between East and West, we also have shrinking towns and communes in the West. They are in some way distributed all over Germany which leads to the general conclusion that the times when we could say that for instance the rural

---

3   Bundesamt für Bauwesen und Raumordnung (ed.), Aktuelle Daten zur Entwicklung der Städte, Kreise und Gemeinden. Ausgabe 2003. Berichte Band 17. Bonn 2004. Print edition and CD-ROM. Cf. also www.bbr.bund.de.

areas were the losing areas and the urban areas were the winning areas are gone. Every region has to be looked at individually, but on the other hand it has to be compared with other towns or regions in order to get a clearer analytical picture about what is going on – referring to its very case. In this way, our endeavour to discover disparities or homogeneities is a powerful tool to pinpoint a development and its possible explanations.

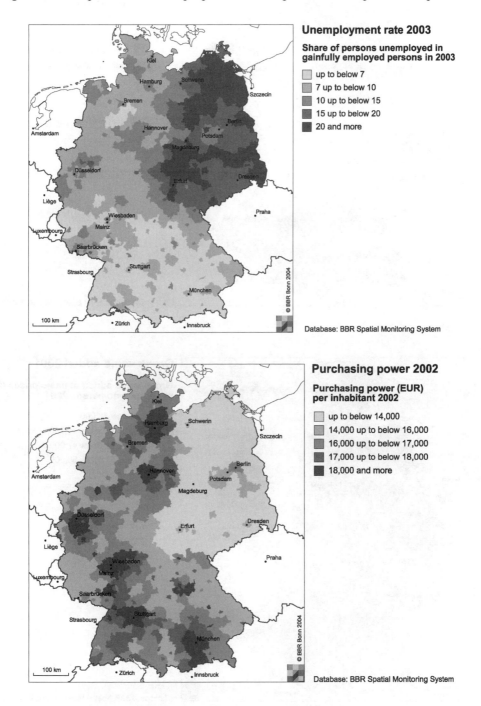

Unemployment rate 2003

Share of persons unemployed in gainfully employed persons in 2003

- up to below 7
- 7 up to below 10
- 10 up to below 15
- 15 up to below 20
- 20 and more

Database: BBR Spatial Monitoring System

Purchasing power 2002

Purchasing power (EUR) per inhabitant 2002

- up to below 14,000
- 14,000 up to below 16,000
- 16,000 up to below 17,000
- 17,000 up to below 18,000
- 18,000 and more

Database: BBR Spatial Monitoring System

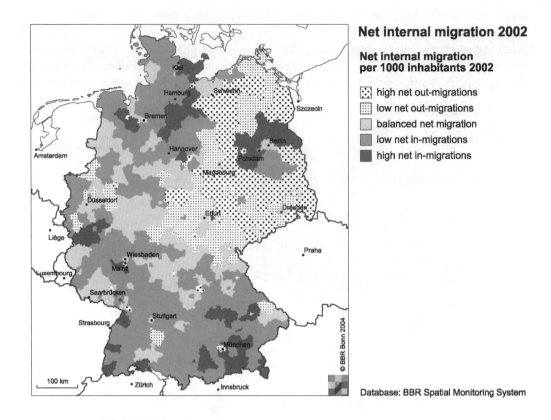

Net internal migration 2002

Net internal migration per 1000 inhabitants 2002

- high net out-migrations
- low net out-migrations
- balanced net migration
- low net in-migrations
- high net in-migrations

Database: BBR Spatial Monitoring System

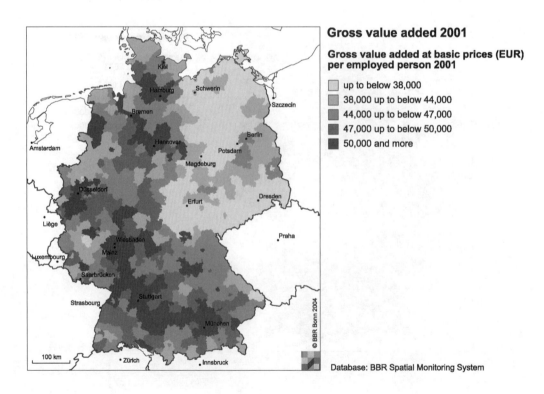

Gross value added 2001

Gross value added at basic prices (EUR) per employed person 2001

- up to below 38,000
- 38,000 up to below 44,000
- 44,000 up to below 47,000
- 47,000 up to below 50,000
- 50,000 and more

Database: BBR Spatial Monitoring System

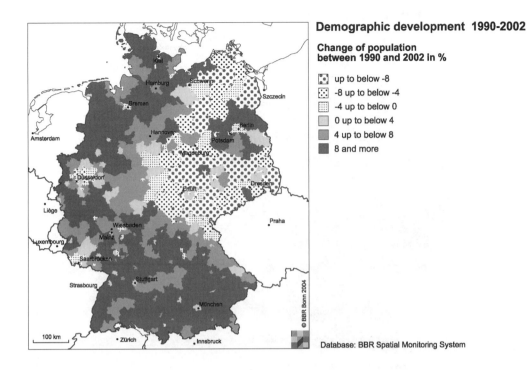

Demographic development 1990-2002

**Change of population
between 1990 and 2002 in %**

- up to below -8
- -8 up to below -4
- -4 up to below 0
- 0 up to below 4
- 4 up to below 8
- 8 and more

Database: BBR Spatial Monitoring System

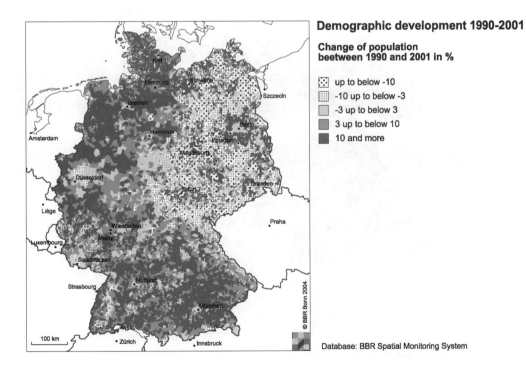

Demographic development 1990-2001

**Change of population
beetween 1990 and 2001 in %**

- up to below -10
- -10 up to below -3
- -3 up to below 3
- 3 up to below 10
- 10 and more

Database: BBR Spatial Monitoring System

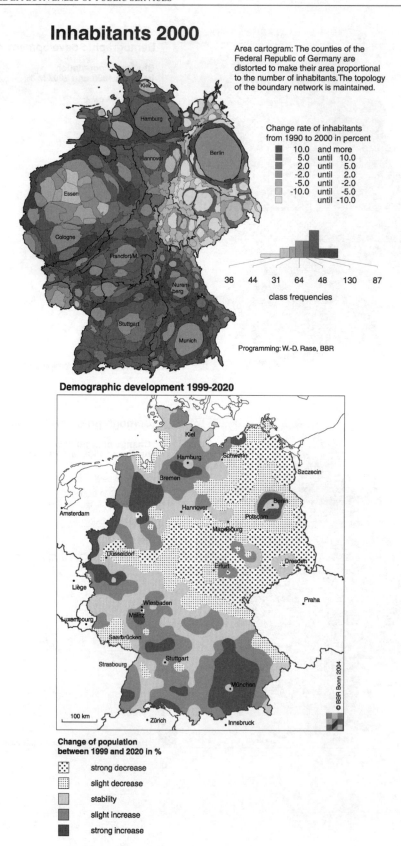

Inhabitants 2000

Area cartogram: The counties of the Federal Republic of Germany are distorted to make their area proportional to the number of inhabitants. The topology of the boundary network is maintained.

Change rate of inhabitants from 1990 to 2000 in percent

- 10.0 and more
- 5.0 until 10.0
- 2.0 until 5.0
- -2.0 until 2.0
- -5.0 until -2.0
- -10.0 until -5.0
- until -10.0

class frequencies

36   44   31   64   48   130   87

Programming: W.-D. Rase, BBR

Demographic development 1999-2020

© BBR Bonn 2004

100 km

Quelle: BBR-Bevölkerungsprognose 2002-2020 / Exp

Change of population between 1999 and 2020 in %

- strong decrease
- slight decrease
- stability
- slight increase
- strong increase

In contrast to these overall pictures of the East-West disparities, which are in some way real challenges for the transformation processes which still have to be tackled, we can also observe a lot of positive signals, which show that the change of East Germany towards an adjustment to the level of living standards of the West is already on the way.

Let's take for instance the case of infrastructure. This is important because infrastructure, as we all know, is a prerequisite for further development into many directions, into the direction of regional development but also into the direction of tourism. In this way, the investment in the traffic infrastructure e.g. is one of those developments which have quite easily been recognised from the outside. Thus, our analysis e.g. of the **accessibility of highways** has shown that it has improved quite considerably, for enterprises and for the population as well. Especially in the Länder of Mecklenburg-Western Pomerania (east of Rostock), Saxony-Anhalt (south of Magdeburg) and Thuringia (south of Erfurt) we can see that the access to the highways is easier and faster than ten years ago. In many regions of these Länder you need today about twenty minutes less to get to the next highway. If you consider that the factor of time is one of high value we can see that the quality of locations in these regions has considerably improved. For all the new Länder we can altogether say that from 1992 to 2003 the percentage of the population who at least needed thirty minutes to get to the next highway access has considerably declined from 20.3 per cent to 10 per cent. This means that for about 1.7 million people living in the new Länder, their access to highways connecting them to the national system of highways has considerably improved. And according to the continuing growth of this infrastructure we expect a continuing improvement of the accessibility for the coming years (until 2015). Accessibility has, of course, also improved in West Germany, but to a quite smaller degree owing to the fact that the highway system in West Germany has been improving for a long time by establishing one of the most efficient highway systems in Europe. However, this also has the result that in the future, Germany will be one of the most intensively used transit countries in Europe.

These two examples might give you some insight into the possibilities of the spatial monitoring system we have developed with so-called objective data, which means with data from official statistics.

In addition to these so-called objective indicators, we have developed so-called subjective indicators. These stem from survey research we conduct annually with standardised questions concerning the social and economic background and with special questions on different aspects we are interested in. Since the unification, we have been doing this survey research covering both East and West Germany. This has given us good insights into the development of the transformation process we can observe in East Germany.[4] As an example, I want to show you the reactions to a survey on the satisfaction **with the condition of buildings** people live in. You can see that in West Germany the level of the judgment that the maintenance is of good standard has been on a relatively high level all over the nineties. But if you look to East Germany you can easily see that the level of satisfaction in the beginning of the nineties, which means immediately after unification, was very low. It was almost half of the amount of percentage points of the West but then it slowly continued to grow and finally it reached almost the level we can observe in the West. So the little difference in regard to the

---

4   Bundesamt für Bauwesen und Raumordnung (ed.), Lebensbedingungen aus Bürgersicht. Berichte Band 15. Bonn 2003.

positive evaluation of the maintenance of houses between East and West shows that high investments in the rehabilitation of the building stock or in new houses had very positive effects. This shows that, as far as possible, not only regarding accessibility but also in regard to the housing stock quite a lot of investments in East Germany had positive impacts which are recognised by the people.

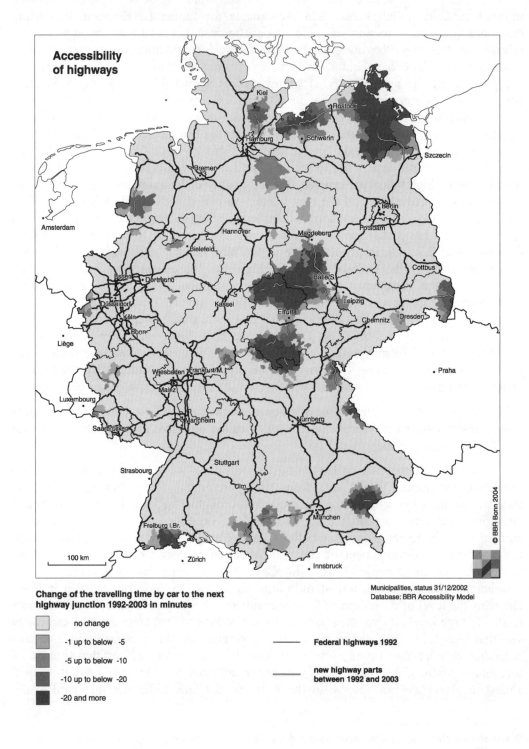

Accessibility of highways

Municipalities, status 31/12/2002
Database: BBR Accessibility Model

© BBR Bonn 2004

Change of the travelling time by car to the next highway junction 1992-2003 in minutes

- no change
- -1 up to below -5
- -5 up to below -10
- -10 up to below -20
- -20 and more

—— Federal highways 1992

—— new highway parts between 1992 and 2003

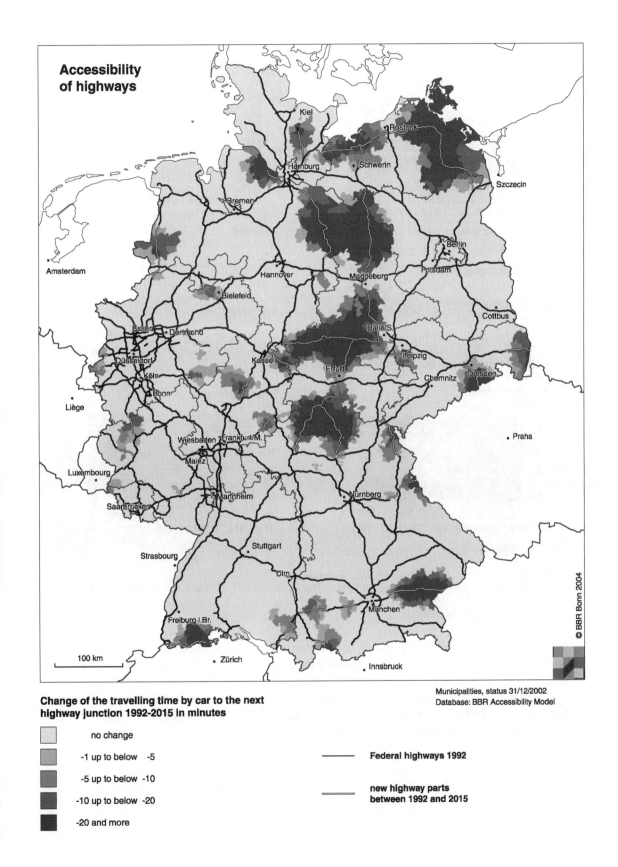

Accessibility of highways

Change of the travelling time by car to the next highway junction 1992-2015 in minutes

- no change
- -1 up to below -5
- -5 up to below -10
- -10 up to below -20
- -20 and more

Municipalities, status 31/12/2002
Database: BBR Accessibility Model

——— Federal highways 1992

——— new highway parts between 1992 and 2015

© BBR Bonn 2004

100 km

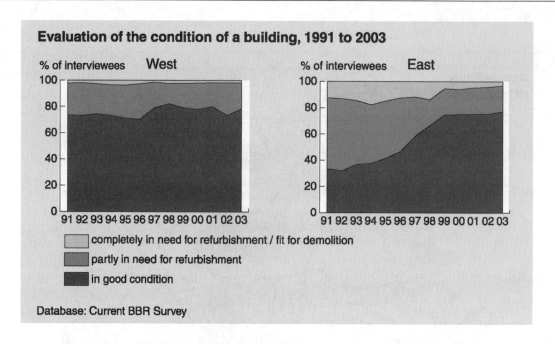

Evaluation of the condition of a building, 1991 to 2003

completely in need for refurbishment / fit for demolition

partly in need for refurbishment

in good condition

Database: Current BBR Survey

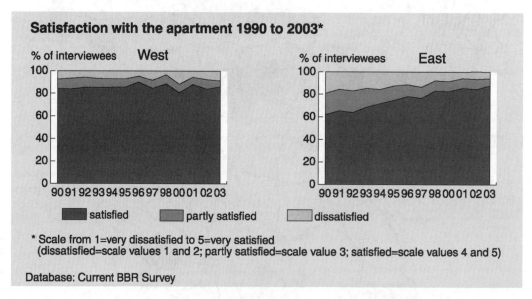

Satisfaction with the apartment 1990 to 2003*

satisfied   partly satisfied   dissatisfied

* Scale from 1=very dissatisfied to 5=very satisfied
(dissatisfied=scale values 1 and 2; partly satisfied=scale value 3; satisfied=scale values 4 and 5)

Database: Current BBR Survey

This can be also seen if you look at another topic of interest, namely the **satisfaction with the apartment**. And another positive development in the East can be observed in regard to the development of the **environmental situation**. If we look e.g. closer to the evaluation of satisfaction with the environment we can see that in West Germany over the nineties about half of the population was satisfied with the environment but in the East in the beginning it was only less than 20 per cent and at the end of the century or the beginning of the new century it had reached almost the level of the West.

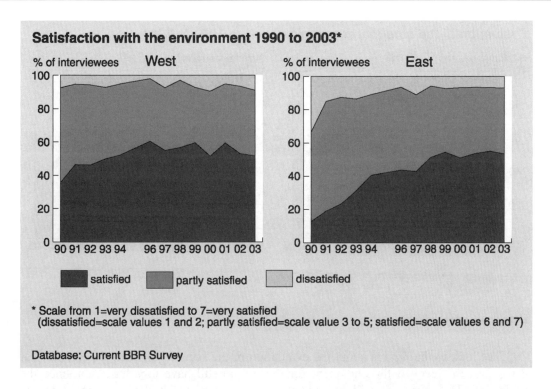

Satisfaction with the environment 1990 to 2003*

satisfied   partly satisfied   dissatisfied

* Scale from 1=very dissatisfied to 7=very satisfied
(dissatisfied=scale values 1 and 2; partly satisfied=scale value 3 to 5; satisfied=scale values 6 and 7)

Database: Current BBR Survey

The other side of the coin is the fact that, measured by official objective statistics, East Germany has an **unemployment rate** which is considerably higher than in the West, as shown on a previous map. However, by looking at our subjective indicators, namely the judgment of the people we asked concerning the evaluation of their **personal economic situation**, we can observe that in 2003 the people evaluate their personal situation much better than they have done in the nineties. That means improvements are at least on the way. At the beginning of the nineties, there were 33 per cent who evaluated their personal economic situation with "good" but this percentage has risen at the end of the nineties to 40 per cent and in 2003 there were about 42 per cent of people in the East who said that their economic situation was quite good in comparison to 47 per cent in the West. Neglecting the regional differentiation we can say that to some degree the equality between East and West has been reached. This information is quite important beyond all day-to-day political discussions reflecting the overall picture of present and pressing complaints.

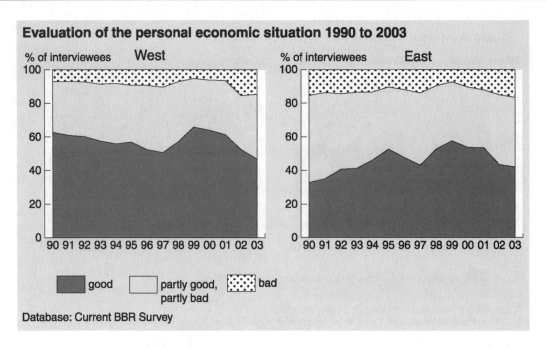

If we look to the figures about the evaluation of the **security of jobs** we can see that in the East the level of this judgment for those who still have jobs has risen since the unification. But there are still considerable differences to the West in regard to the presence of "very secure" jobs. On the other hand we can see that the share of those who evaluate their jobs as "rather secure" is even slightly larger in the East than in the West. Thus, when we look at these figures, we can see that in general the level of satisfaction in the East is in many fields equivalent to that one in the West, even in contrast to the figures from the official statistics, e.g. in regard to unemployment. Additionally, the feelings are much better than those expressed in the public or received and reflected in the mass media. This is quite impressively documented by the fact that the subjective feelings about jobs and job security have improved since the unification started. If we also take the so-called hard facts of infrastructure, improvement and modernisation into account, we can even say that by now in many fields East Germany has at least reached the point of West Germany – contrary to the overall picture of complaints in the mass media.

The fact that there is still some sort of overall dissatisfaction, a landscape of complaints in East Germany by the people living ignores on the one hand that there has been considerable success but on the other hand it reflects the aspirations people have. And there still seems to be a lot of unfulfilled aspirations. But the quarrels and complaints have to be taken seriously. Altogether we can see that the combination of indicators from objective data with those from a subjective background (survey research) allows for substantial analyses about the regional situation or the general situation between East and West.

Thus far I have given my initial arguments in regard to the status and the abilities of the spatial monitoring system within the context of the Federal Office for Building and Regional Planning. In the following, I would like to be a little bit more fundamental that means I want to reason the situation of the monitoring system to give you a little bit more insight and finally I would like to show you the further development of this monitoring system in regard to new approaches in the context of spatial analyses and spatial planning.

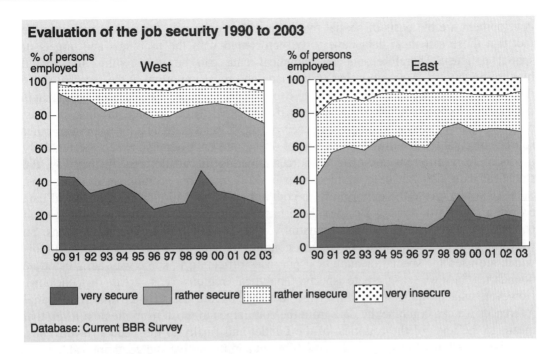

Evaluation of the job security 1990 to 2003

very secure | rather secure | rather insecure | very insecure

Database: Current BBR Survey

The spatial monitoring system of the BBR

Our spatial monitoring system started with the idea that co-ordination as an approach is the central duty of regional planning and regional analysis in the context of a federal system as a system where no central directing actor exists but rather interconnected independent ones. Every actor on one of the different levels has to take the interacting effects of attitudes or positions of those on the other levels into account. This interconnected or intertwined federalism,[5] which includes many aspects of intertwined politics, evidently needs early information about regional disparities and their development in order to develop strategies for action or to influence the regional development which is at disposal. Having such a basic information there is a good chance to discuss and to decide if and where action is needed and which strategy can be used and how this could be co-ordinated and finally to evaluate if the targets were reached. Spatial monitoring as an instrument of information is gifted to take notice of the way in which regional or spatial policy is developing or even if there are some misdevelopments. In this way, spatial monitoring has two sides: on the one hand it can evaluate the success of some politics and on the other hand it can deliver some prognosis about future developments. In this way it may draw the attention to areas where action is needed. With spatial monitoring and its indicators we can combine the discussion of targets with ideas about new programmes and the choice between different strategies to reach improvements in these policy areas. By continuing the monitoring process we can also judge how the targets are reached and if the policy is implemented or how its implementation has to be improved.

The main instrument of spatial monitoring is as already shown indicators based on different sources of regular objective statistics. They are the most important instrument to measure, compare and evaluate spatial development. Statistical data about regional

---

5   Scharpf, Fritz et al., Politikverflechtung. Theorie und Empirie des kooperativen Föderalismus in der Bundesrepublik. 2 vols., Kronberg/Ts. 1976.

development are the basis of spatial monitoring. A prerequisite for such a system is the fact that those statistical data have to be confronted with the problems and targets of spatial policies. Therefore, not all statistical data can be used within the spatial monitoring system. A selection has to be made and most important is the fact that those data covering regional differentiations have to cover the whole area under analysis (that is the national context) and that the statistical data have to be updated in short periods, mostly annually. Besides the data we receive from official statistics, there are also other sources of data about infrastructure, use of space and environment which are regularly produced from different non-official sources covering the whole area. In this way, the statistical data also can be combined with basic data from geographical data systems. Such GIS data create the opportunity to combine geographical data with statistical data covering regions or spaces. Besides these basic geographical data there is the need to connect the statistical data with administrative data (boundaries) of spatial divisions. So we can connect our data with communes, counties or with other territorial (spatial) units which are used for special or analytical purposes reflecting in some way administrative boundaries but we also create special analytical regions (e.g. areas of cohesion). However, what is quite important is the fact that by the use of such different spatial references we can combine the data from the communes to those from the next level, that means to the level of the counties, of the Länder and finally to the Federal level. Thus, there is a possibility to use these data on different administrative and geographical levels.

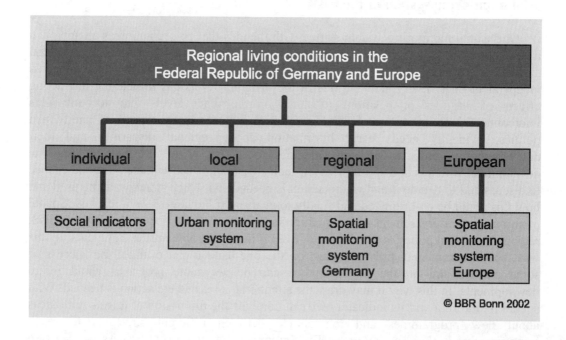

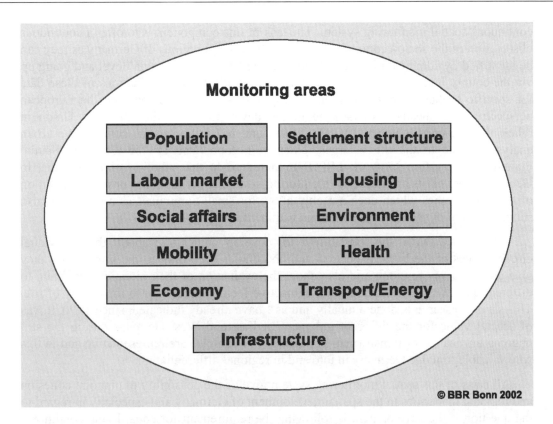

The main tool for the analysis and presentation of the results of spatial monitoring are maps and diagrams. Regional disparities, regional structures and regional interconnections can be made quite visible through such cartographic or graphic design. Therefore, for the presentation and analysis of our data we need quite sophisticated programmes to produce maps and diagrams related to our spatial monitoring system. From the seventies on, we had been developing these tools ourselves. Nowadays, we use software programmes with public access.

Our system, the spatial monitoring system of the BBR, is used by Federal policy-makers in relation to spatial planning. Although it has for a long time been the basis for regular spatial reports,[6] it is now required by law. The spatial law now demands that our agency keeps this sort of spatial monitoring in order to have a continuing flow of data about the current position of spatial development and its change and the consequences of the change over time as a description and as a basis for analysis. But what is most important is the fact that the results of this monitoring system are not kept secret or kept as an administrative arcanum. They are reported to other policy levels and public users as well. That means the standard indicators of our system are not only accessible to administrators or politicians but also accessible to "ordinary" people like researchers, planners, teachers and students, policy-makers on different levels or even businessmen.[7] The chart gives you an overview about the whole spatial monitoring system of the BBR. Generally it is a system of four different interconnected components. The first and the main component was and is the so-called "Laufende Raumbeobachtung"i.e. the

---

6   The last report dates from 2000. Cf. Bundesamt für Bauwesen und Raumordnung (ed.), Raumordnungsbericht 2000. Berichte Band 7. Bonn 2000. Print edition and CD-ROM. The next report will appear this year.

7   This is especially true for the CD-Roms we publish with the essential data of our regional monitoring system.

continuous spatial monitoring system. The task of this component is to offer a continuous observation of the socio-economic living conditions in all regions of Germany as they can be identified by administrative boundaries starting from the communal level and going up via the county level to the state level and allowing different combinations of these data for specific spatial units. In addition, this system is now combined with the European perspective that means with data about the development of the European Union in relation to the units which EUROSTAT uses and in addition to the comparative urban analysis related to the thirty largest cities in Europe (also cf. the European Spatial Planning Observation Network ESPON). In regard to the situation of large cities in Germany there exists an additional monitoring system about the inner-city differentiation of the largest cities which does not only allow for small communes as a target but also subdivisions of or spatial differentiations within cities.

Finally, we have the possibility to develop indicators about the individual circumstances of the lives of persons and households according to the information they give us via survey research and also about the evaluation of their situation according to different questions we ask about their subjective feeling in relation to the quality of life. This survey research is done annually and as I have already indicated, since 1990, it was of special value for the different judgment of East and West Germans during the still ongoing unification or transformation process. The samples are representative and in this way valuable to judge Germany in toto and in regional differentiation.

All parts of this spatial monitoring system give us the possibility to pinpoint cohesion and regional disparities in the spatial development of Germany and especially in regard to the question if the development is following the requirement for equal living conditions. Most important for this spatial monitoring system is the tendency to have an overall picture about spatial development in the Federal Republic of Germany. Its target is not the case study or a very detailed analysis of a local or other special spatial development but it rather has the target to have a tool for comparisons of different regions of Germany in toto. It allows us to describe spatial developments and to analyse the background of such developments by empirical analysis and to lay the foundations for policy actions. This spatial monitoring system thus is a tool which can be used for active spatial policies which must not always be congruent. By showing the development of problematic disparities, politics and special policies we have the chance to take direct influences based on facts. The confrontation between these facts and the effects of policy may have some sort of dialectic relationship between the creation of policies and the analysis of their effects and the facts of figures of urban and regional observation and analysis. Having such a system at hand, it is also the duty of our institute and of the Government to report regularly on these developments. This is done, as already mentioned, by reports about spatial development which are now published every four year. In addition, as I have already said, we publish our data annually. We started twenty years ago by printing them and now we publish them on CD-ROM. All in all we can say that the spatial monitoring system has improved the information we have about different spatial policies on different spatial levels. Today we have very efficient information about regional development which can support the task of different spatial policies on different spatial levels. On account of the fact that there are growing regional disparities and a continuing struggle for different funds to be distributed over the regions and being confronted with diminishing natural resources, the instruments of spatial monitoring may even be more valuable in the future than they have been in the past.

Future perspectives

Having described the possibilities of our spatial monitoring system, especially in regard to the measurement of the equality of living conditions, I do not want to forget to pinpoint at the developmental side of our system which is now going towards the measurement of **sustainable spatial development**. This strategy to develop indicators measuring sustainable development follows again the same approach we have followed in the past. We do not develop an abstract and theoretical system of analysis of sustainable development with all the indicators you can wishfully use and then look for them and finally realise that you cannot find most of them or you find them only covering various specific areas (regions) or only over a very short time, sometimes even discontinuously.[8] We rather tried to use our existing structure to analyse sustainable development with indicators we had at hand or we could develop by looking at the official statistics. This strategy is connected with the national strategy for sustainable development which has been favoured by the Federal Government since 2002. The strategy has a long-term orientation in regard to the economic, social and the ecological development of our country. This orientation towards sustainable development also had a heavy impact on the overall general orientation of spatial development because the general target of sustainable development has now overruled the old orientation of equal living conditions.[9] This was done by including the target of equal living conditions into the context of sustainable development. By creating this new overall general target, our institute has developed a concept of indicators which will tackle the problem of sustainable development.

We have done this by selecting three different dimensions which reflect the targets of sustainable development that means economic competitiveness, social and spatial cohesion (justice) and the protection of the natural resources. When combining these three sides of sustainable development, the so-called magic triangle, we have to pay attention that none of these aims is overruled by the other. Rather the social and economic development has to be evaluated or to be developed in the context of ecological prerequisites.

We have tried to tackle the requirement to analyse the status of sustainable development in the context of spatial development by selecting seventeen indicators.

---

8   Bundesamt für Bauwesen und Raumordnung (ed.), Rio +10: Nachhaltige Siedlungsentwicklung. Reflexionen aus dem BBR. Informationen zur Raumentwicklung, Heft 1 / 2. Bonn 2002.

9   Bundesamt für Bauwesen und Raumordnung (ed.), Rio +10: Nachhaltige Siedlungsentwicklung. Reflexionen aus dem BBR. Informationen zur Raumentwicklung, Heft 1 / 2. Bonn 2002.

Core indicators of sustainable spatial development of the BBR

Target dimension/Target	Indicator
Economic competitiveness	Gross added value Research and development Employees with higher vocational education
Social justice	Income from employment Income from transfer payments Activity rate Female activity rate Unemployment rate School-leavers without completed secondary modern school Foreign pupils at high schools Housing space Municipal debts
Protection of natural resources	Use of new settlement areas Protected areas Energy consumption Domestic waste Rivers and streams with biological quality level II

© BBR Bonn

The first area is **economic competitiveness** measured by three indicators. The first one is economic efficiency, the second the improvement of innovation and the third one is future-oriented qualification.

In relation to **social justice** we have selected indicators measuring the income and the dependence on public transfer money, the percentage of people working, the percentage of women working, the adequate supply of working places, the improvement of education and the improvement of the integration of foreign citizens, the supply of housing and the adequate supply with financial resources for the communes.

With regard to the **protection of natural resources** we have operationalised this by indicators measuring the reduction of the use of space, the protection of species and the economic use of energy, the reduction of waste production and the maintenance of water quality.

If you look closer at the indicators used you can see that we tried to get as close as possible to the target of measuring these different perspectives of sustainable development by using existing statistical data, and by interpreting them as indicators in the intended direction. By using these different indicators, however, we have to take into consideration that by now we do not have an elaborate positive definition of sustainable development pinpointed or concentrated by concrete targets. Our indicators can be used for differentiation in order to evaluate if something has failed or does not exist by now. There are no valid and accepted thresholds for sustainable development. But what we can do is to measure non-sustainable development i.e. we can judge the sustainable spatial development by pinpointing ex negativo at non-sustainable developments. By showing the deficits of sustainable development we can try to have some orientation. But we do not have by now exact perspectives and the deficits in one area do not reflect the deficits in other areas. In addition some deficiencies are compensated in other areas. These methodological approaches mean the measurement of deficits will show in which areas the sustainable development has not proceeded beyond some sort of minimal prerequisites.

I do not want to go into the details of the technologies of measuring these deficits of possible sustainable development but e.g. for the area of economic competitiveness we argue that the development of a region is non-sustainable if it does not reach 75 per cent of the national value in GNP, or in relation to research and development, and to the percentage of working people with higher qualifications.

If you look at the maps which show these deficiencies of sustainability in the dimension of **economic competitiveness**, we can see the dominant role of the agglomeration areas in regard to competitiveness and we also can see the growing deficits if you go from the centre to the periphery, or if you go from the south to the north. Especially in large areas of East Germany, these deficiencies appear quite clearly. If we take all the three indicators together we can see that especially the north of the new Länder, i.e. the former GDR, has clear deficits in all three fields. If we look at the **development** of deficits in economic sustainability we can see that all regions have improved and in some way the regions around the agglomerations more than the agglomeration itself. However, in many regions which are showing now some sort of economic deficiency the differences to the other regions have aggravated in the last years.

Average sustainability deficit of the "economic competitiveness" dimension

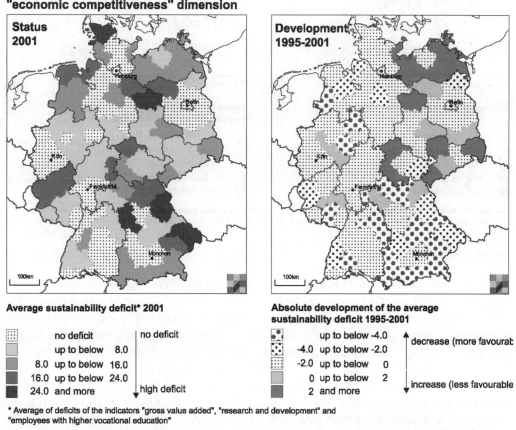

Average sustainability deficit* 2001

⠿	no deficit	no deficit ↑
░	up to below 8.0	
▒	8.0 up to below 16.0	
▓	16.0 up to below 24.0	
■	24.0 and more	high deficit ↓

Absolute development of the average sustainability deficit 1995-2001

●	up to below -4.0	decrease (more favourab ↑
◌	-4.0 up to below -2.0	
⠿	-2.0 up to below 0	
░	0 up to below 2	
■	2 and more	increase (less favourable ↓

* Average of deficits of the indicators "gross value added", "research and development" and "employees with higher vocational education"

Database: BBR Spatial Monitoring System

Spatial planning regions, status: 31/'

If we look at **social and spatial justice** we have also developed some thresholds for the indicators selected. If we look at the maps we can see that in almost all regions there is some deficit, but the largest deficits are situated in the north of the Republic. However, there is some differentiation between the old and the new Länder because in the old Länder and the northern parts there is a large percentage of people depending on social security, a low rate of women working and a low percentage of students going to higher education. In the new Länder, the share of people working is below the average employment and consequently unemployment is higher.

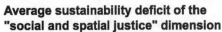

Average sustainability deficit of the "social and spatial justice" dimension

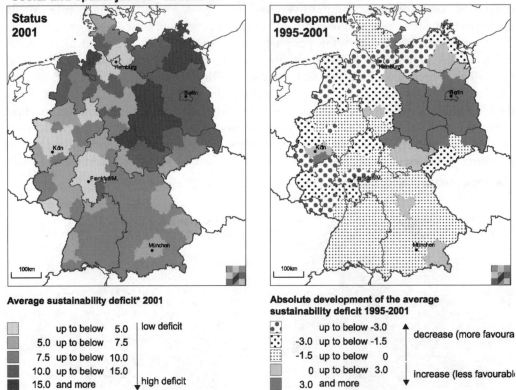

Average sustainability deficit* 2001

	up to below	5.0	low deficit
	5.0 up to below	7.5	
	7.5 up to below	10.0	
	10.0 up to below	15.0	
	15.0 and more		high deficit

Absolute development of the average sustainability deficit 1995-2001

	up to below	-3.0	decrease (more favoura
	-3.0 up to below	-1.5	
	-1.5 up to below	0	
	0 up to below	3.0	increase (less favourabl
	3.0 and more		

* Average of deficits of the indicators "income from employment", "income from transfer payments", "activity rate", "female activity rate", "unemployment rate", "school-leavers without completed secondary modern school", "foreign pupils at high schools", "housing space" and "municipal debts"

Database: BBR Spatial Monitoring System

Spatial planning regions, status: 31/12/20

If we look at the **development** we can see that there has been some general improvement. Almost all regions in West Germany could reduce their social deficit. But this is only a relative success because the share of unemployed people and people dependent on social benefits and the debts of the communes have not increased beyond the national average. However, in the new Länder the deficit of sustainability in regard to the social dimension has risen. This is especially valid for unemployment and to the rising number of people depending on social benefits. Also the share of working women has considerably decreased. Problematic developments have also happened in regard to the share of students graduating with a diploma from school.

In regard to the **third dimension** of sustainability, the **protection of the natural resources**, there is some special evaluation in regard to the new national aim of reducing the land use by 20-30 ha per day while we today have a land use of about a little bit over

100 ha. If we look at the general situation we have to state that by now almost all regions have some sort of deficit in the ecological dimension. The least deficit of the ecological dimension have Baden-Württemberg, Hessen, Rhineland –Palatinate (more or less in South-West Germany) and Thuringia (in the middle of Germany) and parts of Lower Saxony (in North Germany). But the most important factor in the context of the ecological development is land use. If we look at the dimension of **development** we can see that there is a tendency of improvement. Some regions could keep their standard and some could even improve. In general it can be said that the development of the deficits in regard to the ecological dimension is producing a very heterogeneous picture.

Average sustainability deficit of the "protection of natural resources" dimension

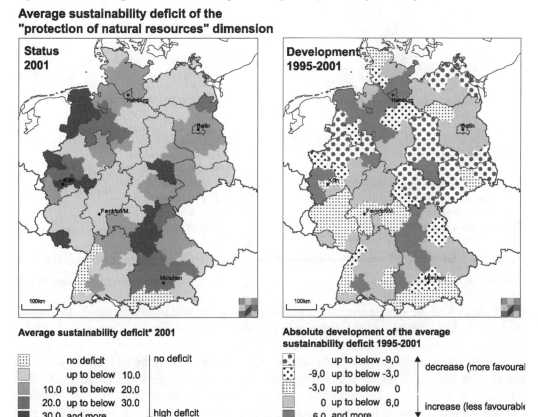

Average sustainability deficit* 2001

:::	no deficit	no deficit
	up to below 10.0	
	10.0 up to below 20.0	
	20.0 up to below 30.0	
	30.0 and more	high deficit

Absolute development of the average sustainability deficit 1995-2001

	up to below -9,0	decrease (more favoural
	-9,0 up to below -3,0	
	-3,0 up to below 0	
	0 up to below 6,0	increase (less favourable
	6,0 and more	

* Average of deficits of the indicators "use of new settlement areas", "protected areas", "energy consumption", "domestic waste" and "rivers and streams with biological quality level II"

Database: BBR Spatial Monitoring System

Spatial planning regions, status: 31/

Finally, let us now take a look at sustainable development with regard to all these three dimensions **(cumulative sustainability deficit)**. Generally we can say that the largest sustainability deficit exists in those places with high deficits in all three dimensions. This is the case especially in East Germany, in some parts of north-west Germany and in some cases also in southern Germany. Regions e.g. with a high share of deficit in the West are dominantly rural areas with a low quality in regard to the environment and with a relatively low share of economic competitiveness. East Germany has a high share in total deficits and in those areas where deficits exist especially in the economic and the ecological dimension. Areas with low deficits are areas from the north to the south right in the middle of Germany. It is interesting to see that some agglomeration areas like Stuttgart or Frankfurt and especially the south-west corner of Germany do not show a big deficit.

Cumulative sustainability deficit

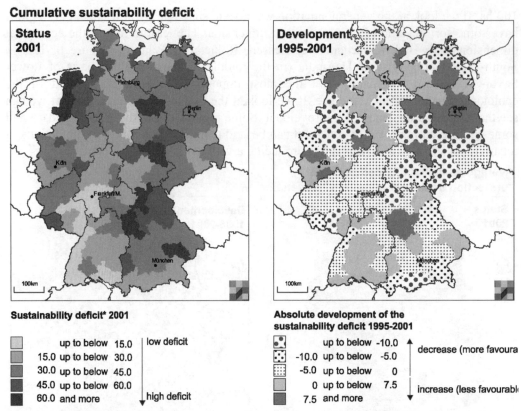

Sustainability deficit* 2001

	up to below	15.0	low deficit
	15.0 up to below	30.0	
	30.0 up to below	45.0	
	45.0 up to below	60.0	
	60.0 and more		high deficit

Absolute development of the sustainability deficit 1995-2001

	up to below	-10.0	decrease (more favoura
	-10.0 up to below	-5.0	
	-5.0 up to below	0	
	0 up to below	7.5	
	7.5 and more		increase (less favourabl

* Sum of average deficits of dimensions "economic competitiveness", "social and spatial justice", and "protection of natural resources"

Database: BBR Spatial Monitoring System

Spatial planning regions, status: 31/12/20(

If we look at the **development** since 1995 we can say that in two thirds of the regions there is a decrease in deficits but there are also other regions with a real increase. However, they include all sorts of regions, meaning regions with a high, low and medium deficit. In other words, a relatively low deficit will not automatically continue in the future. But for every region it is very important to have information about its relative position in relation to sustainable development and in comparison to other regions. Comparing one region to the other creates the possibility to observe its own development track over time. We have visualised this by constructing a cluster or network of deficits and sustainability and these cluster/networks show quite evidently that every region has its own profile of sustainability which can be compared with those of others. If we compare this over time, we can see quite clearly into which direction a region develops. Our spatial monitoring system offers regions some help to look at their own present development and at the development over time in order to understand their own position and development. And by comparing this to other regions this will help them to orient toward directions where they can improve or where they should improve.

If we put all these considerations in relation to sustainable development in regions we can say that there is something to be done politically. We can see that, if we take together economic efficiency, social justice and the economic use of natural resources, agglomerated regions have advantages with regard to disperse settlement structures because there is more efficiency through the concentration of private and public institutions. There is a chance of economies of scale and there is more social justice because the possibilities to keep minimal standards for those who are dependent on social benefits are given. On the other hand, we can see that the use of land and the reduction of traffic in these areas also deliver some sort of protection of natural resources. In general, we can see that one of the main action areas of the Federal Government in regard to the national sustainability strategy and its concrete actions in the area of spatial policy have to do with the sustainable development of settlements. Here the main target will be the reduction of land use.

By constructing and delivering indicators of sustainable development as we try to do, we can open a new field of action for territorial (spatial) policy. These indicators will show individual regions how their policies have improved or how they have failed. In regard to the so-called "Politikverflechtung", that means intertwined politics or federalism, we can say that indicators can help to guide the different levels of spatial duties toward some sort of intertwined optimisation. Beyond these indicators indicating a problem and also evaluating a development, indicators can also help to enlighten the public about the development of a society as comes down to spatial concrete developments. Information as a tool to co-ordinate policies in this important field can be a very powerful one.

Concluding remarks

By giving you an overview about the spatial monitoring system of the Federal Office of Building and Regional Planning with some concrete examples, I hope to have shown you that, beyond any special policy area, we have developed a system of regional indicators in Germany which will help us to better understand the social, economic and natural development we have in our very congested spatial constellation. We know that a lot of influences over those developments are not in our hand. But we also know that if we do not try to tackle and to aim at problem-solving at the local level, in the context of international and national developments, we will not tackle problems at all. But if we know in detail what is going on in our countries, we still need more information what is going on in other ones in order to calibrate our knowledge to European and international standards. We need some comparison beyond our own national spatial system. We need comparison between regions in Germany but we also need comparison within Europe and within the world. At the moment Germany is tackling most of its problems resulting from the transformation of the former GDR into the West German system.[10] But beyond these problems we have the effects of globalisation which have heavy impacts on all regions of Germany. However, this globalisation process also has impacts on other regions in the world and by comparing these different developments especially in regard to sustainable development in its three dimensions we could see at the national and international level into which direction the regional differentiation in the world will go, how it can be measured, how it can be improved, and what we can learn from it. There has been some improvement in the databases of Europe in the context of the European Union. The ESPON (European Spatial Planning Observatory Network) process is very much important for this.[11] On the other hand, we have a clear deficit with indicators e.g. EUROSTAT has been offering by now. I think it should be an important aim to enlarge this international comparison beyond the European scale into the level of the OECD because the problems of these highly developed countries united in this organisation have

---

10   Bundesamt für Bauwesen und Raumordnung (ed.), Regionalbarometer neue Länder. Fünfter zusammenfassender Bericht. Berichte Band 20. Bonn 2004.

11   Bundesamt für Bauwesen und Raumordnung (ed.), Study Programme on European Spatial Planning. Final Report. Forschungen Heft 103.2. Bonn 2001. Print edition and CD-ROM. Cf. also www.espon.lu

an impact, on the one hand general and important for the individual national level, but on the other hand they are regionally differentiated and offer more comparison beyond national borders. By comparing them and following them over time, we can better analyse which factors have impacts, which ones not and what will be the impacts of the future, improvements or non-improvements. I know that the creation of a common database of different national systems is quite difficult. However, having constructed and established a national monitoring-system of regional indicators on the basis of very difficult and not very stable (political and spatial) structures in the context of the German historical development and its federal structure of today, I think, we all could do a better job in the international comparison as well – favouring the understanding of our very national situation and how we are embedded in international developments, between national transformations or reforms and the international globalisation processes.

Planning for the Future

Societal Indicators and Government-wide Reporting in the Government of Canada

Louise Bellefeuille-Prégent, Senior Director and

Tim Wilson, Senior Analyst

Horizontal Results Management, Treasury Board of Canada Secretariat

Abstract

From the perspective of the Government of Canada's management board (the Treasury Board and its Secretariat), key societal indicators can be useful for government-wide analysis. They can be used to achieve a deeper understanding of broad societal trends in order to guide policy and planning, and to provide a context within which government performance can be assessed. The Government's initial explorations of this possibility have led to the production of an annual report, Canada's Performance (http://www.tbs-sct.gc.ca/report/govrev/03/cp-rc_e.asp). The annual report certainly fulfils the latter of these purposes; that is, it provides a context for assessing government performance. However, the explicit link to the planning process is not there yet. This paper outlines the background of the approach to reporting on societal indicators used in the Canada's Performance report as well as possible future directions for this type of reporting in the Government of Canada – namely, the use of societal indicators in conjunction with a government-wide planning process.

The Management Board Perspective

The Treasury Board of Canada is a Committee of Cabinet and manages the Government's financial, personnel, and administrative responsibilities. Considered the general manager and employer of the public service, it sets policy in these areas, examines and approves the proposed spending plans of government departments, and reviews the development of approved programs. The administrative arm of the Treasury Board, the Treasury Board Secretariat (TBS), supports Treasury Board Ministers in fulfilling these roles.

The perspective of the Treasury Board and its Secretariat, then, on key societal indicators is not that of the pure technician or statistician. As the Government's "management board," the Treasury Board of Canada and its Secretariat see reporting on key societal indicators as a primary means of providing a government-wide context for priority planning and for assessing performance. In addition, such reporting is a way in which the Government is accountable to Parliament and to Canadians for the results achieved with the resources allotted.

This paper outlines the experience of the Government of Canada with respect to the use of societal indicators from this management board perspective, that is, for the purposes of government-wide reporting. More particularly, the paper outlines:

- the background of the concept – the roots of the idea of using societal indicators for government-wide reporting in Canada and the objectives this type of reporting is to serve;

- the approach – the steps taken from 1996 to 2001 by the Government of Canada to develop a core set of societal indicators as well as a framework for reporting on those indicators from a government-wide perspective;

- where we are now – the Government of Canada's current vehicle for societal indicator reporting from a government-wide perspective, _Canada's Performance_;[1] and

- possible future directions – the use of societal indicators in conjunction with a government-wide planning process and corresponding report.

Background

Beginning in the mid-1990's, a number of inter-related forces coalesced to form a foundation for societal indicator reporting from a government-wide perspective in the Government of Canada, namely: projects undertaken to "improve reporting to Parliament," the emergence of the Government's commitment to "results-based management," the increasing promotion of and reporting on collaborative or "horizontal" arrangements, and the resurgence of research in "societal or quality of life indicators."

Improved Reporting to Parliament: The Improved Reporting to Parliament Project began in 1994 in collaboration with a parliamentary working group. The objectives of the Project were to improve the Expenditure Management documents supplied to Parliament and to produce and distribute departmental planning and performance information to Parliament and the Canadian public more efficiently and economically, using information technology.

Strengthening accountability to Parliament and to Canadians is a fundamental and on-going commitment of the Government of Canada. Providing Parliament and Canadians with high-quality and timely information about the plans and achievements of the Government "is key to implementing a citizen-focused agenda, since it allows Canadians to engage more effectively in understanding and shaping public policy."[2]

The 2003 and 2004 Budget Speeches re-iterated the Government's commitment to improve its reporting to Parliament. Then, in March 2004, the Government released details of its comprehensive plan to modernize public sector management, entitled Strengthening Public Sector Management: An Overview of the Government Action Plan and Key Initiatives (http://www.tbs-sct.gc.ca/spsm-rgsp/index_e.asp). The plan includes a commitment to improve reporting to Parliament and the public by making it "more timely, clear and useful, based on a 'whole of government' perspective" (p. 19).

These ongoing commitments to improve reporting and to provide information from a government-wide perspective have led to calls for the use of key societal indicators in government reporting. Parliamentarians, for instance, have pointed out that

---

1   Canada. Treasury Board of Canada, _Canada's Performance 2003_, Ottawa: Queen's Printer, 2003; http://www.tbs-sct.gc.ca/report/govrev/03/cp-rc_e.asp.

2   Canada. Treasury Board of Canada, _Results for Canadians: A Management Framework for the Government of Canada_, Ottawa: Queen's Printer, 2000, p. 31; http://www.tbs-sct.gc.ca/res_can/rc_e.asp.

because the outcomes of government efforts are often "borderless," the performance information from individual departments and agencies can be better interpreted if objective context information is also available. For example, the Thirty-Seventh Report of the Standing Committee on Procedure and House Affairs – *Improved Reporting to Parliament Project – Phase 2:* Moving Forward (June, 2000) describes them as "higher-level performance indicators." According to the report, "societal indicators essentially will provide a bridge linking specific government program and policy objectives to broader societal considerations."[3] In that vein, in 2001 a series of seminars entitled "Measuring Quality of Life: The Use of Societal Outcomes by Parliamentarians" took place, bringing together parliamentarians, senior public servants and members of the policy community. The seminars concluded that societal outcome reporting could more effectively plug parliamentarians and citizens into the policy process, lay the foundation of a better working relationship between parliamentarians and the Public Service and provide a "whole-of-government perspective".[4]

In order for this "higher-level" reporting to be linked to government program and policy objectives, however, public service managers must plan for, monitor and report on the results of their policies and programs. For the Government of Canada, "results-based management" provides the foundation of an improved, comprehensive reporting structure.

Results-based Management: The idea that managers in the public service should manage for results has been around for a long time; it could be said that the Government of Canada started contemplating results-based management as far back as the 1960's with the Glassco Commission study on government organisation and its theme of "letting the managers manage." However, it was during the mid-1990's that the concept started to gain real momentum in Canada – an era in which Canadian governments were faced with budgetary deficits and the public service was called upon to do more with less.

Results-based management is enshrined in the Government of Canada's modern management framework, *Results for Canadians*. At the heart of this management framework are commitments to:

- focus on *citizens*, for example, by using the internet and information technology to provide "one-stop access" for government services;

- adopt a clear set of *values* in four areas – democratic, ethical, professional and people values;

- manage for *results*, for example, provide accurate and timely information on the results achieved by government programs and services, learn from experience, and build public confidence; and

- ensure *responsible spending*, both in individual departments and agencies and from a whole-of-government perspective.

While governments have historically focused on inputs, activities and outputs, the Government of Canada committed itself to a modern management agenda that focuses on actual results. In the public service, "results" "are positive changes in the conditions of

---

3   See http://www.parl.gc.ca/InfoComDoc/36/2/HAFF/Studies/Reports/haffrp037-e.html.

4   Bennett, Carolyn, Lenihan, Donald G., Williams, John and Young, William, "Measuring Quality of Life: The Use of Societal Outcomes by Parliamentarians," Ottawa: Centre for Collaborative Government, 2001; http://kta.on.ca/pdf/cg3.pdf.

Canadian society that occur as a consequence – direct or indirect – of public programs. They are aligned with the societal objectives established by the government of the day."[5] Managing for results involves rethinking the "life-cycle" of a program or policy. "It means clearly defining the results to be achieved, delivering the program or service, measuring and evaluating performance and making adjustments to improve both efficiency and effectiveness. It also means reporting on performance in ways that make sense to Canadians."[6]

Reporting in ways that make sense to Canadians means taking a "citizen focus" to reporting. Just as a "citizen focus" in service delivery means moving beyond the traditional, "inside out" approach – beyond the traditional approach of reflecting government organisations more than the needs and priorities of citizens – so too does citizen focused reporting mean providing information on the outcomes of government efforts at a higher level than that of the department or program. This is another reason, then, that reporting on key societal indicators is important. This is also one of the reasons that the Government of Canada has explored ways of planning for, monitoring and reporting on "horizontal" results.

Horizontality: The social and economic outcomes that are measured by key societal indicators and that form the goals of government activity go beyond individual organisations and involve more than one department or jurisdiction, as well as other partners.[7] Since the mid-1990's, there has been an increased concern with the business of getting this horizontal dimension of government right. It is an open question as to whether or not "horizontality" in the public sector is a new phenomenon or not. It could be said that "Canadian governments have been preoccupied since Confederation with the age-old quest for 'coordinated government.'" However, the case can also be made that over the last decade the complexity of the issue, as well as the awareness of the issue, has increased markedly.[8]

The above mentioned focus on results, as part of the "new public management" more generally, has certainly been one of the drivers for this concern with horizontality. Among the other drivers, one would certainly have to cite the commitment to provide seamless, single-window service delivery to Canadians as well as the development of communications technologies, which facilitate the spontaneous generation of policy and program delivery networks.

An important development in the area of intergovernmental collaboration and reporting occurred in February 1999 when the Social Union Framework Agreement (SUFA) (http://socialunion.gc.ca/news/020499_e.html) was signed by the federal government and all provinces and territories except Quebec. The Agreement builds on earlier arrangements and makes the accountability dimension more visible. SUFA accountability provisions commit governments to:

---

5   Canada. Treasury Board of Canada Secretariat, "Rising to the Challenge: A Statement on Results and Results Reporting for Public Service Executives," unpublished paper, November 2004, p. ii.

6   Canada. Treasury Board of Canada, *Results for Canadians: A Management Framework for the Government of Canada*, Ottawa: Queen's Printer, 2000, p. 11.

7   Canada, Treasury Board Secretariat, Getting Government Right: Improving Results Measurement and Accountability: Annual Report to Parliament by the President of the Treasury Board, Ottawa: Queen's Printer, 1996, p. 2.

8   Bakvis, Herman and Luc Juillet, Horizontal Challenge: Line Departments, Central Agencies and Leadership, Canada School of Public Service, 2004, p. 9-16.

- be accountable directly to Canadians – that is, to monitor, measure and report publicly on social policy outcomes; and

- develop joint accountability frameworks for new Canada-wide social initiatives supported by transfers to the provinces and territories.

This definition of intergovernmental accountability relies on citizen engagement in the agenda setting and policy making process. Reporting on societal outcomes, or "quality of life," "can help inform processes for involving citizens in policy making."[9]

Societal Indicator Research: Over the past decade or so, the standard measures of our progress as a society – such as Gross Domestic Product (GDP) per capita – have been challenged as insufficient for fully capturing our "quality of life." The resurgence of societal indicator research is fundamentally tied to this effort to reconceptualize our "quality of life." Within this context, "quality of life" is distinguished from "standard of living" – the latter being generally understood as a quantitative assessment of economic well being solely. "For example, someone may have a high standard of living but be working odd hours, have no job security and suffer from life-threateningly high levels of stress. These will not be reflected in his or her standard of living."[10]

In Canada, the renewed interest in societal indicator research has manifested itself in efforts to develop quality of life frameworks for research and reporting at the community level, at the provincial level as well as the national level.[11] National level research and reporting is not the exclusive domain of the federal government, however. For instance, the Quality of Life Indicator Project led by the Canadian Policy Research Networks, a private non-profit corporation, undertook the task of creating a prototype set of national quality of life indicators, to reflect the range of issues that truly matter to citizens. After engaging citizens in order to determine the appropriate indicators, in 2002 they released the report *Quality of Life in Canada: A Citizen's Report Card*.[12] The difference between efforts such as this by NGOs and those of the Government of Canada can be summed up basically as follows: the former are designed to inform broad policy processes,[13] whereas the efforts of the federal government are designed to link such reporting to priority setting and the assessment of government performance.

Approach

All of these factors – improved reporting to Parliament, results-based management, horizontality and the resurgence of societal indicator research – seemed to align in the mid-1990's and point to a common goal: government-wide reporting on social outcomes and indicators – the "objective being to achieve a deeper and shared

---

9   Canada. Treasury Board of Canada Secretariat. "Quality of Life - A Concept Paper: Defining, Measuring and Reporting Quality of Life for Canadians," 2000, p. 1; http://www.tbs-sct.gc.ca/pubs_pol/dcgpubs/pubsdisc/qol_e.asp.

10   Bennett, Carolyn, Lenihan, Donald G., Williams, John and Young, William, "Measuring Quality of Life: The Use of Societal Outcomes by Parliamentarians," Ottawa: Centre for Collaborative Government, 2001, p. 13; http://kta.on.ca/pdf/cg3.pdf. See also, "Quality of Life – A Concept Paper," p. 3.

11   See Legowski, Barbara, *A Sampling of Community- and Citizen-driven Quality of Life/Societal Indicator Projects*, Ottawa, 2000; http://www.cprn.com/en/doc.cfm?doc=84

12   Canadian Policy Research Networks, http://www.cprn.com/en/doc.cfm?doc=45.

13   Legowski, Barbara, A Sampling of Community- and Citizen-driven Quality of Life/Societal Indicator Projects, Ottawa, Canadian Policy Research Networks, 2000, p. iv.

understanding of broad societal trends to guide policy and planning, and to provide a context within which government performance can be assessed" (*Accounting for Results 1997*, p. 17). This section of the paper outlines the concrete steps taken by the Government of Canada to reach that destination.

Initial Commitment: In 1996, the President of the Treasury Board's annual report to Parliament on the Government's management control and review functions was tabled.[14] That report recognized the confluence of forces described above and highlighted that other jurisdictions were beginning to explore the concept of government-wide reporting on societal outcomes and indicators: "Different approaches can be used to identify and report on broad social and economic objectives. Establishing a few core indicators of government performance and regularly measuring and reporting on them is becoming a popular approach in other jurisdictions." The report also highlighted some of the benefits this approach to reporting seems to provide, namely:

- A single, comprehensive perspective on the most important information that shapes the government's priorities and decisions;

- A stable and more strategic vision of the government's objectives;

- A persuasive context to show the links between programs, which encourages greater cooperation within and among departments and agencies; and

- A more open and disciplined approach to showing the value of policies and programs, which also provides for public involvement beyond consultation on specific issues. (p. 2)

The 1996 President's report committed TBS to "work with Statistics Canada and other departments and agencies to begin to bring together available information and establish a set of core performance indicators from existing and perhaps new data." This commitment involved "examining the experiences and lessons learned in other jurisdictions on items such as: which indicators are most useful; how they should be selected, measured and reported; how to assure the public that the measurement is reliable; how to link the indicators back to the actual programs and initiatives; and how to involve the public" (p. 2-3).

This commitment was reconfirmed in the President's reports of 1997 and 1998.[15] The "Government-wide Performance Indicators Study" that followed from this commitment involved developing a set of cross-cutting indicators that would be useful for policy direction, fostering horizontal approaches and communicating more clearly with Canadians.[16]

Over these years, in addition to the consultations and indicator research described above, the Government of Canada explored the development of "Horizontal Results Frameworks." "Results" frameworks can take a variety of forms and follow a variety of methodologies – i.e., "performance frameworks," "accountability frameworks,"

14 Canada, Treasury Board Secretariat, Getting Government Right: Improving Results Measurement and Accountability: Annual Report to Parliament by the President of the Treasury Board, Ottawa: Queen's Printer, 1996

15 Canada, Treasury Board Secretariat, *Accounting for Results 1997*, Ottawa: Queen's Printer, 1997, (http://dsp-psd.pwgsc.gc.ca/Collection/BT1-10-1997E.pdf); *Managing for Results 1998*, Ottawa: Queen's Printer, 1998.

16 See Ekos Research Associates, "The Use of Social Indicators as Evaluation Instruments," August 1998, p. 19; (http://www11.sdc.gc.ca/en/cs/sp/edd/reports/1998-000391/siei.pdf).

"evaluation" frameworks, "Results-based Management and Accountability" frameworks[17] – but all are basically tools to plan for, monitor and report on the results of government activity. What makes these "horizontal" is that the frameworks account for results, which go beyond the limits of a single department – and so reflect the contributions of other federal departments, other jurisdictions and/or other sectors of the economy.

A Comprehensive Reporting Framework: In 1999, this work on societal indicators and on horizontal results bore fruit in the form of the "Comprehensive Reporting Framework." Basically speaking, this framework calls for a more holistic approach to reporting, consisting of three elements:

- "departmental reporting" on their priorities, plans and achievements – as typically found in their Departmental Reports on Plans and Priorities and in their Departmental Performance Reports;[18]

- "horizontal reporting" on outcomes that go beyond the efforts of any one department, jurisdiction or sector; and

- reporting on "societal indicators."

"The framework suggests that (quality of life) reporting be considered as part of an integrated and comprehensive performance measurement report that would offer Canadians a comprehensive synthesis of performance in areas of interest to citizens – improvement in our quality of life, the achievement of shared societal goals, and the specific results achieved by national programs and services."[19]

The Comprehensive Reporting Framework recognizes that the purpose of each type of reporting is different. That is, reporting on quality of life or societal indicators "is intended to provide information to citizens in a way that can inform broad policy direction and agenda setting. … Reporting on the outcomes achieved on shared societal goals is intended to provide information to citizens in order to engage them, as well as other players such as governments and non-governmental organisations, in the identification and achievement of shared goals. Reporting on departmental program results and service delivery is intended to allow citizens to hold governments accountable, ideally from the perspective of transparency and learning rather than simply to blame or criticize."[20]

Also, the concept of producing a report, which reflected this framework, was considered. It was suggested at this time that the report be modelled on the President's Annual Reports to Parliament: "a (quality of life) report should be a public report rather than an internal report, which could be released by the federal government and perhaps tabled in Parliament, building on the model of the Managing for Results report which is

---

17   See Treasury Board Secretariat, "Guide for the Development of Results-based Management and Accountability Frameworks," (http://www.tbs-sct.gc.ca/eval/pubs/RMAF-CGRR/rmafcgrr_e.asp)

18   Every year, as part of the documentation produced to support the appropriation of funds from Parliament, the government tables two sets of departmental reports in Parliament. In the spring, departments and agencies produce their Reports on Plans and Priorities for the coming fiscal year. In the fall, they provide Parliamentarians with their Departmental Performance Reports indicating achievements attained over the previous fiscal year.

19   "Quality of Life – A Concept Paper," p. 9. The framework was tabled in Parliament in the President's Annual Report, *Managing for Results 1999*.

20   "Quality of Life – A Concept Paper," p. 2.

tabled annually in the fall. The objective of the report would have to be clearly articulated and the linkages between a new initiative on (quality of life) reporting, the existing Departmental Performance Reports, and other reporting commitments of the federal government would have to be clarified."[21]

As a first step to flesh out this framework, the set of societal indicators in the table below were identified by a task force of senior officials and included in *Managing for Results 1999* and *Managing for Results 2000*. Information for each indicator was available on the Web. This information included a definition of the indicator, presented trend analysis in a graphical form, provided some interpretation of the data, and outlined relevant international comparisons, in particular comparable data from the United States where available.

Health, Environment and Public Safety	Economic Opportunity and Participation	Social Participation and Inclusion
• Air/water quality	• Educational attainment	• Measures of racism and discrimination
• Life expectancy	• Literacy rates	• Voter turnout
• Infant mortality	• Employment rates	• Voluntarism
• Health status	• Per capita Gross Domestic Product	• Cultural activity and outputs
• Crime rates	• Discretionary income	
• Violent crime	• Research and development/innovation	

The Question of Accountability: The idea broached with the Comprehensive Reporting Framework that the federal government should report on broad social and economic outcomes in relation to its own department-level plans and performance raises the "question of accountability": can a government be held accountable for societal-level performance?

It was, and is, recognized that single governments could not be held uniquely accountable (in the strictest sense) for the performance of an economy or society: "Given the difficulty in attributing changes in these kinds of indicators to specific government actions, this type of reporting cannot be considered an instrument for holding governments accountable, although some may seek to use it in this way."[22] Despite these issues of "attribution," such reporting is relevant for an analysis of the "contributions" a government makes.[23] Furthermore, while the societal-level goals that are tracked and reported on in the Comprehensive Reporting Framework are beyond what government is solely responsible for (either in terms of what one can attribute as the effects of government action or in terms of the narrowly-defined constitutional obligations of a

---

21   "Quality of Life – A Concept Paper," p. 7.

22   "Quality of Life – A Concept Paper," p. 2.

23   See Mayne, John, "Addressing Attribution through Contribution Analysis: Using Performance Measures Sensibly," Office of the Auditor General, June, 1999; (http://www.oag-bvg.gc.ca/domino/other.nsf/html/99dp1_e.html).

government) they are, nevertheless, areas where government has a significant role (*Managing for Results 1998*, p. 22).

Where We Are Now: *Canada's Performance* Report

Beginning in 2001, TBS took up the suggestion first broached during the construction of the Comprehensive Reporting Framework: to produce a public report, preferably tabled in Parliament, using societal indicators. The first such report is entitled *Canada's Performance 2001*.[24] The President of the Treasury Board tabled it in Parliament on December 6, 2001.

What is it?: *Canada's Performance* is the President of the Treasury Board's annual report to Parliament on government performance – taking the place of the former *Managing for Results* reports – the 2002 and 2003 installments of *Canada's Performance* have been tabled and we plan to table the 2004 version in late November or early December.

The reports provide information on a core set of societal indicators grouped into four themes: economy, health, the environment and communities. Trend information, international comparisons and disaggregations are provided, when applicable, for all of the indicators. This core set of indicators was built on the original sixteen indicators mentioned above. Consultations with departmental and external experts indicated that we needed to make the themes more "user-friendly" than the original three and that we needed to add three indicators: toxic contaminants, biodiversity and physical activity.

The reports also provide information on certain key governmental programs that contribute to improving the quality of life of Canadians. In doing so, the *Canada's Performance* reports contribute to several of the modern management objectives described earlier:

- supporting parliamentarians who require a context for reviewing the results achieved by individual departments and agencies;

- enhancing the government's citizen focus by serving as a vehicle to engage Canadians in discussion of future policy developments;

- advancing results-based management in the federal government and improving the quality of program performance information available to Canadians and parliamentarians over time;

- supporting horizontal management and policy development by providing an overview of the connections between various issues and between the responses to these issues by different departments and agencies; and

- contributing to the transparency of the federal government's plans and achievements, as well as its accountability to Canadians and parliamentarians.

Consultations: After tabling *Canada's Performance 2001*, TBS consulted with Canadians, think tanks, parliamentarians, governments and other partners on the approach adopted in the report. The consultations and engagement strategies focused on such issues

---

24   Canada, Treasury Board Secretariat, *Canada's Performance 2001*, Ottawa: Queen's Printer, 2001, (http://www.tbs-sct.gc.ca/report/govrev/01/cp-rc_e.asp); *Canada's Performance 2002*, Ottawa: Queen's Printer, 2002, (http://www.tbs-sct.gc.ca/report/govrev/02/cp-rc_e.asp); *Canada's Performance 2003*, Ottawa: Queen's Printer, 2003, (http://www.tbs-sct.gc.ca/report/govrev/03/cp-rc_e.asp).

as: selecting indicators that give a more comprehensive view of the economy, health, the environment and communities; presenting information in a manner that best helps Canadians to contribute to the shaping of government policy; using *Canada's Performance* to promote a growing culture of learning about how to manage for and by results, and engaging Canadians in the identification of themes and indicators that reflect their values and the range of issues that matter to them.

Basically speaking, there are three lenses through which to view the indicators in a government-wide report such as this: in terms of government priorities, in terms of the concerns of Canadians and in terms of the accuracy and relevance of the data.[25] More particularly, the consultations described above confirmed the following set of criteria with respect to the indicators and measures selected for inclusion in the report:

- Information must be **relevant**; indicators must reflect Canadian values.

- Information must be **temporal**; data must highlight trends over time and show progress toward goals.

- Information must be **available**; data must be easily accessible.

- Information must be **comparable**; it must be possible to compare with data from other countries.

- Information must be **understandable**; data must be easily grasped by various audiences.

The indicators and approach used in Canada's Performance were also informed by the work of other organisations, such as National Roundtable of the Environment and the Economy (NRTEE) – which was mandated in 2000 to develop a set of national indicators that decision makers could use to track the impact of current economic practices on natural and human assets26 – as well as by the work on comparable health indicators undertaken by the federal, provincial and territorial governments of Canada.27 The Government is still committed to ensuring that we are tracking these types of societal-level outcomes. For instance, for certain priority areas, such as "Cities" and "Aboriginal peoples," the Government is working on developing, tracking and reporting on key indicators of progress.

There are a few other important reporting principles which the *Canada's Performance* reports hold as sacred: balance (presenting both good and bad news), disaggregations to sub-groups or regional data (primarily through the electronic version),[28] and the inclusion of both subjective and objective indicators (for e.g., self-rated health status in addition to life expectancy).[29]

Evolutions: The coverage of the report has expanded over the last couple of years. In 2003, climate change was added, bringing the core set of indicators up to twenty; for

---

25   "Quality of Life – A Concept Paper," p. 6.

26   See the report released in May 2003, *State of the Debate: Environment and Sustainable Development Indicators for Canada*, available at http://www.nrtee.ca/Publications/PDF/Report_Indicators_E.pdf.

27   See the federal report that ensued from this work: *Healthy Canadians: the Latest Indicators from the National Perspective*, available at http://www.hc-sc.gc.ca/iacb-dgiac/arad-draa/english/accountability/indicators.html.

28   "Quality of Life – A Concept Paper," p. 6.

29   "Quality of Life – A Concept Paper," p. 3.

the 2004 version we plan to greatly expand the coverage by adding two whole thematic areas (Aboriginal Peoples and Canada in the World) and bringing the number of core indicators up to thirty-two.

A key development, starting with the 2002 report, has been the construction of a whole-of-government framework to support the societal-level information (see Figure 1). The framework provides a "logic model" for the Government of Canada – mapping the contributions of government programs and departments to "horizontal" (or, "Government of Canada") outcomes and ultimately to the societal-level theme in question, e.g., "Health." If the framework is the logic model, the report itself provides the "performance story." The meat of the framework, so to speak, is provided in the electronic version of the report, which allows the reader to "drill down" to the more specific department- and program-level information provided in the Departmental Reports on Plans and Priorities as well as the Departmental Performance Reports.

Figure 1: The Whole of Government Framework

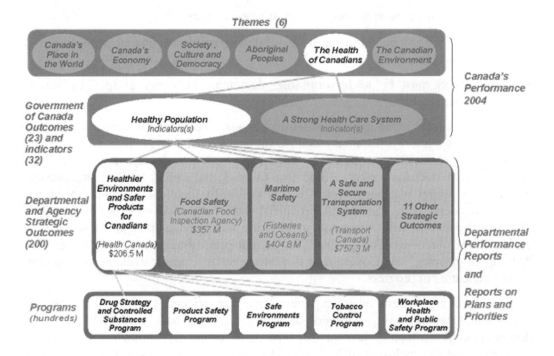

Another key development being planned for this year will be the move to a more rigorous linking of government plans and performance to the societal outcomes and indicators that are tracked – rather than just grouping departments into social issue areas, the 2004 report plans to formulate these areas as "Government of Canada Outcomes" or goals – down the road, these Government Outcomes and indicators could conceivably have targets or benchmarks.

Lessons-learned: Reception on the whole has been good. Public policy experts have been enthusiastic.[30] So too have senior managers in the federal government – who

---

30   See David Zussman, "New tool helps track how our money is spent," April 14, 2003 - Ottawa Citizen; (http://www.ppforum.ca/ow/ow_p_04_14_2003.htm); and CCAF Update: *Canada's Performance 2001*; (http://www.ccaf-fcvi.com/english/documents/canada_performance_2001.pdf).

believe that the "whole-of-government" perspective that the report provides allows them to situate their program or policy in the larger picture. However, there is some room for improvement when it comes to making the report more useful for Parliamentarians; similarly, we need to make the report more well known among Canadians. It could be that the objectives of the report are not always clear to Parliamentarians – since it is purporting to serve many causes. Along these lines, a lesson learned is the importance of targeting a primary audience to ensure a collective perception of the report's purpose. Clearly identifying the primary audience allows us to tailor the information in the report to explicitly meet the objectives of the reader, making the information more meaningful and useful.

Possible Future Directions: Government-wide Planning

During the construction of the Comprehensive Reporting Framework, two general purposes for this type of reporting were discerned: "In particular, the government would need to distinguish between using such reporting to "inform" broad policy processes and making an explicit linkage between QOL reporting and priority setting."[31] As it stands, it is not entirely clear whether *Canada's Performance* is seen as something to "inform" policy or if it is to be rigidly linked to a government-wide planning process. As a result, a possible future direction for the Government of Canada would be to clarify this by making the report more closely aligned with government planning and priority setting.

This move would take place in the context of the current Government's commitment to continually reallocate from low to high priority issues. The links made would have to show, then, how this type of reporting could drive not only priority setting but planning in the context of reallocation – perhaps via its use by Treasury Board and Cabinet Ministers when reviewing allocation and reallocation proposals. A short-term step that could be taken would be to include financials in the report: how much is Canada spending on the environment, or more particularly, on reducing the effects of climate change? This step is also in keeping with the example provided by Alberta's *Measuring Up*, which includes the Alberta Government's Consolidated Financial Statements.

Also, this notion of providing government-wide information on results and spending is enshrined in *Results for Canadians*: in order to "ensure rational priority setting and investment decisions, the government needs integrated, cross-departmental information on expenditures and results." The government-wide view of expenditures and results could serve as a context both for the assessment of the performance of government programming and for the setting of future priorities and plans: "First, it allows decision-makers to assess the integrity of the existing program base. ... Second, the knowledge gained from the broad-based analysis of expenditure supports rational priority setting."[32]

This would also require a formalisation of the government-wide planning process in accordance with the thematic areas (or "Government of Canada Outcome" areas) included in the Canada's Performance framework. One way of formalizing this process would be to pilot interdepartmental planning and budget consultation (at the Deputy Minister level) on one or two of the themes in Canada's Performance.

---

31   "Quality of Life – A Concept Paper," p. 4.

32   Canada. Treasury Board of Canada, *Results for Canadians: A Management Framework for the Government of Canada*, Ottawa: Queen's Printer, 2000, p. 13.

If formalized, this planning process could result in a corresponding government-wide report on plans (*Canada Plans*) – to act as the bookend to the *Canada's Performance* report. In its recently tabled Report on Plans and Priorities, the TBS made public its plan to explore the "development of a whole-of-government planning report that would express the government's targets and provide a clearer basis for reporting on Canada's performance over the medium term."[33]

Conclusion

From the perspective of the Government of Canada's management board, key societal indicators can be useful for government-wide analysis. They can be used to achieve a deeper understanding of broad societal trends in order to guide policy and planning, and to provide a context within which government performance can be assessed. The Government's initial explorations of this possibility have led to the production of an annual report, *Canada's Performance*. The annual report certainly fulfils the latter of these purposes: namely, it provides a context for assessing government performance. However, the explicit link to the planning process is not there yet.

TBS is planning to explore the development of a whole-of-government planning report; that report could complement *Canada's Performance* and could make the link between societal indicator reporting and government-wide planning more explicit. If pursued to its logical end, this report on *Canada's Plans* (along with the existing report on *Canada's Performance*) would be a realisation of the comprehensive reporting framework: with departmental planning and performance information (in the individual departmental reports, accessible through the electronic versions of the government-wide reports), societal-level outcome information (in the annual, government-wide planning and performance reports themselves), and planning and performance reporting around horizontal or "Government of Canada Outcomes." This latter element is the element that still needs the most work. The next step for the Government of Canada in this regard, then, could be to develop a government-wide planning process (that would support the corresponding planning report) based on these Government of Canada Outcomes.

---

33   Canada. Treasury Board of Canada, Secretariat. *2004-05, A Report on Plans and Priorities*, p. 29; (http://www.tbs-sct.gc.ca/est-pre/20042005/TBS-SCT/pdf/TBS-SCT_e.pdf).

Natural Capital: New Measures to Monitor the Economy's Ecological Foundations

Carolyn Cahill

Senior Policy Advisor, National Round Table on the Environment and the Economy, Canada

Abstract

In the 2000 federal budget, Canada's Minister of Finance observed that "we must come to grips with the fact that the current means of measuring progress are inadequate." He then asked the National Round Table on the Environment and the Economy (NRTEE) to develop a set of national indicators that Finance Canada and other decision makers could use to track the impact of current economic practices on the natural and human assets that will be needed by future generations of Canadians.

In May 2003, the NRTEE released the *State of the Debate: Environment and Sustainable Development Indicators for Canada* report[1], which included recommendations in three areas. Specifically, the *State of the Debate Report* recommended:

1. Reporting annually a small set of new, national-level natural and human capital indicators to supplement national macro-economic indicators such as the GDP;

2. Expanding the System of National Accounts to include satellite accounts containing data on all types of capital; and

3. Improving national environmental information systems.

The indicators recommended by the NRTEE illustrate in simple terms some of the key assets that Canadians must maintain to preserve economic options for future generations. That is why they are called indicators of "capital" – they measure the assets necessary to sustain future production. The indicators focus on two types of capital: natural capital and human capital. Natural capital includes land, natural resources, and the services provided by functioning ecosystems. Human capital refers to the knowledge and skills embodied in individuals that facilitate the creation of personal, social and economic well-being.

Five of the selected indicators are linked to ecosystem services that are unvalued in dollar figures, but which nonetheless contribute to the economy. One indicator is linked to human capital.

---

[1] This report can be found on the NRTEE's website: http://www.nrtee-trnee.ca/Publications/PDF/Report_Indicators_E.pdf

The author will describe this indicator initiative, emphasizing the process that was used to develop the indicators. The results of these events, and the challenges encountered throughout the program will also be discussed.

Introduction

Determining whether society is on a desired course requires a measurement system that supplies decision makers with the signals they need to make effective choices. Indicators represent an important part of such a system because they summarize and highlight significant information about complex systems.

Canada's Minister of Finance instigated the Environment and Sustainable Development Indicators (ESDI) Initiative because of widespread agreement in Canada and elsewhere that existing national-level, macroeconomic indicators used to judge a society's success provide only part of the information needed: they exclude many of the factors on which we depend for continued development as a society, particularly the services provided by a clean environment and by our education system. Moreover, macroeconomic indicators emphasize current income rather than wealth, but it is the latter that is the basis for generating income in the future. By neglecting the needs of future generations, macroeconomic indicators ignore the main concern of sustainable development.

In Canada's 2000 budget, the Minister of Finance mandated the Canadian National Round Table on the Environment and the Economy to find ways to track the impact of current economic practices on the natural and human assets that will be needed by future generations of Canadians. Observing that "we must come to grips with the fact that the current means of measuring progress are inadequate," the Minister of Finance stated that the small set of indicators he requested "could well have a greater impact on public policy than any other single measure we might introduce."

An independent federal advisory body, the Round Table identifies issues that have both environmental and economic implications, explores these implications, and attempts to identify actions that will balance economic prosperity with environmental preservation. The Round Table seeks to carry out its mandate by:

- advising federal decision makers and others on the best way to integrate environmental and economic considerations into decision making;

- actively seeking input from stakeholders with a vested interest in any particular issue and providing a neutral meeting ground where they can work to resolve issues and overcome barriers to sustainable development;

- analyzing environmental and economic facts to identify changes that will enhance sustainability in Canada; and

- using the products of research, analysis and national consultation to come to a conclusion on the state of the debate on the issues it examines.

The ESDI Initiative stemmed from the need for national-level indicators and information systems to take better account of those assets that are necessary to sustain a dynamic economy and a healthy society and environment for Canadians. These assets represent the nation's "capital," an economic term first used to designate entities such as buildings and equipment that enable future economic production. The ESDI Initiative's recommendations are based on the notion that other types of capital—such as the environmental assets that provide the "services" that make life possible—are at least as important to the future economy as factories and machinery. To ensure development opportunities for future generations, Canada needs to track and consider all these important types of capital in making economic decisions. Otherwise Canadians risk significantly depleting key human and natural assets without even being aware of it. The Round Table hopes that by expressing the concern for intergenerational equity in terms of "capital," it can provide a link to the economic issues that are the purview of the Minister of Finance.

In addition to the development of a small set of indicators, the Round Table also concluded that, at present, Canada's national information systems do not provide data on the full range of Canada's national capital assets or on the various linkages among environmental, social and economic factors. Canada, like most other countries, relies on various macroeconomic indicators—such as the gross domestic product (GDP)—as well as a System of National Accounts (SNA) to support national-level decision making on economic development. Currently, most economic indicators and the SNA provide little information about natural, human or social capital. As such, they provide only a partial view of the factors that affect development, and they do not account for the true and full costs and benefits of economic decisions. They ignore, for instance, the full cost of paving over fields and burning fossil fuels.

The small set of indicators developed by the Round Table was created to help remedy this asymmetry in the availability of information. It must be noted that these new indicators have been designed to supplement and provide context for macroeconomic indicators such as the GDP, but not to change them.

In addition to developing indicators, the ESDI Initiative's final report also strongly recommended both the improvement and the expansion of data structures on Canada's national capital. Specifically, it proposed that the federal government expand, in a stepwise manner, the System of National Accounts to include new accounts covering natural, human and social capital. It also recommended the investment in improved environmental monitoring and information systems to overcome the paucity of good-quality, national-level information on environmental issues.

A Multistakeholder Process

To guide the ESDI Initiative, the Round Table assembled a 30-member Steering Committee. Members included sustainability indicator experts, non-governmental organisations, academics, government officials, and representatives from business and financial organisations. From the outset, the Round Table collaborated closely with Statistics Canada and Environment Canada to ensure the credibility and applicability of its recommendations and proposed indicators.

Important criteria for selecting the indicators were that they be clear, transparent, as unambiguous as possible, and scientifically credible. Therefore, many different individuals participated in helping to identify and develop the indicators and in commenting on draft recommendations. Included in the indicator selection process were potential audiences for, and users of, these indicators, as well as many experts in indicator development.

The ESDI Initiative unfolded in three phases:

Phase 1 (September 2000 to March 2001) focused on the development of the overall capital model on which to base the indicators. As well, the Round Table convened the first National Conference on Sustainable Development Indicators and a workshop for potential audiences (March 27 and 28, 2001) to review the proposed capital framework.

Phase 2 (April 2001 to June 2002) was devoted to developing suitable indicators. Much of this work was conducted by advisory "cluster groups" of experts, who focused on identifying possible indicators of natural and human capital. From this list of indicators, the ESDI Steering Committee selected a core set of draft indicators and started to develop its recommendations to extend the System of National Accounts.

As well, the Round Table convened a second national conference and workshop for potential audiences (June 19 and 20, 2002) to review the proposed indicators. Following these events, the Steering Committee refined its recommendations.

Phase 3 (July 2002 to March 2003) involved further review of the recommendations, technical refinement of the proposed indicators, and the detailed development of long-term recommendations linked to data collection and reporting.

National Natural and Human Capital Indicators

Supplementing existing economic indicators with the following small set of new indicators will provide Canadians with a more robust picture of the state of our national capital. Like economic indicators, these indicators do not provide the full picture. Rather, they illustrate some important aspects of Canada's natural and human capital.

Air Quality

The National Air Quality Trend Indicator developed within the ESDI Initiative is the first readily available Canadian measure of air quality that weights exposure to a pollutant by population, factoring in the number of people exposed to low-level ozone and the ambient concentrations of ozone in different parts of the country.

Ground-level ozone was chosen for this indicator because of the availability of reliable data linking human health effects to specific concentrations of low-level ozone, and the existence of an extensive ambient concentration time series.

The indicator is not perfect. For instance, problems with respect to data collection and aggregation made it difficult to include other pollutants with significant health impacts, such as fine particulate matter (PM25). However, Environment Canada and Health Canada are currently working on an improved health-risk air quality index, which will inform the methodology for eventual development of a trend indicator based on more than one pollutant.

Freshwater Quality

The Freshwater Quality Indicator provides a national measure of the overall state of water quality in aquatic bodies as measured against major objectives for water use (such as water for drinking, recreation, aquatic life habitat and agriculture).

A preliminary calculation of the indicator provides a first approximation for a national picture of ambient freshwater quality in Canada, indicating that in 2002, approximately 22% of monitored waterways in Canada were classified as "marginal" or "poor".

This indicator is based on aggregated data from existing provincial-level water quality indices, most of which are calculated using a common national methodology developed by the Canadian Council of Ministers of the Environment. Since the national aggregation methodology is new, further work on national consistency (in, for example, data sampling, reporting and assessment), a more extensive monitoring network, and a better aggregation methodology will be necessary.

Greenhouse Gas Emissions

Environment Canada has already developed this indicator to track Canada's total annual emissions of greenhouse gases, including CO_2, CH_4, N_2O, HFCs, PFCs and SF_6. The indicator will report aggregate emissions of all these gases in megatonnes of CO_2 equivalent.

All these gases are linked to global climate change. While a credible indicator directly measuring the impacts of climate change would be ideal, the complex nature of climate change makes the development of such an indicator impossible right now. The proposed Greenhouse Gas Emissions Indicator provides a more indirect gauge of our natural capital by measuring the demand being placed on the atmosphere to accept greenhouse gases.

Forest Cover

Canada's forests represent one of its most valuable natural resource assets because of their production of wood and fibre, as well as their provision of wildlife habitat, recreational opportunities, and mechanisms to clean air and water and sequester carbon. To track changes in the extent of Canada's forests, this indicator will use a combination of satellite remote-sensing data and ground measurements to measure areas of land with a crown closure greater than 10%, a well-accepted threshold that the United Nations defines as constituting a forest. (Crown closure is the percentage of the ground surface that would be covered by a downward vertical projection of the foliage in the crowns of trees. Crown closure is 100% when the forest crown covers all the ground.)

The forest cover indicator represents a new use for existing satellite data and will provide Canada's only regularly updated national indicator of forest cover.

Currently, sufficient data to assess the extent of Canada's forest cover is only available for 1998. That year, Canada was 41% forested, with 392 million hectares of forested land out of a total landmass of 951 million hectares.

The indicator may be refined in the future through higher resolution satellite data, perhaps allowing for the detection and measurement of different types of forest ecosystems and other important factors.

Extent of Wetlands

Wetlands filter and purify water and store large quantities of carbon. They help control floods, reduce erosion and protect shorelines. As well, they indirectly support a range of economic activities such as fishing, farming and recreational activities. Canada is the steward of a large proportion of the world's wetland areas.

Based on satellite remote-sensing data, this indicator will measure the extent of wetlands in Canada as well as the change in this area over time. Because time-series data for all of Canada does not yet exist, this was the only indicator that could not be calculated at the time of the release of the ESDI Initiative's final report. The development of a robust national indicator would take roughly two years. Despite the current lack of data, this indicator has been recommended because of the biological and economic importance of wetlands.

Educational Attainment (Human Capital) Indicator

It has only been in recent decades, with the study of productivity, that the notion of human capital has come to the forefront of economics. As a result, there are no official estimates of human capital in Canada at this time.

Measures of educational attainment are the most commonly used proxies for human capital. This indicator, the only human capital indicator among the six indicators, measures the percentage of the population between the ages of 25 and 64 who have upper-secondary (vocational or apprenticeship training) and tertiary-level (for example, college or university) educational qualifications. This percentage increased from 43% in 1990 to 55% in 2000.

The indicator has limits—it does not, for example, provide information on the quality of human capital being accumulated or lost. But the indicator will reveal our investment trend in an important aspect of human capital—a well-educated workforce—and will help us understand our ability to compete in a global, knowledge-based economy.

An Expanded System of National Accounts

The development of indicators was the ESDI Initiative's primary mandate. However, it soon became clear that these indicators are only as good as the information system from which they are derived. Because of the importance of high-quality data and information, the Round Table strongly recommended the creation of a national information system for capital assets.

The SNA, which has evolved over the past 50 years, serves as the basis for estimating most of our important macroeconomic indicators, including the GDP and the balance of trade. As such, the SNA provides the most widely used framework for structural analysis of the Canadian economy. To provide comprehensive information about Canada's capital assets, the Round Table recommends that the Government of Canada invest in a permanent expansion of its SNA to include explicit measures of natural, human and social capital.

The SNA already provides valuable information to support economic analysis and development decisions. However, there is a clear need to expand the scope of that type of analysis and to base development decisions on a fuller understanding of the long-term implications of current activities. Although it has evolved considerably since it was first published, the SNA continues to focus primarily on market economic activity. It includes, for example, input and output data for about 700 goods and services produced by over 300 types of industries. Currently, however, the SNA excludes data on unpriced natural resource flows into the economic system and unpriced pollutant flows from the economy into the environment. Likewise, the accounts currently include no measures of human or social capital.

Expanding the national accounts will help create a comprehensive, coherent and consistent information system that establishes linkages between environmental, social and economic issues. This will enable measurement of our overall base of capital assets, providing a more complete picture of Canada's total wealth and assisting in policy and decision making. For instance, this information could help clarify the implicit values that we place on such things as clean air. Canadians spend significant amounts of money to prevent, reduce or remediate air (and other) pollution. In doing so, we are attributing an implicit value to the resulting environmental quality. Developing a national information system that would enable us to identify and account for those implicit social valuations will add considerable value to the policy development process.

The following is an outline of the new proposed accounts.

New Natural Capital Accounts

The natural capital information in the System of National Accounts should include:

- natural capital asset stock accounts,

- material and energy flow accounts, and

- environmental protection accounts.

Natural Capital Asset Stock Accounts

The amount and quality of information about natural capital varies considerably. Natural capital can be measured in various ways. The most direct measures are those of the stocks of natural capital assets. Statistics Canada has created basic, if incomplete, accounts for some natural resource stocks (timber, subsoil assets and land) and some land areas, but has very limited information on other natural resource stocks (water and marine resources) and essentially no information about the environmental assets that provide flows of ecosystem services.

The expanded asset accounts will measure quantities of natural capital (natural resources, land and ecosystems) and the annual changes in these stocks due to natural and human processes. These stocks will form the basis for estimates of Canada's natural resource wealth, which could be included in the overall estimate of national wealth in Canada's System of National Accounts to complement traditional measures of produced wealth. The result will be a more complete picture of Canada's total wealth.

Natural capital stock accounts will be closely related to material flow accounts. The annual depletion or harvest of natural resource stocks recorded in physical units in the natural capital stock accounts will represent a portion of the resource flows recorded in the material flow accounts. Also, the integration of both accounts could be used to measure the impact of material use on the stock of "virgin" resources in the environment.

Material and Energy Flow Accounts

Material flow accounts will record, in physical terms, the flows of materials both between the Canadian economy and the "rest of the world," and between the economy and the environment. These flows should include natural resources (e.g. water, energy, minerals), recycled materials (e.g. metals, paper, wood), wastes (e.g. greenhouse gases, solid and liquid wastes) and toxic chemicals (e.g. pesticides, fertilizers). Linking these accounts directly to the economic statistics in the System of National Accounts will provide valuable information about the extent to which the economy places demands on the environment as a source of raw materials and as a sink for waste materials. Moreover, by linking physical measures with data from the input–output accounts based on the industry sector, it should be possible to produce detailed estimates of the resource and waste intensity of various types of economic activities. These intensities will measure the physical quantities of resources (or wastes) used (or produced) per unit of economic activity (a measure of eco-efficiency).

Environmental Protection Accounts

The depletion and degradation of natural capital are recognized as serious problems by society, and a good deal of activity is already devoted to combatting them. Companies spend money to install pollution-control equipment and to clean up the effects of past environmental degradation. Governments invest in treatment plants to reduce the damage done to our lakes and rivers from sewage. Households participate in recycling programs and give money to non-profit organisations with environmental goals.

Most of this activity is already measured in the national accounts, but it is not made explicit. Based on the existing accounts, we cannot say for certain whether environmental protection expenditures are going up or down, or how they are distributed across industries and levels of government. Neither can we say much about the economic growth potential offered by the production of environmental goods and services. Companies making these products want to know whether the demand for them is increasing over time and, if so, where it is originating. Is it mainly businesses that spend money on such products? Or do governments buy a lot of them too? How much of the demand originates in foreign countries and represents an export opportunity for Canadian businesses? The environmental protection accounts will be designed to offer answers to these legitimate and important questions.

Human Capital Accounts

Although Statistics Canada measures many factors associated with human capital, it does not produce official estimates of human capital. The practice of labelling all human development expenditures as (current) consumption misrepresents Canada's overall capital stocks. Saving and investment may be understated, and any analysis of the factors behind economic growth that does not account for investments in education will be incomplete. As human capital is one of the most important assets of a country, it should be included in the national accounts: human development expenditures that have a long-run qualitative and quantitative payoff should be classified as investment and appropriately accumulated into human capital stocks.

Social Capital Accounts

There is an emerging realisation that the formal and informal institutional arrangements, relationships, networks and norms that facilitate collective action are important to a society's ability to function effectively and to the well-being of individuals within that society. Governments trying to promote clean, safe neighbourhoods need well-functioning institutions and a legal system that is respected by citizens. As well, individuals need social networks to feel connected to their community and to have opportunities to express themselves and develop effective interpersonal relationships.

Despite its obvious importance, current understanding of "social capital" is much less advanced than for the other types of capital. Without a clear conceptual understanding of precisely what is meant by social capital, it is not possible to measure or report on it. Nonetheless, work to understand and learn how to measure social capital is accelerating throughout the world. Recent publications by the World Bank and the OECD have highlighted the extensive academic work underway in the United States and Europe in particular. Statistics Canada is conducting research in the area and plans to use the General Social Survey to collect information relevant to social capital.

Reflecting current thinking on this important topic, the ESDI Initiative examined the linkages between human capital and social capital, and developed a capital framework that included a provision for data and indicators on social capital. However, because of the preliminary state of knowledge on this topic, no specific indicators of social capital were developed for short-term use. In order to achieve a system of indicators that provides information on all aspects of Canadian capital assets, it will be important to continue to support this work in the long term, with the objective of incorporating measures of social capital into the expanded System of National Accounts.

A National Wealth Indicator

Over time, the expanded accounts could be used to calculate an expanded estimate of Canada's national wealth, a single measure of the nation's wealth aggregating in one number the full range of capital assets. By increasing the range of capital accounts, this measure would eventually indicate in a theoretically robust fashion whether the nation's capacity to support ongoing development is increasing or decreasing in terms of changes to its overall capital base.

The development of this type of single, aggregated indicator is highly controversial. It raises difficult questions about what types of capital should be monetized, how to estimate the value of non-market assets, and whether it is appropriate to assume that all types of capital are substitutable for one another and can therefore be aggregated into a single overall value.

The Round Table recommends that Canada build on the path-breaking efforts of the World Bank and use an expanded System of National Accounts as the basis on which to work toward the regular publication of an expanded national wealth indicator. As the development of techniques for monetizing non-market assets continues, this national wealth indicator will expand to include a broader range of capital. For the time being, however, the national wealth indicator will be accompanied by additional indicators of natural and human (and, ultimately, social) capital for which monetary estimates are not currently possible or credible.

Improved Environmental Data

Data availability is the third crucial piece of the vision proposed by the ESDI Initiative. The Round Table found the quality of environmental information to be highly varied and its availability patchy. Two problems often emerged. The first was the lack of nationally consistent databases, resulting in little comparability between information collected in different parts of the country and a limited ability to aggregate the data on a countrywide basis.

The second problem was linked to the paucity of relevant time series, with gaps of years existing in the monitoring records of some key environmental quality factors, such as water quality. In other words, few regularly updated national indicators are possible, because of a lack of corresponding information systems.

In this context, progress toward national-level reporting on important types of capital will depend on increased environmental monitoring, as well as improved partnerships among all levels of government and among governmental and non-governmental organisations.

The "State of the Debate"

Most of the Round Table's reports synthesize the results of stakeholder consultations on potential opportunities for sustainable development. One of the unique aspects of the Round Table's work, they not only focus on areas of consensus and recommendations, but also summarize reasons for ongoing disagreement.

This ESDI Initiative's final report was no different. Despite various and inevitable methodological and philosophical disagreements about precisely what and how to measure, most participants agreed that the proposed indicators—of air quality, water quality, greenhouse gas emissions, forest cover, extent of wetlands and educational attainment—all provide important information for Canadians that can be linked to economic activity.

Several important areas of disagreement did arise, however. One of the most contentious issues was whether and how to aggregate information about Canada's overall capital. Much of the discussion here focused on the prospects for developing an aggregated, monetized indicator of the net value of national capital. The benefits of a single, aggregated indicator of national sustainability were weighed against the difficulty of monetizing all types of capital.

More fundamentally, an aggregated indicator is only appropriate if it can be assumed that all types of capital can be substituted for one another and that this is desirable. Because of the controversial nature of this issue, prudence dictates that Canada's information system not assume that all forms of capital are entirely substitutable. Accordingly, the ESDI model includes discrete indicators of some aspects of human and natural capital. The extended SNA will provide the basis both for tracking a broader set of capital assets and for developing an aggregate measure of selected types of capital whose stocks and benefits can be credibly converted to monetary values.

There was widespread support among the participants in the ESDI Initiative for developing indicators based on a capital model to address intergenerational equity issues. Several participants, however, felt strongly that there should have been greater emphasis on measurement of intragenerational equity.

Various participants also argued that the set of ESDI indicators should provide information in addition to that on the state of capital stocks. Because broad indicators such as overall forest cover failed to reveal important qualitative data, some felt strongly that more detailed indicators were required. Also, some program participants recommended including information about the "pressures" faced by the various stocks of natural capital. Some also supported a consumption indicator such as the "ecological footprint." This type of indicator would inform Canadians about the environmental impact, for example, of their driving habits, energy use, consumption patterns, waste production and other types of behaviour.

Putting Recommendations into Action

The Round Table issues the ESDI Initiative's final report in May 2003. Since the Round Table's role is to act in an advisory capacity, it consequently handed the recommendations to the federal government for implementation at that time.

In addition to reporting the indicators on a regular basis and implementing the information system recommendations over the period of time, the Round Table also requested that the Department of Finance take the lead role in using this information for its decision-making.

In February 2004, the federal government's Speech from the Throne noted that "building on recommendations of the National Round Table on the Environment and the Economy, the Government will start incorporating key indicators on clean water, clean air, and emissions reduction into its decision making." The Round Table and its departmental partners continue to work towards promoting the active use of these indicators, the adoption of the three others, and the improvement of information systems.

NOTE: The full report of the ESDI Initiative, titled *Environment and Sustainable Development Indicators for Canada* can be found on the National Round Table on the Environment and the Economy's website (www.nrtee-trnee.ca).

Using Quality of Life Indicators to Inform Policy and Planning: A New Zealand Example

Leigh Gatt

Managing Director Gatt Consulting Ltd

Introduction

The first report on quality of life in urban New Zealand was published in 2001 (Auckland et al., 2001).[1] The report provided the first collection of contemporary social, economic and environmental indicators of conditions in New Zealand's largest urban centres. It provided the first real indication of what effects the previous decade of public policy has had on the well-being of New Zealand's most populated communities. The second report, *Quality of Life in New Zealand's Eight Largest Cities 2003* (North Shore et al., 2003), built on the 2001 report to make a significant contribution to the planning and policy spheres of central and local government. The Quality of Life project used indicators of state to identify key issues to be addressed and then put mechanisms in place to progress those issues. Both the process of developing the indicator programme, and the findings outlined in the report played a critical role in the success of the project.

Key drivers for measurement

Urbanisation and rapid growth

Cities are the economic forces driving growth and development world-wide. "The 21st century will be the century of cities. For the first time, over half the world will live in cities" (Landry, 2001, p. xiii). New Zealand's experience exemplifies this trend, with 46% of the population residing in the eight largest cities. In 2001, out of a New Zealand population of around 3.9 million, the eight largest cities reported a combined population of around 1.8 million. In 2004, four of these cities reported a combined population of around 1.1 million concentrated in a single region - Auckland, which is situated in the north island and is the largest urban region in New Zealand. Over 60% of New Zealand's wealth is generated within the eight cities (Statistics New Zealand 2001). They are also home to some of the nation's most concentrated areas of poverty. The rapid urbanisation in the cities motivated a drive to measure conditions in order to understand the pressures and begin the process of mitigating negative impacts.

Public sector reform

A further driver for measurement was the reform of the public sector. Reform began in New Zealand in 1984 and became known as the "New Zealand Model" (NZ Model). Based primarily on "Public Choice" theory and "Agency" theory, the NZ Model aimed to increase transparency and accountability in the public sector through, among other things, a greater focus on performance measurement (Boston, Martin, Pallot, and Walsh, 1999).

---

1   See www.bigcities.govt.nz

Since that time, measurement has gained momentum, and the understanding of the power of indicators has grown.

Until recently, measurement in the New Zealand public sector was confined to the measurement of inputs and outputs, and focused on efficiency. The New Zealand government is now re-aligning its measurement activity to include outcome measurement and the evaluation of policy impacts. This change is also occurring in local government, with new legislation requiring local authorities to consider and measure their contribution to community outcomes.

Local government legislation

New Zealand has two primary branches of government - central and local government. Local government includes local, regional, territorial and unitary authorities.[2] There are 86 units of local government, comprising: twelve regional councils representing populations of between 32 512 and 1 068 645; fifteen city and fifty-nine district councils, with populations of between 4 040 and 354 532; and four unitary authorities, with populations of between 40 036 and 42 034.[3] These various divisions of local government do not form a hierarchical framework but have a functional relationship.

The Resource Management Act 1991 (RMA) and the Local Government Act 2002 (LGA) are the two pieces of legislation with most influence on local government. The RMA legislates for the management of natural resources, and includes a requirement to report on environmental conditions to monitor sustainable development; and the LGA sets out the role, functions, activities and powers of local government. The LGA requires local authorities to undertake activities that are important to local citizens with the key purposes being:

1. to enable democratic and local decision-making and action by, and on behalf of, communities; and

2. to promote the social, economic, environmental, and cultural well-being of communities, in the present and for the future.

The LGA marks a paradigm shift in the role of local government in New Zealand. The expectation being that the role of local government will broaden considerably and result in greater emphasis on integrated social, economic, environmental and cultural activity. The Act also focuses on citizen choice, accountability, and the effectiveness of local authorities through the quantifiable measurement of community outcomes. Both Acts emphasise monitoring and measurement activity that focuses on understanding the effects of policy and planning on sustainable development and the well-being of citizens. The RMA influenced the establishment of the Quality of Life project, and the LGA reinforced it.

---

2   Hereafter, this paper uses the words local authority and local or city council interchangeably. They are used to encompass all divisions of local government

3   Unitary authorities have both regional and territorial functions.

The Quality of Life project

The report on *Quality of Life in New Zealand's Eight Largest Cities 2003* (North Shore et al., 2003), used fifty-six indicators to assess social, economic, and environmental conditions in these cities. Figure 1 depicts the issues and indicators used in the report.[4]

Figure 1

Health	**Safety**	**People**
Life expectancy	Perceptions of safety	Population growth
Birth weights	Child safety	Ethnicity
Infant mortality	Road casualties	Age
Teenage parents	Crime levels	Families and households
Diseases		
Access to GPs	**Social connectedness**	**Economic standard of living**
Health status	Quality of life	Income
Modifiable risk factors	Diversity	Costs
Mental health and	Community strength and spirit	Household expenditure
emotional well-being	Electronic communication	Social deprivation
Natural environment	**Built environment**	**Economic development**
Waste management and	Look and feel of the	Economic growth
recycling	city	Employment
Biodiversity	Graffiti	Growth in number of
Air quality	City green spaces	businesses
Drinking water quality	Noise pollution	Retail sales
Beach, stream, lake water	Traffic and transport	Building consents
quality	Public transport	Tourism
Knowledge and skills	**Housing**	**Civil and political rights**
Early childhood education	Household tenure	Treaty of Waitangi
School decile ratings	Housing costs and affordability	Involvement in decision
Suspensions - stand downs	Household crowding	making
Qualification levels	Government housing provision	Voter turnout
Community education	Urban housing intensification	Representation

Development processes

Reed (2000) suggests that a rationale or purpose for the choice of indicators is often missing in indicator programmes, and advocates that the purpose should guide the direction of the overall programme. The purpose of the Quality of Life project focused on advocating for quality of life and sustainable development in New Zealand's largest urban centres by applying indicators of social, environmental, and economic conditions (Gatt, 2001). Indicators were used for not only reporting conditions but also for decision-making purposes. This required an approach that would deliver: robust information now and into the future; involve key stakeholders; ensure indicators were linked to key policy-related issues or outcome areas; and enable analysis of independent and interdependent indicators to provide a reasonably holistic assessment of conditions.

---

4   Note that the project makes a distinction between the first category of "People" and other areas – this category was used as contextual information and provided the demographic data against which many other indicators were analysed.

Approach and indicators

Various approaches to structuring the indicators were considered. An issues-based approach was chosen to be consistent with the purpose of the project and the concern about the impact of urbanisation. Issues identified in the report as pertinent to large cities were: health, knowledge and skills, safety, social connectedness, civil and political rights, economic standard of living, economic development, housing, the built environment, and the natural environment (North Shore et al., 2003, p. 10).[5] Identifying issues focused the debate on the concerns expressed by citizens, city councillors and commentators of the day. The approach also meant that indicators were relevant to prevailing policy.

The indicators used tended to be normative and direct. Proxy indicators were used where no direct indicators could be identified. For example, in the natural environment category, where no direct indicators and comparable data were available, a checklist was used to indicate progress toward legislative, national or international standards. The project used composite and aggregated indices sparingly; the economic index of gross domestic product (GDP), and the New Zealand Deprivation Index being examples.[6]

Methods

Indicators were chosen following a stock-take of all the indicators used by the eight local authorities participating in the project. The results of the stock-take were aligned with the identified issues in order to arrive at a broad indicator set. The set was peer reviewed by sector experts, and the views of key stakeholders, such as city council chief executives, were canvassed. The revised indicator set was assessed against agreed criteria to arrive at a final set. These criteria included: relevance to issues and outcomes; measurability; cost effectiveness; validity; comparability; clarity; responsiveness to change; repeatability; ability to be disaggregated (by geographic location, age, sex, ethnicity), and ability to indicate cause and effect (North Shore et al., 2003, p.163). Further research tested the availability of data and a gap analysis identified areas where no data existed. The data were then collected and analysed for reporting.

Data were drawn from both mainstream secondary sources, including government departments and the eight city councils, and primary sources. Primary data were captured through a telephone survey of a representative sample of citizens in each city (4,000 in total across all cities). The survey questions focused on:

- perceptions of own health status and quality of life

- perceptions of air and water pollution, and noise and graffiti as problems in the area

- perceptions of the look and feel of the city

---

5   See also Figure 1.

6   The New Zealand Deprivation Index (Crampton, et al., 2000). (NZDep) uses data from the Census of Population and Dwellings indexed against 9 variables to provide a score of social deprivation in New Zealand. The variables are weighted and are based on the indicators below. The number of people falling within these indicator areas is tallied and a score given, this is then shown on a scale of 1 – 10 to form the index (1: represents areas of least need; 10: represents areas of most need or those experiencing extreme hardship). In this way, zones are identified that require attention. The indicators are: equivalized household income below an income threshold; people aged 18-59 receiving a means tested benefit; people with no access to a private motor vehicle; equivalized household below a bedroom occupancy threshold; people not living in own home; unemployed people aged 18-59; people aged 18-59 without any qualifications; people age <60 yrs living in a single parent family, and people with no access to a telephone.

- perceptions of safety (day and night, at home, in the street, in the town centre)

- perceptions of the affect of increased cultural diversity in the area

- perceptions of neighbourhood strength and spirit

- participation in physical activity and sport

- use of public transport, and perceptions of its affordability, safety and convenience

- understanding and perceptions of city council decision-making, public involvement in this, and the council's effectiveness

Analysis

Trends over time were analysed, along with the relationships between indicators. For example, income levels were linked to housing affordability; unemployment to crime levels; transport use, waste and air pollution to environmental deterioration, and so on. The commentary in the report illustrates the linkages made and the interdependencies of the indicators and issues. This method of analysis allowed key action points and appropriate policy and planning responses to be identified.

The criterion of *disaggregation* had a significant impact on the ability to identify areas for action, and policy and planning responses. Disaggregation by geographical, age, and ethnicity-specific variables allowed issues across and between cities to be highlighted. For example, where monitoring showed a change in crime rates across all cities, disaggregation of the statistics enabled cities where crime rates had changed to be identified, and within these cities affected populations and types of crime to be identified.

Choices in framework and methods

An issues-based approach for the project was selected after considering other approaches, including: goal-based, outcome-based, sector-based, and pressure-state-response based. Discussions on goal-based and outcome-based approaches centred on whether to monitor progress toward existing goals or outcomes, or to monitor and report on current conditions so that new goals or outcomes might be identified from the information gained. As there were no agreed existing goals or outcomes between the eight cities, the second option was chosen. This option avoided a complex and prolonged process of debate to agree goals or outcomes common to all eight cities at the start of the project. The key action points outlined in the report subsequently acted as goals for advocacy purposes.

A sector-based approach aligned to central government policy frameworks to focus on sectors such as health, education, and employment (for example) could have highlighted specific sectoral areas requiring a policy response. The Quality of Life project team supported the view that this approach is not conducive to exploring causal linkages between sectors, and that it is narrower in focus than other approaches (Bennett and James (Eds.), 1999).

The pressure-state-response approach was rejected, as it was difficult to apply to a social and cultural context. Identifying indicators that could be categorised according to whether or not they indicated a pressure on the environment (for example, the social environment), the state or condition of the environment, and the extent of societal responses to pressures, was too complex a process.

When selecting indicators, very little use was made of indices. Extensive use of one-number results, provided by an index, would not have allowed the disaggregation of the findings required for the project. In addition, New Zealand-specific indices were not widely accepted or reliable at the time of the project. Work on indices, as well as composite indicators and the weighting of indicators, is being undertaken for a variety of specific policy areas in New Zealand, and forms the subject of ongoing debate. While this work will improve New Zealand's reporting capability over time, currently there are very few New Zealand-specific composite and aggregate indicators and indices with widespread approval (Patterson, 2002; Statistics New Zealand, 2002).

The method of analysis used by the Quality of Life project to illustrate linkages and interdependencies of indicators and issues was not based on determining cause and effect. A key technical problem with cause-and-effect approaches being the need to balance objective and subjective data to facilitate a more comprehensive source of information, and track how causes are directly attributable to effects (Smith (Ed), 1996). Although a criterion for indicator selection was for indicators to show cause and effect, the issue-based framework adopted by the project was not conducive to this approach. The project overcame this constraint by commenting on research that showed linked sets of factors, rather than suggesting that there were direct cause-and-effect relationships.

Data concerns

Data limitations placed corresponding limitations on the project's ability to contribute to planning and policy. The report (North Shore et al., 2003, p. 163) cites several data issues, such as the availability, consistency and comparability of data. For example, in the environmental section (p. 102) a number of data items were not available, and some indicators lacked standardised data and measures. The costs of research, collection and storage of data, and analysis and reporting of results, also presented a very real barrier for many of the city councils in the project. These factors influenced the final selection of indicators, and so the types of quality of life issues that were analysed and produced for discussion and, as a consequence, the action which informed advocacy on policy and planning.

The concerns about indicators and data described above tend to typify those experienced by other indicator programmes (Barzelay, 2001; Bennett and James (Eds), 1999; Funnell, 1996; Harrision, 1999; Smith (Ed), 1996; United States General Accounting Office, 2003). The following are also seen as commonly experienced concerns (ibid):

- Deciding the issues to be measured
- Selecting the right indicators
- The cost of measurement
- Tracking links between the efforts of an organisation and any change in conditions
- Demonstrating accountability for results.

Inputs to planning and policy

The report suggested action points that emerged from the analysis of results. The action points highlighted specific areas where improvement was sought. They became a set of priority goals, which guided the planning and policy programme for the collective "metro" group of cities when engaging with central government, and their own city councils. The action points in the report are summarised below (North Shore et al., 2003, p. 5).

- The report called for co-ordinated and focused action to plan for growth, manage and minimise waste streams, preserve biodiversity, air and water quality, and increase use of alternatives to private motor vehicles.

- Community safety was reported as having improved in some areas. However, the report called for further work to improve child safety, reduce offending among children and young people, and manage anti-social behaviour.

- The report proposed a strategic approach to manage the impacts of immigration policy, stimulate settlement strategies, facilitate social inclusion, and curb population-based health issues. It also called for action across socio-economic groups, with a focus on housing affordability, health, education and employment.

- Action was called for to promote business and skills, and encourage youth participation in education and training.

- Areas for specific action by city councils were proposed, such as the co-ordination and integration of transport infrastructure, technology for communities, community information, and community engagement and participation in local decision-making.

- A collective approach to monitoring to ensure the availability of data, and alignment of indicators, was also seen as requiring attention.

Benefits of the project

The Quality of Life project has stimulated a partnership between central and local government, with a focus on urban issues. The Prime Minister now meets city mayors to discuss priority issues and action points - these include (Metro Sector Minutes, 2004):

- Transport (especially alternatives to motor vehicles)

- Waste (manage and minimise waste streams)

- Safe communities (reduce offending of young people)

- Settlement (growth and providing support to migrants)

- Economic development (promote business and development that creates sustainable employment)

Several of these priority issues have been incorporated into the government's Sustainable Development Programme of Action (Department of the Prime Minister and Cabinet, 2003).

The project has fostered "joined-up-thinking" by the councils and collaborative activity by the mayors and chief executives. For example, there has been a revitalisation of the Metro Sector group that sits within Local Government New Zealand (the designated voice of local government as a sector). Processes used in the indicator development, reporting, and advocacy phases of the project have promoted a cross-sector, cross-departmental, and across layers-of-government approach to monitoring (for example, a new alliance between the Quality of Life project and the Ministry of Social Development).

The assessment of quality of life in one city depicted against quality of life in other cities has impacted on the planning direction of many of the participating city councils. Both the 2001 and the 2003 Quality of Life project reports illustrated results for each city separately, as well as the cities collectively. Rather than having a negative effect on city councils with below average results, these councils began to adjust their planning in order that results would show improvement in the next round of monitoring. This was a critical success factor in the development of the project; albeit one that was not originally built into the development process.

A further benefit has been the alignment of citizen surveys, survey questions and data sets across participating cities. Indicators and data sets used by the eight cities are beginning to be used by the individual councils in their planning and policy development. The collaborative approach taken in the project has also seen the development of an alliance between the Quality of Life project and the Ministry of Social Development to conduct a New Zealand-wide quality of life survey (in the field in September / October 2004).

The Quality of Life report highlighted the multiple impacts of policies at the local level, and explored links between sectors such as the environment and health. It has also contributed to the debate on sustainability in New Zealand, and placed a focus on urban issues.

Critical success factors

The project's achievements can be attributed as much to the processes of developing the indicator programme, as to applying the findings of measurement. The development of a clear purpose and principles proved to be critical in facilitating the links to planning later in the life of the project. Representatives of the eight city councils initially joined the project with eight different perspectives on the development and application of indicators. The discussion on purpose and principles helped to build trust, a collective view, and consolidate the group. This was the point at which the project direction moved from reporting statistics and indicators showing past conditions, to a report analysing quality of life and proposing key points for future action.

The chief executives of the eight cities participation in the project proved to be a critical success factor in the project's development. The chief executives provided guidance for the project in its decision-making phases, contributed to decisions about the issues to be measured and the choice of indicators. They then sponsored the incorporation of the report findings into planning and action within their own local authorities, and policy advocacy with central government.

The adoption of the project by the elected representatives of the eight city councils also proved to be an important step in ensuring that the councils used the results of measurement and acted on the recommendations in the report. Notwithstanding the administrative logistics and political tensions, the preparation, co-ordination and timing of reports to the various city council's meetings became a necessary pre-curser to stimulating a sense of ownership of the project by the participating councils. This approach and the support of the chief executives helped to gain the sponsorship and commitment of the mayors, and subsequently agreement that the project's findings form a major input to their policy programme. The 2003 report indicates that the mayors had a clear agenda to "work with each other, with (central) government, and with communities to address these issues now and for the future" (North Shore et al., 2003, p. 1). The report also declared that the mayors would continue to use the information contained in the report for planning, and to influence and inform policy decision about urban issues and quality of life in the eight cities.

But has it made a difference?

The Quality of Life project was not designed to assess the effectiveness of specific policy initiatives. Such a purpose would have required an evaluation framework that tracked the links between political decisions, city council performance in the delivery of those decisions, and the impact on communities. The project aimed to highlight areas that required attention. To achieve the sought-after impact in city communities, the project relied on policy makers and planners effecting change. The government's newly established Ministry of Urban Affairs, the Ministry of Social Development's focus on the same issues as the Quality of Life project in its survey work, and each city council's growing awareness of social, economic, and environmental conditions all should have a positive impact on the quality of life of citizens over time.

The project is an example of how to use indicators to plan, prioritise and measure:

- Plan – using indicators to determine gaps

- Prioritise – using research based on indicators to determine what is most important

- Measure – using indicators to see whether the plans and priorities have been effective.

Conclusions

The past four years have seen a significant increase in the use of indicators in New Zealand. Central and local government have both developed indicator programmes that focus on measuring whether policy has 'made a difference' in the public sphere. In New Zealand, the Quality of Life project has led the way in implementing an indicator programme that provides a holistic perspective, and direction for policy improvement. The project has focused on identifying key issues to be addressed, and establishing mechanisms and channels to progress those issues.

The indicators themselves are not the success factor – the indicators are the means, or tools, by which information can be brought into the public domain and into the policy debate. "Creating successful indicators relies far more on focusing on how they are integrated into the processes of urban governance and far less on devising, designing and tweaking particular indicator sets." (Rydin, Holman and Wolff, 2003, p. 558). The Quality of Life project has put this principle into practice.

References

Auckland, Christchurch, Manukau, North Shore, Waitakere, and Wellington City Councils (2001). *Quality of Life in New Zealand's Six Largest Cities*. North Shore, New Zealand: Auckland, Christchurch, Manukau, North Shore, Waitakere, and Wellington City Councils.

Barzelay, M. (2001). The New Public Management: Improving Research and Policy Dialogue, California: University of California Press.

Bennett, M., and James, P. (Eds.). (1999). Sustainable Measures: Evaluation and Reporting of Environmental and Social Performance. Sheffield: Greenleaf Publishing.

Boston, J., Martin, J., Pallot, J., and Walsh, P. (1999). *Public Management – The New Zealand Model*, Auckland: Oxford University Press.

Crampton, P., Salmond, C., Kirkpatrick, R., Scarborough, R., and Skelly, C. (2000). *Degrees of Deprivation in New Zealand: An Atlas of Social-Economic Difference*, Auckland: David Bateman

Department of the Prime Minister and Cabinet (2003). *Sustainable Development for New Zealand: Programme of Action*. Wellington.

Funnell, S. (1996). Reflections on Australian Practices in Performance Measurement 1980-1995, Evaluation Journal of Australia, Vol. 8, No. 1, pp. 36-48.

Gatt, L. (2001). Measuring Sustainable Communities Through Quality of Life Indicators, *Proceeding of the Society of Local Government Managers Conference*, September 2004. Wellington, New Zealand.

Harrison, A. (1999). A Framework for Measuring Sustainable Development, *Proceeding of the Second OECD Expert Workshop*, 2-3 September 1999.

Landry, C. (2001). *The Creative City – A Toolkit for Urban Innovators*, London: Earthscan Publications.

Metro Sector Minutes (2004). Minutes of the Metro Sector of Local Government New Zealand, Wellington: Local Government New Zealand.

North Shore, Waitakere, Auckland, Manukau, Hamilton, Wellington, Christchurch, and Dunedin City Councils (2003). *Quality of Life in New Zealand's Eight Largest Cities 2003*, Auckland, New Zealand: Auckland, North Shore, Waitakere, Auckland, Manukau, Hamilton, Wellington, Christchurch, and Dunedin City Councils.

Patterson, M. (2002). Headline Indicators for Tracking Progress to Sustainability in New Zealand, Technical Paper No. 71 Sustainability, Wellington: Ministry for the Environment.

Reed, P. (2000). *Developing Civic Indicators and Community Accounting in Canada*, Ottawa: Statistics Canada and Carleton University.

Rydin, Y., Holman, N., and Wolff, E. (2003). Local Sustainability Indicators, *Local Environment*, Vol. 8, No. 6, pp. 581–589.

Smith, P. (Ed). (1996). *Measuring Outcomes in the Public Sector*, London: Taylor & Francis.

Statistics New Zealand (2001). *Census of Population and Dwellings 2001*. Wellington.

Statistics New Zealand (2002). Monitoring Progress Towards a Sustainable New Zealand. Wellington.

United States General Accounting Office (2003). Forum on Key National Indicators: Assessing the Nation's Position and Progress. Washington DC.

Indicators and Benchmarking

Indicators and Benchmarking as a Support to the Decision-Making Process: the Italian Experience in Active Employment Policies

Aviana Bulgarelli

Director General for Vocational Training and Guidance Policies, Ministry of Labour and Social Policies, Italy

Abstract

Benchmarking can be helpful in at least two ways in the decision-making process. It can be used for a coordinated, consistent and systemic analysis of performance, possibly tied to a system of targets. It can also be used to identify the most effective intervention policies, models and instruments for achieving the targets and enabling good/best practices to be pinpointed and transferred in the various scenarios.

The adoption of the benchmarking tool in the European experience inevitably enhances the role of statistical information, not only for monitoring and evaluating interventions, but also for constructing and implementing the policy process. The European Employment Strategy, for example, is conceived as a "guided convergence" process towards quantitative targets and, at the same time, as a reference framework for a complex benchmarking exercise based on the open coordination method.

The paper analyses, first of all, the impact of this approach on the Italian experience in recent years. Reference is made not only to the social and labour policy programming model, reorganised for the first time into a global model, but also to the identification and the orientation of priorities for policies. As a result, the identification of a relevant – and feasible – common system of statistical indicators constitutes a strategic goal that has only been partly achieved to date.

The need to dispose of a vaster and better information capital – in terms of timeliness, comparability, pertinence, etc. – is not the only critical point to be dealt with. How can we obtain information that is really capable of guiding policy choices? How can we overcome the ex-post nature of benchmarking? How can we ensure a system consistent with the relevant level of the decision-making process? Basically, our attempt is to open a debate on how – and to what extent – it would be possible to raise the benchmarking system from a simple tool for comparing and analysing policy performance (*performance gap*) to an input – if not an authentic surrogate – of the evaluation process capable of guiding the decision-making process.

Benchmarking in the public decision-making process

Benchmarking bears at least two meanings and can be helpful in two ways in the decision-making process.

- On the one hand, it can be used for a coordinated, consistent and systematic analysis of performance, possibly tied to a system of targets/objectives; in this case, the choice of indicators is strictly linked to the identification of a system of criteria/targets which are considered relevant by public decision-makers, involving, as a first step, the definition of a set of significant and feasible indicators.

- On the other hand, it can be used to identify the most effective intervention policies, models and instruments for achieving the objectives fixed and enabling good/best practices to be pinpointed and transferred in various contexts.

Clearly, this distinction does not imply that both approaches should be considered separately. In fact, the definition and measurement of performance gaps in a system of targets/objectives is a necessary basis for choosing the most suitable good/best practices for a given policy issue. Likewise, the *ex-post* analysis of results achieved through the policies adopted represents a reference for a possible redefinition of the decision-making process.

However, our intention here is to focus mainly on the first approach, not only because statistical information plays an essential role in this case, but also because, as we shall see, the experience gained over these last years within the European Employment Strategy (EES) appears particularly significant.

To understand better the difficulties encountered and to contribute to a definition of policy-makers' needs, it is important to remember that, in order to provide an effective support for the decision-making process, benchmarking should be integrated in a broader process, which could be ideally summarised in the following subsequent and iterative stages[1]:

1. Identification of macro-objectives and corresponding performances to be considered as really significant for comparing different countries/regions in order to measure the success of implemented policies.

2. Identification of a system of elementary variables/indicators referable to the macro-objectives and representative of the different possible channels (national/regional) through which they can be achieved (different territories, population targets, production sectors, etc., should be given a different weight).

3. Comparison, on this basis, between the national/regional situation examined and the reference benchmark. This is particularly important since performance gaps can be measured with reference to either a system of predefined targets or the values presented by best performers.

4. At this point, it is necessary to understand and explain the reasons for the differences observed in performance, pinpointing those on which it is more important to act, and identifying as well actions to be undertaken. Here, benchmarking is used to find best/good practices with better effectiveness/impact taking into account the current context conditions (sociocultural, political, institutional , etc.).

5. Monitoring policy implementation, analysing benchmarking results and, possibly, correcting the entire process, as a final stage.

Unlike its utilisation in the business field, this approach obviously involves different and particularly complex problems in the case of public policies (for instance in the case of the EES). In fact:

---

1 See Tronti L., "Il benchmarking dei mercati del lavoro. Una sfida per le regioni italiane?"; in Antonelli G. and Nosvelli M., "Monitoraggio e valutazione delle politiche del lavoro per una nuova economia", Il Mulino, 2002.

- multiple objectives and, at the same time, specific intervention instruments and policies make this approach complex and often difficult to "systematise" within a single decision-making model;

- objectives sometimes can be conflicting and it is not always possible to identify the corresponding trade-offs;

- it is often difficult to find connections between individual policies/instruments available and the different objectives identified, which are strongly influenced by the specific context conditions;

- the plurality of actors contributing to the identification of objectives and to the implementation and monitoring of policies (these latter having an impact on expenditure decisions) make this scenario even more complex.

Therefore, the measurement of performance gaps only represents the first stage of a decision-making process based on benchmarking, which requires not only measuring but also understanding, planning, testing, monitoring and, if necessary, reconsidering the policy choices made. Within this framework, the need for good statistical information is only one of the necessary conditions; nonetheless, as the EES experience has demonstrated, benchmarking and its related system of statistical indicators have often become a "surrogate" for evaluation, with an appreciable influence on the decision-making process.

The European Employment Strategy and benchmarking in the Italian experience

The EES is an example of multi-level strategic programming and represents, at the same time, the reference framework of a complex benchmarking exercise based on the open method of coordination. It is, in fact, a process of "guided convergence" which, starting with a reference framework of guidelines, uses benchmarking as an instrument to support a programming process based on objectives that are also defined quantitatively. For non-Europeans, this brief example could be useful[2]:

As a matter of fact, this process is somehow similar to that initiated with the Maastricht stability pact, but inevitably with a greater degree of freedom:

- firstly, because of the greater complexity of social and labour policies (in terms of objectives, targets and effectiveness of intervention tools);

- secondly, because it is part of a particularly complex decision-making mechanism involving a large number of actors, at different decision-making levels with high political, managerial and instrumental responsibility (from the EU level to the local level).

---

2   See "Council Decision of 22 July 2003 on guidelines for the employment policies of the Member States", in Official Journal of the European Union, L. 197/13, 5.8.2003.

Overarching objective: Full employment

Member States shall aim to achieve full employment by implementing a comprehensive policy approach incorporating demand and supply side measures and thus raise employment rates towards the Lisbon and Stockholm targets.

Policies shall contribute towards achieving on average for the European Union:

- an overall employment rate of 67% in 2005 and 70% in 2010,

- an employment rate for women of 57% in 2005 and 60% in 2010

- an employment rate of 50% for older workers (55-64) in 2010

Specific guideline: 4. Promote development of human capital and lifelong learning

Member States will implement lifelong learning strategies, including improving the quality and efficiency of education and training systems, in order to equip all individuals with the skills required for a modern workforce in a knowledge-based society, to permit their career development and to reduce skills mismatch and bottlenecks in the labour market.

In accordance with national priorities, policies will aim in particular to achieve the following outcomes by 2010:

- at least 85% of 22-year olds in the European Union should have completed upper secondary education,

- the European Union average level of participation in lifelong learning should be at least 12.5% of the adult working-age population (25 to 64 age group).

However, by identifying a reference system of objectives anchored to a set of quantified indicators, the EES has had an influence on the action of policy-makers, at a national level in the first place, but also at a regional and, in some cases, at a local/provincial level.

Fabrizio Barca[3] has already explained in his contribution the influence EU policies have had in Italy on the development programming and governance model, fostering a strengthening of instruments – both cognitive and methodological – for defining policy choices. The EU programming model, based on the meta-objective of "economic and social cohesion", has triggered a profound reorganisation of structural policies within a "global" model. This model now also constitutes a benchmark for Italian programming at both national and regional level.

Looking specifically at active labour policies, the constant reference to the EU framework has had a considerable influence on public decision-makers. Some examples seem particularly significant in this regard, but we will consider here only their institutional aspects, leaving aside the more specific, albeit important, political aspects of the decision-making process.

We know there are a large number of indicators proposed for monitoring EES targets. They have been partly changed already and will undergo further modifications over time, thanks to the identification of better quality and more relevant indicators with respect to

---

3   Head of Department for Development Policies, Ministry of Economy and Finance, Italy

identified priorities. In particular, employment indicators are linked to the different key aims defined by the Lisbon European Council referring to strengthening employment levels, equal opportunities for men and women and, more in general, greater participation in the labour market of the older population and women.

A first example of the influence of the benchmark mechanism refers to the recent in-depth reform process of the labour market in Italy, and it is quite significant since it concerns a typically national policy sphere. Many of the targets set by the EES have already been assimilated into the national and often regional context. This resulted in stronger emphasis, for example, on the female component or on the older population, even when – as in many regions in southern Italy – the high priority of the "elderly" component of the workforce does not fully correspond to the local labour-market conditions.

Again, at a national level, this impact has also emerged during the implementation of the labour policy monitoring system, whose reorganisation has been partly inspired by the European benchmark model, with all the difficulties ensuing from the aim of coherently linking up a system involving multiple actors at various levels and with different degrees of involvement. As already mentioned, the Italian labour policy programming, implementation and evaluation process is articulated at many decision-making levels with accentuated forms of subsidiarity, both vertical (central administrations, regions, provinces, etc.), and horizontal (employers associations and trade unions). This complexity also inevitably concerns, both from the producer and the user side, the statistical information system which is necessary to monitor and evaluate the policies adopted. The objective of compatibility with the Lisbon benchmark has inevitably made the entire process more complex and required the creation of a large number of "technical units", involving a multiplicity of actors.

Among the Lisbon benchmark indicators, that concerning lifelong learning represents another emblematic case of how having to comply with a system of indicators (and performance gaps) has acted as a catalyst on the attention of policy-makers, prompting extensive corrections in targeting and rebalancing the policy mix.

In Italy, the indicator used for lifelong learning, represented by the participation rate of population aged between 24 and 65 years in permanent and continuing training, shows a severe structural lag: against the objective set to a participation rate of 12.5% by 2010, our country only reached 4.7% in 2003, compared to an EU average of 9.7%. This context is moreover characterized by strong disparities, not only among generations (mainly to the detriment of older groups) but also among regions (southern Italy is particularly affected). Over and above the interpretative problems that this indicator also presents – and we shall come back to this later – it is clear that public decision-makers are well aware of this fact; however, once integrated within the Lisbon framework, this indicator has had a significant impact on policy makers, who only had little room for manoeuvre. In a situation where resources are limited, redirecting them towards lifelong learning policies means reorganising alternative intervention policies, with consequences:

- not only from the political point of view but also regarding the management of the governance system referring to active labour policies;

- from an organisational point of view, due to the need to redirect the "machine" towards greater needs pertaining to the programming, management and implementation of interventions.

In this context, greater attention has therefore been devoted to adult education and training policies, both in general and specifically addressed to the employed population, by developing new types of training supply. However, it was also clear that, because of the gap with the reference benchmark and given the existing budget and time constraints, it was going to be a "mission impossible". Even with greater financial efforts and making adjustments by redefining the beneficiaries covered by the main policy tools available, the only real "room for manoeuvre" had clearly to be found in trying to make the most of available resources.

The existing statistical information – we refer to CVTS2, Eurostat's survey on continuing vocational training in enterprises – showed that, within the broader adult population target, training activities for the employed population had a particularly negative ranking in the European context: in fact, only one Italian firm out of four (around 24%) carried out any form of training activity, compared to a 62% average participation of European enterprises. An in-depth analysis of the data provided by this survey also showed how this could be explained – at least partly – by the peculiarity of the Italian industrial system, based on small and medium-sized enterprises and on so-called traditional sectors (clothing, footwear, wood and furnishings, etc.).

In particular, the existence of smaller-sized enterprises seemed to be a key factor explaining the low propensity of enterprises to offer training to their employees: investing in human capital – just as in Research & Development – does not usually produce tangible effects in the short term and requires a strong corporate culture and strategic vision. Factors that tend to discourage smaller firms from investing in human capital include a greater incidence of training costs (not only direct costs but also those deriving from missing workers in the production process), a lesser organisational and logistical capacity, and greater uncertainty with regards to returns of training, especially in a context of growing labour flexibility and mobility. Within this framework, introducing innovative forms of intervention seemed more important than financial incentives to ensure greater effectiveness of policies for continuing training.

To achieve such an objective, new bodies have been created ("Interprofessional Funds for continuing vocational training" - *Fondi paritetici interprofessionali per la formazione continua*) where, for the first time, social partners would be directly involved in the programming and management of a significant part of the resources allocated to continuing vocational training. The aim was to encourage a greater dissemination of the training culture, especially with regards to smaller-sized enterprises, and contribute to steer financing towards initiatives expected to be more in line with the real requirements of companies.

Interprofessional Funds are now fully operational. Starting from 2004, they have an independent financing channel as well as a significant supply of resources in addition to those allocated in 2003 by the Ministry of Labour and Social Policies for their start-up. Interprofessional Funds are part of the existing system for financing and managing continuing training initiatives (i.e. the European Social Fund as well as the national/regional programmes and funds). The real difference today is the fact that social partners share responsibility for the operational management, whereas previously, the social partners' role mainly consisted of cooperating with public administrations in order to define intervention strategies and priorities within the framework of concerted actions. They now have actually to manage financial resources, to plan and direct interventions, to organise and reconcile local and sector needs and to monitor the outcomes of activities.

The close link between the funds and the enterprises involved acts as a facilitator, and one can reasonably expect a greater and prompter ability to grasp the needs of enterprises.

Also in the case of lifelong learning, the construction of a system for collecting and producing the statistical information needed for monitoring and evaluating the policies implemented is an important related aspect. In the light of our previous explanations, the promotion of lifelong learning involves a set of particularly complex policies, where not only institutional actors but also other players – such as social partners – are directly engaged in the programming and management of considerable financial resources (i.e. not only the *Fondi Interprofessionali* but also the national funds for the vocational training of temporary workers). As far as continuing vocational training is concerned, the achievement of an integrated monitoring and evaluation system in line with the European benchmarks thus requires significant efforts from the administration.

The example of lifelong learning is undoubtedly emblematic for national policies, but what has happened in recent years at a regional level, for instance during the ESF programming and reprogramming, is equally significant. In addition, it is also worth mentioning the experience gained at a strictly local/provincial level of programming, which I will briefly illustrate.

The Italian Provinces are required to play a leading role in active labour policies and have also been involved, more or less directly, in the benchmarking system proposed with the EES. A typical example is the experience of Local Action Plans for employment, where many local authorities have set up integrated strategic programming tools for training, education and labour, within the framework of EES guidelines. These local entities have directly measured themselves with the European benchmark when defining active labour policies and, more in general, local development policies.

All these are only brief examples and many more could be presented, but they obviously give a positive picture of the "stimulating" role of the benchmarking system. However, the processes involved, currently and in the past, are very complex and require the participation of a large number of both national and local stakeholders, as well as a firm commitment of the administrations concerned. Therefore, the identification of a significant and feasible common system of statistical indicators represents a strategic goal that seems to be however only partly achieved. In fact, the need to dispose of wider and better information – in terms of timeliness, comparability, relevance, etc. – is not the only crucial aspect to be dealt with.

Indicators, benchmarking and evaluation

From the experience I have summarised previously, we can identify some of the main difficulties, methodological and technical, linked to the quality of the statistical information system and to the indicators used for the construction of benchmarking. Since data not only constitute the basis for the knowledge of different phenomena, but also play a key role in steering policy makers' choices, their imperfection is a potential source of serious problems for public decision-makers and could make their work more difficult if not "damaging".

Of course, benchmarking makes sense insofar as the accuracy of data is really significant in terms of **coherence** and above all **comparability**. In particular, when the implicit goal is to evaluate the progress of policies in different countries/regions, it is obviously better to avoid making any comparisons at all than to make "wrong" ones.

Without going into too much technical detail, I would like to give a small example concerning lifelong learning.

Until the recent introduction of the new continuous labour force survey, the number of trained employees was estimated with reference to a four-week period preceding the interviews. As it is well known to statisticians, such choice could potentially produce biases due to the poorer statistical visibility of short training courses. For countries with short average duration of training courses, the shorter is the reference time of interviews, the lower is the probability to observe the phenomenon over a given observation period. It is of course difficult to know how significant these biases can be in the Italian case, but it has to be mentioned that our country has an average duration of training courses decidedly below the European average.

The example of the Local Action Plans also enables us to make some considerations, highlighting another important criterion, i.e. the **relevance** of indicators. Relevance is understood as the ability to take into account the cognitive needs of an often very large number of users, with different systems of targets and context conditions. We know there can be great differences from one country to another, not only because of the existing disparities across countries but also because of internal disparities within each country. In a multi-level programming system like that of the European Union, and, to a greater extent, of Italy, paying attention to bringing statistical information to a correct level means, in turn, analysing the different decision-making levels. In this sense, it is important to understand "who has to decide what" and to provide a suitable cognitive support, especially with a view to evaluation.

The problem **of timeliness** of statistical information is more general. The acceleration of economic processes implies that equal speed is needed to adjust decision-making processes and institutional frameworks as well as statistical information and knowledge on the phenomena. However, indicators inevitably reflect an "out-of-date" vision of the economy: indicators are always *ex-post* and they are often available after a long delay. This problem is also encountered at European level – think of the monitoring process of the EES implementation – but it is even more relevant at a national level. The case of the Italian labour market provides a good example of this: over the last decade, the existing forms of employment contracts have been subject to radical changes, just as their legal and regulatory framework, creating considerable problems linked to the significance of statistical information, especially when used for a diachronic analysis of the phenomena.

The issue of timeliness must be tackled more courageously, opening the debate on the possibility to define common methodologies for constructing scenarios/simulations, or at least common criteria and parameters. If it is true that the acceleration economic processes requires a switch from a reactive approach to a proactive one, also in the field of public policies, then the construction of a system for estimating indicators is more and more becoming as important, in the decision-making process, as the knowledge of the context.

Finally, I would like to tackle briefly an issue which is linked to the connection between the objectives to achieve and the policies to undertake. Here we come to the point of the second meaning of benchmarking, i.e. that of good/best practices, where the problem of **transferability** is determinant. The existing differences between the various national/local contexts in which policies are implemented can have a great impact on their effectiveness. It is difficult to relate one aspect to the other, and statistics can only help up to a certain point. However, this is a decisive point for making the benchmarking approach effectively useful for the decision-making process.

We can see that we have gradually come to the crucial point of the relationship between benchmarking and policy evaluation and I have already mentioned at the beginning of this paper that the benchmarking approach in this case seems still very far from being fully applied within this context. How can we obtain information that is really capable of steering policy choices? How can we overcome the *ex-post* nature of benchmarking? How can we ensure a system consistent with the specific level of the decision-making process? Basically, our attempt is to open a debate on how – and to what extent – it is possible to raise the benchmarking system from a simple tool for comparing and analysing policy performance to an input – if not an authentic surrogate – to an evaluation process capable of guiding the decision-making process.

References

Commission of the European Communities, "Benchmarking the competitiveness of European industry", Bruxelles, 1996.

Commission of the European Communities, "Structural indicators" Bruxelles, 2002.

Commission of the European Communities, "Progress towards the common objectives in education and training: indicators and benchmarks", Commission staff working paper, Brussels, 2004

de la Fuente A. and Doménech R., "Human capital in growth regressions: how much difference does data quality make?", Universidad de Valencia, August 2002.

Groenendijk N. S., "The use of benchmarking in EU economic and social policies", CES, University of Twente, netherlands, presented at "The Future of Europe", DAES, University of South Denmark, Odense, September 24-25, 2004.

Martin J. P. and Grubb D., "What works and for whom: a review of OECD countries' experiences with active labour market policies", Swedish Economic Policy Review 8, 2001, pp. 9-56.

Mosley H and Mayer A., "Benchmarking National Labour Market Performance", Report prepared for European Commission, DG V, 1999.

OECD, "Benchmarking, Evaluation and Strategic Management in the Public Sector", Papers Presented at the 1996 Meeting of the Performance Management Network of the OECD's Public Management Service, Paris. 1997.

Tronti L., "Il benchmarking dei mercati del lavoro. Una sfida per le regioni italiane?"; in Antonelli G. and Nosvelli M., "Monitoraggio e valutazione delle politiche del lavoro per una nuova economia", Il Mulino, 2002.

New Public Management Reform and the Legacy of Developmental State in Korea

Chonghee Han

The Korea Institute of Public Administration, South Korea

Introduction

As a genre of administrative reforms, New Public Management (NPM) has spread around the world, covered a variety of concepts as well as ideas, and has been called by many names. It has been called results-driven government or performance-based management. Whatever it has been called, the main ideas of NPM include businesslike transformation of state policies through privatisation, deregulation, and liberalisation, especially under the influence of neo-liberalism with emphasis on market forces in order to enhance the performance of governments (Osborne and Gaebler, 1992; Peters, 2001).

However, the enthusiasm of the NPM bandwagon since the late 1990s has given way to skepticism about applying its main ideas and strategies to developing countries (Sutch, 1999). Can governments in developing countries use really the concepts of the NPM to actually lead to successful administrative reforms to render the public sector produce more and better results? There are questions about how the NPM ought to be applied in developing countries and how such applications reconcile its promises with both old public management principles and operational realities of bureaucratic agents. These substantial questions should be addressed to assess the usefulness of NPM reforms in developing countries.

With doubt of generalized applicability of the NPM, the critics argue that the usefulness of NPM reforms in developing countries is slight at best. (Farazmand *et al.*, 2001). In a bid to support this argument a case of NPM reform efforts in Korea, especially for the central government during the Kim, Dae Jung administration (1997-2001), is employed to critically assess the suitability of international benchmarking originated in developed countries. In explaining the limited applicability of NPM reforms in the Korean government an emphasis is on the legacy of the developmental state within the bureaucratic elite, where active state intervention guided the economy or society according to the state goal. The legacy is distinct from that of developed countries where liberal democracies, based on market economy featuring free competition, have been consolidated.

There is an underlying logic to the trajectory of administrative reforms towards the principles of market and business management, and there are strong pressures giving voice to this logic from such supra-national organisations as the IMF and WTO. At the same time, the reformers in the Korean government have pursued their aims within a framework of the government officials' embedded beliefs and institutional arrangements. Their battles are with a set of oppositional forces within the Korean administrative reform state and the way in which the government carries out the reform initiatives. Such battles are the primary explanation of the limited applicability of the NPM reforms in Korea. Put it generally, this suggests that administrative reform in a country should take account of his own distinct factors domestically in shaping his program of reform.

From this perspective, this article first outlines the character of the different settings where the NPM reform efforts have been made by contrasting them with those of developed countries. Second, it turns to the major reform measures: administrative reorganisation, executive agency system, open personnel system. The conclusions draw on this survey of the reform issues to critically assess the current achievements and their consequent problems, with a final word on strategies for successful NPM reforms in Korea.

Why the Impact of NPM Reforms Has Been Modest: The Legacy of the Developmental State is Still Prevalent

There seem to be plausible explanations for why NPM reforms in Korea have delivered less than initially claimed. The legacy of the developmental state, however, is one the most crucial factors for limiting the applicability of NPM reforms because it can determine the trajectory of reform process and have an effect on the way public servants and citizens or society in general interact.

The legacy of the developmental state can be derived from export-oriented industrialisation or EOI through effective state intervention between the 1970s and the 1980s in Korea. Such industrialisation strategy was possible by the state's corporatist function associated with a political monism that does not allow interest group democracy and represses independent representation of organized interests in the society (Schmitter, 1975). Under the developmental state, the state is no longer seen as an agent of competing and interacting groups, nor simply as a reflection of broader societal conditions under which competing societal groups operate denying the pluralist view of the liberal state. To put it differently, the state is no longer conceived as a dependent actor in relation to competing societal forces as the pluralist perspective assumes. Rather, it is viewed as one of the primary actors in shaping the formation of societal interests and civil society to produce public policy. The causality is inverted from the liberal state in which societal associations and class actors are producers, not products of public policy, which in turn determine the representation and mode of action of societal associations.

In general, such state-centered analysis as the developmental state pays primary attention to state autonomy, such as the ability of state managers to exercise power even in the face of strong opposition from societal forces. According to Nordlinger (1981, pp. 91-140) the growth of state intervention helps to enhance state autonomy because it provides more chances to disguise policies, insulting the policy-making process from opposition. Seen from this perspective, the state, conceived as an organisation that can claim control over territories and people, may propose his own goals without considering the demands of the society, making it clear that state autonomy has an independent effect in social dynamics (Evans, 1995; Skocpol, 1992).

Given that a country's development path is greatly conditioned by the inherently domestic characteristics of each country, in the context of the embedded state autonomy even after the demise of the developmental state since the 1990s, it is reasonable to say that the limited usefulness of the NPR reforms in Korea can be explained better if the relationships between the state and society distinct from those of the liberal state are understood. As suggested by state-centered approaches, "strong state and weak society" relations have been prevalent through the Korean government and the bureaucracy in spite of domestically growing societal pressures as well as internationally deepening globalisation.

By taking advantage of the legacy of state-society relations, therefore, the Korean government has functioned an efficient bulwark for the government itself and its bureaucracy against the reforms initiated by outsiders in particular, which may undermine their vested own interests. In other words, if reform agendas are in favor of their interests, they will be a first priority, while if they are against their interests, the government and its bureaucracy will be lukewarm to them in order to maintain the status quo. This means that government and its bureaucracy in Korea are still remain one of the most formidable power blocks to formulate and reform policy on the basis of their own interests against the mobilized interests of civil society, while the ability of the government to manipulate the society has increasingly been eroded due to the expansion of democratisation and globalisation since the 1990s.

In short, even though it is true that the exercise of government power has become challenged compared with the developmental state as in authoritarian era, the government and its bureaucratic power is still one of the most significant factors to consider before launching any reform in Korea. If one takes account of the legacy of the developmental state in terms of state-society relations, which is distinct from that of the liberal state as in the so-called developed countries, it becomes uncertain whether the NPM reforms in Korea are successful.

Two State Perspectives on the Relationships between Public Administration and Society

As governments in the 1970s, 1980s, and 1990s have become less hierarchical and more decentralized, they are willing to cede their role to the private sector (Kettl, 2000). The rise of the "hollow state," a metaphor for government that reduces its role as a direct supplier of public goods by contracting public service provision out to private or nonprofits organisations, witnesses the collapse of orthodox public administration that bureaucracies within centralized policy jurisdictions could no longer be considered as a dominant policy actor (Frederikson and Smith, 2003, pp. 207-208). Such changed government roles have blurred the boundary between the public and the private. However, in order to analyze the NPM reforms, it is essential to identify the relationship between public employees and ordinary people derived from the relationship between the state and society.

Table 1.   An Overview on the Developmental and the Liberal State

State	Developmental	Liberal
Nature of the State	Paternalistic, Sacred	Competitive, Secular
State-Society Relations	State Dominance	Society (Market) Dominance
Interest Emphasis	State-led Economic Development (Collectivism)	Market-driven Economic Development (Individual Liberty)
Role of the State in Market	Guide (Protection, Support)	Referee (Fair Competition)
Power Orientation in Bureaucracy	Centralized with Powerful Pilot Agency	Decentralized without Powerful Pilot Agency

Again, as discussed in the above, Korea has a developmental state tradition with the strong state-weak society relationship, which has been derived from ideological weapons of Confucianism and anti-communism. This facilitated state-led development strategy. The authoritarian governments between the 1970s and the 1980s were preoccupied with rapid economic growth as compensation for a lack of political legitimacy in order to buy popular support. Economic growth was possible not only by the state's coercive power to guide the economy but also by the insulation of the pilot economic bureaucracy such as the Economic Planning Board (EPB) and the well-coordinated institutional mechanism policymaking and implementation (Koo, 1993). Using the powerful institutional mechanism, the holder of state power, the pilot economic bureaucracy, in particular, has played a monopolistic role in public affair and quickly succeeded in demobilizing civil society.

Considering this context, it is hard to deny that the bureaucratic power is still formidable in relation to civil society and that the administrative culture may be seen as hierarchical, paternal, and authoritative in Korea. This is difficult to be compatible with the principles of the "new public management" in the current governance era.

However, developed or Western countries, which have embraced the ideas of "new public management" and have already established the reform initiatives, have more strong tradition of the liberal state characterized by pluralism. State actions are explained by the interplay of interest groups. Government may thus be considered as an arena within which interest groups struggle in the governmental setting to insure the success of their own particular preferences (Frederickson, 1997, p. 3; Almond, 1990, p. 197). Consequently, the major function of public employees is to make sure that the game is played fairly, supporting the notions of individualism and private ownership. If public institutions are seen as a referee or figurative cash register, the state could not be designated as monopolistic actor with autonomous preferences capable of manipulating and even restructuring its own society, as found in the developmental state.

Specialisation, as evidence of supporting pluralism, is a key tenet of public administration. The designation of governmental agencies is based on specialties, and effective interest groups will try to find allies in particular specialized governmental agencies and to work closely with them or will sometimes pressure them to maximize their own interests. Due to this nature, unlike the developmental state, a powerful pilot agency is irrelevant; the autonomous decision-making capacity of governmental institutions is clearly limited. Since that compatible interests groups and governmental agencies often form friendly networks, so-called policy community, consensus building process is essential before implementing any reform or public policy. Thus, it should be no surprise that civil society cannot accept strong bureaucratic control designed to effectively yield the public good, in the traditions of the liberal state characterized by pluralism.

Again, given that triggers for the evolution of NPM are increasing cynicism regarding government bureaucracies' responsiveness to citizen concerns, as well as dissatisfaction with governmental programs (Aucoin, 1995; Manning, 2000), one of the prerequisites for successful NPM initiatives is that there must be a continuing source of pressure from politically natured civil society for public sector performance improvements (Romzek, 2000). From this point of view, western or developed governments, whose major function is to insure the transformation of citizens' preferences, not state own preferences into results, often find considerable common ground in explaining why NPM reforms are necessary. Accordingly, the reforms have delivered more than implemented in governments that have the strong traditions of the developmental state whose overdeveloped bureaucracies hindered the activation of the society.

To summarize, for countries with the legacies of the developmental state that do not trace back to the liberal state on the basis of society-centeredness to public affairs, it is difficult to transplant western NPM reforms and to have a full effect of the reforms. In other words, a "cultural preparedness" for appropriate applications matters before carrying out NPM reforms because they, by their nature, are constrained by the embedded state-society relationship.

Are NPM Reforms on the Right Track in Korea?

Direction of Reform

In the midst of the so-called Asian Crisis in 1997, Kim Dae Jung administration launched reform with a philosophy of "parallel development of democracy and the market economy." The administration set three objectives for performing Korea's pubic sector restructuring program. The three objectives are as follows: 1) to realize "a small but efficient government" by streamlining government functions and reducing its size; 2) to achieve "a highly competitive government" by introducing the principle of competition among civil service organisations and personnel; 3) to bring about "a better-serving government" by fostering desirable actions and attitudes of civil servants (Kim, 2000, p. 147). These are in line with NPM tenets characterized by providing flexibility, devolving authority, ensuring performance, and developing competition in the public sector (Kickert, 1997).

However, such market-driven reforms have finally led to the reduction of the state influence in providing public service. The businesslike reform has diminished the "publicness" of public service as an authentic public domain. This growing concern for the status of public service has reflected a broader international discourse over NPM reforms (Haque, 2001).

Reorganization

Wide-ranging reshuffling programs were undertaken in the name of streamlining the structure and functions of government organisations. The programs for the central government structure were launched in February 1998. Thanks to them, the number of cabinet numbers was reduced from 21 to 17, with 20% reduction of staff and the Ministry of Government Administration and the Ministry of Home Affairs were merged to form the Ministry of Government Administration and Home Affairs (MOGAHA). By taking advantage of tradition of developmental state, the powerful bureaucrats of the MOGAD have imposed diverse charters on local governments. The proliferation of characters was possible because of coercive institutionalisation. This reform made the MOGAD reinforce its control over local governments and other ministries.

Kim Dae Jung administration tried to reform the government by newly establishing a regular government agency that takes charge of administrating reform. Therefore, the Planning and Budget Commission was set up in 1998. The agency has been renamed Ministry of Planning and Budget (MPB) to play a key role in government reform. In this sense, the government's reform strategy was based on bureaucratic-centered one whose reform agenda was monopolized by the MPB and implemented in a top-down manner. Additionally, the Kim government undertook management consulting in all 17 ministries and agencies in the central government, which was done by foreign consulting firms such as Anderson Consulting and AT Kearney. The management review was carried out from

October 1998 to February 1999. Based on the final report of this management review, the government reshuffled governmental organisations in May 1999.

Combined with the privatisation of eight Social Enterprises, as of 2001, the Kim government reduced the number of public employees in the central government by about 16% or 22 400 persons (Ministry of Planning and Budget, 2002, p. 43, and p. 93). At a glance, these results seem to be consistent with the main ideas of NPM reforms. But the structural reform did not meet the public's expectations that render inefficient agencies shape a small government or give autonomy to the privatized organisations. According to the original proposal made by the Planning and Budget Commission, the Ministry of Information of Communication, the Ministry of Science and Technology, and the ministry of Industry and Resources were to be combined but the plan could not be realized. Rather, the consecutive reshuffling plan newly established the Ministry of Women Affairs and additionally created the two positions of the Deputy Prime Minister for Economy and Human Resource Development in 2000. This development means that the government itself violated the logic of making the small government while pushing the private sector for restructuring. For that reason, it is no more than a "political rhetoric."

Executive Agency System or Agencification

Korea adopted the British style of executive agency to be shifted out of the ministerial organisations. Twenty-three administrative offices were designated as executive agencies including the National Hospital, Driving and Vehicle Agency, and National Theatre. Obviously, the designation of the executive agencies was designed to promote autonomous and responsible for operational management independently of the ministry. As a result, this development will enhance customer-oriented service provision and facilitate a performance-centered culture in the government with increased autonomy for agencies in terms of flexibility in resource use.

However, the concept of an executive agency, which separates executive functions from the policy-making role, is not clear to Korean bureaucrats. The determination of the services transformed into agencies was influenced by power game within the government bureaucracies. The so-called "powerful ministries" such as the Ministry of Economy and Finance and General Affairs and Decentralisation were not affected by this reform; only one service became magnified from the two ministries respectively and the ministries, who officially supervise the agencies, continued control over them (Imp, 2003, p. 95).

Open Position System (OPS)

The system was designed to recruit competent personnel through open competition among the applicants from public and private sectors. In particular, for highly specialized positions, candidates with outstanding talent and expert were to be sought both inside and outside of the public sector. The Civil Service Commission (CSC), an agency newly established in May 1999, exercised an overriding power during the OPS position selection phase. The CSC finally selected 129 OPS positions in spite of opposition from most of the Ministries that are reluctant to open core policy planning positions to the private sectors. For example, such positions as Assistant Minister for Economic Policy Coordination (grade 1) of the Office for Government Policy Coordination, Direct General for Trade Policy (grade 2) of the Ministry of Commerce, Industry and Energy are the core policy planning positions. In the midst of such unwillingness, the appointments were taken up; among the appointments as of December 2002, 95 officials were from the same

Ministry and five officials coming from other Ministries (4.2%) and 18 civilans (15.3%) were appointed. The total of the appointments from outside is only 19.5% (Among, 2003, p. 57).

The statistics suggests that the OPS should be no more than a policy tool to justify the existing promotion system. This is a good example why the market principle of competition does not work in terms of higher civil servant appointments in Korea. The rate of the civilian appointments was low because qualified non-governmental candidates did not apply for the positions. Barriers preventing horizontal job transfer between the public and private sector, the closed culture of the bureaucratic organisations, and the low level of payment made competent civilians reluctant to apply for the OPS positions.

In addition, in a response to the OPS each ministry made relatively less important positions become open positions and continued to keep the more important positions under the existing personnel system. This is designed to minimize the effect of introducing open positions and to retain their embedded bureaucratic power. Seen from such a formal response it is hard to say that the initial intention of OPS to invite qualified civilians to the government organisations is successfully done.

Summary and Implications for Administrative Reform

Depending on the nature of the reform, the bureaucrats have reacted to the NPM reforms. Nevertheless, in Korea where strong state-weak society relations have been embedded because of the experience of developmental state, the bureaucracy in particular, the MPB have retained their dominance over the reforms. Society or market has not developed to the point of keeping powerful ministries from registering their own bureaucratic interests in the process of the reforms and has benefited from powerful bureaucrats.

Table 2. Summary of Reform Effects

Reform	Official Results	Bureaucrats' Response
Reorganisation	20% Retrenchment of Staff 8 SOEs Privatized	Increase the Size of Powerful Ministries Keep indirect influence
Executive Agency	23 Agencies Changed Legal Status	Exclude Powerful Agencies Keep Controlling Power
Open Position	129 Positions Opened	Exclude Key Positions Only 15% more Civilians Recruited

Source: Reorganized from Im (2003), Table 3, P. 96.

Consequently, the NPM reforms themselves have paradoxically reinforced bureaucratic power. Why were the true effects of reform contrary to originally expected ones? To answer this puzzle, it is helpful to recall the experiences of Korean bureaucrats in times of developmental state as summarized in the table 1 above. Korean bureaucracy has enjoyed relative high degree of independent bureaucratic power from market or social forces. The administrative culture different from that of western advanced countries should be the driving factor in determining the suitability of NPM reform.

In reforming the public sector the construction of small, efficient or businesslike government that is a tenet of NPM represents the language of the market, competition, performance and entrepreneurial management that originate from the West. In considering the embedded experiences of developmental state in which the state dominates the market, it would be successful for the administrative reform movement in Korea to build on some ideas that have come from foreign countries? The point here is to filter the public management reform approaches suitable for Korean administrative soils before simply following them. In other words, it is imperative that Korean scholars and practitioners should see their problems from their own point of view with taking their own historical experiences into account.

In addition to considering historical experiences, what should be done to achieve administrative reform appropriately? Korean government needs to build managerial capacity and confidence as well as to engage the public in businesslike practices in government without maddening bureaucracy. For the successful administrative reform the promotion of democratisation of administration and politics with robust markets is necessary in advance, instead of concentration of sheer increase in efficiency in the operation of government.

Market-based reforms have produced tangible changes in the way government provides public service in Korea, but the questions remain about how much, in what ways, and whether the provision of public service should be done as western countries should. A number of adjustments should be made before the way western countries reform the public sector is embraced.

Composite Indicators - The Controversy and the Way Forward

Andrea Saltelli, Michela Nardo, Michaela Saisana and Stefano Tarantola

European Commission

Joint Research Centre of Ispra

Abstract

In this paper we first present an example of how Composite Indicators "naturally" emerge in a context where country performance is being benchmarked, we discuss some salient aspect of the Composite Indicators Controversy, pitting "Aggregators" and "Non-Aggregators" against one another, and showing Pros and Cons to the use of composite indicators. We offer next some examples of JRC experience in the quest for a methodology for ensuring quality of composite indicators including the use of uncertainty and sensitivity analysis. Finally, we analyse two crucial issues in composite indicator building such as correlation and compensability, which have not received the necessary attention.

The Composite Indicators Controversy

"Composite indicators are confusing entities whereby apples and pears are added up in the absence of a formal model or justification."

"Composite indicators are a way of distilling reality into a manageable form."[1]

Conflicting views on the merits on the use of indicators are increasing at the same pace as the role of indicators in public life has become more evident, as testified by the present conference. Among indicators, composite indicators (CI) have also experienced a surge in popularity, possibly because of their use to capture complex (someone would say poorly defined) concepts such as sustainability, welfare, achievement of an internal market, progresses toward the Lisbon goals, etc.

Whether or not one likes or accepts CI for the purpose of comparing countries performance, one might find itself exposed to a CI even when unwilling. An anecdotic evidence of this was early this year, when the Financial Times, purportedly commenting the EU Spring report 2004, and citing the European Commission as source, titled "Brussels points the finger at EU lax states", under a graph showing EU countries rated with stars (one for laggards, three for leaders) in relation to the Lisbon Goals (Financial Times, January 22, 2004). In fact the European Commission had done nothing of the sort, and the star rating had been entirely created by the Financial Times analysts based on the table of colour-coded 14 key or headline structural indicators contained in the Spring Report (Figure 1). Star rating, a crude but effective way to summarise sets of variables, is used in the UK health system (NHS) to rank hospitals performance and can be considered as a form of composite indicator.

Figure 1. Extract from the EC Spring report 2004. Assessing policies: Dark shading – Country policy on a good path; Light shading – Country policy on a bad path (expert judgment done by the EC services).

Levels	Y	AT	BE	...
Labour productivity (EU 15=100)	2003	97.9	114	...
Employment rate (%)	2003	69.3	59.9	...
Employment rate of older workers (%)	2003	30	26.7	...
...	...	...	...	...

The morale of the anecdote would be that one having to benchmark countries performance, as increasingly the case on issues ranging from the quality of health system to the quality of welfare, would be better advised to find a composite index or else risk being found by one ("Find God before God finds you" was a semi-serious preacher's slogan).

And yet the composite indicators controversy is there to stay. Andrew Sharpe, of the Centre for the Study of Living Standards, Ottawa, notes in its 2004 review [2]:

"The aggregators believe there are two major reasons that there is value in combining indicators in some manner to produce a bottom line. They believe that such a summary statistic can indeed capture reality and is meaningful, and that stressing the bottom line is extremely useful in garnering media interest and hence the attention of policy makers. The second school, the non-aggregators, believe one should stop once an appropriate set of indicators has been created and not go the further step of producing a composite index. Their key objection to aggregation is what they see as the arbitrary nature of the weighting process by which the variables are combined."

Saisana et al., 2005 we similarly observe [3]:

"[…] it is hard to imagine that debate on the use of composite indicators will ever be settled […] official statisticians may tend to resent composite indicators, whereby a lot of work in data collection and editing is "wasted" or "hidden" behind a single number of dubious significance. On the other hand, the temptation of stakeholders and practitioners to summarise complex and sometime elusive processes (e.g. sustainability, single market policy, etc.) into a single figure to benchmark country performance for policy consumption seems likewise irresistible."

The European Commission, whose services at times use composite indicators, made an effort to review what is good and bad about them, producing the attached table (From Saisana and Tarantola, 2002 [4]).

Table 1. Pros and cons of composite indicators adapted from Saisana and Tarantola, 2002

Pros

- CI can be used to summarise complex or multi-dimensional issues, in view of supporting decision-makers
- CI provide the big picture. They can be easier to interpret than trying to find a trend in many separate indicators. They facilitate the task of ranking countries on complex issues.
- CI can help attract public interest by providing a summary figure with which to compare the performance across countries and their progress over time.
- CI could help to reduce the size of a list of indicators or to include more information within the existing size limit.

Cons

- CI may send misleading, non-robust policy messages if they are poorly constructed or misinterpreted. Sensitivity analysis can be used to test CI for robustness.
- The simple "big picture" results which CI show may invite politicians to draw simplistic policy conclusions. CI should be used in combination with the sub-indicators to draw sophisticated policy conclusions
- The construction of CI involves stages where judgement has to be made: the selection of sub-indicators, choice of model, weighting indicators and treatment of missing values etc. These judgements should be transparent and based on sound statistical principles.
- There could be more scope for disagreement among Member States about CI than on individual indicators. The selection of sub-indicators and weights could be the target of political challenge
- The CI increase the quantity of data needed because data are required for all the sub-indicators and for a statistically significant analysis.

As discussed in Table 1, composite indicators are much easier to interpret than trying to find a common trend in many individual indicators. Composite indicators have proven to be useful in ranking countries in benchmarking exercises. However, composite indicators can send misleading or non-robust policy messages if they are poorly constructed or misinterpreted. The simple "big picture" results which composite indicators show may invite politicians to draw simplistic policy conclusions. An index of industrialisation might for instance be read overlooking the fact that increased industrialisation might or might not coincide with an improvement of living conditions or of well being depending on a country's position on the development curve. The construction of CI involves stages where subjective judgement has to be made: the selection of sub-indicators, the treatment of missing values, the choice of aggregation model, the weights of the indicators, etc. These subjective choices can be used to manipulate the results. A country unhappy of its position on a competitiveness scoreboard might fight to have additional dimensions included which would raise its ranking. On the other hand, if a CI were to rise controversy more than shed light on an issue, that composite would have perhaps failed its purpose.

For all their merits and demerits, composite indicators can be seen as component of a wider analytic framework. Take for instance the structural indicators (SI) used in the European Union to gauge progresses toward Lisbon Goals. The full SI list, which contains 107 yearly revised variables (considering disaggregations, e.g. by gender,), is extensively visited and used by the commission services and by external users, the EUROSTAT SI web site being one of the most visited of the EC[1]. The EU Council found this list too detailed for effective reporting, and wanted a short list of 14 so called

---

1   http://europa.eu.int/comm/eurostat/structuralindicators

headline indicators to be used. These headline indicators, used by the European Commission in the Spring 2004 report, were further aggregated by the Financial Times to a star rating. Thus, depending on the level of analytic rigour, on the audience, and on the purpose, different resolution levels of the information can be adopted.

- Practitioners   107 indicators

- Spring Council   14 headline indicators

- The public   one-three star rating

The composite indicators' controversy can perhaps be put into context if one considers that indicators, and a fortiori composite indicators, are models, in the mathematical sense of the term. Models are inspired from systems (natural, biological, social) that one wishes to understand. Models are themselves systems, formal system at that. The biologist Robert Rosen (1991, Figure 2, [5]) noted that while a causality entailment structure defines the first system, and a formal causality system entails the second, no formal rule of encoding the second system given the first, i.e. to move from perceived reality to model, was ever agreed. The scientific method does without it, and some scientists accept modelling as a craftsmanship as opposed to modelling as a science.

Figure 2, From Rosen 1991.

As argued in a forthcoming OECD-JRC handbook of good practices for composite indicators building, the quality of a composite indicator is in its fitness or function to purpose. The economist A. K. Sen, Nobel prize winner in 1998, was initially opposed to composite indicators but was eventually seduced by their ability to put into practice his concept of "Capabilities" ('the range of things that a person could do and be in her life', Sen A. 1989 Development as Capabilities Expansion, Journal of Development Planning vol.19, 41-58) in the UN Human development index. This Index is defined as a measure of the process of expanding people's capabilities (or choices) to function. In this case, composite indicators's use for advocacy is what makes them valuable.

Although we cannot tackle here the vast issue of quality of statistical information, there is one aspect of the quality of composite indicators – of their fitness for purpose – which we find essential for their use. This is the existence of a community of peers (be these individuals, regions, countries, facilities of various nature) willing to accept the composite indicators as their common yardstick based on their understanding of the issue. In discussing pedigrees matrices for statistical information Funtowicz and Ravetz note (in Uncertainty and Quality in Science for Policy, 1990 [6])

"[…] any competent statistician knows that 'just collecting numbers' leads to nonsense. The whole Pedigree matrix is conditioned by the principle that statistical work is (unlike some traditional lab research) a highly articulated social activity. So in 'Definition and Standards' we put 'negotiation' as superior to 'science', since those on the job will know of special features and problems of which an expert with only a general training might miss".

We would add that, however good the scientific basis for a given composite indicator, its acceptance relies on negotiation.

We would like to close this section by pointing to the several recent reviews on the use of composite indicators [2,4, 7-10]. More links are available at a recently opened composite indicators web site[2].

Open issues on Composite Indicators building

Among the many open questions in the application of composite indicators which are treated in the forthcoming handbook of good practices in composite indicators building [11] there are two issues that we would like to touch upon here: correlation among indicators and compensability between indicators. Both these issues pop up frequently when debating composite indicators, yet they have not received the attention they deserve.

The first one is the existence and the role of **correlation among input variables** in the CI The user of a CI should look for the correlation matrices of the underlying variables. A composite constructed on the basis of underlying indicators with high internal correlation will give a very robust CI, whose values and ranking are moderately affected by changes in the selection of weights, the normalisation method and other steps involved in the analysis (see next section). This composite indicator could be appropriate or not appropriate depending on the theoretical framework.

When building composite indicators using automated tools such as factor analysis, one seeks to obtain a set of totally uncorrelated new variables. While this can be a powerful tool to benchmark countries performance, the interpretation in terms of original variables becomes more difficult. One may want to eliminate the effect of correlations by weighting less the correlated variables (this is also a possible practice [11]). At the same time, it would be very difficult to imagine a composite indicator made of truly orthogonal variables. In a multicriteria context, one would consider the existence of correlation among the attributes of an issue as a feature of the issue, not to be compensated for. A car's speed and beauty are likely correlated with one another, but this does not imply that we are willing to trade speed for design. Note that on this speed-beauty point there is no agreement among the experts. The e-business readiness index, developed by the European Commission, is criticised by EU official statisticians because of the important correlations among the input variables.

The second problem we want to discuss briefly is that of **compensability**. Munda, and Nardo, 2003 [12], noticed how weights, customarily conceived as "importance" measures, act in practice as substitution rates, e.g. w_i/w_j is the ratio of substitution (or compensation) of indicator "i" with indicator "j". This may be perceived as an important limitation of a CI. Imagine for example that an index of development is being created and that literacy is one of the input variables. One might argue that literacy should not be traded with GDP per capita. When one is not willing to accept this kind of trade offs, e.g.

2   http://farmweb.jrc.cec.eu.int/ci/

when the variable cannot be compensated with another, a multi criteria approach can be applied. We illustrate this briefly in the following.

The **multi-criteria** procedure (MCA) tries to resolve the conflict arising in countries comparisons as some indicators are in favour of one country while other indicators are in favour of another. This conflict can be treated at the light of a non-compensatory logic and taking into account the absence of preference independence within a discrete multi-criteria approach (Munda, 1995, [13]). The approach employs a mathematical formulation (Condorcet-type of ranking procedure) to rank in a complete pre-order (i.e. without any incomparability relation) all the countries from the best to the worst after a pair-wise comparison of countries across the whole set of the available indicators [12]. We offer here a "hand waving" description of the algorithm. Imagine we have three countries, A, B and C and we aim at ranking their overall performance according to N indicators. We build to this effect an "outranking matrix" whose entries e_{ij} tells us how much country "i" does better than country "j". e_{ij} is in fact the sum of all weights of all indicators for which country "i" does better than country "j". e_{ji} will likewise be the sum of all weights for which the reverse is true. If the two countries do equally well on one variable, its weight is split between e_{ij} and e_{ji}. As a result $e_{ij} + e_{ji} = 1$ if weights have been scaled to unity. We now write down all permutations of county order (ABC,ACB,BAC,BCA,CAB,CBA) and compute for each of them the ordered sum of the scores, e.g. for ABC we compute $Y = e_{AB} + e_{AC} + e_{BC}$. We do this for all permutations and take as the multicriteria country ranking the one with the highest total score Y. Note that this ordering is only based on the weights, and on the sign of the difference between countries values for a given indicator, the magnitude of the difference being ignored. With this approach no compensation occurs, to exemplify, a country that does marginally better on many indicators comes out better than a country that does a lot better on a few ones because it cannot compensate deficiencies in some dimensions with outstanding performances in others.

Note that the MCA method provides results in terms of country rankings, and not of an index, so we can only follow the country rankings though time.

Between the full compensability of additive aggregations and the non-compensability of the multicriteria method an intermediate solution is the geometric aggregation, in which indicators are multiplied and weights appear as exponents. For example if an hypothetical composite were formed by inequality, environmental degradation, GDP per capita and unemployment, two countries, one with values 21, 1, 1, 1; and the other with 6,6,6,6 would have equal composite if the aggregation was additive. Obviously the two countries would represent very different social conditions that would not be reflected in the composite. Using instead a geometric aggregation the first country of our simple example would have a much lower composite than the second (2.14 versus 6).

We have touched in this section just a couple of the many critical issues for CI building, i.e. correlation and compensability. The forthcoming handbook [11] has more. Our next section is devoted to one of the key issues addressed by the authors in the field of composite indicators building: this is the use of uncertainty and sensitivity analysis in the investigation of the robustness of the message conveyed by the CI.

Robustness analysis

One of the points more thoroughly treated in the handbook is how to improve the CI by robustness analysis. The iterative use of uncertainty and sensitivity analysis during the development of a CI can contribute to its well-structuring.

Doubts are often raised about the robustness of the results of the CI and about the significance of the associated policy message. For instance, Mathis Wackernagel, father of the "Ecological Footprint" and thus an authoritative source in the Sustainable Development debate, concludes a critique of the World Economic Forum Environmental Sustainability Index presented at Davos in 1991 by noting[3]:

"Overall, the report would gain from a more extensive peer review and a sensitivity analysis. The lacking sensitivity analysis undermines the confidence in the results since small changes in the index architecture or the weighting could dramatically alter the ranking of the nations."

Uncertainty analysis (UA) and sensitivity analysis (SA) is a powerful combination of techniques to gain useful insights during the process of CI building, including a contribution to the indicators' quality definition and an assessment of the reliability of countries' ranking As noted, the construction of CI involves stages where judgment has to be made, which introduces issues of uncertainty in the construction line of a CI: selection of data, data quality, data editing (e.g. imputation), data normalisation, weighting scheme, weights' values and aggregation method. All these sources of subjective judgment will affect both the ranking - changes are more likely among middle-of-the-road performers - and the message brought by the CI in a way that deserves analysis and corroboration [11, 14]. In fact, UA focuses on how the sources of uncertainty propagate through the structure of the CI and affect its values. SA studies how much each individual source of uncertainty contributes to the CI value/ranking variance. Despite that a synergistic use of UA and SA has proven to be more powerful (Saisana et al., 2005 [3]; Tarantola et al., 2000 [16]), UA is more often adopted than SA (Jamison and Sandbu, 2001, [15]) and the two types of analysis are almost always treated separately.

The types of questions for which an answer is sought via the application of UA&SA are:

1. Does the use of one construction strategy versus another in building the CI provide actually a partial picture of the countries' performance?

2. Which constituents (e.g. countries) have large uncertainty bounds in their rank (volatile countries)?

3. Which are the factors that affect the countries rankings?

All things considered, a careful analysis of the uncertainties included in the development of a CI can render its building more robust. A plurality of methods (all with their implications) should be initially considered, because no model (CI construction strategy) is a priori better than another, provided that internal coherence is always assured, as each model serves different interests. The CI is no longer a magic number corresponding to crisp data treatment, weighting set or aggregation method, but reflects uncertainty and ambiguity in a more transparent and defensible fashion. More details on quantitative sensitivity analysis are available in succinct form in Saltelli et al., 2004 [17]. The handbook has an application of it to the Technology Achievement Index [11].

We have also applied this methodology in a series of ongoing co-operations between the JRC and the services of the European Commission (Economic and Financial Affairs, Internal Market, Enterprise, Research, Information Society) on composite indicators and,

---

3   Notes by M. Wackernagel, Redefining Progress, February 10, 2001,   http://www.anti-lomborg.com/ESI%20critique.rtf

last but not least, the Yale and Columbia Universities for the World Economic Forum's Environmental Sustainability Index.

Application to examples

The section is devoted to the discussion of the two key issues of correlation and compensability. To this end, we will first deal with the choice of weighting of the indicators using the example of e-business readiness index, and then we will consider the choice of the type of aggregation and study how the latter affects the resulting country rankings in the Environmental Sustainability Index.

Test case: E-business readiness (e-BSN)

The e-business readiness defines the degree of preparation of enterprises to participate and benefit from the information and communication technologies. The eEurope 2005 Action Plan (COM(2002) 263 final)[4] calls for a benchmarking of the target that "by 2005, Europe should have (…) a dynamic e-business environment". It proposes general guidelines for the benchmarking exercise and sets out a number of indicators to monitor progress. The European Commission has selected 12 indicators from that list and aggregated them into an "e-business readiness index". Six indicators are considered measures of *"Adoption of ICT by business"* and six indicators of *"Use of ICT by business"* (see Table 2).

Table 2. List of indicators for the e-BSN index.

Indicator	Description
Adoption of ICT by business	
a1	Enterprises that use Internet
a2	Enterprises that have a web site/home page
a3	Enterprises that use at least two security facilities at the time of the survey
a4	Total number of persons employed using computers in their normal work routine (at least once a week)
a5	Enterprises having a broadband connection to the Internet
a6	Enterprises with a LAN and using an Intranet or Extranet
Use of ICT by business	
b1	Enterprises that have purchased products / services' via the internet, EDI[5] or any other computer mediated network where these are >1% of total purchases
b2	Enterprises that have received orders via the internet, EDI or any other computer mediated network where these are >1% of total turnover
b3	Enterprises whose IT systems for managing orders or purchases are linked automatically with other internal IT systems
b4	Enterprises whose IT systems are linked automatically to IT systems of suppliers or customers outside their enterprise group
b5	Enterprises with Internet access using the internet for banking and financial services
b6	Enterprises that have sold products to other enterprises via a presence on specialised internet market places

The set of 12 indicators has a mean absolute correlation coefficient equal to 0.48 and 12 pairs of indicators (total 66 pairs) with a correlation coefficient greater than 0.70 in

---

4   http://europa.eu.int/information_society/eeurope/news_library/documents/eeurope2005/eeurope2005_en.pdf

5   Electronic Data Interchange

absolute value (Table 3). The highest correlation is found between (a1, a2), (b1, b2) indicators (r = 0.87) pointing to the redundancy of one of the two indicators. In the context of this Index, however, it has been considered that the indicators measuring "enterprises that use Internet" (a1) and "enterprises that have a web site/home page" (a2), despite their high statistical correlation, actually express different aspects of the phenomenon, and therefore, they have both been included. The same conclusion holds for the pair (b1, b2).

Table 3. Spearman correlation coefficients for the indicators' set in the e-BSN index.

	a1	a2	a3	a4	a5	a6	b1	b2	b3	b4	b5
Adoption of ICT											
a2	0.87										
a3	0.69	0.78									
a4	0.78	0.79	0.74								
a5	0.47	0.37	0.44	0.64							
a6	0.62	0.61	0.46	0.82	0.43						
Use of ICT											
b1	0.33	0.67	0.48	0.64	0.12	0.53					
b2	0.49	0.71	0.53	0.80	0.23	0.66	0.87				
b3	0.42	0.23	0.20	0.53	0.39	0.67	0.10	0.41			
b4	0.01	-0.02	-0.09	0.04	0.01	0.23	0.14	0.27	0.74		
b5	0.76	0.62	0.55	0.62	0.35	0.58	0.38	0.50	0.38	-0.12	
b6	0.31	0.48	0.53	0.60	0.43	0.63	0.64	0.70	0.63	0.43	0.43

The presence of high correlated pairs of indicators belonging to two different groups Adoption and Use of ICT has been claimed as a reason to revise the grouping of indicators. Actually, 17 out of 36 pairs of indicators have a correlation higher than 0.5 and 3 higher than 0.7. Ideally these two groups should convey a distinct dimension of ICT in business and therefore should display little correlation. However, high correlation is a necessary but not sufficient condition for redundancy: in the e-BSN is somewhat natural the high correlation between internet connection (a1) and the use of more sophisticated applications (b5). Dropping one of the two indicators claiming a high correlation would imply dropping an important aspect of the ICT in enterprises.

Table 4. Alternative weights for the e-BSN

weights	a1	a2	a3	a4	a5	a6	b1	b2	b3	b4	b5	b6
Panel of Experts	0.09	0.08	0.05	0.08	0.11	0.10	0.08	0.09	0.10	0.10	0.06	0.06
Equal weighting	0.08	0.08	0.08	0.08	0.08	0.08	0.08	0.08	0.08	0.08	0.08	0.08
Factor Analysis	0.09	0.10	0.07	0.08	0.08	0.08	0.09	0.10	0.07	0.06	0.11	0.08

Table 4 shows that the importance of an indicator in explaining the e-readiness is sometimes different from its information content. If, for example, factor analysis (FA) suggests a weight of 0.11 for b5, a panel of experts only assigns 0.06 to it. The reverse happens for a5 and a6 which have been assigned more importance than the information content indicated by FA. The overall correlation between weights derived from FA and from a panel of expert is -0.2, indicating that the weights assigned to the e-BSN indicators from FA are based on correlations that do not correspond to their perceived importance for the phenomenon being measured. In spite of the difference in weights the result in countries' ranking is rather stable except for the middle-of-the-road performers, i.e. Austria Iceland, Norway and UK.

Test case: Environmental Sustainability Index (ESI)

The ESI aims at measuring the overall progress towards environmental sustainability. It uses 20 indicators each of which combines two to eight variables for a total of 68 underlying data-sets. These 20 indicators are further combined in five core components:

1. Environmental systems

2. Reducing stresses

3. Reducing human vulnerability

4. Social and institutional capacity to cope with environmental challenges

5. Global stewardship.

With a view to discuss the compensability issue we will apply to ESI three different aggregation approaches: linear (LIN), geometric (GME), multi-criteria (MCA). We will assume equal weighting for all indicators in any case.

Table 5 highlights the dependence of the country rankings on the aggregation method used. Already, in the group of the top 10 performers, there are some interesting results. Finland ranks on the top based on a LIN or a GME aggregation scheme, however it is found at the 8th position with MCA. Switzerland is an even more extreme case: 1st under MCA, 5th under LIN, but 21st under GME.

An interesting case that emphasises **compensability** is given by the comparison between Switzerland and Uruguay. The ranking of Uruguay is not affected at all by the aggregation scheme (always ranked 6th). Switzerland, on the other hand, is ranked 1st under MCA, 5th under LIN, but 21st under GME. Going back to the indicators level, one would notice that Switzerland has six indicators much below the average and the remaining 14 ranging from good to very good. Uruguay, on the other hand, performs very well in 17 indicators, and slightly below the average on the remaining three. The greater variability of the indicators for Switzerland with respect to Uruguay is, therefore, highlighted in the geometric aggregation scheme, whilst totally hidden in the linear aggregation scheme. Interestingly, the MCA approach would place Switzerland at the 1st position, despite the country's deficiencies in six dimensions of the phenomenon. This is partly explained by the fact that Switzerland performs better than Uruguay in 12 indicators (more than half), and it is also related to the pair-wise comparison pattern in the countries set.

Further work

As mentioned, several of the points touched upon in this brief discussion of open issues in CI building will be tackled in a forthcoming joint paper from OECD and JRC on composite indicators building. The plan of this work, which aims to be an easy to use guide to the construction and use of CI, is to cover several aspects of the problem. The flavour is given by the outline:

*   **Theoretical framework** - What is badly defined is likely to be badly measured.

*   **Data selection** – The quality of composite indicators depends largely on the quality of the underlying indicators.

- **Multivariate analysis** – Multivariate statistic is a powerful tool for investigating the inherent structure in the indicators' set.

- **Imputation of missing data**– The idea of imputation is both seductive and dangerous.

- **Normalisation** – Avoid adding up apples and pears.

- **Weighting and aggregation** – Relative importance of the indicators and compensability issues.

- **Robustness and sensitivity** – The iterative use of uncertainty and sensitivity analysis during the development of a composite indicator can contribute to its well-structuring.

- **Link to other variables** – Correlation with other simple indicators or composite indicators.

- **Visualisation** – If arguments are not put into figures, the voice of science will never be heard by practical men.

- **Back to the real data** – Deconstructing composite indicators for analytical purposes.

Our society is changing so fast that we need to know as soon as possible when things go wrong. Without rapid alert signals, appropriate corrective action is impossible. This is where composite indicators could be used as yardstick. The handbook will hopefully provide us with a structured way of thinking for the design and construction of composite indicators.

Table 5. Rankings obtained using alternative aggregation schemes: linear aggregation (LIN), geometric aggregation (GME) and multicriteria analysis (MCA).

Country	Ranking LIN	Ranking GME	RankingMCA
Finland	1	2	8
Norway	2	1	4
Sweden	3	3	2
Canada	4	4	3
Switzerland	5	21	1
Uruguay	6	6	6
Austria	7	8	9
Iceland	8	5	10
Costa Rica	9	7	13
Latvia	10	14	7
Hungary	11	9	12
Croatia	12	10	23
Botswana	13	13	15
Slovakia	14	12	14
Argentina	15	16	16
Australia	16	11	17
Estonia	17	15	11
Panama	18	18	18
New Zealand	19	67	5
Brazil	20	17	24
...			
Denmark	31	104	41
...			
France	33	26	40
...			
Spain	44	37	37
United States	45	28	35
...			
Germany	50	50	47
...			
Japan	78	71	69
...			
Italy	83	66	66
...			
United Kingdom	91	105	81
...			
Belgium	125	140	103
...			
China	129	135	134
...			
United Arab Emirates	141	141	139
Kuwait	142	142	138

References

[1] Euroabstracts (2003) Mainstreaming Innovation. Published by the European Commission, Innovation Directorate, Vol. 41-1, February 2003. The full quote is: "Our lives and societies are becoming more complex and bewildering. How can we measure and track the important factors that affect us all? Composite indicators are a way of distilling reality into a manageable form."

[2] Andrew Sharpe, 2004, Literature Review of Frameworks for Macro-indicators, Centre for the Study of Living Standards, Ottawa, CAN.

[3] Saisana M., Saltelli A., Tarantola S., 2005, Uncertainty and Sensitivity analysis techniques as tools for the quality assessment of composite indicators, *Journal of the Royal Statistical Society A*, 168,(2), 1-17.

[4] Saisana, M. and Tarantola, S., 2002, State-of-the-art report on current methodologies and practices for composite indicator development, EUR 20408 EN, European Commission-JRC: Italy.

[5] Robert Rosen, 1991, Life Itself - A Comprehensive Inquiry into Nature, Origin, and Fabrication of Life, Columbia University Press.

[6] S.O. Funtowicz and J.R. Ravetz, 1990, Uncertainty and Quality in Science for Policy, FUNTOWICZ S. O. and Ravetz J. R. Kluwer Academic Publishers, Dordrecht, NL

[7] Michael Freudenberg, 2003, Composite indicators of country performance: a critical assessment , OECD, Paris.

[8] Rowena Jacobs, Peter Smith, Maria Goddard, 2004, Measuring performance: An examination of composite performance indicators, Centre for Health Economics, University of York, UK.

[9] Andrew Sharpe Julia Salzman, 2003, Methodological Issues Encountered in the Construction of Indices of Economic and Social Well-being

[10] Julia Salzman , 2004, Methodological Choices Encountered in the Construction of Composite Indices of Economic and Social Well-Being, Center for the Study of Living Standards , Ottawa, CAN.

[11] OECD - JRC joint handbook of good practices in composite indicators building, provisional title, in progress (2004).

[12] Munda, G. and Nardo, M. (2003) On the methodological foundations of composite indicators used for ranking countries. In OECD/JRC Workshop on composite indicators of country performance, Ispra, Italy, May 12, http://webfarm.jrc.cec.eu.int/uasa/evt-OECD-JRC.asp. See also Munda, G., M. Nardo (2003), "On the Construction of Composite Indicators for Ranking Countries", mimeo, Universitat Autonoma de Barcelona.

[13] Munda G. (1995) - Multicriteria evaluation in a fuzzy environment, Physica-Verlag, Contributions to Economics Series, Heidelberg.

[14] Stefano TARANTOLA, Roman LISKA and Andrea SALTELLI, 2004, Structural Indicators of the Lisbon agenda: robustness analysis and construction of composite indicators, Report EUR 21287 EN, Luxembourg.

[15] Jamison, D. and Sandbu, M. (2001) WHO ranking of health system performance. Science, 293, 1595-1596.

[16] Tarantola, S., Jesinghaus, J. and Puolamaa, M. (2000) Global sensitivity analysis: a quality assurance tool in environmental policy modelling. In Sensitivity Analysis (eds A. Saltelli, K. Chan, M. Scott) pp. 385-397. New York: John Wiley & Sons.

[17] Saltelli A. Tarantola S., Campolongo, F. and Ratto, M., 2004, *Sensitivity Analysis in Practice. A Guide to Assessing Scientific Models*, John Wiley & Sons publishers.

Cross-Country Comparisons

Millennium Development Goals: Measuring and Monitoring Global Progress

Paul Cheung

Director, United Nations Statistics Division

The Millennium Declaration

In September 2000, at the United Nations Millennium Summit, 147 Heads of State or Government (and 189 Member States) adopted the Millennium Declaration committing to a global partnership to make the right to development a reality for everyone. They affirmed the determination to free their "fellow men, women and children from the abject and dehumanizing conditions of extreme poverty".[1] Poverty reduction was recognized as the most daunting of all the problems facing the developing world in the new century. The objective of the Millennium Declaration was to promote "a comprehensive approach and a coordinated strategy, tackling many problems simultaneously across a broad front."[2]

Setting out in details the commitments of the world leaders, the Declaration included a series of clear time-bound development goals and targets. Most of the goals set by the Millennium Declaration were not new. They derived from the global conferences of the 1990s and from the body of international norms and laws that had been codified over the previous half-century. Collectively these conferences represented an enormous effort in terms of time, political and financial resources to define and agree on the main issues and policy objectives in development. In the Millennium Declaration, a synthesis of the conference goals and objectives was carried out with global consensus. This global consensus, on both the objectives and the means, provided the platform on which the Declaration would be implemented.

With the adoption of the Declaration, the responsibility falls on the countries to carry out the commitments and to implement appropriate development strategies. As stated in the road map by the Secretary-General, the Millennium Declaration marked the transition from the era of commitments to the era of implementation.

Monitoring the Millennium Development Goals

In order to track progress towards the development goals set out in the Millennium Declaration, consultations were held to develop a system of monitoring and reporting on the progress made over time in countries and regions of the world. A comprehensive framework of goals, targets and indicators was then developed to provide the road-map for the monitoring efforts.

---

1   United Nations, Resolution adopted by the General Assembly, 55/2, United Nations Millennium Declaration, 18 September 2000 (A/RES/55/2).

2   United Nations, Road map towards the implementation of the United Nations Millennium Declaration, 6 September 2001 (A/56/326).

Eight Millennium Development Goals (MDGs) were identified as set out in the Declaration. The first seven Goals range from halving income-poverty and hunger; achieving universal primary education and empowering women; reducing under-5 mortality by two-thirds and maternal mortality by three-quarters; to reversing the spread of HIV/AIDS and other diseases; and ensuring environmental sustainability. These goals are to be achieved by 2015, as measured against their levels in 1990. The eighth goal— "a global partnership for development" — comprises a set of commitments by developed countries to support these efforts through increased aid, a non-discriminatory trading system and debt relief, and to provide work opportunities, access to affordable drugs and new technologies.

The MDG framework represents a new approach to development, which recognizes that development is not exclusively macro-economic, but covers human and social dimensions as well. More importantly, it sets specific measurable and time-bound targets for each goal. With few exceptions, all targets specify the exact objective and define in numerical terms how far countries need to go to achieve the goal. For instance, to ensure environmental sustainability, among other targets, countries will need to halve by 2015 the proportion of people without access to safe drinking water and sanitation. The MDG framework includes a total of 18 targets for the 8 goals.

Progress in attaining the targets is measured on the basis of a list of internationally agreed indicators. Extensive technical consultations were held to identify the appropriate indicators to help monitor the trends towards meeting each of the targets. This also helps countries and international agencies to set priorities in their development programmes and to harmonize the monitoring and reporting at both the international and the country level. Statisticians and technical experts from international and national statistical services were asked to provide technical specifications on the indicators needed to measure the targets. These extensive technical consultations, working within guidelines and rules established by the political process, led to a set of 48 indicators now endorsed by the General Assembly. The same set of indicators is being used as the basis for assessment of progress towards the MDGs as presented by the Secretary-General to the General Assembly every year. For the purpose of monitoring progress, the normal baseline year for the targets was fixed at 1990, which was the baseline used by the global conferences of the 1990s. (See Annex 1 for a complete list of Goals, targets and indicators)

The MDG indicators, based on established principles and practices of official statistics, are now widely accepted and used in national, regional and international programmes for monitoring and evaluating implementation of the MDGs. Supplemented by more detailed national data, and with appropriate adaptation to national needs and circumstances as appropriate, they are increasingly being used to help design and manage national policies aimed at achieving the Goals.

The development of the MDG indicators represents an important step in the work towards harmonizing and streamlining monitoring and reporting on socioeconomic development. It provides a compact and comprehensive framework summarizing many dimensions of development adopted unanimously at the national and international levels by all parties involved.

Over the years, the list of indicators has been slightly refined to adjust it to policy priorities and data availability in specific areas. These changes are generally minor and do not undermine the overall framework which is supposed to remain stable over the years to ensure continuity and consistency in the monitoring exercise. For instance, the indicators to monitor progress under the HIV/AIDS target were modified to reflect the importance of strengthening prevention programmes-- two behavioral indicators on young people are now included in the list. Clearly, there were issues of conceptual relevance and interpretability, as in the case of the unemployment indicator. Unemployment is a difficult concept when applied to workers in the poorest countries where a large part of the work is either unpaid or in the informal sector. For this indicator, it was agreed that responsible agencies would work to identify a suitable alternative.

There have been, however, attempts to expand the list of indicators or to substitute current indicators with alternatives. Some discussions are still on-going in areas that are more problematic, involving a number of measurement issues and policy implications. For instance, should the contraceptive prevalence rate be under the maternal health goal rather than an indicator on progress to reverse the spread of HIV/AIDS? There is as yet no consensus on this.

It is now clear that no new indicators will be included in the current list and no modifications will be considered until after the 2005 Millennium Summit, as any discussion and changes prior to the forthcoming Summit would only distract from the debate by decision makers and member States on the actions to be taken to achieve the goals.

Implementing global assessment of the progress towards the MDGs

Systematic and sustained tracking of the indicators is the prerequisite to ensure a common assessment of the status of the MDGs and to identify areas for intervention. The monitoring process keeps the spotlight firmly on the MDGs, informing global and national campaigns and turning the goals and targets into widely recognized measures of development benchmarks.

Monitoring the indicators at the global level has required the full collaboration of the international agencies and continuous consultation with national experts and statisticians. The work is undertaken through the Inter-agency and Expert Group (IAEG) on MDG Indicators, coordinated by the United Nations Department for Economic and Social Affairs, to ensure full consultation and collaboration across the UN system, international agencies, and national statistical services. The group met for the first time in 2001 and has successfully worked together ever since, with regular meetings—generally twice a year—and extensive collaboration in all areas, including data compilation, methodological development and statistical capacity building initiatives. All specialized agencies, regional commissions and other international statistical services are members of the group, together with representatives from national statistical offices and ad hoc experts on selected areas. For each indicator, the office of the Secretary-General has designated one or more agencies responsible for being data providers and for leading the data and methodological developments.

Given the strong focus of IAEG's work on data development at the national level, which includes statistical capacity building, bilateral and multilateral donors are also represented in the meetings. The United Nations Statistics Division maintains the public-access website of the IAEG, which contains documents and reports of their regular meetings and background material and reports of the thematic sub-groups.

The strong collaboration and coordination efforts carried out by the IAEG on MDG Indicators represent an important achievement of the international statistical community. For the first time, international agencies have come together in a fully concerted way to compile and analyse the necessary data for the global monitoring. Agencies producing the same or similar indicators have agreed to use a common methodology and issue one common set of data and estimates.

The assessment of progress towards the MDGs produced by the IAEG represents the official view of the whole UN system and is used in the annual report by the Secretary-General to the General Assembly on progress made in the implementation of the Millennium Declaration. The data and analysis prepared by the group every year are compiled in a comprehensive report consisting of extensive analysis of the current situation around the world, trends and expected progress by the target year of 2015 on each target. The report also presents analysis of supplementary "non-official" indicators, some discussion on policy implications and examples of successful strategies as indicated by the responsible agencies. The report is posted on the website of the United Nations Statistics Division and is linked to a number of other informative web pages maintained by the Division, as well as to the Millennium Indicators Database—a database containing all official country series and regional and global estimates on the 48 agreed indicators. Links are also provided to all background documents and official General Assembly reports and resolutions on which the IAEG work is based.

The MDG indicators have also provided a unique opportunity for the international statistical community to raise their awareness on the importance of statistics to inform policies. For the first time the international statistical community has come together and work towards measuring progress towards human development. These efforts have also led to the recognition of the urgent need to build national capacity for monitoring and reporting on goals and targets. **MDGs as national goals: country level monitoring**

It is crucial that the millennium development goals are being adopted by the countries and serve to increase the coherence and consistency of national policies and programmes. Active country participation and ownership of the MDGs are critical to their effectiveness. By adapting the global MDG framework to national priorities and mobilizing local resources to prepare the necessary data and analysis, the national monitoring of the MDGs, including the preparation of country reports, has emerged as an important results-oriented counterpart to the Poverty Reduction Strategy Papers (PRSPs) and Country Assistance Strategies (CASs). Country reports provide a concise overview of objectives and results for intra-governmental mobilisation and analysis and public understanding and debate.

The assessment of progress in countries is based on data produced by the national statistical authority and is presented in MDG country reports. MDGs national reports have now been produced in 76 countries and widely used to inform national debate and promote the production and use of statistics for policy making and monitoring.

While the MDGs themselves set out overall social and poverty objectives, the PRSPs bring together the macroeconomic framework and the detailed policies which comprise the country's development programme. The MDG country reports provide the operational framework and key benchmarks for describing and monitoring local progress towards these objectives. Even in countries in special circumstances, such as those in conflict and post-conflict situations and countries affected by humanitarian, refugee and displaced persons crises, the MDG framework has proven useful for planning assistance, support and redevelopment.

In some countries, there could be is the existence of social and geographical inequality which creates pockets of deprivation. To address this, some countries have taken the MDGs to the community level, i.e., have set disaggregated targets for sub-groups or sub-regions within the country; some have set targets for reducing disparities within the country. MDG indicators have been disaggregated to address these priorities, by geographical areas and by population groups. The MDGs have thus extended the scope of the anti-poverty strategies contained in PRSPs.

Monitoring the MDGs at the country level often include procedural, qualitative and quantitative activities related to the preparation of country indicators and reports. These processes engage governments in national debates to discuss priorities and to tailor the MDG targets to these priorities and national circumstances. National statistical services have become increasingly involved in the preparation and analysis of MDG indicators. This has resulted in a stronger sense of national "ownership" and also caused national policy decisions and planning efforts to gradually coalesce around a defined set of development aspirations. In many cases, the global MDGs and indicators have been adjusted to countries' individual development conditions. For example, several middle-income countries have adopted more ambitious targets and goals and are now referred to as "MDG-plus countries".

Producing statistics for monitoring the MDGs

More than three years later, the Millennium Development Goals have succeeded in raising awareness that a sound quantitative knowledge of progress achieved is an important element in reaching the final goals set by the Millennium Declaration. The monitoring requirements however have also clearly uncovered important shortcomings in the availability of data to monitor development efforts. Producing the necessary data to monitor the MDGs in countries where resources are limited is obviously a significant challenge. Aggregating the data up to a meaningful regional and global level is another complex task.

Data requirement and statistical capacity building

It is clear that in many countries, existing data are insufficient to assess trends in a number of indicators. Also, for some of the indicators, technical specifications and methodologies need to be further developed. For instance, in the 2004 Report to the General Assembly on the Implementation of the Millennium Declaration, there were no trend data or inadequate trend data for 8 of the 48 MDG indicators and problems of uncertainty for some others.[3]

The availability of reliable statistics and the capacity of the governments to systematically measure and monitor indicators is a critical success factor for the achievement of the MDGs. The lack of statistical capabilities in some developing countries makes it difficult to obtain good and reliable data. Out of 56 countries and areas in Africa, for instance, 19 have not conducted a population census during the last ten years, and nearly twice as many in the previous ten years. Many countries do not have a sustainable, coherent programme of household surveys, or administrative data systems which can be used to produce basic statistics routinely.[4] Where basic statistical systems are not available, the global monitoring may have to rely on national and international

---

3 United Nations, Implementation of the United Nations Millennium Declaration, Report of the Secretary-General, 27 August 2004, A/59/282.

4 See, for example, the case studies and international study of the PARIS21 Task Team on Improved Statistical Support for Monitoring Development Goals, available from www.paris21.org.

estimates of widely varying quality and reliability. This may lead to misjudgments regarding progress and may undermine the effectiveness of policy interventions at national and sub-national levels.

Recognizing that quantitative monitoring of progress is easier for some targets than for others and that good quality data for some of the indicators are simply not (yet) available for many countries, the Inter-agency and Expert Group has agreed that their monitoring task cannot be fulfilled without addressing the need to assist countries in building national capacity.

Shortcomings in national capacities for maintaining sound statistical programmes in developing countries and economies in transition have long been a concern of statisticians and development practitioners. However, until recently, it has been difficult to mobilize sufficient national and international commitments to provide adequate and well-coordinated resources to have a lasting impact on the development of national statistical services. Over the past three years, as commitments to the MDGs have crystallized, governments, agencies and donors have identified the statistical programme requirements for effective and sustained monitoring as a priority in development assistance.

A major step in turning this recognition into action for statistical development was the endorsement of "The Marrakech Action Plan for Statistics—Better Data for Better Results, An Action Plan for Improving Development Statistics", by the Second International Roundtable on Managing for Development Results, held in Marrakech 4-5 February 2004.[5] The United Nations Statistical Commission added its endorsement at its session in March 2004.[6]

The Marrakech Action Plan for Statistics makes a number of specific recommendations aimed at donors and the international statistical community to support the development of national statistical programmes and to ensure funding and technical support for statistical capacity building.

The data collection programmes required to fulfill the monitoring needs, are in large part the standard tools employed by statistical services around the world:

- Household surveys covering sex-disaggregated data on income and consumption, economic activity and employment–including formal and informal–unemployment, population characteristics including education, reproductive and child health, issues of health prevention (especially for major diseases such as HIV/AIDS, malaria and TB) and demographic, household and dwelling characteristics;

- Vital registration systems;

- Administrative records, including education enrolment;

- Population censuses.

Ongoing efforts to strengthen countries' capacity to produce data are generally targeted at the improvement of these basic programmes. But the MDGs also focus on important aspects of social and human development that are often not entirely addressed by existing data collection instruments. Statistical systems need to turn their attention to areas that are in some countries very little developed, such as: environment statistics;

---

5 The Marrakech Actions Plan for Statistics is available from http://worldbank.org/data/results.html .

6 See the report of the Statistical Commission at its 2004 session (United Nations document E/2004/24, section 5D, available from http://unstats.un.org).

statistics of new technologies especially information technologies and research and development; a sound health information system that harmonizes household survey data with vital and administrative records–including data on preventive and public health, and access and use of services. Among the greatest technical challenges, national statistical systems also need to further develop and harmonize disaggregation methods especially for gender, urban/rural and cities, sub-national areas, and national and ethnic groups. Finally, a key prerequisite for a coherent result-oriented MDG reporting is an improved collaboration among various branches of the national statistical services and improved ways of analyzing, presenting and disseminating statistics.

Improving methods

The second challenge is improving the standards and methods for compiling and analysing MDG indicators, including finding ways to aggregate country data in a meaningful way, overcoming problems of comparability and, even more importantly, providing a meaningful analysis of the aggregate figures that represents the local situation.

The development and application of standard statistical concepts and methods for national and international use in compiling data for the MDG indicators has been an important preoccupation of the statistical community since the monitoring of MDGs started in 2001.

The political importance attached to the MDG indicators has created a number of significant challenges for international agencies. The international statistical community has the responsibility of ensuring the credibility of the MDGs by providing every year a sound basis for assessing progress and for focusing the international debate and the development of strategies for the achievement of the goals. Valuable initiatives have been undertaken to improve and standardize monitoring methods, provide guidelines to countries and prepare coherent sets of data and analysis for specific targets/indicators. International agencies and programmes have created specialized working groups on monitoring and indicators development—such as for instance the Roll Back Malaria, the Monitoring and Evaluation Reference Group (MERG) on HIV/AIDS, the Joint Monitoring Programme for Water and Sanitation, the Slums Expert Group and the Child Survival Initiative-- and a number of sub-groups on thematic areas of the MDGs— including environment, gender, poverty and hunger, slums and employment. Many of these groups are working directly within the framework of the United Nations Inter-Agency and Expert Group on MDG Indicators, which serves as an overall coordinating body for international monitoring of achievement of the MDGs.

These groups work to improve existing international standards and guidelines for the preparation of MDG indicators, and to provide guidance to countries on their national data collection programmes. They have reviewed existing data sources and alternative ways of conducting the analysis and assessing trends. They have also addressed the need to refine the existing indicators to better measure progress towards the target and goals and adequately reflect the situation of poorest countries, where large part of work is informal or unpaid, gender differences are significant, major diseases are still unabated and education and health systems poorly working and difficult to monitor.

Another important preoccupation of the Inter-agency and expert group on MDG indicators has been identifying methods to estimate missing data and aggregate country figures to produce regional and global estimates, to ensure coherence across the international system and transparency, while at the same time providing sets of estimates of reasonable quality even for indicators where country data are very scarce.

Data in international series compiled by the designated specialized UN agencies and other international organisations are primarily national data adjusted for international comparability. When national data are not available or considered of poor quality, models are used to produce series of estimates. In some instances, assessment of trends is not possible as national data are available only for one point in time.

Methodologies for regional estimates and aggregates vary with the indicator. In most cases, there are missing values for several countries for one or more years and data are explicitly or implicitly imputed for the calculation of the aggregated figures. Important initiatives to estimate data are carried out by all international agencies engaged in the monitoring exercise and efforts have been initiated to review methods and modeling technique and improve existing documentation on methodologies used.

The challenges ahead

The MDGs have succeeded in raising awareness of the importance of a sound quantitative knowledge of what has been achieved and the remaining distance. The monitoring requirements have also contributed to the launching of a number of important initiatives aimed at strengthening data production both at the national and international levels. However, the present gaps in the availability of data for effective monitoring clearly show that much work remains to be done. There is little doubt that the MDGs monitoring process has had a positive impact on the international statistical community as well as at the country level.

The availability of data necessary to compile the indicators depends on the capacities of national statistical services. Strengthening national statistical services and improving the use of data in countries represent the most urgent area of work. Donors must work with the developing countries in a coordinated fashion in planning and implementing support to the national statistical services and ensuring the development of underlying statistical capacities. Sufficient government and donor support to ensure the development and maintenance of these capacities must be an integral part of PRSP planning relating to MDGs. Some of the activities could include the following:

1. The improvement of basic statistical infrastructure and data collection programmes to produce a sustained flow of reliable and timely social and economic statistics.

2. Funding and technical support for population and housing censuses.

3. Increased financing for statistical capacity building based on the implementation of national statistical development strategies.

4. International support to regional and sub-regional training centres in statistics to provide a regular flow of qualified statistical staff to work in national statistical services.

Continuous efforts are needed by the international statistical community to further strengthen their coordination and collaboration to avoid duplication, ensure consistency and overcome problems of comparability across different sets of data. The international availability of comprehensive, reliable and well-documented statistics and indicators on the Millennium Development Goals must be further improved. The data on indicators, together with the methodologies, should be made as widely available as possible.

ANNEX 1

Millennium Development Goals (MDGs)

Goals and Targets (from the Millennium Declaration)	Indicators for monitoring progress
Goal 1: Eradicate extreme poverty and hunger	
Target 1: Halve, between 1990 and 2015, the proportion of people whose income is less than less than one dollar a day	1. Proportion of population below $1 (PPP) per day[1] 2. Poverty gap ratio [incidence x depth of poverty] 3. Share of poorest quintile in national consumption
Target 2: Halve, between 1990 and 2015, the proportion of people who suffer from hunger	4. Prevalence of underweight children under-five years of age 5. Proportion of population below minimum level of dietary energy consumption
Goal 2: Achieve universal primary education	
Target 3: Ensure that, by 2015, children everywhere, boys and girls alike, will be able to complete a full course of primary schooling	6. Net enrolment ratio in primary education 7. Proportion of pupils starting grade 1 who reach grade 5[2] 8. Literacy rate of 15-24 year-olds
Goal 3: Promote gender equality and empower women	
Target 4: Eliminate gender disparity in primary and secondary education, preferably by 2005, and in all levels of education no later than 2015	9. Ratios of girls to boys in primary, secondary and tertiary education 10. Ratio of literate women to men, 15-24 years old 11. Share of women in wage employment in the non-agricultural sector 12. Proportion of seats held by women in national parliament
Goal 4: Reduce child mortality	
Target 5: Reduce by two-thirds, between 1990 and 2015, the under-five mortality rate	13. Under-five mortality rate 14. Infant mortality rate 15.Proportion of 1 year-old children immunised against measles
Goal 5: Improve maternal health	
Target 6: Reduce by three-quarters, between 1990 and 2015, the maternal mortality ratio	16. Maternal mortality ratio 17.Proportion of births attended by skilled health personnel
Goal 6: Combat HIV/AIDS, malaria and other diseases	

Target 7: Have halted by 2015 and begun to reverse the spread of HIV/AIDS	18. HIV prevalence among pregnant women aged 5-24 years
	 19. Condom use rate of the contraceptive prevalence rate[3]
	   19a. Condom use at last high-risk sex
	   19b. Percentage of population aged 15-24 years with comprehensive correct knowledge of HIV/AIDS[4]
	   19c. Contraceptive prevalence rate
	 20. Ratio of school attendance of orphans to school attendance of non-orphans aged 10-14 years

Target 8: Have halted by 2015 and begun to reverse the incidence of malaria and other major diseases	21. Prevalence and death rates associated with malaria 22. Proportion of population in malaria-risk areas using effective malaria prevention and treatment measures[5] 23. Prevalence and death rates associated with tuberculosis 24. Proportion of tuberculosis cases detected and cured under directly observed treatment short course DOTS (Internationally recommended TB control strategy)

Goal 7: Ensure environmental sustainability	
Target 9: Integrate the principles of sustainable development into country policies and programmes and reverse the loss of environmental resources	25. Proportion of land area covered by forest 26. Ratio of area protected to maintain biological diversity to surface area 27. Energy use (kg oil equivalent) per $1 GDP (PPP) 28. Carbon dioxide emissions per capita and consumption of ozone-depleting CFCs (ODP tons) 29. Proportion of population using solid fuels
Target 10: Halve, by 2015, the proportion of people without sustainable access to safe drinking water and basic sanitation	30. Proportion of population with sustainable access to an improved water source, urban and rural 31. Proportion of population with access to improved sanitation, urban and rural
Target 11: By 2020, to have achieved a significant improvement in the lives of at least 100 million slum dwellers	32. Proportion of households with access to secure tenure

Goal 8: Develop a global partnership for development	
Target 12: Develop further an open, rule-based, predictable, non-discriminatory trading and financial system Includes a commitment to good governance, development and poverty reduction – both nationally and internationally Target 13: Address the special needs of the least developed countries Includes: tariff and quota free access for the least developed countries' exports; enhanced programme of debt relief for heavily indebted poor countries (HIPC) and cancellation of official bilateral debt; and more generous ODA for countries committed to poverty reduction Target 14: Address the special needs of landlocked developing countries and small island developing States (through the Programme of Action for the Sustainable Development of Small Island Developing States and the outcome of the twenty-second special session of the General Assembly) Target 15: Deal comprehensively with the debt problems of developing countries through national and international measures in order to make debt sustainable in the long term	*Some of the indicators listed below are monitored separately for the least developed countries (LDCs), Africa, landlocked developing countries and small island developing States.* Official development assistance (ODA) 33. Net ODA, total and to the least developed countries, as percentage of OECD/DAC donors' gross national income 34. Proportion of total bilateral, sector-allocable ODA of OECD/DAC donors to basic social services (basic education, primary health care, nutrition, safe water and sanitation). 35. Proportion of bilateral official development assistance of OECD/DAC donors that is untied 36. ODA received in landlocked developing countries as a proportion of their gross national incomes 37. ODA received in small island developing States as a proportion of their gross national incomes Market access 38. Proportion of total developed country imports (by value and excluding arms) from developing countries and least developed countries, admitted free of duty 39. Average tariffs imposed by developed countries on agricultural products and textiles and clothing from developing countries 40. Agricultural support estimate for OECD countries as a percentage of their gross domestic product 41. Proportion of ODA provided to help build trade capacity Debt sustainability 42. Total number of countries that have reached their HIPC decision points and number that have reached their HIPC completion points (cumulative) 43. Debt relief committed under HIPC Initiative 44. Debt service as a percentage of exports of goods and services
Target 16: In cooperation with developing countries, develop and implement strategies for decent and productive work for youth	45. Unemployment rate of young people aged 15-24 years, each sex and total[6]
Target 17: In cooperation with pharmaceutical companies, provide access to affordable essential drugs in developing countries	46. Proportion of population with access to affordable essential drugs on a sustainable basis
Target 18: In cooperation with the private sector, make available the benefits of new technologies, especially information and communications	47. Telephone lines and cellular subscribers per 100 population 48. Personal computers in use per 100 population Internet users per 100 population

The Millennium Development Goals and targets come from the Millennium Declaration, signed by 189 countries, including 147 heads of State and Government, in September 2000 (http://www.un.org/millennium/declaration/ares552e.htm). The goals and targets are interrelated and should be seen as a whole. They represent a partnership between the developed countries and the developing countries "to create an environment – at the national and global levels alike – which is conducive to development and the elimination of poverty".

Note: Goals, targets and indicators effective 8 September 2003.

[1] For monitoring country poverty trends, indicators based on national poverty lines should be used, where available.

[2] An alternative indicator under development is "primary completion rate".

[3] Amongst contraceptive methods, only condoms are effective in preventing HIV transmission. Since the condom use rate is only measured among women in union, it is supplemented by an indicator on condom use in high-risk situations (indicator 19a) and an indicator on HIV/AIDS knowledge (indicator 19b). Indicator 19c (contraceptive prevalence rate) is also useful in tracking progress in other health, gender and poverty goals.

[4] This indicator is defined as the percentage of population aged 15-24 who correctly identify the two major ways of preventing the sexual transmission of HIV (using condoms and limiting sex to one faithful, uninfected partner), who reject the two most common local misconceptions about HIV transmission, and who know that a healthy-looking person can transmit HIV. However, since there are currently not a sufficient number of surveys to be able to calculate the indicator as defined above, UNICEF, in collaboration with UNAIDS and WHO, produced two proxy indicators that represent two components of the actual indicator. They are the following: a) percentage of women and men 15-24 who know that a person can protect herself/herself from HIV infection by "consistent use of condom"; b) percentage of women and men 15-24 who know a healthy-looking person can transmit HIV.

[5] Prevention to be measured by the percentage of children under 5 sleeping under insecticide-treated bed nets; treatment to be measured by percentage of children under 5 who are appropriately treated.

[6] An improved measure of the target for future years is under development by the International Labour Organisation.

Indicators for EU Policy Making: The Example of Structural Indicators

Pedro Díaz Munoz

Eurostat

Introduction

In the European Union there has been a recent trend towards an increased use of indicators to define, monitor and assess policy. As a result a somewhat proliferation of sets of indicators or scoreboards have been developed. At the summit of these collections stands a specific set, the Structural Indicators. These are used to measure progress towards the Lisbon Objectives.

Every year, the European Commission presents to the Spring Council of the European Union a Synthesis Report that discusses the achievement of the Lisbon objectives. An important element of this report is its statistical annex which includes the data for all EU countries of the Structural Indicators.

Furthermore, Eurostat publishes on its Web site a page devoted to this statistical annex in which the set of indicators are continuously updated for public free access (Annex 1 and 2). The present paper reviews the process of creation of the Structural Indicators and evaluates the main challenges that have to be faced by statistical Institutions for the establishment of the list; for the production of the actual data and for the evaluation of their quality.

A new political context with a key role for indicators

A reconsideration of the way to define public policies, to increase the legitimacy of the public

Institutions to enhance democracy have been going on since some years in the EU. This has lead, among others, to the publication in the summer of 2001 by the European Commission of a White Paper on European Governance and has also lead to the definition of the Open Method of Coordination (OMC). That method has had a considerable impact on the role of statistics in decision making. It was formally established by the Lisbon European Council (23–24 March 2000), even if it was used previously without being formalised.

The OMC involves:

- Fixing guidelines combined with specific timetables for achieving specific goals in the short, medium and long terms;

- Establishing, where appropriate, quantitative and qualitative indicators and benchmarks against the best in the world and tailored to the needs of different countries and sectors as a means of comparing best practice;

- Translating these European guidelines into national and regional policies by setting specific targets;

- Periodic monitoring, evaluation and peer review organised as mutual learning processes.

The increasing role of the OMC, used in areas like the Broad Economic Policy Guidelines, the European Employment Strategy, the social inclusion and innovation policies, to name a few, has provoked not only a more systematic use of statistical information but also, and mainly, a more explicit reference to quantitative information in the justification of political initiatives. And this broad use of indicators is, of course, not restricted to areas where the OMC is applied as illustrated by the role played by statistical indicators in the EMU, in the stability and growth pact, in the sustainable development strategy, in regional policies, for instance.

The necessity to base policy decisions and to monitor programmes with statistical information stems from different considerations:

- New, and more limited, role of law

- New approach to problem solving with iteration, mutual cooperation and standard settings

- Participation of different instances (regional, national, supranational or private and public) and necessity of a public dialogue

- Preservation of diversity and subsidiary

- Accountability of public authorities

The example of Structural Indicators

The use of Structural Indicators is an example of this new way to design common policies at the European level and to promote convergence among Member States through, among others, a common definition of objectives and a common set of indicators to monitor the progress and the convergence.

The Lisbon agenda and the use of indicators

In its 2000 Lisbon meeting, the European Council launched the challenge of making the EU "the most competitive and dynamic knowledge-based economy in the world, capable of sustaining economic growth with more and better jobs and greater social cohesion" and invited the Commission to draw up an annual synthesis report on progress on the basis of structural indicators to be agreed relating to employment, innovation, economic reform and social cohesion. This decision puts an incredible pressure on official statisticians.

Following this commitment, each of the last three years, the Commission and the Council agreed a set of structural indicators which were used in the Commission's Spring Report and other Commission documents to provide statistical support for policy messages and to measure progress towards the Lisbon objectives.

The structural indicators were chosen according to different criteria. They should be:

1. Easy to read and understand;

2. Policy relevant;

3. Mutually consistent;

4. Available in a timely fashion;

5. Available for most, if not all Member States, acceding and candidate countries;

6. Comparable between these countries and, as far as possible, with other countries;

7. selected from reliable sources; and

8. Do not impose too large a burden on statistical institutes and respondents.

Necessity of a framework

However, even with this set of criteria, the number of structural indicators has tended to increase over the years thus making it more and more difficult to draw a clear picture on progress towards the Lisbon objectives. Recognising this issue, the Spring 2003 European Council Conclusions noted the Commission's intention, in close co-operation with the European Statistical System, *"to report in time for the 2004 Spring European Council on how the use of structural indicators and other analytical tools for assessing progress on Lisbon strategy could be strengthened"* (§18).

As a first response to this request, the Commission proposed to structure the set of indicators into two subsets: a shortlist of fourteen core indicators and a database of about 100 other indicators.

A **shortlist of indicators** had several advantages. First, the main purpose of the structural indicators, as stated in the Lisbon European Council conclusions, is to allow for an assessment of progress towards the Lisbon objectives in the Commission's Spring Report. A shortlist of indicators makes it easier to present a clear picture of the Member States' positions relative to the most important Lisbon targets. This clarity helps to maintain the momentum of the Lisbon strategy. Using a smaller number of indicators it is also possible to achieve a better coverage of the acceding and candidate countries and to present information on both levels and changes in performance more easily. Second, the proposed list of indicators includes well-known and easy-to-understand indicators. These indicators are more understandable by the general public as they are familiar and their drawbacks are also better known. Third, the shortlist of indicators has a clearer logic. Therefore the policy messages drawn from the progress assessment based on the structural indicators will be soundly based. Finally, the stability of the list will be ensured by agreeing it once every three years.

It should be noted that different responses can be given to the concern raised in the European Council conclusions. The necessity to structure sets of indicators used for policy making has for instance been addressed differently in the area of Sustainable Development Indicators.

Another framework proposed for Sustainable Development Indicators

In that area of Sustainable Development (SD), as well, a large number of indicators were needed to properly assess the multidimensional nature of SD. In order to facilitate communication about SDI, the indicator set was built as a three-level pyramid. The different levels can be used in order to match the needs of different types of users. The hierarchical framework itself lends readily to an indicator pyramid, especially as the three levels of the framework also correspond to the headline objectives and implementation measures to be monitored by the SD indicators.

- Level 1: consists in a set of 12 high level indicators allowing an initial analysis of the theme development (Economic development, poverty and social exclusion, ageing society, public health …). These indicators are aimed at a high-level policy-making and general public and can therefore be seen as a set of headline indicators.

- Level 2: corresponds to sub-themes of the framework and monitor, together with Level 1 indicators, progress in achieving the headline policy objectives. These 40 indicators are aimed at evaluation of the core policy areas and communication with general public.

- Level 3: corresponds to various measures implementing the headline objectives and facilitate a deeper insight to special issues in the theme. These 84 indicators are aimed for the further policy analysis and better understanding of trends and complexity of issues associated with the theme or inter-linkages with other themes in the framework. They are intended for a more specialised audience.

The short list of structural indicators

The short list is based on the political priorities of the Lisbon strategy and is balanced to reflect the importance that Lisbon and Gothenburg placed on the domains of employment, innovation and research, economic reform, social cohesion and the environment.

The structural indicators proposed for the Spring Report 2004	
Indicators	Country coverage
1. GDP per capita	Full coverage[1]
2. Labour productivity	Full coverage
3. Employment rate*	Full coverage
4. Employment rate of older workers*	Full coverage
5. Spending on human resources (public expenditure on education)	15 MS + 12 ACC
6. Research and Development expenditure	15 MS + 12 ACC
7. Information Technology expenditure	15 MS + 11 ACC
8. Financial market integration (convergence in bank lending rates)	Not applicable (measured by the variation across available countries)
9. At risk-of-poverty rate*	Full coverage
10. Long-term unemployment*	Full coverage
11. Dispersion of regional employment rates	12 MS + 6 ACC[2]
12. Greenhouse gases emissions	Full coverage
13. Energy intensity of the economy	Full coverage
14. Volume of transport	15 MS + 11 ACC

* Indicators disaggregated by gender.

---

1   "Full coverage" means data are available for all 15 Member States (MS) and all 13 acceding or candidate countries (ACC).

2   Calculated using NUTS2 regions and hence not applicable for 3 MS and 6 ACCs.

A new kind of quality assessment

As already written, the provision of structural indicators put a huge pressure on statisticians which entailed not only an important work load for statistics in Europe but also a new role for statistics in the EU decision making. The key role and the visibility given to the indicators called for in depth study of their fitness for the Lisbon agenda. For Official statistics, this role was not new but the emphasis put on the assessment was. But part of the information did not come from the ESS. Who was supposed to guarantee its quality? As some indicators were produced by the services whose activities had to be assessed, they were not eligible candidates. Official statisticians were ideally placed to play that new role: statistical institutes as clearing houses and as more general service providers.

A procedure was designed to quality profile the Structural Indicators within the ESS. This quality profile can be considered as a kind of technical certification of the information. It is supposed to inform the policy maker on the technical properties of the indicators and to help him in the selection of the most appropriate ones.

The design of the procedure raised numerous interesting questions as well: should the assessment result in a "Yes" or a "No"? Should at least a kind of overall evaluation, with a grade, be proposed? Should relevance be part of that grade? How does this link with the existing approach of quality (ESS definition of the 6 quality components for instance)? How to present the result of the assessments in a readable way? How to approach the quality of a set as something different from the quality of the parts?

After discussions with the Member States, the services of the Commission and after different tests and feasibility studies, a method for assessing the quality and a procedure to involve the ESS were designed.

Features of the Eurostat quality profile

The criteria used in the quality profile are derived from the joint Eurostat and ESS definition of quality in statistics and have been tailored to the characteristics being most important to users of structural indicators given their objectives.

The following **user-oriented quality criteria** are covered.

1. **Feasibility** by looking at **timeliness** and **coverage**: The indicator has to be available in time for Member States, Candidate Countries and as far as possible the United States and Japan. It should cover, in principle, two target reference years, of which one is the year prior to the Lisbon European Council 1999 and the other, if possible, the year preceding the annual Spring Reports. Moreover, longer time series are required to allow for a dynamic analysis.

2. **Technical soundness**, comprising overall **accuracy**, **comparability** (over time and across countries), is assessed as far as possible on the basis of existing quality information in the domain: the indicator should stem from reliable sources meeting high standards and involving statistical expertise as regards the technique and methodology applied; the indicator should be comparable between Member States, Candidate Countries as well as with the United States and Japan; the indicator has to be comparable from one year to another.

For each of these components a brief overall assessment (high/restricted) is provided, substantiated by further qualitative information, if considered useful.

Moreover, room is provided to describe (3) **other characteristics** which may lead to restricting the use of this indicator in the Spring Report, relating e.g. to the complexity of an indicator, a lack of an unambiguous scientific basis or to the coherence with other existing indicators, lack of comprehensive metadata etc....

The quality profile discusses (4) the **relevance** which is considered here in a broad sense, comprising not only the content and suitability for a clear normative interpretation of the indicator but also possible restrictions with regard to describing the characteristics of interest (target population).

The quality profile also includes a (5) **systemic criterion** aiming at – as far as possible - an assessment of how well the indicator contributes to an integrated analysis of the whole set. This part of the quality profile is to be distinguished from the other criteria. It requires looking at the whole set at one time rather than at a single indicator. Moreover, it introduces a notion of relativity of indicator quality. Depending on which other indicators feature on the list, the qualities of one indicator may be seen in a different light. Its inclusion has been motivated by the fact that the database of structural indicators has become, over time to some extent, a collection rather than an organised set of indicators stemming from all kinds of different sources. To deal with the contribution of an indicator to the quality of the set the following three approaches have been identified: to explore the internal logic of the data set by means of statistical analysis, to consider whether an indicator qualifies for an integrated policy analysis provided through European Statistical System's accounting frameworks and to assess how far an indicator is suited to identify spill-over effects between the policy domains. For the time being, this approach has an explorative character. It will be further developed in the framework of the Eurostat structural indicators working group.

Finally, information on (7) the **development perspective** for improving the quality of an indicator is provided, including, as far as possible, a qualitative estimation of the related additional costs in terms of implications for the producers of data and burden for the respondents.

A last paragraph lists – if applicable - (8) relevant European legislation that may be consulted for further reference.

The quality profile provides also an overall quality assessment of each indicator according to 4 quality grades (AA, A, B, C). A fifth category has been added to qualify an indicator as to be (further) developed. See Annex 3 for an example of a quality profile.

The procedure used to produce the quality profiles

The drafting of the quality profile involves the National Statistical Institutes (NSI) of the Member States during the various steps of the process from gathering basic quality information until circulating the final draft to the relevant ESS working groups.

To arrive at a common ESS understanding of the quality of an indicator, Eurostat has proposed to have the quality profiles per indicator "officially recognised" by the European Statistical System as a final step prior to their release on the Eurostat website. This joint recognition is in particular important with regard to the quality grades, the development perspective for an indicator and the qualitative assessment of the related costs.

There are several arguments for this approach, among them to promote

1. Horizontal consistency and comparability of the assessment of different indicators by involving on a continuous basis a "neutral" instance, other than the domain concerned. This holds not only for the set of structural indicators but as well for other (sets of) indicators subject to user-oriented quality reporting, like e.g. the sustainable development indicators.

2. Vertical consistency of producer- and user-oriented quality reporting for one and the same indicator (or data source)

3. Consistency with regard to quality reporting by Eurostat and by the National Statistical Institutes on national level

4. Visibility of the work within the European Statistical System

Creation of a new kind of solidarity among Official Statistical Institutions

The use of indicators to benchmark countries and to monitor convergence has also an impact on the way the "global system" has to be organised:

Harmonised definitions are necessary.

Solidarity is indispensable as the force of the system could be the force of the weakest, Agreement on the information to use for National and Community analysis has to be reached to guarantee coherence of the conclusions drawn at different levels and their credibility.

On the other hand, the experience of Structural Indicators puts in evidence the need of actions from the statistical institutions in order to respond jointly to the information demands of policy makers. This ensures that the indicators retained are relevant; but also feasible and that their production is included as a priority in the statistical work programmes. The dialog –and tension!- between policy makers and statisticians, if well managed, is a good example of adapting statistical development to user needs while guaranteeing data quality.

Finally, use of indicators for long term perspectives like in the Lisbon agenda (10 years) and in the SDS calls for sustainable systems that can be best provided within the official statistics framework. Indeed, sustainability, credibility, neutrality are key characteristics that can only be ensured by statistical institutions. They can explain the increasing demand placed on official statistics, they should justify the trust put on these institutions by the policy makers.

Annex 1

http://europa.eu.int/comm/eurostat/structuralindicators

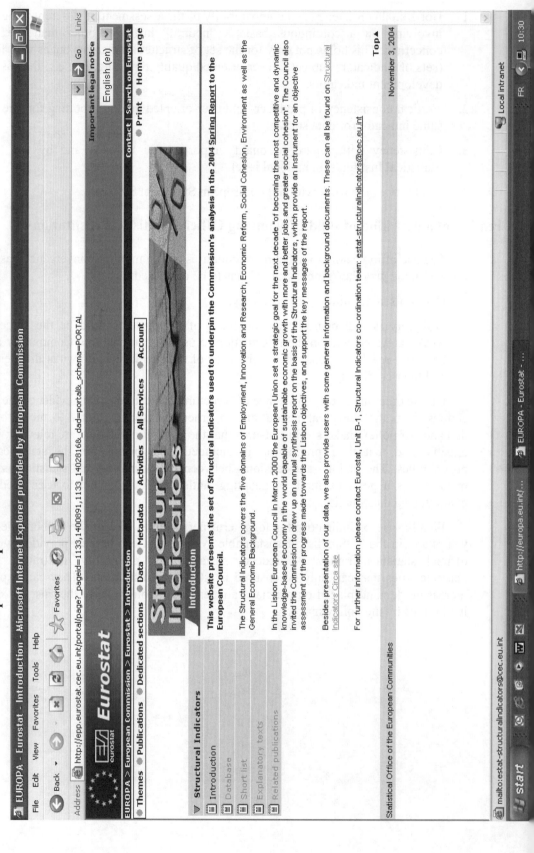

EUROPA - Eurostat - Introduction - Microsoft Internet Explorer provided by European Commission

File   Edit   View   Favorites   Tools   Help

Back

Address   http://epp.eurostat.cec.eu.int/portal/page?_pageid=1133,1400891,1133_14028168&_dad=portal&_schema=PORTAL

Important legal notice

English (en)

Eurostat

EUROPA > European Commission > Eurostat > Introduction

Themes   ● Publications   ● Dedicated sections   ● Data   ● Metadata   ● Activities   ● All Services   ● Account

Contact | Search on Eurostat
● Print ● Home page

Structural Indicators

Introduction

▼ **Structural Indicators**

- Introduction
- Database
- Short list
- Explanatory texts
- Related publications

This website presents the set of Structural Indicators used to underpin the Commission's analysis in the 2004 Spring Report to the European Council.

The Structural Indicators covers the five domains of Employment, Innovation and Research, Economic Reform, Social Cohesion, Environment as well as the General Economic Background.

In the Lisbon European Council in March 2000 the European Union set a strategic goal for the next decade "of becoming the most competitive and dynamic knowledge-based economy in the world capable of sustainable economic growth with more and better jobs and greater social cohesion". The Council also invited the Commission to draw up an annual synthesis report on the basis of the Structural Indicators, which provide an instrument for an objective assessment of the progress made towards the Lisbon objectives, and support the key messages of the report.

Besides presentation of our data, we also provide users with some general information and background documents. These can all be found on Structural Indicators Circa site

For further information please contact Eurostat, Unit B-1, Structural Indicators co-ordination team: estat-structuralindicators@cec.eu.int

Top▲

Statistical Office of the European Communities

November 3, 2004

mailto:estat-structuralindicators@cec.eu.int

Local intranet

start   EUROPA - Eurostat - ...   http://europa.eu.int/...   EUROPA - Eurostat - ...   FR   10:30

Annex 2

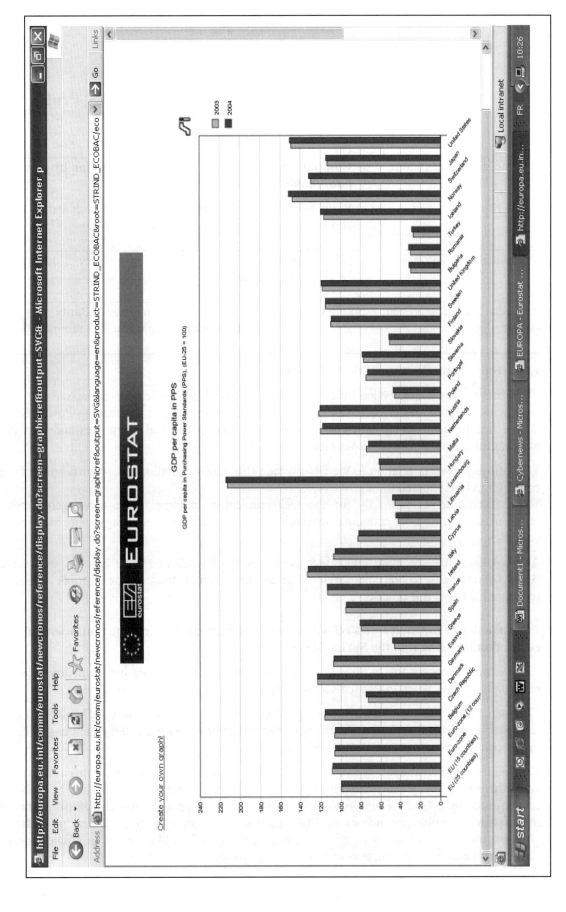

Annex 3 Eurostat Structural Indicators Quality Profile

Indicator (definition)	Comparative price levels of final consumption by private households including indirect taxes: Ratio between the respective Purchasing Power Parities (PPPs) and the market exchange rate for each country.	
Eurostat Unit: C5-Prices	Other Commission DGs: DG ECFIN; DG MARKT	Date: June 2004
European Statistical System Working Group (WG):	WG on Purchasing Power Parity European Comparison Programme	

1. Objective and relevance of the indicator:

PPPs are currency conversion rates that convert economic indicators expressed in national currencies and national price levels to a common currency, called Purchasing Power Standard (PPS), which equalises the purchasing power of different national currencies and thus allows meaningful comparison across countries.

The ratio is shown in relation to the EU average (EU=100) and allows the general price level of countries to be compared for a given year.

The indicator serves primarily for the measurement of nominal price convergence between economies. It is used for economic research and policy analysis requiring comparison between countries.

As markets tend to be more integrated, as the result of weakened trade barriers and increased flows of resources, goods and services, prices in different countries tend to be closer. The indicator measures this process.

2. Restriction of the indicator's relevance and other characteristics which may lead to restriction for using it in the Spring Report

PPPs is not a concept that is immediately understood by users. This has sometimes generated misunderstandings when PPPs are used for purposes for which they are not suited.

The indicator is indexed to the EU average (EU-15=100) what may cause difficulties to use the indicator in statistical analysis. Rescaling of the indicator following enlargement has to be taken into account when comparing it with previous releases.

The indicator is constructed primarily for spatial comparison and not for comparison over time. Nevertheless, for many analytical purposes, it is important to observe the evolution of PPPs and of related indicators. However the usage of these series for inter-temporal comparisons should be made with particular precautions as PPPs time series capture both price and price structure changes. In addition sampling of items and price collection for PPPs are not specifically designed to capture the pure price change over time but price differentials over space.

Taking this into account, inter-temporal analysis could be either based on different sets of PPPs or a set of PPPs for a reference year and then extrapolating the indicator for other periods by applying the inflation rates (from the CPI) for each country (OECD).

Given the error margins related to PPPs, attention has to be paid in interpreting the relative position of a country in time.

Inclusion of non-tradable goods limits pertinence of the indicator for policy monitoring.

2a Data availability: overview

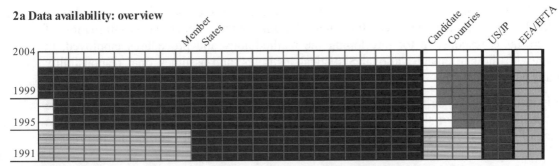

In general, data availability prior to 1995 cannot be expected for the new Member States and Candidate Countries

2b Data availability: details
(t_1: earliest reference year available; t_2: latest reference year avail. in Dec. 2004)

	Member States	Candidate Countries	US and Japan	EEA-EFTA[3]
t_1	1991- 15 MS 1995- 9 new MS 1999- MT	1995-BG, TR 1998- RO	1991	1991
t_2	2002	2002-BG, RO, TR	2002	2002

Comments (including information on time series): Data for the period 1995-2000 have been revised to incorporate all new developments in the methodology and to harmonise some aspects that were not fully harmonised.

3. Overall assessment of accuracy and comparability
short summary explanation:

☒ A
☐ B
☐ C
☐ Indicator to be developed

Data is collected from reliable sources applying high standards with regard to the methodology. Restrictions in comparability over time are related to the construction of the indicator as such rather than to shortcomings with regard to data production and are well documented and explained.

---

3   While being a member of the EEA, Liechtenstein has complete or partial exemptions from several statistical requirements due to its size. Thus, Liechtenstein is excluded from this overview as most of the data for structural indicators are missing.

4. Overall accuracy
High   ⊠

PPPs are calculated by Eurostat in strict collaboration with the OECD in the framework of the European Comparison Programme (ECP) whose aim is to make annual volume comparison of the main national accounts aggregates.

Accuracy of the indicator is ensured during the harmonisation of the compilation process. Prices are collected by the National Statistical Institutes of each country, under the co-ordination of Eurostat. Eurostat is responsible for developing the methodology and procedures employed, in collaboration with the participant National Statistical Institutes, and assumes final responsibility for the results which are published.

Accuracy is restricted in so far as the PPPs methodology establishes that the surveys have to be carried out in the capitals of the countries and at the specific month fixed by Eurostat. As a consequence of that, it is necessary to apply some regional and temporal coefficients in order to calculate the national and annual average prices.

While harmonisation of methods and data revisions since 1999 have considerably decreased its size for the EU Member States, OECD roughly estimates a +/-5% error margin for the other OECD countries (which can be considered to be even higher at disaggregated levels).

The reason is that PPPs are statistical constructs rather than precise numbers. The error margins surrounding PPPs depend on the reliability of the expenditure weights and the price data as well as the extent to which particular goods and services selected for pricing by participating countries truly represent the price levels in each country.

Restricted (sources, errors,   ☐
methodology etc.)

5. Comparability across countries
High   ⊠

Guidelines concerning the preparation and production of input data are prepared and updated by Eurostat in co-operation with the participant countries and international organisations to harmonise the methods and to achieve comparable data.
Minor comparability problems may arise due to the differences in the representativeness of the products priced.

There are still some drawbacks in the process of data collection outside the ECP carried out by Eurostat which reduces its usability as an indicator for international comparisons, especially if comparisons entail countries that belong to different continents as they have different habits and expenditure patterns.
Restricted   ☐

6. Comparability over time
High   ☐
Restricted   ⊠

The indicator is constructed primarily for spatial comparison and not for comparison over time.

PPP samples are planned to maximise comparability of items across countries at a given point in time- not over time. Because PPP samples change over time, the comparison over time should be made with a necessary caution.

Besides as the indicator is calculated by dividing the PPP by exchange rate, these types of comparisons depend on the development of the exchange rate. For countries outside the euro-zone this needs to be taken into account and may make such comparisons in times of erratic exchange rate even meaningless.

Although the indicator is not constructed for comparisons over time, the consistency is guaranteed by the data revisions 1995-2000.

7. Development perspective for improving quality of this indicator (including as far as possible an indication of burden on Member States and respondents.)

The PPPs produced by Eurostat are designed to cover the whole expenditure included in final consumption by private households and its sub-aggregates. Therefore this indicator, that allows analysing the price convergence, includes all products consumed by households including non-tradable items.

The theory (e.g. "the law of one price") tells that price differentials between countries are not sustainable in the long run as market forces will equalize prices between countries. Whereas there are many factors why the theory does not hold the main point is that, basically, only tradables could be liable for price convergence. One should not expect the price level differentials of non-tradables to disappear as the price levels of those products (especially services) are highly related with the income differences between the locations where they are sold.

In order to satisfy this need, Eurostat, together with the other interested COM services, will study the possibility to produce a set of comparative price levels data that includes only tradable products.

Although Purchasing Power Parities are highly complex, the basket of products representing all Member States to enable comparability across countries could be improved. The highly detailed level of breakdown of GDP components on the demand approach that is required to compile this indicator often makes for a dearth of information for estimation, thus impairing reliability. Improvements in this area imply very high costs for the participating countries.

Further improvements could encompass a regular update of spatial coefficients thus increasing representativeness of prices collected in the cities.

8. Contribution to quality of the set/potential to qualify for an integrated policy analysis

Comments/ Assessment:

> **Relevant European legislation:** Purchasing Power Parities are not currently governed by a legal act (data is provided under a gentlemen's agreement). A draft regulation of the European Parliament and of the Council concerning the production of Purchasing Power Parities has been prepared and is currently undergoing the regular legal procedures. The adoption of the regulation is not expected before 2005.

Description of Eurostat quality grades:
overall technical assessment of the indicator based on accuracy and comparability

Grade "A"   An indicator is graded "A" when all of the following conditions are fulfilled:
-    Data is collected from reliable sources applying high standards with regard to methodology/accuracy and is well documented in line with Eurostat metadata standard.
-    The underlying data is collected on the basis of a common methodology for the European Union and, where applicable, data for US and Japan can be considered comparable; major differences being assessed and documented.
-    Data are comparable over time; impact of procedural or conceptual changes being documented.

Grade "B"   An indicator is graded "B" if
-    data is collected from reliable sources applying high standards with regard to methodology/accuracy and is well documented in line with Eurostat metadata standard.
-    there are   EITHER some serious shortcomings with regard to comparability across countries (including the lack of data)
      OR breaks in series for several countries which seriously hamper comparison over time (including the lack of data).
Deficiencies with regard to assessing and documenting the impact of these shortcomings might be identified.

Grade "C"   An indicator is graded "C", if one or both of the following conditions is fulfilled:
-    Data might have to be interpreted with care as methodology/accuracy does not meet high quality standards.
-    There are some serious shortcomings with regard to comparability across countries (including the lack of data)
      AND breaks in series for several countries which seriously hamper comparison over time (including the lack of data).

Indicator to be developed   The indicator is not ready to be used for the Spring Report.

Politics and Statistics

The Use of Indicators for Better Policy Making

Lorenzo Bini Smaghi
Director General for International Financial Relations
Italian Ministry of the Economy and Finance
Department of the Treasury

Gian Paolo Ruggiero
Head of Division in the Directorate General for International Financial Relations
Italian Ministry of the Economy and Finance
Department of the Treasury

Introduction: the role of indicators for policy-making

Statistics have always provided a key input to good policy making[1].

In the past years, statistics have gained an even greater role for policy making. To a large extent, this is linked to globalisation, one of the major drives of the complexity of today's world[2]. This ever increasing complexity requires more articulated policy responses and adequate inputs to policy making as those provided by statistics and indicators.

Providing information about international developments is just one example on the role that statistics can fulfil in the face of globalisation. Other increasingly important tendencies accrue the importance of statistical indicators in our globalised world.

One very distinctly observable trend is benchmarking. Comparing the performance across countries is a useful tool to assess policy needs and outcomes and to learn lessons from the extremes (the very successful or unsuccessful countries).

Another increasingly important feature of policy making is the need to be accountable. In this case, as well, statistics have become a key element by allowing the public to hold policy makers accountable in view of the measurable results they achieve or are supposed to achieve.

All of these factors lead to mounting pressure for more statistics of higher quality and easier of use. Therefore, there is an increasing demand for indicators which are simple enough to be understood by public opinion and comparable internationally. The challenge

---

1   Thanks to the use of synthetic indicators policy makers are better placed to spot policy issues; the quality of policy choices is enhanced; communication amongst policy-makers and between the latter and public opinion is facilitated; making judgements about whether a policy produces positive results or not is made much easier.

2   Globalisation implies that national policy makers must increasingly take action to respond to developments occurring in other parts of the world. In addition, in all circumstances national policy making must be carried out taking into account international interdependencies.

is that at the same time these indicators must be able to catch complex phenomena and are partly affected by national contexts.

In the following sections, remarks are organised around three main themes: (i) the increasing usefulness of indicators in a globalised context, (ii) the risks related to their inappropriate use and, last but not least, (iii) a few possible enhancements that could improve the current situation.

The growing need for indicators in an increasingly globalised context

Statistical indicators share many features with the notion of public good and bear great externalities. Nowadays, these characteristics are magnified with the rise of international interdependencies. Therefore, greater efforts and cooperation are needed in order to enhance clarity and comparability of indicators.

The mounting utility of statistical indicators derives from three major circumstances.

- First, there is an increasing need to capture effects and implications of globalisation. For example, statistics show that new important players are emerging in the international economy, the major one being China[3].

- Secondly, there is a greater demand for more comparable indicators. In a globalised context, countries engage in a continuous dialogue where it is important to know their relative position or their contribution to selected global phenomena. This can be done only thanks to indicators that are consistent across different countries[4].

- Finally, better statistics are increasingly required in order to augment accountability of both national statisticians and policy makers. The availability of terms of comparisons in other countries exposes national practices to a sharper judgement both in statistics and policy making.

Comparability and accountability considerations just mentioned also allow greater and more effective international surveillance, often taking the form of peer review and benchmarking. For example, indicators take a special place in EU processes whereby discipline and policy objectives are pursued thanks to the reference to common indicators[5].

The focus of the public sector to improve availability and quality of statistics is not driven only by the need to improve official policy making. It rests also on the awareness

---

3   Even though this is an already easily recognizable phenomenon, selected indicators provide a clearer view of its magnitude and prospects. The share of world exports by China has grown from about 2 per cent in 1990 to more than 5 per cent last year. Official reserves of its central bank account for more than 500 billion dollars. This is an extraordinary amount of money also considering that it represents 14 per cent of total world official reserves. The rate of growth of the Chinese economy is close to double digit figures. If sustained at this rate, China could soon claim to seat with the other largest industrialised economies gathering in the G7. From the above and other more specific indicators, policy makers in other countries have precious information to lead them in an appropriate policy response to such an inescapable secular trend.

4   For example, international competitiveness can be grasped through a number of selected indicators relating to exchange rates, prices, labour costs, administrative efficiency and so on. These are all relevant indicators for countries both individually, as a way to enhance their own competitive position, and collectively, in the debate over the relative international adjustment process.

5   While this has been common for several years in the realm of fiscal policy, it is increasingly used also in the Lisbon process to assess progress made by the EU and its members in several areas of structural policies.

that more informed economic agents support a better functioning of the international economy and of the international financial markets.

For example, it should not be forgotten that in the context of the repeated international crisis in the second half of the nineties, one major policy response at the international level was to make sure that sufficient and timely information be ordinarily available to individual market players. The Special Data Dissemination Standard (SDDS) agreed within the IMF was elaborated with a view to foster national authorities to publish relevant economic and financial statistics in a regular, transparent and timely fashion. The compliance of IMF members with such standards is regularly assessed by IMF staff.

Admittedly, once statistics are indeed available, an equally important policy issue was (and is) to make sure that private agents have adequate incentives to make good use of them[6].

In conclusion, the relevant question is: how can the production of statistics be governed in the new internationally challenging outlook? Clearly, the work and efforts in isolation of national statistical institutes are not any longer sufficient. A new and already developing approach is needed, mainly based on the increasing role of international institutions and on stricter cooperation amongst national institutes.

To enhance availability and comparability of statistics, international institutions play a key role by performing two possible functions. First, thanks to their work, methodological guidelines are issued so that individual countries can follow uniform rules to arrive at broadly comparable results. The ESA95 or the IMF balance of payments handbook are good examples. Moreover, in certain cases, international institutions can go even further and compile internationally comparable and aggregated statistics based on national sources[7].

In addition to the role of international organisations, international cooperation is also increasing. This takes place on a regular or on a project basis with regard to many different sectoral areas. This does not conflict with the function of international organisations. Quite the opposite is true as shown, for example, by the creation of a Statistics Committee within the OECD. This is important also because it opens the way to an all-round process of cooperation extending at 360 degrees. Until now, international cooperation has often been driven by the need to build statistical indicators in certain policy areas with the risk of losing sight of trade-offs in the use of scarce resources. By bringing together the top management of national institutes and by its broad mandate, the OECD statistics Committee may support a more general approach useful to jointly assess costs and benefits of various sectoral initiatives. In addition, the OECD can catalyse further international cooperation in policy areas, such as labour, education, science and even fiscality, where it is relatively more difficult to gather internationally consistent indicators.

---

6   Unfortunately, this cannot be taken for granted because herding behaviours, costs related to the processing of information and short sightedness may indeed imply that publicly available statistics are disregarded or not sufficiently accounted for. However, this could be the topic of another entirely new roundtable.

7   For example, the Bank for International Settlement performs this function with respect to statistics about international financial and exchange markets. That is how we know that every day 1.9 trillion dollar of transactions are carried out in foreign exchange markets, an incredible amount which is yet another sign of the magnitude of globalisation.

Risks involved in a un-cautious use of statistics

It is clear that the focus on and the usefulness of statistics can only grow over time along with greater globalisation.

However, this also calls for greater caution against an inappropriate design and use of statistical indicators. Before highlighting certain risks, it should be stated that it is not always clear where any misgiving might lie. Sometimes, indicators simply distort reality because they are not technically sound or because they are based on inaccurate/incomplete information. Sometimes, the fault does not lie with indicators but in their inappropriate use, either unconsciously or - worse – consciously. Sometimes, even though conveying in principle the right information, the message provided by indicators may be misinterpreted by the audience to which they are addressed.

A first issue to be wary about is the risk that statistics lead policy making rather than the opposite being the case. While exceptions may exist, as a rule, policy makers ought to provide the necessary orientation to the work of statisticians in view of their policy requirements. This avoids that efforts are wasted in unnecessary work and that certain indicators provide inaccurate or non relevant input for action to policy makers.

Simplicity is another issue calling for great caution in the use of statistics. Only a relatively simple indicator guarantees comparability across countries, accountability for policy makers and proper communication to public opinion. However, simplicity is hard to reconcile with the complexity of phenomena that increasingly face policy makers[8].

In addition, this issue often lies at the heart of communication difficulties between policy-makers and public opinion. For example, it is not an easy task for a government to explain to citizens that, even though the current public deficit might be relatively moderate, projected government liabilities measured with reference to rising interest rates or to demographic patterns call for pre-emptive rigour in public expenditure[9].

A superficial use of statistics may also bring about overconfidence on the "precision" of indicators. This is dangerous for two main reasons. The first is that statistics are subject to measurement errors and ex-post revisions. Of course, revisions can either be planned or unforeseen. In both cases, policy-makers run the risk of acting on the basis of misleading information. Whereas this may often be unavoidable, such a risk should always be very well clear in the minds of policy makers. It is also a responsibility of statisticians to clarify *ex ante* the level of confidence that can be associated with an indicator.

A second more fundamental problem has to do with the impossibility of providing accurate measures for certain phenomena. As an extreme, let's just dare here to recall the notion of utility and welfare, for which monetary measures such as income and GDP can only provide approximations. The reading of these indicators must be integrated by politics with an assessment of other intangible elements.

Admittedly, quite often policy makers and public opinion fall easy prey of an excessive manic use of numbers. For example, if any EU country were to reach a public deficit of 3.1%, policy makers, media and public opinion would point at it as being

---

8   The possibility of measurement errors and inaccuracies increases the simpler is the indicator chosen and the more complex is the phenomenon to be measured.

9   Likewise, it is hard communication for a central bank to tighten monetary policy when headline inflation is still low but greater inflationary expectations embedded in financial asset price indicators rise for whatever reason.

excessive. A decimal point less, which could easily be due to trivial measurement errors or rounding procedures, would spare that country a good deal of institutional and political trouble.

Over-reliance on individual indicators at one point of time should also be resisted. Albeit fundamental and emblematic, certain statistics should always be read in a dynamic way and jointly with other related indicators. If, for whatever reason, an excessive focus is attached to a certain indicator on a static basis, there is a serious risk that policy makers will act taking wrong decisions just in order to achieve a mere statistical goal.

This leads to a few final considerations on the possible "endogeny" of indicators. This expression refers to the possibility that once an indicator is chosen as reference, behaviours affecting the measured phenomenon may change as a result. In other words, indicators may become endogenous within the context they are applied to, in a similar way as claimed by the so-called Lucas critique in relation to parameters in econometric models. Many examples can be made and can entail both positive and negative aspects.

On the positive side, it means that if agents know that a certain variable under their control or influence will be measured with certain consequences, they may have incentives to act so that the measure turns out to a good reading. For example, since the entry into force of the Maastricht Treaty, the ongoing benchmarking vis-à-vis the famous 3 and 60 per cent thresholds for public deficit and debt have exerted a powerful influence on EU governments to implement virtuous and sustainable fiscal policies.

On the negative side, endogeneity may imply that such efforts to influence the turn-out of a certain measures are un-orthodox. Again, with reference to the EU framework, in some occasions EU governments have strived to remain within the Maastricht criteria through accounting work-around and cosmetics.

As a further example, this is also one powerful argument against the simple transposition of the golden rule in the Stability and Growth Pact. If investment expenditure were to be excluded from the required fiscal balance, apart from objective statistical difficulties, one can also be sure that governments would have the strong temptation to disguise certain current outlays as capital expenditure.

Selected considerations on how to improve statistics and their use

Let us now finally make a few considerations on how to avoid mistakes and strive for statistics to remain a valuable tool for policy makers.

Of course, both policy makers and statisticians have to make their own best efforts to enhance the quality and use of indicators. The key for such a process to be successful is ongoing and fruitful dialogue between policy-makers and statisticians. Both categories may face different constraints and have different desiderata. While this is unavoidable, it is absolutely necessary that such differences are reconciled in a consistent way[10].

---

10   Policy makers should endeavour to appropriately select the relevant phenomena to be measured for policy needs by making clear and realistic requests to statisticians. In turn, statisticians should strive to design indicators, which are sufficiently simple, comprehensive, timely and comparable. Left on their own, statisticians may well produce technically sound indicators which are of difficult use and communication by policy makers and public opinion. On the other hand, without any dialogue with statisticians, policy makers may well ask for straight and immediate indicators, which would require just too many oversimplifying assumptions to be de facto reliable.

Only through a continuous interaction between policy makers and statisticians it is possible to arrive at satisfactory results. Moreover, the final shape of selected indicators will not coincide in any case with the theoretical optimum. Also in this case, only dialogue can make sure that both statisticians and policy makers are well aware of this and take it into consideration in their behaviours and policies.

This dialogue could and does take place in several ways.

Clearly international organisations are a first natural forum. Here, member countries are represented both with policy and statistical expertise so that the two can interact and be made compatible. In addition, ongoing interaction must be engaged by and within working groups gathering national representatives with the mandate of either producing or using certain indicators. Finally, let us stress that events such as this OECD World Forum favour exactly the type of interaction that would be needed[11].

In addition to dialogue, it's useful to recall two further elements on how a proper design and use of indicators can support better policy making.

The first refers to the need for further efforts in the direction that the international community has already taken since a few years. The usefulness of reliable indicators for the functioning of the international economy and financial markets is already consolidated in the statistics and policy making community. There is a need for a follow-up to initiatives already taken to enhance the aggregation and comparability of existing indicators as well as to ensure the introduction of new indicators that become necessary for policy-making in an increasingly globalised context.

A second more innovative concept that could guide future initiatives is the need to reinforce both independence and accountability of statisticians. This would be desirable both in the private and public sectors to increase the unbiasedness and reliability of indicators. Focusing on the public sector, to which we belong, there is certainly an inclination to mix conflicting objectives in the production of statistics in a way that is little transparent. Side by side with the overarching virtuous objective of having reliable indicators, policy makers and politicians do have sometimes the less noble temptation to distort statistics for their own short term needs. Making statistical offices more independent from government could be a valuable tool to enhance the quality of statistics, provided that this goes hand in hand with greater accountability of statisticians and that their final objectives are still dictated by policy makers. A similar option has been adopted by many countries, including the EU, with regard to monetary policy, which is independent, accountable and bound by price stability. It is hard to say to what extent it will be possible to follow this example for statistical offices but the direction of the way forward is quite clear.

Concluding remarks

In addition to trade, finance and society, globalisation reverberates strongly also on statistics. Indicators are a powerful tool to support policy makers provided that they adjust to the evolving global reality.

---

11   Indeed, apart from the dialogue we are engaging in these four days, this Forum will enable us to better realise and single out issues of common interest. Probably and hopefully, these will be the subject of further deepening in separate fora.

Looking forward, the importance of indicators is bound to grow even further due to mounting international pressure for national transparency in terms of both quantity and quality of information disclosed. In addition, a parallel pressure is developing to increase the availability of indicators that are comparable and extend to all range of policy areas.

However, in such a globalised environment, efforts needed in order to make indicators a valuable tool for policy making are greater than usual. Achieving and preserving the usual desired characteristics of statistical indicators (such as comparability, clarity, timeliness, comprehensiveness, etc.) are complicated by the need to reach international consistency. In addition, the risks of a misuse or misinterpretation of statistics cannot be minimised.

The key to ameliorate indicators and their use lies in a continuous dialogue between producers and users of indicators, i.e. primarily statisticians and policy-makers respectively. Greater accountability of both categories would be highly beneficial. For statisticians this may imply the need for more independence accompanied by appropriate arrangements to avoid undesirable self-reference.

As a final remark, this paper started by saying that reliable indicators are a key tool to deal with policy issues. In the end, given the importance of the matter, let's rather say that the availability of reliable indicators represents itself a key policy issue to be addressed.

Sustainable Development Indicators for Policy Making

Thorvald Moe

Deputy Secretary General, Norwegian Ministry of Finance

Introduction

In Norway, the Prime Minister has asked The Ministry of Finance to coordinate policies to enhance sustainable development which is considered to be a key political priority for the Norwegian Government.

To that effect, a Norwegian Action Plan (National Agenda 21) was presented to the Parliament in The National Budget 2004 which is the main economic policy document in Norway. The follow up to the Action Plan is coordinated by a group of State Secretaries chaired by The Ministry of Finance.

Since the Second World War, developing indicators for economic policy making has been an important activity by establishing national accounts, leading to GNP and other indicators for economic developments like prices, employment, public expenditures and so on. Such indicators are no longer controversial and widely used in economic policy making nationally and internationally. In Norway, Statistics Norway plays a key role in producing and refining statistics and indicators for economic policymaking, as well as statistics regarding social developments, the environment and so on.

Since the Harlem Brundtland Commission presented its report "Our Common Future" in 1987,[1] and after the Rio Summit in 1992, sustainable development has been an important part of the longer term policy agenda nationally and internationally. I will here focus on how we go about making indicators for policy making regarding sustainable development in Norway, and not go into a broad discussion of the wide ranging topic of sustainable development more generally.

National Wealth as an Indicator of Sustainable Development[2]

According to The World Commission for Environment and Development, WCED, "Sustainable development is development that meets the needs of the present without compromising the ability of future generations to meet their own needs", ibid. page 43.

The concept is intuitively fairly easy to comprehend, but in practice more difficult to make operational.

---

1   See WCED 1987

2   This section and the next one draws on current work in an Expert Group on Indicators for Sustainable Development in which I am deputy chair. I am grateful to Knut H. Alfsen for comments to an earlier draft.

For an economist, it seems natural to define sustainable development as non-declining welfare (pr. capita) over time. What constitutes welfare is, of course, controversial, but since maintaining or enhancing welfare over time is a main goal of policy making requiring almost daily political decisions, we have tried to adapt a pragmatic approach to measuring sustainable development (hereafter SD)

One may ask if SD is a meaningful concept on the national level. The Norwegian Government argues that it is, and that a main purpose is to pursue national policies that contribute to global sustainability. If all OECD countries pursue sound long term SD policies, notably eliminating trade and non-trade barriers *vis a vis* developing countries, achieving SD globally will be facilitated. It is probably a large measure of agreement that the main challenge for SD globally is poverty and the uneven distribution of resources and development between relatively rich and relatively poor nations and parts of the global population. A set of indicators for global SD world thus have the fight against poverty as a key focus.

But most policy decisions are still taken at the national level,[3] and many countries (including Norway) have adopted national policies for SD. In Norway it is as already mentioned called National Agenda for the 21st Century. Thus, I will focus on indicators for NA21 policies.

A point of departure is to ask the question: What can we expect to realize regarding future welfare, given our present point of departure? This points to the present resource base, widely defined, and how we can maintain, and possibly enhance, the future resource base. I think here not only of economic resources such as real capital and financial resources, it also covers natural resources, renewable and non-renewable, and human capital. In principle, social capital is included in the residual when one estimates National Wealth, but no effort is made to identify social capital and its contribution to welfare. That does not mean that we exclude social indicators as briefly elaborated on in section 3 below.[4]

The total national resource base I call our National Wealth (hereafter NW), which consists of:

- Real- and financial capital

- Human Capital

- Natural- and Environmental Capital

These components of NW provides us as consumers and producers with rates of return, which directly and indirectly produces welfare. NW, furthermore, consists of components which have a market price and components which are not subject to market transactions. The value of NW is determined by the welfare the use of these respective components may produce over time. In other words, the value of NW is equal to the discounted value the wealth components will yield over time. If you accept my definition of SD assuming that our total welfare should not decline over time, and preferably increase, then the assessment of SD for a country is fairly straight forward. If NW, as

---

3   The present difficulties of solving global problems through international action can, inter alia, be illustrated by the difficulties of implementing international agreements to combat climate change. And each party of the Kyoto protocol has to implement national policies in addition to participating in international trading schemes.

4   The best discussion I have seen on social issues and SD is given by Mira d'Ercole and Salvini, OECD 2003

broadly defined above, increases over time, developments have the potential of being sustainable and vice versa.

I will not go into an extended discussion on strong versus weak sustainability. But I will argue that not all of the components of our resource base, NW, are necessarily substitutable. For example, all services received from the environment, defined for simplicity as Environmental Capital, may not be substituted by increased income (rates of return from real-, financial, natural and human capital). One example may be that a fundamental condition for future welfare is a reasonably stable climate. And if global warming gets out of control, the foundation for the welfare of future generations may be threatened.

One could add an ethical dimension. Some question our rights to exploit the natural and environmental capital base in a very detrimental way, even if – at least in the short run – it could enhance NW. In Norway, this is a very real and practical challenge. We extract our petroleum wealth, a non-renewable resource, but try hard not to spend the money now. Rather it is transformed into building up financial resources abroad through our Petroleum Fund.[5]

Be this as it may, I will argue that whether one wants to pursue weak or strong SD, is basically a political question. As an economist, I want to establish indicators so that our politicians can judge for themselves whether SD is weak or strong as a basis for the policies they as democratically elected decision makers want to pursue.

A Core Set of SD Indicators for Policy Making

As we move from concepts to actual practice, it is probably broadly accepted that systems are complex, and that we do not know enough about how economic activities depend on and impact environmental and social systems and relations. The large number of humanly produced chemicals released to the environment, and our limited knowledge on their effects on nature and human beings, may be a case in point.

There are also a number of well known practical challenges in estimating NW. When the above mentioned capital components are to be aggregated, one needs shadow prices which are hard to estimate when services needed are not traded in perfectly functioning markets. And a number of environmental services are not traded in markets at all.

But a well founded and consistent strategy, nevertheless, is to chose indicators that reflects values, understood as effects on welfare, of the main components of NW.[6] With this point of departure, and given that we are to establish indictors for policy making regarding NA21 (our national action plan for SD), we focus on the six main policy areas identified in NA21:

- Climate, ozone and long range transport of pollution to air

- Biological Diversity

---

5   A key operational guideline for economic policies in Norway is that we should only spend the rate of return on our Petroleum Fund, estimated at 4 per cent pr. year, and not touch the capital base, which is growing presently and approaching 70 per cent of GDP.

6   This is much the same approach as chosen by Canada, i.e. the capital approach. See Smith, Simard and Sharpe (2001)

- Health and environmentally dangerous chemicals

- Natural resources

- Sustainable economic development

- Sustainable social development

The first three can be seen as indicators of Environmental Capital.

Furthermore, to be of practical use for policy makers, and in order to facilitate regular monitoring, the core indicator set must be compact and relatively small. I will strongly argue that many of the other SD indicators sets available that use of large number of indicators, and often without a systematic theoretical foundation, are impractical and thus of little use to policy makers.[7]

Table 1: Preliminary Core set of Indicators for Sustainable Development Policies.

	Main Indicators	Main Policy Areas					
		A Climate Change	B Biological Diversity	C Natural Resources	D Chemicals	E Economic SD	F Social SD
1.	Norwegian Climate Gas Emissions	X					
2.	Water conditions	X		X			
3.	Conditions for birds		X				
4.	Status for fisheries		X	X		X	
5.	Ecological status in costal areas		X	X			
6.	Ecological status in inland waterways		X	X			
7.	Use of energy as a share of GNP	X		X			
8.	National Wealth					X	
9.	Public Finances. Generational Accounts					X	
10.	Employment						X
11.	Human Capital. Level of education						X
12.	Expected life length at birth					X	X
13.	Imports from African countries						X
14.	Official Development Assistance, ODA						

Source: Expert Group on Indicators of SD

---

7   For a useful overview of the different approaches, see Brunvoll et.al. (OE CD 2002)

In table 1 a preliminary core set of indicators for SD polices is set forth.

As mentioned above, National Wealth (line 8) is the key indicator in the set giving an overall indication of whether economic developments have the potential of being sustainable nationally or not.

It is well known that in standard practice of computing NW, environmental, human and social capital are arrived at as residuals. Thus the rather crude NW estimates should be supplemented as far as possible with indicators of these three types of the national capital base.

The statistical basis for assessing Environmental Capital, in general, and biological diversity in, particular, is surprisingly weak in Norway as probably in most other OECD countries. Indicators 3, 4, 5 and 6 in Table 1 should therefore be seen as preliminary and with considerable room for improvement. However, it is important to use such indicators to supplement NW as part of an overall assessment of SD. They are meant to illustrate that specific environmental areas key to SD need to be looked at specifically in addition to an overall assessment facilitated by regularly producing and presenting NW estimates. One could argue that (at least) a minimum level of biological diversity is a necessary condition for SD in the long run, even if NW increases in the short term.

The level of education, and the amount of Human Capital more generally, is important for both economic growth (as documented in the OECD Growth Study) and longer term SD. It is a dominant component in NW estimates, but estimated residually. The level of education is included as indicator No. 11 in Table 1, and I hope much more work will be put into developing and refining future direct indicators for Human Capital.

Notions of social capital are controversial, and the meaning of trying to develop indicators for social capital is unclear. Nevertheless, most would agree that social developments are important for SD, not least in developing countries.

Mira d'Ercole and Salvini discuss how social conditions and developments are important for longer term SD, notably relationships between experiences during childhood and investments in human capital, education systems, transition from school to work, changing working conditions, poverty and exclusion, sustainable retirement, income systems and illness and disability in old age.

As can be seen from Table 1, indicator 10 Employment, indicator 11 Level of Education and indicator 12 Expected life length at birth are included as important for social SD (as well as economic SD).

In most OECD countries, sustainable public finances in the longer term is a challenge often discussed by Ministers of Finance these days. It is important for economic and financial sustainability, even though the possibility of reduced public expenditures or increased taxes in developed countries may not be of great importance for SD in the developing world.

In Norway, generational accounts are produced and presented by the Ministry of Finance regularly in key economic policy documents[1]. Indicator 9 in Table 1 is Generational Accounts as a summary indicator of the long term sustainability of public

---

1   See "Challenges and Choices for the Norwegian Economy", White Paper No. 8 (2004-2005), section 5.4.3, pages 93-95.

finances in Norway. Alternative and model based analyses of this challenge are also presented by The Ministry of Finance in White Paper No. 8 (2004-2005).

Indicators 1 (National Emissions of Climate Cases), 13 (Imports from African countries) and 14 (ODA) refers to our direct contribution to global sustainability. Developments of national emissions of climate gases refer to our commitments to implement the Kyoto Protocol according to our targets, a concrete polity obligation. Indicators 13 and 14 should tell us something about the contribution our policies to reduce global poverty. Firstly and most importantly to reduce trade barriers *vis a vis* developing countries. Secondly, our level of ODA.

The strategy is thus to supplement NW estimates with a small number of indicators in the six main policy areas identified in NA21. Limiting the set to 14 indicators for these six main areas hopefully will make it easy to handle and practical to policy makers. 14 is not of course a magic number, and this set should certainly not – as underlined above - be seen as written in stone. The objective is to start a dynamic process in which the statistical base for these indicators is continually improved, and in which new and refined indicators can replace the present ones. To summarize, overriding considerations have been to:

- Have a consistent and theoretically sound point of departure, the capital approach.

- Make the indicators policy relevant, relating them to the six main policy areas of NA21.

- Keep the set small so as to make the production of indicators manageable and easily understood by policy makers.

Another practical consideration we emphasize is to use Statistics Norway as the key producer of the indicators. As this institution is responsible for official statistics in Norway, it should develop both the statistical and the analytical/theoretical base for measuring SD. Setting up separate institutions and sources of data, as done in some other OECD countries, would seem unfruitful and uneconomical.

Last, but not least, SD policies with the core SD indicator set as an aid, will be regularly presented in the Government's National Budgets.

The Policy Setting

As mentioned, in Norway, estimates of NW and generational accounts are regularly presented in main policy documents such as the National Budget and a recent White Paper of Long Term Economic Perspectives. Estimating NW and Generational Accounts – which should be carried out by The Ministry of Finance - is well established along with policy discussions both within the Government and in the Parliament of the longer term policy implications of such estimates. Of course, these estimates have not yet gotten the same prominence as measures of GNP, but the ambition is to more closely connect debates and policies to enhance SD to economic policy debates. That would, in the event, move the SD closer to the centre of policy making.

A next step would be to include a closer look at main challenges like Environmental Capital (e.g. biological diversity) in such a context. Although the relationships between economic developments and biological diversity are imperfectly understood, both biologists and economists would have to take a closer look at these relationships if indicators of biological diversity would be seen as important to SD, and not only looked at in isolation by natural scientists and environmentalists. If the main indicator of SD,

NW, seems to go in the right direction, but the biological diversity indicators show a significant deterioration, this could contribute to a debate and possibly policy measures by the Cabinet, not only arguments from the Ministry of Environment outside the centre of policy making.

Although The Norwegian Ministry of Finance now coordinates SD policies in Norway, a note of caution is probably in order. Short term economic and political concerns and considerations are still fairly dominant in policy making in Norway. One reason may be that our NW estimates indicate that economic developments in Norway are potentially sustainable, at least in the weak SD sense. The focus now is mainly on the generational accounts and the sustainability of our pension system, not on long term environmental sustainability. Nevertheless, I will argue that integration of long term economic and environmental (and social) policies is greatly facilitated by:

- Relating SD indicators closely to economic developments.

- Discussing and presenting SD policies in key economic policy documents.

It is beyond the scope of this paper to discuss international developments and considerations of statistics and indicators of SD. The present state of affairs seems diverse with a number of different approaches, and no apparent consensus.

OECD work in this area has in my opinion been disappointing in recent years. Despite given a clear and strong mandate from the OECD Ministerial Meeting in 2001, OECD did not deliver the product it was asked to deliver to the Ministerial Meeting in 2004 regarding the development of indicators for SD.

However, given the important international role that the OECD plays in the statistics area generally, and the organisations competence regarding economics, the environment and development, the OECD should be well placed to take the lead in establishing – perhaps in cooperation with the World Bank – an authoritative set of global indicators for SD. That set should in my opinion be based on consistent economic thinking, the capital approach, focus on global poverty, and be a small set that is manageable to maintain and update and thus easily understood by policy makers.

References

Sustainable Development. Critical Issues. OECD, Paris 2001

Smith, Simard and Sharpe: "A Proposed Approach to Environment and Sustainable Development Indicators Based on Capital". Canada, 2001.

Brunvoll, Hass and Høie: "Overview of Sustainable Development Indicators used by National and International Agencies." OECD, Paris 2002

Mira d'Ercole and Salvini: "Towards Sustainable Development: The Role of Social Protection".
OECD Social, Employment and Migration Working Papers no. 12. Paris 2003

The Norwegian National Budget. White Paper no. 1 (2003/2004). Oslo, 2003

Norway's Action Plan for Sustainable Development. Norwegian Ministry of Finance. Oslo, 2004

"Challenges and Choices for the Norwegian Economy". White Paper No. 8 (2004-2005).

Norwegian Ministry of Finance, Oslo, 2004.

The Role of Central Banks

Statistics, Accounts and Key Indicators Compiled by Central Banks: The Case of the ECB

Steven Keuning, Director-General

Alda Morais, Senior Economist-Statistician

ECB's Directorate-General Statistics [1]

Introduction

The European Central Bank (ECB) was set up in June 1998 with the primary objective of maintaining price stability in the euro area.[2] Its key task is the definition and implementation of the monetary policy for the euro area, which is seen as a single economic territory. In addition, the ECB shall support the general economic policies of the European Union (EU). Such tasks can only be performed effectively with recourse to data that are 'fit for purpose'. As Mr. Trichet stated in his speech opening the second ECB conference on statistics[3], *"Statistics are like the glasses through which policy-makers and all other economic agents view macroeconomic reality. If the glasses are totally reliable, well polished and easy to handle, we may hardly notice that we are wearing them (...)".*

This paper describes the experience gathered by the ECB in developing a *range of statistics, accounts and key indicators* for the euro area. Detailed statistics and accounts are more commonly used in models, forecasts, simulations, etc., both for analytical purposes and for policy preparation. Key indicators are in turn also of great value to the general public, to the media and to those policy-makers who want to obtain an insight into the economy at a glance.[4] They are moreover particularly useful as a communication tool, for example, in ECB data press releases; however, they only serve their purpose if they are internationally and intertemporally comparable and if their concept can be understood by the general public.

The core issue in the data compiled by the ECB is probably not so much a lack of statistics as a lack of their integration. For this reason, one of the ECB's main priorities for the medium term is to set up a fully integrated system of quarterly institutional sector accounts for the euro area. Integrated statistics enable further use of existing statistics,

---

1   Comments on an earlier version by Frank Mayerlen, Reimund Mink, Paolo Poloni, Patrick Sandars and Caroline Willeke are gratefully acknowledged.

2   Cf. article 105 of the Treaty. The euro area is currently composed of 12 EU countries: Austria, Belgium, Finland, France, Germany, Greece, Ireland, Italy, Luxembourg, the Netherlands, Portugal and Spain.

3   See J-C. Trichet (2004a). The full set of documentation presented at the Second ECB Conference on Statistics can be found under http://www.ecb.int/events/conferences/html/eastats2.en.html.

4   For a concrete application of these principles, see Keuning (1997).

may have a positive feedback effect on the quality of the source data, and allow the computation of useful key summary indicators.

The rest of this paper is structured as follows: Section 2 describes the statistics and accounts compiled by the ECB, while Section 3 outlines the key indicators. Section 4 briefly refers to some ongoing projects at the ECB which are designed to close remaining gaps in ECB statistics. Section 5 presents the medium to long-term perspectives for ECB statistics. Section 6 examines the development of statistics subject to limited resources. Finally, Section 7 presents some conclusions.

ECB statistics and accounts

According to its Statute, the ECB is entitled to collect statistical information that is necessary to perform its functions and tasks. To the extent possible, the ECB relies on national central banks (NCBs) to collect national data (on the basis of legal acts describing in detail their reporting requirements for the purposes of euro area statistics) and to transmit these data to the ECB's Directorate General Statistics (DG-S), where they function as a building block for the compilation of euro area statistics.

The ECB uses a wide range of detailed statistics and accounts in making its economic and monetary analyses. In many cases, the development of these statistics and accounts began before the start of Economic and Monetary Union.[5] ECB statistics and accounts can be grouped into the following main areas: (i) monetary, financial and operational statistics for the euro area (on monetary aggregates and counterparts, interest rates, securities issues, investment funds, other financial market operations, minimum reserves, etc.); (ii) euro area external statistics (balance of payments (b.o.p.), the international investment position (i.i.p.), external reserves and effective exchange rate statistics); (iii) euro area quarterly financial and non-financial accounts for institutional sectors (balance sheets and transactions); and (iv) some other general economic statistics (government finance statistics, the house price index, seasonally adjusted price indices, etc.). Other important statistics that the ECB uses for policy-making are the general economic statistics which it mainly receives from Eurostat. The most important of these is the Harmonised Index of Consumer Prices (HICP), which was adopted by the ECB to 'operationalise' the definition of price stability in the euro area. Besides this, additional statistics widely used at the ECB include other prices and costs statistics, labour market statistics and national accounts, as well as all kinds of business tendency surveys conducted by the European Commission and by commercial sources.

The achievements in the development of euro area statistics would not have been possible without the very fruitful cooperation with all EU NCBs, in particular in the context of the ECB's Statistics Committee and its working groups. Another success factor is the excellent cooperation between the ECB (DG-S) and the Commission (Eurostat), based on the most recent Memorandum of Understanding signed by the two institutions in March 2003. This agreement has worked very well in avoiding any duplication of statistical work at the EU level. While DG-S has prime responsibility for money, banking and financial markets statistics, Eurostat is the main responsible party for general

---

5   Data compiled by the ECB are released via monthly or quarterly press releases and are published in the ECB's Statistics Pocket Book, the Monthly Bulletin and the statistics section of its website (www.ecb.int). For a detailed description of the development of ECB statistics, see Bull (2004).

economic statistics. The responsibilities for b.o.p. and financial and non-financial national accounts by institutional sector are shared by the two institutions.

In addition, the ECB values its good relationships with the euro area national statistical institutes (NSIs) (e.g. via the Committee on Monetary, Financial and Balance of Payments Statistics (CMFB)) and with other international organisations such as the International Monetary Fund (IMF), the Organisation for Economic Co-operation and Development (OECD) and the United Nations (UN). This is particularly important because of the need to maintain and enhance the worldwide comparability of economic and financial statistics and accounts.

Currently, many efforts in this direction concern the recently initiated updates of the System of National Accounts 1993 (SNA 1993) and the 5th edition of the IMF's Balance of Payments Manual (BPM5). These handbooks codify the worldwide accounting rules for macroeconomic statistics, and lay down what can be seen as *a universal language of economics*. Few people fully realise the tremendous efficiency that has been achieved in terms of communication and decision-making simply because the media, market participants and policy-makers around the world now all speak the same language, namely the language of the SNA 1993, when they discuss economic performance and measures to improve it.

The current review of the SNA 1993 and its European peer, the ESA 95, is limited to methodological issues that may need to be amended or clarified in the light of new developments. In Europe, where the economic policy framework is to a large extent based on rules that utilise national accounts figures, even more may be at stake than in the rest of the world. Precisely because of the high practical importance of the SNA 1993 and the ESA 95 for policy-makers, the transparency of the national accounting system should be one of the overriding principles guiding the current review. Whereas a macroeconomic accounting system has its own specific features, e.g. a focus on the interrelations between economic agents and the need to record the same type of transaction in the same way for all types of economic actors, it should also stay close to the (monetary) reality of the economic agents themselves. In particular, imputing monetary values to transactions that were not actually settled in monetary terms, as well as the re-routing of flows to economic agents that in reality do not behave as if they actually had such receipts, should be limited in the core accounts. Similarly, all computations that require complex estimation techniques, which necessarily introduce large margins of uncertainty and rely heavily on assumptions made by statisticians, are better performed in supplementary accounts for specific purposes (e.g. sustainability analyses). Of course, it remains desirable to achieve consistency between the updated SNA 1993 and the revised ESA 95.

Despite its importance for monetary policy-making, central banks are generally not greatly involved in reviewing the SNA 1993. However, the ECB is represented in the Advisory Expert Group, which plays an important role in this updating process. Issues such as the treatment of implicit pension liabilities, guarantees, non-performing loans and reinvested earnings are some of the topics currently at the heart of the methodological debate. For government accounts, a highly useful link with the development of worldwide financial reporting standards for governments has been established.[6] Unfortunately, there is hardly any relationship at present between international standard-setters for national accounts and for business accounts.

---

6   See Keuning and van Tongeren (2004) for a further elaboration of this link.

The ECB statistics and accounts (including meaningful historical series of such data for model-based analysis) help monetary policy-makers understand both the structural characteristics and the current state of the euro area economy. To give an example, detailed euro area data on monthly monetary and credit developments and financial asset data broken down by instrument are extensively used to assess the portfolio decisions of euro area residents, including instrument shifts between banks and investment funds. The euro area harmonised interest rate statistics are important for assessing the transmission mechanism of monetary policy and, more generally, for measuring the sensitivity of economic agents to interest rate changes. They also serve to monitor financial stability. Policy-makers also need to understand the shifts in the financing of non-financial corporations, between self-financing from retained earnings and financing through loans and securities issues and, within the latter category, between equity and debt securities.

Nonetheless it should be emphasised that ECB statistics and accounts are not only used for monetary policy-making, but are also intended for a wide variety of other tasks at the ECB (e.g. payment systems, financial stability, operations and research), for economic policy-making in general, for market participants, and for the general public (i.e. including the reporting agents themselves, as the latter may also rely on ECB data for their own economic decisions). This highlights the *importance of disseminating key indicators for the euro area.*

Key indicators

Key macroeconomic indicators are usually derived from existing statistics and accounts and therefore do not involve an extra burden on reporting agents. Referring back to Mr. Trichet's analogy between statistics and glasses, key indicators can be likened to powerful magnifying glasses. Obviously, they typically try to catch billions of economic events in a single number and, therefore, cannot cater for all conceivable requirements.[7]

The ECB's Monthly Statistics Pocket Book, available in hard copy free of charge since August 2003 to all interested parties (and additionally posted on the ECB website), presents the key economic and financial indicators for the euro area. Harmonised indicators compiled by the ECB include:

- monthly monetary aggregates (M1, M2 and M3) and their counterparts (e.g. loans to households and non-financial corporations);

- monthly deposit and lending (retail) interest rates on new business and on outstanding amounts, money market interest rates and government bond yields;

- monthly debt securities and quoted shares issued and redeemed;

- the monthly total value of the outstanding amount of quoted shares;

- annual structural banking indicators (e.g. assets and number of employees);

- the monthly b.o.p. current account balance (seasonally adjusted), net direct and net portfolio investment, and reserve assets, plus the monetary presentation of the b.o.p.;

- daily nominal effective exchange rates and monthly real effective exchange rates;

---

7   See Keuning (2003) for an elaboration of this caveat.

- quarterly financing and financial investment of non-financial corporations, households, and insurance corporations and pension funds; and

- the quarterly indebtedness of households and non-financial corporations.

The Statistics Pocket Book also presents indicators compiled by Eurostat, such as key inflation rates, GDP per capita, unit labour costs and short-term business indicators. The b.o.p. current account balance, HICP and GDP are good examples of more complex indicators that are key to understanding the current economic situation. This also underlines the importance of the timely and orderly availability of the so-called Principal European Economic Indicators (PEEIs).[8]

The experience of the ECB has shown that the dissemination of the indicators contained in the Statistics Pocket Book provides a good service to policy-makers and euro area citizens alike. These indicators also serve the purpose of providing the media and citizens of the euro area with an understanding of the euro area economy in general and its most recent developments in particular. This is all the more relevant because the euro area is a relatively new economic entity, and many people only have a hazy idea of its size and structure. The indicators should thus be presented in such a way that their meaning can also be grasped by those who do not have a strong background in economics or statistics.[9] This is also in keeping with the importance that the ECB attaches to "open and transparent communication with investors, savers, market participants and the public at large." (Trichet, 2004b)

The euro area indicators must naturally also be "fit for purpose" in terms of their frequency, timeliness, reliability and adequacy for the phenomena they are intended to capture. Particularly for the purpose of the ECB's monetary policy, they must be based on maximally harmonised figures and be made available at a rather high frequency (monthly or at least quarterly[10]) soon after the reference period (i.e. before the end of the next month for monthly data and in the middle of the next quarter for quarterly data). However, the ECB does not strive for timeliness at any cost, and much importance is also attached to the reliability of the indicators. This is related to the so-called debate on the activism of central banks. As ECB Chief Economist Issuing (2002) notes, "central banks should moderate the responsiveness of the policy instrument when underlying data are expected to be subject to measurement error. The reason is that, when a measurement error occurs, a strong policy response to mismeasured data will induce unnecessary fluctuations in the economy. In fact, the weight given to the individual information variables should depend on how precisely those variables are measured". Similarly, ECB President Trichet (2004b) recently remarked: "Constantly faced with economic news, a

---

8   This Eurostat initiative, which the ECB is involved in, aims at the timely release of key euro area and EU indicators that are essential for short-term economic analyses (e.g. monthly consumer prices, quarterly national accounts aggregates, monthly and quarterly business and labour market indicators, and monthly external trade balances). The first European releases should be made on the same day as the first data for the most important countries become available (the "First for Europe" principle), and should be based on a sufficient (but not necessarily complete) coverage of national contributions.

9   For an in-depth discussion on the "need to communicate better with the regular man in the street", see Randzio-Plath (2004).

10   The US Federal Reserve publishes data on bank credit and the monetary aggregates at a weekly frequency, based, respectively, on a sample of commercial banks and the reporting of a limited range of deposit items. Therefore, they involve some degree of estimation, whereas euro area statistics are generally based on a census, and contain a high level of detail.

central bank risks being swamped by the latest indicator and by its conjectures concerning markets' likely reaction to the latest indicator. This mechanism can gradually steer monetary policy away from its foremost role of providing a firm medium-term anchor for the economy."

Ongoing projects

In general, the ECB data supporting monetary policy analysis are reasonably well-developed. Nevertheless, improvements are still needed and work is ongoing to fill a number of gaps identified by the main users.

For example, statistics on *non-monetary financial institutions* are currently only available for investment funds, and even these are compiled on the basis of non-harmonised national data (and only for stocks). Data on non-monetary financial institutions provide important information which can develop and deepen the analysis of monetary and credit developments (e.g. by providing evidence on counterpart transactions, on portfolio shifts between monetary and other financial assets, and on the substitution of bank loans with loans granted by non-monetary financial intermediaries). These statistics should also incorporate much more elaborated data on insurance corporations and pension funds, if only because the monitoring of these institutions is becoming increasingly important from a financial stability point of view. However, the situation is complicated by the fact that the ECB currently has no legal powers to address reporting obligations directly to insurance corporations and pension funds (unfortunately, this sub-sector is not particularly well-covered by Eurostat either).

Another challenging project deals with the establishment of a *centralised securities database*, which should contain all statistically relevant information on individual securities, starting with their issuance and subsequently extending to their holding. Without any increase in the reporting burden for business, this database should significantly improve the quality of b.o.p./i.i.p. statistics, monetary statistics, security issues statistics (including further detail about maturity, geographical breakdown, type of instrument and institutional sector) and quarterly institutional sector accounts for the euro area. In addition, it will be of use in the analysis of financial stability and financial integration.

The growing importance of financial integration issues has led to increasing interest in *financial integration indicators for the euro area*. First of all, indicators on the average price of homogeneous financial asset categories can reveal the extent to which the "law of one price" holds.[11] Besides this, indicators are also compiled on the volume and pattern of cross-border activity (trade and financial investment). Harmonised and easily accessible financial integration indicators should also be useful to market operators when taking their business decisions.

Medium-term perspectives for ECB statistics

Notwithstanding the progress achieved since the first stages of Economic and Monetary Union much remains to be done if a comprehensive statistical system for the

---

11   In an integrated market, assets with identical risk and return features, but located in different regions, should have the same price. For further details, see Baele et al. (2004).

euro area is to be achieved. In view of the long lead times involved, the ECB has therefore established a medium-term plan for its statistics.

The most important challenge for ECB statistics is the design and compilation of a *system of quarterly institutional sector accounts* for the euro area, together with Eurostat, the NCBs and the NSIs. The sectors covered consist of households (including non-profit institutions serving households), non-financial corporations, financial corporations, government and the rest of the world. Compiling such accounts enables a further and better use of existing statistics without entailing extra costs for respondents and implying only limited costs for compilers. They reveal the interrelations among the different sectors (and the rest of the world) and between the financial and the real side of the economy.[12]

At the moment, certain sub-sets of the financial accounts are published by the ECB, namely the so-called table on financing and investment for the non-financial sectors, and for insurance corporations and pension funds. Furthermore, detailed quarterly data are also published for the b.o.p. and several financial sub-sectors such as the money-creating sector and investment funds. Recently, a comprehensive set of quarterly non-financial and financial accounts for the government sector has become available, based on regulations adopted in the context of the EMU Action Plan.[13] Work has already started to integrate these pieces into timely quarterly sector accounts, which should initially become available after 90 days. In particular, if a sufficiently long and recent time series of such sector accounts becomes available, the impulses of monetary policy can be traced from the financial sector to the non-financial sectors of the euro area and, more generally, the impact of economic shocks on the euro area can be analysed. Besides this, such time series will allow the quality of the underlying statistics to be checked, as inconsistencies between the various data sources can be detected and the harmonisation of the concepts, definitions and methods used for these statistics can be enhanced. Finally, this will enable a wide range of other analyses, such as fiscal policy analysis and conjectural analysis in relation to various key indicators that are embedded in the system.[14]

Another important ECB priority for statistics is the *enlargement of the statistical framework for financial stability analysis*. In view of the Asian crises and other recent events, central banks and governments have been urged to pay increasing attention to macroeconomic and institutional developments that pose potential risks to financial stability. Data for financial stability analysis primarily refer to the banking sector, but also encompass information on non-bank financial corporations, on the financial positions of households and non-financial corporations, and on asset markets.[15] So far, most of the indicators concerned are compiled from (non-harmonised) national supervisory sources, in addition to the already available macro-prudential indicators. The number of market-based indicators is relatively low but is nevertheless constantly growing. Regarding the banking sector, a principal aim is to ensure appropriate links between the statistics on banking sector stability and macroeconomic statistics, and to harmonise definitions and consolidation methods across the euro area. In particular, this means that national

---

12   See Keuning (2003) for a further elaboration of this subject.

13   See ECOFIN (2000).

14   More details on an initial pilot exercise carried out at the ECB to develop an accounting matrix for the euro area can be found in Jellema et al. (2004).

15   See also Remsperger (2004).

supervisory data and harmonised macroeconomic statistics should be better integrated in two dimensions: 1) applying statistical concepts and classifications when aggregating micro-prudential data; and 2) enhancing macroeconomic statistics with additional breakdowns needed for macro-prudential analysis. In this field, the ECB works closely with the IMF (developing a number of financial soundness indicators) and the Bank for International Settlements (BIS) (on consolidated banking statistics).

Developing statistics subject to limited resources

In an economic environment that is permanently changing and becoming increasingly complex, new statistical needs continue to emerge. As the resources for statistics are not unlimited, the ECB, in coordination with the EU NCBs, has established a so-called *merits and costs procedure* to evaluate such needs. When deciding on whether to introduce new or substantially changed statistics, the additional benefits of statistics for users must be balanced against the additional costs for reporting agents and data compilers. The involvement of NCBs and reporting agents (either directly or indirectly via their associations) in this process ensures that the ECB complies with the Treaty provisions that this must not entail an excessive burden on economic agents. In this context, users must clearly justify their requirements for new or enhanced statistics.

The concern with the obligation to *minimise the burden of reporting institutions* and the need to *streamline reporting requirements* is also reflected in the ECB's interest in promoting a closer alignment of reporting requirements between the International Financial Reporting Standards (IFRS)[16], supervisory returns and the statistical standards (the SNA 1993, ESA 95 and BPM5). Many, although not all, of the statistical implications of the IFRS that are intended to be implemented in the EU are welcome. Unfortunately, unnecessary deviations between statistical and accounting standards may remain.[17] Moreover, the ECB would like to avoid a situation whereby differences in the approaches and timing of implementation of the IFRS by EU countries have a negative impact on the quality of euro area statistics.

The approach of streamlining ECB reporting requirements has already yielded some results. A clear example of this is that the same data are now used for compiling monetary aggregates as well as for calculating the minimum reserve requirements of credit institutions in the euro area. In addition, some data collected from credit institutions in order to monitor monetary developments are also used to compute macro-prudential indicators for the euro area.

Conclusions

The ECB has gradually developed and compiled a wide range of statistics, accounts and indicators for the euro area for use by policy-makers, economic analysts, researchers, the media and the general public. Among the ECB's main priorities in the medium term is the regular compilation of a fully-fledged system of quarterly euro area financial and non-financial accounts for institutional sectors. The building blocks for the compilation of these integrated accounts will use euro area statistics and accounts that are already

---

16   Formerly the International Accounting Standards (IAS).

17   See, for example, the CMFB's opinion on the Fair Value Option under IAS 39, published on its website (www.cmfb.org).

compiled by the ECB, such as monetary statistics, security issues, statistics on investment funds and external statistics (b.o.p. and the i.i.p.), on top of additional national statistics that need to be supplied by NSIs and NCBs. Other important statistical projects already underway are the setting up of a centralised securities database and a financial markets database. Furthermore, the ECB will soon publish a geographical breakdown of the euro area b.o.p. statistics.

The current legal and institutional environment within the European System of Central Banks (ESCB) is no doubt supportive of the development, compilation and dissemination of euro area statistics by the ESCB. One possible lacuna, however, could be the lack of legal basis for the collection of data from insurance corporations and pension funds by the ESCB.

In addition, the ECB's cooperation with the EU NCBs and international organisations (primarily with Eurostat, but also with the OECD) is particularly effective. This may also pave the way for the further development of euro area statistics that are already partly available at the NCBs. For example, a number of central balance sheet offices are already up and running in the EU NCBs. Their integration into a more comprehensive European Office might imply a considerable improvement in the provision of corporate data for balance sheet analysis.

Last, but not least, a few comments on the quality of statistics should be made. The quality framework for ECB statistics builds on good practices that already exist (e.g. at the IMF) and looks not only at the output of statistics, but also at the processes whereby ECB statistics are produced. In this context, the possibility of regularly publishing *quality indicators for euro area statistics* is being explored (indicators on revisions, consistency, etc., are already provided for b.o.p./i.i.p. statistics).[18] In order to enhance the serviceability and accessibility of the data, DG-S has also identified the dissemination of its statistics as a medium-term priority. For example, the ECB is developing a more easily accessible website on statistics and has already set up a dedicated statistical information service for users. These and other improvements all aim at providing a better service to our users. Indeed, there is no point in producing good and comprehensive statistics if those who need them are not sufficiently aware of their availability or assured of their quality.

References

Baele, L., Ferrando, A., Hördahl, P., Krylova, E. and Monnet, C. (2004): "Measuring Financial Integration in the Euro Area", ECB Occasional Paper No 14 (May 2004).

Bull, P. (2004): "The Development of Statistics for Economic and Monetary Union", ECB (July 2004).

ECB/European Commission (2004): Report of the Task Force on Quality, CMFB (July 2004).

ECOFIN (2000): "Action Plan on EMU Statistical Requirements", ECOFIN Council (September 2000).

Issuing, O. (2002): "Monetary Policy in a World of Uncertainty", speech delivered at the Economic Policy Forum, Paris, 9 December 2002.

---

18   Cf. ECB/European Commission (2004).

Jellema, T., Keuning, S., McAdam, P. and Mink, R. (2004): "Developing a Euro Area Accounting Matrix: Issues and Applications", ECB Working Paper No 356 (May 2004).

Keuning, S. (1997): "SESAME: An Integrated Economic and Social Accounting System", *International Statistical Review*, Vol. 65, No 1, pp. 111-21.

Keuning, S. (2003): "European Structural Indicators, a Way Forward", *Economic Systems Research*, Vol. 15, No 2 (June 2003).

Keuning, S. and van Tongeren, D. (2004): "The Relationship between Government Accounts and National Accounts, with Special Reference to the Netherlands", *Review of Income and Wealth*, Series 50, No 2 (June 2004).

Randzio-Plath, C. (2004): "Statistics' Ultimate Purpose: Serving European Citizens", paper presented at the Second ECB Conference on Statistics - "Statistics and Their Use for Monetary and Economic Policy-making", ECB, Frankfurt am Main, 22-23 April 2004.

Remsperger, H. (2004): "Statistics for Financial Stability Purposes", paper presented at the Second ECB Conference on Statistics - "Statistics and Their Use for Monetary and Economic Policy-making", ECB, Frankfurt am Main, 22-23 April 2004.

Treaty establishing the European Community (consolidated version, December 2002).

Trichet, J-C. (2004a): "Euro Area Statistics and Their Use for ECB Policy-making", speech delivered at the Second ECB Conference on Statistics - "Statistics and Their Use for Monetary and Economic Policy-making", ECB, Frankfurt am Main, 22-23 April 2004.

Trichet, J-C. (2004b): "Key Issues for Monetary Policy: An ECB View", speech delivered at the National Association of Business Economics, Philadelphia, 5 October 2004.

Financial Stability Policy and Statistics

Toshio Idesawa

General Manager for Europe, Bank of Japan

A general view on financial stability policy and statistics

Policy and statistics are two sides of the same coin. Statistics give objectiveness to policy. Any policy in a democracy needs to be objective. And policy gives meaning to statistics. Any statistics need to be linked with the policy target.

A good example is the relationship between inflation targeting monetary policy and the consumer price index. The policy objective is the stability of the value of money. Price stability, a synonym of the stability of the value of money, can be expressed by some statistics, in most cases the consumer price index, or its rate of change. Once statistics are defined, monetary policy is objectively exercised. When monetary policy takes the style of inflation targeting, the policy is said to be quite transparent and objective.

This relationship between policy and statistics holds true with financial stability policy no less than monetary policy. Financial stability policy, however, has some difficulty when we try to set its policy target linked with statistics. The policy objective can be described in various ways. Let me define it as maintaining the function of money. The money in this context is deposit money that functions as an instrument of payment and settlement run by the banking industry. To put it differently, the financial stability policy objective is to maintain a state in which payments and settlements are executed across the accounts of banks without disruption. Then the policy target is no bank failure or even no anticipation of bank failures. Describing the degree of the anticipation of bank failure in terms of statistics is technically difficult and sometimes politically inappropriate.

Anticipating a bank failure can be self-fulfilling. If any statistics related to the probability of a bank failure are released to the public, a bank failure would actually occur with a higher probability than the originally measured probability. This is why the bank supervising authorities very cautiously handle the disclosure of banks' financial states in any form. Private rating agencies also face similar difficulties when they lower the rating of a bank.

Bank supervising authorities would rather look at the banks' financial soundness indirectly and multilaterally than approach directly the probability of a bank failure. They would not, even if they could, try to calculate the probability of a bank failure. They try to figure out the banks' financial soundness through data like capital ratio, liquidity ratio, and coverage ratio of bad loans by provisions. When completed, IMF's work on "Financial Soundness Indicators" will provide a framework of a set of data relevant to banks' financial soundness.

Objectiveness in financial stability policy may be somewhat different from that in monetary policy. Monetary policy affects a whole economy in a general way and it is not involved in any individual conflict of interests. Monetary policy is objective, provided the authorities explain logically why the policy measure could attain the policy target which is expressed by statistics. Financial stability policy, however, is more often than not involved in an individual conflict of interest when the policy measure is exercised to attain the policy target. To maintain financial stability the authorities sometimes need to rescue a failing private bank by public funds. That policy measure definitely needs objectiveness to prove fairness as well as objectiveness. Objective statistics help the authorities claim fairness.

"Prompt Corrective Action" is one of the bank supervisory measures to enforce recapitalisation in weak banks. The authorities trigger the PCA when weak banks fail to keep a certain capital ratio. To make the policy measure objective, the threshold capital ratio is stipulated by a law and the capital ratio is a well- defined statistic. The Basel Committee on Banking Supervision has been contributing to providing a framework for the capital ratio.

The Committee recently proposed a new framework for banks' risk management. The new framework, so-called Basel 2, encourages banks to build a reliable and extensive database related to their risk profiles so that a more meaningful capital ratio can be established.

Japan's case study of statistics for financial stability policy

Japan's economic conditions in the 90s and after

In the late 80s an unprecedented boom occurred in Japan. The boom took place prominently in the stock market and the real estate market while the general inflation rate remained moderate around 3% per annum.

Some say that a boom was inevitable. Japan witnessed a miracle recovery after the last war and by 1970 it grew to be one of the world economic powers. It overcame the oil-shocks twice, which made people feel the country's resilience. Japanese money and goods started to outflow overseas in the 70s and 80s. A kind of euphoria caught Japan. People simply believed that stock prices and land prices could never be too high for an ever-growing country like Japan.

Others say that the boom was nothing but a result of miss-conducted economic policies. Facing the unprecedented sharp appreciation of the Japanese yen after the Plaza Meeting in 1985, the Government and the Bank of Japan continued to employ stimulating economic policies for too long. The Government and the Bank of Japan overreacted to the exporting industries' depression due to the appreciation of Yen.

The boom occurred for whichever reason. And it burst when the Bank of Japan tightened monetary policy in 1989. First stock prices nosedived, and two years later real estate prices collapsed. The banking industry gradually suffered deterioration in its loans. The deterioration came in two ways; borrowers' bankruptcies and insufficiently collateralised loans due to decreasing value of the real estate submitted as collateral against the loans.

The Bank of Japan soon geared up to the crash. The economy seemed to hit bottom around 1993 but the recovery was sluggish. Real estate prices continued to fall and the banks' loans deteriorated further. The slump in the real estate market affected not only the banking industry but almost all the sectors, corporate and household alike. The stock market continued to crawl. Investors stayed away from the market, suffering heavy capital losses. Japan was in depression after the crash (see Figure 1).

By the way, two myths prevailed in Japan at that time; banks were immortal and real estate prices never fell (see Figure 2). Banks were rigorously supervised by the authorities. Failing banks, if any, could be bailed out before it was too late. In other words failing banks could well expect a rescue in due course. Its corollary was that immortal banks could decide the fate of failing borrowers. Borrowers never go bankrupt as long as the lending bank provides liquidity. And real estate was believed to be the most reliable asset to possess because Japan had long been facing over–population and real estate had always been in short supply.

Given these myths, people naturally hesitated to cut a loss. They could well anticipate that the time would come when they could sell what they possessed without a loss as long as they were protected by the immortal banks. Businesses postponed selling stocks and land they held at a loss. Banks postponed writing off non-performing loans they lent to businesses. The Government postponed enforcing the recapitalisation of failing banks. From time to time the economy seemed to get out of the depression and only to realize that it was too early to say so. This continued till 1997 and finally a financial crisis came.

Once the crisis occurred, the Government and the Bank of Japan decisively took action; the Government poured public funds into the banking industry and the Bank of Japan lowered the interest rate to zero, which meant infinite provision of liquidity, if necessary. Structural reform has been tried everywhere, public and private. It took a long time for these measures to make a visible impact on the economy but at last Japan is now out of the depression.

Statistics related to financial stability policy

The target of financial stability policy in Japan may appear to be "no bank failure". The target has been deliberated from time to time in relation to other social and economic concerns in the era; efficiency of banks, moral hazards, depopulated local economies. Still that target seems to be widely shared by people, explicitly or implicitly.

To measure the soundness of banks the bank supervising authorities monitor financial data; liquidity ratio, capital ratio, and others. Besides disclosed financial data, banks are required to report more detailed data to the bank supervising authorities. Financial data of banks are made according to the Japanese Accounting Standards and rules and regulations are stipulated by the Banking Law. Statistics are well defined and are accurately calculated.

The Relevancy of data, however, was not necessarily guaranteed before. Bad loans, for example, used to be recognised only as legally defaulted loans. This recognition was narrow, compared with the current one that includes doubtful loans and special attention loans. Nonetheless it had some relevancy in the era when the tax authorities regarded only legally defaulted loans as deductible. In theory banks were free to make any provisions or write-offs when they believed them prudent. But in practice they dared not to do that because of the unfavourable tax treatment for loans that had not gone under yet. Therefore banks did not focus on doubtful and special attention loans as much as they should have done if they had been more prudent.

When banks were in a position to virtually decide the fate of failing borrowers, disclosing possible default loans was regarded as an irresponsible action on the side of banks. Therefore banks were not required to disclose data on bad loans, but only report to the regulatory authorities (see figure 3).

The two myths about real estate and bank failure had been already dead when a financial crisis occurred in 1997. The bank supervising authorities no longer kept public confidence as much as they once did. Their concern was how to respond to scepticism about Japanese financial stability. The scepticism prevailed both at home and abroad. At last the authorities let statistics replace the role of myths, hoping the banks would regain public confidence.

The authorities revised the regulatory definition of bad loans so that statistics could cover bad loans extensively. Bank examiners introduced the cash discount approach to identify non-performing loans when they visited banks for on-site examination. Despite the unfavourable treatment in taxation with regard to provisioning and writing-off against any loans other than legally defaulted loans, the regulatory authorities ordered bank to cover credit risks by more prudent provisioning and writing-off. Banks started to disclose data on bad loans comprehensively under the new regulation in 1998. Ahead of Basel 2 implementation in 2006, banks started in 2004 quarterly disclosure of banks' financial data relevant to bad loans.

Along with the series of reforms of banks' prudential policy, the Government launched an unprecedented recapitalisation program for weak banks. Rigorous classification of loans would possibly get weak banks into fatal trouble; insufficient capital or even deficit. Measures that were intended to enhance financial stability in the long run could cause financial instability in the short run. The objective of financial stability policy at that time was to avoid a financial catastrophe.

Today we seem to be back from the merge of a financial catastrophe. The Financial stability policy objective is to make the banking industry more resilient. The bank supervising authorities encourage banks to build a framework for better risk management.

By 2006 the Basel 2 will be implemented in Japan. Basel 2 encourages banks to build a reliable and extensive database related to their risk profiles. Major Japanese banks are steadily preparing for Basel 2.

During the last decade we learned a lot of things. The most important thing was that we should be always on alert with a historical perspective to perceive instinctively a structural change taking place in financial circumstances. We must review the policy objective if the perception tells us to do. We need to redefine, if necessary, statistics so as not to lose their relevance to the reviewed policy objective. Then the appropriate relationship between policy and statistics would be restored.

(Views in this paper are personal and do not represent those of the Bank of Japan or the Japanese Government)

Figure 1. The Crash and After

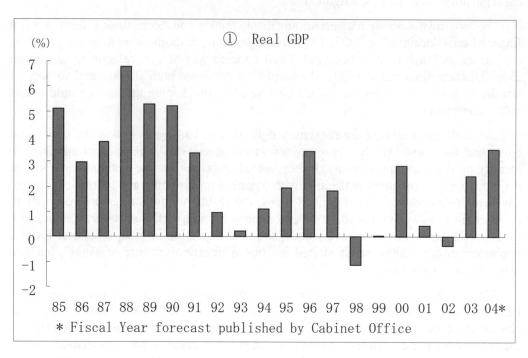

① Real GDP

* Fiscal Year forecast published by Cabinet Office

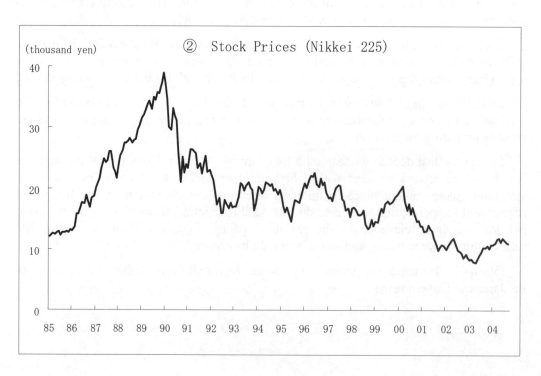

② Stock Prices (Nikkei 225)

Figure 2. Two Myths prevailed till the Crash

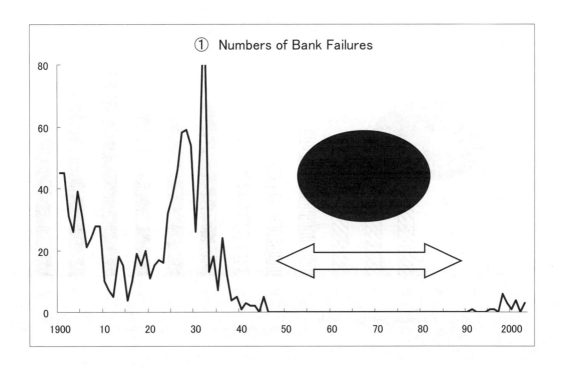

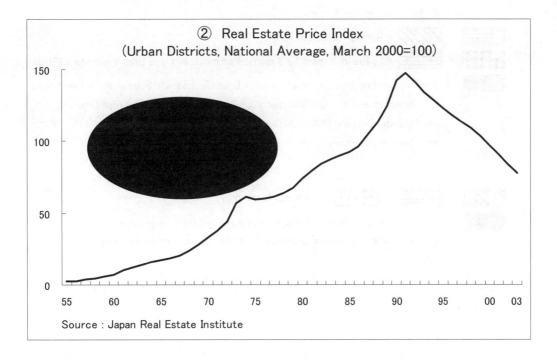

Figure 3 Non Performing Loans of Japanese Banks

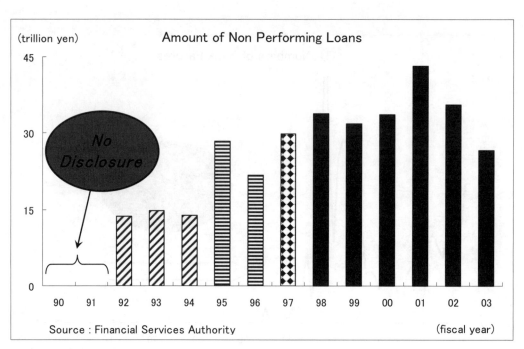

 = Loans to Borrowers in Legal Bankruptcy (LBB) + Past Due Loans in arrears by 6 months or more (PDL)

 = ▨ + Restructured Loans

= ▨ + Loans in arrears by 3 months or more and less than 6 months (3PDL)

= Bankrupt and de fact Bankrupt Loans + Doubtful Loans + Special Attention Loans

   * Bankrupt and de fact Bankrupt Loans = LBB + de fact Bankrupt Loans

   ** Doubtful Loans = PDL − de fact Bancrupt Loans

   *** Special Attention Loans = 3PDL + Restructured Loans

▨ , ▤ , ◈ = covers loans only

= covers securities loaned, foreign exchanges, interest receivable, suspence payments and customers' liabilities for acceptances and guarantees as well as loans

The Role of Civil Society

Collaborating with Civil Society: Reflections from Australia

Jon Hall, Chris Carswell, and René Jones, Australian Bureau of Statistics

David Yencken, Professor Emeritus at the University of Melbourne and convenor of the Australian Collaboration.[1]

Abstract

There are many reasons why those working on indicator initiatives have an interest in civil society. But two reasons stand out as particularly important. First, representatives from civil society can play a key role in shaping an initiative and are often important users of the indicators themselves. Second, the health of a country's civil society can impact on the progress a nation makes in many areas of economic, social and environmental concern. This paper discusses both aspects, though we focus on the former.

We begin by discussing the role civil society has played in developing three significant, but rather different, indicator initiatives in Australia: the Australian Bureau of Statistics' *Measures of Australia's Progress*; the Victorian State Government's *Growing Victoria Together*; and the Tasmanian State Government's *Tasmania Together*. As well as discussing why governments and civil society collaborate, we reflect on the styles of collaboration that work best from both parties' perspectives. We go on to present material that highlights Australian thinking around indicators of progress in the areas of *social cohesion* and *governance, democracy and citizenship:* areas that are intimately related to the health of our civil society.

What is Civil Society?

We should begin by defining what we mean by *civil society*. Britain's Institute for Development Studies noted, "Definitions of 'civil society' are bewilderingly diverse" (Manor, Robinson and White 1999). After spending five minutes browsing the web it is clear that many definitions are plain bewildering.

The World Bank's definition is one of the more appealing "the groups and organisations, both formal and informal, which act independently of the state and market, to promote diverse interests in society" (World Bank 2002). The London School of Economics' definition provides more detail in a similar vein "*civil society* refers to the

---

1   We'd like to thank the following people, whose comments on this paper strengthened it considerably: Dennis Trewin, Ken Tallis, Lee Prince and Marion Frere.

The views in this paper are those of the authors and do not necessarily represent the views of the Australian Bureau of Statistics or the Australian Collaboration. Where quoted or used they should be attributed to the authors.

arena of uncoerced collective action around shared interests, purposes and values. In theory, its institutional forms are distinct from those of the state, family and market, though in practice, the boundaries between state, civil society, family and market are often complex, blurred and negotiated … Civil societies are often populated by organisations such as registered charities, development non-governmental organisations, community groups, women's organisations, faith-based organisations, professional associations, trades unions, self-help groups, social movements, business associations, coalitions and advocacy groups"(LSE 2004).

Three Important Australian Indicator Initiatives

In recent years, Australia has seen a growing interest in measuring progress, wellbeing or sustainability. Initiatives have come out of Commonwealth, State and local government, academia and beyond. We focus on three significant projects in this paper. The initiatives are significant in their size and impact. They make an interesting selection because they differ quite substantially in how they were run and the outcomes they were designed to achieve.

Measures of Australia's Progress

The Australian Bureau of Statistics (ABS) released the first issue of Measures of Australia's Progress (MAP) in 2002. MAP is a facts-based publication that is built around indicators spanning key aspects of Australia's economic, environmental and social progress. It focuses on outcome measures and is designed to inform public debate.

In the foreword to the publication, Dennis Trewin (the ABS head) noted, "This publication does not purport to measure every aspect of progress that is important. Nor does it consider all of the many different ways that parts of Australia and groups of Australians are progressing. But it does provide a national summary of many of the most important areas of progress, presenting them in a way which can be quickly understood. MAP will, I hope, inform and stimulate public debate and encourage all Australians to assess the bigger picture when contemplating progress in all its forms" (ABS 2002).

Although there was a good deal of consultation about MAP's content within government and the community, the ABS took the final decisions about which dimensions of progress to include, and which indicators best measured them.

Tasmania Together

In 1999 the Tasmanian Premier challenged residents to come together to plan the future of the State into the new century. The *Tasmania Together* plan, published by a Tasmanian community leaders group in 2001, sets out a social, environmental and economic plan for Tasmania. It includes clear goals for the state, half of which are benchmarked with indicators that have baseline-data, interim targets and a final target for 2020. The ABS assisted with its statistical development.

The intended outcome is for Tasmania to achieve the goals set in the plan: "through the process of community participation…establish broad goals and specific and concrete benchmarks for the plan, and develop detailed indicators, and an ongoing process, for open, transparent and ongoing measurement of the achievement of the goals" (Salvaris et al 1999). Moreover, the initiative might also be viewed as an attempt to embed social capital and community capacity into policy making.

Tasmania *Together* is a process that reflects - and depends - on the collaborative and collective actions of civil society, business and government. A board has responsibility for monitoring the plan's progress. It is an independent statutory authority and has made three reports direct to parliament, and through parliament, to the people of Tasmania. Government has a particular interest in the reports, because budgets and policies are linked to the plan. Civil society is keenly interested too, because the plan reflects both the aspirations of, and contributions from, the Tasmanian people.

Growing Victoria Together

In 2001, the Hon. Steve Bracks M.P., Premier of Victoria, launched Growing Victoria Together (GVT), a document that expresses a broad vision for the future of Victoria through a list of goals and priority actions. This Victorian State Government document also lists indicators and targets that will be used to demonstrate progress towards the articulated goals.

GVT has its origins in the public policy environment of 2000. The initiative aimed to develop policy that integrated the economic, social and environmental; and draw upon the knowledge within civil society to formulate and implement policy. It aims both to communicate the Victorian government's priorities to the public, and to help the public sector deliver a whole of government approach.

Like Tasmania Together and MAP, GVT is a "live" initiative. The first publication made clear that "the priority actions and measures of progress will continue to be developed to ensure that they are responsive to community concerns". A second, updated version of GVT is being prepared. This version will be based on input from Ministers, all departments and research into community attitudes. The updates are likely to focus on re-examining the issues and measures covered in GVT; and improving the way government works at all levels to achieve the GVT outcomes.

Civil Society's Role in Developing Australian Indicator Initiatives

Section 1 described the background to three significant Australian indicator initiatives. Each project differed in purpose, and each project had a different approach to collaborating with civil society. This section describes those approaches.

Measures of Australia's Progress

The ABS began work on the MAP project in early 2000, with the first issue of the publication released in April 2002. Most of 2000 and 2001 was spent developing and discussing thinking around progress and its measurement – rather than preparing the actual document *per se*. The publication itself took about 6 months to write, peer review and publish. The consultation around its development took nearly two years.

Before and during MAP's development a range of Civil Society Organisations (CSOs) had called for new and better measures of progress to supplement Gross Domestic Product. In the mid-1990s the ABS began discussions with academics, scientists and policy makers about ways to measure progress. And in 1997 the Bureau co-sponsored an important conference "Measuring National Progress: Is Life in Australia Getting Better, or Worse?", the proceedings of which were published (Eckersley 1998). Another notable call came from the Australian Collaboration, (a group of major national non-governmental organisation peak bodies) in 2001. The third section (Reflections from David Yencken) of this paper talks in more detail about the work of the Collaboration.

Strengths and weaknesses of the ABS approach

Progress is a nebulous, subjective and potentially controversial topic for a national statistical agency to try to measure. And so, at the beginning of the MAP project, the ABS recognised a need to consult very widely within and outside government. Those consultations needed to take account of the views of civil society if the publication was to resonate with a broad Australian audience.

The ABS is fortunate in having comprehensive links with civil society. The Bureau has a systematic program for consulting users of statistics. Through this program, hundreds of government agencies, academic researchers, businesses and business councils, community organisations and individual Australians have told the ABS what they think it is important that it measures. And so, during the design of MAP, the selection of progress dimensions and indicators were guided by past and current ABS consultations. The choices were tested through several further rounds of consultation undertaken specifically for MAP (and 20 or so members of CSOs attended those consultations). The final choice of indicators was made by the ABS after taking account of the full spectrum of views.

The ABS invited a small group of external advisors to sit on an "expert reference group" to inform MAP's development and provide a sounding board for ABS ideas. This group comprised several academics, a scientist and the heads of two prominent civil society organisations: the Australian Council of Social Services (ACOSS) "the peak council of the community services and welfare sector and the national voice for the needs of people affected by poverty and inequality"(ACOSS 2003); and the Australia Institute, an independent public policy research centre, "concerned about the impact on Australian society of the priority given to a narrow definition of economic efficiency over community, environmental and ethical considerations in public and private decision making" (Australia Institute 2004).

The group met three times, and played several roles. Individually, their expertise in several areas with which the ABS was less familiar helped guide the selection of indicators and potential sources of non-ABS data that could be used to populate those indicators. Collectively, their diverse backgrounds helped ensure that the ABS view of progress was palatable to a broad cross-section of Australia. And, almost as important as the advice they provided, their involvement in the process of developing MAP helped to ensure that they supported the final publication. The group's links with civil society meant that they were able to draw on wide range of opinions when commenting on the MAP project. These links also helped to ensure that news of the MAP project was passed back to civil society who became increasingly interested.

There was, however, at least one weakness to the ABS approach that on reflection might have been avoided. It involves the importance of perception: perception around the role of, and perceived bias in the expert group, even though the ABS head made the final choices on dimensions and indicators.

Some dimensions of progress attract more debate than others. There is, for example, a good deal of discussion about what changes in the distribution of income mean vis-à-vis progress. Some people equate a move to a more equal distribution of income with progress. Others feel that progress is achieved if people are earning more on average, even if the distribution of income widens. It is important that those designing an indicator initiative are aware of these areas of potential controversy and make a special effort to consult with people of all persuasions. Simply relying on responses to invitations to public consultations and the like might not be enough. And so an organisation might need to go out of its way to ensure that sufficiently diverse viewpoints are represented when it consults stakeholders.

Nearly all of the coverage about MAP has been favourable. But the first issue attracted one quite prominent critic from Australia's Centre for Independent Studies (CIS), a leading independent public-policy think tank that is "actively engaged in support of a free enterprise economy and a free society under limited government where individuals can prosper and fully develop their talents" (CIS 2004). The CIS is an organisation that fits within our definition of "civil society".

The critic claimed that the ABS had fallen unwitting victim to a broadly green and left wing agenda (Saunders 2002). He cited a number of pieces of evidence to back up his claims, including "The ABS selected its indicators on the advice of a "panel of experts' whose composition was skewed towards people concerned with environmental and/or social inequality issues." (Saunders 2002).

Could the ABS have avoided this criticism? Perhaps not. But with hindsight a couple of actions might have tempered it. First, the critic may have thought that the expert group had more control in the selection of indicators than they actually did. If the Bureau had been more explicit about the group's role in developing the publication, some criticism might have been avoided. Second, and perhaps more importantly, the ABS might have thought more carefully about the perceived balance of the group's political persuasions. Members were selected for their expertise in measuring progress, or aspects thereof: the Bureau didn't take account of the overall balance of political views among the group, or the perception thereof. It might have been both politic and useful to the publication's development to have ensured the full political spectrum was perceived to have been better covered by the group.

Tasmania Together

Tasmania Together describes itself as a people's plan based on shared ideas and dreams. Civil society has had – and continues to have - a very significant role in its development. Although all the major political parties contributed, the initiative engaged the community from the outset. *Tasmania Together* wanted to generate a plan that extended beyond the government of the day to include input from civil society. And that input went beyond the planning phase to encompass the implementation and achievement of long-term policy objectives. The involvement of civil society is critical to the success of *Tasmania Together* - in both its development and achievement. *Tasmania Together* requires collaboration among all sectors of the community to achieve its goals and benchmarks. It also sits outside the electoral process.

When the initiative began, a public nomination process led to the appointment of 22 community-based people (the leaders group) who led the plan's development. A conference in 1999, conducted by the leaders group and involving 60 other members of the Tasmanian community, drafted a vision statement. The consultation on the draft plan included 60 community forums and consulted 100 community organisations. A database recorded the views presented at forums, along with 679 responses to an attitudinal survey; 4,000 comments about particular goals; 2,500 postcard responses from householders; 6,200 web-forum messages; and 160 detailed written submissions from business, not-for-profit organisations and individuals. Results from the database were analysed, and published in October 2000. They provided a solid foundation for the plan.

The community leaders group formed benchmarking committees to cover the broad domains of community, economy, governance, culture, sustainable development and nature conservation. Members were drawn from peak business and labour organisations, community groups and interested individuals. The benchmarking process prepared concrete *standards* that reflected the goals of the plan; selected *indicators* to evaluate progress; and set the interim *targets* required to achieve the Year 2020 goals. The initiative also depends on community involvement to achieve those goals.

Strengths and weaknesses of the Tasmanian approach

The *Tasmania Together* plan was developed after extensive community consultation at every stage. Engaging the community in broad-based planning helped to ensure the indicator set reflects progress towards the community's aspirations: the plan provided an opportunity for all Tasmanians to discuss the State's future. The goals and benchmarks of the plan can be linked directly to the issues raised in the community consultation, and the target setting exercise involved representatives from the government (state and local), business and community sectors. The plan offers common ground for partnerships between civil society and government to meet the benchmark targets. The government has aligned budget processes with the plan and made provision for regular reports to the community on progress.

Civil society has been able to use the profile of benchmarks and indicator reporting to support funding applications and proposals for policy change. One indicator – whose goal calls for an end to clear-felling old-growth forest by 2010 – has generated a particularly large amount of debate. This is one of only three indicators (all environmental) about which there was no consensus when the plan was published, reflecting the apparently irreconcilable social and nature conservation values that surround native forest use in Tasmania. People debate both the way in which civil society contributed to the development of the benchmark, and the likely outcomes of policy to meet the target.

The Board continues to engage civil society in partnerships and forums to help achieve the benchmarks and long-term goals. Five-yearly reviews involving community consultation will be conducted to update and refine the goals and benchmarks. But, despite what, by most reckoning, was an exceptional amount of consultation, the Tasmania Together Progress Board recognize that some sectors and individuals did not have sufficient input to the plan. The plan does not include issues specifically relevant to people with disabilities, older Tasmanians, families with very young children, and sport and recreation participants. This will be addressed. Moreover, the issues that were of greatest concern to the Tasmanian community in 2001 are not identical to those of 2004. Housing affordability has emerged as a significant topic, now rivaling the prominence given to unemployment (unemployment has declined sharply in recent years).

Community involvement has to be a continuing commitment if indicators are to remain relevant, and this is reflected in legislation that provides a mechanism to amend, delete or add to the goals and benchmarks to reflect changes in community aspirations. This can be done at any time, but the legislation requires reviews every five years and stipulates public consultation. It is important, though, to recognize that while some things could have been done differently, a different approach would have had costs as well as benefits. Broader or more frequent community input would have cost time and money.

Growing Victoria Together

Civil society had a much more limited role in designing GVT than it had in Tasmania Together, reflecting the two initiatives' very different purposes. *Tasmania Together* allowed the community to set the State's goals and monitor progress towards them. *Growing Victoria Together* was designed by government to set government direction: one of its primary aims was to encourage government departments to work better together when tackling crosscutting issues of concern.

Civil society was involved early in the initiative's life. Consultation was broad and included community forums, policy summits and round table discussions between the government and a range of people from civil society including trade unionists and those with an interest in social and environmental concerns. In March 2000 the Growing Victoria Together summit, chaired by former Prime Minister Bob Hawke, brought together 100 participants from business, unions, community organisations and local government.

In November 2001 the Premier launched the GVT document. It set out the Victorian Government's vision for the medium-term (5-10 years), balancing the government's economic, social and environmental responsibilities through a triple bottom line approach.

Strengths and weaknesses of the Victorian approach

One important determinant of civil society's role in GVT was the balance the Victorian government decided to strike between "top down" and "bottom up" direction setting. There have been various Australian and international experiments in developing integrated, whole of government strategies and progress measures. These range from centrally managed models, to highly decentralised community consultation initiatives (such as *Tasmania Together*). GVT took a middle path. It drew on an extensive consultation but did not establish an ongoing community consultation process. As a result, GVT's main engagement with civil society has been to communicate the Government's priorities to Victorians.

One potential weakness of the initiative is a lack of "buy-in" from communities and line departments. Most community input into the measures has come from research into community attitudes. While this provides useful insight into the pulse of a community, it doesn't generate a high degree of ownership.

If communities fail to give adequate support to an initiative it is, perhaps, not unsurprising that government departments are less enthusiastic than they might be. It might be argued that whole of government approaches are most enthusiastically implemented when they have the support of voters. But voters are unlikely to care greatly about whole of government policy formulation and delivery per se. Rather, they are concerned with the tangible outcomes of better policy making and delivery, outcomes that can be proven through indicator initiatives. But that proof is not particularly useful if the public isn't aware - or supportive - of the indicators. Perhaps the tension between the document's two aims – communicating government priorities to the public, and a tool to drive public sector performance and management towards more joined-up government – is difficult to overcome. To overcome this potential problem and get buy-in, the Victorian government see the future challenges for GVT include: strengthening planning and delivery on whole-of-government issues and improving performance information, management and reporting; delivering and communicate positive outcomes on important issues; and improving community and stakeholder engagement.

The View From the Other Side of the Fence: Some Reflections From David Yencken on Civil Society's Perspective

Community groups take a vital interest in monitoring and reporting regimes.

They put great store on regular, comprehensive and independent reporting of social, cultural, environmental and economic conditions and trends. One illustration is the work of the Australian Collaboration. The Australian Collaboration is a collaboration of seven of the most influential national community organisations in Australia. When the Collaboration first came into being in July 2000, the heads of the various member bodies met to consider what it should first do. The Steering Committee decided to prepare a report on social and environmental issues facing the nation and what should be done about them. This was eventually published as *A Just and Sustainable Australia* (Yencken and Porter 2001). Significantly, the Collaboration also determined to prepare a report on monitoring and reporting regimes at all levels of government and across all sectors. This was eventually published as *Where are we Going: Social, cultural, environmental and economic reporting* (Yencken 2001).

Why the interest in monitoring and reporting? In its report the Collaboration argued that without good reporting, key trends aren't known to citizens and their governments and there is an inadequate basis for decision-making. Where reporting regimes are well-established, trends and issues are given media attention, and they are kept in the forefront of the consciousness of citizens. In this way they gain standing in public opinion and in political debates. These are the essential preludes to action. Where reporting is poor or non-existent, issues are buried, neglected by the media and given scant attention by politicians.

Of particular concern to community organisations such as the Australian Collaboration is unbalanced reporting since, by weighting some forms of human activity highly and ignoring or paying insufficient attention to others, the community remains poorly informed and policy is distorted. In Australia as in other countries there are long established regimes for reporting economic conditions and trends. Only recently have state-of-the-environment reporting programs been established. While there is a well-developed national program and regimes of some kind in all States and Territories, they are hampered by inadequate funding. Full independence for the reporting bodies is also the exception rather that the norm. Full independence requires the establishment of a Commissioner, Commission or other body appointed by statute and dedicated staff reporting directly to the Commissioner or Commission rather than to a host department.[2]

By far the greatest deficiency is social reporting. There are now long-term studies under way such as the Household Income and Labour Dynamics in Australia (HILDA) survey and the Longitudinal Survey of Australian Children, but there is no independent national body equivalent to the Australian State of the Environment Committee charged with overall social monitoring and reporting. As a consequence, there is not a strategic understanding of, and approach to, poverty and disadvantage in Australia.

---

2   Although not a commission per se, the Australian State of Environment Committee operates under a legislative provision which ensures that it operates independently of the government of the day. The Australian Statistician has been appointed to the last two Committees to reinforce this independence.

Another groundswell of community and expert concern has related to the use of Gross Domestic Product (GDP) as the standard summary measure of progress, despite its many distortions of social and environmental progress. Dennis Trewin the Australian Statistician's response was immediate. The options for him were to use another summary measure such as the Genuine Progress Indicator or to take a different course. He judged that the Genuine Progress Indicator had too many subjective components. His solution was to prepare a composite list of separate social, environmental and economic indices of progress as is described in the discussion of the MAP project in this paper.

From the perspective of an academic and head of a group of community organisations, the model had two attractions. The first was that Australia at last had a full set of indicators that put the social and environmental conditions and trends on an equal footing with economic indicators and forced attention to be paid to them. The second attraction of the model was the way it was developed. The overall consultative approach has already been described. Small working meetings formed part of that consultation. Those who had previously shown an active interest in reporting regimes were invited to take part in discussions about the way the indicators might be developed. Later when the Bureau of Statistics wanted feedback about the first edition of MAP and ideas about the development of a strong conceptual framework for the choice of the individual indicators, the absence of which had been a criticism of the first edition, the ABS hosted a workshop of experts.

Although the detailed work on the MAP program had been done by others, in each instance the Australian Statistician was present and thus able to hear the view of the advisory group personally. Thus when radical ideas about the framework were put forward he did not hear about them second or third hand. There was, furthermore, great openness and willingness to listen from all the Bureau staff. When therefore the proposal for the new framework was jointly developed by the original proposer (an external member of the advisory committee) and the manager of the MAP project, despite objections to it, there was a fertile environment for its adoption.

Membership of an advisory body to government can be a very frustrating experience. All too often the views of the advisory body are ignored. Often they are seen to be too adventurous. This is particularly a problem with middle management in bureaucracies when they are uncertain about the views of the head of the department or agency or the minister. Hence the great importance of leadership and the openness of the institutional environment in which government employees work. In passing, it is a reason why monitoring and review tasks are best done by statutory bodies. The way expert consultation for the MAP project was carried out was exemplary. This is to put a somewhat different perspective on the so-called failings of the expert consultation program reported earlier in this paper. It is true that there were attacks on the Bureau for, as it was claimed, exceeding its mandate, listening to too many so called 'greenies and lefties' and including indicators for which there was inadequate statistical validity. These attacks were, however nonsensical. No person on any of the advisory committees had any other motive than the most accurate description of environmental, social and economic trends in Australia. Even if any one had had an ulterior ideological motive, a national statistical agency would have given such attitudes short shift.

The Bureau acted carefully and responsibly to ensure that the prominent and influential critic and others like him were fully consulted the second time round. An important concession was made. The indicators were no longer presented under the title *Measuring Australia's Progress* but under the title *Measures of Australia's Progress*.

Readers of the document were therefore left to make their own choices about the measures that that they thought mattered.

The best initiatives, and MAP is an outstanding and widely praised one, usually require courage and risk. Smart operators also know how important it is to respond quickly and effectively to any criticism. The Australian Statistician and the managers of the program had the courage and took the risk and then acted quickly to deal with them. This is an example of expert public consultation. There are many other forms of public consultation and participation which there is no space to explore in this paper. Suffice it to say that public consultation by government bodies is a very complex matter and that it can be done for many different reasons and in many different ways. There are rules of thumb that need to be recognised. They include that the smaller the group of people involved the less representative it will be, that there is unequal opportunity to participate for reasons of access, education, confidence and the like and that consultation without genuine commitment to listen and respond is quite counterproductive. The MAP consultation served its purpose well and produced a good outcome. A different project might need an entirely different approach.

Lessons in collaboration

The benefits of collaboration

There are many reasons why government and civil society collaborate on indicator initiatives.

From civil society's perspective, the benefits of collaborating on an indicator initiative include having a structured conversation about how progress (or wellbeing etc) should be measured. Such conversations, lead - almost inevitably - to a discussion about what progress actually means; that is, people begin to get a clearer understanding of what progress amounts (or should amount) too. This benefit potentially goes much wider than the indicator initiative itself.

First, a publication can provide an important reference document. The information within MAP has helped inform debate within civil society. Indicators in Tasmania Together have provided civil society with the facts and platform to advance particular causes. And second, indicator initiatives often influence – directly or indirectly - government policy. Tasmania Together set out to provide a framework to guide government policy. Growing Victoria Together sought to promote inter-governmental cooperation to better achieve key outcomes. And MAP was influential (both directly and indirectly) on policy-maker's thinking. In each case, civil society had a vital interest in the initiative, because civil society is (nearly) always particularly concerned with government policy.

From a government, or statistical agency, point of view, the benefits from collaborating with civil society include tapping into some a nation's leading thinkers and experts who often seem to be involved with civil society organisations (CSOs). Collaborating with them provides access to their skills, knowledge and resources. Moreover, when trying to understand and measure something as nebulous as progress it is important to recognise that there are many ways to look at the world. Understanding the opinions of civil society organisations can help ensure that the indicators do not reflect the potentially narrow viewpoint of the statistician or bureaucrat.

Working alongside CSOs can foster a wider level of ownership and support for a project, which can help to ensure it achieves its outcomes. And collaboration with CSOs can help ensure that the publication is promoted and reaches its intended audience. And, finally, projects like MAP need to evolve as views or thinking about progress change. CSOs can provide a source of inspiration and information on ways in which a publication should improve.

Successful mechanisms for collaboration

We have demonstrated that there are often good reasons for collaboration between government and civil society. But what things help to ensure that that collaboration works well? It is wise to pay attention to the choice of collaborators, the pace of collaboration and the ways in which collaborators interact.

Choice of collaborators

Collaboration on an indicator initiative can take many forms. Many initiatives undergo some form of public consultation. These are useful in many ways: as a source of ideas; a way to foster support; a means to promote the initiative; and a way to defend the initiative against accusations of bias. It is important though, that such consultations, even if not truly 'public', seek the views of a broad range of stakeholders. Simply relying on an open invitation may not attract a particularly diverse audience, and care should be taken to ensure that a range of opinions and population groups are involved. Tasmania Together, for instance, undertook a massive consultation exercise. But still there is evidence that some stakeholders – such as the elderly, disabled or those with young children – were not well represented (it is perhaps not a coincidence that these groups are among those least able to have attended open consultation sessions).

The diversity of collaborators is particularly important if an indicator initiative appoints – as with the MAP project – some sort of *expert group* to help guide the publication. Such a group provides most benefit when its combined membership provides expertise across a range of aspects of progress and a diversity of backgrounds and political philosophy. And finally, as the ABS found, the perception of the style and diversity of consultation is important too.

Pace of collaboration

Anecdotal evidence suggests that the pace of collaboration can be a significant determinant of success. The speed of an initiative's development should depend on many factors, such as the diversity of stakeholders, the political environment, and the complexity of the topic. But, because the process of collaborating can inculcate a sense of ownership of in a project, it shouldn't be rushed. We're aware of initiatives that have foundered because consultation and collaboration was initiated too late in the piece or undertaken too quickly. That said, consultation on a prototype version can provide a more focused discussion than something more open-ended. Moreover, one needs to guard against over consultation, which is expensive, can lead to stakeholder "fatigue", and create frustrations that a project is stagnating.

Interaction between collaborators

Many of the *dos and don'ts* that determine the effectiveness of collaboration between government and civil society apply equally to successful relationships. In successful collaborations, government and civil society listen to one another; are open to new ideas and act on them; and understand the wider systems in which their partners operate. These facets in turn help build a shared trust. And when collaborators feel they have genuine influence over an initiative, they bring a greater energy and enthusiasm to the collaboration.

A useful handbook is the OECD's *Citizens as Partners: A handbook on consultation and public-participation in policy making* (OECD 2001). It discusses ten tips for government officials wanting to strengthen government-citizens relationships (See Annex 1).

Finally, it is important to recognise, that collaboration should be ongoing. Issues important to indicator initiatives change over time, and continued collaboration can ensure that such issues are recognised and measured as they arise.

Measuring Progress: The Strength and Health of Civil Society

This paper is primarily about the ways in which government and civil society can best collaborate to develop indicator initiatives. But it also provides an opportunity to discuss current thinking in Australia around measuring the contribution civil society makes to national progress.

In recent years, the ABS and others in Australia have begun to pay more attention to understanding and measuring the impact that civil society has on the quality of national life. It is an area of statistics that is still in its formative years. ABS work has not focused on the role of civil society *per se,* but it has touched on key aspects of civil society: most notably *social capital, social cohesion* and *governance, democracy and citizenship*. Both the *Tasmania Together* project and the Victorian Government have worked in this area too.

The ABS Social Capital Framework

Considerable ABS effort has been focused on social capital. Social capital can potentially make a positive contribution to outcomes in diverse areas of social concern such as health, community safety and education. This has led to a demand for statistics that measure the concept of social capital, and that can be applied to policy development and research. There is a strong interest in understanding the links between social capital and why some communities adapt better to change than others, why some communities are able to do better with a given set of resources, and what influences community confidence in achieving goals. The ABS has produced a conceptual framework, in which dimensions of social capital have been defined and described, and possible indicators suggested for each element (ABS 2004a). The ABS has chosen to use the OECD definition to guide work on the development of measures of social capital: "networks, together with shared norms, values and understandings which facilitate cooperation within or among groups".

Measures of Australia's Progress

The second and latest issue of MAP (ABS 2004b) includes statistics and commentary around two dimensions of progress closely linked to the health of Australian civil society: *Family, community and social cohesion* and *Democracy, governance and citizenship*.

These sections were among the more difficult parts of MAP to write. The difficulty stemmed in part from the paucity of available data with which to measure aspects of the dimensions. But, more importantly, there appears little consensus around the relationship of these areas to progress: that lack of consensus made it quite difficult for the ABS to select indicators that were unambiguous measures of progress (i.e., measures which (almost) everyone would agree reflect progress).

Moreover, the area is sometimes shrouded by impenetrable academic language that can hinder understanding by the general reader. MAP tries to present information about key aspects of progress in an accessible way, and one that resonates with a general readership. Terms like social attachment, social capital and even social cohesion and civil society are quite poorly understood, but there seem few "plain English" alternatives that might be used to describe these quite difficult concepts in a way which the public might identify with.

MAP: Family, community and social cohesion

The 2002 issue of MAP included a dimension entitled "Social attachment" that included indicators of people's participation in social events, along with information about marriage, divorce and suicide rates. This was one of the more experimental sections in MAP, and the ABS recognised that future editions would be informed by the growing ABS and international work on social capital.

By the time the second issue of MAP was released in 2004, the ABS social capital framework had been published. MAP 2004 built on this work to describe progress in a dimension entitled *Family, community and social cohesion*. MAP moved away from the term *social attachment* because few readers seemed to understand it. MAP adopted *social cohesion* as its focus because – conceptually - it covered both social capital and social exclusion.

The commentary presents indicators of aspects of family and community life in Australia, particularly those that are important to social cohesion. The discussion covered two broad areas: *families and family functioning*, and *community support*.

Indicators include the proportion of adults undertaking voluntary work, and donations to charity. Annex 2 includes some more information.

MAP: Democracy, governance and citizenship

Another section of MAP relevant to civil society is a progress dimension entitled *Democracy, governance and citizenship*. Again, this was new territory for the ABS. MAP 2002 simply noted the importance of the area, and said the ABS hoped to develop this section in future editions of the publication. MAP 2004 includes four pages of indicators and commentary.

The Bureau's starting point for the commentary was a framework for democracy assessment developed by the Swedish-based Institute for Democracy and Electoral Assistance (IDEA 2004). But the ABS commentary did not cover every aspect of progress in the *governance, citizenship and democracy* dimension: "The discussion that follows needs to be read with some qualification. It is not intended as a comprehensive discussion of all the elements of democracy set out in the IDEA framework (partly because data are not available for some elements, and others are not regarded as significant issues for Australia). It is intended only to illustrate some issues where reasonably good data already exist; it does not imply that these issues have a higher priority than others not discussed. Issues such as corruption in public life, and the availability of social and economic rights are also important" (ABS 2004b).

The commentary covers nationhood and citizenship; political participation; and civil society and civic participation. Annex 3 includes some more information.

Tasmania Together's Indicators of Community and Democracy

Several of *Tasmania Together's* goals identify key roles for civil society's contribution to Tasmania's progress. Relevant goals from the plan include recognising and valuing the contributions of volunteers and unpaid workers; increasing the participation of young people in community groups; and providing more opportunity to participate in decision-making. Benchmarks and indicators have been set up to measure progress in these areas.

The Victorian State Government's Indicators of Community Strength

The Victorian State Government has also undertaken work in the area of social capital/cohesion and produced indicators of community strength. The Department for Victorian Communities (DVC) considers that "a strong community is one constituted by people that understand its social, economic and environmental assets and are working towards sustainability…. [and that] to do these things, members of a strong community need to engaged, feel involved, feel capable of working through issues and be supported through external partnerships" (DVC 2004).

The DVC has developed an outcomes framework "based on research that has shown successful community strengthening strategies deliver benefits to communities in three ways: *improved services*, *improved community connectedness* and *improved community strength*" (DVC 2004). The indicators are drawn from the Victorian Survey of Population Health. Questions of particular relevance to civil society include whether people are members of community or professional groups, and whether those groups have taken any local action on behalf of the community, together with a question that asks whether people have opportunities to have a real say on issues that they find important.

A role for the OECD

The organisers of this forum asked us to consider what role the OECD might play in this area. Events such as this one, which seek to share best practice, are clearly important, as is the fact that representatives from civil society have been invited. The OECD could also provide a forum for pooling concepts and measures that might assess the health of civil society and perhaps develop some international measures in this area. In the longer term, a project that sought to assess the economic and social benefits that are thought to flow from social capital would be of considerable interest, and might perhaps be run across different countries.

Another area where the OECD might seek greater involvement is around designing frameworks and indicators to measure progress or wellbeing for specific - potentially controversial - areas.

It is often the case that CSOs are actively involved in key political debates. Australia is not alone in experiencing considerable public debate around areas like poverty; the trade-offs between economic activity and environmental protection; the treatment of our Indigenous peoples; and policies towards refugees and asylum seekers. It is very often the case (indeed almost by definition) that the debates that attract most attention from civil society are the most controversial. Such debates are often areas that an indicator initiative would feel most reluctant to develop measures of progress for, because the debate that ensued would likely generate more heat than light.

The ABS sees a good progress measure as having an unambiguously 'good/bad' direction of movement: ideally nearly all would agree that a movement in one direction represented progress (and a movement in the other regress), other things kept equal. Such agreement is most difficult to find when an area is subject to controversy. Although many members of civil society can understand the need for caution in these areas, that caution can prove disappointing to those who want to see a suite of indicators that portray all the key aspects of progress. A set of internationally agreed measures that portray progress in some of these more controversial areas would provide a useful way for an indicator initiative to venture into more difficult waters. In the face of criticism, reference to an international standard can be of great assistance.

Conclusions

Collaboration with civil society seems almost a necessary condition for an indicator initiative to get broad acceptance. Not only can collaboration strengthen the content of the indicators, the process itself can build a solid foundation of support. Those in government wishing to collaborate with civil society, might do well to ensure that the collaboration begins at an early stage; that the pace of development is appropriate; and that a diverse range of collaborators express their views and become involved.

Without indicators, arguments are often based on anecdote rather than fact. Moreover, indicators can have a positive effect on civil society: the reports can become agents of change. It is arguably their main purpose. As Gahin et al (2003) say in Do Indicators Help Create Sustainable Communities? "Indicators build connections between people, foster discussion in the community, and provide a powerful educational tool to raise awareness. As a source of data about the community, indicators empower community members, leading to positive change in planning, advocacy, and decision-making. Clearly, indicators are not a substitute for action, but help to create the social knowledge, connections, and inspiration for meaningful action. In this way, indicators can lead to progress, albeit slowly and incrementally, toward community sustainability and well-being".

Annex 1. Ten Tips for Government – Civil Society Interaction

These ten tips for government officials wanting to strengthen government-citizens relationships come from the OECD's Citizens as Partners: A handbook on consultation and *public-participation in policy making* (OECD 2001).

- Take it seriously
- Start from the citizen's point of view
- Deliver what you promise
- Watch timing
- Be creative and dynamic
- Balance different interests
- Be prepared for criticism
- Involve your staff
- Develop a coherent policy
- Act now

Annex 2. Extracts from Measures of Australia's Progress - Family, Community and Social Cohesion

Progress and this dimension

Measures of Australia's Progress noted: "Family and community are important aspects of society, but the way in which they contribute to progress is difficult to define and measure. The quality and strength of people's relationships and bonds with others — their family, friends and the wider community — are important ingredients of the level of social cohesion. And a more cohesive society is one in which communities are strong and inclusive, and where fewer people fall through the cracks."

Civil society's role

On civil society's role, the ABS said, "Strong community bonds can be formed through things like volunteering and donating money to groups and organisations in the community. Such networks may involve people who do not normally associate with one another and in this way help to form bridging relationships between these community members. When the support offered by people's families and communities declines or is absent, it can contribute to serious social exclusion and problems such as homelessness, suicide and deaths from drug taking.

The likelihood that people will voluntarily give their time to do some work for an organisation or group might be regarded as one of the stronger expressions of social capital, as it involves providing assistance, fulfilling needs and providing opportunities in the community. Participation in voluntary work also reinforces networks and adds to the richness of community life."

Annex 3. Extracts from Measures of Australia's Progress - Democracy, governance and citizenship

Progress and this dimension

Discussing the links between this area and progress, the ABS wrote: "National life is influenced, not just by material qualities such as economic output, health and education, but also by many intangible qualities such as the quality of our public life, the fairness of our society, the health of democracy and the extent to which citizens of Australia participate actively in their communities or cooperate with one another. For a long time these qualities, although often publicly agreed to be of critical importance, were seldom measured statistically. This was partly because they were harder to measure than more concrete statistics, e.g. the value of goods produced or the rate of infant mortality; and partly because they were regarded as more controversial … The strength and health of our democracy in practice is the product of many factors, such as the effectiveness of political institutions like Parliament, fair elections, an independent judiciary, equal laws and a free press. Other important factors include the trust that citizens have in government and public institutions, and the degree to which they participate in civic and community life and value and understand their rights and duties as citizens" (ABS 2004b).

Civil society's role

On civil society's role, the ABS said: "Civic participation describes activities reflecting interest and engagement with governance and democracy, such as membership of political parties and trade unions/professional associations, or serving on committees of clubs and associations. It has been defined as a two way communication process between the government and citizens. The overall goal is for better decisions, supported by the public and fostering the increased wellbeing of the population (World Bank 2002b). Some people suggest that active citizen engagement is important for better government. Researchers and commentators, such as Robert Putnam, argue that civic engagement is associated with better government in two ways: citizens in civic communities expect better government, and (in part through their own efforts) get it, and that the performance of representative government is improved by the social infrastructure of civic communities and by the democratic values of both officials and citizens (Putnam 1993). Civic participation involves both collective and individual activities, including the membership of civic organisations, such as political parties and trade unions, and serving on committees of clubs, voluntary organisations and associations. More recent forms of civic participation include support for global or local advocacy groups or campaigns, email networks, or one day activities such as 'Clean Up Australia' events ... These activities extend social networks of those participating, and help people develop important skills for participating in democracy and governance."

References

ABS 2002, *Measuring Australia's Progress*, catalogue number 1370.0. Australian Bureau of Statistics, Canberra.

ABS 2004a, *Information Paper: Social Capital, An Australian Framework and Indicators*, catalogue number 1378.0. Australian Bureau of Statistics, Canberra.

ABS 2004b, *Measures of Australia's Progress,* catalogue number 1370.0. Australian Bureau of Statistics, Canberra.

ACOSS 2003, *Strategic Plan*. Australian Council of Social Services, Sydney. http://www.acoss. org.au/about/strategicplan2003.pdf last viewed 18 August 2004.

Australia Institute (2004), from the 'About Us' page on their website. www.tai.org.au, last viewed 18 August 2004.

CIS 2004, from the 'About Us' page on their website. www.cis.org.au , last viewed 18 August 2004.

IDEA 2004, International Institute for Democracy and Electoral Assistance (IDEA), *Democracy Assessment: The Basics of the International IDEA Assessment Framework*. <http://www.idea.int/ publications /sod/demo_ass_ inlay_eng_L.pdf> last viewed 10 February 2004.

DVC 2004, *Indicators of Community Strength in Victoria*. Department for Victorian Communities, Melbourne, Victoria.

Eckersley, R. (ed) 1998, *Measuring Progress: is life getting better.* CSIRO publishing, Collingwood, Victoria.

Gahin, R., Veleva, V., and Hart, M. 2003. *Do Indicators Help Create Sustainable Communities?* Local Environment, Vol 8. No. 6, 661-666.

London School of Economics 2004, *What is civil society?* http://www.lse.ac.uk/collections /CCS/what_is_civil_society.htm last viewed 13 August 2004.

Manor J., Robinson M., and White G. 1999. *Civil Society A concept Paper.* Institute of Development Studies, University of Sussex website. http://www.ids.ac.uk/ ids/civsoc/public.doc last viewed 12 August 2004.

OECD 2001 *Citizens as Partners: A handbook on consultation and public-participation in policy making.* http://www1.oecd.org/publications/e-book/4201141E.PDF last viewed 19 August 2004.

Putnam, R.D. 1993, *Making Democracy Work, Civic Traditions in Modern Italy.* Princeton University Press, Princeton, New Jersey.

Salvaris M., Hogan D., Ryan R. and Burke T. 2000, *Tasmania Together, Benchmarking Community Progress.* Final Report for Department of Premier and Cabinet, Tasmania.

Saunders, P. 2002, *Whose Progress? A response to the ABS report Measuring Australia's Progress.* Centre for Independent Studies report no 25, Sydney, Australia.

World Bank 2002a, What is Civil Society?, <http://www.worldbank.org/poverty/scapital /sources /civil1.htm> last viewed 9 March 2004.

World Bank 2002b, Draft module on *Civic Participation in National Governance,* <http://www.worldbank.org/wbi/communityempowerment/Modules/Natgov_Module. doc> last viewed 10 February 2004.

Yencken, D. 2001, *"Where are we going: Comprehensive social, cultural, environmental and economic reporting."* Published on behalf of The Australian Collaboration by The Australian Council of Social Services, Sydney, Australia.

Yencken, D. and Porter, L. 2001, *A Just and Sustainable Australia.* Published on behalf of The Australian Collaboration by The Australian Council of Social Services, Sydney, Australia.

Measuring and Monitoring Economic and Social Well-Being: Comments from a Labour Perspective

Andrew Jackson

Senior Economist, Canadian Labour Congress,
Social and Economic Policy Department, Canada

Abstract

It is now very widely recognised that GDP is a highly incomplete indicator of economic let alone social well-being, that summary labour market statistics such as the unemployment rate must be enriched through a wider range of indicators of labour market performance, and that social indicators are an important tool for analysis and policy-making. Accordingly, the OECD and some national statistical agencies have begun to make widely available a very wide range of indicators of economic and social well-being and progress.

Richer indicators have enriched policy analysis and debate, and some innovative and welcome attempts have been made (mainly by civil society organisations) to develop new aggregative indexes of well-being. However, beyond inherent conceptual and technical difficulties, wider reception of such efforts has been bedevilled by the absence of an underlying consensus on what constitutes social progress. We have a plethora of indicators, but little agreement on which ones deserve the closest attention and which ones should drive economic and social policy. At root, this is because the selection and privileging of social indicators is inevitably a political process, informed by interests and values.

It is argued that existing indicator systems developed by national and international statistical agencies are improving but tend to relatively discount some key issues which are highly relevant in measuring well-being and social progress from the material perspective of working people, and from the values perspective of democratic social citizenship. For example:

Societal averages and medians tend to be stressed in national reporting and international comparisons, as opposed to comparisons of distributions of outcomes. This is commonplace in comparisons of economic performance as between Canada and the US, and the US and the social market and social democratic countries of continental Europe; even though we know that the relative degree of inequality of income and wealth shapes a range of important social outcomes.

Issues of security and subjective well-being, especially with respect to the quality of working life, tend to be underplayed in monitoring and assessing labour market performance, helping privilege issues of job creation over issues of job quality. This is particularly the case in North America.

Issues of poverty and social exclusion tend to be stressed over issues of social inclusion, and we have largely failed to develop good indicators of social inclusion (e.g. weak connection of life-chances to social class origins; use and development of skills and capacities at work; active citizenship; spatial sorting and social distance by social class.)

From a gender equity perspective, there is a tension over use of individual versus family-level data, and under-reporting of what happens in households and communities, as opposed to outcomes from labour markets and social programs.

Introduction: A Trade Union Perspective on Statistics

Trade unions very much welcome the fact that the OECD has taken the initiative to organize this conference and to invite our participation.

As users of data and statistics in both collective bargaining and in public policy debates, we are fully aware of the importance of accurate and conceptually well-grounded data to informed dialogue with employers and governments. We note that statistical categories, not least those used for comparative national analysis, are constructed rather than simply given. The OECD regularly provides a wide range of economic and social statistics derived from national sources, which are harmonised or standardised and regularly presented on the basis of standard categories (e.g., incidence or part-time work or temporary work, defined in a specific fashion). The development of such statistical categories and indicators is complex given wide diversity of national circumstances (e.g., in forms of employment, patterns of working time), and differing views on what it is important to measure and monitor. This process of selection and definition of indicators should involve a much wider group than technical experts. It is certainly appropriate that unions should be closely involved in the development of statistical surveys, new sources of data and new indicators, and we hope that trade unions (through TUAC) will continue to be involved closely in this area of OECD activity.

A major topic of discussion of this conference is how to develop and use comprehensive indicator systems as a basis for national benchmarks, and as a means to evaluate the relative economic and social performance of countries. There is a continuing strong focus by national statistical agencies and the OECD on the production of conventional, long-standing economic (national accounts) and labour market statistics. While this activity is important, it is now also very widely recognised that GDP is a highly incomplete indicator of economic, let alone social, well-being; that summary labour market statistics, such as the employment and unemployment rate, must be enriched through a much wider range of indicators of labour market performance and workplace conditions; that summary population indicators must be disaggregated by gender, age, and other key characteristics; that comprehensive social indicators are needed to supplement traditional measures of economic performance; and that more and better data generally are important tools for analysis and policy-making. The OECD and national, statistical agencies have begun to make available a widening range of indicators of economic and social well-being and progress.

Richer indicators have enriched policy analysis and debate, and some innovative and welcome attempts have been made (mainly by civil society organisations) to develop new aggregative indexes of well-being. For example, Osberg and Sharpe (2002) have developed a theoretically well-grounded and rather comprehensive index of economic well-being for OECD countries. However, beyond the inherent conceptual and technical difficulties, wider reception of such efforts to develop comprehensive indicator systems to judge economic and social progress has been bedevilled by the absence of an underlying consensus on what constitutes social progress. We have a plethora of data and indicators, but little fundamental agreement on which ones deserve the closest attention, and which ones should be most important in measuring the success or failure of economic and social policy. At root, this is because the selection and privileging of social indicators are inevitably a political process, informed by interests and values.

From a trade union perspective, social progress could be defined very summarily as movement towards a substantively democratic society which ensures that all citizens enjoy the full range of minimum human and social rights as embodied in the core international covenants, promotes a broad equality of outcomes and life chances, and allows all persons to develop their talents, capacities, and capabilities to the fullest extent possible.

While there would be little disagreement over the proposition that we should be concerned about issues of human rights, social inclusion, and distributional outcomes, this short paper argues that the indicator systems developed by national and international statistical agencies still tend to relatively discount some key issues which are highly relevant in measuring well-being and social progress from the material perspective of working people, and from the values perspective of democratic social citizenship. Trade unionists believe that we need much more comprehensive indicator systems than are currently used if we are to adequately benchmark economic and social performance, and judge the relative performance of countries in terms of economic and social progress

The main purpose of this paper is to selectively note some particularly significant gaps and silences in current statistical indicators from a trade union perspective. The final section presents some suggestions for future OECD activity.

Work and Employment Indicators from a Labour Perspective

Trade unions understandably have a keen interest in labour market and workplace data and statistics. While increasingly rich data sets are available from the OECD, ILO, the LIS/LES, Eurostat, and other sources, some major deficiencies remain.

Earnings and Earnings Distributions

Sophisticated international measurements and comparisons of economic welfare go beyond GDP per capita to explicitly take income distributions into account. Such analyses typically focus on the growth and distribution of annual after-tax/transfer or disposable income at the family level as the key measures of economic welfare. While this is reasonable for many purposes, it is often hard to separate out the relative contribution of wages and social transfer income sources to family incomes in different countries and over periods of time within countries, and comparative data on the structure of earnings are limited.

Redistributive social transfers and progressive taxes can and do significantly offset inequality in the distribution of market and wage income. However, it remains the case that national wage structures are of decisive significance in shaping the distribution of family disposable income (Smeeding 2002). For example, greater final income inequality in the US compared to most European countries is driven more by a much more unequal structure of earnings than by a less generous system of social transfers. In short, if we take the issue of income equality seriously, at least as much attention has to be paid to earnings distributions as is given to social transfers. Earnings distributions are also highly relevant to assessing trends in gender and intergenerational equality.

Such data are relatively hard to find (though they can be found in analytical studies based on the dynamic Luxemburg Income Study database). Standardised earnings data tend to be provided on an annual basis, conflating hours worked in the week, weeks worked in the year, and hourly wages. And, data are most often provided at the family rather than individual level. The OECD has usefully published standardised comparative data on hourly wage distributions for men and women, and on the incidence of low hourly pay (OECD 1996). These data show that, for all of the talk about the harmonizing effects of "globalisation" and technological change, there are still huge differences between advanced industrial countries which are shaped by labour market institutions. (For example, the ratio of the top to bottom decile of full-time male earners is well over 4:1 in the US compared to just over 2:1 in Sweden, and about one in four workers in the US earn less than half the median hourly wage compared to just 1 in 20 in Sweden.) However, these important data are published only on an episodic basis, and decompositions are not readily available by occupation, sector, gender, form of employment, etc. In sum, it would be useful if the OECD developed standardised indicators of wage distributions, making clearer trends within countries as well as differences in earnings distributions between countries.

Better comparative data are needed on the non-wage components of compensation in order to facilitate international comparisons.

Wage and Unemployment Dynamics

The increasing availability of panel data in some countries has been drawn upon by the OECD to examine wage dynamics and the dynamics of employment and unemployment. Wider use of such data should be encouraged. Low pay is clearly more of a concern if workers are trapped in lifetime trajectories of low-paid, non-developmental work, and short-term unemployment is of concern from a social inclusion/exclusion perspective if it is concentrated among workers who move frequently between short-term, low-paid jobs. The concept of precarious work is grounded in the observation that low pay and instability in employment frequently overlap, and that many workers (particularly women, minorities, and those with limited formal education) are excluded from stable employment and progressive job ladders. The incidence of precarious work appears to be significantly higher in the relatively deregulated labour markets of North America and the UK than in much of continental Europe (where long-term unemployment is much more serious).

It would be useful if the OECD considered developing and regularly publishing a set of standard indicators of labour market performance in a dynamic context, disaggregated by age and gender. For example, it would be useful to have data on the incidence of individual unemployment over a year (which is much higher than the annual average rate where unemployment durations are relatively short) as well as over longer periods, and summary data on transitions from low-wage to higher wage work.

TUAC has recommended that the OECD should build upon and further develop the Key Indicators of the Labour Market (KILM) developed by the ILO to present a core set of labour market indicators on a regular basis. (Details available from <http://www.ilo.org/public/english/employment/ strat /kilm/indicats.htm>.)

The Security Side of "Flexicurity"

Trade unions have long been critical of the loose use of the concept of "labour market flexibility" and of the mainstream OECD Economics Directorate view that there exists a

NAIRU (non-accelerating inflation rate of unemployment) which is mainly determined by labour market institutions and the structure of unemployment benefits. In the mainstream view, structural unemployment will be higher and "flexibility" lower if there is a compressed distribution of wages and a high wage floor due to statutory minimum wages or widespread collective bargaining, and if unemployment benefits replace a high proportion of earnings. The construction of the NAIRU indicator — estimates of which are regularly published by the OECD for OECD countries — is an interesting example of how theory underlies the development of seemingly objective statistical indicators which are far from neutral in terms of their policy implications. In practice, the NAIRU concept and indicator has led to acceptance of high levels of unemployment as the supposedly necessary price for low inflation. (For an excellent theoretical and empirical critique of the view that protective labour market institutions are a key determinant of the unemployment rate, see Baker *et al.* 2002.)

The International Labour Organisation (ILO) and European Commission (EU) have both recently highlighted the experience of some smaller European countries to suggest that high employment and low inflation can be achieved even with relatively compressed wage distributions, high wage floors, and generous unemployment benefits (Auer 2000; ILO 2003; European Commission 2001 and 2002). The fundamental policy message has been that highly deregulated labour markets, such as the US, can give rise to unacceptable levels of wage inequality and social exclusion, while a "flexicurity" model can achieve high employment rates along with high levels of equality, security, and inclusion. The flexibility side of such a model involves acceptance of limited job security (as opposed to employment security), tolerance of job creation in non-standard forms of employment, and pro-employment wage bargaining outcomes; while the security side involves relatively equal wages and benefits in different forms of work, access to career ladders, decent unemployment benefits, and swift access to new and higher quality jobs for unemployed workers. Training, active labour market policies and workplace co-operation all help make equitable labour markets employment-friendly.

The mainstream view of how labour market institutions intersect with job creation — namely that there is a dismal trade-off between job creation and job quality — has underpinned lack of sufficient attention to worker security issues in monitoring and assessing labour market performance. This is particularly the case in North America and at the OECD. The European Commission Directorate-General for Employment and Social Affairs has, by contrast, published explicit comparisons of national performance in terms of job quality measured by pay, working conditions, subjective job satisfaction, and opportunities for advancement (European Commission 2001, Chapter 4). Denmark is found to have the highest rate of job quality in the EU, as well as a very high rate of employment and employment growth, undermining the conventional view of a trade-off between job quality and job quantity.

A particularly significant gap is in the availability of good comparative data on worker perceptions of employment security, which is arguably at least as important as objective data on unemployment incidence and duration in measuring and monitoring worker well-being. Survey evidence for Canada from the Personal Security Index of the Canadian Council of Social Development shows that fear of job loss is significantly higher than unemployment incidence, and that many workers fear that, in the event of job loss, they would have a great deal of difficulty finding comparable employment. (See <http://www.ccsd.ca>.) Measured by such subjective variables, the level of employment insecurity in Canada is significantly greater than in Denmark, despite quite comparable rates of unemployment and job turnover.

Workplace Conditions and the Quality of Working Life

From a worker perspective, there are multiple dimensions to job quality, which goes beyond wages and job security to include access to opportunities for skills development and mobility, and conditions of work. The quality of work is crucial to mental and physical health, and to the development of individual talents and capacities. Critical variables include the pace and intensity of work; degree of control over the job; access to training and to internal job ladders; hours of work, including variability of hours, long hours, shift work, unsocial hours, and paid vacation time; health and safety, and physical working conditions; ability to balance work, family, and community activity; information and consultation at work, and access to union coverage; and, harassment in the workplace. All of these dimensions and others are regularly monitored in EU countries though the excellent European Survey on Working Conditions (conducted by the European Foundation for the Improvement of Living and Working Conditions) but comparable data do not exist for other OECD countries, and limited use has been made of the quality of work data in comparing the labour market performance of different countries.

Trade unionists also need better international comparative data on collective bargaining coverage, especially comparative data broken down by industry, occupation, gender, and age, in order to facilitate comparative work on union impacts on wages, benefits, job quality, productivity, etc.

OECD labour and employment Ministers last year invited the OECD to carry out further work regarding "the analysis of the issue of job quality and its implications for productivity and growth: cross-country analysis of how labour and product market reforms have affected job quantity and quality and work organisation, and the consequences for productivity and growth." (The full communiqué of the meeting, entitled *Towards More and Better Jobs*, is available at <http://www.oecd.org/document/30/0,2340,en_2649_34487_15519454_1_1_1_1,00.html>.)

Generally speaking, we lack good data on the functioning of internal labour markets and the demand side of the job market. Other countries might learn from Statistics Canada's Workplace and Employee Survey which has two, matched components: a survey of employers and a survey of employees.

Measuring the Relative Economic and Social Performance of Countries

The OECD makes extensive use of economic and social data to benchmark the economic and social performance of member countries and to make systematic comparisons between them. However, despite the wealth of data available, attention still tends to focus on economic growth (growth of GDP per capita); macro-economic outcomes; and, broad indicators of labour market performance, such as employment and unemployment rates. Successful countries tend to be seen as those with high rates of GDP growth and high rates of employment. While this is reasonable so far as it goes, equality and inclusion concerns tend to take second-place in evaluations of national success or failure. This results in some important misperceptions of social and economic progress and levels of well-being.

By most accounts, the US was a successful performer through much of the 1990s, turning in relatively high rates of GDP and employment growth compared to most other OECD countries. However, distributional variables present a different picture. Much of the income growth in an already highly unequal US society has taken place at the top extreme of the income distribution. The income share of the top 1% of tax filers in the US has doubled from 9% to 17% since the mid-1980s, in contrast to relative stability in continental European countries for which data are available (Atkinson 2004). Averages are clearly misleading in making comparisons of national well-being if distributions are not explicitly accounted for. For example, US GDP per capita at PPP is about 15% higher than in Canada, but median disposable family incomes are comparable, and the US income advantage over Canada is enjoyed only by the top one-quarter or so of households, with much of that advantage going to the very top layer of US households. The bottom quarter of Canadian households have significantly higher disposable incomes than the bottom quarter of US households (Wolfson and Murphy 1998). Similar points could be made comparing US disposable incomes to those in European countries.

At least two other key areas of well-being tend to be omitted or obscured in conventional national comparisons. First, hours worked to earn incomes are frequently ignored, understating economic welfare in many European countries to the extent that they have consciously opted for shorter work weeks, longer vacations, and earlier retirement in preference to more material consumption. Second, inequality of income tends to be understated since it is conventionally measured with respect to post-tax/transfer incomes, and does not take into account the fact that claims upon disposable income differ greatly depending upon the level of provision of public services and subsidies. Canada and Sweden have more equal disposable income distributions than the US, and higher levels of public compared to private consumption. Relative inequality in the US is clearly understated by disposable income measures since lower income households commonly lack access to a range of free or highly subsidised public goods, from health care, to child care, to housing subsidies, to quality education, which are provided in other countries. This is a serious omission since countries with high levels of disposable income equality also tend to have high levels of public consumption, and vice versa.

Understating real differences in the level of inequality between countries is a serious issue since economic inequality is closely linked to valued substantive outcomes, such as population health, basic capabilities, such as literacy and numeracy, and inter-generational mobility. Too much inequality of conditions clearly undercuts genuine equality of opportunity and equal life-chances for all citizens. These comparisons will be missed if we do not consciously attempt to measure and monitor equitable outcomes.

Societal averages and medians tend to be stressed in summary national reporting and international comparisons, as opposed to comparisons of distributions of outcomes. Yet, the latter are at least as important. For example, young adults from a higher socio-economic status background have similar (high) literacy levels across advanced industrial countries, but young adults from lower socio-economic status families in Scandinavia (defined by both parental education and income) score much higher than young adults from similar backgrounds in the US. More equal societies also tend to have not only higher average literacy levels, but also a much narrower distribution of literacy levels among young adults (OECD and Statistics Canada 2000). More equal societies tend to have better aggregate health outcomes among the relatively less affluent and less skilled, and a "flatter" overall relationship between socio-economic status and health. Surprisingly to some, more equal societies also seem to have higher rates of intergenerational income mobility, meaning that the life-chances of children are less directly shaped by the socio-economic status of their parents (Fortin and Lefebvre 1998).

The key point is that if social inclusion is taken to mean equality of opportunity to develop capacities and capabilities which lead to equitable life-courses, then the OECD and other statistical agencies should be devoting more time and attention to measuring, monitoring, and highlighting trends in economic inequality and distributions of key social outcomes.

Suggestions for Future OECD Work

OECD country reviews typically review a wide range of macro-economic and labour market variables and outcome, but pay little or no systematic attention to job quality and distributional issues in assessing national performance. This partly reflects the fact that the Economics Department is responsible for such reviews. The Directorate of Employment, Labour and Social Affairs has undertaken a great deal of useful statistical and analytical work on many of the issues identified above, particularly in the annual *Employment Outlook*, but little of this work is reflected in country reviews.

It is suggested that the OECD, in consultation with TUAC and others, develop a broader set of social indicators to be used on a continuing basis in country reviews, and that consideration be given to measuring and monitoring national performance on the dimensions identified above.

Further, the OECD should support innovative attempts by independent researchers and civil society organisations to develop comparative synthetic indexes of economic well-being.

The OECD has considerable experience in developing standardised and harmonised statistical data bases. It is suggested that the organisation could do much more to make this rich data base available and useful to trade union and other researchers.

Statistics Canada has undertaken some important recent initiatives which could be emulated. First, an enormous amount of standardised data, most notably from the *Census*, is now readily available free, on line, in 20/20 format, and a great deal of labour market and household income information is now made available in CD ROM 20/20 format at a modest charge. The capacity of trade unions and civil society organisations to undertake quantitative research has been greatly enhanced as a result. Micro-data files from several major national surveys have been deposited in university centres to facilitate free access to academic researchers under the Data Liberation Initiative.

Second, Statistics Canada has recently supported an extremely interesting database development project, the *Gender and Work Database*, in co-operation with a team of academic, trade union, and other researchers. (The project is led by Dr. Leah Vosko of York University, Toronto, and information is available from <http:www.genderwork.ca>.) Statistics Canada has provided large amounts of data from household surveys according to categories developed by the research team, such that large, searchable databases now exist on line in 20/20 format. One module, the union module, provides access to a huge amount of information on union coverage and union impacts on wages, benefits, hours of work, etc. by form of employment, detailed occupation, and industry, age, gender, racial status, and at different levels of geography. Another module focuses on precarious employment, and links individual and family level data. Some categories, for example, the dimension of form of employment, have been built from micro-data to meet the research needs of the project and differ somewhat from the standardised ways in which labour market data is presented in standard Statistics Canada products.

The key point is that Statistics Canada has been quite accommodating and innovative in providing data to researchers and to civil society organisations to facilitate independent research on economic and social well-being. Labour researchers have also been appointed to Statistics Canada expert advisory committees. These experiences could serve as a useful model for the OECD and national statistical agencies.

References

Atkinson, A.B. Income Inequality in OECD Countries: Data and Explanations. Working Paper. 2004.

Auer, Peter. Employment Revival in Europe: Labour Market Success in Austria, Denmark, Ireland and the Netherlands. ILO. Geneva. 2000.

Baker, Dean, Andrew Glyn, David Howell, and John Schmitt. *Labor Market Institutions and Unemployment: A Critical Assessment of the Cross-Country Evidence.* Centre for Economic Policy Analysis Working Paper 2002-17. 2002. Available at < http://www.newschool.edu/cepa >.

European Commission (Employment and Social Affairs). Employment in Europe. 2002. 2001.

Fortin, Nicole, and Sophie Lefebvre. "Intergenerational Income Mobility in Canada" in Miles Corak (ed.) *Labour Markets, Social Institutions and the Future of Canada's Children.* Statistics Canada. 1998.

International Labour Organisation (ILO). Decent Work in Denmark: Employment, Social Efficiency and Economic Security. 2003.

Osberg, Lars and Andrew Sharpe. "An Index of Economic Well-Being for OECD Countries." *Review of Income and Wealth.* Series 48, Number 3, September 2002.

Organisation for Economic Cooperation and Development, OECD *Employment Outlook.* 1996. "Earnings Inequality, Low Paid Employment and Earnings Mobility."

Organisation for Economic Cooperation and Development and Statistics Canada. Literacy in the Information Age: Final Report of the International Adult Literacy Survey. 2000.

Smeeding, Timothy. Globalisation, Inequality and the Rich Countries of the G-20: Evidence from the Luxemburg Income Study. Luxemburg Income Study Working Paper No. 320. July 2002.

Wolfson, Michael and Brian Murphy. "New Views on Income Inequality Trends in Canada and the United States." *Monthly Labour Review.* US Department of Labor. April 1998.

Using Indicators to Engage Citizens: The Oregon Progress Board Experience

Jeffrey Tryens

Executive director of the Oregon Progress Board[1]

Abstract

In May 1989 Oregon's then Governor Neil Goldschmidt unveiled *Oregon Shines: An Economic Strategy for the Pacific Century*, a strategic vision that recommended a series of initiatives meant to transform the state's economy to meet the challenges of the twenty-first century. The vision was a holistic one that considered social and environmental health vital contributors to a healthy economy. In 1989, the state legislature created the Oregon Progress Board (Board) to identify and monitor a set of indicators, called Oregon Benchmarks, designed to track progress toward achieving the Oregon Shines' vision.[2]

Since then the Board has issued biennial reports on the state's progress toward the goals. Unlike public-sector performance systems in other states and localities, Oregon's system has not assigned responsibility for meeting specific targets to any state agency. The benchmarks and the vision they embody are theoretically the responsibility of all Oregonians

Chaired by the governor, the Progress Board is made up of business, community and political leaders intended to represent the ethnic, cultural, social and economic diversity of the people of the state. The Board has little statutory authority over state agencies and none over other sectors of society. As respected leaders of the community, the Board's influence comes primarily from its association with the governor and other members' standing in their respective communities.

Engaging civil society in the Oregon Shines planning process has been a key ingredient since its inception. In its third biennial report, the Board declared "Never before has a state brought together so many public, private and non-profit organisations to pursue a shared vision and measure progress toward that vision." In the fifteen years since its creation, the Progress Board has engaged civil society in many ways. This paper will address five components of the Board's work that best illustrate its successes and challenges in that engagement. They are:

1.   Articulate a Vision for the Future;

2.   Identify What Matters;

1   Thanks to Rita Conrad and Zoë Johnson for their assistance in preparing this report.

        The views in this paper are those of the author and do not necessarily represent the views of the Oregon Progress Board.

2   The Board's current authorizing statutes can be found at its website – www.oregon.gov/DAS/OPB.

3.   Encourage Collaboration;

4.   Assess Progress; and

5.   Improve State Government Performance.

A Short History of the Oregon Progress Board

Many believe Oregon's most noteworthy accomplishment in this arena is keeping the same strategic vision and indicators in place for fifteen years. The Oregon Benchmarks have survived four governors and eight legislatures. While a noteworthy accomplishment, the Board has had its share of ups and downs.

The development and use of benchmarks has involved civil society since their beginning. Governor Goldschmidt personally enlisted nearly 200 business, labor, education, and government leaders to help plan a strategy for Oregon's development over two decades. *Oregon Shines* outlined an economic development strategy to: (1) transform Oregon's population into a world-class, 21st-century workforce; (2) create an "international frame of mind" to position Oregon as the gateway to the Pacific Rim; and (3) emphasize the comparative economic advantage of Oregon's extraordinary environmental amenities. The benchmarks flowed out of that process.

In 1991 the state legislature reviewed and revised a package of benchmarks proposed by the Progress Board, ultimately approving 158 indicators grouped into three categories: exceptional people, outstanding quality of life, and diverse, robust economy. Seventeen of the 158 indicators were designated as "lead benchmarks" representing key state problems identified in *Oregon Shines*.

The 14-member board is chaired by the governor with nine citizen leaders reflecting the geographic breadth and cultural complexity of the state, two legislators appointed by the legislature and two ex- officio members - a university student representing young leaders and the director of the state's Department of Administrative Services. An executive director appointed by the governor manages day-to-day board activities.

The Board's history can be divided into three overlapping periods: high expectations; disillusionment; and rebuilding and rethinking.[3]

High Expectations

When Governor Goldschmidt chose not to run for re-election in 1990, the recently issued *Oregon Shines* was in danger of becoming the classic study that sits on a shelf collecting dust. However, his successor, Governor Barbara Roberts, enthusiastically supported the project. The 1990 election was noteworthy for another reason: Oregonians approved Measure 5, a property tax limitation initiative that shifted the primary responsibility for funding primary and secondary education from local to state government, leaving fewer resources for other state programs and services.

The evolution of the benchmarks and the passage of Measure 5 intersected in 1992 when Governor Roberts prepared her 1993–95 budget. The property tax limitation caused a 15 percent cut in funding for state programs other than education. The Governor ordered cuts in all state agency budgets but allowed restoration of part of those cuts if

---

3   The history section of this paper draws heavily from Achieving Better Health Outcomes: The Oregon Benchmark Experience by Howard M. Leichter and Jeffrey Tryens.

agencies linked their budgets to specific, high priority benchmarks. The Governor herself described one result: "Agencies of government who hadn't been paying enough attention to the benchmarks suddenly took the benchmark documents, and they [the documents] became dog-eared while those agencies searched for things in the benchmarks that applied to their work.[4]"

As a result of this new importance, the Board was pressured to add benchmarks that reflected the issues of particular segments of the population and of state agencies that felt unrepresented. In 1993 the Board increased the number of benchmarks from 158 to 272. Consequently the Board's 1995 report to the legislature was so long that it required an index to find a benchmark on a particular issue. During this period, many community collaborations oriented toward achieving benchmark targets were initiated.

Disillusionment

The 1995 legislative session was difficult for the Progress Board. Although the legislature appropriated funding for the Board, it allowed the Board's authorizing statute to expire. The newly elected governor, John Kitzhaber, had to rescue the Progress Board by recreating it through executive order.

Like Tolstoy's families, each legislative critic was unhappy with the Progress Board and benchmarks in his or her own way. Some argued that, in its desire to satisfy constituents, the Progress Board had adopted so many benchmarks that they no longer served a useful purpose. Others said the unachievable targets left legislators vulnerable to constituent criticism when unrealistic goals were not met. Still others called it "a Democratic program with a Democratic agenda.[5]"

In response Governor Kitzhaber ordered a top-to-bottom review of the process by a 46-member blue-ribbon task force of community, business and political leaders as part of the 1996 *Oregon Shines* update. After extensive community consultation, the task force recommended that: 1) the Progress Board be continued; 2) the number of benchmarks be reduced to 100 or less; and 3) that state government take a greater leadership role in using the benchmarks.

The changes had the desired effect. The 1997 legislature voted overwhelmingly to make the Progress Board a permanent part of state government.

Rebuilding and Rethinking

The late 1990s marked a turning point for the Board. Oregon leaders no longer needed convincing that a comprehensive strategy was necessary to help shape Oregon's future. While continuing to keep an eye on Oregon's future, the Board would have to make the benchmarks tools for public sector accountability if it was to survive. In 2001, the legislature moved the Progress Board from the state's economic development agency to the Department of Administrative Services and established new responsibilities for guiding agency performance.

In 2002, the Board faced another setback when a severe revenue shortfall caused the legislature to rescind all Board funding for the remainder of the 2001–03 fiscal year.

---

4   Varley, Pamela. 1999. The Oregon Benchmarks Program: The Challenge of Restoring Political Support. Cambridge, Mass.: Case Program, Kennedy School of Government, Harvard University, 11.

5   For a more complete discussion of Republican and Democratic criticisms, see Varley 1999, 17–9.

Once again, gubernatorial intervention was necessary to allow the Board to continue operating. During this fiscal crisis, over 50 community leaders wrote to the legislature imploring them to continue funding for the Board.

Today, Board staff divides its time between tracking and reporting on benchmark trends and institutionalizing a performance measure framework for state government. Funding is assured through June of 2005 and relatively certain beyond that date. Funding for the now overdue *Oregon Shines'* update, however, will have to come from non-government sources.

The Role of Benchmarks in Civil Society

In *Oregon Shines* and the benchmark system embody two cherished and celebrated traditions in Oregon politics. The first is the pride Oregonians take in their state as an innovator. Oregon was the first state to adopt the citizen initiative and referendum process, the first to have a bottle deposit law, the only state to establish a prioritisation process for allocating scarce health care resources for its low-income residents and the first to legalize physician-assisted suicide.

The second tradition is reliance on participatory democracy to initiate, legitimize, or ensure citizen oversight of public policy. Through its initiative and referendum process, citizens can pass new laws, nullify existing laws and change the state's constitution. Citizen involvement is also an expected part of deliberation at all levels of government.

The development and use of the Oregon Benchmarks exemplifies both traditions. From its inception the Progress Board has engaged Oregonians in developing the benchmarks. The Board has two primary ways to interact with the public regarding benchmarks and targets. First, community meetings are held all over the state whenever Oregon Shines is updated. In 1996, more than 500 Oregon community leaders were involved in the review and comment process. Second, the Board holds public hearings on the benchmarks every two years. Until recently, the input came primarily from agency staff, experts and advocates. Using an Internet-based format for the first time in 2004, the Board received comments and suggestions for benchmark improvements from 275 citizens.

Articulate a Vision for the Future

At their core, the benchmarks represent the Board's attempt to quantify the vision that is laid out in *Oregon Shines*. They tell citizens what Oregon will be like if that vision becomes reality. They put meat on the bones of phrases like "world-class, 21st-century workforce."

In the early years, the benchmarks were primarily used to describe this preferred future. Visionary leaders and citizens thought big thoughts and honed in on a list of indicators that would describe the preferred future put forth in *Oregon Shines*. By developing future targets for the many indicators that emerged, the Board painted a vivid, optimistic picture of the state's future.

For the most part, the benchmarks logically flow from the vision articulated in *Oregon Shines*. The Oregon Shines' vision has clearly influenced how benchmark targets were set. As the process matured, however, the benchmarks have tended to become the vision. Now in its fifteenth year, the state's twenty-year vision, with its inspirational phrases like "create an international frame of mind to position Oregon as the gateway to the Pacific Rim," has faded into the background.

Today's civic leaders generally know that *Oregon Shines* exists. While acknowledging its importance, most would be hard pressed to describe its contents beyond a few key phrases and concepts. Without the benchmarks, *Oregon Shines* would probably not exist today as an instrument of change in Oregon. On the other hand, benchmarks would be less useful in the long run if they were not tied closely to a strategy for achieving a preferred vision for the state.

Oregon's Experience – Using indicators to articulate a community-driven vision for the future is a necessary part of the process.

Identify What Matters

Settling on a set of indicators that identified what mattered most in creating the *Oregon Shines'* future took over five years. Hundreds of indicators were proposed. A churning period between 1991 and 1995 saw the introduction of nearly 300 "benchmarks," although many had neither clear definitions nor data. In 1996, the Board settled on 92 benchmarks after an extensive citizen-led review process.

Civic leaders and interested Oregonians were deeply involved in the development and refinement of benchmarks. Board staff estimate that over 8,000 Oregonians have helped create or refine the benchmarks.

The benchmarks are generally accepted as the single best set of measures of overall quality of life in the state.[6] They are used extensively as guideposts in many different policy arenas from child well being to economic prosperity. Even critics would agree that benchmarks are legitimate for this purpose.

Approximately 20 percent of Oregonians say they are familiar with Oregon Benchmarks.[7] As strategic plans go, 20 percent familiarity is impressive. Unfortunately, this figure has not increased in four years. The lack of improvement is probably a by-product of the Board's increasing focus on state government performance rather than community outreach.

Since their inception, benchmarks have been prioritised, but the importance of that differentiation has diminished over time. First called "lead" and "urgent," these high priority benchmarks played an important role in budgeting in the early 1990s. Now called "key," the chosen benchmarks receive little more attention than a greater weight when the Board tallies overall grades in its biennial report to the Oregon legislature.

Oregon's Experience – Using indicators to identify what matters has worked well.

Encourage Collaboration

In the second phase of the benchmarks' evolution, the Board encouraged the development of partnerships that could drive change. Benchmarks became known as "magnets for collaboration" with numerous joint efforts launched. This phrase, coined by local official (and subsequent Progress Board member) Beverly Stein, was the battle cry

---

6   Benchmarks are limited to policy sensitive topics so some quality of life measures, such as spiritual health or interpersonal relationships, are absent from the set.

7   Preliminary estimate from the 2004 Oregon Population Survey.

of benchmark true believers during the mid-1990s. Over the years, many community leaders have taken notice of the benchmarks, realizing that the indicators could be used to focus disparate interests on a particular commonly held result.

Despite their economic origins, the benchmarks engendered many new collaborations around social issues including child health, early childhood education, childcare and juvenile crime. Benchmarks were also enlisted in structural reform efforts. Probably the most famous of those was a federal-state-local collaboration called Oregon Option developed during the Clinton Administration. The simple premise of this approach was the federal government would provide regulatory relief and fiscal flexibility to Oregon's state and local governments in exchange for a focus on improving benchmark trends. Numerous collaborations came out of this effort.

One of the best current examples of collaboration including benchmarks is an effort known as Partners for Children and Families (PCF).[8] A 1999 law, drafted by then-Senator and current Progress Board member Neil Bryant, requires five state agencies to work with one another, their local counterparts and related community organisations to develop a single comprehensive, coordinated delivery system for children and families statewide. In its fifth year, PCF has used disaggregated benchmarks (using sub-state data) to good effect in focusing local efforts on particular topics. While supporters would argue that it's too early to judge, a dispassionate observer would find little evidence that benchmark trends, either positive or negative, have been significantly affected by PCF-driven efforts.

In searching for proof of effect, leaders of collaborations can sometimes overstate the relationship between high level outcomes trends and those efforts. Teen pregnancy in a rural Oregon county is a case in point. In 1991 a broad-based, community-led effort was initiated to reduce a particularly high teen pregnancy rate. Partners ranging from conservative churches to family planning organisations worked for three years to put new procedures in place to provide education and health-related services to teens that were aimed at reducing the risk of teens becoming pregnant. By 1994, the teen pregnancy rate had been halved to the lowest in the state. Subsequent changes in community leadership and shifting priorities caused the teen pregnancy focus to wane and, sure enough, the teen pregnancy rate shot back up to earlier high levels. Leaders of the collaboration and researchers commissioned by the federal government all agreed - the collaboration was effective while it lasted.

Revisiting the issue three years later, Progress Board staff found that the teen pregnancy rate in the county had dipped to a similar statewide low in 2001, dropping precipitously from near the state's highest rate the year earlier. When queried, county leaders could point to no intervention that had occurred to cause the reduction. With the total number of pregnancies averaging 19, the reduction was, apparently, simply a function of small number variability. The earlier intervention no doubt had a positive effect on reducing teen pregnancy, but the strength of that effect is unknown when the longer data series is considered.

Oregon's Experience – Some success, but collaboration results can be difficult to determine.

---

8   See http://www.oregonpcf.org/

Assess Progress

The Board's "bread and butter" activity is its periodic assessment of progress. All the periodic Progress Board reports – *The Benchmark Performance Report, Oregon Benchmarks: A Progress Report on Oregon's Racial and Ethnic Minorities* and the *Oregon Benchmarks County Data Book* – are aimed at educating and informing citizens and community leaders. Press coverage is sought when reports are released and community leaders are notified of their availability.

Different aspects of the data motivate particular groups in civil society. Advocates of particular positions, like supporting the cause of disadvantaged groups, are particularly interested in using Board reports to buttress their cases for more attention or more resources. Naturally, the data is more appealing when it supports the arguments a particular group is making. Advocates inclined to "cherry pick" only the data that supports their case have, perhaps, a harder time in Oregon because of the widely accepted legitimacy of the benchmarks.

As the keeper of the benchmarks, the Board prides itself in presenting "just the facts." Remarkably, the benchmarks have remained above politics when assessments of progress are released. Citizens who care about the state's future trust the Board to tell the truth about Oregon trends. This perceived independence from government influence, despite the Board's ties to government, is key to its success in the long term.

Finding a proper forum for presenting progress assessments to the state legislature has been challenging. No single committee or group within the legislature holds the responsibility for assessing progress over the broad range of issues covered by the Progress Board. Informing legislative leaders about Board findings has been a hit or miss affair for quite a few years.

While the veracity of the data is unchallenged, its real life, everyday use in decision-making is difficult to discern. While many would argue that benchmark data is important to decision-making in the state, evidence of systematic application of the Board's analysis to policy making or resource allocation is in short supply. The most common use of the data/analysis is to establish a general context within which decisions are made.

Over the years the Board has tried different formats for assessing progress that were digestible by the public. After using trend line-driven letter grades for three reporting cycles, the Board moved to a more nuanced approach in 2003. Looking over a ten year time period, the Board answered the question "Is Oregon Making Progress?" The Board has found that citizens are more interested in knowing whether things are getting better or worse than knowing exactly how Oregon is doing in relation to a predetermined target.

Oregon's Experience – The data generated by the Board is good but policy makers and opinion leaders in the state do not fully utilize it.

Improve Government Performance

Since their inception, benchmarks have been used by agencies to improve performance. The most persistently used avenue is the budget development process. In the early years, agencies received preferential treatment in the budget process by showing linkages to key benchmarks.

In 1993, the Oregon legislature required state agencies to develop performance measures that linked to the Oregon Benchmarks. Initial results were less than satisfactory. Performance measures changed frequently and often had little relevance to benchmarks.

In 2001, the legislature assigned responsibility for performance measure development to the Progress Board. In 2002, the Board issued criteria-based guidelines for performance measure development and reporting that were incorporated into the budget development process.

All executive branch agencies now develop performance measures in the same manner and produce an annual performance reports that document progress toward achieving performance measure targets.[9] These reports are intended to inform policymakers and citizens about state agency performance. The Progress Board is currently working with a group of citizens on developing a set of recommendations that would make state government performance reports more "citizen-friendly."

By requiring linkages to benchmarks and annual self-assessments, the Board hopes to encourage public servants to "look up" to the benchmarks. In this way, agency planners and administrators must look beyond their day-to-day worlds to consider how they are changing things for the better for Oregonians.

Today, Board staff focus on using benchmarks and performance measures to improve government performance. The legislature's willingness to relent on eliminating Board staff positions was predicated on the understanding that staff would focus primarily on improving government performance. While high-level indicators like Oregon Benchmarks are not necessary for developing a functioning performance measurement system, they provide a real world context that makes them more meaningful to citizens.

Oregon's Experience – Incorporating high level indicators into the state's performance measure system holds substantial promise for engaging civil society in improving government performance.

Have the benchmarks made a difference?

To answer this question, benchmarks must be considered in the larger the Oregon Shines' context. Without the vision, Oregon's indicators would not exist.

A quantitative case cannot be made for Oregon Shines' success. After six years of "pedal to the metal" economic growth in the mid -1990s, the state's economy took a nosedive that caused Oregon's unemployment rate to rise to the nation's highest. Actions emanating from Oregon's strategic vision did little to soften the blow of recession. When a 2002 assessment sought evidence that the Oregon Shines' process had positively affected health outcomes, hard evidence was inconclusive.[10]

Some of the key policy initiatives put into place in conjunction with *Oregon Shines*, like reform of primary and secondary education, remain. Others, like a "key industries" initiative, have come and gone.

While less than hard, evidence abounds that the Oregon Shines' process has significantly contributed to a culture change in Oregon. Many leaders will unequivocally state that this process, and especially the Oregon Benchmarks, have made the state more results oriented in the way it develops and implements policy. When a cross-section of state leaders was queried about the impact of the Oregon Shines' process on health

---

9   See http://egov.oregon.gov/DAS/OPB/GOVresults.shtml

10   Leichter, Howard M. and Jeffrey Tryens, 2002, Achieving Better Health Outcomes: The Oregon Benchmark Experience. New York, N.Y.: Milbank Memorial Fund.

outcomes, respondents said the most important effect was allowing them to engage with others from different walks of life around developing the vision and exploring ways of achieving benchmark outcomes. Outside observers believe that the longevity and continuing vitality of the process are evidence enough of the difference *Oregon Shines* and the benchmarks have made in Oregon.

Critics of the process say the benchmarks have had little meaningful impact on life in Oregon. One legislator calls the Board a "feel good operation." However, the promising practice of using benchmarks to improve government performance has silenced many critics, at least temporarily.

On balance, the author believes that Oregon civil society is better off for having had the benchmarks in place for the last 13 years. As one out-of-state observer put it, "Maybe the existence of the benchmarks does not automatically solve your problems but at least you know how you're doing on the things that matter."

Over their life, Oregon's benchmarks have evolved from the numerical manifestation of an idealistic future to tools for improving strategic alignment, especially for state government. Putting a set of indicators in place that can be both inspirational and practical is a challenge that every indicator project must address when engaging civil society.

Making Governments Accountable

China's Economic Indicator System and Government Auditing

Li Jinhua

Auditor General of China

Abstract

Every year, over one thousand economic indicators are published in China of which GDP (gross national product) is the one most often referred to. Other major indicators in China include "registered urban unemployment rate", "citizen's consuming price index", "fixed assets investment", "residents income" and "international revenues and expenditures" et al.

The government must ensure the accuracy and effectiveness of national economic indicators and the development of the economy depend heavily on the reliability of these indicators. Auditing institutions, though not directly involved in making economic indicators, play an important role in ensuring the accuracy and usefulness of the indicators. This can be achieved first through ensuring the reliability of the indicators by disclosing any untruthful economic operations. Secondly, audit institutions can bring those indicators incompatible with each other to the attention of the government so that timely measures may be taken for the health of the economy. Moreover, auditing institutions can detect such problems in terms of the quality of economic development as unsustainable development and highly risky monetary operations and promote the adoption of more scientific and reasonable development concepts.

The practices of the National Audit Office of China (CNAO) in the past years have made audit institutions' role in the above areas widely recognised by both the government and the general public.

The Economic Indicator System Framework in China

A large number of economic indicators are used in China; each year several thousand statistical indicators are published in the "China Statistical Annual Book" alone. Countries in the world are yet to establish a universally accepted macro-economic indicators system to assess the macro economic development. Based on its years of exploration and by referring to experiences of other countries, China has defined promoting the growth of the economy, increasing employment, stabilizing the price and keeping international balance of payment as its main objectives of macro control.

The growth of the economy is a major indicator in measuring the development of the economy and is a broad and comprehensive concept reflecting the growth of the national strength and the improvement of the people's living standards. For these reasons, nearly all countries have made growth of the economy a primary objective of macro control.

The Gross Domestic Product (GDP) and the rate of GDP increase are the most widely used indicators for assessing the growth of economy. GDP is the monetary value of all goods and services produced by an economy over a specified period. It is the gross value of wealth created in the given period including both the tangibles and the intangibles. GDP is a summarizing measurement of the overall performance of an economy and is internationally comparable. It is also the most important gross value indicator in the United Nations System of National Accounts (SNA) and is extensively used in all economies as a basis for international comparison.

As an important indicator for macro economic assessment, GDP still has its limitations and is far from a panacea. There are some factors this indicator can not reflect such as the social costs; the means of economic growth and the price for the growth achieved; the efficiency, value for money and the quality of the economic growth; and the gross accumulation of the social wealth, nor by which the social distribution and social justice can be assessed. If our attention is only paid to the gross economic value and the rate of economic growth and not to the loss of resources, environmental pollution, biological destruction, we may very likely face a situation where the economy keeps growing yet the quality of people's livelihood becomes less satisfactory, or even worse, the economy does not grow at all. Therefore we should take a more scientific attitude toward GDP. Its importance should be highly valued on the one hand, and on the other hand we should never be engaged in one-sided pursuit of a high GDP growth rate.

Other important indicators in China besides GDP include "Registered Urban Unemployment Rate", "Residents Consumption Price Index", "Fixed Assets Investment", "Total Volume of Social Consumption Goods Sales", "Industry Increase Value", "Residents Income" and "International Balance of Payment" et al.

The Role of Government Audit in Promoting the Objectivity, Accuracy and Effectiveness of the Economic Indicators

Unlike the statistical institutions, government audit institutions are not directly involved and cannot intervene in the compilation of the economic indicators. In practice however, government auditing has a unique role to play in promoting the objectivity and effectiveness of these indicators.

Audit institutions' role in finding and disclosing the untruthful factors while the indicators are compiled

Budget making and implementation are closely linked with the national economic indicators. While the level of social economic development serves as the basis for budget making, the budget also, to a large degree, influences the national economic indicators. For years, SAI of China has carried out budget implementation audit following the principle of ensuring truthfulness and has put forward many recommendations regarding regulating bank accounts of budget units, further increasing the details of the departmental budgets, ensuring the completeness and accuracy of the fiscal budget and reforming the special transfer payment system and insisted the implementation of the recommendations. It has greatly promoted the reform of the national fiscal system with a high degree of budgetary completeness and transparency. Enterprises are cells of the economic life and the truthfulness of their accounts, the quality and performance of their operation directly affects the quality of bank assets as well as the performance of major national economic indicators. Since 1999, the National Audit Office of China (CNAO) has directly organised and participated in auditing of over 2,000 enterprises including some super large scale state owned enterprises (SOEs). About one month ago, we published the fourth Audit Announcement of this year disclosing in details audit findings regarding the taxation payment situation of over 788 enterprises. By revealing problems such as loss of tax revenues and practices of accounts falsification, the report served indeed as a warning about the credibility and accuracy of some national economic indicators and has received great attention from the State Council and other relevant departments.

The SAI's role in bringing to the attention of the government departments any findings of uncoordinated factors in the development of the national economy

China's government audit system was re-introduced and enjoyed fast development in the course of the reform and opening up of China, witnessing the changes of China's economy taken place in the past 20 years. In China's transition from a planned to a market economic system, its economy faces many challenges and some uncoordinated factors. The CNAO while centering around the core task of government reform and development, paid much attention to exploring and studying those problems of universal and tendency features from the unique perspective of auditing and has provided much useful information to the government as the basis for decision making. For example, excessive use of arable land in China has become an evident problem in recent years, which if not properly controlled will directly lead to many social problems. Moreover, over heated growth of fixed assets investment as the result of uncontrolled use of land may bring about the problem of sharp decrease of grain. In a country like China with a population of 1.3 billion shortage of food may lead to disastrous results if left unsolved. As early as two years ago, CNAO became aware of these dangerous signals with its keen insight and conducted a special investigation on the land issue and submitted a report to the State Council. This report later was seen as the beginning of a round of large-scale rectification of land using control in China. Other views and comments raised by the CNAO have also received high attention from the National People's Congress (NPC, China's parliament) and government. These include for example, recommendations by CNAO based on special investigations on the financial condition of 49 counties in the western and middle regions of China and on social security funds from the perspectives of guarding against financial risks and promoting a coordinated development of social-economic development.

Audit institution's role in disclosing problems regarding the quality of the economy

Statistics show that wealth achieved at the price of excessive consumption of resources and destruction of the environment now accounts for 12% of China's net GDP. This means that China's economic growth mode is still an extensive one featuring high input, high consumption, high growth and low efficiency. For a country like China with a huge population and low per capita resource level, this fast growth will not last long. In recent years, China practiced an expanding fiscal policy, the massive economic expenditures successfully fuelled great power to the economic development, yet the system itself faces such problems in terms of funds management and utilisation to which the CNAO has attached due attention. In the past 5 years since 1999, we followed and audited the utilisation of public debt funds and public works funded by public debts. Irregularities such as losses and wastes, embezzlement of public debt funds and low performance of public debt funds were detected and dealt with, as a result funds management was improved and safety and value for money of funds was better safeguarded. At present, the government of China has gained an increasingly thorough understanding about the GDP measuring system and has put forward an objective of establishing a scientific development concept, realizing a sustainable development. China has started a pilot green GDP system where resource consumption costs and environmental losses will be gradually deducted from the current GDP level. This reform will have a deep influence on government auditing, especially the contents and standards of Value for Money auditing, moreover, our environmental audit and accountability audit work will include new contents and will be further strengthened. Furthermore, the banking industry as a barometer reflecting the level and quality of the national economy has always been a center of attention of China's SAI. Every year, some important banking institutions are audited for the purpose of improving management and preventing operational risks of the auditees.

Indicators and Public Accountability in India

Vijayendra N. Kaul

C&AG of India

Abstract

Use of indicators and the establishment of an infrastructure for gathering statistical information have been integral to the process of planned development in India. Ad hoc indicators have been developed and used for planning and evaluating public interventions. A major initiative was taken towards developing a comprehensive set of 70 indicators and three composite indices in the Human Development Report of 2001. Despite its contextual significance in aptly capturing the concerns of our people this effort was not able to address the growing importance of environmental issues and sustainability. The Government of India is now working on a comprehensive set of sustainable development indicators which will address the specific circumstances of the Indian reality.

In deference to stakeholder interests, SAI India has progressively been devoting greater attention to performance auditing which also evaluates the effectiveness of government programmes and schemes in relation to their objectives. Presence of a widely accepted system of indicators in economic, social and environmental areas would provide a uniform set of criteria for such performance audits. This will reduce the possibility of divergence of conclusions regarding efficacy of the success of government interventions, thereby enhancing the usefulness of performance audits.

Indicators play a more critical role in organisations which have progressed to result based budgeting. Since the key identifying feature in such a context is the emphasis on the outputs to be produced and the consequent outcomes, clarity and consensus on indicators becomes extremely necessary. Furthermore, since indicators become integral to stakeholder reporting, their independent external verification becomes essential. In its external audit assignments of UN agencies, SAI India regularly reviews indicators and their underlying assumptions and statistics.

Once a comprehensive set of indicators is adopted in India, we see a distinct role for SAI India in enhancing their reliability and usefulness. The indicators can themselves be subjected to audit scrutiny to seek an assurance on their policy relevance, analytical soundness, measurability, ability to aggregate information and capture the context and process, sensitivity, reliability and manageability. If targets and associated indicators are found to be technically sound then audit can examine achievements, reasons for delays and their consequences, costs and efficiencies of the policies used and forecast whether targets are likely to be met if current trends continue.

SAIs will need to address competence and capacity building issues *vis a vis* indicators and decide whether they should get involved in the process of their formulation.

Public accountability and Audit

In India public accountability entails accountability not only of the executive to the elected legislative bodies but also of the subordinate public agencies to the executive. In particular, financial accountability is realised through budgetary control including proposals for taxation and public debt and demands for grants being voted in the legislatures and reporting of expenditure in the form of accounts.

Accountability and Performance auditing

There has been a progressive shift of stakeholder concerns beyond budgetary control and regularity of public expenditure to the outcome and impact of State's interventions in the development process. In deference to stakeholder interests, SAIs have also started devoting greater resources to performance auditing. Apart form the economy and efficiency in use of resources in government programmes and schemes, performance audits also evaluate effectiveness of performance in relation to the achievement of the objectives of the audited entity and audit of the actual impact of activities compared with the intended impact.

Performance auditing and indicators

Critical to evaluation of the effectiveness of government programmes and activities is the adoption of appropriate criteria for evaluating performance. Presence of a widely accepted system of indicators in economic, social and environmental areas would provide a uniform set of criteria not merely for performance audits by an SAI but also evaluation by other agencies (external and internal). Unfortunately there is no comprehensive system of performance indicators available in many countries. Divergent practices continue to be followed by independent evaluators, nation governments and multilateral agencies. The inconsistent quality of statistical information within and across countries currently leaves scope for divergence of views on performance evaluation. This leads to widely divergent conclusions regarding the extent of success of government interventions. Therefore, there is need for development and acceptance of a selected set of indicators to inform civil society and support wider communication with the public.

Such a set of indicators would facilitate the understanding of the mutual inter-dependence of various policies/programmes; assessing the position and progress of the economy over time, across the countries and across the regions within a country; providing crucial guidance for decision making in identifying and transition towards sustainability, and providing information to general public in forms that non-specialists can relate to and thus strengthen the accountability mechanism of governance.

Need for indicators: SAI India's case

The Comptroller and Auditor General of India is mandated to audit all the expenditure and receipts of both the federal and provincial governments, all commercial enterprises where government have a majority equity stake and all other organisations which are substantially financed by grants form the government. The audit is not restricted to regularity and compliance and has progressively been oriented towards evaluating performance of the various programmes and schemes undertaken or funded by the Government.

In order to prioritise its activities and audit efforts, SAI India has formulated a Strategic Plan 2003–08 which is premised on evaluation of the various programmatic interventions of Government so as to promote accountability and encourage effective utilisation of resources. The five themes selected for this Plan reflect the priorities of the Tenth Five Year Plan adopted by the Government of India. The theme of human development incorporates social sector programmes of poverty alleviation, health services, population stabilisation, literacy and education, nutrition, food security, and improvement of disadvantaged and vulnerable groups. The theme of economic liberalisation includes fiscal management, tax reform, management of subsides and privatisation. The theme of infrastructure modernisation includes power sector, ports, roads railways, communications and hydrocarbons. The theme of technology up-gradation covers information technology and biotechnology. The theme of sustainable development includes environmental legislation, multilateral environmental agreements, air and water quality, waste management etc.

The primary objective of the audit efforts of SAI India will be on assessing the efficiency, effectiveness and economy of the various schemes and programmes funded by the government and make recommendation for improving performance. Presence of a set of key indicators in each of these areas would go long way in making the performance audit results more reliable and acceptable.

Indicators and result based budgeting

Indicators play a critical role in organisations that have moved to result based budgeting e.g. UN agencies. The key identifying feature of results-based budgeting is that the emphasis is on the outputs to be produced (reports, studies, conferences, etc.) and consequent outcomes, as opposed to input budgeting where the defining feature is an emphasis on the inputs (staff, materials, equipment etc.). The orientation towards either outputs or inputs is important at all stages of the budget process (programming, budgeting, implementation, monitoring and evaluation). However, the most important determining factor here is the initial budget proposal stage as this sets the output pattern and framework for all subsequent stages.

Almost all the UN agencies have moved to result based budgeting. A similar trend is also evident among national governments. In such contexts, clarity and consensus on indicators is extremely necessary. Furthermore if indicators become integral to stakeholder reporting, independent and external verification (equivalent to assurance on financial statements) should become essential. A comprehensive system of indicators would in fact supplement accounting standards and disclosure norms in such an environment.

Nature of Indicators being used in India

In its aspiration to quicken the pace of development and to raise the economic well being of its people the Government of India has been following a path of centralised economic planning. This entailed planned commitment of resources to realize objectives on which there was political consensus. Both, the establishment of goals and evaluation of the success of the plans needed indicators and reliable statistical information on those indicators. Hence, ad hoc indicator sets were developed early in the country and used for monitoring government expenditure. However, no system for comprehensive monitoring of the economy through a reliable indicator based system was in place.

Indicators and statistical information was generated at two levels. At the first level, information on the performance of the Government is generated and disseminated by economic and social ministries and departments of the national and provincial governments by way of either an administrative by-product or specifically designed periodic or ad-hoc surveys. In addition, there are centralised agencies such as the Central Statistical Organisation (CSO) and the Programme Evaluation Organisation which compile, collate and analyze information about a host of parameters of national importance both as policy inputs to planning and development interventions or as the outcome of past programmes. The issues of symmetry of information by this centrally located evaluation agency and the requirements of better cooperation with the implementing departments are addressed through Coordination Committees, set up for each evaluation exercise, which have representatives form line ministries/departments and other stake holders and subject matter specialists as their members.

Another source of statistical information on national indicators has been the decadal population census, which has been in vogue in India since 1881. It has emerged as one of the most comprehensive sources of demographic information down to the village level. Besides the head count of population, the census also collects and provides information on status of houses as residential and non-residential, information on occupation by age, sex, marital status, social status, educational level attained, economic activity, fertility trends and migration. Census also validates the data generated by Central Registration System (CRS), which makes registration of births and deaths mandatory. Population is used as a common normalizing factor to make parameters like revenue, expenditure, income, infrastructural availability etc., scale neutral.

Social indicators

Comprehensive indicators have been designed and are in use in health and education sectors. Annual Health Information Index by the Department of Health and Family Welfare provides information on vital statistics, infant mortality rates, life tables, prevalence of communicable disease, coverage of population under family welfare programmes, number of health care units at primary, referral and speciality and super-speciality level, medical and paramedical persons, etc. National Samples Survey Organisation (NSSO) of the CSO in its consumption expenditure surveys of households also provides information on expenditure of a household for health related aspects. Ministry of Human Resource Development provides information on teaching institutions, teachers, examination results, enrollment, educational inputs and physical facilities. Information is also provided by NSSO on household expenditure on education and literacy levels. However, there has yet been no move to adopt International Standard Classification of Educational Statistics proposed by UNESCO and as such international comparability of many education related indicators is still absent.

Economic Indicators

NSSO through their quinquinial surveys undertaken every five years since 1972-73 provides most comprehensive set of data on employment. It provides estimates of number of employed according to the activity status and their social, demographic and economic characteristics. Director General Employment and Training also provides information on employment in organised sector, but for informal and unorganised sector, NSSO surveys are the ultimate source.

NSSO generates household consumption expenditure data akin to the Family Living Surveys in most other countries though specific surveys since 1950-51. These are extensively used in studies on levels of living, disparities in levels of consumption, cross section and time series analysis of consumer behavior, incidence of poverty, etc. In recent years, the survey data have become extremely important for the measurement of absolute poverty and head count poverty ratios. Department of Rural Development had initiated Below Poverty Line surveys for their poverty alleviation programmes to assess their numbers. The consumption surveys for selected class of population have also been in vogue. The Labour Bureau in the Ministry of Labour has been conducting Family Living Surveys since 1958-59 for industrial workers to draw their weighting diagram for Consumer Price Index (CPI-IL), which is also used as an inflation index for organised sector wage indexation.

Environmental Indicators

In addition to the two broad groups of social and economic indictors, some institutional and environmental indicators are generated. Environmental indicators relate to pollution levels, pollution control measures, air and water quality, forest cover, etc.

Human Development Report 2001

A major initiative was undertaken by the Planning Commission of India in 2001 to put together seventy indicators and three composite indices to evaluate the development process. The Report focused on three critical dimensions of well being, namely, ability to live a long and healthy life; the ability to read write and acquire knowledge; and the ability to enjoy a decent standard of living and have a socially meaningful life. An extensive state level data base was prepared covering around seventy indicators. The entire data set has been compiled for at least two points of time; early eighties and early nineties.

An attempt was made to capture the process of development from two perspectives-conglomerative perspective, capturing advances made by the society as a whole and the deprivational perspective, assessing status of the deprived. Statistics was also compiled for the elderly, working children, disabled and violence and crime against women. Similarly separate information was captured for women, people residing in rural areas and those belonging to so called lower castes. For most indicators gender and Rural-Urban gaps were estimated.

The Report also attempted three composite indices. A Human Development Index which incorporated inflation and inequality adjusted per capita consumption expenditure, a Human Poverty Index encompassing longevity deprivation captured by the indicators, persons not expected to survive beyond age 40 years; composite indicator on educational deprivation and composite indicator on economic deprivation and a Gender Equality Indices using the same methodology as HDI.

The data has been presented in a unique manner, through 'development radars', which gives a snapshot view of the structure, the growth and the gaps vis-a-vis desired normative levels, in respect of eight different indicators converting attainments on education, health, economic well being and access to amenities. It not only helps in simultaneously assessing attainments in different aspects of quality of life, but is equally useful in identifying the areas of gaps for facilitating an informed policy focus at the State level. The development radars overcome the criticism often directed at the use of subjective weighing techniques to combine diverse social indicators into composite indices of human development.

Despite its contextual significance in aptly capturing the concerns of our people, the Human Development Report and its indices were not able to address the growing importance of environmental issues. They were also not able to integrate several aspects of sustainability. A mapping of the indicators used in the NHDR with those of OECD and CSD is place at Annexure I and II respectively.

Developing a preliminary sustainable Development Indicators framework for India

In another initiative, the task of formulating a comprehensive set of Sustainable Development Indicators has been taken up by the Government of India. This has been a follow up to the decisions taken at the Rio and Johannesburg summits. The formulation of a comprehensive set of indicators takes on a great complexity in the Indian context. The first major problem is definition of a set of indicators, which are relevant throughout the country, especially in view of different socio-economic and environmental concerns in the urban, rural and other geographical regions. The second issue is addressing data requirements for aggregation of local indicators at the national level.

Work has already been done by several agencies across the world in formulating indicators of sustainable development. These would provide some guidance but the final framework will need to address the specific circumstances of the Indian reality. The alternative models are presented in the succeeding table.

Initiative	Organisation	Framework
World Development Indicators	World Bank	Six section: Worldview, People, Environment, Economy, States and Markets, and Global links
State of the Environment (SoE) report	United Nations Environmental Program	SoE framework based on PSR approach
World Resources	World Resources Institute	Assessment and analysis of the state of various ecosystems
Human Development Report (HDR)	United Nations Development Program	Critical analysis of a specific theme each year to assess the state of human development
World Health Report	World Health organisation (WHO)	Presentation and expert analysis of indicators of health systems and status
International Development goals-indicators of progress	OECD in partnership with the UN, world Bank and IMF	Indicators that gauge progress towards development goals selected form a series of UN Conferences held during the decade of 90s.
Indicators of sustainable development	Commission on sustainable Development (CSD), united Nations	134 indicators organised in driving force-State-Response (DSR) framework-replaced by 4 dimensions (economic, social, environmental, institutional)

While most attempts capture indicators relating to specific themes, the indicator programme undertaken by the UN CSD has a larger mandate of developing a framework for "indicators of sustainable development". This programme was initiated in 1995 in response to Agenda 21 which called for harmonised efforts towards developing indicators of sustainable development that could provide a basis for decision making at all levels. The main objective of the CSD Work Programme was to make SDI (sustainable development indicators) accessible to decision-makers at the national level, by defining them, elucidating their methodologies, testing them and providing training and other capacity building activities.

Audit of Indicators

The CAG of India has been making use of indicators widely in international audit assignment particularly in cases where resulted based budgeting has been adopted. However, use of indicators for audit in the domestic context has not been on a systematic basis. This is primarily because a comprehensive set of key indicators have not been determined for purposes of reporting, planning, clarifying policy objectives and for budgeting and assessing performance. As stated earlier there is a proposal to adopt a comprehensive set of sustainable development indicators. We envisage a distinct role for a SAI once this is done.

Apart form the usefulness of indicators to SAIs in discharge of their performance audits, indicators could themselves be objects of audit scrutiny of SAIs. For instance, SAIs might look to see whether indicators:

1. Have policy relevance, which means that they must be easy to interpret; show trends over time; respond to changes in driving forces; and have threshold or reference values against which progress can be measured.

2. Are analytically sound, for example based on a clear understanding of the goal of sustainable development.

3. Are measurable, that is no matter how attractive the theoretical construct, if an indicator cannot be measured at reasonable cost, it is not useful.

4. Are able to aggregate information. The list of potential sustainability indicators is endless but for practical reasons, indicators that aggregate information on broader issues may be more manageable.

5. Are able to capture the context and process. The relevance of any indicator lies in the context that it captures-an augmented agricultural productivity and decision making, it should be able to capture the underlying processes and context which can be made possible only through the involvement of stakeholders.

6. Are sensitive enough to detect a small change in the system. Even where indicators represent stock values such as literacy level, these should be chosen such that these are sensitive to tracing developmental changes on an annual basis as against those, which capture only the accumulated attainments.

7. Use reliable data, from a credible source, and

8. Consist of small set, which is manageable.

Performance audits using indicators and targets

If targets and associated indicators are found or thought to be technically sound, comparisons between them should reveal the progress that has been made. The scope of audit can be as under:

1. If the deadline of the target has already passed, an audit can simply comment on whether the target has been achieved. Audit attention can then shift towards explaining why the target has or has not been achieved, or the cost and efficiency of

the policies used to attain the target, or any unintended consequences of those policies, and

2.   If the deadline is still some way off, then an audit should focus on whether the target is likely to be met if current trends continue.

Indicators – Issues for the Auditor

SAIs will need to address the following issues while taking up this new challenge:

1.   Role of SAI in developing indicators: should Audit take proactive action like Government Accountability Organisation (GAO) of USA or review them after they have been developed? GAO organised a Forum associating academics and other stakeholders on the issue of key national indicators. This will have the advantage of a prior consultation and consensus between the auditor and auditee.

2.   The extent of reliance to be placed on indicators in devising performance audit plans and in assessing performance of government programmes. For instance, rather than audit a specific programme or scheme, SAI could select all the programmes and schemes related to a key indicator.

3.   Should performance indicators be reviewed as a part of financial audit, particularly if audited entity adopts results based budgeting and discloses information on performance indicators as a part of financial statements?

4.   How much reliance should the audited entity and audit place on quantitative performance indicators vis-à-vis qualitative evaluations?

5.   Should the SAI review the process of developing performance indicators or comment on the relevance and appropriateness of the indicators?

6.   How should an SAI deal with situations where there are disagreements among experts regarding indicators, reliability of statistical information and the resultant performance evaluations?

7.   Should an SAI restrict itself to validating the process involved in achieving targets of a key indicator rather than the value of the indicator? The latter may require techniques and resources not available with an SAI.

8.   SAI will need to be cautious in using indicator values in drawing inferences regarding efficacy of government programmes since several programmes and extraneous factors would impact indicator values.

ANNEX 1.

Mapping of NHDR with OECD indicators

Goals	OECD Indicators	Reference to NHDR indicator
Economic well being	1. Incidence of extreme poverty	Incidence of poverty
	2. Poverty gap ratio	******
	3. Inequality	Inequality adjusted per capita consumption expenditure Inflation and inequality adjusted per capita consumption expenditure
	4. Child malnutrition: prevalence of under weight under 5s	Nutrition
Universal Primary Education	5. Net enrolment in primary education	Net enrolment ratio
	6. Completion of 4th grade of primary education	Drop out ratio
	7. Literacy rate of 15-24 year olds	Adult literacy ratio
Gender equality	8. Ratio of boys to girls in primary and secondary education	Literacy rate (contains details for boys and girls separately)
	9. Ratio of literate females to males	Adult literacy rate (contains details for boys and girls separately)
Infant and Child mortality	10. Infant mortality ratio	Infant mortality ratio
	11. Under 5 mortality ratio	Under 5 Mortality ratio
Maternal Mortality	12. Maternal mortality ratio	Maternal mortality rate
	13. Births attended by skilled health personnel	Births attended by health professionals Birth delivered in medical institutions
Reproductive health	14. Contraceptive prevalence ratio	Couple Protection ratio
	15. HIV prevalence in 15 to 24 year old pregnant woman	******
Environmental sustainability and regeneration	16. Countries with effective process for sustainable development	******
	17. Population with access to safe water	Access to safe drinking water
	18. Forest cover as a % of national surface area	Forest cover
	19. Biodiversity: land area protected	******
	20. Energy efficiency – GDP per unit of energy use	Per capita consumption of electricity
	21. Carbon dioxide emission	Air Pollution

ANNEX 2.

Mapping with CSD indicators

Theme	CSD Indicators	Reference to NHDR indicator
SOCIAL		
Equity	% of population below poverty line	Incidence of poverty
	Gini Index of income inequality	Inequality adjusted per capita consumption expenditure
	Unemployment rate	Incidence of unemployment
	Ratio of average female to male wage	******
Health	Nutritional status of children	Nutrition
	Mortality rate under 5 years old	Under five mortality rate
	Life expectancy at birth	Life expectancy at birth
	Population with access to safe drinking water	Access to toilet facilities
	Percent of population with adequate sewage disposal facilities	
	Immunisation against infectious childhood diseases	Fully vaccinated child aged 12-23 months
	Contraceptive prevalence ratio	Couple protection rate
Education	Children reaching Grade 5 of primary education	Gross enrolment ratio Net enrolment ratio
	Adult Secondary Education Achievement level	Intensity of formal education
	Adult Literacy rate	Adult Literacy rate
Housing	Floor area per person	Distribution of households according to number of rooms occupied
Security	Number of recorded crime per 100,000 population	Rate of total cognizable crime
Population	Population growth rate	Population growth rate
	Population of urban formal and informal settlements	******
ENVIRONMENTAL		
Atmosphere	Emissions of greenhouse gases	******
	Consumption of ozone depleting substances	******
	Ambient concentration of air pollutants in urban areas	Air pollution
Land	Arable and permanent crop land area	******
	Use of fertilizers	******
	Use of agricultural pesticides	******
	Forest area as per cent of land area	Forest cover
	Wood harvesting intensity	******
	Land affected by desertification	******
	Area of urban formal and informal settlements	******
Oceans, Seas and coasts	Algae concentration in coastal waters	******
	Percent of total population living in coastal areas	******
	Annual catch by major species	******
Fresh water	Annual withdrawal of ground and surface water as percentage of total available water	

	BOD in water bodies	******
	Concentration of faecal coliform in freshwater	******
Biodiversity	Area of selected key ecosystems	******
	Protected areas as a % of total area	******
	Abundance of selected key species	******
ECONOMIC		
Economic structure	GDP per capita	Per capita net state domestic product
	Investment share in GDP	******
	Balance of Trade in goods and service	******
	Debt to GNP ratio	******
	Total ODA given or received as percent of GNP	******
Consumption and production and patterns	Intensity of material use	******
	Annual energy consumption per capita	Per capita consumption of electricity
	Share of consumption of renewable energy sources	******
	Intensity of energy use	******
	Generation of industrial and municipal solid waste	Urban solid waste
	Generation of hazardous waste	******
	Management of radioactive waste	******
	Water recycling and reuse	******
	Distance travelled per capita by mode of transport	******
INSTITUTIONAL		
Institutional framework	National sustainable development strategy	******
	Implementation of ratified global agreements	******
	Number of internet subscribers per 1000 inhabitants	******
	Main telephone lines per 1000 inhabitants	******
	Expenditure on research and development as a percent of GDP	******
	Economic and human loss due to natural disasters	******

Enhancing Public Accountability
National Performance Indicators and the Role of the Board of Audit of Japan

Muneharu Otsuka

Commissioner, Board of Audit of Japan

Abstract

In recent years, public accountability to evaluation of public policy achievement and performance has been playing increasingly important role due to the shift of emphasis from input toward output and outcome in the public sector management. This past development of public accountability implies that indicators have increasingly added its value. Recently, indicators have expanded its coverage and now play a bigger role than ever. In some countries indicators measure nationwide socio-economic progresses, stimulate public debates, and help Government decide on important issues. Here, I tentatively call this National Performance Indicators.

In Japan, the Government has established its major indicators such as "People's Life Indicators". These are living standard indicators other than economic indicators like GDP. And recently the Japanese Government has developed "Life Reform Index" to evaluate the results of the incumbent cabinet's Structural Reform Program directly influencing Japanese people's living condition. However, so far there has been no move to establish holistic National Performance Indicators in Japan.

Like other countries, Japan has a possibility to develop National Performance Indicators. If they are developed, the Board of Audit of Japan would take much interest in the processes of the Japanese Government's indicators development because it would much contribute to upgrading quality of Government activities and eventually enhance people's living standards.

SAI should shift priorities in viewpoints of audit, audited bodies, audit areas, as the country's socio-economic conditions change. The SAI audit of National Performance Indicators I believe will be sooner or later one of the top priority areas in future not only in Japan but also in many other countries in the world.

National Performance Indicators from public accountability aspects

Public Accountability

The word "public accountability" means that public servants are held "totally accountable" for their management and disposal of money and assets they collected from the general public. The word's meaning, content, and social systems, however, have changed as time passed. But it is generally understood that the word "accountability" originally meant, as exemplified in the medieval Europe, that King's retainers who worked in rural areas were held responsible for reporting to the King how much money they collected from local people, and how much they spent for what purposes. And as time passed, persons or bodies to report to changed from King to the general public and the Parliament.

In recent years, public accountability to evaluation of public policy achievement and performance has been playing increasingly an important role in the public sector. This may be due to the fact that private sector's free market principles have been gradually introduced to the public sector, and emphasis has accordingly shifted from "input and procedures" to what we call "output, outcome and results". Consequently, "Public Accountability" today requires submitting not only monetary statements such as Statement of Accounts, but also performance evaluation reports, to the Legislative body.

Indicators and Public Accountability

It is clear that the past development of the "Public Accountability" proves that indicators have increasingly added its value in the past decades. This is because the indicators have enabled the Government to do fair and more effective policy evaluation, and thus have enabled the Government to explain the results of the evaluation to the general public and the Legislative body more concisely and comprehensibly. Today, indicators have expanded its coverage and play bigger role compared with the indicators developed in 1970s, which were but narrow "social" indicators. The indicators recently introduced in some countries measure nationwide socio-economic progresses, publish the measurement results, stimulate public debate, and thus help Government decide on important issues. Here, I tentatively call this type of indicators "National Performance Indicators". The National Performance Indicators are epoch-making for fulfilling Public Accountability which emphasizes results and outcome.

Three Key Points in Developing and Using National Performance Indicators

In my view, there are three important points in developing and using National Performance Indicators and thus maintaining Government's public accountability.

One, the Government should make its National Performance Indicators logically and practically consistent with its policies, through scientific and impartial analysis. This is clear because the Government by using the Indicators should achieve its accountability for management and disposal of National assets. This consistency between policies and indicators is necessary also because the Government should reflect the results of its performance evaluation, which is conducted by using indicators, on present and future policies. And this consistency should be achieved through objective and scientific analysis.

Two, the process of indicator development plays a vitally important role. For the National Performance Indicators to serve the Government's accountability, credibility to the Indicators among the general public and the Legislative body is indispensable. However, it is also clear that there is no National Performance Indicator which is flawless and everyone agrees to. Also, setting and/or weighing individual indicators often entails problems caused by difference in views and values among the general public. To overcome this difficulty, it is necessary to ensure involvement of general public and the Legislative body in the indicator development process to the extent possible. The Government also should disclose the indicator development processes and keep their highest transparency.

Three, Supreme Audit Institution, SAI, should constantly check and evaluate the National Performance Indicators, and thus maintain credibility of the Indicators. As British administrative scientist E. L. Normanton's book "The Accountability and Audit of Governments" said "Without audit, no accountability. Without accountability no control; and if there is no control, where is the seat of power?" SAI audit plays a vitally important role in maintaining Government's accountability. But on the Government side, National Performance Indicators, however simple and clear they are, require wide and varied information and high technicality in their development processes. Also, these Indicators may change as social conditions and people's living conditions change. The indicators being such changeable and complex by nature, Supreme Audit Institution importantly should maintain their credibility through its independent audit.

Major Indicators in Japan

Outline

In Japan, public sector agencies establish statistical indicators in various fields such as economy, education, and environment. These indicators are shown as unemployment rate, high-school entrance rate, per household garbage collection and so on. Ministries and Agencies form their policies mainly based on these indicators. Japanese taxpayers also give great credit on these indicators. The Diet deliberates on Government policies and performances based on these indicators. Mass media also report and analyze incumbent issues based on these indicators, and so do many academicians in writing their theses. This proves that these indicators, established in Japan either by Central or local governments or by any other public bodies, have had widespread credibility throughout the Japanese society.

The Japanese Government has established its major indicators such as "People's Life Indicators" based on these statistical indicators. These indicators are living standard indicators other than economic indicators like GDP and per capita income. The Japanese Government also has shown these indicators in concise and comprehensible manner to the general public and policy makers by showing coefficients such as up and down rates against previous years.

As one of these indicators, the Japanese Government established People's Life Indicator, PLI, in 1992. The PLI was established against following backgrounds of the late 1980s: One, despite Japan's per capita income having statistically risen to nearly top of the world in late 1980s, people could not really sense such high level of living conditions in their daily life, and because of this, the Japanese Government needed more realistic indicators. Two, the Japanese Government needed indicators to measure varying and good living conditions in provincial areas amid people's growing yeaning for, and over-population of, the capital city of Tokyo.

However, the purpose of the People's Life Indicators, or PLI, was not to evaluate achievement of set policy goals of the Japanese Government. The only indicator the Japanese Government so far has developed to evaluate accomplishment of its policy is "Life Reform Index" which was made by the incumbent Koizumi Cabinet. The Index is to evaluate the results of the implementation of the "Structural Reform Program". The Index was made public in February 2003.

The "Life Reform Index" is to quantify the results of the Japanese Government's "Structural Reform Program" implementation in the area directly influencing Japanese people's living conditions. The Index divides each of the Structural Reform Program's indicators into 10 Indexes, such as "creating good living conditions", "creating good learning conditions", and "creating good working conditions". These 10 Indexes further divide themselves into sub-Indexes. For example, "Creating good living conditions" divides into "Fair and free competition in housing market", "Shorter commuting time", "Better house purchasing conditions". The accomplishment of these policies are shown, as "Number of used house selling and purchasing cases", "Average commuting hours", "Average floor square measures of newly purchased houses" and "average annual income versus house purchasing cost ratio".

However, having just started this type of policy evaluation, the Japanese Government is yet to make it clear whether it will continue this effort or not.

Challenges Facing Japan's Major Nationwide Indicators

As I have explained thus far, the Japanese Government has established several nationwide indicators on Japanese people's living standards. But these indicators still have several challenges.

One, it is getting difficult to select or set indicators amid changing societal and ethical values among Japanese people. For example, in case of divorce rate indicator, people are increasingly divided over whether divorce is good or bad in present social conditions. The Japanese Government therefore is now facing a challenge how to select indicators acceptable to the majority of the Japanese people amid varying societal and ethical values.

Two, there have been complaints among people that they cannot really sense the Japan's "high living standard" the indicators show. This means there are considerable gaps between what indicators show and what people feel. The Government therefore presently needs to meet public expectation by reexamining the statistical value of the indicators.

Three, these indicators intend to evaluate people's living standards in changing Japanese society, but do not necessarily intend to evaluate the Government's performance and policy goal achievements. The Government therefore needs to further strengthen its recent effort to evaluate its policy goal achievement and its effects.

Audit of National Performance Indicators in Japan

Present Status

As I have mentioned a moment ago, the Japanese Government established the "People's Life Indicators", and "Life Reform Index". However, so far there has been no move to establish National Performance Indicators, which are indicators to measure nationwide socio-economic progress.

Also, the answer to the question "Has the Board of Audit audited the adequacy and accomplishment of People's Life Indicators and Life Reform Index?" is "No". Reasons are: One, the Japan Board of Audit so far has mainly focused on financial and accounting side of the Government activities in its audit. Two, neither of the "People's Life Indicators", PLI, and the "Life Reform Index" is established based on broad consensus among Japanese people, and national indicators are still in development stage.

Future Prospect

While the governments implement various policies in various fields such as economy, community life, culture, environment and try to upgrade people's life, SAIs are responsible for encouraging the Government to implement such policies effectively and efficiently and improve their activities, and eventually responsible for enhancing peoples' living standards. And SAIs' audit so far has very much contributed to the people's better quality of life. Therefore, if a holistic National Performance Indicators to measure nationwide socio-economic progress are established, SAIs would very much contribute to upgrading quality of Government activities in various fields by deliberately and carefully examining each of the National Performance Indicators.

Like other countries, Japan has a possibility to develop such comprehensive and total indicators. These National Performance Indicators should reflect each country's scope of Government activities, economy, community life, culture, environment and so on.

The "People's Life Indicators" and the "Life Reform Index" which the Japanese Government so far has developed would become parts of the National Performance Indicators in future. In that case, the Board of Audit of Japan would take much interest in the processes of the Japanese Government's setting the Indicators, indexes, and target values. This is because there may be some common purposes between the Government setting such indicators and indexes, and the Board of Audit auditing them, despite the fact that such indicators and indexes are not part of Government's accounting activities the Board presently audits.

Viewpoints of Auditing National Performance Indicators

How the Board of Audit would audit National Performance Indicators, or how the Board of Audit would use these indicators for its audit, is presently unclear, because the contents of these indicators are yet to be clarified.

However, generally speaking, the viewpoints of SAI's auditing National Performance Indicators would be as follows:

One, regarding selection and establishment of indicators, the SAI audit would examine:

1. Does the Government properly create and maintain consistency among indicators in various fields such as economy, community life, environment and so on, and do such coordination efforts accurately reflect country's present socio-economic conditions?

2. Do the established indicators accurately measure national performance in each field, and produce accurate statistical values?

3. In establishing a synthesised single indicator in each field, does the Government fairly weigh and balance each of the individual indicators in individual areas?

Two, regarding targeted values, the audit would examine:

4. Are targeted values sufficiently high and justifiable, and reflect actual policy goals to be achieved?

5. Does the Government fairly measure external socio-economic elements which influence indicator accomplishment?

Conclusion

Perhaps like SAIs in many other countries, the Japan Board of Audit up to now has shifted its viewpoints of audit, audited bodies, and areas of audit from time to time taking people's changing demands into consideration. In order to effectively use limited resources and thus meet people's needs, SAI should shift priorities in viewpoints of audit, audited bodies, audit areas, as the country's socio-economic conditions change.

The SAI audit of Government's performance indicators I believe will be sooner or later one of the top priority areas not only in Japan but also in many other countries in the world. This is because both Governments who set the indicators, and SAIs who check them, share the common goal – to achieve higher living standards of the people.

I believe this Forum will certainly bear fruit through useful discussions on this theme.

Advocacy, Numeracy and the Role of Media

Agree on Numbers While Discussing Words. Or is it Just the Opposite?

Luca De Biase

Journalist and Writer, Italy

Abstract

Numbers are objective. Words are difficult to define. Thus goes the common sense. And this makes numbers a perfect tool for sharing ideas, while words are tricky and easily misconstrued. Economic and general journalism share this notion: adding numbers in any way possible to an article will make it more credible. But discussing too much the meaning of those numbers would spoil the effect. Using some examples from real life, this paper discusses the role of statistics as a communication tool and the power of the sources of these numbers in the media: which is more important, the quality of numbers or their ability to fit in prevailing journalistic frames?

Numbers are credible, aren't they?

When a non-specialized weekly newsmagazine hired me, my new editor in chief told me: "You are graduated in economics. So you'll write for the economy section. But remember: writing for the economy section means that you have to add numbers to your articles. Understand?"

Numbers meant credibility and serious information. It was about 20 years ago. Today, numbers' credibility is in serious trouble.

It is a small aspect of a more general credibility crisis in the media and the communication system. It is also a consequence of an easier availability of numbers and of a proliferation of different sources of data. But it is also a consequence of a crisis of statistical concepts and meanings: there are some telling episodes. Here is one.

The case with inflation

After the introduction of the euro, some countries have experienced a very clear crisis of the official inflation rate. While people in Europe were complaining about an incredible growth in prices, official statistics about inflation seemed unable to register any significant change. The notion of "perceived inflation" has been proposed by some sources as opposed to "official inflation".

No solution is in sight. Every time new data is published the same argument comes back. Wages have grown 2.5 percent in September 2004 on September 2003. Prices have grown, officially, by a mere 2.1 percent in the same period. That should calm down the request for fatter salaries. But trade unionist Giorgio Santini comments: "I don't believe this. Wages have not outgrown inflation. Perceived inflation is much higher than what is shown in Istat's figures". (*La Repubblica* – October 28, 2004). And he is a voice that speaks for a majority of Italians.

Once, numbers were accepted by almost everybody and the discussion was about words used to explain those numbers: some thought that profits were to blame; some other thought that wages were to blame. But everybody accepted the numbers. Now numbers are part of the discussion. It is a consequence of what has happened to numbers and their sources when they started to be massively used by the media. And it is a problem that must be solved.

Reality is described by both research and perception. It is true that after the introduction of the euro in Italy, as in other European countries, some prices greatly increased. The euro was worth about two thousand liras but some businesses succeeded in getting their prices to a new level setting a sort of new rate of change at about one euro for one thousand liras. The price for a cappuccino used to be something like 2 thousand liras, but after the introduction of the euro, its price changed to about 1.5 euro. A taxi ride from the airport to the center of Rome was worth 50 thousand liras, but the price was changed to 40 euro. Many prices went the same direction. As statistical authorities in Italy continued to assess a real inflation at about 2.5 per cent, the notion of "perceived" inflation was proposed. Official inflation was 2.5 percent but perceived inflation was at 80-100 percent. The truth, everybody seemed to think, was to be somewhere in between.

What could the press do? Not being able to do its own statistical research and attributing a relative value to perception, the press that wanted to be "objective" had only one choice. To publish both inflations: the official and the perceived one. This meant that the most radical and different interpretations of the phenomenon were possible and published, and that there was no agreement about the real meaning of inflation and its causes.

Italians had no more common data to accept and the discussion was no more limited to their causes. The facts – ie. the numbers – were to be discussed as well as their causes. Potentially, it was the end of a general contract that had stabilized the economy for a decade.

This was already bad. But there was something even worse: the credibility crisis of the numbers didn't lead to any important consequence. Why?

That's because a solution would probably be a disaster. Everyone understands that if the official rate of inflation continues to be under control so will be interest rates, mortgage rates, wages and other fundamental data: a dramatic change in those variables would destabilize the Italian macroeconomic situation.

This explains why critics didn't make any difference. Truth about inflation was less important than a more general understanding of reality. Thus, numbers such as the inflation rate have become a mere agreement. And the media have helped this to happen.

The media could have done more for finding the truth. But what the people wanted was not the truth: it was a tool for the community to decide together about some very important behaviors. Italians wanted stability in some fundamental variables. And they got this from their media.

The consequence: as objectivity becomes a matter of a social agreement about what it is to be considered the truth, then the truth becomes less important than credibility. But as most people understand this and as credibility is more and more separated by the truth, the result is a general credibility crisis.

Credibility and the information ecosystem

Carlo Goldoni, a very successful play writer of the XVIIIth century, used to say: "some critics accuse my characters for not being real enough. My answer: if I wrote the truth people in theaters wouldn't believe me. I prefer to write what is credible and not what is true: thus I can tell a little bit of the truth and the public understands, believes, and gets the message."

Goldoni knew that credibility is more important than truth in the media business. Of course, the media want attention and consensus from the public. But when it comes to assessing the quality of information, the most important criteria are about credibility and are not necessarily about truthfulness. In the media business success doesn't result from telling the truth but from being believed. This conclusion can seem to be sad and cynical, particularly if we think at those mythical old times in which the epistemology of the media repeated that "objectivity" was the concept that was more linked to the one of "truth" and that "truth" was what we all should believe in.

But a reality check of the notion of "objectivity" in the media gives a different picture. Practice has clearly bypassed epistemology in defining what is to be considered "objective" information. News is "objective" if articles report all the existing different opinions about facts or if sources are "credible".

Credibility has a few different causes. Here are some:

- What powerful people say is usually credible

- Information that ends up being useful is credible

- Information that everyone seems to think is right is credible

- News that is easily understandable is also credible

- Information that is gathered with an accepted methodology is credible.

Media looking for credibility have some research to do by themselves with the last of those five causes. But most credibility that they use for publishing comes from the other four causes. And this is true with numbers and statistics, too. Is this a matter of scarce competence? Or is it something else? The answer cannot be found if we do not think of the whole system of information as a sort of ecosystem.

Scientists and specialized observers of economic and statistical matters often smile about the lack off accuracy in economic journalism. This has, by the way, probably improved quite a bit since some decades ago. Some think that it does not matter because they conceive journalism only as a sort of extension of communication, with no real cultural meaning. Some think that it is a problem that statistical sources have to solve. Very few seem to understand that it is a real systemic problem: there is a sort of ecosystem of information, with sources, media and the public all interacting in a very complex way.

Credibility is a strange kind of resource. It is easy to lose and hard to build. So most players in the ecosystem try to specialize in the least risky business they can find. Serious statistical sources cultivate the quality of their data and give a lot of attention to communicating all the scientific precautions that prevent them from losing face with inevitable errors. The media respond by putting all responsibility of the quality of information on the sources' shoulders. The media quote the sources and if the sources are many, the media quote them all. Only in the long run bad sources will be thrown out of the game. But in general, credible sources will always be quoted. The media will not be able to remove the information overload.

Instead of risking their credibility, the media will act in a conservative and conformist way. They will publish all sources. And if sources will understand this mechanism, they will be able to manipulate it, for better or for worse.

An ecosystem can be conservative or innovative, it can be stable or it can generate new life. Or it can be polluted. Cleaning it is a must if someone wants to save both the media's and the sources' credibility.

Numbers in the information ecosystem: the media point of view

Numbers are objective. Words are difficult to define. Thus went the common sense. This is why numbers have always been seen as a perfect tool for sharing ideas, while words have been considered tricky and easily misconstrued. In many contexts, from science to management, this is a sort of rule. The right thing to do in case of crisis in the perceived quality of data is to improve the quality of numbers and to better share their meaning.

What does usually happen in journalism?

Economic journalism shares this notion with a peculiar twist: adding numbers to an article will make it more serious and credible. But discussing too much about the meaning of those numbers would spoil the effect. Credibility counts, but immediate comprehension is even more important. Of course, these speed limits are different in different media: television news needs less of an explanation than newspapers. In reality, reasoning happens before publishing, but what is published applies to intuition more than reasoning.

Why is that? Is it because the media lack competence? Or is it a way not to bore the public? Both are true: and they are both continually changing realities. Journalism is navigating in a very difficult sea.

The context is changing. Numbers have long meant credibility and serious information but in the last decades they have become both less rare and less reliable. Numbers are everywhere in the news, not only in the serious economy sections. Politics is made of numbers as much as of words, as the recent polling inflation for the American presidential election has shown. Sports sections are full of numbers, as they want to look more and more technical. Society sections use a lot of numbers from any kind of sociological source for their new-trend-seeking articles. Even cultural pages rely on numbers for building their influence on the publishing and media business. Numbers are *per se* less serious than language.

At the same time, numbers in economics have moved into different media as the media geography has changed. Television and radio financial news are the media of the life news about what is worth a bet: and they give financial information with the same style, a flow of numbers with very little historical and critical information. It's the latest results that count. Newspapers seem to be more interested in discussing the numbers and, even more importantly, the creation of some sort of consensus about their interpretation. While the operative use of numbers is gone to the Internet: businessmen and traders think they can find more objective and functional numbers on the Web. And it is often true, as the OECD Web site or as the Stock Exchange numbers feeds demonstrate.

All these phenomena have changed the public approach to numbers. Numbers seem more available for those who want to work on them. But at the same time they seem too easy to find, as if they were just part of the show. And the public seems to think that they are becoming much more a part of some sort of manipulative machine.

From the media point of view, there is not much that journalist can do about this.

Journalists live on deadlines. They have to sell their news not when information is best gathered and controlled but at the time their news must be published. And the first rule of the media is that content must be easily accessible.

But journals live on credibility. There is no way for the public to know if a newspaper is worth the euro that is needed to read it: the only way to know is to buy it, read it and afterwards decide if the money was well spent. And credibility is the only means for journalists to convince people to spend their money in this way. Publishers could invest in improving the credibility of their newspapers. But they can do it in very different ways: and they seem to think that investing in regular advertising is much more effective in sustaining their credibility than investing in improved research capability of their journalistic teams.

It is a strange business: a lot of reasoning is dedicated to editorial projects, while a very small amount of time is spent on their implementation. Credibility is slow. Content production is fast. Even the best journalists cannot do a perfect job of controlling everything and in writing with all the information that is needed for the best possible understanding of statistical information.

A solution has been found and it is defining the relationship between the media and the sources of statistics: writing and style will be what journalists worry about, while control and quality of the research will be done by sources. If the writing and style is clear and smart enough, the risk for credibility will not be the journalist's problem: credibility will be entrusted to the sources.

But this solution is tricky. Time constraints become the leading force and content must adapt. If some sources will refuse to give their statistical information on time and their comments on it, journalists will find other, easier sources.

Is this ok? If sources are really good, they give the right answer at the right moment and the public is happy. But is this possible? No: it is a perfect mechanism for generating mistakes.

The technology bubble has demonstrated this in a perfect way. The Nobel laureate Daniel Kahneman writes about his research with Amos Tversky: "We examined systematic errors in the casual statistical judgments of statistically sophisticated researchers. Remarkably, the intuitive judgments of these experts did not conform to statistical principles with which they were thoroughly familiar (…). We were impressed by the persistence of discrepancies between statistical intuition and statistical knowledge, which we observed both in ourselves and in our colleagues". In fact, time constraints determine a clear reaction in both knowledgeable and amateur commentators: they tend to use more intuition than reasoning. And they make mistakes.

There is a sort of automatic reasoning that is used when time constraints are the law. And automatic reasoning means less controlled reasoning.

Both the sources and the media have a problem with this. The media seem less and less able to cope: they respond, at best, only by asking many sources the same questions and putting them all together in their articles. But even this is not always possible.

Sources should respond in a more sensible way: but they often seem to be more interested in being quoted by the media than in preserving their credibility.

In this context, information is objective when it comes from a source that everybody thinks is able to tell the truth. Prejudgment, authority and power are all means for achieving this general agreement on source's credibility. If there is no time for an epistemological discussion about the way information is collected, controlled and published, an automatic reasoning will prevail. The best that is done is what journalists call "framing": a sort of pre-built reasoning that applies to all matters, for some time.

Frames: what sources can do

The media call good news the growth in GDP and bad news the growth of inflation. And this seems to be quite a stable frame that is related to the general macroeconomic reasoning.

They also call good and bad what is alternatively most important in the public's agenda: in some cases they define deregulation as part of the "good" news, in some other cases they define a growth in employment as part of the "good" news. These are also frames.

Frames are pre-digested reasoning that create an interpretation for facts. They make some facts go up in the agenda and some others go down. They even make the media actually see – or not notice – something. Outsourcing in India was important even during the technology bubble; but the media noticed only when jobs in Silicon Valley became less easy to find for Americans.

This pre-digested reasoning could be better than mere intuition. And it could give some space for improvement. The ecosystems can only be cleaned with a more developed ecological consciousness.

The media know that credibility means selling their products. They can work on education for their journalists, and some do. But they cannot do the whole job by themselves. They badly need statistical sources to help.

What should sources do? They already clarify – often too much – the statistical meaning of their numbers. And sometimes help to understand the right way to interpret them. But they can do more. They can understand that numbers have meanings that go beyond their statistical value. Numbers send messages. Statistical sources should know what the message is that their numbers send and help correct it if possible.

"Percentage" abuse is an example.

Again from Daniel Kahneman's prospect theory we have learned that we judge by difference. Given a situation we understand the change in it or the comparison with other situations. We tend to have a worse understanding of the absolute value of that situation.

The answer to this has been an inflation of percentage data. GDP growth is much more known than GDP level. This has many consequences. An easy one: Europeans are scared because their growth is slower than the Chinese one, but they tend to forget that their absolute level of wealth is many times higher than that of China. A more interesting consequence: the growth of the growth rate is considered "going ahead" and a slowdown of growth is considered "going backwards".

The growth of growth is "good" and the slowdown is "bad". This is exactly the way bubbles work.

If we thought more in absolute terms we would better remember some lessons from history.

Sources should always give the absolute numbers to educate the public and the media to think historically and ecologically. Comparing percentages between different variables is often impossible. If we want to improve our understanding of sustainability we have to think in absolute numbers and not only in percentages.

Sources should think the existence of this information ecosystem and act coherently. They should stop thinking the media as the place where the incompetent live: because even if this judgment can be true, it doesn't result in any practical consequence. Understanding the media is the only way to make it better.

Journalism is not only about facts

Journalism is, of course, information over what is happening; but it is even more about creating a community and even leading to common action.

Agreement about general ideas and knowledge in the community is pivotal to the success of the media.

Journalism is not about competence in statistical matters. Statistical sources are those that specialize in that kind of research: they can criticize the media for not being able to understand the data but they should also understand the professional knowledge of the media people. Even journalism is a very specialized culture: time constraints and accessible language are some of its peculiarities; interface design is its true specialization, while credibility risk management is its special knowledge. Shared prejudgments are to be kept in mind while writing journalism, sometimes to develop on them, sometimes to change them. But in any case success means attention, agreement, alignment, and consequent action.

Frames and intuitions are more important to media credibility than controlled reasoning about sources and concepts.

Statistical sources that want to contribute with some improvement in this ecosystem of information should know how the media work and ask what is possible while addressing the only space that the media leave to reasoning: frames and pre-digested reasoning. It is a long time strategy: but it is worth a try.

References

Luca De Biase, *Obiettività?*, in «Problemi dell'informazione», Il Mulino, a. XXVIII, n. 4, dicembre 2003, pp. 417-426.

Daniel Kahneman, Map of bounded rationality: a perspective on intuitive judgment and choice, Nobel Prize Lecture, December 8, 2002.

Giorgio Meletti, *Il ricatto dell'obiettività*, in «Problemi dell'informazione», Il Mulino, a. XXIX, n. 1, marzo 2004, pp. 19-24.

David Randall, *The Universal Journalist*, Pluto Press 2000

John Seely Brown and Paul Duguid, *The Social Life of Information*, Harvard Business School Press 2000

Good and Bad in Britain and What the Press Makes of It

Simon Briscoe

Statistics Editor, Financial Times

Abstract

Statistics-based performance measures have been creeping up on Britons for years but they mushroomed in their number and grew in importance after the 1997 election of a Labour government. We were flooded with all sorts of measures and did not know what to make of it. Now we can look back at that experience and see what was good and bad – there are plenty of examples of both – and look to the future.

This paper will look at the institutional, cultural and statistical changes that are required in the years ahead if the current arrangements are going to be materially improved. There are some signs of hope but until there is a fair and reasoned framework for the debate on targets and performance indicators, it is hard to be sure that society is benefiting and the right policies are being pursued. When the framework is good, the media coverage will improve and one of the foundation stones for increasing trust in the democratic and political process will be in place.

Introduction

A debate about targets and related data is possible now in a way that was not so a decade ago - no society has ever been measured quite as much as ours at this time. We have never before had the computing power to allow us to collect and analyse these numbers. And the internet makes the figures readily available and generally they are free. Despite the adverse publicity that data often gets, Britain benefits from a rich supply of numbers - indeed it is probably only because so much data is available that the criticism is at the level it is - but of course it could be much better and presented more usefully.

A good range of statistics has a vital role to play in helping to rescue politics and the democratic process from distrust and apathy. Poor data, politically manipulated will feed the skepticism of the press and public. We have a mixed bag in the UK at this time – partly statistical and partly political. The difficulties reflect a range of problems - a complicated cocktail of errors, revisions, biased or skilful presentation, spinning and leaking, stupid targets and benign neglect of data quality. Many problems could be resolved with the desire and some money but neither are in great supply.

The public mistrust and poor use of figures by government is a shame as we were promised a big cleanup of data after the 1997 election following the pledge to introduce an independent statistical service. But it is very slow in coming and its implementation is half-hearted. While there are many success stories of new and better statistics, a few highlighted problems tarnish the good work and undermine confidence in the system, not only in the data but in the whole process of government. We are yet to see political independence for official statistics. Indeed, the governing Labour Party's own website contains one of the most perfect examples of statistical manipulation and sleight of hand, showing how close such dark skills are to the heart of power. (See annex for details)

While many of the individual number crunchers in government are scrupulous in their attention to detail and impartiality, there are examples of figures that suggest that some statistical work in government departments falls short of the ideal. Statisticians working in the Office for National Statistics, the powerhouse of the British official statistical system, have day to day freedoms to do the best job possible, yet the organisation reports to the Chancellor and depends on his goodwill for funding. This link might distort the priorities of the senior statisticians and the work programme of the office. At least half of central government's statisticians – and often those producing important data – work in other departments and more directly report to ministers. This has been likened to giving an alcoholic the keys to a pub.

Targets

Against this background, the measurement culture has become an increasingly important feature of public services over the last 10 or 15 years as more and more organisations began to have data that could be used as the basis for measurement. Targets were given a kick start and given increased political importance by the new Labour government in 1997 with its election pledges on jobs and hospital waiting lists and became especially important in 1998 following the first comprehensive spending review and the original publication of public service agreements. Both the 2004 Budget and spending review emphasised the government's continued enthusiasm for them.

Most people agree that performance indicators have managerial, democratic and research value. Organisations need to have a means of measuring their own performance internally (often between people or groups doing the same job) and in comparison (as an organisation) with others in order to learn and develop. Taxpayers and users of public services have a right to know how well their services are being delivered and who is accountable for them. And there is a genuine research role in discovering "what works".

Despite the general support for the government's use of targets many people have serious reservations about their operation in practice. There are allegations of cheating, perverse consequences and distortions in pursuit of targets, along with unfair pressure on professionals. League tables and ranking lists are often seen as untrustworthy and misleading. The increase in accountability and transparency which targets in theory bring and should be invaluable, has been marred by insufficient heed being given to the risks of over interpretation in the presence of large, often inadequately reported uncertainty.

As the Royal Statistical Society said, "Good performance monitoring is productive for all concerned but done badly, it can be very costly, ineffective, harmful and destructive." A subsequent report from the RSS offered practical solutions for resolving critical issues in target setting and in the design, analysis and reporting of performance indicators, against which current and future performance monitoring of the public services could be judged.

The government set out its own aspirations for the targets. It said they should be SMART - specific, measurable, achievable, relevant and timed. Laudable as these aims are, in many cases there has been a failure to connect between the politicians at the centre setting the targets and the employees on the front-line whose job it is to deliver them.

Targets can be of different types and importance. The most important group are public service agreements made between the Treasury and government departments. But beyond that there are targets announced by the Prime Minister, other ministers or heads of non departmental bodies, those included in white papers and other reports, those set by Labour in opposition or at party conferences or other political events. The government said in March 1999 that it had set 350 policy targets and 175 efficiency targets. Research by the Liberal Democrats found many more - 8600 - and that did not to include any set for the Scottish, Welsh or Northern Ireland offices, the regional development agency, and most of the Best Value targets set for local authorities. The number of targets has since been cut.

The Public Administration Committee made a number of recommendations in its 2003 report, including ensuring greater local autonomy to construct more meaningful and relevant targets, making sure they are as few as possible and focus on key outcomes, widening the targets consultation process to involve professionals and service users, and reforming the way in which targets are set to move away from the simplistic hit or miss approach. The committee also called for common reporting standards on targets and an independent assessment by the National Audit Office of whether and how far targets have been met. These hopes along with the committee's desire to see a more mature political debate about the measurement culture based on a better understanding of targets as tools to improve performance has yet to be fulfilled.

There are a number of failings:

1. A lack of clarity about what the government is trying to achieve and risks to equity

There is no guarantee that a reliance on national targets will promote greater equity. A national target can be met in more than one way and some of them promote greater equity than others. For example, a 10% improvement in services can be achieved if all providers improve equally. It can also be achieved if some units do disproportionately well while others fail. If top performers improve most, the gap in the available service quality will widen between citizens in different parts of the country.

2. Failure to provide a clear sense of direction and a clear message to staff

Targets can never be substitutes for a proper and clearly expressed strategy and set of priorities - they can be good servants but are poor masters. Targets should drop out of the business plan and not the other way round. Local people need to feel the centrally imposed targets reflect sensible aspirations if they are not to be counterproductive. Professionals need to feel ownership of the targets - they have often expressed concern that targets fail to take account of their special expertise and judgment. Many have felt undermined by targets with the late 1990s obsession with cutting hospital waiting lists frequently cited, by doctors who say they distorted medical treatments, as the most damaging example.

Another problem is the tendency for central government sometimes to appear to pluck targets out of the air in support of the latest initiative. Such targets tend not to command respect or credibility. The aim to reduce school truancies by 10% by 2004 compared to 2002 is relevant and highly desirable but the target figure was seen as quite arbitrary - 5% or 20% would have had just as much rationale.

It is also usually inept to set extreme value targets, such is "no patient shall wait in accident and emergency for more than four hours" because as soon as one patient has waited more than four hours, the target is forgone and seen as irrelevant to staff. Typically, avoiding extremes consumes disproportionate resources for an organisation. It would have been far wiser to have the target as "95% of patients will wait in accident and emergency for under four hours" but it was presumably not deemed as politically desirable.

3. *Failure to focus on delivering results*

Even if the government is achieving the majority of the PSA targets it has set itself that does not mean that results are also being delivered. There are documented cases where the measurement ceases to be a means to an end and becomes the end in itself - more effort is being directed into ensuring that the figures produced have hit the targets than to improving services. There is evidence that targets for ambulance response time were jeopardising the effective delivery of services and with it clinical outcomes. The national targets for ambulances require them to respond to incidents defined as life threatening emergencies within a certain number of minutes. There has been no uniform standard of measurement of ambulance response times within the many ambulance services. The clock starts at different times - the time the call was made, was answered, classified to a particular grade of emergency, dispatch of the ambulance, or the ambulance leaving - which may vary by several minutes. Similarly the classification of what is a life threatening emergency differs between ambulance services and ranges from less than 10% of all emergencies to about 50%. These differences in measurement of starting points and definition of a 'life threatening emergency' cast doubt on the usefulness of their targets.

Another danger with the measurement culture is that excessive attention is given to what can easily be measured at the expense of what is difficult or impossible to measure quantitatively even though this may be fundamental to the service provided. The quality of patient care or the time devoted by a teacher to a difficult child's needs is not easily measured.

Hospital consultants have explained that the waiting time targets for new outpatient appointments at their hospitals have been achieved by canceling and delaying follow up appointments for existing patients often with damaging consequences for those patients whose treatments had not been completed.

A more direct threat to the public service ethos is the deliberate falsification of information and failure to follow proper procedures, amounting at times to cheating. Targets for accident and emergency maximum waiting times were being circumvented by imaginative fixes where trolleys either had their wheels removed or were redesignated as "beds on wheels" and corridors and treatment rooms were redesignated as "pre-admission units". Evidence of deliberate manipulation of figures has come to light in other parts of the NHS, perhaps most notoriously the case of hospital waiting lists - which comprise the people who have been referred by a GP to a hospital consultant and, having seen the consultant, are waiting for the start of the treatment. The figures for hospital waiting lists were vital for the government as the promise to reduce waiting lists by 100,000 was a key pledge of Labour in the 1997 election.

4. *Failures in reporting and monitoring*

The NAO has noted the absence of either centrally accepted standards for reporting performance or of any general audit requirements for validation of results reported. Many of the NAO's value for money reports have examined departments' performance measurement systems or validated performance data. The NAO reported that in over 80% of such first-time validations, they found that the organisation had materially misstated their achievements or had failed to disclose potentially material weaknesses with their data. In over 70% of validations there were material inaccuracies in performance data used to track progress against one or more key targets.

According to the NAO the reason for these problems was a lack of attention to, or expertise in, performance measurement and reporting techniques. But the absence of any routine external validation of the measures meant that there was no external discipline of reporting, and no routine independent review of the quality of information. There has been little central guidance on how such reporting should be carried out but the situation jeopardises the credibility of the whole policy of government by measurement.

Difficulties in monitoring and reporting have also sometimes been the result of poorly thought out targets. The Statistics Commission has pointed out that in some policy areas targets have been set without consideration of the practicalities of monitoring and what data do or do not already exist. Many people feel that performance targets need to be independently validated if they are to be credible. At the moment, all such assessments are based on departments' own judgments of how well they have performed against their targets.

Institutions can appear out of line with others in rank orderings based on performance indicators for various reasons other than their true performance, one of which is poor quality of data. For example, in one piece of research based on official data, the university given the title "the worst university" in 1997 found itself in that position because of incorrect data. It had accidentally included 267 students who had enrolled on a single year course as students on the traditional three year course. Naturally their progression rates to a second year course were very low - about 11% - compared to the national average of 77% for those on three year courses. But the incorrect inclusion of these students in the aggregates caused the averages for that institution to plummet.

5. *Confused accountability*

A major cause of confusion over accountability is the fact that the centre does not have a strong enough sense of the importance of the structure of service delivery. Although the Westminster system tries to centralise the responsibility for the performance of all public services, the delivery of services is dispersed and often devolved. Departments do not have their hands on the management of programs - they supervise policies for which ministers answer to Parliament, while others deliver them.

A decade and more of structural reforms in public administration has increased the complexity of what is in effect multi-layered government. At the top is a layer of Whitehall departments, in the middle are a set of institutions such as local authorities and health bodies supervising the delivery of public services, who are working with others, often contractors, who are organising the manpower and at the bottom are individuals who meet the public when they go to a school, the surgery or a library. This complex geography has a profound effect on accountability and motivation and means there are fundamental problems with the accountability of any target that is set centrally without proper reference to those on the front line.

As long as targets are being met, the centre and local providers can happily claim ownership and credit. However, if the targets are missed this may well lead to acrimonious dispute about where the blame rests. The setting of impossible targets is a recipe for the growth of blame culture.

6. The problems with presentation - league tables and other simplistic measures

There is also a danger that any achievement short of 100% success is classified as failure. Simplistic approaches of this kind, with political and media charges about failure to meet fully the targets, can be profoundly demoralising to schools, teachers, police officers and hospital staff who have worked hard to achieve progress in the face of local difficulties. Crude league tables and star ratings can be particularly misleading and demotivating, as they tend to make everybody except the "league champions" look and feel like failures.

Crude ratings tend to take no account of the particular features of local communities which can go a long way in explaining the different performance of areas. For example, it might be expected that the school exam success in English for a London Borough such as Tower Hamlets, where two thirds of the population is Bangladeshi, might well be lower than the national average even if the efforts of the teachers and pupils are above average. Even so there have been press reports that ministers had seriously considered using such naive information to help decide on the fate of head teachers.

League tables also usually fail to take account of uncertainties due to the quality and variability of the data. For many purely statistical reasons the performance of a hospital's surgeons or a school's pupils will fluctuate from year to year.

League tables are best avoided if there is no measurements of ranking uncertainty included. Star ratings - essentially presenting a series of categories or leagues rather than a straight ranking in one league table - are generally deemed preferable but they also need to explain the uncertainty involved in the categorisation. The star ratings system for hospitals (first published in 2001, it graded each of the hospital trusts between zero and three starts) has suffered particular criticism.

Many practitioners have advocated the use of so-called funnel plots, which can identify outliers, in preference to league tables. If there are several or many performance indicators available for analysis, and amalgamation into a single summary figure can be avoided, information can be illustrated by means of a so-called "spider web", sometimes known as star plots. The advantage of this presentation is that it precludes overemphasis and distortion often inherent in single measures.

The measurement culture adapts

There is no doubt that the management culture has been adapting fast during the 1990s and is continuing to adapt. The number of PSAs has been reduced since they were first introduced in 1998 and an increasing number of targets are now outcome or output related. Some key targets have been changed (for example the switch between waiting list numbers to waiting times in health) or abandoned as unhelpful or unrealistic (examples are drugs and traffic congestion). Some targets have become less rigid and more aspirational. There is also a greater emphasis from the centre on consultation. The publication of the pan-government FABRIC report in 2001 provides guidance to government departments on setting targets. The report stressed the importance of reliable data and recommended the use of National Statistics where appropriate, on the grounds that these data are more likely to meet the expected standards in terms of transparency, quality and integrity – but NS are still only used for a minority of the targets.

There has been a call for the provision of measures of progress that can give a more rounded and accurate picture of how schools, hospitals and other public services are performing - in direct contrast to the 1990's fashion for "naming and shaming". Such measures would be much closer to what most people want from public services.

Access to data about targets used to be very hard to find. But the latest figures relating to the major public service agreements can now be found on the Treasury web site.

The required cultural change

If the practice of targeting is to improve then a few changes will be required – the first in the list are on the part of ministers and the others by statisticians. A growing acceptance of shortcomings by the centre will also need to be matched by an acceptance among professionals that government by measurement is here to stay.

Fairer presentation

Most politicians love quoting figures. It suggests they have grasped the detail of policy and they come over hard-nosed and unanswerable. Politicians naturally present existing data in the best possible light but they have to be a bit more even-handed in their presentation, perhaps reducing the extent of boasting. Politicians rarely lie but they are often economical with the truth. We might well be told that personal tax rates have not risen under Labour - and indeed they have not. But that does not mean that most people are not paying more personal tax or that the total tax burden on people has not risen - it has. Britain is currently experiencing a period of historically very low inflation and long-term interest rates, but is due to the actions of the current government? Since the trend was established under the previous administration and is pretty much a worldwide phenomenon, it might be strange if our government were to take particular credit for the achievement. In the public spending review of 1998, the Chancellor announced that spending on education, for example, would be rising by £19 billion. Close examination of the figures showed that what he meant was that it would be rising by £3 billion in the coming year and by £6 billion and £10 billion in two years after. The sum of these three incremental increases being £19 billion. This unusual way of presenting public expenditure increases – which did not represent particularly high real terms increases going forward compared to the past – probably contributed to the setting of (too) high expectations that voters had of improvements in public service.

Leaking and spinning

Government ministers and their senior officials have access to data up to three days prior to its release. They say they need this pre-release access in order to be while briefed when the data are released so that they can respond to any questions they might be asked. Unfortunately some ministers and officials occasionally find the temptation to leak the data – usually in a very subtle form – irresistible. The Statistics Commission's 2004 annual report listed a number of instances during the previous year when the data had been leaked and expressed its dissatisfaction with the practice. Both the commission and the National Statistician would like to see an end to pre-release access but they are powerless to bring this about unless ministers agree.

Try not to move targets

In the late 1990s the government set hundreds of targets will variety of public services. Although some of these targets have been met, many have been dropped and some redefined. Where some form of redefinition has taken place, this can either be a rewording or recalibration of the target itself or a change to the data that is going to be used to measure against the original unchanged target. The government set a target for a sharp reduction in childhood poverty. Originally the definition of childhood poverty that was chosen was the number of children living in households where the income was less than 60% of the median. Initially including, and then excluding, housing costs as it would be an easier target to hit in a period of rising house prices.

Ensure proper funding

When government wants to move rapidly it can. Regarding animals used in scientific tests, most people would like to know either how many animals die in the testing process or what their suffering is. The current data - and only available data - show instead the number of animals in the latest year which have been used for animal experiments for the first time. A review was announced in 2003 and yet by the end of 2004 there was still no response. If there was a real desire within government to have proper data surely the recommendations would have been produced more quickly. In contrast, where government decides it does want to move quickly it does so regardless of the pressures is government statisticians find themselves under. Examples from the last couple of years would include the Treasury-led Allsopp Review, on the statistical needs associated with regional policy, and the Atkinson Review, on measuring productivity in the public sector. Both these reviews were carried out very swiftly and the many and complex recommendations are being funded by the Treasury.

Get the right data

Many questions that we would like answered remain unanswered because the right data do not exist. There are no regular surveys, for example, of the number of illegal immigrants in the country, the scale of the black economy or most other illegal activities. If there is no data, there will be less substance to any debate on the associated issue. Revisions and errors need to be minimised.

The problem of data from administrative systems

Most data come from surveys conducted by the government but in an increasing number of areas figures are being produced as a by-product of administrative systems. Statisticians ought to tell us when such figures are being distorted by changes in administration.

The government is very keen to remind us at every opportunity that the New Deal for young people has effectively eradicated long-term youth unemployment. But armed with a clearer understanding of what the New Deal actually requires of the young people and how long-term unemployment is defined, the value of these figures is thrown into doubt. Participation in the New Deal is compulsory for all young people under 25 years of age once they have been in unemployment for six months. They are then required to engage in one of the New Deal options such as training or workplace experience for a period of some weeks. At the end of the training period, a number of the young people will find work, while those that do not will return to claiming unemployment benefit, i.e. jobseeker's allowance. Those returning to benefit will count as newly unemployed even if immediately prior to that short period of training they had been unemployed for a period of six months. The terms and conditions of the New Deal have been skillfully crafted in such a way that the scheme has effectively made it impossible for a person under 25 to be long-term unemployed - as long-term unemployment is defined as being unemployed for over six months. The few thousand people currently in the statistics as long-term youth unemployed are either a small minority who have slipped through the net or will be people in the seventh or eighth month of unemployment awaiting the start of their New Deal option. This is not to say, of course, that there are no young people who are effectively permanently unemployed. It is just that their long term of unemployment is punctuated by placements on New Deal options (or off benefit for another reason). But so far as the record book shows, the Labour government has done away with the problem of long-term youth unemployment.

The act of counting makes things worse

There are many cases of the statistics starting to show the rising trend there has been panic about something rather than before it. Classic examples might be the reporting to police of racially inspired attacks (for example, the number of racist attacks reported to the Metropolitan Police increased fivefold in the year after the death of Stephen Lawrence) and the number of sex attacks on children (when more are reported after a wave of publicity). Again our statisticians ought to warn of these problems.

Keep data changes to a minimum

It is inevitable that definitions will change over time. Generally such changes are for the better as new, improved sources of information become available they will make the estimates of variables more accurate. But these changes are not always advertised in advance, thoroughly signalled when they occur or properly explained at the time. Sometimes there is a hint of political involvement driving the change.

In the summer of 2004, after much political and public comment that the large injections of spending into the health service did not seem to be delivering extra outputs, the Office for National Statistics published largely out of the blue new figures for health service productivity. These had the effect of doubling the rise in health sector output over the previous six years. It seemed strange to many observers that there was so little forewarning about such a large change when normally much smaller changes are thoroughly publicised. Also in 2004, the ONS changed the methodology used to calculate the monthly inflation figures. They introduced the use of so-called "hedonics" to better measure quality change in some areas of the RPI. This had the happy consequence of reducing the inflation rate thereby saving the Treasury millions of pounds a year in payments (for index-linked benefits and savings products) and taxes (by up rating allowances by less).

All of these issues which make our lives with statistics harder than they should be are compounded by some other unfortunate "facts of life" that statisticians should rally against. For example, data for the right geography (United Kingdom, Great Britain, England and Wales together and sometimes for England on its own) is not always available. And often data is almost impossible to find! Different government departments have different ways of presenting data. Some are free, others are not. Some are only in books, others are in databases. Most are on line but many are not. Some have customer service people to help while others positively discourage contact with users.

Conclusion

It is unclear how much of the problem is due to conspiracy and how much to cock-up. We will probably never know. But our politicians and government statisticians have some way to go if they are to be trusted and inspiring useful public servants.

The idea that counting things could abolish politics altogether and usher in a reign of facts wasn't true when pioneering statisticians thought it two centuries ago, and it isn't true now, but I am convinced that the quality of today's political debate in parliament and the media would be higher – and the policies followed better – if we had stronger factual foundations. Britain does not even have a key indicators report as found in many other countries. It is a sensible target for the country to have robust, accessible, trusted and reliable figures on the key issues of the day within a decade.

Annex - "Things can only get better" - a case study in data manipulation

This song was the theme tune for the Labour Party in the 1997 general election. A kind interpretation of this choice of music would be that it simply reflected the Labour Party's enthusiasm to do a good job. From a statistical point of view, however, the definition of "a good job" led to the presentation of an Orwellian database showing that the government had been successful in improving all aspects of the lives of everyone in Britain everywhere, all of the time.

The evidence is drawn directly from the statistics on "What Labour's done in your constituency" made available on the Labour party web site. (At the time of the 2001 election, the web site was www.labourparty.org. It is now www.labour.org.uk and the data can be found by clicking on "making life better" and then "in your area".) In essence, the methods that Labour adopted meant that a picture of general, but modest and variable, social improvement was transformed into a picture of universal improvement. The web site contains thousands upon thousands of apparently relevant performance indicators, every one of which the party can claim illustrates the success of its policies. In fact the database is the result of a certain amount of sleight of hand designed to provide a somewhat distorted picture of the local geography of Britain. (Source: "A good place to bury bad news? Hiding the detail in the geography on the Labour party's web site", Political quarterly 73, 2002)

In the months leading up to the 2001 general election the Labour Party's web site included certain statistical indicators for each of the 641 Parliamentary constituencies in England, Wales and Scotland. The constituency profiles were designed to indicate how conditions have improved in each local area after four years of Labour. If they had not improved, then the data being shown was changed, to make them improve. The profiles of each constituency were arranged in several categories - for example, economic stability, families and children, pensioners, schools standards, crying and rebuilding the NHS - and each category contained a number of indicators, up to 28 in total. For example, under the crime category, data included the increase in police force numbers and the percentage fall in crime since 1997.

It is extremely unlikely that the many thousands of indicators improved for all constituencies. However, the Labour Party reported the figures in such a way as to make it appear that they did. For example, if an indicator had not improved for one timescale than the timescale was changed for that constituency to one in which conditions had improved. Indicators are also reported on different spatial scales - if conditions had not improved at the constituency level, for example, then a larger scale - such as the region - was deployed at which things has improved.

In the case of crime figures, for example, one third of constituencies had indicators given in terms of averages for the whole of England and Wales, not by police force area, if those constituencies were in areas where crime had increased. Crime fell in England and Wales overall, but in only two thirds of police force areas. Thus, on this web site, crime had fallen under Labour everywhere and police numbers had similarly risen everywhere, even though to show this both the spatial and temporal scale had to be altered to ensure universal improvement.

Additional reading:

2004 Budget, www.hm-treasury.gov.uk/budget

2004 Spending review, www.hm-treasury.gov.uk/spending_review along with the PSA White Paper published at the same time

"Measuring government performance", Conference proceedings, Statistics Users' Council, November 2003

Source: "Performance monitoring in the public services", Journal of the Royal Statistical Society, A-167, 2004

www.hm-treasury.gov.uk/performancedocs

www.hm-treasury.gov.uk/performance

"Choosing the right FABRIC", a framework for performance information, www.hm-treasury.gov.uk/fabric, March 2001

"Targets in the public sector", Audit Commission, September 2003

"Performance indicators: good, bad, and ugly", RSS, 2003

"Public services for the future: modernisation, reform, accountability", Cm 4181, 1998

"On target? Government by measurement", fifth report, July 2003, HC 62-1, www.parliament.uk

National Audit Office, "Inpatient and outpatient waiting in the NHS", HC 221 and HC 452, 2001

Statistics Commission memorandum to the PAC, 2003

"Performance indicators in UK higher education", Journal of the Royal Statistical Society, A-167, 2004

The Growing Demand for Statistics: Challenges and Opportunities

Pilar Martín-Guzmán

Vice President, International Statistical Institute

Abstract

The last years have witnessed a dramatic increase in the demand for statistical information. This fact is putting the institutions responsible for the production of official statistics –mainly national statistical systems and international organisations- under great pressure. For one thing they have been obliged to increase the amount and quality of their production. For another they also have had to modify methodologies and to establish new systems of definitions and classifications.

The challenges arising from these new demands have been faced by the official statisticians with the scarcity of human and budgetary resources in which the statistical world usually works. Being aware that challenge is also an opportunity, official statisticians are managing to cope with them quite successfully -at least in the developed countries- and making the most of these opportunities: filling the continuous gaps created by the quick social and economic changes, adapting methodologies and definitions to these changes, improving the quality of the information provided and finding more efficient and friendly ways to disseminate this information. As a result, the development of official statistics that has taken place during these last years has been outstanding, to the point that it has been described by some qualified stakeholders as the "silent revolution" of statistics (Domingo Solans, ECB, 2003).

A number of reasons account for this increase in the demands for statistics. To start with, new segments of users have appeared on the stage as a result of political or social changes. But also the traditional groups of users are growing in number and diversity, and extending their activities to new fields, covering new interests and demanding more attention. Globalisation and the ICT revolution are also a source of challenges when it comes to providing the accurate description of the world that can be expected from a reliable statistical system. And, last but not least, users of statistics are now more exacting on quality issues that they had ever been.

Official statisticians are now everywhere involved in a major effort to satisfy all these demands. But there is something to keep in mind to this effect: satisfaction is primarily a perception of the user. A user will be satisfied when the statistical information provided fulfils his/her expectations. The new user-oriented policy adopted by the more developed statistical offices has to take this into account. This implies, for one thing, to get to know these expectations, but also to make sure that expectations are within reason, in the sense that the users have a good understanding not only on the correct use of statistics, but also on its possibilities and limitations as well. Training the users in developing the correct expectations, which ultimately means increasing the statistical literacy of the different segments of them is now an essential task in which the cooperation of all professional statisticians, producers of data, researchers or academics is needed.

This paper intends to comment on some of these new challenges, and to point up to some policies and instruments that could help coping with them.

The traditional segments of users

Statistical information is an essential tool for the healthy development of a democratic society. No real democracy can exist without a system of reliable, independent statistics that guarantee the correct development of institutions, encourage political debate and provide a basis for rational decision making (Malaguerra, 2004).

In long established democracies statistics are demanded on a regular basis by several segments of users. Among them, international organisations, policy makers, financial markets and enterprise leaders, researchers and the public at large are the most relevant.

Completely different has been the situation in non-democratic countries with centrally planned economies, where only the two first groups made a significant use of the statistical information, to the point that most of this information was very often considered as confidential, and not subject to dissemination to the society at large. (Korolev and Ivanov, 2003). For the so-called transition countries most of the present users of statistics are really newcomers. Providing these new customers with information that could be roughly comparable, both in quantity and quality, with what can be usually obtained in democratic countries has been a major challenge for their national statistical systems.

Then there is a third group of countries that, although they were never subject to a centrally planned economy, enjoy a comparatively short record of democratic performance. Most of these countries are now in the process of consolidating their initially weak, labile democracies, by creating organisations and institutions meant to reinforce the democratic culture and organisation, and these institutions are still very often in a learning-by-doing process, trying to identify which is the role that they are expected to play in the democratic game.

International organisations are not producers, but users of statistics, that they compile and disseminate. Although they are great supporters of the producers, they are also very exacting in their demands that have increased considerably during the last years, both in quantity and in quality. A paradigmatic case is the IMF: reaching the standards set by this organisation has been a major challenge for many countries, but also a unique opportunity to improve their dissemination practices.

Also policy makers need more and more information, as they tend to make an increasing use of statistics in their decision processes. In long established democracies there are also a number of bodies that play an important role in the democratic game: members of parliament at large, opposition parties, trade unions, the different associations -of employers, consumers, and the many others related to professional or social activities- in which civil society usually clusters, social and economic councils and several other commissions meant to guarantee a balanced distribution of powers. All of these organisations are regular users of the statistical information, which they need in order to carry out studies and get to conclusions that will lead them to support, influence, criticise or oppose the government policies. In the new democracies many of these bodies do not exist yet, or have been recently created. As soon as they start working, they usually become an additional source of pressure on the national statistical system of the country with their new demands.

Researchers are an important segment of users. As any phenomena can be a subject for research, and as the number of researchers increases everywhere, the demands of this group are potentially unlimited. This certainly is a permanent challenge for official statisticians. Also, the last years have witnessed a growing trend in the use of statistics by researchers in a number of new fields, such as history, geography or law, who might not be endowed with the high level of numeracy that can be expected from the statisticians. For the producers of statistics it is a must to devise dissemination systems that direct them towards a correct use of the data and help them understand the possibilities and limitations of the statistical techniques.

The public at large receives statistical information through the media. Citizens are generally interested in the main indicators of the economic and social trends measuring the effectiveness of policies. And households tend to increasingly concentrate on the optimisation of their resources as their wealth grows, so developing a new interest in the framework described by the current economic indicators. The impact of changes in tax or social benefit measures on the income and wealth of households and on their consumption patterns, their portfolio shifts as a result of variations in interest rates or their investment in housing are important economic issues that have to be accurately described with statistical figures.

Some newcomers

In the recent years a number of political changes have taken place that have introduced some newcomers in the circle of users of statistics. The transition of non-democratic centrally planned economies to democratic, market economy countries is undoubtedly the most important of these changes, and has already been mentioned. Still, there are several more, of which two certainly deserve a comment.

One of them, concerning for the time being only the European space, is the start of a common monetary policy strategy for the Euro countries, and the foundation of a European Central Bank in charge of implementing this strategy. The ECB enters the statistical stage as a user, as well as a producer. The demands of this newcomer have widely surpassed the requirements of the ongoing harmonisation process among the statistics of the E.U. countries that Eurostat has been undertaking for so many years. Now new indicators for the Euro area as a whole are necessary.

The Harmonised Consumer Price Index is an example of a new demand that has already been fulfilled. But several more have already been explicitly formulated, among which the Quarterly Financial and non Financial Euro area Accounts by economic sectors and the Principal European Economic Indicators –within the framework of the first-for Europe principle-, aiming to meet in some cases the standards of timeliness adopted in the United States (Domingo Solans, 2003). The production of these statistics will mean a significant challenge for most of the countries involved, but a huge improvement in the short term economic information, from which the financial markets and business leaders will also greatly benefit.

As other common policies for the Euro area will presumably be implemented in the near future, referring to issues like the tax system or the social security benefits, it can be foreseen that new European institutions will soon join the group of users of statistics, bringing new demands and challenges. Also, how rapidly other supranational organisations like Mercosur, or Nafta, will follow on this path, adopting common policies and, consequently, demanding new supranational indicators, remains to be seen.

A second segment of newcomers, also significant in many countries, is the one formed by the new regional and local policy-makers. The spread of a democratic culture, together with a trend to devolve powers to local entities with the intent to apply the subsidiary principle to the benefit of citizens has given ground to the development of administrative units at regional and local level with considerable powers for decision making. These new customers will naturally demand specific information for the geographical units on which they have to take their decisions.

This is a most challenging issue for official statisticians, particularly in the countries in which administrative registers do not satisfy the basic requirements that would allow to extract from them reliable information. Fortunately, this problem is being dealt with the very valuable support of researchers in theoretical statistics. As a result of this co-operation, new methods on small area estimation are now in a very advanced stage, and basically ready for application. Still, there are also limitations in the use of these methodologies that policy makers should be aware of. As is sometimes the case with the newly created social bodies in new or consolidating democracies, the members of these local governments are learning from experience their new assigned roles, and may not be as experienced in the use of statistics as the civil servants in central governments. Improving their level of statistical literacy is an important task to be mainly undertaken by the official statisticians, but in which co-operation from other branches of the statistical group –researchers, academics, teachers- is most welcome.

A new scenario: globalisation and the ICT revolution

Globalisation pervades practically all aspects of human activity, and accounts for a number of dramatic changes covering a wide spectrum, from the increasingly multinational organisation of many productive branches to substantial modifications in the everyday life patterns of the population. All of these changes have to be accurately described with figures, which implies a permanent challenge for the producers of statistics.

It is also a mark of our time that these changes take place at a much quicker pace than they did in the past. So it very often happens that when a new system of definitions and classifications able to describe a new scenario has been agreed upon and is ready for use, this scenario has already been left behind as the result of subsequent changes, and the classification system becomes obsolete even before it has been adopted. The world-wide harmonisation process that usually takes place before one of these changes is introduced, and which is highly advisable from many points of view, can eventually be a hindrance for the most advanced countries in this particular issue.

A complete description of the changes induced by globalisation and affecting the statistical production would be impossible. But some of the most important ones deserve to be mentioned.

The massive migration inflows now taking place in most developed countries are an important challenge for statisticians, and this for several reasons. To start with, when these inflows are significant it is not easy to keep population registers with a high level of accuracy, which means that the figures and trends finally produced might not be a good picture of the real demographic situation of the country. On the other hand, new immigrants, particularly if they are illegal, tend to be extremely reluctant to co-operate with the interviewers, both in population censuses and in surveys, so aggravating in many countries the already significant problem of non-response. Also, these new immigrants are very often involved in non-registered activities, so that these activities increase quickly in a country as soon as an immigration wave arrives. When this is the case, the traditional methods of collecting information usually produce a blurred view of the economic performance of the country, and indicators of activity, employment and productivity become less and less reliable.

Another fact associated with globalisation is the gradual but steady increase in the internalisation of the markets for goods, services and capitals. As this process advances, it becomes more and more difficult for the enterprises to collect and provide information at national level, as that means in many cases producing figures that would result from distributing among the countries, on the basis of ad-hoc criteria, the global figures, that are the ones that the enterprise accurately knows. Whether the GDP calculated with these estimated national figures still remains a good picture of the economy of the country is something open to research.

A third point, also connected with globalisation, is the growing demand for statistical information about countries that would seem remote some years ago, but are now a subject of interest from several points of view. In many of these countries statistical systems are weak, and information scarce and of low quality.

Although most of the transition countries are doing very well on this point, there are still some in which the end of the totalitarian regime was followed by a collapse of the register system from which information was obtained in the former times, and are now in the process of painfully reconstructing their statistical information from scratch.

As concerns the so-called developing countries, most of them suffer from a lack of administrative infrastructure and an endemic scarcity of material and human resources, with the result that the improvement of their statistics is following a slow and somehow hazardous pace, and the gap between the statistical production of the developed and the developing countries is increasing. This is an issue of major concern for international organisations, as they are aware that globalisation is for developing countries a two-folded weapon: it helps in the provision of funds and the support for capacity building, but at the same time it facilitates an increasing flow of qualified migration towards the richer countries, so reducing the human resources available, and rendering more difficult the improvement of their statistics

And then there is the ICT revolution to consider. With the information society new organisational forms have developed everywhere, inducing a change in every field of human activity: organisation of work, activity planning, relation with administration bodies, commerce, education, culture and entertainment.

Identifying the statistics that would accurately reflect these changes is already a hard task, for which narrow co-operation between official statisticians and experts in the different fields is proving essential. But this will solve the problem only to a certain points. As has been pointed out (Jeskanen-Sundström, 2003) it is not only that new statistics have to be implemented, but also, that many of the macro-economic statistics that are being collected now are loosing their relevance as a result of these changes. That gives rise to the additional task of reviewing all the traditional concepts, definitions and methodologies to see how they perform in the new scenario.

Quality as perceived by the user

Users of statistics are becoming increasingly exacting about quality issues. This is a matter of concern for official statisticians, as the credibility of the statistical system depends basically on a positive image of quality among the users, that in turn will develop the so-called "virtuous circle" of statistics: the informant will be more ready to co-operate with an institution that enjoys a high reputation, which will finally result in better statistics.

Presently, both producers and users are interested in quality issues. But what the producers understand as good quality does not necessarily coincide with the appreciation of the users. As it has been stated (Platek and Sarndäl, 2001) everybody agrees on the quality of a Rolls-Royce because every driver knows what kind of services to expect from a good car. But for many users it is not clear what can be expected from a good statistic.

A high correlation between the quality appraisal of the producers and that of the users could reasonably be expected. But this is not necessarily the case. Actually, it seems that this correlation varies considerably from one country to another, and this can be accounted for by two facts.

First of all, as the perception of the users depends to a great extent on their expectations; and their level of statistical literacy plays an essential role. And then the statistical literacy of some segments of users differs greatly among countries.

The second fact to consider is that one of the main aspects of quality, just the one to which producers pay the highest attention, the accuracy of the data, can hardly be appreciated by the users, as they are not usually in a position to replicate a survey, or to actually check the information in the registers. This is a point in which the users simply have to trust the producer, and that emphasises how important it is for statistical agencies to keep an image of quality.

Several definitions of quality have been provided, among which the better known are those used by Statistics Canada and Eurostat. Actually, they come to identify basically the same elements: relevance, coherence, timeliness, interpretability, accessibility and accuracy (Brackstone, 1999, Trewin, 2002).

For policy makers and the financial markets timeliness is usually the strongest demand. But there is normally a pay-off between timeliness and accuracy, and the producers tend to keep on the safe side by guaranteeing a high level of accuracy at the cost of a delay in the dissemination of the product. They are usually the more conservative in the countries where the level of statistical literacy of the population at large, and of the media in particular, is comparatively low, for they know that it is in these countries where significant revisions of the data can really put into jeopardy the credibility of the office.

Benchmarking on timeliness issues is one of the greatest challenges that these countries have to face in this communication era, as frequently users cannot understand that different NSO should follow their path towards improvement at different speed, depending of the resources available and of the statistical literacy of the population to which they serve. Also, competition with private enterprises that specialize in producing very quick statistical results and which are not that much concerned about quality and credibility issues is another significant source of pressure for national and supranational statistical systems.

This trade-off between accuracy and reliability has been a usual subject for debate. An interesting point of view has been expressed by Sir Claus Moser (Moser, 2003), who thinks that in this framework of desirable dominance of the user timeliness should have the preference, for what is important about accuracy is not so much increasing it as measuring it. So, he believes that timeliness could be improved at the cost of some accuracy on condition that it will be possible to attach reliable error margins to the data for all major public figures.

Researchers are a very different type of users. In general they are not particularly pressed, and coherence and accessibility are for them more important than timeliness. They put special emphasis on the quality of data, consistency of time series, links between data when methodological changes are implemented and accessibility of microdata. This last issue can be a problematic one, to the extent to which it can collide with the very sensitive issue of confidentiality. Once again, national cultures are very different in this point, so that it is difficult to devise common policies at international level. Each national statistical system has to find the right balance that both the users and the informants of that particular country are ready to accept.

Also the demands for quality and consistency of the series can be a source of challenges. Full aware that they have no means to replicate the surveys, the researchers are increasingly pressing official statisticians to produce technical assessments on the level of quality of each of their products. On the other hand, researchers very often feel unhappy when changes of definitions and methodologies take place breaking the consistency of the series, and request timely links. As a result, the statistical systems are faced with the problem of finding a good balance between consistency and innovation.

But the group of researchers using statistics is extending to new fields, some of which do not include a strong training in statistics in their university curricula. This is a high risk for the producers of statistics. The publication and eventual dissemination in the media, of wrong, illogical results obtained through an incorrect use of official data are not rare in some countries. This is something that should be avoided at all costs, as it will badly damage the image of statistics. The NSO´s have to implement a really good metadata system, which would help to turn information into the correct kind of knowledge. And they also should be very careful about giving out the microdata files, which should always be accompanied by some elementary operating instructions, a sort of manual for the users.

Finally, there are two segments of users that require particular attention. One of them consists on the members of all these new regional and local governments, or of these new democratic institutions and forces within the civil society that have been mentioned before. As newcomers to their roles, they sometimes lack the background and practice in dealing with statistics that can be assumed in top level government officials. When this is the case, they have to get some information about the essentials of statistical techniques, and be trained to understand the possibilities and limitations of the different sources of statistical data. In order to cope with this additional challenge, many NSO have created, in co-operation with researchers and academics, a school of statistics for public administrators, in which not only these new users, but also civil servants and clerks in charge of running the administrative registers from which statistical information is extracted, are trained and updated in basic and new methodologies.

The second segment to consider here are the media. Their level of statistical literacy varies greatly among countries. But also, it can be very diverse within the same country, as local newspapers and radio stations -and even television stations- tend to proliferate now in the most remote provinces. And, as they are the link between the producers of statistics and the users at large, the credibility of the statistical system is mainly in their hands.

Organising specific courses for the media is a regular practice nowadays in most countries, particularly when a new statistic is started, or a new methodology implemented. Also, the NSO's have to allocate resources and concentrate efforts in having a good press office, friendly, open to consultation and capable of producing press releases that are accurate, but also easy to understand by the public at large. This facilitates the work of the journalists while preventing at the same time misinterpretations of the data appearing in the media.

Also, co-operation of all the highly literate statisticians, including those not necessary involved in production, such as academics, researchers or teachers, by opening debates in the press whenever statistical data have been misinterpreted and the resulting information published, would be most welcome. This is unfortunately a rather unusual practice in most countries, and should be encouraged. Creating bridges between the different groups of professional statisticians, as well as including some knowledge on official statistics in the university curricula would certainly help in this point.

Conclusions

We are going through a time in which the number of policy makers is growing as a result of democratic processes being developed through more complex networks, new supranational, regional and local structures are created, statistical information is increasingly becoming a major instrument in new fields of research and globalisation and the ICT technologies are dramatically changing the scenario in which social and economic development takes place. As a result, the demand for statistics grows at a quicker pace than ever.

The producers of statistics have to cope with the challenge of satisfying this demand within the framework of a user-oriented approach.

Much has been done in the line of providing new statistics, and also, in improving their quality; and this result is clearly assessed and praised by the most qualified stakeholders. Still, the perception of satisfaction of the users at large, of those who shape the public opinion on quality depends, to a great extent, on the expectations of these users, and this is very much related to their level of statistical education and their numeracy. As not only the number of users, but also their diversity, extends, it is necessary to make an effort to improve the statistical literacy of the several segments of them. And this responsibility is not restricted to the official statisticians: it should be made extensive to all statisticians. Researchers, academics and teachers can play an essential role in imparting their students a solid knowledge of official statistics, and co-operation of the governments is also necessary, as they should provide universities and secondary schools with the means and the impulse to promote the study of statistics at large –basic concepts and methodologies as well as official statistics- and to include it in their curricula.

References

Brackstone, G. (1999) *Managing Data Quality in a Statistical Agency*, Survey Methodology, vol 25

Domingo Solans, E, ECB (2003) *Official Statistics for a Global Economy*, Invited presentation at the 54th session of the International Statistical Institute, Berlin, Germany

Korolev, M. and Ivanov, Y (2003) The Development and Achievements of the Conference up to the 1990's: the Point of View of Countries of Eastern Europe, 50 Years of the Conference of European Statisticians, U.N. publication

Jeskanen-Sundström, H. (2003) ICT Statistics at the New Millennium –Developing Official Statistics-Measuring the Diffusion of ICT and its Impact, International Statistical Review, Vol 71,1

Malaguerra C. (2004) *Official Statistics, Globalisation and World Democracy, A Challenge?,* The 2004 ISI Special Conference, on The Vital Role of Statistical Science in Assuring National Prosperity, Daewon, Korea

Moser, C. (2003) *The Conference of European Statisticians: Past, Present, Future*, Keynote Address in 50 Years of the Conference of European Statisticians, U.N. publication

Platek, R. and Särndal (2001) *Can a Statistician Deliver?,* Journal of Official Statistics, Vol 17, nº 1.

Trewin, D. ((2002) *The Importance of a Quality Culture*, Survey Methodology, vol 28

New Software Brings Statistics Beyond the Eye

Hans Rosling, Division of International Health, Karolinska Institute, Sweden.

Anna Rosling Rönnlund and *Ola Rosling*, Gapminder, Sweden

Abstract

Swedish medical students were found to know less than the Chimpanzee about World Health. When ranking countries according to child mortality they scored below random. The reason was that they have preconceived ideas about the State of the World that correspond to the situation as it was 30 years ago. These students never had access to updated development statistic in a visual format that could challenge their preconceived ideas. Starting from users need we therefore developed software for interactive animated visualization of development statistics.

The aim is to enable broad target groups of computer users to acquire an evidence based world view using MDG and other basic socio-economic indicators for all countries. The representation of time by movement in scattergrams with carefully designed interfaces has proven to bring statistics beyond the eye to hit the brain. Using latest versions of program compilators for visual format (FlashMX2004) we will provide the software in free modules. These can be used for interactive visualization of large databases on websites with *aha-effects* and for making thematic animated presentations with considerable *wow-effects*. Free prototypes are available www.gapminder.org, and in collaboration with UN Statistics Division we are developing more advanced formats for visualization of databases directly on websites. The ultimate aim is to contribute to Internet search mechanisms for digital time series in standardized format. As have happened with other forms of digital information a standard format for powerful visualization may drive the process of standardized XML format for time series.

Background

When teaching global health and socio-economic development to Swedish university students we found they lacked even the most basic evidence-based understanding of the State of the World. Their perceptions about the life expectancy, fertility rate, literacy rate and other basic development indicators for countries reflected the situation in the world more than one generation ago. This is so in spite of the availability of data with relatively good quality for these variables for most countries of the world.

Updated international statistics are annually published in yearbooks by UN organizations. UN Statistics Division and the Development Data Group of the World Bank provide the most comprehensive datasets with time series on the Internet, but these are only accessible against a fee. Specialized UN organizations and regional as well as national statistical agencies also provide time series statistics in various interactive visual formats on the Internet; some free and some against fee.

In spite of the existence of available data of relatively good quality we found that Swedish students, even those that graduated from secondary school with the highest grades, were unaware of the considerable decrease in child mortality that has occurred in the last generation in most countries in Asia, Middle East and South America. When asked to rank pairs of countries by child mortality they surprisingly scored statistically significantly worse than random, i.e. they would have answered better if they had guessed. We thus found that the Swedish medical students start University knowing less than the Chimpanzees about World Health. This is paradoxical as the data is available in digital format on the Internet and that the students we tested were very interested to learn about world development. Yet one of the most important indicators of development statistics, child mortality, has not reached the brains of a Swedish generation that grew up with full access to computers and the Internet. This finding was the starting point for the software development by the non-profit company Gapminder. The free software enables inter-active animation of development statistics in enjoyable and understandable graphic interfaces. The aim is to improve the use and understanding of development statistics.

The aim of this paper is to review the prototypes developed and the future plans. Gapminder is owned by the Karolinska Institute together with the authors. Six software developers presently work at Gapminder in Malmö, Sweden. Gapminder's software is developed in Flash modules in collaboration with Swedish universities, and UN organizations, especially the UN Statistics Division. The plans are to provide the modules as free software for public institutions to be used both for visualizations of databases on the Internet and for production of thematic presentations (Figure 1). We make use of the amazingly fast development of program compilators of animated graphic (www.macromedia.com). This now enables cost-effective animation of statistics in ways that were impossible only a few years ago. However, the challenge is to create animated graphics that not only reach and please the eyes, but that also transform statistics into understanding, i.e. goes beyond the eye to hit the brain.

Figure 1. How Gapminder's software may facilitate the path from data repository to the understanding in the brain of the TV viewer.

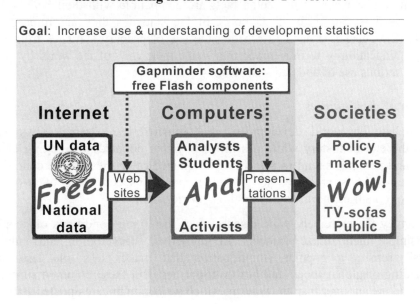

Statistics for an evidence based world

United Nations Millennium Development Goals (MDGs) are set to base monitoring of world development on sound statistics. The MDG´s highlight the need for evidence based policy and decision-making at both national and international level. This requires more and better provision, use and understanding of development statistics. The MDG process reveals the urge for more resources for the statistical system; from the primary data collection in the household, through several levels of compilation, to data documentation, repository management and communication by statistical agencies at local, national and international level.

The financing of national and international statistical systems and provision of statistics has gone through policy changes in widely opposite directions in the last decades. The policy switched from free provision to sale of statistical information as a commercial good, and thereafter in several countries back to provision of statistics as free public goods. In parallel to these policy changes the IT & Internet revolutions have profoundly changed the context for statistical services. The contemporary challenge is to apply policies for public statistics that make optimal use of the fast advance of Information Technology.

In this context we wonder why Sweden's educational system fails to provide an evidence-based worldview by use of international development statistics. In addition to the fact that teaching often reflects the State of the World one generation ago when teachers were young, we find two special factors that may explain why preconceived ideas about the world totally dominate over the evidence-based worldview that is easily obtained from development statistics.

Rhetoric selection

The media and advocacy organizations select the global development statistics for the public with precise purposes. Most of the global development statistics that reach the public in OECD countries is incorporated in rhetoric campaigns, where feelings and facts are merged in reach for the audience's empathy and wallets. For political purposes the selections may be even more selective. The audiences often react to development statistics in similar ways. If presented facts are compatible with their beliefs, they will trust the statistics, but if the facts don't fit the statistics they are refused as being unreliable (2). There is a need to broaden the use of primary statistics from providing agencies in education to form a public that shape their view of the world by continuous critical but serious use of updated statistics.

Attraction of dichotomies

The debate on world development is dominated by extreme views. Optimists proclaim the end of history while pessimists say that doomsday is getting close. Both optimists and pessimists tend to present dichotomized categories for the countries of the world. The world is presented to the wider public as consisting of two simplistic categories of countries; north/south, we/them, or rich/poor.

To convey the extremely wide disparities of the living conditions of people in the World, simple dichotomized models are attractive. "Developing and industrialized countries", remain a popular simplification that makes less and less sense for understanding of global social and health disparities. But these common simplifications of the World are stronger than the ways in which we communicate updated statistics from each country. Based on life expectancy most of the world population today lives in countries with intermediate values of this basic indicator. There is a need provide comprehensive views of data from all countries.

Development statistics in graphic interfaces

Development statistics can be purchased from homepages of public agencies as PDF-publications, and occasionally as downloadable digital datasets to be used for modern data mining. Some agencies provide all data freely; others only provide a minor selection of the data for free. It is a fact that available statistics are used by relatively few, both in relation to the growing amount and quality of statistical data and to the explosive use of the Internet. Is this because the interest for world development is limited? Is it because data access is too costly and cumbersome? Is it because the format and interfaces in which statistics is provided makes it difficult to use and understand?

We think that improved graphic interfaces for animated presentation of statistics can greatly increase the demand and use of statistics. It is interesting to compare to meteorology that has gained a central place in the TV media by the graphic presentations used for weather forecast. Will better graphic user interfaces and animations be a driving force for increased flow of statistics from under-utilised databases to the public in the TV sofa? The full force of the IT revolution has not yet been used for improving the understanding of development statistics. Will the new interfaces be more successfully developed from the user-end rather than from the provider-end of the flow of statistics?

"For information to become knowledge it must be assessed, interpreted, and put into a context. We believe that the ability to interpret statistics is under valued in current educational curricula" (1)

Data in spreadsheets are meaningless to most people. Most statistics are communicated as if musicians stand in front of the audience showing the sheet music instead of playing. We believe the number of users of international development data could multiply by millions if the data was distributed freely on the Internet in interactive and enjoyable graphic interfaces. A much bigger and less skilled audience could thereby understand more complex images of the world.

"For those who grew up in a world dominated by the technologies of print, writing and reading constituted literacy. As the technologies of communication and information change, the requirements for literacy also change." (6)

Visualization in moving graphics is an intuitive method for understanding relationships and it is an excellent way to exhibiting patterns. Our objective is to turn the already existing development statistics into meaningful knowledge by displaying the time series as easily understandable moving graphics. We have had surprising success when displaying development statistics in moving graphic interfaces in lectures. However, even after trying hard, we conclude that it is not a simple task to get the middle-aged computer users to explore data themselves in modern graphic user interfaces. This is simply because most of them are not yet sufficiently computer literate for graphic interfaces. They just do not feel comfortable to click in the graphic interfaces. To see animations they expect the computer to do the job, as when watching a video. In front of the non-linear inter-active interfaces in our software many middle-aged users wait for something to happen.

In sharp contrast, young audiences are highly computer literate mainly because they have played computer games. This is true in OECD countries and elsewhere in the world. This literacy provides a unique new opportunity to provide statistics directly as moving inter-active animated graphics, rather then as numbers and static graphs. We can change how the young generation understands the state of the world if we provide IT-tools that give them a more complex and relevant moving images of world development in the form of animated statistics. We think the main challenge is to find teachers and providers of statistics to bringing such tools into the hands of young students in the young generation of Internet users. We are far from sure that our attempts to develop software for animated interactive displays of statistics will be successful. But we are convinced beyond all doubt that new software will come that will convert the way we use and understand development statistics! We are also convinced that this new digital technology will change the way collection and provision of development statistics are financed.

New and free software

It started in 1998 from an idea to enhance the understanding of world health. We developed the World Health Chart 2001 prototype with WHO and Dollar Street prototype with Save the Children Fund. Gapminder thereafter developed the free software Trendalyzer that turns boring time series of development statistics into attractive moving graphics. The software imports data from excel and shows moving graphics on the screen, as exported Flash files or as images in PowerPoint. The prototype of Trendalyzer is provided as World Development Chart 2003 with data sets from the UN Statistics Division.

Beneath follow short descriptions of some of Gapminder's pilot projects. The text and image format cannot give a fair picture of the interactive interfaces. We recommend the reader to download prototypes from www.gapminder.org.

World Health Chart 2001

The "World Health Chart 2001" displays 50 to 100 years of health development for all the countries in the world. WHO provided time series for the 35 included indicators. World Health Chart is developed in collaboration with World Health Organization (WHO), and the two Swedish universities Karolinska Institute and Lund University; and Sida (Swedish International Development Cooperation Agency) funded it. Time is shown as movement of the bubble-shaped country icons. The size is population and the color is the continent. The historical development paths for the countries are animated by smooth tweening. The user can change any setting at any time and get an animated change to the new position. Use the control panel, rewind and play to see the historical development.

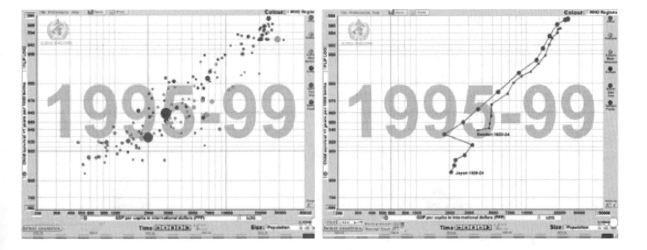

Figure 2: World Health Chart. Default image is displayed automatically. X-axis: GDP per Capita, Y-axis: Child Survival up to 1 year per 1000 live births. Each bubble is a country. Size: population, Color: WHO-region. Each data point is an average of five years.

Figure 3: World Health Chart. A comparison between two countries with trails. GDP per Capita on the x-axis and Child Survival up to 1 year of 1000 live births at the y-axis. Japan (red) and Sweden (blue) 1920-2001.

World Development Chart 2003

World Development Chart is a prototype for stand-alone software that can import datasets and export images in PowerPoint and Flash. It is an extended version of the World Health Chart regarding the graphic interface, but it has more functions added: Import and Export data; Export animations to PowerPoint or Flash; Multiple languages, Zoom and other goodies such as different icon shapes instead of bubbles.

World Development Chart was first developed in Director/Lingo but is now rewritten in Flash/Action Script. The Beta Version is available for pilot testing. Sida (Swedish International Development Cooperation Agency) also funded the World Development Chart. UN Statistic Division has provided data set for the test version.

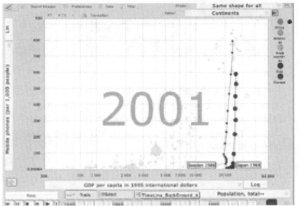
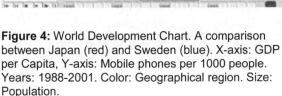
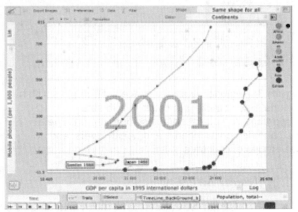

Figure 4: World Development Chart. A comparison between Japan (red) and Sweden (blue). X-axis: GDP per Capita, Y-axis: Mobile phones per 1000 people. Years: 1988-2001. Color: Geographical region. Size: Population.

Figure 5: World Development Chart. Development Show the same variable as in Figure 10, but with other view settings. **NOTE, the value of these software can only be seen live when the graphics move with time!!**

Human Development Trends 2003

This linear thematic Flash presentation is developed with United Nations Development Program (UNDP) for the release of the Human Development Report 2003. Major conclusions of the report are displayed in animated charts, such as: Setbacks in income end health 1960-2001, Development crisis in the 1990´s and Regional differences. (www.undp.org/hdr2003/flash.html).

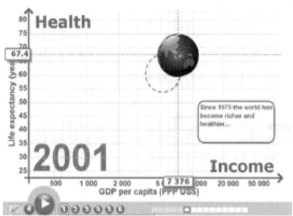

Figure 6: Human Development Trends 2003. Since 1975 the World on average has become richer and healthier... as shown by GDP per Capita on the x-axis and Life expectancy on the y-axis.

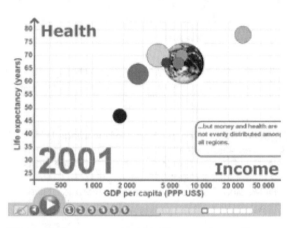

Figure 7: But money and health are not equally distributed among geographic regions.

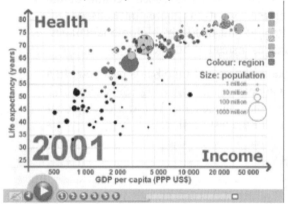

Figure 8: Regional averages conceal differences within regions. Each bubble is a country, with size proportional to population and color to region. There are countries on all income and health levels, and not two groups of countries

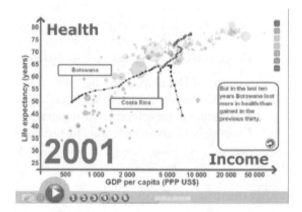

Figure 9: Botswana and Costa Rica makes remarkable progress during the 1960s, 70s and 80s. But in the last ten years, due to HIV/AIDS Botswana has lost more in health than gained the previous thirty.

Dollar Street

Dollar Street displays the world as a street. The street number is the daily income per person in the family. All people of the world live on Dollar Street. The poorest live in the left end and the richest in the extreme right end. All other people live in between on a continuous scale of daily incomes.

What does it look like in a household with a daily income of $1-$2 per person per day, compared with a household with a daily income of $10 or $100? By clicking the houses on Dollar Street a smaller window opens where it is possible to make home visit and walk around in all rooms. Each room is a 360-degree photo panorama that provides the full view. Some video documentation is also available. Vital functions of the households can be selected from a list above the street. These are basic functions such as electricity, water supply, toilet and sofa. Several houses can be open at the same time. If the word "Sofa" in the Menu is clicked all open windows will automatically display the sofa of the current households. Dollar Street is developed in collaboration with Save the Children Sweden.

World Income Distribution

The World Income Distribution is an interactive display of statistics on household income distribution for Bangladesh, Brazil, China, India, Indonesia, Japan, Nigeria, Pakistan and USA and the World as a whole in each year from 1970 to 1998. Each graphic distribution represents one country. The shape show how the population is distributed across different income levels. Countries are selected/deselected by click on the country names to the right. Drag the time bar at the bottom to see how the shapes have gradually changed between 1970-1998. Prof. Xavier Sala-i-Martin, Colombia University, has kindly provided the data sets.

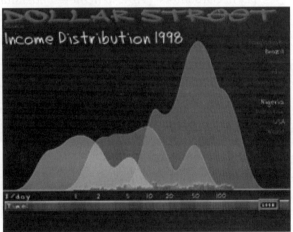

Figure 10: Dollar Street. Three households are displayed above the street: 1-2 $/person a day in Mozambique, 2-5 $/person a day in Uganda, 10-50 $/person a day in South Africa.

Figure 11: World Income Distribution. From left to right: Nigeria, Brazil and USA in 1998. The richest group of Nigeria's population overlaps the middle-income group in Brazil and the poorest group in USA.

The Future

The key to successful exchange of digital information on the Internet has proven to be new ways of combining free access with innovative financing. In short; few pay for the free use by millions. It is rarely effective to charge all end users. The reason is that the marginal cost for an additional user is negligible. The cost is instead recovered from the provider, from advertisements or from a smaller group of highly specialised users that are willing to pay for a very advanced function. Prominent examples of free software are Internet Explorer, Acrobat Reader, and the Google search engine.

Another example is the successful free sharing of genetic data as global public goods using free software on the Gene Bank servers for DNA sequences. It has also proved productive to combine the virtues of open source and commercial software in new ways; as shown by the data base system MySQL.

The full force of the IT revolution has not yet reached World Development Monitoring. It seems as if this force will only serve the international statistic system when innovative software are combined with innovative and sustainable ways of financing the software maintenance and development as well as the management of the statistical databases. Standardization of data format in XML will greatly facilitate the necessary software development, and vice versa successful software for provision will drive the process of data set standardization. The future software may emerge in the form of combinations of free and commercial modules with open source code for a joint development by interested partners. It may also emerge as one single commercial alternative that is part of major software systems.

Independently of which way new software will emerge the stage is now set for major improvements of the understanding of development by providing international development statistics in new animated graphics that will increase the number of users from thousands to millions!

References

[1] P. Gärdenfors; *"How to achieve understanding with the aid of e-learning"*, e-Learning 2nd WBLE Conference, Proceedings, Lund, Sweden, 2001, pp. 51

[2] B. Lomborg, The Skeptical Environmentalist: Measuring the Real State of the World, Cambridge University Press, 2001

[3] J. Manninen, *"eMyths and eReality"*, e-Learning 2nd WBLE Conference, Proceedings, Lund, Sweden, 2001, pp. 111-120.

[4] M.S. Meadows, *Pause and Effect – the art of interactive narrative,* New Riders, Indianapolis, Indiana, 2003

[5] A. Naeve, *"The Concept Browser – A new form of knowledge management tool"*, e-Learning 2nd WBLE Conference, Proceedings, Lund, Sweden, 2001, pp. 151-161.

[6] S. Papert, The connected family, bridging the digital generation gap, Longstreet Press, Atlanta, Georgia, 1996

[7] S. Seiple, M. Lindkvist, *"Simulation based collaborative experiments for interactive learning in virtualized classroom environments"*, e-Learning 2nd WBLE Conference, Proceedings, Lund, Sweden, 2001, pp. 347-355.

Workshops

Measurement of Social Capital in the UK

Penny Babb

Social Analysis and Reporting Division, Office for National Statistics

This paper presents the context for the development of statistics on social capital in the UK, the approach taken for measuring social capital, and the UK position on international work in the area.

In terms of the reasons for work on measuring social capital, it is helpful to first consider the political context for these developments. In 1997 a new government came to power in Britain. It was the first Labour government for 18 years and they brought with them a shift in thinking and approach to policy development.

There was a new interest in evidence-based policy – drawing on social research to inform the nature, implementation and evaluation of policies. There was also a desire to address social inequalities – looking for ways to reduce the gap between the advantaged and disadvantaged of UK society. This focus resulted in the development of community policies, to regenerate neighbourhoods and promote cohesive communities. The principal aim of the community policy is to:

develop strong and active communities in which people of all races and backgrounds are valued and participate on equal terms…

This was also a period of great change for government statistics. The UK national statistics office was created from the Central Statistics Office and the Office for Population Censuses and Surveys. There was a move also to become more responsive to policy needs for data. However, at the same it was recognised that we needed also to be more proactive in identifying pertinent issues and ways that we could inform the development of policy through the collection and dissemination of statistics.

Alongside this was a desire to expand our analysis and reporting of social change. Part of this was in looking for new ways of describing the trends and issues of particular societal interest. But also there was an increased awareness of the need to examine the impact of factors operating at an areal level, as well as individual characteristics.

A number of topics emerged of central concern – these were ethnicity and identity, e-society and social capital. These were each areas that required developments in the collection of data to assist in the formulation of appropriate policies. Social capital was an issue of tremendous interest in numerous government departments – particularly those covering education, health, crime and citizenship but also through to the central policy strategy and delivery areas.

However, social capital is a nebulous concept and one that required definition and operationalising for use in the policy context. It is multifaceted and operates at both individual and areal levels. It is also culturally sensitive and so needed understanding as experienced within the United Kingdom.

ONS has a key role and responsibility to provide the tools for the data collection – part of this is to ensure that harmonised questions for use on surveys are developed and used to support the cross-government initiatives.

There has been much debate both within the UK and internationally over the definition of social capital. It encapsulates a new way of looking at old problems. However there is now general consensus that social capital is to do with networks and norms. The OECD definition of social capital presented in *The Well-Being of Nations* describes it as:

networks together with shared norms, values and understandings that facilitate co-operation within or among groups

This embodies both networks and norms and so was adopted in the UK to form the basis of our data collection and analysis.

To measure social capital, we first needed to identify the key dimensions that underpin it. Five main aspects form the basis of the UK work:

- civic participation – the propensity to vote, to take action on local or national issues

- social networks and support – such as contact with friends and relatives

- social participation – involvement in groups and voluntary activities

- reciprocity and trust – which include giving and receiving favours, as well as trusting other people and institutions such as the government and the police

- views about the area – although not strictly a measure of social capital, it is required for the analysis and interpretation of the social capital measures, and includes satisfaction with living in the area, problems in the area.

This framework is based on earlier work carried out in the UK and international studies. Our aim has been to produce a standardised set of questions that can be used in national and local studies to describe the patterns of social capital within the UK, and to help inform the development of national governmental policies, as well as local community action.

Two forms of the harmonised question set were developed – the full or main set which takes around 20 minutes to complete and the core question set which takes about 5 minutes to complete. The question set is currently being run on the General Household Survey in Great Britain. Results will be available in 2006. It is also being adopted on other household surveys within the UK, including the Citizenship Survey and the Survey of English Housing, which is currently in the field.

The UK harmonised question set was originally designed for computer-assisted interviewing and work is now underway to develop a self-completion version. Alongside this is the preparation of a guide or tool-kit to provide the information needed to help design and run the postal surveys that will use these questions.

Questions on bridging social capital that represent networks that help us get ahead in life couldn't be included within the first stage of the development. However, work is now planned to develop and then test these questions in order to extend the question set.

We are also in the process of investigating the nature of the social capital of young people. Earlier work highlighted that this age group had surprisingly low levels when measured on the same indices as used for all adults. In the course of the analysis the question arose whether this difference was due to genuinely low levels of involvement or whether the measures used failed to pick up the actual activities undertaken by young people. This is an example of one way in which social capital is context specific. New questions were developed to test this hypothesis and the results are currently being examined.

The GHS 2004 data will be analysed – probably in early 2006 when the data become available – to describe the national picture of social capital and provide a baseline for comparisons into the future and against local studies.

These data will also be used to model local level estimates of social capital indicators. This modelling work is currently underway using the British Crime Survey to produce estimates of indicators such as helping each other, tight knit community, friendly place to live and fear of crime. We hope to include these estimates on our web site showing neighbourhood statistics across the UK.

There is a general desire within national statistical offices to be able to compare with other nations. Many of the problems that are encountered are not unique to social capital measurement. However, the problems of conceptualisation are magnified with social capital. The problem is compounded as we look at the varying nature of different societies and their experience of social capital. Add language into the mix and the measurement becomes even more challenging.

There is much to be gained from striving for a common understanding of the facets of social capital. We have learnt much from the experience of other countries, both in terms of their particular experience of social capital, as well as their means of approaching its measurement. However, it is important that we appreciate the differences when defining indicators, for example, voting becomes less useful as a measure when it is mandatory, as in some countries.

We also need to recognise that the social capital experience within one country is impacted by the events in other countries. This may be through, for example, migration, and the interaction of differing cultures. It may also be through economic and social events – the recent events in Iraq will have had a tremendous effect in other countries on the views of individuals and the experience within communities, depending on their religious beliefs, ethnicity or country of birth.

These problems are further compounded by the dynamic nature of social capital, such as changes in networks and the impact of technological developments, leading to shifts in lifestyle, and also to problems in comparing indicators over time. For example, cohort differences are likely to be observed following the uptake of texting and emailing as ways of keeping in touch with friends and relatives.

It is important to acknowledge the work of the OECD and the Siena group, and their member countries, for their work over the past few years in addressing these key issues. The OECD raised four possible options regarding international comparisons at their conference on social capital measurement in Budapest in 2003.

The first presents a non-flexible module that is agreed at an international level. The second provides a flexible list with perhaps a core set of indicators, plus a series of optional questions run on a variety of surveys rather than one dedicated survey. The third option covers internationally agreed concepts, but without specific questions. It would involve having specified the underlying dimensions of social capital and established agreed definitions and categorisations. These would be supported by defined indicators and guidelines on the ways to conduct the survey, such as on sampling methods and response rates. While being responsive to local needs and experience, it would limit to a degree the comparability between countries.

The last option is to agree to disagree – this would exacerbate international comparability problems and limit possible comparisons and sharing of experience.

Our preference is for something between options 2 and 3. We feel it is vital to reach a common understanding of the key concepts of social capital but also to appreciate that these will be played out differently between different countries. This will allow us to still learn from others to inform our own measurement and policy development.

The guidelines would also allow us to identify best practice but wherever possible to use common indicators. However it won't always be meaningful to do so and different indicators may be needed to reflect the local experience.

The efforts to achieve standardisation are already underway. For example the European Union Survey of Income and Living Conditions has included indicators of social participation, such as contact with relatives and friends, and informal volunteering. While there was some debate over the appropriate phrasing, a version of these questions will be included when the questionnaire is adopted. It will be some years before the data will be obtained, when we will have an opportunity to be able to make the first comparisons. However, this is a useful experience and can help inform our further efforts to achieve comparability.

The UK harmonised question set is presented on the UK National Statistics web site: www.statistics.gov.uk/socialcapital

Towards an Atlas of Social Capital and Institutions in Italy: Strategy, Developments and Open Issues

Alessandra Righi,

Senior Researcher, National Institute of Statistics, Italy

Abstract

In the late 90's social capital gained wide interest among researchers and policy makers. This interest developed together with the results of some promising reports that showed how social capital could help to explain not only the differences in productive organisation and economic development, but also the differences in other sectors of social life (health, housing..). Furthermore, the attempts to incorporate the relational aspects into the economic development theories in the past few years have produced some interesting practical consequences in Italy (territorial pacts, business incubators, etc). In this framework, the importance of being able to analyse and measure the relational aspects on a disaggregated territorial level increases, in order to be able to define and explain the deep territorial differences that exist in Italy. The need to measure social capital is becoming a more urgent one, as the term seems to be frequently used in the strategic policies of many local authorities or non-profit associations. In fact some local networks are already active, aimed at experimenting new ways to give value to civil society organisations for local development, by using practices of restoring social cohesion or strengthening institutions on a local level. These projects are now in progress and have not enjoyed a homogeneous or comparable information and inquiry framework.

Likewise, following the growing information demand to define and explain the differences among various areas of Italy from both the scientific world and from the political world, national institutes of statistics as well as some international organizations (with Eurostat and OECD in the first place) have given more attention to this problem. What is more, it has aroused the interest of the Siena Group, the permanent forum of statistic institutes and research organizations in the social-statistical field under the protection of the United Nations. Numerous projects pertinent to this matter have been started in the past years, leading to an increasingly urgent need to obtain comparison measurements on an international level and for as many countries as possible.

In this paper, after a brief overview of the concept framework within which the project operates and of the international and national experiences gained or still in progress, some developments of the Istat Project of the Atlas of Social Capital and Institutions will be outlined further on. As already mentioned, the specific interest of our approach lies in the relations between social capital, institutions and local development. A biunique relation appears indeed to exist between institutions and social capital since the institutions influence the behaviour of individuals and modify their predispositions towards cooperation and reciprocity while the social capital can determine the efficiency and efficacy of the institutions. Thus, both are important for the development.

We will explain the operations for choosing the work definitions, for identifying all the dimensions of the concept, together with the relative themes and sub-themes that define it in the specific key indicators. We will moreover describe the first products of the Project, a matrix of social capital main dimensions in Istat data sources and a question databank, that are relevant work tools for researchers who want to work on this subject (nationally and internationally). These databases allow for a flexible approach to the studying of the social capital, a controversial subject and multi-dimension by nature. We will conclude by indicating the phases yet to be realised, the relations with other institutions that are interested in developing this type of studies, the problems that remain open and possible future evolutions.

Social capital: theoretical framework and measurement experiences

There have been several attempts at theoretically defining the social mechanisms that determine or aid the economic development of a country or an area. For our purposes, the most interesting are those that call intangible and relational aspects into play, referred to each time, as social capital, relational assets, or spontaneous sociality.

Very briefly, the concept of social capital began to be used in the 1970s, but it was only in the 1990s that it became truly popular. Loury, in the 1970s, began to use this concept to explain the different degree of success of young people in increasing their human capital. For the author, social capital indicated the networks of family and social relations that can increase human capital. In the 1980s, Bourdieu expressly distinguishes social capital from economic and cultural capital, defining it as personal relations that can be directly mobilized by an individual to pursue his own ends and to improve his social position. Granovetter demonstrated the importance of social networks in the labour market. He does not speak of social capital, but shows how the social networks influence the possibility of finding employment. In addition, Granovetter underlines how the networks of relations that link entrepreneurs offer a fundamental resource for the organisation of production that is trust (Granovetter, 1973).

Coleman refers to a more relational conception of social capital. This would be made up of social relations that an individual has and would be a set of resources that the individual can use together with other resources to better pursue his own ends. Individuals, therefore, start up long-lasting relations to achieve their own interests, so relationships of authority, trust, rules of reciprocity, come into being. These are all structures that can become resources for action, i.e. social capital. In his attempt to correct the individual distortion of neoclassic economics, Coleman separates the resources that an individual has at his disposal into physical capital, human capital and social capital. In social capital however, structural dimension (structural characteristics of the social system, institutions, organisations, norms) and subjective dimension (relationship resources that each person inherits and develops alone in his family and in social circles) cross over and interact (Coleman, 1988).

An important methodological contribution came from R.D. Putnam. For Putnam, the Italian regions with the highest degree of civicness are subject to economic dynamism and better administrative operations than those regions with a lack of civic virtues. In the latter, the lack of generalised trust is at the basis of a negative ethos that prevents cooperation between individuals and therefore economic growth. "For social capital – says Putnam – we mean the trust, the rules that govern our living together, the civic association networks, elements that improve the efficiency of social organisation, promoting commonly agreed initiatives". The measure to which a consistent structure of more symmetrical mutual connections exists is the only matter through which one can reasonably presume that these take on the form of a resource for social change and economic exchange. "The networks of civil commitment, such as local area associations, choirs, cooperatives, sports clubs, mass parties and other similar groups are the expression of horizontal interaction and are a crucial component of social capital. The more a community has, the more likely it is that the citizens will collaborate to everybody's advantage" (Putnam, 1993).

In the mid-1990s, Fukuyama corresponds social capital with the possibility of using relationships of trust. It therefore becomes a resource that arises from the prevalence of trust in society or a part of it. It can be allocated in the family or in small or large groups and differs from other types of capital as it is transmitted by religion, tradition, or historical habits. Social capital is within a community, it is a part of human relations, it is a part of "virtuous" behavioural codes that represent the culture of a people and can be summarised as trust and spontaneous sociality, both of which are attitudes to the service of economic growth (Fukuyama, 1996).

Forms of social capital are therefore information channels, rules and efficient endorsements, relationships of authority, mutual trust. A decisive element therefore appears to be trust, which has various overtones in the various authors. For Putnam and Fukuyama, trust is not intentionally created, but comes from a process inherited from a historical dynamic process. Others consider trust to be an asset that can be intentionally and rationally created, and on which it is possible to build a prescriptive theory (Gambetta, 1989). Primary groups and particularistic communities, but the institutional political system too can be potential producers of trust. According to Coleman, they are therefore trust brokers. Trust has the function of stimulating sociality to generate social relations and also carries out control and social regulation functions.

Other important characteristics of social capital also emerge, even though they have different overtones from the work of the various authors. Social capital is created, maintained and destroyed; therefore it needs continuous investment, like any other form of capital. It is an intangible good and not completely fungible. Its benefits can be used not only by those who have contributed to its creation, but also by the general public. Furthermore, in the approach that mainly belongs to political scientists, social capital is considered a property of the entire social system that aids democracy and economic development.

Several criticisms have been made on social capital studies on various angles. One of the most important is that the theory of social capital shows the difficulty moving from the micro level to the macro-social dimension. The institutional and systemic set-ups cannot only be explained, in fact by the nature of the relationship networks under them (Mutti, 1998). More, we need to consider the fact that one form of social capital that aids a certain action in one context, can be found to be a hindrance in another context. Social capital is incorporated into social relations, which are not the same thing, however. Particularly dense networks can have such a strong control on individual behaviour that they discourage economic innovation. It has emerged from more recent studies how the contradictions that were seen in institutionalist approaches (Putnam and Fukuyama), but also those of Coleman, can be overcome by simply considering social capital as a situational and dynamic concept (Piselli, 2001). That means, that is appropriate for grasping the innovation of forms of social development and cooperation.

Social capital has not just been an object of interest for sociologists. One of secrets of its success is in fact that of setting up a common ground for sociology, political science and economics. Converging collaboration of different disciplines seems possible on this ground; the use of simplifying models to be treated with mathematical techniques is hoped for (Bagnasco, 2001). It should be pointed out that in their dealings, economists prefer the term relational goods to social capital. In models of economic growth, the production capacity of factors depends on the way in which they combine and development differences can be explained by the collective capacity to combine and coordinate inputs in the best way, in addition to production inputs (including some intangible elements such as human capital and production knowledge). A different culture, a different system of relations and interconnections, in other words a different supply of relational goods, influences growth rates. Naturally, each author grasps some different overtones of this concept.

For Gui, relational goods are "an intangible capital good, that lies in long-lasting interpersonal relationships and that produces both intrinsic and instrumental benefits" (Gui, 1995). One may think of reciprocal familiarity, friendship, trust, cooperation - values and relations that seem to be created and which are less likely to be preserved in modern societies than in traditional ones. The high mobility of modern production systems tends to interrupt long-lasting ties and to discourage investing in relationships, thus creating a loss of collective well-being or a slow-down in its growth.

According to a different approach, relational goods are goods "that can only be produced and used optimally by their same producers and consumers, via relationships that connect the players involved. These are therefore those goods whose essence is provided by the quality of the relationship that is created between producer and consumer (educational, health, cultural services and so on)" (Zamagni, 1996). For economic growth purposes, it is vital to make a change to social and productive organisation, that determines an increase in consumption time by the players, via the re-modulation of work time and/or the sustained increase in non-paid work activity (producer of relational goods), made possible by new technologies .

Brunetta, Tronti and Scandizzo considered the existence of intangible relational elements, that they call "relational goods", as an independent variable in the process of production. A complex residual factor has been added to capital and work factors, that, each time, have been attributed low or high responsibility on the final effects. Thus, relational goods have been added to human capital, social capital (that increase the disposition of all the factors to enter the production process) and technological capital.

Therefore, relational goods can be defined as that set of cultures, values, relationships, interconnections, synergies that permit a higher productivity than the one that can be obtained by individuals with the same human and physical capital but who operate alone or in another relational set-up. Thus, relational goods allow each worker to exploit his own human capital in the same other environmental conditions (Fondazione Giacomo Brodolini, 1995). This is therefore a system of relationships that has an economic effect, but which will only be effective if the potential users are aware of its existence and its importance, and if they are know how to exploit it.

Therefore, the debate on which types of factor relational goods are is still open. In particular, an attempt is made to try to understand how far these goods actually favour development and whether, beyond a certain point, they do not represent a limit for further development, as they are however, the result of a culture and a traditional social fabric. It is still not clear if they have a direct or indirect effect on economic development and, consequently, whether their production can be aided with public policies or whether, instead, they come from spontaneous processes.

Recently, the Banca d'Italia (Bank of Italy) has also focused on the concept of social capital, adding it in its own thoughts on economic productivity and on how new technologies have determined a profit of the so-called "total factor productivity" (TFP) and an increase of work productivity (Desario, 2000).

Anyway, one of the most critical points in social capital studies, together and consequently to the one of adopting an appropriate working definition, is that of measurement. In contrast to the emerging need to develop new measures of social capital, there are theoretical arguments over whether or not social capital is actually something that can be measured at all. Opinions range from being totally unapproachable to more reconcilable ones, although they are aware that this is not an easy task.

Harsh criticism has been made on the experience of measurement carried on by the main studies on social capital. For example, according to some authors, the experience of Putnam has been judged as being theoretically naive, as available data define the interpretation of social capital. Furthermore, research carried out by Inglehart (1997) shows that unless the context and way of measuring social capital is specified, differing results are obtained. In fact, statistical examination of Putnam's correlations on a world scale has led to contrasting results.

Some of the attempts to overcome the many definition difficulties encountered in these studies have resulted in progress being registered in the OECD framework. Analysing the specific role of human capital and social capital on well-being, it has been proposed a new definition of social capital. According to this definition, social capital is "networks together with shared norms, values and understanding that facilitate cooperation within or among groups" (OECD, 2001). It is undeniably difficult to find the right balance between theoretic aspects, always very extensive and complex, and the need to operationalise the definitions when trying to obtain exact measurements of the concept. Many subsequent studies have decided to adopt this definition as it can sufficiently be used in measurement phases.

Some open issues remain however: first, if the indicators are collected afterwards (and not using specific surveys), they may lack a clear definition and the researcher will no longer know what he is measuring. Secondly, sometimes research on social capital confuses the unit of measurement, adding information on individual social capital to a measurement that should represent a wider collective unit. The benefits of social capital coming from individual networks can be rather different to those available on a social level (those of institutions and government).

Many studies, especially in Anglo-Saxon countries, have tried to measure social capital or its action in some specific fields, such as the labour market or productive organisation. These are studies that varying degrees of flexibility, both methodologically and in terms of indicators considered. Some are inquiry approaches coming from ad hoc surveys, as is the case of the strategy adopted by the World Bank (see Rossing Feldman, Assaf, 1999). Others, especially the ongoing attempts by national statistics institutes, have an ex post approach of reconsidering the sources and the indicators produced, or are of a mixed type.

It is worth briefly remembering some of the most important experiences in progress in other national statistics institutes. The Office for National Statistics (ONS) in the United Kingdom is coordinating a project for the development of a measurement and analysis framework for Social Capital. Other ongoing attempts are conducted by Statistics New Zealand and Australian Bureau of Statistics (ABS). Other experiences to be mentioned include the "General Social Survey on Social Capital 2003" carried out by Statistics Canada on a sample of about 25 thousand persons and The Social Capital Community Benchmark in the US.

In Italian experiences (all smaller experiences from the point of view of effort in collecting data than the international ones), the indicators to measure relational goods were calculated at provincial level referred to 3 main areas: civic environment, cultural vitality and global relations (Sessa, 1998a; Sessa, 1998b). Barbieri (1997) has studied the link between social capital, intended as the support received from relational and family networks, and the job search. The actual social resources of individuals are not so much grasped by indicators built to reveal the morphological aspects of the network, but more by indicators that can measure the specific weight and the overall social evaluation of the importance of contact, i.e. social capital. Other recent Italian researches on institutions and local development have shown how widespread civicness is largely influenced by the intensity of the presence of intermediate institutions and collective associations. One other study that refers to the issue of job search wants to use the concept of individual social capital. A survey among 35-40 year olds in Turin allowed the dwelling location (proxy of social capital) to be related to indicators of different relations according to professional sub-groups. An attempt was also made to distinguish between potential social capital and social capital actually activated in the job search (Bianco, 2001).

More recently, the "European Social Survey", which counts the participation of 24 countries, has realised a questionnaire on social capital that is submitted in Italy to a sample of about a thousand interviewees. The survey, which provides for a module on social engagement and democracy, enables to measure voluntary activities, social trust, political trust, political participation trough behaviours or attitudes. Finally, an issue of the sociological review "Inchiesta" was dedicated to the presentation of different definition and measurement experiences regarding the social capital on a national level (AaVv., 2003).

The Istat Project

Strategy

Given the large scientific interest and the pressure exercised by statistical institutes and international organizations on this matter, the National Institute for Statistics also felt the urgent need to start a project on social capital with the final intent of realising an Atlas of Social Capital and Institutions. This project presents two peculiarities: first, the local dimension; second, putting together institutions and social capital. Because of the delicacy of this subject and the extent of all the possible methods, it was decided to realise this Atlas by dealing first with a documentary phase and subsequently by proceeding with the measurement phase. Since, in the past decade, Istat has substantially increased its informative offer on social statistics and in particular on networks, social participation and engagement, perception and control of personal sphere and public sphere, it considered necessary, in starting up the project, to begin from a re-examination of its currently produced statistics from the point of view of social capital concept.

Other NSIs also adopted this method before deciding whether some informative or definition gaps had to be filled in through the introduction of an ad hoc survey. The informative contribution deriving from a critical examination of the data produced seemed a preliminary step for any measurement method whose purpose was to present a determined sharing as well as the following characteristics: reproducibility, reliability and quality.

In order to identify the indicators that define the various dimensions and themes, we made a critical analysis of the experience of sets of indicators that have already been collected in other countries and by expanding them and adapting them to the Italian situation in order to have a basis of indicators that can be identified in existing surveys or to be used with later in-depth studies.

Searching for social capital dimensions in several surveys and administrative sources, it quickly became clear that it was possible to find the same dimension or even the same questions in different sources. This has thus become one of the key elements of the project, which is we are searching for the most appropriate data source for each dimension. The vastness and the diversity of data sources that constitute the puzzle of this Atlas brings about the following by-products: 1) a careful assessment of the need to carry out new processing of existing data source, that has never been validated at that territorial level; 2) to assess the possible need to avail of or identify new sources to fill the existing information gaps.

Other key element of the atlas is searching for the most appropriate territorial level for the various aspects that contribute to the definition of Social Capital. Indeed, with the aim of proceeding with mapping of the area from the point of view of the presence/absence of institutions and of how this presence is compensated or not by social networks, and of how this interacts with socio-economic development, we will try to identify for the most appropriate territorial level for each type of indicators. The problem of measuring the dimension of social capital, which is already a difficult operation in itself, is complicated by the need to identify indicators that take into account the various territorial dimensions of the country in a flexible way. To do this it is possible to resort to the current administrative limits (boroughs, provinces, regions), and to the re-groupings of such bodies (productive districts, local work systems, mountain communities, local health authorities etc...).

One of the most important decisions of the Project so far is that of forming a collaboration with the Bank of Italy and the Ministry of Economy. Our three institutions consider it indeed strategic the carrying out of a study on social capital and its main economic consequences, collaborating throughout the various development phases of the Project. In addition to exchanging researchers between these three institutions, new informative needs are emerging though this partnership, such as time series viewpoint, the even more systematic use of administrative sources for obtaining more punctual indicators on the performances of public institutions (e.g. intra-institution collaboration indicators), a better definition of the non-administrative territorial areas of analysis, the functions and the services provided by economic organisations on a desegregated territorial level, as indicator of the middle society's development on a local level.

Developments

Before describing the main achievements of the Atlas Project until now, let us summarise the mains phases that have led to these achievements.

We have started on this Project by reviewing the main attempts made or still in progress at studying and searching the social capital nationally and internationally (Australian Bureau of Statistics - ABS, Statistics New Zealand, Office for National Statistics of the United Kingdom, Statistics Canada, World Bank, OECD). This phase was also useful for creating an international and national research network on which one may share study activities on the theme. We then participated in the activities of a Working Group in the framework of OECD, whose purpose is to improve the measurement of the social capital on an international level, through the drawing up of a core of questions shared and used in all countries, thereby establishing the most harmonised and comparable approach. After having identified four main areas of social capital measurement, the objective is to identify the formulation of questions for each area, that makes it possible the most comparable possible measurement on an international level (if implemented in all countries).

Subsequently, an adequate work definition was chosen through a debate, taking into account the researches carried out by scholars from various countries within the Social Capital Project of the OECD. The already mentioned definition drawn by the OECD in 2001 and generally used in the past years was consequently adopted. Despite the fact that the international debate highlighted the numerous facets that characterise the concept of social capital and which have not made it possible to establish a universally shared definition until now, that definition was adopted because it appeared it could easily be used and because it limits the concept's field of action in such a way that the predefined set is not too narrow as to forget the important dimensions of the concept, nor excessively wide as to moderate the measurement's meanings.

Once identified the work definition, the next phase was to identify the dimensions gathering the different levels of the social capital: micro (individual prospective: this is an individual's potential of mobilising resources through a social network), meso (structural prospective: it concentrates on the development and distribution process of the social capital in the network) and macro (how the network takes root in the economic and social political system). These three levels are nevertheless inter-related; by establishing relationships of interpersonal trust, the actors contribute at strengthening the systematic trust, which in turn will favour them (Coleman 1990, Bagnasco 1999).

Next, the social capital dimensions were identified among the twenty sources considered (all the main Social Surveys and the numerous administrative sources since 1993). Questions pertaining to each dimension were subsequently distinguished from various surveys. These questions, as we will see in the next paragraph, were gathered (according to their exact wording and their evolution over time) and added to a computerised matrix of sources and questions.

Finally, the next step was to found an ulterior matrix with the dimensions and indicators that will integrate the Atlas, such as: individuals' characteristics and human capital; socio-economic integration; communications; local economic actors; public institutions.

The present phase, that is the elaboration phase, provides for the gathering of quantitative information and of the indicators identified in Istat sources together with their territorial desegregation. A comparative study is being carried out on the quality of the indicators in order to determine the most valid source from which an indicator can be drawn and what is the territorial level at which we must stop in order to maintain high the meaning of the indicator. We are also currently studying some methods for producing synthetic indicators regarding the social capital's various dimensions, leading us to measurements that could be produced in forms of maps realised from geographic systems, where the level of territorial aggregation and the presentation of the measurements are as simple as possible.

This is indeed related to the need of diffusing the indicators for both the matrix of the social capital's main dimensions and the matrix of the other dimensions. The data will be diffused though various channels, while some web pages will be created, relating the Project's main achievements.

Istat Social Capital Matrix of Sources and Questions DataBank

The matrix of sources and the questions databank are the main products until now achieved by the Project. As already mentioned, these products should enable to analyse the evolution over time and the level of territorial desegregation provided by the information produced. The various sources provide indeed information with either greater or lower level of territorial detail. These differences are determined by the level of territorial meaning of each survey and go from the finest levels of census or administrative surveys to the most aggregated ones of the surveys.

This type of matrix enables also to use different methods for measuring the social capital, either in terms of dimensions, or in terms of choosing the sources and the indicators for the measurement. It becomes therefore possible to choose not only the best question for representing each dimension identified, but also the best source from which the interesting question will be drawn. Besides making it easier to gather information from very different types of sources (surveys, administrative sources, censuses), it enables to choose the themes and the indicators, which have extensively been tested in literature by now, and experience them with other ones that are less used. It enables a time comparison of the answers to the individual questions, survey by survey; it allows one to choose, among the different surveys, the one with the most appropriate wording for accepting the social capital one has in mind and finally, it enables to compare the different indicators that come from different sources, although from identical or similar questions.

With the purpose of providing indicators comparable on an international level, a careful analysis of Istat surveys pointed out to themes according with the OECD criteria; these themes were then adequately integrated in order to enrich and preserve the specificities characterising the Italian situation. Some references were made to the results of a workshop, organised by the Hungarian Ministry of Education and by the OECD (with the participation of 13 OECD countries, the European Commission and Eurostat), held in Budapest in May 2003. Four main social capital dimensions were identified as well as some possible indicators. The dimensions identified are: 1) Participation, Social engagement; 2) Civic participation; 3) Social interactions, social networks and supports; 4) Trust, reciprocity, social values.

Other dimensions were added: "Control and self-efficacy" and "Perception of social structures and public services". The Istat surveys dedicate particular attention to these two dimensions, especially to the subjects relating to the personal sphere (satisfaction for life, health, work, economical situation, etc.), the quality of public services and of the area where one lives. Each dimension is divided in a greater or lower number of sub-themes that, together, express the dimension's meaning. These themes include topics to which the questions pertain materially.

Subsequently, a computerised matrix was created, gathering questions on the dimensions identified and surveys considered, according to its exact wording and evolution over time. Each question was codified according to some characteristics (survey, year, number of section and questions, type of questionnaire). In the 400 questions gathered, some dimensions result particularly rich in contents, such as "Social interactions, social networks and supports" with 137 questions pertaining to it and "Perception of social structures and public services" with 82 questions pertaining to it. These areas relate to social behaviours, to which Istat has particularly dedicated itself over the past decade. Some areas result to be much less rich in questions, such as "Trust, reciprocity and social values", as Italy does not have a great tradition of study compared to the Anglo-Saxons (internationally well-known questions regarding trust were adopted in a survey only last year). Questions relative to the areas "voting and political participation" also results to be scanty, where the measurement experiences obtained by means of surveys have given different results (at least in the field of voting, joining a party, etc) from those of administrative sources. It was therefore decided to propose both possibilities.

Table. 1 – Questions according main dimensions and themes of social capital

DIMENSION	THEME	QUESTIONS (nr.)
1) Participation, Social engagement	Participation in groups, Formal Volunteering, Religious practice	65
2) Civic participation	Voting, Political participation, Funding	26
3) Social interactions, social networks and supports	Parental, neighbour and friend networks, Receipt of unpaid help, Provision of unpaid help	137
4) Trust, reciprocity, social values	Trust in other people and in public services, Perceived fairness of life, discrimination, Positive attitudes toward the future, Perception of social values	27
5) Control and self-efficacy	Subjective aspects	62
6) Perception of social structures and public services	Quality of public services and of local area, Importance of environmental variables and of protection against crime	82

Table 2 shows the synthesis of the matrix with the main social capital dimensions, where the rows present the social capital's dimensions and themes and the columns indicate the Istat sources considered (those that present a significant number of questions). Due to the lack of space, sub-themes are not indicated for each theme, as more than 60 sub-themes have been identified. The results offer starting points for some considerations. First of all, there are two groups of themes: 1) those that present a great number of questions held in one single survey, but that do not allow for a wide comparison on several sources; 2) those characterised by their small number of questions for each survey (often similar surveys or even identical) but for which it is possible a comparison among different surveys.

Table. 2 – Matrix of main dimension and themes of social capital in Istat surveys and administrative sources

Dimension	Theme	Surveys										Administrative source		
		Aspects of daily life	Family, social subjects and childhood condition	Health conditions and use of health services	Leisure time and culture	Citizens' safety	Time Use	ECHP	HBS	Survey on Birth	School to work transitions (upper sec. and univ.grad.)	No profit institutions Census	Administrative source	Volunteering Organization Survey
Participation, Social engagement	Participation in groups	10	4	-	2	-	2	2	-	-	-	-	-	-
	Formal Volunteering	10	6	-	1	-	6	1	-	-	-	7	-	6
	Religious practice	1	1	1	1	-	5	-	-	-	-	-	-	-
Civic participation	Voting	6	-	-	-	-	-	-	-	-	-	-	1	-
	Political participation	9	-	-	8	-	-	1	-	-	-	-	-	-
	Funding	1	-	-	-	-	-	-	-	-	-	-	-	-
Social interactions, social networks and supports	Parental, neighbour and friend networks	13	32	2	23	2	16	4	-	-	1	-	-	-
	Receipt of unpaid help	-	13	3	-	-	-	4	2	10	-	-	-	-
	Provision of unpaid help	1	4	-	-	-	3	3	-	-	-	-	-	1
	Trust in other people and in public services	9	1	-	-	4	-	-	-	-	-	-	-	-
	Perceived fairness of life, discrimination	1	-	-	-	-	-	-	-	-	-	-	-	-
Trust, reciprocity, social values	Positive attitudes toward the future	1	-	-	-	-	-	1	-	-	-	-	-	-
	Perception of social values	2	1	-	-	-	-	7	-	-	-	-	-	-
Control and self-efficacy	Subjective aspects	10	4	10	3	-	11	12	1	4	1	6	-	-
	Quality of public services and of local area	35	3	-	-	30	-	-	2	4	-	-	-	-
Perception of social structures and public services	Importance of environmental variables and of protection against crime	6	-	-	-	-	-	2	-	-	-	-	-	-

The first case refers in particular to the area of "Perception of social structures and public services", for which 22 questions were chosen, relating to the theme "Quality of public services" and to the sub-theme "Perception of crime safety, victimisation", all added in the Citizens' safety survey. The questions regard the degree of safety persons feel when walking alone in the evening in the area where they live, the fear of criminality in general or of suffering from violent acts. A similar situation can be observed for the 14 questions that characterise the sub-theme "Problems in local area", with questions that dedicate greater attention to criminality and to the conditions of the housing area.

Moreover, the Time use survey and Family, social subjects and childhood condition survey and Leisure time and culture survey contribute, by means of a discreet presence of questions, at characterising some sub-themes inherent to the dimension "Social interactions, social networks and supports", which regard socialisation and free time activities (to visit, to be visited, to go to the cinema/theatre, etc.), the frequency of the activities carried out in the free time and contacts with parents, neighbours and friends, expressed in terms of numbers of times a week or a month.

A first examination of the matrix points out to the fact that right now, it is possible to identify the greatest gaps in the gathering of the data on the dimension of the Reciprocity and Trust in its specific connotations (trust in institutions, neighbours, etc). Moreover, the fact that most of the questions is held in surveys, rises the methodological problem of evaluating the opportunity of acting ex-post on the weights held in some surveys in order to increase the territorial detail. Finally we must note the opportunity this matrix provides, in other words the use that the ONS has made of a similar matrix; it enables to improve the questions held in the surveys and to select those that provide the best results in order to add them in possible ad hoc modules on the social capital of the "General Social Survey".

The matrix is made up of an on line database. Thus it makes it possible to best gather the potentials of comparison among scholars from the ICT. In the international contest this database was considered as a very useful tool for a reciprocal knowledge, as the current experiences regarding the gathering of questions on these dimensions were realised until then only in English-speaking countries (Righi, 2003). These countries though are interested in comparing the wording of their questions with the one used in Latin-language countries, in order to understand better the differences in the questions that could lead to differences in comparing the results.

Open issues

We consider the production of the matrix of social capital data sources and questions, with the gathering in a database of about 400 questions, a necessary effort for starting a very clear definition and measurement path on the social capital, a much-debated and controversial concept. It appears evident that the use of this new informative tool will be complete when quantitative information relative to each questions or indicator will be available. It will then be possible to carry out a first synthesis of the indicators in order to obtain the measurements of the social capital.

Many issues still remain open for discussion: our work definition able to take into account both relational aspects and those regarding the institutional type approach. Secondly, which is the best approach to measurement, in order to guarantee greater statistical reliability and to allow reproducible measurements by all the researchers that will have access to the quantitative database? Thirdly, are we able to fully exploit the interpretational potential doming from the diversity of the areas in which the indicators will be measured? Finally, how to best use the levels of territorial aggregation offered by the possibility of reasoning according to a geographical system in order to manage to understand the interactions between institutions-social capital and local development.

All these are themes that Istat try to compare with those people inside and outside its own organisation that wish to work on the soft aspects, relational and cultural ones, of development. The challenge will only be won by adopting an approach that can be shared by as many as possible and if it will be possible to find enough forms of the necessary financing of the activities.

References

Aa.Vv. (2003), *Inchiesta*, Rivista trimestrale, Anno XXXIII, n. 139, gennaio-marzo, Dedalo.

Australian Bureau of Statistics (2000), "Measuring Social Capital: current collections and future directions", *Discussion Paper*, Australian Bureau of Statistics, November, Belconnen.

Bagnasco A. (1999), "Teoria del capitale sociale e political economy comparata", *Stato e mercato*, n°57.

Bagnasco A. (1999), *Tracce di comunità*, Il Mulino, Bologna.

Bagnasco A., Piselli F., Pizzorno A., Trigilia C. (2001), *Il capitale sociale. Istruzioni per l'uso*, Il Mulino, Bologna.

Banfield E. C. (1976), Le basi morali di una società arretrata, Il Mulino, Bologna.

Barbieri P. (1997), "Non c'è rete senza nodi. Il ruolo del capitale sociale nel mercato del lavoro", *Stato e mercato*, 49.

Bianco M.L. (2000), "Ricercare il capitale sociale. Problemi di analisi", paper presented at *Workshop on Social Capital*, Trento 1-20 oct. 2000.

Bourdieu P. (1986), "The Forms of Capital", Richardson J.G. (ed.), *Handbook of Theory and Research for the Sociology of Education*, Greenwood Press.

Brunetta R., Tronti L. (1994), Capitale umano e Mezzogiorno. I nuovi termini della questione meridionale, Il Mulino, Bologna.

Bryant C.A., Norris D. (2002), *Measurement of Social Capital: The Canadian Experience*, Country Report for the International Conference on Social Capital Measurement, 25-27 September, London.

Capitale Sociale (2000), Notiziario del progetto Capitale Sociale nell' area pisana, n. 19, maggio.

Cersosimo D. (a cura di) (2001), *Istituzioni, capitale sociale e sviluppo locale*, Rubbettino, Catanzaro.

Coleman J. (1990), *Foundations of Social Theory*, Harvard Univ. Press, Cambridge.

Coleman J. (1988), "Social Capital in the Creation of Human Capital", *American Journal of Sociology*, 94, supplement.

Desario V. (2000), "La Banca d'Italia e lo sviluppo dell'e-banking", intervento per l'assemblea annuale della Convenzione Interbancaria per i Problemi dell'Automazione (CIPA), Frascati, 19 settembre.

Field J. (2003), *Social Capital*, Routledge, London.

Fondazione G. Brodolini (1997), Sviluppo economico e beni relazionali: una prima ricognizione teorica, *Economia and Lavoro*, Gennaio-giugno

Fukuyama F. (1996), *Fiducia*, Rizzoli, Milano.

Gambetta D. (a cura di), (1998), *Le strategie della fiducia*, Einaudi, Torino.

Granovetter M. (1973), "The Strength of Weak Ties", *American Journal of Sociology*, no.78.

Gui B. (1995), "On "Relation Goods": Strategic Implications of Investment in Relationship", *Working Paper*, Università di Venezia.

Hudson L., Chapman C. (2002), "The Measurement of Social Capital in the United States", paper for the International Conference on Social Capital Measurement, 25-27 September, London.

Inglehart R., Granato J., Leblang D. (1997), The Impact of Culture on Economic Growth, in Modernization and Postmodernisation, Princeton U.P., Princeton N.J.

Mutti A. (1998), Capitale sociale e sviluppo, la fiducia come risorsa, Il Mulino, Bologna.

OECD/OCSE (2001), The Well-being of Nations. The role of human and social capital, Paris.

OECD, UK ONS (2002), Social Capital: The challenge of international measurement, Report for the International Conference on Social Capital Measurement, 25-27 September, London.

Office for National Statistics, Social Analysis and Reporting Division (2001), *Social Capital A Review of he Literature*, October, National Statistics, London.

Portes A. (1998), "Social capital: its origins and applications in modern sociology", *Annual Review of Sociology*, vol. 24, pp. 1-24.

Piselli F. (2001), "Capitale sociale: un concetto situazionale e dinamico", Bagnasco A., Piselli F., Pizorno A., Trigilia C., *Il capitale sociale. Istruzioni per l'uso*, Il Mulino, Bologna.

Putnam R.D. (1993), La tradizione civica nelle regioni italiane, Mondadori, Milano.

Putnam R.D. (2000), Bowling *Alone. The collapse and revival of American Community,* Simon and Schuster, New York.

Righi A. (2002), "Toward an Atlas of Social Capital and Institutions in Italy", paper presented at 2002 General Meeting of the Siena Group on Social Statistics, November 4-6, London.

Righi A. (2003), "Il Capitale sociale tra implicazioni per le politiche sociali ed esigenze di comparazione internazionale", Seminario Istat, 20 Gennaio, Roma.

Righi A. (2003), "Toward an Atlas of Social Capital and Institutions: a draft of the Italian Social Capital Matrix of Surveys and Question Bank", paper presented at

Measurement for Policy: a Workshop on Social Capital, OECD-Hungarian Ministry of Education, Budapest, May 21-23.

Rossing Feldman T., Assaf S. (1999), "Social Capital: Conceptual Frameworks and Empirical Evidence. An Annotated Bibliography", *Social Capital Initiative Working Papers*, no. 5, January, World Bank.

Scandizzo P.L. (1997), "Beni relazionali e crescita endogena", *Economia and Lavoro*, n. 1-2.

Sessa C. (1998a), "I beni relazionali nelle province italiane: una metodologia di misurazione", *Economia and Lavoro*, n.2.

Sessa C. (1998b), "I beni relazionali e le politiche industriali territoriali", *Economia and Lavoro*, n.3.

Spellerberg A. (2001), Framework for the Measurement of Social Capital in New Zealand Statistics, New Zealand, Wellington.

Stone W. (2001), "Measuring Social Capital", *Research Paper* No. 24, Australian Institute of Family Studies, Melbourne.

Stone W., Hughes J. (2000), "What role for social capital in family policy?", *Family Matters*, No.56, pp. 20-27.

Stone W., Hughes J. (2002), "Social Capital – Empirical meaning and measurement validity", *Research Paper* No. 27, Australian Institute of Family Studies, Melbourne.

Trigilia C. (2001), "Social Capital and Local Development", paper presented at Euresco Conference Social Capital: Interdisciplinary Perspectives, Exeter, 15-20 September 2001.

Tronti L. (1997), "Il mercato del lavoro come sequenza di stati. Spunti analitici e ipotesi di intervento", Vitali L., Brunetta R. (a cura di), *Mercato del lavoro: analisi strutturali e comportamenti individuali*, Franco Angeli, Milano.

Uhlaner C. J (1989), "Relational Goods and Participation: Incorporating Sociability into a Theory of Relational Action", *Public Choice*, n. 62.

Zamagni, S. (1996), Nuove tecnologie, disoccupazione e regole di organizzazione del tempo, Accademia Nazionale dei Lincei, Roma.

Gender Statistics and the Work of the National Development Plan Gender Equality Unit, Ireland[1]

Mark P. Manto

Statistician, National Development Plan Gender Equality Unit, Ireland

Introduction

In this paper, I will focus specifically on the activities of the National Development Plan Gender Equality Unit in which I work and which is based in the Department of Justice, Equality and Law Reform in Ireland. But first let me begin with a little history.

In 1973, Ireland joined what was then the six member European Economic Community, along with the United Kingdom and Denmark. At that time, when examined by GDP per capita, Ireland was the poorest member of the expanded community of nine member states. It had an economy in which primary agriculture remained a significant component along with low-skilled, low value-added manufacturing. It was an economy which was experiencing major and apparently intractable emigration and unemployment problems. Compared to our new partners in Europe, jobs were scarce and incomes were low.

In the field of gender equality, Irish women then faced some serious inequalities in daily life and in the opportunities available to them. For example, at that time, women were obliged to leave work in the public service when they got married. Women's average industrial earnings were half those of men, and there could, quite legally, be different pay scales for men and women, even when doing the same job.

It is fair to say that Ireland's membership of the European Union has provided the stimulus to a social, economic and political transformation of our country. Though it should be pointed out that contrary to the widely held perception, this did not happen immediately following membership and indeed until the middle of the 1990's Ireland remained one of the 'poorer' members of the European Union.

It is perhaps in the area of social change that the EU has had its greatest impact on Ireland. To consider labour market participation: in 1971, two years before accession, female participation in the Irish labour market was less than 20%. It is now almost 50% of all women aged over 15 years, which compares favourably with many of our European partners. Indeed over the last seven years there has been an increase of over 30% in the number of women in employment. This huge increase is also a cause of wider social transformation in that there are now a greatly increased number of mothers in the workforce, with important implications for childcare and also for eldercare. It is also likely to have an impact on birth-rates. Birth rates have generally fallen in Ireland over recent decades (though they remain among the highest) in line with the rest of the EU. Intriguingly, the birth rate has increased significantly over the past decade. Increased

---

[1]   The views expressed in this paper are those of the author and do not necessarily reflect the views of the NDP Gender Equality Unit or the Department of Justice, Equality and Law Reform.

employment rates amongst mothers also have implications for time use through the division of labour in households and decisions involving work / life balance.

There is no doubt that progress towards gender equality in Ireland has been encouraged and facilitated by the significant body of legislation developed in the EU and implemented in member states. Irish women benefited from the anti-discrimination and equal pay directives of the mid 1970s, which underpinned their right to participate equally in the labour market. Nevertheless, it should also be pointed out that whilst EU membership has benefited Ireland in terms of promoting equality (and providing in instances a stimulus for legislation); it is also the case that Ireland has been at the forefront in a number of equality developments in Europe. For example, our national equality infrastructure in Ireland is extremely well developed and predates the directive in this area. Irish legislation outlaws discrimination in employment and in the supply of goods and services on nine grounds: gender, marital status, family status, age, disability, race, religion, sexual orientation and membership of the Traveller Community.

But it is not just in the area of legislation that the EU has had a positive effect on equality in Ireland. Debate on equality often distinguishes between apparent anomalies of policies aimed at equality of opportunity and those aimed at equality of outcome. Equal opportunities means equal rights, responsibilities and opportunities for women and men to pursue work which provides economic independence; to care for children and the home; to participate in politics, unions, and other societal activities; and to pursue personal growth and development. Equality of outcome may be described as where the Government attempts to ensure through policies and programmes that everyone achieves the same outcome. In the past, legislation to ensure equal access to opportunities has been introduced, and positive action to address gender inequalities through small-scale projects focused particularly on women. Despite these important steps, it is still sometimes difficult for all people to access opportunities equally.

None of us, I believe, would disagree that people of similar abilities, who take the same risks, and put in the same effort, should enjoy the same outcomes. And policies aimed at equality of opportunity can assist this. In its pursuit of equality of opportunity, the State must in the first instance intervene to ensure that everyone has the same chance of fulfilling their potential. It can intervene through laws that ban discrimination. It can also intervene to mitigate the disadvantage suffered by some from birth, through its welfare systems, including health, education and housing. Taxation policy and public expenditure programmes could also be designed to benefit society as a whole and address disadvantage. In this way, Government can create the conditions for equality, and ensure real equality of opportunity for all.

There is recognition of this important role at EU level. To quote from the European Commission's Communication on the EU Community Framework Strategy on Gender Equality (2001-05):

"Considerable progress has been made regarding the situation of women in the Member States, but gender equality in day-to-day life is still being undermined by the fact that women and men do not enjoy equal rights in practice".

In recognition of this, the Framework Strategy espouses a dual-approach: gender mainstreaming and positive action. Positive action is a "reactive" intervention, which seeks to address gender inequalities and disadvantage that are currently found to exist. This paper will examine gender mainstreaming and the role of gender statistics rather than the Irish approach to positive action. However, I will mention that the Irish Government funds an "Equality for Women" measure, under which a wide range of projects address barriers to women's equal participation in society. Further information may be found at: www.ewm.ie

In describing gender mainstreaming and the role of gender statistics, this paper will cover five topics:

- Gender mainstreaming and the role of gender statistics in the Irish National Development Plan (NDP)

- The NDP Gender Equality Unit and the supports it provides, focussing particularly on gender statistics

- Gender issues illustrated with gender statistics in some policy areas

- How to "gender mainstream" a policy, using example of funding for services for young people in the NDP

- Barriers to effective gender mainstreaming, and how to overcome them

Gender mainstreaming in the Irish National Development Plan (NDP)

Gender mainstreaming is the process of incorporating gender equality considerations into all stages of policy planning, development, implementation and evaluation. Put simply it means putting **gender** equality into **mainstream** policies.

The NDP is the largest and most ambitious investment plan ever drawn up for Ireland. It involves a planned investment of over €52 billion of public, private and EU funds (in 1999 prices) over the period 2000-2006. The Plan involves significant investment in health services, social housing, education, roads, public transport, rural development, industry, water and waste services, childcare and local development. Unlike previous Plans, most of the public funding for this Plan (over 90%) will be provided from domestic sources, mainly from the Exchequer. The EU contribution will total €6 billion comprised of:

- €3.8 billion from the Structural and Cohesion Funds

- €2.2 billion under the Common Agricultural Policy (CAP) Rural Development Plan.

It is divided into six Operational Programmes, namely:

- Economic and Social Infrastructure (includes areas like transport, water, housing, health infrastructure)

- Employment and Human Resource Development (covering employment, enterprise, adaptability in the work force, and equality)

- Productive Sector (funding research, industrial development, marketing, fisheries and agriculture)

- Two Regional programmes - Border, Midland and Western Region, and Southern and Eastern region, (funding social inclusion, infrastructure, agriculture and enterprise) and

- Peace programme (to promote peace and reconciliation on our island)

Gender mainstreaming is a requirement for all EU Structural Funds programmes. Though as previously stated, the NDP is funded largely by the Irish Exchequer, nonetheless the requirement of gender mainstreaming was adopted by the Irish

Government for almost all of the 130 measures which are funded through the NDP, not just those funded by the Structural Funds. This means that gender mainstreaming is a requirement in policy areas ranging from industrial development to sports, from arts to community development, from infrastructure to IT provision.

Gender equality and the role of statistics

In order for policy makers and others to identify and then address inequalities, it is crucial to have statistics on the roles and activities of both women and men in society. Such statistics are also important in measuring progress over time in eliminating inequalities and are widely applicable as part of the focus on increased evidence-based policy making and evaluation across Government.

In 1995, 189 countries including Ireland, attending the United Nations Fourth World Conference on Women in Beijing adopted a "Platform for Action" (PfA). This Platform for Action included discussion on the topic of gender statistics. It specifically requires governments to 'generate and disseminate gender-disaggregated data and information for planning and evaluation' as part of any institutional mechanisms to advance women. In particular it called for the following:

- Statistics related to individuals to be collected, compiled, analysed and presented by age and sex

- Staff to be appointed to strengthen gender-statistics programmes

- Data on the full contribution of women to society to be improved, e.g.

    - on unremunerated work, in agriculture for example

    - on the measurement of women's and men's paid employment and underemployment

    - on unremunerated work outside the national accounts, e.g., childcare and housework,

    - on time-use surveys (carry out and develop international classifications)

    - on the measurement of poverty

    - on access to health services, on violence, and on people with disabilities

- Governments to ensure regular production of statistical publications on women and men

- Review of adequacy of official statistical systems for gender disaggregated data to be ensured

- Quantitative and qualitative studies by research organisations, trade unions, NGOs, private sector, etc. to be developed and encouraged

- Such data to be used in policy development and implementation

The NDP commitments on gender mainstreaming

The NDP laid down a number of commitments to implement its gender mainstreaming requirements:

- Include equal opportunities among the **project selection criteria** for all measures

- Specific **indicators** to assess impact on gender equality will be developed where feasible, and **statistics** will be broken down by gender "where the nature of the assistance permits"

- Gender equality is to be incorporated into all **evaluations**

- Monitoring committees will include **equality representatives**

- **Gender balance** will be promoted on all monitoring committees

- A **co-ordinating committee** to oversee progress on equal opportunities and social inclusion

- The Plan will include **gender equality analysis** as appropriate, and summaries of how the various policy interventions will **impact** on equal opportunities

- A **Unit** will be established under the Department of Justice, Equality and Law Reform to **monitor and advise** on gender mainstreaming

- A Unit in the **Department of Education and Science** will carry out similar work specifically in the education sector

In addition, **gender impact assessments** were carried out at an early stage in the Plan. This involved the requirement that the programme complement documents[2] contained a brief description of the baseline position in relation to gender equality and, where appropriate, targets for the anticipated impact; and the completion of a gender impact assessment form for all non-exempt measures at the Programme Complement stage.

The gender impact assessment form contains the following three questions:

1. Outline the current position of men and women in the area which this measure will address (i.e. available data, baseline data, context data).

2. What factors lead to women and men being affected differentially in the area being addressed by this measure? i.e. gender patterns in daily life, time use, access to resources, etc. (availability of statistics?)

3. How can the factors which lead to women or men being affected differentially be addressed **and changed**? (i.e. proactive measures put in place)

These forms were completed for five of the six OPs (the Productive Sector OP in general does not complete them). These commitments were very much in line with those made by other organisations who have introduced gender mainstreaming.

---

2   The Programme Complement documents outline for each measure funded through an Operational Programme:

-The conditions under which funding will be allocated
-The type of funding available (e.g. grant, loan, training course)
-The finance plan for each measure
-The criteria for selection of projects under each measure (where relevant), and the composition of project selection boards
-The organisations which will spend the funding, and who will manage/monitor this spending
-What targets are to be reached (monitored by indicators) – baseline data available at onset relevant to measure.

The NDP Gender Equality Unit

To aid in progressing these commitments, the NDP Gender Equality Unit has been created to provide this support and advisory service. The Unit advises and supports NDP policy makers and implementers in gender mainstreaming. The Unit is funded through the Employment and Human Resources Development operational programme. The Unit has funding of €5.36 million over the period 2000 - 2006.

The Unit carries out work in a number of areas to support gender mainstreaming, including:

- Collecting and analysing data

- Engaging in a research programme to assess and support gender mainstreaming

- Providing advice, training and information on issues relating to gender mainstreaming in the NDP

- Advising on the gender impact assessment of policy proposals drawn up under the NDP

- Advising on and developing appropriate indicators to support gender mainstreaming in the NDP

- Monitoring the extent to which NDP commitments on gender equality are being met

- Providing inputs to the Equal Opportunities and Social Inclusion Coordinating Committee, which reviews how NDP commitments in the areas of equal opportunities and social inclusion are being met

- Providing inputs to the Mid Term Review carried out of the NDP

- Supporting participation by community and voluntary groups in the gender mainstreaming process

The Unit has five full-time staff – a head of Unit (position currently vacant), a statistician (on secondment from the Central Statistics Office (CSO)), a gender equality expert (engaged on contract), and two administrative staff (both on secondment from the Department of Justice, Equality and Law Reform).

Training and guidance for specific, targeted personnel

The Unit has organised over 20 training days, and trained over 700 NDP policy makers and implementing agency personnel. Training has covered both a general introduction to gender mainstreaming, and gender mainstreaming of particular policy areas[3].

The Unit also provides guidance in the form of a "Gender Proofing Handbook", which offers a clear step-by-step approach to gender proofing policies. Other guidance is provided as series of "How To" sheets which offer advice on how to promote gender balance in decision-making, and how to incorporate gender equality into project selection and evaluations.

---

3   These were industry, training, agriculture and rural development, housing, transport, urban development, sports and leisure, tourism and youth services.

Most recently, the Unit has produced a set of "Relevance Guidance Sheets" for all measures of the regional and infrastructure operational programmes, which highlight the relevance of gender equality to the specific measures, and advise on how gender equality can be promoted in each measure.

Research

The Unit has produced 19 fact sheets[4] on gender equality in different policy areas which have been widely circulated. The Unit has also funded research reports on gender equality issues in the following policy areas: NDP evaluations; housing and accommodation need; social welfare reform; valuing care work. The Unit also funded a report on Women in Irish Politics, and a photographic exhibition on women in decision-making, which has been touring Ireland since late 2002. Much of the Unit's statistical research will be described in more detail in the following section.

Statistics

I will make a slight digression before describing our statistical work. In 2002, the Unit developed and launched its own website www.ndpgenderequality.ie. All the Unit's statistical information, reports and research are available to download free of charge from the website. Given the Unit's policy maker target audience, it has been found that the website is a very efficient and effective means of communication and also for dissemination of publications and other resource material, as described below.

Three databanks of gender disaggregated statistics have been complied in 2000, 2002 and in 2004. These have been gathered from all known sources, e.g. Government Departments, State Agencies, NGO's, Universities, etc. The statistics provided are grouped in three separate ways. There are those that are relevant to each particular measure (useful if specific measure managers or implementers wish to do a quick search for highly measure relevant statistics). Secondly the gender disaggregated statistics are arranged by topic (useful if searching for broader context statistics – say in health, education or labour market areas). The third and final means of arrangement is by Ireland's two NUTS2 geographic regions, the Southern and Eastern region and the Border, Midland and Western region.

A new approach taken in the construction of the 2004 databank is that the information presented can be downloaded in both graph and spreadsheet formats to enable more rapid and more flexible use of the data provided, rather than as had previously been provided through flat HTML pages.

When the initial databank was compiled in 2000, a report was produced in conjunction with it which outlined major data gaps relevant to NDP areas. Among the areas identified were:

1. Housing – there has been a large population increase over the past decade, this coupled with a traditionally high percentage of Irish home ownership has created a construction and price "boom"

---

4   On gender equality issues in - industry, training, rural development, housing, transport, urban development, sports and leisure, tourism, arts and culture, film and media, research and development, community development, crime prevention, IT and e-commerce, infrastructure, environment and waste management, refugee issues, youth services, and application to the Peace II programme.

2.   Transport – a large increase in the labour force, coupled with the effect of the Celtic Tiger: "2 car/3 car families" now more common than a decade ago, with a very large increase in commercial traffic

3.   Enterprise – entrepreneurship, emphasis on increasing the number of start-ups by women and men

4.   Training in employment – lifelong learning, "re-training", "up-skilling" and adult education

5.   Flexible working arrangements – family friendly policies and work/life balance

6.   Job seniority and roles – both vertical/horizontal e.g. has the increase in female participation in labour force been reflected in an increased number of women in senior and decision making positions

7.   Progress over time – longitudinal studies

8.   Time use – unpaid work, division of labour in households and decision making / household roles

1.   Housing and   2. Transport

Two nationwide research surveys were carried out in 2001 and 2004 by the Unit. A report was produced entitled ***Women and Men in Ireland: their transport use and their housing tenure*** describing these results. Some interesting patterns emerge in these data. For example in the transport data it was observed that the difference between male and female car ownership rates had narrowed over the survey interval, while differences in housing in both the level (%) and the amount (€) of rent / mortgage paid by women and men also decreased over the survey intervals. Further details of these surveys and all research described in this paper and copies of reports produced are available on the Unit's website.

3.   Enterprises and Entrepreneurship

This research survey was carried out in 2003. A report was produced entitled *"**Women and Men in Ireland as Entrepreneurs and as Business Managers**"*. Among the observations were that a greater proportion of male entrepreneurs exported than female entrepreneurs. Less female than male entrepreneurs used IT for their business transactions. Also more male than female entrepreneurs had previously set up a business, suggesting that should male entrepreneurs initially fail in a venture they are more likely to "bounce back" than are female entrepreneurs. One similarity which caused some concern was the very low numbers of both women and men entrepreneurs who were in contact with State agencies or who engaged in training either prior to or while in the process of setting up their business.

4.   Training in employment and Life long learning

5.   Flexible working arrangements

6.   Job seniority levels and roles

Numbers four and five have been covered by the Central Statistics Office (CSO) through special modules of the labour force survey, which in Ireland is called the QNHS (Quarterly National Household Survey). Number six is due to be covered through the new NES (National Employment Survey) which is also being run by the CSO and for which fieldwork and data collection was carried out last year.

7. Progress over time

This is likely to be best covered by the new EU-SILC (Survey on Income and Living Conditions), carried out by CSO, which is currently replacing the ECHP (European Community Household Panel) EU survey.

8. Time use and unpaid work

Following a public consultation and request for submissions made by the CSO, it is possible that questions on unpaid work will be included in the Census 2006 questionnaire. The questions piloted are:

Q.21 Do you regularly do any unpaid work looking after the home or family?

Examples include: looking after children, cooking, cleaning, gardening, repairs and shopping

1. Yes, 1-14 hours a week

2. Yes, 15-28 hours a week

3. Yes, 29-42 hours a week

4. Yes, 43 or more hours a week

5. No

Q.22 Do you provide regular unpaid personal help for a friend or family member with a long-term illness, health problem or disability?

Include problems which are due to old age.

Personal help includes help with basic tasks such as feeding or dressing.

1. Yes, 1-14 hours a week

2. Yes, 15-28 hours a week

3. Yes, 29-42 hours a week

4. Yes, 43 or more hours a week

5. No

Q. 23 In the last 4 weeks have you done any of the following activities without pay?

Tick all the boxes that apply

1. Helping or voluntary work with a social or charitable organisation

2. Helping or voluntary work with a religious group or church

3. Helping or voluntary work with a sporting organisation

4. Helping or voluntary work with a political or cultural organisation

5. Any other voluntary activity

The CSO are currently assessing the pilot responses and are expecting to have their assessment complete within the next month or so.

This "uptake" of numbers 4, 5 and 6 by the Central Statistics Office highlights the vital importance of ongoing dialogue between the users and the producers of gender statistics (and all statistics!). To encourage this dialogue and to aid in the development of links between the NDP Gender Equality Unit and the Central Statistics Office, briefing sessions were held for CSO staff focused on issues, gaps, policy concerns, use, etc. Presentations were made to middle and senior officials in the CSO. Senior members of staff from the CSO also participated alongside Unit staff from the delivery side of the table. These presentations ranged from an initial "context" presentation on gender equality, to international perspectives and data practices, national perspectives and data practices and finally to data gaps and suggested areas of further interest. Time was also given to an open floor discussion of all issues raised. These training sessions were also of use when set in the context of the increase in evidence based policy and the increased demands on the CSO. One of the points that emerged was that it is very important that those producing the statistics know that what they produce is valued and the uses these data is then put to. This understanding enables a flexibility of response and an easier and more progressive evolution of data collection and production systems rather than a stop/start revolution of acquisition and analysis methods.

Gender statistics and Indicators

When examining indicators in a gender focussed way, the "areas of concern" outlined in the UN Beijing "Platform for Action" are considered amongst the widest ranging and broadest in scope. In 2000, an exercise was undertaken in Ireland to produce a listing of potential indicators relevant to each of these areas of concern. It was found that data were lacking for the majority in Ireland. This simply underlines the need for an agreed, relevant, realistic set of indicators for which reliable, timely data actually exists. While of course wishing to encompass as many areas as possible when dealing with such a listing is may be best to take the maxim "less is more" to heart. Indeed many of the indicators listings developed in recent years, for example the result of the agreement at EU head of government level at Lisbon – the Laeken indicators – are a short and concise grouping. Yet due to the presence of Primary, Secondary and Tertiary indicators (many of which are or have the potential to be gender disaggregated) a flexibility of response and description is available. From a purely national perspective the recent publication by the CSO of "Measuring Ireland's Progress" many of whose indicators are disaggregated by gender show the potential of such a construct, when based on existing data. Further work in 2004 on the indicators listing relevant to the "Areas of concern" identified in the Beijing Platform for Action and on the 2000 indicator listing was carried out to produce just such a small group of "useable" indicators.

Furthermore, there has been major cross Departmental work through the "Steering Group for Social and Equality Statistics" to identify existing data sources, combined with current and potential data needs across Government Departments. Follow up work on the SPAR report ("Statistical Potential of Administrative Records") describes what can be done in and done for each Department through the development of data strategies and the reporting within each Annual Report of a set of indicators measuring performance.

Assistance is also provided by the Unit to organisations with gender disaggregated data holdings, for example the State Railways, Iarnród Éireann, with help provided in analysing, publicising and disseminating gender disaggregated data and also in developing gender disaggregated indicators.

Agriculture

Another major area of work on gender statistics undertaken by the Unit was on the topic of agriculture. The Irish Department of Agriculture and Food produced a report entitled the "Role of Women in Agriculture" in 2000. This report included a large number of recommendations over a wide range of areas of farm life and supports. The NDP Gender Equality Unit undertook to progress two of these recommendations. This work then led to the production of a report *"Assessment of the main gaps in existing information on women in agriculture"* in the spring of 2003. It identified a number of gaps of interest for possible future work. One of the areas identified was an attitudinal survey of the role of women on the farm. The Unit undertook this and following the completion of a research survey carried out in 2003/2004 produced *"Women and Men on Farms in Ireland – their activities, attitudes and experience"*. Some observations from this survey were that more women than men had paid employment off the farm; indeed most of these had full-time employment. Inheritance/succession by a son or "keeping the name on the land" was important consideration for both women and men. Interestingly, men ascribed a higher level of importance to the work of women on the farm than the women placed on their own work! Overall it was found that the responses of women and men were often very similar.

Regional requirement for data in Ireland at NUTS2, NUTS3 and NUTS4 levels

Over the past decade there has been an increasing emphasis placed in Ireland on differences between our regions and also whether the effects of the "Celtic Tiger" have been felt equally across the country. The regional classifications are based on the NUTS (Nomenclature of Territorial Units) classification used by Eurostat. The NUTS3 regions correspond to the eight Regional Authorities established under the Local Government Act, 1991 (Regional Authorities) (Establishment) Order, 1993, which came into operation on 1 January 1994. The NUTS2 regions, which were proposed by Government and agreed by Eurostat in 1999, are groupings of the NUTS3 regions. The NUTS2 regions are the Border, Midland and Western region (Objective 1 region) and the Southern and Eastern region (Objective 1 in transition region). Regional Assemblies and regional Authorities have been established in the NUTS2 and NUTS3 regions and the requirement for data disaggregated by gender to be made available at these regional levels is growing. Consequently the Unit produced a booklet entitled *"Geographic Gender Equality – Women and Men across the regions of Ireland"* displaying an analysis of existing Census and other gender disaggregated data by these regional breakdowns through colour coded maps and tables

Non-specialist topics

The information resources provided by the Unit were not just for specific topics or indeed for policy makers or those in Agencies and NGO's. Taking the example of Statistics Sweden, the Unit produced a small pocket sized booklet entitled *"Women and Men in Ireland: Facts and Figures"* to mark Ireland's EU Presidency between January and June 2004. It presents a statistical snapshot of the relative positions of women and men across a range of different fields, ranging from population, health, education, income from paid employment, paid unemployment, paid unemployment, violence and crime, influence and power, living and lifestyles and transport. This was a highly successful publication with reprints required to fulfil the requests of many Government Departments who included the booklet in their Presidency welcome packs.

All of the Unit's publications and statistical databases and reports are available on our website: www.ndpgenderequality.ie

Support for community and voluntary organisations

The Unit has developed a range of supports to promote the participation of community and voluntary organisations in the gender mainstreaming process. This is strategically important, as within these sectors there is much energy and commitment to promoting gender equality. Supporting these groups can also therefore help to influence statutory organisations in developing good practice. Supports developed for this sector include: training on effective lobbying; training for women in decision-making; a handbook on how to develop and implement a gender equality policy; a fact sheet on men, boys and gender equality; a series of videos on women's activism in Ireland; and a high-profile Ireland/UK conference on partnership working across different sectors (attended by 300 people) in Dublin Castle.

Gender Budgeting Initiatives

The Unit is also piloting two gender budgeting initiatives in locally-based organisations. The aim of these pilots is to develop a gender budgeting template which can be disseminated to similar organisations.

Gender issues in some policy areas

Part of the Unit's work is to provide advice on gender equality issues in various policy areas. What might these be? Examples for Ireland are provided below (statistics sourced from www.ndpgenderequality.ie).

In terms of health, men have lower life expectancy at birth (73.5 years) than women (79 years). A higher percentage of adult males are classified as overweight, with 40% of men overweight, compared to 25% of women. Substance abuse also tends to be higher among men, with 72% of those attending drug treatment centres being male, and only 28% women (although this gender difference in treatment may not reflect actual substance abuse by women and men). Death by suicide is also higher for men – of those committing suicide 81% are men. Men are also much less likely than women to visit their doctor.

Among the homeless, in Ireland, 50% of the homeless are men; while 27% are women and 23% are children. But there are differences in how women and men are homeless – often men are alone, and living rough. Women are more likely to be homeless with their children, and to move from friends to relatives, without actually having a home of their own.

How about crime? Here men are over-represented, and this increases with age. Women are also more strongly represented among those carrying out petty crimes such as larceny; while men are more likely to carry out more serious crimes such as murder. In Ireland 91% of those convicted of a crime are men. However they are also 74% of murder victims, and 80% of assault victims. Women are more likely to be victims of sexual assault (74% of those assaulted) and of domestic violence (86% of complainants are women). Men are the vast majority (89%) of domestic violence offenders. These statistics indicate a gendered pattern in who commits crime, who is a victim of crime and who is convicted for crime.

For transportation, less women than men in Ireland own a car, have a full driving licence, or are insured to drive. Women are therefore more reliant on public transport. Of those travelling to work by bus in 41% were men and 59% women. And 63% of those travelling to work by car were men, while 37% were women. But men drive more dangerously – 75% of those killed on the roads are men, and only 25% women. Men are also 93% of those convicted for drunk driving. Tackling of all these strongly gendered patterns requires policies which recognise and address gender differences.

Gender mainstreaming a policy area

Case study: Youth Services

In considering how to gender mainstream a policy area, what issues should be considered, at what stage, and how will they alter the design and implementation of the policy? The example of the "Youth Services" measure of the NDP which provides funding for a number of schemes, including youth information centres, sports facilities for young people, and funding to youth groups will be used.

What are the gender equality issues for young people?

Early school leaving – almost two-thirds of early school leavers were boys. Girls, however, were more likely to be unemployed than boys.

Substance abuse – there is an increase in drug and alcohol consumption among both boys and girls, but more boys abuse drugs and alcohol. Physiological effects of drugs and alcohol can be different for boys and girls, as can social and psychological consequences of intoxication (e.g. violent behaviour, vulnerability)

Suicide – in Ireland the suicide rate for young men is 30 per 100 000 population (with a seven-fold increase in 20 years), while for young women the rate is 10 per 100 000. However, more young women attempt suicide.

Eating disorders – 90% of those suffering from eating disorders are girls.

Sports – girls' involvement in sport declines sharply with age, with implications for their future health.

Offenders – 80% of young offenders are male; many of those who are victims of assault are young men.

Communication/isolation - girls are generally more likely to use youth services, and to ring help lines. Their socialisation emphasises connection and building relationships, while the socialisation of boys often emphasises relating to or through "things" and activities.

When should these various issues be considered in policy development and implementation?

These issues are important at the following stages:

- Project selection
- Development and agreement on indicators
- Gender impact assessment
- Consultation
- Monitoring
- Evaluation

- Decision making

Project selection

At project selection stage the following factors should be considered (some of these issues apply for all projects, not just those targeted at young people).

First, who is on the project selection committee? Are men and women represented? From a wide variety of organisations?

Secondly, who drew up the project selection criteria? Was the group charged with this representative of women and men, and of statutory and non-statutory organisations?

Thirdly, what are these project selection criteria? Do they consider issues such as targets for under-represented groups (to ensure their representation is increased), and public transport to facilities funded (more important to women as they rely more on public transport and important for all young people)? How about costs/eligibility criteria (can all groups meet these costs/criteria?), and hours of opening? Do the organisations seeking funding have an equal opportunities policy? How is that implemented and monitored? Do the project application forms include a section asking how equality issues will be addressed? Do the projects provide training on equality issues for staff? Do they have indicators broken down by gender? How will they publicise the services they offer? Will the publicity reach both women and men (women are more likely to hear information from the radio, men from the newspaper)?

Indicators

In terms of indicators, the following would yield information on how young women and men are benefiting from the services or facilities provided through the youth services funding.

- Number of young people using the facility, by gender

- Number of single sex and mixed sex groups funded

- Number of girls and boys in youth groups funded

- Number of facilities built, by type (e.g. football pitches, gyms, halls)

Some indicators require a baseline value from which to set targets, and in some cases the baseline data (if it exists) is not broken down by gender. In this case, projects can commit to collecting gender disaggregated data on how many women and men benefit from the service/facility offered, and once a baseline has been gathered in this way, then indicators with targets can be set. Targets should always be realistic – it does not make sense to set a target that male-female participation should increase from 80/20 to 50/50 within five years. There a change from 80/20 to 65/35 might be more realistic over five years.

Gender Impact Assessment

Gender Impact Assessment in this area would help to identify differences in how young men and women use services and facilities, and which services and facilities they would like to access that are not currently available. Sources for this information include gender disaggregated statistics on existing youth services/facilities, and analyses which have been made of these. Another way to identify gender issues is through consultation.

For young people, this can be carried out with local schools, colleges, young people's organisations; and also if necessary through targeted research.

The types of issues which are likely to come up in this area, and their policy implications, are as follows:

- There is a need to provide services on a range of issues relevant to both young men and women - not just employment, transport, and contraception for example; but also eating disorders, suicide, depression.

- There is a need to advertise services and facilities which are available in both girls and boys schools.

- There is a need to find ways of incorporating excluded group, e.g. a programme to involve girls in football, or boys in learning domestic skills.

- There is a need to build facilities used by girls and those used by boys – for example, both football pitches (used by boys) and gyms (used by girls).

Addressing these issues could help to meet targets set to address any gender imbalances which exist.

Monitoring and evaluation

It is important that the commitments to promote gender equality are monitored regularly to ensure that they are being met. Gender disaggregated indicators must not just be collected, but reported and analysed. This is vital for later evaluation of the effectiveness of gender mainstreaming in the policy area.

Women in decision making

A final important issue to consider is the number of women and men in decision making positions, which is relevant to project selection committees, monitoring committees, and those implementing projects (who are the managers?). In general, women are not well represented in these posts. How can the numbers be increased? The following can be considered:

- Who can apply for the posts? Are they publicly advertised?

- Who nominates? Can they be requested to consider gender balance when nominating?

- Are non-statutory representatives paid for their time?

- Are meetings accessible – in terms of transport links, time at which they are held, childcare?

- What changes need to be made in the above in order to allow more women to participate?

Barriers to gender mainstreaming, and how to overcome them

Barriers

Lack of knowledge, information, understanding	Lack of political will
Other priorities	Cultural resistance, attitudes
Failure to perceive relevance of gender equality to policy area	Lack of sanctions
Lack of capacity and resources for gender equality advisors	Lack of time
Lack of public debate, awareness and media profile of gender equality issues	

Solutions

- Provide clear, statistical and practical information as well as practical and relevant guidance.

- Use a wide range of methods, e.g. cartoons, videos, one-to-one meetings, website, databanks, publications.

- Communication: statistical and practical information should be widely disseminated, targeted at the key people and readily available in a variety of electronic and hard-copy formats.

- Raise awareness through high-profile events and initiatives and tie in with publications and data resources.

- Demonstrate how gender mainstreaming improves policies through data and practical personalised steps.

- Support networks for those involved in gender mainstreaming and making available data resources.

- Prioritise certain measures for "special attention" – develop good practice models and describe how action can be taken at specific "micro" level – do not just consider from a wide "macro" level where it can be lost.

- Bring learning from positive action programmes into gender mainstreaming.

- Offer "rewards" (e.g. "equality marks") for good practice organisations.

I hope that this has given you a flavour of how gender statistics can be incorporated into gender mainstreaming and how work on gender statistics is being implemented in the National Development Plan Gender Equality Unit in Ireland. Both gender statistics and gender mainstreaming are still relatively new concepts in Ireland, and it is true that whilst our provision is developing, there is some way to go in terms of implementation and in particular the wider uptake and use of gender disaggregated statistics. This is just part of a wider trend to an increased level of evidence based policy making across Government in Ireland.

Gender Equality Statistics and Indicators: The Canadian Experience[1]

Brigitte Neumann, Nova Scotia Advisory Council on the Status of Women

Sheila Regehr, Status of Women Canada

Leroy Stone, Statistics Canada

Abstract

The need for gender equality indicators has been emphasized by a number of international conventions and declarations. However, many countries, including Canada, while doing fairly well in collecting gender statistics, still face challenges in using statistics as effectively as possible to provide the indicators needed to understand how conditions in society are changing for women and men. This paper will review the institutional framework within which gender equality statistics and indicators are developed. It provides examples of collaboration between federal, provincial and territorial governments, women's machinery, non-governmental organizations and academic institutions Canada that allows for the creation and use of these statistics in activities such as gender-based analysis, monitoring and reporting. Key examples of best practices from a variety of agencies and future directions will be discussed.

Introduction

This paper begins with a brief discussion of the difference between gender "statistics" and gender "indicators". It then describes essential features of the Canadian context; i.e., the arrangements within federal and a sample of provincial jurisdictions for the production and use of gender statistics. Then, examples from the federal jurisdiction are presented, followed by examples from four of the provincial jurisdictions. The paper concludes with a summary of accomplishments and challenges for the production of gender equality indicators.

Gender "Statistics" and Gender "Indicators"

Among the recommendations of the 1st United Nations World Conference on Women, held in Mexico City in 1975, was that governments should ensure that all their statistical products should be available with gender breakdowns.

---

1   The authors gratefully acknowledge the contributions of Suzanne Cooper, Status of Women Canada; Aisling Gogan, Newfoundland and Labrador Women's Policy Office; Hélène Massé, Sécretariat à la condition féminine, Gouvernement du Quèbec; and Mireille Kantiebo, Bureau of Women's Health and Gender Analysis, Health Canada. This paper does not express the official position of any government or organization with whom the authors and contributors are affiliated. The presentation in Palermo by Brigitte Neumann was made possible through funding support from Status of Women Canada and Statistics Canada.

Since that time, there has been an explosion of information in every field. And that explosion does include statistical information on a wide range of subjects, including matters related to the equality of women.

It is in part to make the statistical information explosion manageable, and to turn data into useful information–information useful to measuring where we are, setting milestones for where we want to be, defining our long-range goals and outcomes–that we share an interest in moving beyond statistics toward "indicators".

Gender equality indicators would tell us where women are in comparison to men in a concise but comprehensive manner. The comparisons of interest relate to central policy concerns, such as the paid and unpaid work situation of women and men, their economic status, their vulnerability to certain types of violence, their health and well-being, with due attention to cultural diversity and social inclusion. *Good* indicators would be concise and intuitively meaningful to the public and to decision-makers. *Excellent* indicators would be those where we had a clear understanding of what drives them, so that legislative, policy and program initiatives might be designed to affect them.

What are Canada's institutional arrangements for gender equality and for the production and use of gender statistics and indicators?

The Canadian Context

Canada is a confederation, with a constitutional division of powers between the federal government and the provinces and territories. Matters such as foreign affairs are in the sole jurisdiction of the federal government. Provinces have jurisdiction in education, health service delivery, social services and the administration of justice. Many responsibilities are shared: for example, the federal government has responsibility for the Divorce Act, but other areas of family law are in the jurisdiction of the provinces. It is necessarily a complex state of affairs, with many areas of overlapping responsibility of particular concern to women.

Canada's "machinery for the advancement of women" is headed by Status of Women Ministers in each of Canada's jurisdictions; i.e., fourteen of them. The Ministers are supported by status of women offices, which serve as focal points for both conduct of and training for gender based analysis and the use of statistics and indicators related to that effort within each jurisdiction. Since the early 1980s, Status of Women Ministers have met annually as a Federal/Provincial/Territorial (FPT) Forum to address matters of common concern, including work on economic gender equality indicators and violence against women indicators.

With increased success in "main-streaming" gender-based analysis, other government departments and agencies have increased their demand for and use of gender statistics: some examples will follow.

Activities related to gender statistics and indicators, particularly in the analysis work, are also found in some non-governmental organizations, including a large number of women's groups, think tanks, and universities: these linkages frequently feed back into grassroots organizations.

Within these networks, no one has over-arching authority for the creation of gender equality indicators, and therefore collegial collaboration and consensus-building are of critical importance, not only within and between governments, but also between governments and the communities they serve.

Examples from the Federal Jurisdiction

Statistics Canada

Statistics Canada has a long history of collecting and publishing gender-disaggregated data through both Census and survey techniques, as well as administrative sources. A special guide, *Finding Data on Women: A Guide to Major Data Sources at Statistics Canada*[2], is produced as a navigational aid to users by Status of Women Canada.

Statistics Canada has published a compendium of gender statistics since 1985. The most recent edition[3] contains 12 chapters, with topics including health, education, paid and unpaid work, income and earnings, criminal justice and housing. Chapters on immigrant and aboriginal women are also included. This publication is a statistical compendium, an excellent source of gender statistics at the national level, but the production of more complex indicators is not attempted.

A major contribution through Statistics Canada to the development of gender equality statistics is through the collection of census data on unpaid work–work in the home, looking after children and caring for elders. Analysis of these data promises to inform the further development of gender equality indicators, making both conceptual and technical innovation possible.

One area of needed innovation is that of reflecting population diversity in the design of any given indicator. There has been concern that indicators reflect not only the global average for a population, but that they also take into account the variation of its values among diverse population sub-groups, thus yielding an *adjusted* global index. The design of the adjusted global index should be such that as the dispersion of sub-population values increases, the adjusted value of the global index will fall; because it means that many segments of the population fail to share the level of the index that is indicated by the unadjusted global value. Thus, one single indicator will reflect both the overall level for the general population and diversity as indicated by the dispersion sub-population levels. In addition to the adjustment of the global value of an index, this approach would allow one to measure the overall degree of downward divergence (propensity to show below-average values) shown by one specific sub-population across several indicators. Its overall degree of downward divergence would be a statistical reflection of the group's level of social exclusion.

The development of gender indicators that take the diversity of Canada's population into account will be further encouraged by the federal government's current commitment to the development of an Aboriginal "report card" that is to include gender-relevant indicators and benchmarks, and is being designed through collaboration among governments and representatives of Aboriginal women's organizations.

---

2   Status of Women Canada. Finding Data on Women: A Guide to Major Sources at Statistics Canada. Ottawa: 1998 Also available for download at http://www.swc-cfc.gc.ca/pubs/0662266315/index_e.html January 2005

3   Statistics Canada. Women in Canada 2000: a gender-based statistical report (Catalogue number 89-503-XPE). Ottawa: 2000

Economic Gender Equality Indicators

The first effort to develop a set of economic gender equality indicators was published in 1997 by the FPT Status of Women Ministers[4], with the development work done by Statistics Canada in extensive consultation with Status of Women Canada and provincial officials.

Economic Gender Equality Indicators is notable because its conceptualization in general terms and in many details was done with active collaboration between statisticians and partners in policy-oriented agencies of the federal and provincial governments. As a result, some methodological decisions and frameworks for interpreting patterns in the data were influenced by the results of explicit attention to the perspectives and concerns of the key parties that would be using the statistical outputs.

The design of *Economic Gender Equality Indicators* was marked by an unusual degree of attention paid to some strategic questions concerning the values that should guide the construction of an index of gender equality. The work was premised, for example, on

> *"the importance of gender equality to other social goals, the need for social and economic policy integration and the need for balance in measuring and valuing male and female experience".*

This means that measures of sex differences were not immediately computed on variables for which data was already available for men and women. Instead, certain questions were first addressed, such as the following:

- What kind of gender equality matters – is it equality of opportunity or equality of outcomes?

- If the pertinent behaviours of men and women are greatly influenced by gender differences in values, whose value system should the indicator design accept as the standard against which performance is to be measured?

It is easy, for example, to inadvertently adopt male perspectives as the standard when computing equality indicators pertaining to work and income. *Economic Gender Equality Indicators* presented conceptual and technical innovations in connection with the design of measures of equality in the field of work. This development involved paying explicit attention to unpaid work, and allowing measures of the volume and distribution of unpaid work to enter into the construction of the indicators.

The Economic Gender Equality Indicators were widely publicized in the national media. Within governments, officials engaged in a variety of knowledge exchange activities with officials in other relevant government departments and agencies. A symposium was held to further discuss both national and international approaches to such indicators. And, finally, a subsequent update of the indicators was published in 2000.

Nevertheless, despite being technically innovative, the Economic Gender Equality Indicators are not yet established as a regular product, widely reported, understood and used, to provide direction to policy or program design.

---

4   Federal-Provincial-Territorial Ministers Responsible for the Status of Women. Economic Gender Equality Indicators. Ottawa: Status of Women Canada, 1997. Also available for download at http://www.swc-cfc.gc.ca/ January, 2005

Women's Health Indicators

The Bureau of Women's Health and Gender Analysis of Health Canada (formerly the Women's Health Bureau) has been leading the development of Women's Health Indicators since 2002, an initiative designed to address the key commitments and strategic directions adopted by the Bureau of Women's Health and Gender Analysis through Health Canada's *Women's Health Strategy*[5]. The goal of the project is to provide baseline information for monitoring women's health and to facilitate knowledge transfer to policy decision-makers, potential users and the public.

To date, a synthesis report, *A Profile of Women's Health Indicators in Canada*[6], has been produced, and ongoing stakeholder consultations held. To fill identified gaps in women's health indicators, research proposals focused on socio-cultural roles and responsibilities, social exclusion, the environment and health services–all in relation to women's health–have been solicited. Two successful research projects are currently underway on the following topics:

- "Measuring Health Inequalities Among Canadian Women: Developing a Basket of Indicators"

- "Psychotropic Drug Use as a gender-sensitive marker of emotional health for women in Canada".

Health Canada seeks to use this information to assist in the further development of policies, programs and services that reflect the health needs and concerns of women. The long-term aim is to improve ways that women's health is measured, to more accurately monitor changes in women's health status and outcomes, with attention to both gender and cultural diversity. The women's health indicators will inform health policy decision-making, enabling an adequate surveillance and policy response to women's diverse health needs, and enabling compliance with the Health Canada policy requirements for gender based analysis in all its policy initiatives[7].

Mandated Statistical Reporting and Monitoring: National and International

At the federal level, Canada has a number of important pieces of legislation that require monitoring of gender differences in program utilization and impact. Two important examples are the utilization of Employment Insurance, and the monitoring function of the Employment Equity Act.

The Employment Insurance Monitoring and Assessment Reports[8] are important to women both because they provide detail on income replacement after job loss, and because they show what proportion of women were able to access maternity, parental and compassionate care benefits.

5   Health Canada. Health Canada's Women's Health Strategy, 1999. Cat.H21-138/1997. Also available for download at http://www.hc-sc.gc.ca/english/women/womenstrat.htm

6   Colman, Ronald. A Profile of Women's Health Indicators In Canada, 2003. Prepared for the Women's Health Bureau, Health Canada.
     http://www.gpiatlantic.org/whbreport.pdf

7   Health Canada. Health Canada's Gender-based Analysis Policy, 2000. Cat. H34-110/2000E-IN.
     http://www.hc-sc.gc.ca/english/women/gba_policy.htm

8   Human Resources Development Canada. Employment Insurance Monitoring and Assessment Reports. 1997-2003. Available for download at http://www.hrdc-drhc.gc.ca/.en/ei/reports/eimar_2003.shtml January 2005

The Employment Equity reports[9] are mandated in legislation, and provide information on hiring, promotion and retention of women, visible minorities, aboriginal persons and persons with disabilities in those sectors of the work force governed by the Act.

Canada also has gender-disaggregated data for income security and pension programs, student loans and taxation. Such statistics are useful in measuring the relative impact on women and men of, for example, tax and transfer policies in relation to dependent care.

Canada's Performance[10], published by Treasury Board Canada, is the Government of Canada's annual report to Parliament and the public. Discussed in more detail at this World Forum, the report does include reference to gender differences in various domains.

Finally, the federal jurisdiction assists equality-seeking women's organizations in their work in international contexts, such as reporting for the Convention on the Elimination of all Forms of Discrimination (CEDAW) through an alternative report to CEDAW[11] in response to Canada's submission. The alternative report uses a wide range of publicly available data to analyze the situation of women in Canada, shedding further light on gender equality at the national level from an advocacy perspective.

Examples from the Provinces

Newfoundland and Labrador

The Newfoundland and Labrador Women's Policy Office works closely with its Statistics Agency and other provincial government departments to ensure that statistical information along with qualitative evidence is used to assess gender impacts of legislative and policy initiatives.

Newfoundland and Labrador has also developed a Community Accounts[12] system, an online data retrieval system for statistical information available for 400 communities, 80 census subdivisions, 20 economic development zones, 6 planning regions and the province as a whole. The system can generate tables for a wide variety of social and economic indicators, including one termed Well-Being. In most cases, the data can be broken down by gender, age and family status.

Currently, a new section or "account" is being added, on community safety. The intention is to integrate indicators for such variables as the incidence of family violence as an important tool for issue identification and tracking.

---

9   Human Resources Development Canada. Employment Equity Annual Reports 1999-2003. Available for download at http://www.hrdc-drhc.gc.ca/asp/gateway.asp?hr+en/lp/lo/lswe/we/ec_tools/reports/annual/index-we.shtmlandhs=wzp January, 2005

10 Treasury Board of Canada Secretariat. Canada's Performance 2002. Available for download at http://www.tbs-sct.gc.ca/report/govrev/02/cp-rc_e.asp January 2005

11 Canadian Feminist Alliance for International Action. Canada's Failure to Act: Women's Inequality Deepens. Submission to the UN Committee on the Elimination of Discrimination Against Women, January 2003. Available for download at http://www.fafia-afai.org/Bplus5/natFAFIAreport012103.pdf January 2005

12 Newfoundland and Labrador. Community Accounts. http://www.communityacounts.ca January 2005

The information in the Community Accounts is used in many different ways both as a gender-based analysis tool and to identify issues that affect women at the community level. Some specific policy and program applications have included:

- The Department of Health and Community Services determined communities to target for youth at risk programs. The community accounts allowed for detailed analysis by gender and other relevant factors at the community level so that programs could be properly tailored for community needs;

- The Labrador Strategic Social Plan Regional Planning Committee used the Accounts to determine the best location for a new Family Resource Centre. As a result of using the Accounts' dynamic output features the Regional Planning Committee recommended that two Centres were required.

- The WPO is currently using the Accounts as part of its Annual Report. Community Accounts will allow WPO to report on women's economic and social status, including their overall well-being. Over time, WPO will be able to track changes and assess progress.

Over time, the Women's Policy Office will use the Community Accounts system to track changes and monitor progress on women's economic status and well-being. However, at this time, a specific set of gender equality indicators has not been identified or implemented.

Nova Scotia

Nova Scotia has produced gender equality indicators in the form of statistical compendia since the late 80s[13], bringing together Census data and other public domain statistics relevant to women's equality, with a focus on trends in a wide range of issues of concern to women and to society as a whole. The current statistical series[14] includes demographic issues; income and earnings; education and training; paid and unpaid work; and family violence and personal safety. These publications are immensely popular, reaching a wide variety of audiences including government officials, women's groups, educators and students, and the media, for example.

At this time, Nova Scotia is also adapting the Community Counts system developed by Newfoundland and Labrador to our own province, with leadership from the Department of Finance. As a development partner, the NS Advisory Council on the Status of Women will work toward a system that reflects a commitment to gender equity, cultural diversity and social inclusion.

While the statistical reports show significant progress for women as a totality, they also show that progress is not equally shared by all women. Aboriginal women, women of African descent, immigrant women, low income women and others face multiple sources of discrimination and disadvantage. In order to consistently address these issues, they are considered "up front" in our work.

---

13   Nova Scotia Women's Directorate. Women in Nova Scotia: A Statistical Handbook. Halifax:1st edition, 1990; 2nd edition, 1995

14   Sandra McFadyen. Family Matters; Money Matters; Family Violence and Personal Safety; Learners and Teachers: Women's Education and Training; Women's Paid and Unpaid Work. Parts 1-5 of Women in nova Scotia: A Statistical Series. Halifax, NS: Nova Scotia Advisory Council on the Status of Women. Available for download at http://www.gov.ns.ca/staw

For example, the NS Advisory Council on the Status of Women is currently a lead partner, with the Atlantic Centre of Excellence for Women's Health, in the Healthy Balance Research Program, funded as a Community Alliance on Health Research by the Canadian Institutes for Health Research. The research program investigates the relationship between women's paid work and unpaid caregiving to their health status. Four research teams, two focused on qualitative work and two, on quantitative are at work. At the beginning of the program, four Equity Reference Groups[15] were set up: women of African descent; Aboriginal women; women with disabilities; and immigrant women. This helped immensely in developing appropriate questions, recruiting participants, helping to interpret findings and providing feedback to communities.

The approach taken in Healthy Balance is a model to follow in indicators work, work that depends on consensus-building and the possibility of disaggregation of indicators to reflect the realities of various subgroups of women.

Quebec

In February 1997, with the publication of the *1997-2000 Action Plan for Women Throughout Quebec*[16], the Government of Quebec acted on commitments made at the United Nations' Fourth World Conference on Women, held in Beijing, in 1995. In doing so, it adopted, initially on a trial basis, a developmental project aimed at introducing Gender-based Analysis (GBA) into its laws, policies, programs and public services.

"Gender-based Analysis" quickly gave way to "Gender-based Approach," a more appropriate description of the set of processes that underlie the initiative. As a result, Gender-based Approach is the term used throughout the work.

The "gender based approach" trials performed by the Government of Quebec have now been completed and a final report is being prepared[17]. The report will present information drawn from the entire trial period, from 1997 to 2003, with the participation of 11 departments and organizations in the introduction of GBA into the Government of Quebec.

From the beginning of the project, "gender based approach" was defined as a management approach aimed at identifying, in a preventive manner, during the design or evaluation of government initiatives, the specific effects that such initiatives might have on women and men, taking their particular socio-economic conditions into account. This approach thus shed light on decisions to be made in respecting the principle of equality between men and women in Quebec.

---

15   Nasser, S., Neumann, B. and Amaratunga, C. The Puzzles of Partnership: Creating Common Ground so that Research Makes a Difference, presented at the Annual Conference of the Canadian Evaluation Society, Vancouver, British Columbia, June 2003 . Available for download under "publications" at http://www.healthyb.dal.ca/

16   Secrétariat à la condition féminine. Programme d'action 1997-2000 pour toutes les québecoises, dans le cadre de La politique en matière de condition féminine, Un avenir à partager... Québec : Gouvernement de Québec, 1997

17   For further background, see Massé, H., Laberge , M. and Massé, G., L'Analyse differenciée selon les sexes au gouvernement du Québec : vers une mobilisation interne et des alliances stratégiques pour l'égalite. Management International 7(1) : 79-88 Also available for download at http://www.scf.gouv.qc.ca/pdf_fr/Ads.pdf

It must be emphasized, as specialists of many international organizations have done, that the "gender based approach" can in no way replace the "women-specific approach." The "gender based approach" is an additional measure. The women-specific approach is intended to put in place measures to correct demonstrated and persistent cases of discrimination. Such measures will continue to be necessary so long as systemic discrimination continues (e.g. the Pay Equity Act).

The targeted objective throughout this initiative, including nine trial projects in seven departments, has been to determine the best method for developing and proposing flexible and adaptable means of ensuring its adoption into government practices. The Institut de la statistique du Québec (ISQ) has been a major player in the development of the "gender based approach" from the very start of the project.

ISQ involvement in this large government project reinforces ISQ policy that, where it is possible and relevant, statistical programs should report data by gender. In the sectors for which it is responsible, ISQ produces statistics by gender; in other sectors, ISQ asks the relevant government departments and organizations to provide it with statistics disaggregated by gender.

Departments and organizations use these statistics in the design and evaluation of their programs. The initial stage of the development of planned governmental measures requires rigorous analysis based on reliable data. As a means of supporting the introduction of the gender based approach, the ISQ Internet site[18] identifies in the "Society" section of the Official Statistics on Quebec, the business lines for which data reported by gender is available. It is from this type of data that gender equality indicators can be developed to measure progress towards equality between men and women during a specific period of time.

In 2003, the government of Quebec approved a change in name and the "approche différenciée selon les sexes" [Gender-based Approach]" became the "approche intégrée de l'égalité" [Gender mainstreaming]. The report to be tabled in the coming weeks will help the government to make appropriate decisions regarding the measures needed in this area.

Accomplishments and Challenges

Although Canada has not yet established a set of gender equality benchmarks and indicators, the process toward such an accomplishment has begun. One of the impacts of a decentralized government is that it is difficult to achieve consensus on one universal set of gender equality indicators. However, the institutional framework that has been established in Canada allows for collaboration among federal, provincial, and territorial governments, universities, and NGOs at both national and community levels in the production and use of gender equality indicators.

An important challenge facing those who will do this work is theoretical: what assumptions will we make about how gender inequality arises and is maintained? What decisions will we make about the proper measures to reflect the role of the state, the family and individual, the community and the market? How will we incorporate an adequate reflection of the unpaid work of caring for children, persons with disabilities and the aged, so central to women's societal contribution? The biggest challenge

---

18   http://www.stat.gouv.qc.ca/default_an.htm

confronting indicator development is not necessarily technical: it is to develop clear and compelling understandings of substantive equality, and how these can be operationalised to reflect the realities of women in all their diversity. The 1997 publication, *Economic Gender Equality Indicators,* began to address these issues and provides a baseline for further efforts.

A further challenge arises from the need to position the further development of gender equality indicators in such a way that trends can be established through retrospective analyses and change can be meaningfully interpreted. For example, a commonly used statistic, the ratio of earnings between women and men commonly referred to as the wage gap, has serious interpretive problems in that apparently positive change–a narrowing of the gap–can arise from falling male incomes as well as from rising female incomes. Thus while "equality" might be achieved in an arithmetic sense, the broader question addressed by Australian colleagues at this Forum, "Is life getting better?" must also be considered.

In short, while much progress has been made in the design and use of gender equality indicators, important innovations need to be pursued in future work. Such work includes not only technical innovation, but also methodologies that enable participation in indicator development by the constituencies about which we wish to generalize, and that in turn foster the consensus on which successful indicators depend.

Rewarding Jobs: Government Policy and Work Incentives[1]

Christopher Heady, Head of Tax Policy and Statistics Division, OECD

Herwig Immervoll, Directorate for Employment, Labour and Social Affairs, OECD

Introduction

There is widespread concern around the world about "benefit dependency" and the need to provide incentives for people of almost all skill levels to participate in the labour market. This concern is particularly focussed on low-skilled people who command low wages when they do participate. These low-skilled people are generally observed to have lower employment rates than higher skilled people, and it is widely believed that this is partly explained by the tax and benefit systems placing them in a situation where the financial return to work is inadequate.

This concern naturally leads to a wish to design policies that improve the financial return to work and to the search for indicators that can measure the effect of policy on work incentives. Such indicators could be used for several purposes: the identification of sub-groups in the population for whom policy has seriously reduced work incentives; the measurement of progress in improving incentives; and the comparison across countries of the disincentives created by the tax and benefit systems, as in the "open co-ordination" approach of the European Union.

The OECD produces two regular publications that provide such indicators for its member countries: *Taxing Wages* and *Benefits and Wages*. The first concentrates on measuring the taxation of labour – personal income taxes, social security contributions and payroll taxes – but also takes account of family cash benefits that are effectively equivalent to family-related tax reliefs that some countries provide. It presents tax indicators for households earning in a range either side of average earnings. *Benefits and Wages* concentrates on a lower range of in-work incomes and also examines the income situation of unemployed individuals and their families. It incorporates social security and welfare benefits into its analysis, to obtain a full picture of the effects of both taxes and benefits on the incentive to work.

Of course, tax and benefit systems have other objectives apart from providing incentives to work. Taxes are designed to raise revenues for government programmes in a way that takes account of a broad range of social objectives, including income distribution. Social benefits are primarily aimed at either income maintenance or poverty avoidance. Thus, indicators of work incentives alone would give insufficient guidance for

1   The results reported here represent output from a joint project between the OECD and the European Commission which is partly financed by the European Community. The views expressed herein are those of the authors and do not implicate the European Commission, the OECD or the governments of respective member countries.

policymakers. Therefore, both of the OECD publications provide information that can be used to measure progress in a fuller range of objectives.

Following this introduction, the next section provides a brief outline of the methodology behind these two publications. The section following provides illustrations of the indicators that are included in, or can be derived from, these publications. Finally, the last section contains some concluding comments.

Methodology

The methodologies of Taxing Wages and Benefits and Wages are fundamentally similar, but the inclusion of detailed benefit information in the latter results in some differences. To avoid confusion, this section first outlines the Taxing Wages methodology and then moves on to Benefits and Wages. Full details of the methodologies can be found in the respective publications.

The Taxing Wages methodology

The basic approach is conceptually straightforward: a small number of "typical families" are chosen and the tax rules for each country are applied to them in order to calculate both the average and the marginal effective tax rates. For the purpose of these calculations, universal family benefits paid in cash in respect of dependent children are treated as negative taxes. This is to permit comparisons between those countries that mainly assist families through the tax system and those that mainly assist them with cash benefits.

It is assumed that each employee's annual income from employment is equal to a given fraction of the average gross wage earnings of adult, full-time workers in the manufacturing sector of each OECD economy – referred to as the average production worker (APW). The taxes considered are personal income tax, social security contributions and more rarely payroll taxes, payable on gross wage earnings. Consequently, any income taxes that might be due on non-wage income, as well as all other kinds of taxes —e.g., corporate income tax, net wealth tax and consumption taxes — are not taken into account.

In calculating taxes, it is necessary to model various tax reliefs that reduce the amount of tax that would otherwise be paid. Two broad categories of reliefs may be distinguished: *Standard tax reliefs*, which are unrelated to the actual expenditures incurred by the taxpayer and are automatically available to all taxpayers that satisfy the eligibility rules specified in the legislation; *Non-standard tax reliefs*, which are wholly determined by reference to actual expenses incurred and are neither fixed amounts nor fixed percentages of income. Standard tax reliefs are taken into account in calculating taxes, but non-standard reliefs are disregarded. Tax reliefs and family cash transfers universally paid in respect of dependent children between five and twelve years of age who are attending school are included. If tax reliefs or cash transfers vary within this age range, the most generous provisions are taken. The case of twins is explicitly disregarded.

The present methodology identifies eight types of taxpayers:

- a single individual with no children earning 67, 100 and 167 per cent of APW earnings, respectively;

- a lone parent with two children earning 67 per cent of APW earnings;

- a married couple with two children and a single earner at the APW level;

- two-earner married couples, with earnings split between the two partners at 100–33 per cent of APW earnings, both with and without children; and finally

- a couple with children with the earnings split 100–67 per cent of APW earnings.

In cases of families with children, the children are assumed to be aged between five and twelve. The family is assumed to have no income source other than employment and — depending on family-size — universal cash benefits.

The main measures of average effective tax rates provided in *Taxing Wages* are the personal taxes and the overall "tax wedge" for each of the typical families. In addition, the corresponding marginal tax rates are provided, taking account of the fact that these rates can be different for the two workers in a two-earner household. The tax wedge is the sum of income tax, social security contributions (employer's and employee's) and payroll taxes minus universal family benefits, expressed as a proportion of total wage cost (wage plus employer's social security contribution and payroll tax). The personal taxes, on the other hand, ignore employer's social security contributions and payroll taxes and simply report income tax and employee's social security contributions minus universal family benefits as a proportion of the wage. It can, therefore, be thought of as that part of the taxation of labour that is visible to the employee.

In a competitive labour market, the division of the tax wedge between the amount that legally falls on the employee (the personal taxes) and the amount that legally falls on the employer is irrelevant to any economic outcome in terms of employment, hours of work and after-tax income. This suggests that the personal taxes are a less useful measure than the tax wedge. However, for workers who are paid a legally defined minimum wage, the personal taxes are important in terms of determining their after-tax income in employment although it will be the employer's social security contributions and payroll tax that affects how many are employed. It may also be important for workers whose wages are determined by trade union agreements, at least until the agreement is renegotiated.

The *Taxing Wages* approach is not the only way in which the taxation of labour income can be assessed. One alternative is to calculate the implicit average effective tax rate, by estimating the total amount of tax paid on labour earnings in a country and dividing that by an estimate of total wages or labour costs. Pioneering work of this sort was undertaken by Mendoza, Razin and Tesar (1994). This stimulated a substantial literature including OECD (2001). Another alternative is to use a micro-simulation model (based on publicly available sample survey data) to calculate labour taxes for a representative sample of a country's population. An interesting recent example of this has been the construction of the European tax-benefit model, EUROMOD, described by Sutherland (2001).

There are four major differences between these approaches.

- First, they differ in the amount of detail they provide. An implicit average effective tax rate calculation for any one country in one year produces just one tax ratio. The *Taxing Wages* methodology generate results for a small number (currently 8) of different typical families, while micro-simulation models can produce results for each of the households or stratified groups in the database that it uses.

- Second, they differ in the extent to which they are based on "real" data. Implicit average effective tax rates have the advantage of being based entirely on observed quantities (although there are disputes over whether these are exactly the appropriate quantities), and thus reflect all the factors that influence the amount of taxes actually paid. Micro-simulation models are based on real households and the results are therefore capture the variability of tax burdens in a heterogeneous population, but the taxes paid are usually simulated in a similar way to the *Taxing Wages* calculation (for instance, they usually assume full tax compliance and cannot take account of all relevant non-standard tax reliefs). The calculations in *Taxing Wages* take no account of observed data.

- Third, they differ in the tax rate information that they provide: both micro-simulation models and *Taxing Wages* are able to provide marginal and average effective tax rates, but implicit effective tax rate calculations yield only an average rate.

- Fourth, *Taxing Wages* takes account of cash benefits to families, as can micro-simulation models. This is not done with the currently calculated implicit effective tax rates, and would only be possible if data on aggregate cash benefits to families were available.

The value of the approach that lies behind each measure depends on what is being studied, so that different approaches are likely to be most suitable in attempting to answer different questions. The particular strength of the *Taxing Wages* approach is comparability between countries: the typical households are the same in each country (with the wage received bearing the same relationship to the APW) and so differences between effective tax rates are always due to differences in the tax systems and not to differences in the structure of the population. In contrast, differences in implicit average effective tax rates between countries or over time reflect a combination of differences in tax systems (both policy and administration) and differences in population structure (in terms of income distribution, demographics and other factors that affect tax liability).

This source of strength for some purposes is also a limitation for others. For example, the limited range of incomes considered in *Taxing Wages* makes it impossible to obtain an overall picture of how labour is taxed. In contrast, the implicit average effective tax rate takes account of the taxation of all workers. This is useful in analysing how the tax base is allocated between labour, capital and consumption. In principle, it is the micro-simulation model that can produce the combination of comprehensive coverage and individual detail. However, although there have been considerable advances at the European level (EUROMOD), the complexity of microsimulation models can cause problems in terms of timeliness and comparability across large numbers of countries.

The Benefits and Wages methodology

Similar to *Taxing Wages*, the *Benefits and Wages* series presents calculations for selected "typical" income and family situations. Advantages and limitations that apply to this methodology in general are therefore also relevant for indicators shown in this publication. While the tax rules used as part of the calculations are the same as in *Taxing Wages*, the range of earnings considered is different and includes both low in-work incomes below 67 per cent of APW and, most importantly, non-employed individuals with no earnings at all.

In order to characterise the income situation of these individuals, the calculations need to adopt a wider scope taking into account not only taxes and universal benefits but also income-related and unemployment benefits. These include unemployment insurance and assistance payments, social assistance and housing benefits, employment-conditional "in-work" benefits as well as family and childcare benefits. The focus is on the effects of taxes and benefits on current household incomes and this implies two differences vis-à-vis the *Taxing Wages* approach. While employer social security contributions and payroll taxes can be included if desired, they are not generally part of the analysis. At the same time, mandatory employee insurance contributions, such as payments to private insurance companies, are taken into account (and thus reduce calculated net incomes) even if they do not correspond to the formal definition of a tax.

Calculated net incomes can be used to assess the levels and adequacy of net incomes across family circumstances and countries. By comparing incomes of different income and labour market situations, it is possible to examine the financial incentives of moving between them. For instance, the results provided in *Benefits and Wages* include measures of net replacement rates and marginal effective tax rates for a range of different family types, at different earnings levels and at different stages during a given spell of unemployment.

Examples

The purpose of this section is to provide examples of policy-relevant indicators that can be generated by the OECD's methodology for modelling taxes and social benefits. The examples presented here relate to: the taxation of low-paid workers, the tax treatment of families, tax advantages for two-earner couples, the financial gain of additional work efforts (marginal effective tax rates), the degree of income maintenance provided by existing tax and benefit systems in the event of unemployment (net replacement rates) and the adequacy of incomes available to low-wage workers and benefit recipients.

Taxation of low-paid workers

There has been considerable recent interest in reducing the barriers to the employment of low-paid workers. The tax barrier to employment can be summarized by the "tax wedge", the proportional difference between the costs of a worker to their employer (wages and employer social security contributions) and the amount of income that the worker receives (wages minus personal income tax and social security contributions, plus any available family benefits). This tax wedge can be an "average wedge" (measuring the tax burden as a percentage of labour costs for a particular worker) which affects the likelihood of the worker being employed or a "marginal wedge" (measuring the increase in the tax burden that results from an increase in income that costs the employer one unit of currency) which affects the amount of work effort that the worker supplies.

Table 1 presents data on the 2003 values of the average and marginal wedges for a single worker with no children earning 67% of APW in each OECD country, as well as the amounts by which these numbers have increased since 2000. The average wedge shows a considerable range: from about 12% in Mexico and Korea to about 47% in Belgium and Germany. The marginal wedges are almost always higher, for each country, than the average wedge, reflecting the progressive nature of taxes on labour in OECD countries. Generally, countries with a high average wedge also have a high marginal wedge but the correlation is not perfect: France has the highest marginal wedge but has an average wedge that is much nearer the average.

Table 1. Tax Wedge for Low-income Workers in 2003

	2003 Values		Increase since 2000	
	Average wedge	Marginal wedge	Average wedge	Marginal wedge
Australia	24.70	35.38	n.a.	n.a.
Austria	40.15	55.23	0.02	3.31
Belgium	47.48	69.74	-2.47	3.85
Canada	30.69	35.30	n.a.	n.a.
Czech Republic	42.04	44.91	0.42	0.00
Denmark	39.86	43.31	-1.38	-7.37
Finland	39.47	51.05	-2.99	-3.20
France	37.65	74.07	-1.93	1.59
Germany	46.68	59.80	0.20	-0.36
Greece	34.28	34.28	0.00	0.00
Hungary	41.01	55.34	-5.21	-0.91
Iceland	23.76	40.42	3.14	1.44
Ireland	16.69	29.95	-1.42	1.84
Italy	41.27	52.60	-2.00	2.45
Japan	26.14	28.11	3.02	3.02
Korea	12.85	15.68	-2.35	-1.95
Luxembourg	27.34	36.45	-3.03	-5.19
Mexico	12.39	17.44	2.50	0.53
Netherlands	37.56	54.07	-3.07	-0.19
New Zealand	18.94	21.00	0.26	0.00
Norway	33.72	43.09	-0.52	0.00
Poland	41.64	45.33	-0.25	0.00
Portugal	29.62	37.78	-0.76	-1.62
Slovak Republic	40.32	43.13	0.78	-1.26
Spain	32.75	49.62	-0.08	5.94
Sweden	44.78	51.43	-2.94	-2.13
Switzerland	26.56	31.19	-0.40	-0.91
Turkey	41.15	44.53	2.07	1.60
United Kingdom	26.20	40.60	0.91	1.21
United States	27.12	34.11	-1.86	-0.45

Note: n.a. indicates that data are not available because of break in the time series.

Because of the concerns about unemployment of low paid workers, a number of countries have taken steps to reduce their tax wedges, as is shown by negative entries in the last two columns of table 1. Hungary, the Netherlands, Finland and Sweden show particularly large reductions in the average wedge. These countries all have fairly large wedges and, indeed, there is a pattern of larger reductions in countries with higher wedges. Marginal wedges have also fallen substantially in some countries, but there is only a weak relationship between the reductions in the marginal and average wedges, and no pattern of larger reductions for countries with larger wedges. This perhaps reflects the fact that average wedges have been seen as a more important concern than marginal wedges.

The tax treatment of families

While work incentives are an important aspect of tax design, broader social issues are also important. One very widespread feature of tax systems in OECD countries is the preferential treatment given to families. This is illustrated in Figure 1, which reports personal taxes (personal income tax and employee social security contributions, less family cash benefits) for a single worker with no children and a family consisting of a single-earner couple with two children. Both households are earning the APW wage. It should be noted that the subtraction of family cash benefits in computing personal taxes is very important for comparability, as some countries provide assistance to families mainly through the tax system while others mainly use cash benefits.

Figure 1: Personal Taxes by Single Individuals and Families

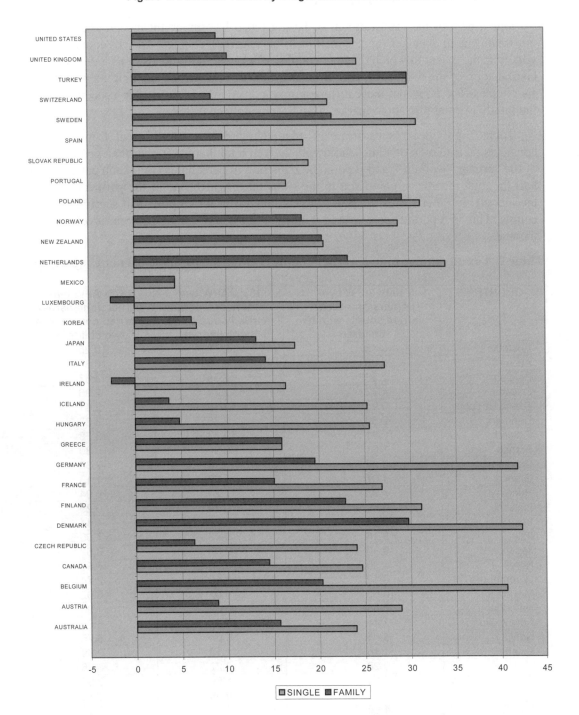

Figure 1 shows that there are very wide differences between OECD countries in the size of the preference they give to families. At one extreme, Greece, Mexico and Turkey give no preference at this income level. At the other, Ireland and Luxembourg give such large preferences that the personal taxes are negative: family cash benefits outweigh the sum of personal income tax and employee social security contributions.

Tax advantages for two-earner couples

One aspect of the tax treatment of families also has important incentive effects: the tax treatment of married (and, sometimes, un-married) couples. OECD countries vary widely in the extent to which they tax couples as separate individuals or as a unit, or some combination of the two. They also differ in whether they provide explicit tax preferences for couples. The effects of these different provisions on the incentive for a second adult in the family to enter the labour market have been widely analysed.

Table 2 provides results from an approach that is a bit different from usual. It considers the situation of a household with a given total income (rather than given income of the "primary worker"), and reports the reduction in personal taxes if each partner earns half the total income as compared to the situation in which one of the partners earns all the income. In other words, it shows the tax incentives for employment sharing within a couple. This is reported for a couple with two children, at three different levels of total income.

Table 2. Tax advantage of two-earner couples compared to single-earner couples, 2002

COUNTRIES	100% APW two-earners/one-earner married couple with two children	133% APW two-earners/one-earner married couple with two children	167% APW two-earners/one-earner married couple with two children
Australia	3.18	6.59	10.25
Austria	6.98	6.00	10.85
Belgium	2.88	2.35	3.87
Canada	4.77	2.21	2.96
Czech Republic	0.94	1.19	2.41
Denmark	-2.50	2.75	6.83
Finland	10.91	10.33	13.78
France	3.01	0.94	0.30
Germany	0.94	0.18	-2.35
Greece	1.07	5.82	11.13
Hungary	7.93	12.24	16.94
Iceland	0.41	0.34	0.29
Ireland	2.84	1.24	4.14
Italy	5.16	5.49	7.68
Japan	-0.36	-0.08	0.62
Korea	1.36	4.66	7.60
Luxembourg	0.12	0.10	2.74
Mexico	10.55	9.02	10.92
Netherlands	6.58	-0.09	1.98
New Zealand	2.44	5.17	8.08
Norway	3.65	5.04	8.75
Poland	1.46	1.12	0.90
Portugal	0.28	3.27	3.36
Slovak Republic	1.95	1.54	2.57
Spain	1.00	0.58	3.72
Sweden	4.06	4.33	9.02
Switzerland	1.65	1.75	1.46
Turkey	2.76	2.86	4.13
United Kingdom	5.64	7.71	5.70
United States	0	0	0

Table 2 shows that almost all OECD countries provide some fiscal incentive for partners to share employment, but that it varies substantially across countries and earnings levels. Denmark and Japan penalise employment sharing at lower incomes, but support at higher incomes. In contrast, Germany only penalises it at higher incomes.

Financial gain of working more (marginal effective tax rates)

Marginal tax rates caused by income taxes and social contributions provide a good measure of the financial incentives to increase wages or working hours for employees with moderate to high wages. For low-wage earners, however, transfer payments are often more important driving factors of financial work incentives. Benefits that are reduced as earnings increase can severely compromise the ability of low-wage earners to improve their economic circumstances by working more. For these groups of employees it is therefore essential to bring benefits into the analysis. Regardless of the wage level, detailed information about benefits is also required to assess the financial incentives relevant for moving between employment and non-employment.

One useful approach for illustrating relevant mechanics of tax-benefit systems is by means of so-called "budget-constraint" graphs. These graphs show the feasible combinations of gross and net incomes given the tax-and benefit rules that apply to a specific type of household. They can be used to identify so-called "low-wage traps" where higher earnings result in no, or only very small, net income gains. To analyse which taxes and benefits determine net incomes (and contribute to "low-wage traps"), the budget constraints can be broken down to separately examine the impact of each tax and benefit instrument.

The graphs in Figure 2 show the relationship of work effort and net income gain by plotting net incomes (NET) against pre-tax-benefit incomes (GROSS) for gross earnings between 0 to 133% of APW (with working hours between 0 and 133% of full-time hours). Net incomes are shown as the sum of gross earnings plus benefits minus taxes. Gross earnings, social assistance (SA), housing benefits (HB), family benefits (FB) and in-work benefits (IW) are shown as positive income components above the horizontal axis while income tax (IT) and own social security contributions (SSC) reduce net income. Results relate to a lone-parent household with two children aged 4 and 6 and not entitled to unemployment benefits (social assistance benefits are available to those on low incomes). For illustration purposes, and in order to examine the characteristics of some recently-introduced "make work pay" policies, we focus on countries operating employment-conditional benefits (the full set of budget-constraint graphs for six family types and 28 countries is available on the Internet at www.oecd.org/els/social/workincentives).

The rate at which any additional gross earnings are "taxed away" by the combined effects of taxes and benefit withdrawals can be seen by comparing the *slope* of the budget constraint to that of the GROSS line. The budget constraint graphs therefore present useful summary pictures of these marginal effective tax rates (METR). If a small increase in gross earnings results in no change in net income, the NET line is horizontal (METR=100%) while parallel GROSS and NET lines indicate that the full amount of additional earnings amount adds to net income (METR=0). Similarly, the distance between NET and GROSS indicates the size of the net tax burden (taxes minus benefits). Where the lines cross, net tax burdens are zero.

Figure 2. Net incomes, taxes and benefits at different earnings levels

Lone-parent household with two children, 2002, selected countries[2]

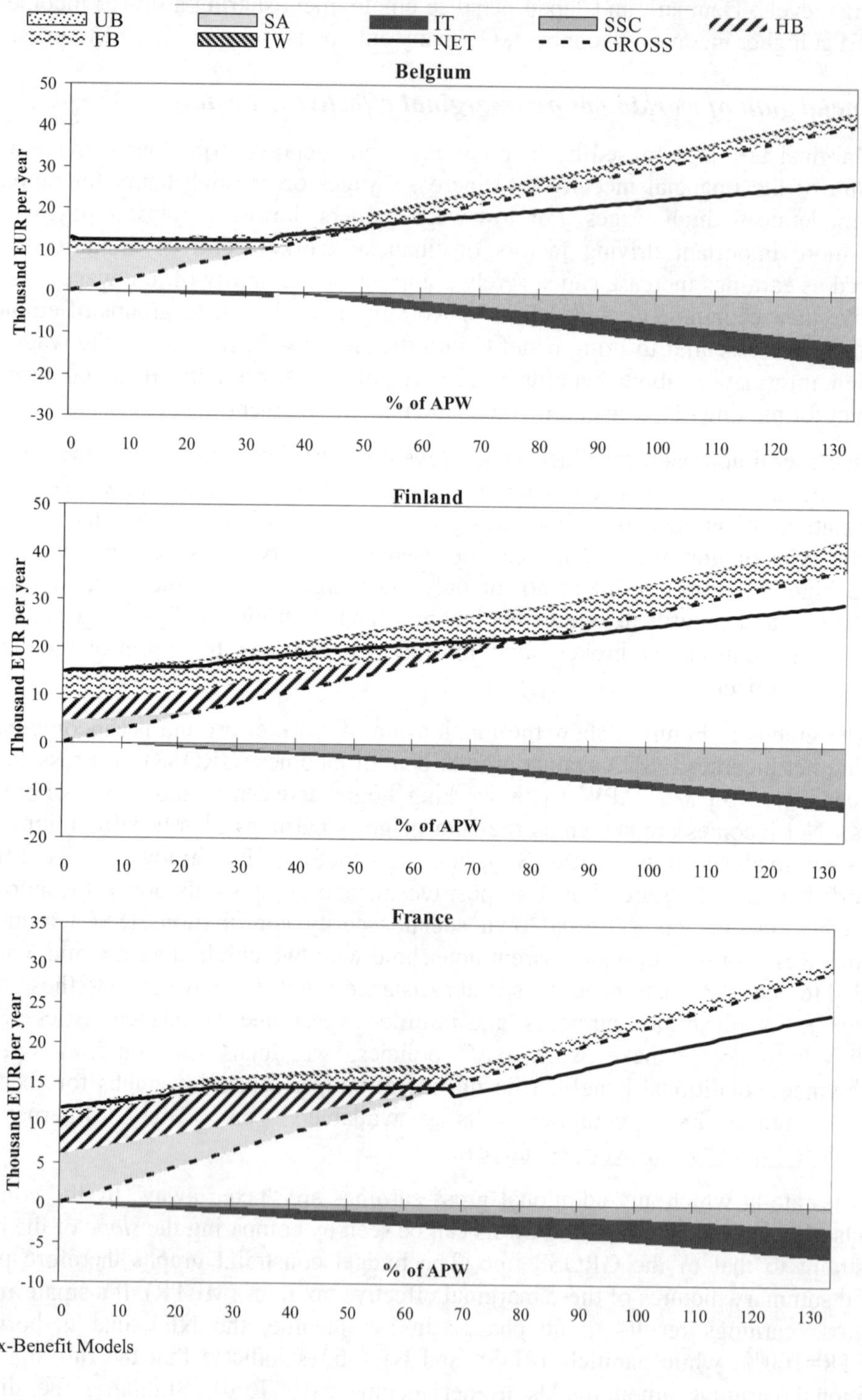

Source: OECD Tax-Benefit Models

---

2 UB stands for unemployment benefits, SA for Social assistance, IT for income tax, SSC for social security contributions, HB for housing benefits, FB for family benefits, IW for in-work benefits (employment conditional benefits), NET for net income (after tax and social contributions), GROSS for gross income

Figure 2: (continued)

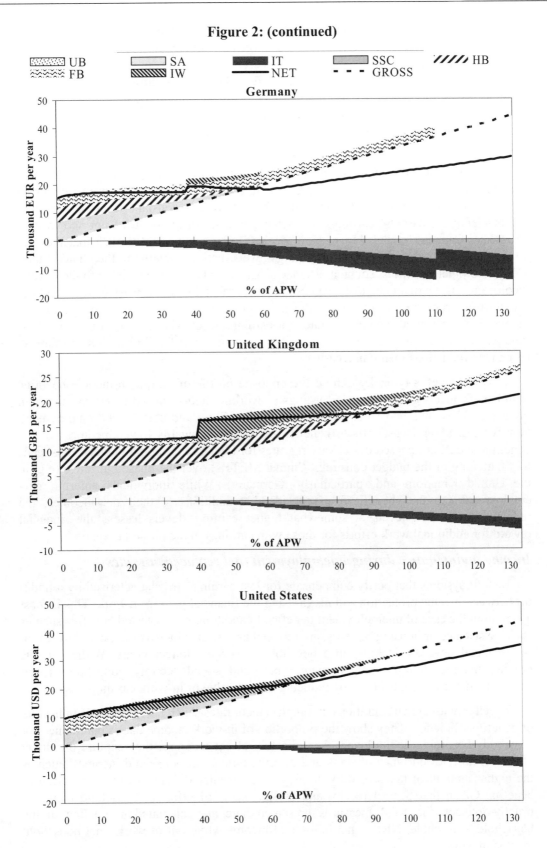

For all countries, the net income line is flat at low levels of gross income: the phasing-out of means-tested benefits absorbs large parts of any additional earnings so that a change in work effort results in no or only very small changes in net income. Earnings disregards, as in the United Kingdom, can reduce benefit withdrawal rates at very low earnings levels and hence increase net incomes for those combining benefit income with small amounts of in-work earnings. Once social assistance and housing benefits are withdrawn completely, net incomes increase at faster rates as indicated by a steeper slope of the NET line.

In the majority of countries shown, family benefits (including lone-parent benefits plus any cash childcare benefits that are available independently of the use of childcare services) are not income-related and therefore provide a constant level of resources independently of parents' earnings or working hours. Other countries not shown here (Australia, Canada, Ireland, Japan, New Zealand) phase out benefits such that they are already severely reduced at average earnings levels. Family benefits in the United States are akin to other countries' social assistance schemes and are only available to the lowest-income groups. German taxpayers can opt between receiving a non-wastable tax-credit or a deduction from taxable income – the latter being more advantageous for taxpayers facing higher marginal income tax rates (at earnings levels above 110% of APW in the lone-parent case). This illustrates the possible equivalence of family benefits and family-related tax reductions mentioned earlier.

In-work benefits typically exhibit the opposite profile of minimum income benefits, with benefit levels going up once earnings or working hours exceed a certain minimum threshold. They thus boost net incomes for those willing and able to find employment. However, in several cases, these benefits are targeted towards lower incomes so that benefit amounts are phased out at varying rates for higher-earning individuals. This leads to a flattening of the budget constraint (higher METRs) over the phase-out range (e.g. in the United Kingdom and, particularly, Germany). While individuals entering new employment can thus benefit from considerable additions to their net incomes, the reduction of benefit levels at somewhat higher earnings levels lessens the financial reward for additional work efforts for those with earnings in the phase-out range.

Income maintenance during unemployment (net replacement rates)

Benefit systems that partly compensate for lost earnings are characterised by a trade-off between income protection and maximising the financial gain from work. This is most apparent in the case of unemployment benefits. In addition, means-tested benefits, such as social assistance or housing benefits, are reduced as earnings increase and can thus lessen the financial reward of taking up a new job or working longer hours. While benefits provide income during unemployment, taxes and social security contributions can adversely affect work incentives by reducing the net value of in-work earnings.

Together with benefit durations, net replacement rates (NRR) are important indicators of benefit sufficiency. They show the proportion of in-work income that is maintained for somebody becoming unemployed. As indicators of net incomes, they capture the direct effects of all relevant types of taxes and benefits on current household incomes, such as the higher amount of taxes paid by employees or country differences in the taxation of benefits. Given that benefit receipt and tax payments of different household members usually interact, the NRR measures presented here are calculated in relation to the household as a whole: NRR = net household income while out of work / net household income in work.

Table 3. Net Replacement Rates for six family types: initial phase of unemployment

2002, different earnings levels

| | 67% of APW | | | | | | 100% of APW | | | | | | 150% of APW | | | | | |
| | No children | | | 2 children | | | No children | | | 2 children | | | No children | | | 2 children | | |
	Single person	One-earner married couple	Two-earner married couple	Lone parent	One-earner married couple	Two-earner married couple	Single person	One-earner married couple	Two-earner married couple	Lone parent	One-earner married couple	Two-earner married couple	Single person	One-earner married couple	Two-earner married couple	Lone parent	One-earner married couple	Two-earner married couple
Australia	48	42	53	60	79	68	34	30	44	56	69	56	25	22	36	42	52	48
Austria	55	58	80	75	78	86	55	57	76	72	73	81	55	56	72	65	66	76
Belgium	83	73	96	79	74	96	63	55	82	63	58	84	46	41	67	48	45	70
Canada	63	65	81	68	69	88	63	65	78	75	76	85	45	47	62	58	58	69
Czech Republic	50	50	77	56	55	78	50	50	72	55	55	75	50	50	67	55	53	70
Denmark	85	91	93	96	96	93	60	67	77	76	77	78	45	52	64	61	61	66
Finland	74	81	81	89	87	86	61	69	75	82	81	80	48	54	66	67	65	70
France	83	87	92	91	91	92	71	67	82	78	78	83	70	69	79	70	69	79
Germany	63	61	90	89	82	99	61	54	85	82	78	96	62	51	80	78	70	91
Greece	63	66	74	72	72	76	45	45	62	49	49	62	32	32	49	35	35	49
Hungary	65	65	81	73	73	85	47	47	68	58	57	73	35	35	57	46	46	63
Iceland	63	54	81	77	69	86	46	41	68	63	57	75	33	30	55	49	45	62
Ireland	40	59	71	60	67	80	29	44	59	54	54	68	21	31	47	41	40	55
Italy	50	50	77	54	57	81	52	56	71	60	62	76	46	49	63	57	60	67
Japan	73	71	89	81	71	88	63	62	80	74	62	81	62	61	75	63	62	76
Korea	54	54	77	55	54	77	55	55	72	56	55	72	47	47	62	47	47	62
Luxembourg	85	82	90	90	90	94	85	84	89	89	89	92	87	85	88	92	89	91
Netherlands	80	88	85	86	89	85	71	73	83	76	77	83	61	63	74	66	64	74
New Zealand	55	81	57	77	83	65	38	54	46	62	67	52	27	39	37	45	49	42
Norway	66	68	83	90	87	87	66	67	80	85	74	83	53	53	69	66	59	72
Poland	68	69	76	70	62	77	47	48	62	49	51	63	32	33	48	34	35	50
Portugal	86	84	95	86	86	92	78	76	88	76	76	87	83	79	88	80	78	87
Slovak Republic	72	73	81	77	78	84	64	68	78	72	75	83	47	49	64	56	56	69
Spain	76	72	88	77	77	89	72	72	84	76	74	87	49	50	66	63	63	76
Sweden	82	82	91	92	90	92	78	78	87	89	82	88	56	56	71	69	61	72
Switzerland	79	79	89	81	81	90	71	71	82	82	82	88	72	71	80	82	82	87
UK	64	63	63	48	50	72	45	45	53	46	46	60	31	31	42	35	35	49
US	62	63	81	53	53	83	58	60	75	56	55	78	58	41	59	40	39	63

1. Initial phase of unemployment but following any waiting period. No social assistance "top-ups" are assumed to be available in either the in-work or out-of-work situation. Any income taxes payable on unemployment benefits are determined in relation to annualised benefit values (i.e. monthly values multiplied by 12) even if the maximum benefit duration is shorter than 12 months. See Annex A for details. For married couples the percentage of APW relates to one spouse only; the second spouse is assumed to be "inactive" with no earnings in a one-earner couple and to have full-time earnings equal to 67% of APW in a two-earner couple. Children are aged 4 and 6 and neither childcare benefits nor childcare costs are considered. Comparability with 1999 results (OECD, 2002, Benefits and Wages): for some countries, calculation models have been revised in line with clarifications received from country experts and this introduces a break in the time-series. Details are provided in Annex A and need to be kept in mind when interpreting observed changes as some of them are due to clarifications of the calculations rather than policy reforms.

Table 3 shows NRRs during the initial phase of unemployment (*i.e.* following any benefit waiting period) for somebody who was previously employed on a full-time basis with earnings at 67, 100 and 150% of APW. Given benefit floors and ceilings, replacement rates are frequently higher for low levels of previous earnings. However, as a result of progressive tax systems, higher earnings levels are taxed more heavily. This reduces the denominator for high-wage workers in the above equation and can cause NRRs to be higher for better-paid individuals (e.g. Italy, Luxembourg, Portugal).

Comparisons between family types show that NRRs tend to be higher for larger families since family-related additions to unemployment benefits and other benefit entitlements combine to reduce the relative drop in household resources. Some benefits (e.g. family benefits) may be available in both the in-work and out-of-work situations while others (e.g. housing benefits) may be income-related. In both cases, benefit payments increase NRRs although the effect is stronger for benefits targeted towards low-income groups.

NRRs compare total family resources across two different work situations of one particular household member. They thus capture the degree of income protection provided by both the tax-benefit system and any incomes of other household members. As a result, NRRs for two-earner married couples are, to a large extent, driven by the employment income of the second earner (whose employment status and hours of work are assumed to remain unchanged following the job loss of the other spouse), particularly in countries where unemployment benefits are low. In these cases, the earnings of the second earner can serve an insurance function and represent an important complement of unemployment benefits, which would, by themselves, maintain only relatively small proportions of in-work earnings.

In 2002, low-earning lone parents (67% of APW) in six OECD countries face net income losses of 10% or less during the initial period of unemployment (NRRs of 90% or higher). Clearly, replacement rates of this magnitude result in very limited short-term gains from work. Yet, when interpreting them, it is important not only to focus on NRR measures in isolation but to also consider the income situation prior to the transition into unemployment. From an income security point of view, both relative income maintenance and absolute income levels are relevant. Hence, even high replacement rates may leave households below the poverty line if they are poor while in work. For instance, in the case of lone parents with low levels of previous earnings (67% of APW), Table 3 shows that NRRs in 19 OECD countries exceed 70% during the initial phase of unemployment. At the same time, results reported in OECD (2004) indicate that in about half of these countries, earnings higher than 67% of APW are required to ensure family income above the poverty line. In these countries, the lone-parent family considered here would therefore be at high risk of poverty both with and without work. Given a concern with income poverty, this limits the scope for reducing NRRs through reducing out-of-work benefit levels and suggests an important role for measures aiming to increase net incomes of working lone parents.

Overcoming benefit dependency – and poverty

Data in OECD (2004) show that, across OECD countries, income from market activities or from benefits other than social assistance is needed to ensure family incomes above commonly-used poverty thresholds (50 and 60% of median household income). But the work efforts required to bring family resources up to a given minimum level vary markedly. Low-wage or part-time employment is a potentially effective route out of poverty in countries allowing benefit recipients to complement benefits with in-work earnings. In addition, low levels of income taxes and, particularly, social security contributions for these types of employment increase the financial attractiveness of low-paid jobs by increasing the part of any employment income that adds to family resources. Where earnings levels make a noticeable difference to family budgets, low-skilled workers and those with limited work experience will find employment to be a more feasible route out of poverty and benefit dependency.

In most countries, in-work earnings required to escape income poverty are found to be around 50 to 60% of APW in the case of single-person households. Yet, a few countries, through a combination of low tax burdens and limited benefit clawback rates for those seeking to supplement their benefit income with income from work, succeed in making even very low-wage employment, below 40% of average earnings, viable as a strategy to exit poverty. Country differences are even larger in the case of multi-person households and this is shown in Figure 3 for married couples with two children. To ensure net income above the poverty line, families in countries as diverse as Hungary, Spain, Sweden or the United States require earnings that are, relative to each country's average earnings, up to three times as high as in Australia or New Zealand.

Figure 3. In several countries, above-average wages are required to escape poverty[1]

Earnings required for income above the poverty line, % of APW, married couple with two children, 2001

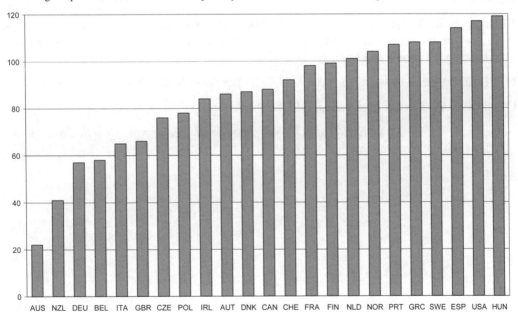

1. It is assumed that there is only one earner per family. Results are shown in relation to the "60% of median income" poverty threshold. The selection of countries is limited by the availability of recent income data required for computing these poverty lines.

Source: OECD Tax-Benefit Models, and calculations based on Förster, M.F. and M. Mira d'Ercole (2004), "Income Distribution and Poverty in OECD Countries in the Second Half of the 1990s", *Social, Employment and Migration Working Paper*, OECD, Paris, available at http://www.oecd.org/dataoecd/48/9/34483698.pdf.

Conclusions

This paper has demonstrated that the two OECD publications, Taxing Wages and Benefits and Wages, provide a range of policy-relevant indicators of the effect of government policy on work incentives and other economic and social objectives. The use of example households implies that these indicators are not capable of describing economic circumstances for all household situations. However, it permits international comparisons and focuses attention on the structure of the tax and benefit systems. Calculations based on household types that do not change over time provide a stable point of reference and are therefore particularly useful for policy monitoring purposes.

A key feature of the modelling approach described in this paper is that it is not limited to the indicators presented here and in the two publications. Rather, it provides a framework that can readily generate additional indicators as the need arises. For example, the indicators reported in Table 2 are not part of the Taxing Wages publication, but were devised for a separate (so far unpublished) report and calculated using the same standard models used for the publication. Similarly, the tax-benefit calculation models used as a basis for the Benefits and Wages publication are employed by the European Commission to derive a number of work-incentive measures used for policy monitoring purposes.

As with all indicators, the relevance of particular results will depend on the policy issue to be addressed and a careful choice of appropriate indicators is therefore critical. Given the heterogeneity of populations and the strong influence of household structures and circumstances on tax burdens and benefit entitlements, it is desirable to monitor tax-benefit policies for a wide range of family circumstances. Yet, no set of circumstances can be appropriate for all purposes. A modelling framework that is sufficiently flexible and can be adapted to satisfy different needs is therefore useful.

References

Mendoza E G, A Razin and L L Tesar (1994), "Effective tax rates in macroeconomics: cross-country estimates of tax rates on factor incomes and consumption", *Journal of Monetary Economics*, 34 (3), pp. 297-323.

OECD (2001), *Tax Ratios: A Critical Survey*, OECD Tax Policy Studies No. 5. Paris: OECD.

OECD (2004), *Benefits and Wages*, OECD, Paris.

Sutherland, H. (2001), *EUROMOD: An Integrated European Benefit-Tax Model*, EUROMOD Working Paper No. EM9/01.

Opening Remarks to the Workshop on FDI Statistics for Policy Making

William H. Witherell

Director, Financial and Enterprise Affairs, OECD

Introduction

The Investment Committee has as its mission "to enhance the contribution of investment to growth and sustainable development by advancing investment policy reform and international co-operation". The Committee's work covers matters relating to foreign direct investment, other capital movements and the activities of multinational enterprises. Investment statistics is one of the core activities under the purview of the Committee. Its on-going work in this area seeks to assist in "better informed decision-making due to improved international investment statistics". The title of today's workshop is thus particularly timely and relevant.

Direct Investment

FDI promotes international economic integration and sustainable growth. It has a recognised impact on the development of international trade. FDI can contribute significantly to poverty reduction in the developing world. However, economies are faced with various policy challenges to attract FDI, such as securing an enabling regulatory environment, providing for transparent government practices, maintaining non-discriminatory investment policies and appropriate fiscal or tax policies, obtaining international co-operation for expanding market and investment opportunities, etc. Statistical data are essential to assess the performance of these policies in attracting FDI and determine the need for future changes in policies or regulations.

Direct investment differs from other types of cross-border investment. It is primarily defined by the motivation of the investor, a motivation which is not the same as for portfolio investments. FDI is undertaken to create direct, stable and long-lasting relationships between economies and is an important additional source of capital. It contributes to the development of local enterprises and competitive markets as it allows the transfer of technology and know-how between entities and the countries in which they are located. FDI has an impact on labour markets, in particular when the investment is in the form of a "greenfield"[1] investment or the extension of capital of existing enterprises as opposed to mergers and acquisitions (MandA). The latter do not necessarily lead to job creations but are more focused on the governance of corporations.

Major FDI players are traditionally large multinational enterprises (MNEs) although in the recent years there is an increasing involvement of small and medium-size enterprises (SMEs). Large transactions account, to a large extent, for the spectacular increases in FDI. But, at the same time, the number of smaller transactions has also

---

1   Creation of new corporations through foreign direct investment.

grown. Also, the economic sectors attracting foreign investors are becoming more diversified. For example, in recent years, significant increases are recorded in investments in the service sector. Another observation is the emergence of new "home" (of the investor) and "host" (of the direct investment enterprise) countries. Some countries which were traditionally only recipients of FDI have also become important investors. In sum, the geographical and sectoral penetration of FDI has increased around the globe.

As a complement to information on FDI flows and stocks based on balance of payments data, which form the bulk of the statistics used for direct investment analysis, it is also important to look at the activities of multinational enterprises. Among the analytically useful data for MNEs are statistics on the value added, gross output, sales or turnover, gross operating surplus, taxes on direct investment income, number of employees, number of enterprises, etc. These data are compiled more and more in member countries but they are, in the majority of the cases, enterprise statistics which do not provide a basis comparable with FDI flows and stocks. Another related set of statistics is on the cross-border trade by MNEs. The United States provides one of the rare country cases of harmonisation between the various types of statistics relating to MNEs. That is why the case study of the United States was selected as the main focus of this Workshop.

A statistical framework for FDI

As legal and regulatory restrictions on cross-border operations were lifted over the past several decades, the task of statisticians became more and more complicated. Traditional statistical systems depending largely on reports from national financial institutions were no longer fully adequate to analyse investment activities as investors had increasing recourse to overseas markets. This development contributed to divergences between statistical outputs and the needs of the analysts. It has, in consequence, led the international organisations to establish better adapted statistical frameworks accompanied by comprehensive guidelines. As a part of this international effort, OECD *Benchmark Definition of Foreign Direct Investment* (*Benchmark Definition*) was first published in 1983 to provide operational guidance to national statisticians to compile and disseminate internationally comparable and comprehensive FDI statistics. While it remains totally compatible with the IMF guidelines, the objectives of the *Benchmark Definition* is primarily to avoid inconsistencies between the statistics of member countries; to reduce discrepancies with partner countries and to allow a meaningful exchange of data; and to achieve consistent statistical series over time.

OECD countries account for a large share of the world-wide cross-border investments. For this reason it is the member country national agencies dealing with FDI statistics that have taken the largest steps for implementing more adequate statistical systems that approach the international benchmark. Yet, while notable progress has made, compliance with international standards is not completely fulfilled by all countries. The reliability of FDI policy analysis based on the statistics is closely related to the reliability and the comprehensiveness of the underlying indictors. OECD regularly monitors the extent of the progress in member countries through its joint exercise with the IMF, the "Survey of Implementation of Methodological Standards for Direct Investment" (SIMSDI). [2]

---

2   The latest SIMSDI results were published in the joint IMF/OECD publication Foreign Direct Investment: How countries Measure FDI.

FDI Trends

OECD publishes regularly articles on trends in FDI, which are disseminated through the internet and published in our periodical *International Investment Perspectives.* This work relies heavily on the analytical FDI database of the OECD[3] which allows a comprehensive geographical and sectoral analysis of FDI flows and stocks.

Let me therefore add a few words on some recent FDI trends. It is important to recall that in 2001 FDI flows to and from OECD recorded the largest drop of the recent decades. This decline followed the "investment bubble" of 1999-2000 when FDI stood at around six times higher than the levels reached at mid-90s. The increase in FDI also accounted for other factors such as the introduction of large scale privatisations in the second half of 90s. The drop in 2001 essentially eliminated two-thirds of the increase by reducing the flows to twice the levels reached at mid-90s. 2001 has marked a correction towards more sustainable levels of investment. This contraction of FDI does not imply that FDI activity is low by any longer-term historic standard. Both OECD inflows and outflows compare favourably with the early and mid-1990s.

The most recent analysis confirms, to a large extent, the forecast of a year earlier. In 2003, FDI investment into the OECD declined for the third consecutive year when it dropped by 28 per cent to USD 384 billion. It is too early to make a firm assessment of FDI trends for 2004. Anecdotal evidence points to a recovery in cross-border mergers and acquisitions. It must be said that this is not visible in FDI balance of payments data available for the first months of the year.

The decline in the inflows in 2003 is in part due to sluggish macroeconomic performance and weak economic recovery and the concerns about international security. On the other hand, some sectors of the economy where large scale cross-border investment were realised in the late 1990s had yet to finalise the consolidation of their acquisitions and applied more cautious corporate strategies. This drop in FDI inflows in 2003 affected all major regions but particularly North America. FDI inflows to European countries were 23 per cent lower than in 2002 but distributed differently across the countries.

In contrast, FDI outflows from the OECD held up better and even marked a slight increase reaching USD576 billion in 2003. With net outflows of USD 190 billion in 2003 (six times more than in 2002), OECD countries continue to maintain their traditional role as providers of FDI. In 2003, China overtook from the United States the position of the largest FDI recipient, attracting USD 53 billion. In contrast USD 4 billion was invested by OECD countries in India and only USD 1 million in Russia.

The way forward

Today's workshop is expected to allow a useful exchange of experiences amongst the experts from OECD and other countries. I hope that the discussion will contribute to both a better understanding of the present state of FDI statistics and their further improvement of FDI statistics as these data are essential for policy analysis.

Two international organisations, the IMF and the OECD, have started working on the revision of the international statistical standards in this area. It is with great satisfaction

---

3   See International *Direct Investment Statistics Yearbook*, OECD

that I welcome this close co-operation between the two institutions as well as the valuable contributions of European institutions and of the UNCTAD to this effort.

Finally I might mention one specific area of immediate policy interest. Most OECD governments have included in their high priority agendas improving their understanding of the practice of "outsourcing" by MNEs. Nevertheless, the phenomenon is difficult to analyse or to project in the absence of appropriate statistical information. So, analysing "outsourcing" remains as one of the major challenges of the statistical systems for the near future, one to which the OECD is seeking to contribute. We would welcome suggestions on this subject in the course of this workshop.

Measuring Foreign Direct Investment

Ayse Bertrand

Manager, International Investment Statistics, Directorate for Financial and
Enterprise Affairs, OECD

Introduction

Closely related the presentations of previous speakers is the conceptual work by the international organisations for the statistical measurement of foreign direct investment (FDI) as well as the compilation, the dissemination and the analysis of these statistics. Very frequently we see references to direct investment and to the accompanying statistics in our professional readings or simply in the daily press. A number of fundamental questions come to mind in relation to the analytical information: What are the data sources? How are the statistics estimated? What do they really represent or cover, i.e. what do they tell us? Are they comprehensive and are they properly interpreted by the analysts? How reliable are they? Are they comparable over time or across the countries or between various sectors of the economy? Do they represent the most recent estimates? All these questions are central to the statistics which normally provide an objective measurement of the direct investment activity. In fact, the degree of satisfaction of the responses to these questions provides an evaluation of the data quality and gives indications on the analytical relevance of the statistics.

The statistical measurement of direct investment relies on standards set by international organisations, the IMF and the OECD. The *OECD Benchmark Definition of Foreign Direct Investment, 3rd* edition (the *Benchmark Definition*) is entirely devoted to direct investment statistics. It is complementary to the *IMF Balance of Payments Manual, 5th* edition (BPM5) which deals with the overall balance of payments and, in consequence, with direct investment which one of the five functional categories of the financial accounts (see Box 1). Both IMF and OECD guidelines are developed to coincide, as much as possible, with the more general accounting principles of the *System of National Accounts* 1993 (SNA).

All three set of guidelines (the *Benchmark Definition*, BPM5, SNA93) have started a new revision cycle of the underlying concepts and definitions. An important feature of the current revision process is the increased efforts of the international statistical community to co-ordinate the discussions of different groups with a view to achieving consistency across the various sets of guidelines in the most transparent way.

I will briefly discuss the following points:

- An overview of FDI statistics

- Statistical standards to measure FDI

- Revision of the Benchmark Definition of FDI

An overview of FDI statistics

FDI statistics are initially compiled by national entities. In the majority of OECD countries the central banks assume this responsibility while in other countries data are compiled by national statistical offices. Most of these statistics follow the standards set by the OECD *Benchmark Definition* and the *IMF BPM5* even if full compliance is not always achieved. The institutions which are the producers of the statistics usually are not directly involved in the policy decisions for investment although they analyse regularly the data and disseminate the results.

Box1 . Balance of Payments: Current account and Capital and Financial Account	
Current Account	**Capital and Financial Account**

A. **Goods and Services**
      1. Goods
      2. Services
 	
   B. **Income**
      1. Compensation of employees
      2. **Investment income**
         2.1 **Direct Investment**
         2.2 Portfolio investment
         2.3 Other Investment
 	
   C. **Current transfers**
      1. General government
      2. Other sectors
	A. **Capital Account**
	      1. Capital Transfers
	      2. Acquisition/disposal of non-produced non-financial assets
	
	   B. **Financial Account**
	      1. Direct Investment
	      2. Portfolio investment
	      3. Financial Derivatives
	      4. Other Investment
	      5. Reserve assets

In most of the countries, there is a second set of administrative data compiled by policy entities, depending on each countries governmental and administrative structures and responsibilities. These data generally represent investment intentions and are not based on international standards set by IMF/OECD. On the other hand, they usually have the merit of timeliness for providing guidance to policy makers. We believe that the exchange of information between the two sets of data varies from one country to the other although the large majority of the countries relay primarily on other data sources.

Direct investment statistics disseminated by international organisations are based on national statistics (the first set of data mentioned above). FDI statistics compiled and disseminated by the IMF and the OECD have different purposes. In consequence, they are organised and presented differently, i.e. the level of detail and breakdowns are not the same.

Direct investment as a part of balance of payments (BOP) statistics and the international investment positions (IIP): Balance of payments summarises symmetrically for a specific time period the economic transactions of an economy with the rest of the world while the IIP indicates the related claims on and the liabilities to the rest of the world at a given point in time. As a part of this general matrix, FDI components are presented as aggregate amounts (See boxes 1 and 2). In addition, regional entities, such as the European Central Bank, also compile FDI as a part of BOP data for regional analysis.

Box 2. Direct Investment Financial Flows: Basic Components

Direct Investment abroad	Direct Investment in reporting economy

Equity Capital
    Claims on affiliated enterprises
    Liabilities to affiliated enterprises
	Equity Capital
	    Claims on direct investor
	    Liabilities to direct investor

Reinvested Earnings	Reinvested Earnings

Other capital
    Claims on affiliated enterprises
    Liabilities to affiliated enterprises
	Other capital
	    Claims on direct investor
	    Liabilities to direct investor

Direct investment statistics: In the 90s, OECD and Eurostat have adopted jointly a questionnaire to collect detailed FDI statistics. The questionnaire is designed according to the basic BOP components of direct investment but has further breakdowns by partner country and industry sectors. It is however to note that, detailed breakdowns of FDI are more vulnerable to confidentiality rules than the aggregate BOP statistics.

Detailed FDI statistics are greatly appreciated by analysts who are not only interested to know the global amounts of FDI transaction or the amount of outstanding investments but they are more and more interested in complementary information likely to explain the reasons: e.g. the attractivity of countries or economic sectors; the reasons for disinvestments; the distribution of dividends/reinvested earnings, etc. .

OECD-Eurostat FDI statistics:

1. **Data coverage and components**: inward and outward FDI financial flows, income flows and stock positions.

    1. **FDI financial flows**: Equity income (claims, liabilities), Reinvested earnings (net) Other capital (claims, liabilities),

    2. **FDI income flows:** Income on equity (credits and debits - Dividends and distributed branch profits; and Reinvested earnings and undistributed branch profits); Income on debt (interest – debits and credits)

    3. **FDI stock positions**: Equity income and reinvested earnings (claims, liabilities); other capital (claims, liabilities).

2. Breakdowns:

    1. By partner country [individual countries and economic or geographical zones]; data include all regions and the coverage of individual partner countries is currently being expanded to all countries of the world.

    2. By industry [based on ISIC 3 see also Annex 1]

    3. By country and industry sector [data sets are not yet developed]

UNCTAD also compiles and disseminates FDI aggregates as time series by country based on their own statistical reports. The reporting country coverage of UNCTAD is wider than the OECD/Eurostat databases.

Statistical standards to measure FDI

Direct investment relates to one of the most complicated statistical concepts, a feature which does not facilitate the tasks of national data compilers and of analysts. Statistical standards recommended by international organisations are intended to address a wide range of issues. Some choices had to be made when setting these standards, namely (i) to ensure the comparability of the data; (ii) to limit the reporting burden of respondents (data providers to national authorities); (iii) to provide comprehensive statistics to users.

The comparability of direct investment statistics refers, in the first place to the extent of data harmonisation across the countries. If national compilers apply similar methodologies, it is expected that the discrepancies between partner country statistics will be reduced in consequence.

FDI statistics are mostly derived from the information received from resident companies for both inward and outward investments while legislations are limited to data collection from entities resident in their own jurisdictions but not from the entities abroad. Most OECD countries rely more and more on quarterly or annual enterprise surveys. It is, however, necessary to train the respondents in order to obtain good quality information from the surveys. A clear description based on comprehensive statistical standards is an integral part of this exercise.

Let me give a few simplified examples to demonstrate how significant discrepancies between partner country data are likely to occur. In other words, if similar methods are not applied, transactions covered by Country A – country of the direct investor (outward investment) will not be the same as the transactions covered by Country B – the country of the direct investment enterprise (inward investment). For example:

1. If the compiling countries do not apply strictly the 10 per cent threshold of ownership of equity or voting stocks when identifying the direct investor and the direct investment enterprise, their estimates will not cover the same sample of enterprises. The statistics of Country A and Country B be will be different.

2. Two reporting countries may use different methods for geographical allocation for the same transaction where funds invested by Country A may be channelled through Country X which in return will transfer the funds to Country B. Statistics will show the following asymmetries unless same principles are used by both countries:

    Outward FDI statistics of Country A will attribute the transaction to Country B

    Inward FDI statistics of Country B will attribute the transaction to Country X (but not A)

3. Two reporting countries may use different methods for the industry allocation for the same transaction. Direct investor in Country A is a manufacturing enterprise. The direct investment enterprise in Country B is in the service sector. Country A may record in its outward investment the transaction according to the economic activity of the direct investor, i.e. manufacturing. Country B records the same transaction in its inward investment according to the economic activity of the direct investment

enterprise, i.e. services sector. The same transaction is analysed differently in the statistics of each country.

Metadata is essential to inform the analysts on the deviations from the standard methodology. However, if a critical limit in the compatibility with basic concepts and definitions cannot be achieved, the interpretation of the statistics will naturally be quite misleading and of little value.

Since 1997 OECD and IMF have undertaken jointly the Survey of Implementation of Methodological Standards for Direct Investment (SIMSDI which has gone beyond the initial objectives of monitoring the extent of implementation of recommendations by member countries. SIMSDI provided, in addition, a realistic demonstration that some of the existing standards are difficult to apply.

Box 3. The Survey of Implementation of Methodological Standards for Direct Investment (SIMSDI)

SIMSDI is a comprehensive study of methodological practices as well as data sources, collection and dissemination methods for foreign direct investment statistics. It is also intended to facilitate the exchange of information between reporting countries. It provides information on the methods used by partner countries that, to some extent, may help explain the discrepancies in the bilateral comparison of national statistics.

SIMSDI was conducted for the first time in 1997 jointly by IMF and OECD and covered 114 countries. The exercise was repeated in 2001 for 61 countries. The results of the 1997 and 2001 SIMSDI surveys have been analysed in reports prepared by IMF and OECD secretariats. Main results of the study measuring the progress since the 1997 survey are outlined in Annex 2.1 A survey of more than 100 IMF countries including 30 OECD members was conducted at end-2003.

1. See Foreign Direct Investment Statistics – How countries measure FDI, IMF/OECD, 2003.

Information for OECD countries will be available by end-2004 at the OECD web site www.oecd.org/daf/investment

---

Revision of the Benchmark Definition of FDI

Revisiting statistical standards at regular intervals is a good practice. The decision of the OECD to revise the *Benchmark Definition* coincides with similar exercises undertaken for the revision of the SNA93 and the BPM5.

As a part of the international co-ordination effort, IMF and OECD have jointly created the Direct Investment Technical Expert Group (DITEG)[1]. The main objective of DITEG is to make recommendations to the IMF Committee on Balance of Payments Statistics (BOPCOM) and to the Workshop on International Investment Statistics (WIIS) of the OECD Investment Committee on the revision of the international standards for direct investment. DITEG scheduled three meetings: June and December 2004 and March 2005. Both OECD and IMF attach an importance to a wide consultation and to the transparency of the revision process. All DITEG discussion documents and

---

1 DITEG is co-chaired by IMF and OECD. The representatives are from Australia, Belgium, Canada, Colombia, France, Hong Kong-China, Japan, the Netherlands, the Russian Federation, Tunisia, the United Kingdom, the United States, European Central Bank, Eurostat, UNCTAD. Participants underlined are also members of the OECD Benchmark Advisory Group.

recommendations are posted on both OECD and IMF web sites where comments are invited. www.oecd.org/daf/investment

To accommodate the very tight revision timetable, WIIS held exceptionally a second meeting on 12-13 October 2004 to review the first set of DITEG recommendations and informed the BOPCOM of the outcome in advance of its meeting on 26-29 October 2004. WIIS will review the remaining recommendations at end-April 2005. Thereafter, the drafting of the revised version of the Benchmark Definition will commence with the assistance of the OECD Benchmark Advisory Group A draft version of the revised 4th edition of the *Benchmark Definition* is scheduled for the review/approval of the Investment Committee by end-2006 and for clearance by the OECD Council for publication by end-2007.

A joint list of items was identified by IMF and OECD for the revision FDI statistical standards (see Annex 3). Some of them are purely technical issues while others are more related to policy analysis. A question which is central to the revision of the standards is "what should direct investment statistics measure". Discussions to date show that some issues require further research while others are difficult to conclude due diverging views and where theory and practice are difficult to reconcile.

I will discuss only a few of the issues which bear direct linkages to policy analysis, namely the 10 per cent threshold, SPEs and MandAs and Greenfield investments.

One of the decisions already agreed both by the WIIS and BOPCOM is to maintain the 10 per cent threshold applied to the definition of direct investment as opposed to 20 per cent which was recommended by the DITEG for practical purposes (aligning FDI to International Accounting Standards). The decision to maintain the 10 per cent threshold takes into account that (a) in practice the statistical differences in the results when applying 10 per cent and 20 per cent are minimal and (b) if 20 per cent is used, inconsistencies will be enhanced between statistical analysis and policy analysis where many countries do in practice make reference to 10 per cent including in their tax analysis and corporate governance considerations. In short, the decision to maintain the 10 per cent threshold demonstrates the willingness of the statisticians to align the statistics as much as possible to policy analysis.

The current treatment of SPEs in FDI statistics is a major concern for OECD's FDI policy analysts. Similar concerns were expressed by UNCTAD analysts as well. As compared to early 90s, MNEs have substantially more recourse for their overseas investments to special organisational structures, most of which are not involved in production. Statistics based on current recommendations for the treatment of SPEs do not necessarily reflect the FDI reality which is defined as the "establishment of a lasting interest" between two entities located in different economies. (see Box 4).

The example of Luxembourg, although not unique, is the best translation of the concerns of analysts. In 2003 China was listed as the leading FDI recipient although technically Luxembourg was in the first position. Luxembourg is systematically excluded from the OECD trends analysis. Funds passing through holding companies and SPEs located in this country are reflected in inward and outward FDI statistics of Luxembourg. This exclusion from the analysis is not satisfactory while the Luxembourg economy as a whole is ignored even though it does have genuine FDI which cannot be segregated form the data largely overstated by SPEs and holding companies.

> **Box 4.**
>
> **Special Purpose Entities (SPEs):** are (1) generally organised or established in economies other than those in which the parent companies are resident and (2) engaged primarily in international transactions but in few or no local operations. SPEs are defined either by their structure (e.g., financing subsidiary, holding company, base company, regional headquarters), or their purpose (e.g., sale and regional administration, management of foreign exchange risk, facilitation of financing of investment). SPEs should be treated as direct investment enterprises if they meet the 10 per cent criterion. SPEs are an integral part of direct investment networks as are, for the most part, SPE transactions with other members of the group.
>
> For SPEs that have the sole purpose of serving as financial intermediaries:
>
> - All transactions except those with affiliated banks and affiliated financial intermediaries should be recorded in the direct investment data.
>
> - Transactions with affiliated banks and affiliated financial intermediaries should be excluded from the direct investment data, except transactions in equity capital and permanent debt.
>
> (IMF and OECD)

FDI statistics of the Netherlands are disseminated to the public, as well as to the IMF and the OECD, excluding SPEs according to their national definition. Even if this solution is not fully satisfactory, data can be used as a part of the overall analysis

The most recent SIMSDI results inform that more than 20 OECD countries have SPEs established in their economies and their residents establish SPEs abroad. In other words, SPEs are no longer a phenomenon relating to only a handful of countries but have become globally integrated within the investment landscape, at least in the OECD area.

DITEG has not yet finished its work on SPEs. The subject is vast and not so easy to tackle. OECD is taking the lead in further research and has plans to organise a special session with interested parties back –to-back with the March 2005 DITEG session.

In line with the developments since the last revision of statistical standards, OECD is proposing to introduce an additional breakdown to FDI statistics by type of FDI, namely greenfield investments, extension of capital, and Mergers and Acquisitions (MandAs). The economic impact of each type of investment is different, in particular for the host economy. Existing data on MandAs are based on enterprise statistics and are difficult to use along with the official FDI statistics. On the other hand it cannot be neglected that MandAs have a large share of the overall FDI and should be a part of the fDI analysis. Some countries such as Canada, the United Kingdom, the United States have some experience in such data collections which are, in principle, compatible with their official FDI statistics.

Conclusions

Revised standards which are being developed for the 4th edition of the *Benchmark Definition* will have to be forward looking. The process involves not only to the revision of the standards but also to their practical implementation in the statistics of member countries. It will, therefore, take some years between now and the time when the actual results of new or revised standards will be available to users. We look forward to your contributions and suggestions for this difficult but very challenging task.

Annex 1. ISIC/NACE codes used in OECD-EUROSTAT questionnaire for industrial activities

	ISIC Rev.3	NACE Rev.1	OECD / EUROSTAT
AGRICULTURE AND FISHING	sections A and B	sections A and B	0595
MINING AND QUARRYING	section C	section C	1495
of which: Extraction of petroleum and gas	division 11	division 11	1100
MANUFACTURING	section D	section D	3995
of which: Food Products	divisions 15, 16	subsection DA	1605
Textiles and wearing apparel	divisions 17, 18	subsection DB	1805
Wood, publishing and printing	divisions 20, 21, 22	subsections DD and DE	2205
Total textile and wood activities (*)			**2295**
Refined petroleum products and other treatments	division 23	division 23	2300
Chemicals and chemical products	division 24	division 24	2400
Rubber and plastic products	division 25	division 25	2500
Total petroleum, chemical, rubber, plastic products (*)			**2595**
Metal products	divisions 27, 28	subsection DJ	2805
Mechanical products	division 29	division 29	2900
Total metal and mechanical products (*)			**2995**
Office machinery and computers	division 30	division 30	3000
Radio, TV, communication equipment	division 32	division 32	3200
Total machinery, computer, RTV, communication (*)			**3295**
Motor vehicles	division 34	division 34	3400
Other transport equipment	division 35	division 35	3500
Total vehicles and other transport equipment (*)			**3595**
ELECTRICITY, GAS AND WATER	section E	section E	4195
CONSTRUCTION	section F	section F	4500
TRADE AND REPAIRS	section G	section G	5295
HOTELS AND RESTAURANTS	section H	section H	5500
TRANSPORTS, COMMUNICATION	section I	section I	6495
of which: Land transport	division 60	division 60	6000
Sea and coastal water transport	group 611	group 61.1	6110
Air transport	division 62	division 62	6200
Total Land, Sea and Air transport (*)			**6295**
Telecommunications	group 642	group 64.2	6420
FINANCIAL INTERMEDIATION	section J	section J	6895
of which: Monetary intermediation	group 651	group 65.1	6510
Other financial intermediation	group 659	group 65.2	6520
of which: Financial holding companies	part of class 6599	part of class 65.23	6524
Insurance and activities auxiliary to insurance	division 66 and group 672	division 66 and group 67.2	6730
Total other fin. intermediation + insurance activities (*)			**6795**
REAL ESTATE AND BUSINESS ACTIVITIES	section K	section K	7395
Real Estate	division 70	division 70	7000
Computer activities	division 72	division 72	7200
Research and development	division 73	division 73	7300
Other business activities	division 74	division 74	7400
of which: Business and management consultancy	group 741	group 74.1	7410
of which: Management holding companies	part of class 7414	class 74.15	7415
Advertising	group 743	group 74.4	7440
OTHER SERVICES	sections L, M, N, O, P, Q	sections L, M, N,O, P, Q	9995
UNALLOCATED			9996
SUB-TOTAL			9997
PRIVATE PURCHASES AND SALES OF REAL ESTATE			9998
TOTAL			9999

* OECD-EUROSTAT classification.

Annex 2. The Survey of Implementation of Methodological Standards for Direct Investment (SIMSDI)[2]

Summary of results of 2001 exercise as compared to 1997

Areas where there have been marked improvements since 1997:

1. Availability of FDI statistics, particularly:

    –   Position data

    –   Income data (including reinvested earnings)

    –   Geographic and industrial sector breakdowns

2. Coverage of the FDI statistics, particularly the inclusion of:

    –   Non-cash acquisitions of equity

    –   Inter-company loans and financial leases

    –   Real estate owned by non-residents

    –   Activities of Special Purpose Entities (SPEs)

    –   Activities of offshore enterprises in the outward FDI statistics

    –   Expenditure on natural resource exploration

Areas where more than 75 per cent of countries surveyed follow the international standards applicable to their economy:

*   Use of the 10 per cent ownership rule as the basic criterion for defining FDI relationships

*   Equity capital transactions between affiliated banks and between affiliated financial intermediaries

*   Recording of reverse investment equity transactions when two FDI relationships have been established

*   Inclusion of data on real estate owned by non-residents

*   Inclusion of data on activities of SPEs

*   Inclusion of data on activities of offshore enterprises

---

2   See Foreign Direct Investment Statistics – How countries measure FDI, IMF/OECD, 2003.

Areas where, despite improvements, the majority of countries do not yet follow the international standards:

- Inclusion of activities of indirectly-owned direct investment enterprises – the Fully Consolidated System

- Use of the Current Operating Performance Concept to measure direct investment earnings

- Time of recording FDI income on equity and income on debt

- Recording of reverse investment transactions when the FDI relationship is in one direction only

- Inclusion of data on quasi-corporations involving construction enterprises and mobile equipment

- Valuation of FDI positions (assets and liabilities)

Annex 3. IMF Committee on Balance of Payments Statistics and OECD WORKSHOP OF INTERNATIONAL INVESTMENT STATISTICS

Consolidated List of topics for the Direct Investment Technical Expert Group (DITEG) as Revised at diteg meeting, June 17, 2004

Topic[3]	Agency responsible[4]	Related Group[5]	Meeting[6]/ Priority
1. Valuation of (i) direct investment equity	US, ECB, Australia		June 2004
(ii) branches	IMF		June 2004
2. Direct Investment – 10 percent threshold of voting power/equity ownership, employment	Luxembourg, OECD (Luxembourg)		June 2004
3. Indirect investment -- FCS, USM, or 50 percent ownership	IMF, ECB/Eurostat, Japan (Netherlands[7])		June 2004
4. Mergers and Acquisitions	Canada, OECD (France, United Kingdom[5])		Dec. 2004
5. Reinvested earnings:			

---

3   Where a topic is italicized, it is to indicate that another technical expert group has primary carriage; the topic has been included here as DITEG will have an interest in the issue.

4   The agency shown is to prepare an issues paper for consideration by DITEG. Some issues papers are not yet assigned.

5   Indicates which other group(s) are involved in the subject: BOPTEG = Balance of Payments Technical Expert Group, CUTEG = Currency Union Technical Expert Group, TFSITS= Task Force on Statistics on International Trade in Services

6   Indicates whether the topic is scheduled for initial discussion at the first DITEG meeting (June 2004 in Paris), the second DITEG meeting (December 2004 in Washington, DC), or the third DITEG meeting (March 2005 in Paris).

7   For those issues where DITEG has primary carriage, countries shown in italics have indicated that they will be preparing background papers.

Topic[3]	Agency responsible[4]	Related Group[5]	Meeting[6]/ Priority
A. as it affects national saving	Australia	BOPTEG	June 2004
B. of indirectly owned direct investment enterprises	IMF		
6. Bring together all direct investment issues (stocks, flows, income, between affiliates) in an appendix to the Balance of Payments Manual	IMF		June 2004
7. Directional principle	**United States (new issues paper for December 2004)** IMF (Ireland[5])		**For reconsideratio n in Dec. 2004**
8. Reverse investment – classification	**United States (new issues paper for December 2004)** IMF		**For reconsideratio n in Dec. 2004**
9. SPEs, shell companies, holding companies, off-shore enterprises (units, sectorisation, residence, transactions)	**Netherlands to prepare paper** IMF, Australia	BOPTEG (CUTEG for information)	**For further consideratio n in Dec. 2004**
10. Rules for identification of branches (for information)	IMF	BOPTEG	June 2004
11. SPEs[8] (i) Inclusion in direct investment of transactions between nonfinancial DIE and affiliated financial SPE	ECB (Netherlands[5])		Dec. 2004
12 (i). Country identification (Ultimate beneficial owner/ultimate destination and immediate host/investing country) 12 (ii). Geographic classification principles (debtor/creditor or transactor principle) (for information)	Eurostat United States	TFSITS (for information) BOPTEG CUTEG	Dec. 2004
13. Round tripping	Hong Kong SAR		Dec. 2004
14. Permanent debt between affiliated financial intermediaries	IMF, Japan		Dec. 2004
15. Land and buildings owned by nonresidents	IMF		Dec. 2004
16. Use of maturity and full instrument split for direct investment	IMF		Dec. 2004
17. Multi-territorial enterprises	IMF	BOPTEG (CUTEG, for information)	Dec. 2004
18. Application of direct investment to government (for information)	IMF	BOPTEG (CUTEG, for information)	Dec. 2004
19. Bring together all direct investment-related issues (transactions in goods and services, income, financial flows, stocks, between affiliates) as an appendix to the Balance of Payments Manual	IMF		June 2004

8   For further clarification of issues relating to SPEs (and similar units) as they relate to direct investment, after discussion of broader issues in paper #9.

Topic[3]	Agency responsible[4]	Related Group[5]	Meeting[6]/ Priority
20. Define terms more clearly, including: Direct investor; Affiliated DI enterprise; Parent company; Majority ownership and control; Multinational enterprise; Loan guarantees; Debt forgiveness	Canada (excluding guarantees and debt forgiveness)	BOPTEG (for loan guarantees and debt forgiveness)	Dec. 2004
21. Various special cases, including Banking activities; Natural resource exploration; Construction; and Shipping companies	Belgium: Banking Greece: Shipping Russia: Natural resource exploration, and Construction		Dec. 2004
22. Other capital (focusing on short-term instruments)	Netherlands		Dec. 2004
23. Inter-company transactions and amounts outstanding with fellow subsidiaries	Italy		Dec. 2004
24. FDI stock (financial versus economic measurement)	Belgium		Dec. 2004
25. Valuation of real estate	France		Dec. 2004
26. Accounting methods and IAS	Russia		Dec. 2004
27. Principles for classification by industry (according to direct investor or direct investment enterprise)	Eurostat		Dec. 2004
28. Greenfield investments	OECD		Dec. 2004
29. Extensions of capital	OECD		Dec. 2004
30. Mutual funds (units, sectorisation, residence, transactions)	Japan		Dec. 2004

Annex 4. Glossary of foreign direct investment terms and definitions[9]

Aggregate basis: Data collected on this basis show the total transactions made by respondents during specified reporting periods, such as information obtained through enterprise surveys.

All-inclusive concept: The application of this concept is one of the two main approaches to measuring earnings. The concept is explained in the *International Accounting Standard No.8, "Unusual and Prior Period Items and Changes in Accounting Policy"*. When earnings are measured on the basis of this concept, income is considered to be the amount remaining after all items (including write-offs and capital gains and losses, and excluding dividends and any other transactions between the enterprise and its shareholders or investors) causing any increase or decrease in the shareholders' or investors' interests during the accounting period, are allowed for. (See also the entry for *Current operating performance concept.)*

Asset/liability principle: The Financial Account of the balance of payments records an economy's transactions in external financial assets and liabilities. The transactions are classified by (1) functional type of investment (*direct investment, portfolio investment, other investment*, and *reserve assets*); (2) assets and liabilities or, in the case of direct

---

9   Source: IMF/OECD Survey of Implementation of Methodological Standards for Direct Investment.

investment, direction of investment; (3) type of instrument; and, in some cases, (4) domestic sector and (5) original contractual maturity. This distinction between external assets and liabilities is of primary importance for the functional types of investment other than direct investment. Transactions should be recorded on a straight asset/liability basis. Even when a net basis is used for recording the Financial Account of the balance of payments, transactions in financial assets should be shown separately from transactions in financial liabilities.

Balance of payments: A statistical system through which economic transactions occurring during specific time periods between an economy and the rest of the world can be summarised in a systematic way. The fifth edition of the IMF *Balance of Payments Manual (BPM5)* provides conceptual guidelines for compiling balance of payments statistics according to international standards.

Bonds and money market instruments: include bonds, debentures, commercial paper, promissory notes, certificates of deposit, and other tradable nonequity securities (with the exception of financial derivatives). For the purposes of the questionnaire, the category also includes Treasury bills.

Book value: is the value at which an equity or other capital asset or liability is recorded in the balance sheet of an entity. Book value can reflect one of the following valuation methods:

- Historical cost
- Replacement cost
- An interim adjusted price, which is not the current market price
- Fair market value
- Current market price

Business register: A register of enterprises or establishments involved in foreign direct investment, which is maintained by countries to assist in the compilation of their direct investment data.

Compulsory reporting requirements: Situation where legislation creates a legal obligation (and usually an appropriate penalty for non-compliance) for reporters to provide the requested information.

Current operating performance concept (COPC): The application of this concept is one of the two main approaches to measuring earnings. The concept is explained in the International Accounting Standard No.8, "Unusual and Prior Period Items and Changes in Accounting Policy". When earnings are measured on the basis of this concept, such earnings consist of income from normal enterprise operations before non-recurring items (such as write-offs) and capital gains and losses are accounted for.

Data dissemination: refers to all the means by which data are made available to the public, including dissemination on the Internet.

Debtor/creditor principle: There are two principles that may serve as the basis for geographic allocation of direct investment financial flows: the debtor/creditor principle and the transactor principle. Under the debtor/creditor principle, transactions resulting from changes in financial claims of the compiling economy are allocated to the country or residence of the non-resident debtor, and transactions resulting in changes in financial liabilities are allocated to the country of residence of the non-resident creditor, even if the amounts are paid to or received from a different country (See also the entry for the *Transactor principle*.)

Debt securities: cover all tradable securities, except those classified as equity securities. Debt securities include bonds, debentures, notes, etc., money market or negotiable debt instruments.

Direct investment: is a category of international investment made by a resident entity in one economy (direct investor) with the objective of establishing a lasting interest in an enterprise resident in an economy other than that of the investor (direct investment enterprise). "Lasting interest" implies the existence of a long-term relationship between the direct investor and the enterprise and a significant degree of influence by the direct investor on the management of the direct investment enterprise. Direct investment involves both the initial transaction between the two entities and all subsequent capital transactions between them and among affiliated enterprises, both incorporated and unincorporated.

Direct investment enterprise: is an incorporated enterprise in which a foreign investor owns 10 per cent or more of the ordinary shares or voting power for an incorporated enterprise or an unincorporated enterprise in which a foreign investor has equivalent ownership. Ownership of 10 per cent of the ordinary shares or voting stock is the guideline for determining the existence of a direct investment relationship. An "effective voice in the management", as evidenced by an ownership of at least 10 per cent, implies that the direct investor is able to influence, or participate in, the management of an enterprise; absolute control by the foreign investor is not required.

Direct investment enterprises are defined as those entities that are either directly or indirectly owned by the direct investor and comprise:

- subsidiaries (an enterprise in which a non-resident investor owns more than 50 per cent);

- associates (an enterprise in which a non-resident investor owns between 10 and 50 per cent) and;

- branches (unincorporated enterprises wholly or jointly owned by a non-resident investor);

When the 10 per cent ownership requirement for establishing a direct investment link with an enterprise is met, certain other enterprises that are related to the first enterprise are also regarded as direct investment enterprises. Hence the definition of direct investment enterprise extends to the branches and subsidiaries of subsidiaries of the direct investor (so-called "indirectly owned direct investment enterprises"). The OECD *Benchmark Definition of Foreign Investment* and the IMF *Balance of Payments Compilation Guide* describe the scope of enterprises, both directly and indirectly owned, that should be included in the definition. The OECD's specification of this group of enterprises is referred to as the "Fully Consolidated System". (See also the entry for the *Fully Consolidated System*.)

Direct investment income: comprises income on equity and income on debt. (See also the separate entries for these two elements.)

Direct investment relationship: A direct investment relationship is created when an enterprise resident in one economy owns 10 per cent or more of the ordinary shares or voting power for an incorporated enterprise, or the equivalent for an unincorporated enterprise, that is resident in another economy. Direct investment enterprises that are considered to be in a direct investment relationship with a direct investor are also considered to be in direct investment relationships with each other.

Direct investor: is an individual, an incorporated or unincorporated public or private enterprise, a government, a group of related individuals, or a group of related incorporated and/or unincorporated enterprises that has a direct investment enterprise (that is, a subsidiary, associate or branch) operating in an economy other than the economy or economies of residence of the foreign direct investor or investors.

Directional principle: Unlike other financial investments, direct investment is not recorded in the balance of payments on a strict asset/liability basis. Direct investments are recorded on a directional basis (that is, as resident direct investment abroad, or non-resident direct investment in the reporting economy). Capital invested by the direct investment enterprise in its direct investor (reverse investment) is regarded as an offset to capital invested in the direct investment enterprise by a direct investor and its related enterprises. That is, such capital is regarded as disinvestment by the direct investor rather than as an asset of the direct investment enterprise, except when the equity participations are at least 10 per cent in both directions and two direct investment relationships are therefore established. (See also the entry for *Reverse investment.*)

Dividends: are the distribution of earnings allocated to shares and other forms of participation in the equity of incorporated private enterprises, co-operatives, and public corporations. These can be recorded on the date they are payable, on the date they are paid, or at some other point in time.

Equity capital: comprises: (i) equity in branches; (ii) all shares in subsidiaries and associates (except nonparticipating, preferred shares that are treated as debt securities and included under direct investment, other capital); and (iii) other capital contributions.

Exchange rate gains or losses: can be either realized gains/losses or unrealized gains/losses.

Financial derivatives: are financial instruments that are linked to another specific financial instrument or indicator or commodity, and through which specific financial risks can be traded in financial markets in their own right. The value of a financial derivative is based on the price of an underlying item, such as an asset or index. Unlike debt instruments, financial derivatives do not require the advancement or repayment of principal amounts and do not generate investment income. Financial derivatives are used for a number of purposes including risk management, hedging, arbitrage between markets, and speculation. In accordance with the 2000 revision of the fifth edition of the IMF's *Balance of Payments Manual (BPM5)*, income from financial derivatives (such as interest rate swaps) is no longer considered to be Income on Debt (Interest) in the balance of payments.

Financial intermediary: For the purposes of balance of payments data, financial intermediaries are defined as being: (i) other depository institutions (banks, other than the central bank); (ii) other financial intermediaries, except insurance companies and pension funds; and (iii) financial auxiliaries. The definition would therefore include Special Purpose Enterprises (SPEs), whose sole function is financial intermediation, and enterprises such as security dealers, whose function is the provision of services auxiliary to financial intermediation.

Fully Consolidated System (FCS): The fifth edition of the IMF *Balance of Payments Manual (BPM5)* and the OECD *Benchmark Definition of Foreign Direct Investment (Benchmark)* consider that inward and outward direct investment statistics should, as a matter of principle, cover all directly and indirectly owned subsidiaries, associates, and branches. *BPM5* and the OECD *Benchmark* recommend the following definition of these enterprises:

1. Subsidiary companies

    Company X is a subsidiary of enterprise N if, and only if

    1. enterprise N either

        (i) is a shareholder in or member of X and has the right to appoint or remove a majority of the members of X's administrative, management or supervisory body; or

        (ii) owns more than half of the shareholders' or members' voting power in X; or

    2. company X is a subsidiary of any other company Y which is a subsidiary of N.

2. Associate companies

    Company R is an associate of enterprise N if N, its subsidiaries and its other associated enterprises own not more than 50 per cent of the shareholders' or members' voting power in R and if N and its subsidiaries have a direct investment interest in R. Thus company R is an associate of N if N and its subsidiaries own between 10 and 50 per cent of the shareholders' voting power in R.

3. Branches

    A direct investment branch is an unincorporated enterprise in the host country that:

    1. Is a permanent establishment or office of a foreign direct investor; or

    2. Is an unincorporated partnership or joint venture between a foreign direct investor and third parties; or

    3. Is land, structures (except those structures owned by foreign government entities), and immovable equipment and objects, in the host country, that are directly owned by a foreign resident. Holiday and second homes owned by non-residents are therefore regarded as part of direct investment, though few, if any, countries actually include such investment in their direct investment statistics; or

    4. Is mobile equipment (such as ships, aircraft, gas and oil drilling rigs) that operates within an economy for at least one year if accounted for separately by the operator and is so recognized by the tax authorities. This is considered to be direct investment in a notional enterprise in the host country.

Statistics based on those definitions should, as a matter of principle, cover all enterprises in which the direct investor has directly or indirectly a direct investment interest. For convenience, this approach is referred to below as the Fully Consolidated System.

To illustrate the above definitions, assume enterprise N has the following investments:

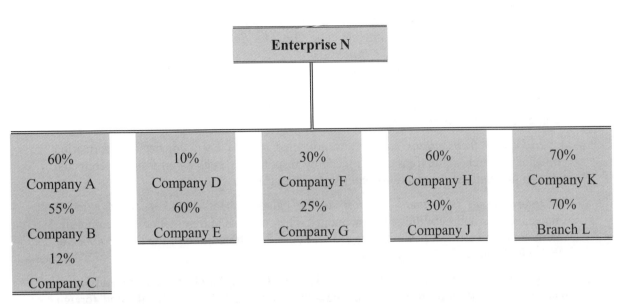

Under the Fully Consolidated System, Company A is a subsidiary of N. Company B is a subsidiary of A and thus a subsidiary of N even though only 33 per cent of B is indirectly attributable to N. Company C is an associate of B and, through the chain of subsidiaries A and B, of N as well, even though only 4 per cent of C is indirectly attributable to N. Company D is an associate of N, Company E is a subsidiary of D and thus an associate of N even though only 6 per cent of E is indirectly attributable to N. Company F is an associate of N and G is an associate of F, but G is not an associate of N. Company H is a subsidiary of N and Company J is an associate of H and thus an associate of N. Company K is a subsidiary of N and L is a branch of K and thus of N. Thus direct investment statistics based on the Fully Consolidated System would cover A, B, C, D, E, F, H, J, K and L.

Immediate host/investing country: Geographic analysis of direct investment transactions is complicated by holding companies; that is, when the ultimate parent enterprise's investment in a foreign country is held through another subsidiary in a third country. Because the principle of classification used in balance of payments regional statistics is based on the change of ownership, direct investment flows should be compiled only in respect of the immediate host/investing country. The same rule applies for the international investment position statement; liabilities should be classified by the country of residence of the owner of the claim, and assets should be classified by the country of the liability holder. However, it is suggested that the stock of net assets of direct investment could also be compiled in respect of the ultimate host or controlling country, as supplementary information.

Income on debt (interest accrued): consists of interest payable on intercompany debt to/from direct investors from/to associated enterprises abroad. It covers interest on the borrowing and lending of funds (including debt securities and suppliers' credits) between direct investors and direct investment enterprises.

Income on equity comprises: (i) dividends and distributed branch profits; and (ii) reinvested earnings and undistributed branch profits. (See also the entry for *dividends*.)

Indirectly owned direct investment enterprises: As a matter of principle, foreign direct investment statistics cover all enterprises in which direct investors have, directly or indirectly, a direct investment interest. The OECD's *Benchmark Definition of Foreign Direct Investment* and the IMF's *Balance of Payments Compilation Guide* describe the scope of enterprises, both directly and indirectly owned, that should be included in the definition. The OECD's specification of this group of enterprises is referred to as the "Fully Consolidated System" (FCS). (See Annex I of this questionnaire for more a more detailed description of the FCS.)

Individual transactions basis: Data collected on this basis consist of information collected for each of the transactions made by respondents, such as information collected from an international transactions reporting system (ITRS).

International investment position: is the balance sheet of the stock of external financial assets and liabilities of an economy. The concepts and guidelines for compiling international investment position data are set out in the fifth edition of the IMF *Balance of Payments Manual*.

International Transactions Reporting System (ITRS): An ITRS measures individual balance of payments cash transactions passing through the domestic banks and foreign bank accounts of enterprises, and noncash transactions and stock positions. Statistics are compiled from forms submitted by domestic banks to the compilers and from forms submitted by enterprises to the compiler.

Inward: refers to direct investment in the reporting economy.

Land and buildings: All land and buildings located within an economy, except that owned by foreign governments (such as embassies) are, by convention, regarded as being owned by residents. If an actual owner is a non-resident, the owner is treated as if the ownership had been transferred to a resident notional institutional unit that is deemed to own the land and buildings. The non-resident has a financial investment in this notional unit, which is therefore a direct investment enterprise.

Market price: is the amount of money that willing buyers would pay to acquire a financial asset from a willing seller. The use of market price for valuation of assets and liabilities is one of the key principles of balance of payments compilation.

Most comprehensive data: This term refers to the direct investment statistics that are disseminated and based on the most comprehensive regularly available data sources. These data may be preliminary and subject to revision. Note that if your country compiles and disseminates data that are always based on the same sources and coverage, the "most comprehensive data" are the same as the "most timely data", and the answer to the questions regarding the "most comprehensive data" should be "N.A". (For many countries "N.A." will be the correct answer.) The issue of "data revision policy" is dealt with later in this questionnaire.

Most timely data: The term refers to the direct investment statistics that are first disseminated; that is, the data with the shortest lapse of time between the end of the reference period (or the reference date) and dissemination of the data. Although disseminated, such data may be preliminary and subject to revision.

Natural resources exploration: When a direct investment enterprise is set up for the exploration of natural resources, inward direct investment flows provided to the direct investment enterprise by the direct investor located abroad that are used for exploration should be recorded as *direct investment, equity capital.*

Nomenclature generale des Activites economiques dans les Communautes europeennes (NACE): refers to the industrial classification as defined in Revision 1 which is used by EUROSTAT. (See Annex II of this questionnaire for more details.)

Non-voting stocks are equity/shares that do not give voting rights to the holder. The category includes participating preference shares. (See also the entry for *Voting stocks*.)

Off-shore enterprises: In balance of payments accounts, the residency of so called "off-shore enterprises" is attributed to the economies in which they are located without regard to the special treatment they may receive by the local authorities, such as exemptions from taxes, tariffs, or duties. This treatment applies to enterprises such as those engaged in the assembly of components manufactured elsewhere and in the processing of re-exported goods, to those engaged in trade and financial operations, and to those located in special zones (e.g. special trade zones, free-trade zones, or tax-havens).

Other capital: covers the borrowing or lending of funds between direct investors and subsidiaries, branches, and associates - including debt securities, suppliers' credit, and non-participating, preferred shares (which are treated as debt securities).

Outward: refers to direct investment abroad.

Periodicity: refers to the frequency with which the data are compiled. Periodicity specifications for flow data are given in terms of the longest interval to be represented by a single data point; those for stock data are given in the form of the longest interval between compilations. For example, the specification of quarterly periodicity for balance of payments data means that one quarter is the longest interval that may be represented by a single estimate.

Perpetual inventory method: The process of deriving data on stocks from transaction data is known as the perpetual inventory method. Under this method, for which a stock estimate for some base point in time is required, the compiler may calculate the value of a stock at the end of a period as being equal to the value of the stock at the beginning of the period, plus the impact of transactions and non-transaction changes in the value of the stock during the period.

Quasi-corporations: are enterprises that produce goods and services in an economy other than their own, but do not establish separate legal corporations in the host country. Quasi-corporations that are in a direct investment relationship with the parent enterprise are deemed to exist if:

- Production is maintained for one year or more.

- A separate set of accounts is maintained for the local activities.

- Income tax is paid in the host country.

Quasi-corporations are often involved in construction or the operation of mobile equipment in another economy. The fifth edition of the IMF *Balance of Payments Manual (BPM5)* recommends that quasi-corporations be included in the direct investment data.

Reinvested earnings and undistributed branch profits: comprise direct investors' shares in proportion to equity held of earnings that foreign subsidiaries and associated enterprises do not distribute as dividends, and earnings that branches and other unincorporated enterprises do not remit to direct investors.

Reinvested earnings of indirectly owned direct investment enterprises: are treated as follows under the Fully Consolidated System. Assuming that: (a) Company A in Country 1 owns 51% of Company B in Country 2, which in turn owns 51% of Company C in Country 3, and (b) The reinvested earnings of Company B is 500 and the reinvested earnings of Company C is 100, the income of Company A from reinvested earnings is 281, that is:

51% of the reinvested earnings of Company B: .51x500 = 255
51% of 51% of the reinvested earnings of Company C: .51(.51x100) = 26
(Table 4 of Annex I of the OECD *Benchmark Definition of Foreign Direct Investment* gives a more detailed example.)

Reverse investment: refers to the acquisition by a direct investment enterprise of a financial claim on its direct investor. Because direct investment is recorded on a directional basis, capital invested by the direct investment enterprise in its direct investor (reverse investment) is regarded as an offset to capital invested in the direct investment enterprises by a direct investor and its related enterprises, except in instances when the equity participations are at least 10 per cent in both directions.

Such reverse investment transactions are recorded based on the direction of the direct investment relationship.

When the claims are not sufficient to establish a second, separate direct investment relationship, the reverse investment transactions should be recorded according to the directional principle of the direct investment relationship as follows:

- As *direct investment in the reporting economy, claims on direct investors* in the data for the economy in which the direct investment enterprises is resident.

- As *direct investment abroad, liabilities to affiliated enterprises* in the data for the economy in which the direct investor is resident.

When the equity participations are at least 10% in both directions, two direct investment relationships are established. In these circumstances, equity and other capital transactions between enterprises are recorded as direct investment claims and liabilities in both directions, as follows:

- As *direct investment abroad* for transactions on assets.

- As direct investment in the reporting economy for transactions on liabilities.

Special Purpose Entities (SPEs): are (1) generally organised or established in economies other than those in which the parent companies are resident and (2) engaged primarily in international transactions but in few or no local operations. SPEs are defined either by their structure (e.g., financing subsidiary, holding company, base company, regional headquarters), or their purpose (e.g., sale and regional administration, management of foreign exchange risk, facilitation of financing of investment). SPEs should be treated as direct investment enterprises if they meet the 10 per cent criterion. SPEs are an integral part of direct investment networks as are, for the most part, SPE transactions with other members of the group.

For SPEs that have the sole purpose of serving as financial intermediaries:

- All transactions except those with affiliated banks and affiliated financial intermediaries, should be recorded in the direct investment data.

- Transactions with affiliated banks and affiliated financial intermediaries should be excluded from the direct investment data, except transactions in equity capital and permanent debt.

Time of recording: The time of recording for transactions and, hence, for holdings is governed by the principle of accrual accounting. For financial claims and liabilities, changes of ownership are considered to have taken place at (or be proxied by) the time that the parties to the transactions record them in their books or accounts. If no precise date can be fixed, the reporter may use the date on which the creditor received payment or the date on which some other financial claim was satisfied. For direct investment income data, dividends should be recorded as the date they are payable and income on debt as it is accrued.

Timeliness: refers to the speed with which the data are disseminated; that is the lapse of time between the end of a reference period (or a reference date) and dissemination of the data. Note that if new data are disseminated only once a year, but the periodicity of the data is quarterly, the timeliness of the data refers to the lapse of time between the end of the first of the four newly disseminated quarters and the time of dissemination. For example, if at the end of March 2000 data are disseminated for the four quarters of 1999, the timeliness is "up to 12 months"; that is, the lapse of time between the first quarter of 1999 and end-March 2000.

Transactor principle: There are two principles that may serve as the basis for geographic allocation of financial flows: the debtor/creditor principle and the transactor principle. Under the transactor principle, transactions resulting from changes in the claims and liabilities are allocated to the country of residence of the non-resident party to the transaction (the transactor), even if this is not the country of residence of the direct investment enterprise or direct investor. (See also the entry for the ***debtor/creditor principle***.)

Ultimate host/investing country: Geographic analysis of direct investment transactions is complicated by holding companies; that is, when the ultimate parent enterprise's investment in a foreign country is held through another subsidiary in a third country. The compilation of foreign direct investment statistics on income and financial flows based on the ultimate source of such flows would require a basis for the recording of transactions other than the change-of-ownership principle that is recommended in the fifth edition of the IMF *Balance of Payments Manual*. Therefore, direct investment flows should be compiled only in respect of the immediate host/investing country. The regional allocation of the international investment position statement should also be compiled on the basis of the immediate host or investing country. However, it is suggested that the stock of direct investment net assets could also be compiled in respect of the ultimate host or controlling country, as supplementary information.

United Nations International Standard Industrial Classification for all Economic Activities (ISIC): refers to the industrial classification as defined in the third version of ISIC. (See Annex II of this questionnaire for more details.)

Valuation of stocks: The fifth edition of the IMF *Balance of Payments Manual (BPM5)* and the OECD *Benchmark Definition of Foreign Direct Investment* recommend using market price as the basis for valuation. However, it is recognised that, in practice, book values from the balance sheets of direct investment enterprises (or investors) are often used to determine the value of the stock of direct investment. (See also the entry for ***Book value)***

Voluntary reporting requirements: Situations where there is no legal obligation for reporters to provide the requested information.

Voting stocks: are equity/shares that give voting rights to the holder. These can either be "listed voting stocks" (that is, equity/shares that are listed on an official stock exchange), or "unlisted voting stock" (that is, equity/shares that are not listed on a official stock exchange. (See also the entry for ***Non-voting stocks.***)

Multiple Indicators for Multiple Uses: United States Statistics on Foreign Direct Investment

Obie G. Whichard

Bureau of Economic Analysis, U.S. Department of Commerce

Abstract

The United States has a lengthy history as a direct investor and as a host of direct investment. It has developed an extensive data system to track this investment and the related operations, and over time it has made numerous improvements to the system as policy and other needs have created new demands. This presentation gives a general overview of the system and discusses selected need-driven data improvements. The improvements singled out for discussion relate to the development of current-price measures of investment stocks, supplemental current-account measures based on ownership, unduplicated measures of production by direct investment enterprises, and data on services delivered through the commercial presence mode of supply. Use of the data to address topical issues is illustrated through a discussion of offshore outsourcing by U.S. multinational companies. The presentation concludes with a discussion of two situations that have created difficulties in the interpretation of U.S. data on direct investment—(1) the interposition of holding company affiliates between U.S. parent companies and their foreign operating affiliates, and (2) corporate inversions.

Introduction

Foreign direct investment has a lengthy history in the United States. From its 18th-century beginnings, the country has been both a host of foreign-owned enterprises and a source of capital for business ventures located overseas.[1] However, its systematic collection of statistics on this investment is of much more recent advent. Some information on direct investment was collected by the U.S. Government in the early 1900's, but regular and systematic data collection did not start until about 1950. Over time, the data collected have become more detailed and comprehensive, and today the nation has what many regard as the world's most fully developed data system on foreign direct investment. It covers not only stocks and flows of investment, but also extensive information on the financing and operations of the enterprises involved.

Over time, numerous data improvements have been made, and to a substantial extent, the directions taken in improving and expanding the data have reflected responses to changing policy and other user needs and to changes in the U.S. and world economies.

---

[1]   For an account of these early ventures, see Mira Wilkins, The Emergence of Multinational Enterprise: American Business Abroad from the Colonial Era to 1914 (Cambridge, Massachusetts: Harvard University Press, 1970).

Not only do the data serve as critical components of the balance of payments accounts, but they also have been called upon for such diverse purposes as helping gauge the nation's position as a net debtor or creditor, supporting the negotiation of trade agreements and investment treaties, investigating responses to tax regimes, and—most recently—addressing the issue that has come to be known as "offshore outsourcing". In this paper, I will describe the major improvements that have been made in these statistics and identify some of the needs they were meant to address. To give a sense of perspective, it will be helpful first to review a few key facts about direct investment in and by the United States.

The United States is both the world's largest direct investor and the host of the world's largest stock of inward direct investment. Recent United Nations estimates based on book values indicate that the United States accounted for almost one-fifth of the global stock of inward direct investments in 2003, and for about one-fourth of the global stock of outward direct investments.[2] Estimated at market value, the U.S. direct investment position abroad at yearend 2003 was $2.7 trillion, while the foreign direct investment position in the United States stood at $2.4 trillion. Although these positions are not components of gross domestic product, it may give a sense of the magnitudes involved to observe that U.S. current-dollar GDP in 2003 was $11.0 trillion, or a little more than double the combined value of the inward and outward direct investment positions. The income generated by these investments also is significant. In 2003, receipts of income on U.S. direct investment abroad were $188 billion, and payments of income on foreign direct investment in the United States were $67 billion.

Direct investors and their affiliates account for a substantial share of U.S. international trade in goods. In 2002, U.S. exports and imports of goods associated with multinational companies headquartered or investing in the United States totaled over $1.0 trillion and accounted for over half of U.S. imports and two-thirds of U.S. exports. U.S. parent companies, their foreign affiliates, and U.S. affiliates of foreign companies together employed about 34 million people in the United States and abroad in that year (26 million were in the United States, of a total private workforce of about 113 million). The combined value added of U.S. parents and U.S. affiliates accounted for over one-fourth of U.S. GDP.

The U.S. data on direct investment are collected in two distinct groups: (1) Balance of payments and direct investment position data and (2) financial and operating data. The former include the various categories of income and capital transactions that may occur between parent companies and their affiliates, as well as the transactions that occur between parents and third parties when parents acquire or sell ownership interests in affiliates. They also include the related investment positions. These data conform closely to those called for by the 5th edition of the IMF *Balance of Payments Manual (BPM5)* and by the 3rd edition of the OECD *Benchmark Definition of Foreign Direct Investment (BD3)*. Of particular importance, they use the same 10 percent ownership criterion that is recommended by those international standards as the threshold for categorizing an

---

2   United Nations Conference on Trade and Development, World Investment Report 2004, Annex tables B.3 and B.4.

international investment as "direct".[3] The most recent annual estimates are shown in table 1.

The financial and operating data include such items as balance sheets, income statements, sales of goods and services, employment and employee compensation, U.S. trade in goods, research and development expenditures, taxes, and external financial position. Unlike the balance of payments and direct investment position data, they pertain to the entire operations of the affiliates, not just the parent company's share. Some financial and operating data are available on a 10-percent ownership basis, but to an increasing degree, both data collection and data presentation have been more focused on data for majority-owned affiliates.[4] The most recent annual estimates for these affiliates are shown in table 2.

While the United States has compiled both direct-investment-related balance of payments and financial and operating data for many years, the data have not always been as useful in addressing policy questions as they are now. In the section that follows, I would like to describe selected improvements that have been made in recent years in response to user needs and demands. The subsequent section will comment upon how BEA has brought its data to bear on the issue of offshore outsourcing, which has attracted considerable public interest in recent months. A final section discusses two issues that pose challenges for the future—holding companies and corporate inversions.

Improvements

BEA continually strives to improve its data on direct investment, and almost every year brings with it some data improvement or enhancement. Typical of these improvements would be the modernization of industry classifications or changes in methodology that improve alignment with international recommendations. Cataloguing and describing these improvements would easily provide material for a separate paper. However, consonant with the orientation of this conference toward policy uses of the data, I have chosen to focus here on four improvements that have played key roles in making the data BEA provides more useful for policymakers. The improvements singled out for discussion relate to the development and provision of (1) current-price measures of investment stocks, (2) supplemental current-account measures based on ownership, (3)

---

3   With regard to outward investment, where the U.S. ownership interest is indirectly held, all the ownership percentages (based on voting equity) between the U.S. investor and the indirectly held foreign company are multiplied together to determine whether the 10-percent criterion has been met. (For example, if a U.S. company's share in Firm A is 60 percent and that firm, in turn, owns 40 percent of Firm B, then Firm B would be considered a foreign affiliate of the U.S. company, since the product of the two ownership shares linking it to Firm B—24 percent—is in excess of 10 percent.) This implementation of the 10-percent rule is somewhat different from that called for by BPM5 and BD3, which include as foreign affiliates any firm in an unbroken chain of majority ownerships. From a practical standpoint, this difference in implementation probably does not have a major impact on the overall categorization of investments.

4   Because of the presumption of control, majority ownership is viewed by many as the preferred basis for selecting firms for the analysis of the economic role and importance of foreign-owned firms. It is also recommended as the primary basis for the compilation of statistics on the operations of foreign-owned firms by the OECD's forthcoming Handbook of Globalisation Indicators and for the compilation of statistics on "foreign affiliates' trade in services" (or "FATS") by the international Manual on Statistics of International Trade in Services. Finally, majority ownership appears to be the most relevant concept for the support of trade agreements, such as the General Agreement on Trade in Services, and it can be viewed as a practical statistical implementation of the concept of "foreign-controlled enterprise" found in the System of National Accounts (which, however, may admit other firms based on subjective assessment of the degree of actual control).

unduplicated measures of production by direct investment enterprises, and (4) measures of services delivered via the commercial presence mode of supply.

Table 1. Key Indicators of U.S. Direct Investment Abroad and of Foreign Direct Investment in the United States, 2003

(Billions of dollars)

U.S. Direct Investment Abroad	
Position at year end:	
Historical cost	1 788.9
Current cost	2 069.0
Market value	2 730.3
Balance of payments flows:	
Financial outflows	173.8
Equity capital	24.6
Increases in equity capital	45.3
Decreases in equity capital	20.7
Reinvested earnings	141.1
Intercompany debt	8.1
Income receipts	187.5
Income on equity	181.5
Income on debt (net U.S. receipts)	6.1
INTRAFIRM SERVICES TRANSACTIONS:	
Royalties and license fees, net receipts	29.8
U.S. parents' receipts	32.5
U.S. parents' payments	2.7
Other private services, net receipts	9.1
U.S. parents' receipts	27.7
U.S. parents' payments	18.6

Foreign Direct Investment in the United States	
Position at yearend:	
Historical cost	1 378.0
Current cost	1 554.0
Market value	2 435.5
Balance of payments flows:	
Financial inflows	39.9
Equity capital	62.2
Increases in equity capital	74.1
Decreases in equity capital	11.9
Reinvested earnings	12.0
Intercompany debt	-34.4
Income payments	68.7
Income on equity	50.3
Income on debt (net)	18.3
Intrafirm services transactions:	
Royalties and license fees (net payments)	10.3
U.S. parents' receipts	13.7
U.S. parents' payments	3.4
Other private services, net	3.9
U.S. parents' receipts	16.9
U.S. parents' payments	20.8

Table 2. Key Indicators of the Operations of Majority-Owned Nonbank Foreign Affiliates of U.S. Companies and of Majority-Owned Nonbank U.S. Affiliates of Foreign Companies, 2002

	Foreign affiliates of U.S. companies	U.S. affiliates of foreign companies
Total assets	6 209.8	4 556.6
Sales	2 548.6	2 043.5
Goods	2 034.5	1 548.0
Services	420.2	416.2
Investment income[1]	93.9	79.3
Net income	204.8	-51.2
U.S. exports of goods[2]	177.2	137.0
U.S. imports of goods[3]	199.3	324.6
Compensation of employees	269.3	307.1
Employment (thousands)	8 813.9	5 420.3
Value added	611.5	453.6
Capital expenditures	113.2	111.9
Research and development expenditures	21.2	27.5

[1]Investment income reported by companies, primarily those in finance and insurance, that record such income as operating revenue.

[2]For foreign affiliates, shows goods shipped to affiliates. For U.S. affiliates, shows goods shipped by affiliates.

[3]For foreign affiliates, shows goods shipped by affiliates. For U.S. affiliates, shows goods shipped to affiliates.

Current-price measures of investment stocks

In the mid-to-late 1980's, concerns began to arise about the shift in the net international investment position (IIP) of the United States from positive to negative and about the possible implications of that shift, such as for receipts and payments of interest income or a vulnerability of the economy to capital flight. However, public debate on the issue was hampered by limitations of the statistics and, in particular, by the mix of valuation methods used by BEA in deriving the IIP. Although many of the assets in the position (such as portfolio investment and most reserve assets) were being valued at current-period prices, other assets, including direct investment, were valued at the historical cost at which they were purchased. In 1990, BEA suspended publication of the IIP and announced that it was undertaking a review of alternative methods of valuing international investment to reflect current-period prices.

As a result of its review, BEA developed two new alternative methods—current-cost and market value—to revalue its estimates of direct investment in terms of current-period prices. The *current-cost* method revalues the U.S. and foreign parents' share of their affiliates' investment in plant in equipment using a perpetual inventory model; in land, using general price indexes; and in inventories, using estimates of their current replacement cost. The *market-value* method revalues the owners' equity portions of the inward and outward direct investment positions using indexes of stock market prices.

As expected under inflationary conditions, the revalued estimates on either basis were higher than the historical-cost estimates, for both outward and inward investment. However, the differences were relatively larger for outward investment, which tended to be of older vintage than inward investment. Furthermore, the increase over historical cost was greatest for the market-value measure, which reflected changes in the price of *all* the assets of the firm, rather than only its tangible assets. In the initial estimates for 1989, the current-cost measure exceeded the historical-cost measure by 43 percent for outward investment and by 14 percent for inward investment; for market value, the comparable figures were 115 percent and 36 percent, respectively.[5] When these current-price measures were substituted for the historical-cost measures in the computation of the net U.S. IIP, the position remained negative, but by a significantly lesser amount. By placing these components of the IIP on a consistent valuation basis, this exercise provided sounder statistical underpinnings for the public dialog with regard to the nation's international claims and liabilities.

Since the release of the initial estimates more than a decade ago, a variety of developments have affected the relative current-price valuations of inward and outward direct investment—the two types of investment flows have grown at different rates, exchange rates have changed, and equity prices in the United States and abroad have changed at different rates. As a result, the adjustments to value the positions in current prices no longer uniformly raise the outward position more than the inward position. For 2003, on a current-cost basis, the adjustments raised the U.S. direct investment abroad position by 16 percent and the foreign direct investment in the United States position by 13 percent. For market value, the comparable figures were 53 percent and 77 percent, respectively.

Supplemental current-account measures based on ownership

In the early 1990's, demands arose from several sources—including a blue ribbon National Academy of Sciences study panel—for the traditional balance of payments presentation to be supplemented by a presentation that reports more fully the dimension of ownership.[6] These demands arose simultaneously with, and probably to a large extent because of, the increasing interdependence of world economies that occurred as multinational firms assumed a more prominent role in the delivery of goods and services to international markets and the appearance of commercial presence as an issue to be addressed in multilateral negotiations.

In 1993 and 1995 articles, BEA proposed a framework that responded to the need for added detail on ownership while at the same time maintaining consistency with the conventions of the national and international economic accounts.[7] An objective of the framework is to better recognize the role of foreign affiliates as a means of delivering goods and services to international markets and as a contributor to the nation's economic performance in world markets. Under this framework, "trade" is construed broadly to include not only cross-border exports and imports of goods and services, but also deliveries through affiliates. However, the latter are entered in the accounts, not at their full value, but in a way that reflects only the return to the capital ownership by the parent firm. An alternative trade balance is introduced that reflects both channels of delivery,

---

5   Both the initial estimates and the methodology that would subsequently be used in constructing the official estimates of the IIP are given in J. Steven Landefeld and Ann M. Lawson, "Valuation of the U.S. Net International Investment Position," Survey of Current Business 71 (May 1991): 40-49.

6   See Anne Y. Kester, ed., Behind the Numbers: U.S. Trade in the World Economy, National Research Council, Panel on Foreign Trade Statistics (Washington, DC: National Academy Press, 1992).

7   For detailed information on the sources and methods used to prepare the supplemental accounts, see Obie G. Whichard and Jeffrey H. Lowe, "An Ownership-Based Disaggregation of the U.S. Current Account, 1982-95," Survey of Current Business 75 (October 1995): 52-61. For a general review of issues relating to ownership relations in international transactions, see J. Steven Landefeld, Obie G. Whichard, and Jeffrey H. Lowe, "Alternative Frameworks for U.S. International Transactions," Survey 73 (December 1993): 50-61. In recent years, the supplemental accounts have been updated each year in the January issue of the Survey.

thus capturing the effects on the U.S. economy of sales that originate both within and beyond its geographical boundaries.

The conventional measure of the trade balance reflects a country's performance in international markets in terms of the net value of goods and services transactions between firms and persons residing in that country and those residing abroad. Sales of goods and services by foreign affiliates of investing companies to other foreign persons, and sales by foreign affiliates in host countries to other persons in those countries, are not regarded as exports and imports and are therefore excluded from the trade balance.

In the ownership-based framework, in contrast, sales by foreign affiliates are entered in the accounts in a way that reflects the return to the direct investor's ownership interest in the affiliate (which, in conventional balance of payments accounts, may be labelled "direct investment income"). Returns to U.S. direct investors generated by the sales of goods and services by their foreign affiliates are added to the conventional measure of U.S. cross-border exports, to yield a measure of total U.S. receipts arising from cross-border sales and sales by foreign affiliates. Similarly, returns accruing to foreign owners of affiliates located in the United States are added to U.S. cross-border imports, to yield a comparable measure of total U.S. payments. Entering the effects of affiliate sales in this way recognizes these sales as a separate and distinct method of supplying foreign markets, while at the same time ensuring that only the portion of sales revenues that accrues to the benefit of the home country is included as revenue from that country's foreign sales. The grouping of these items recognizes that cross-border trade and sales through affiliates both are methods of active participation in international markets for goods and services.

To show the linkages between the returns to direct investors and the activities of affiliates that generate these returns, details obtained from the financial and operating data are added showing the gross sales and expenses (as well as any profits accruing to local or third-country investors) that, when netted against one another, give rise to this return. Expenses are further broken down to show compensation of employees, thus providing a more detailed picture of the activities generating and underlying the return to direct investors. Having constructed these more comprehensive measures of receipts and payments resulting from international sales and purchases, a balance is calculated equal to the difference between them.

Accounts compiled on this basis have been presented periodically in the United States since the early 1990's. The basic structure of the accounts and key figures for the years 2001 and, in less detail, 2002 are shown in table 3. The table shows that, for those years, the U.S. deficit on goods, services, and net receipts from sales by affiliates is smaller than the deficit on goods and services alone, reflecting the fact that U.S. investors had higher returns on their direct investments abroad than foreign investors had on their direct investments in the United States.[8] In addition to the items discussed above, the table adds details on whether the cross-border trade is with unrelated parties or with affiliated parties and, for the latter, on whether the trade is with foreign parent companies or with foreign affiliates. In more detailed tables published by BEA, trade in goods and trade in services are separately identified for each of these ownership categories.

---

8   Rates of return for foreign-owned U.S. companies have been persistently below those of both other U.S. companies and foreign affiliates of U.S. companies. For a discussion of the gap in rates of return between foreign-owned and U.S.-owned U.S. companies, see Raymond J. Mataloni, Jr., "An Examination of the Low Rates of Return of Foreign-Owned U.S. Companies," Survey of Current Business 80 (March 2000): 55-73.

Table 3. Ownership-Based Framework of the U.S. Current Account, 2001-2002

(Billions of dollars)

Line		2001	2002
1	**Exports of goods and services and income receipts**	**1 284.9**	**1 229.6**
2	Receipts resulting from exports of goods and services or sales by foreign affiliates	**1 131.9**	**1 117.0**
3	Exports of goods and services, total	**1 007.6**	**974.1**
4	To unaffiliated foreigners	693.9	....
5	To affiliated foreigners	313.7	....
6	To foreign affiliates of U.S. companies	230.4	....
7	To foreign parent groups of U.S. affiliates	83.3	....
8	Net receipts by U.S. companies of direct investment income resulting from sales by their foreign affiliates	**124.3**	**142.9**
9	Nonbank affiliates	121.7	140.7
10	Sales by foreign affiliates	2 929.6	....
11	Less: Foreign affiliates' purchases of goods and services directly from the United States	256.8	....
12	Less: Costs and profits accruing to foreign persons	2 032.4	....
13	Compensation of employees of foreign affiliates	308.3	....
14	Other	1 724.1	....
15	Less: Sales by foreign affiliates to other foreign affiliates of the same parent	518.7	....
16	Bank affiliates[1]	2.7	2.3
17	**Other income receipts**	**153.0**	**112.6**
18	**Imports of goods and services and income payments**	**1 632.1**	**1 651.7**
19	Payments resulting from imports of goods and services or sales by U.S. affiliates	**1 383.2**	**1 441.6**
20	Imports of goods and services, total	**1 365.4**	**1 392.1**
21	From unaffiliated foreigners	859.9	....
22	From affiliated foreigners	505.5	....
23	From foreign affiliates of U.S. companies	198.5	....
24	From foreign parent groups of U.S. affiliates	307.0	....
25	Net payments to foreign parents of direct investment income resulting from sales by their U.S. affiliates	**17.8**	**49.5**
26	Nonbank affiliates	15.1	47.0
27	Sales by U.S. affiliates	2 354.1	....
28	Less: U.S. affiliates' purchases of goods and services directly from abroad	393.5	....
29	Less: Costs and profits accruing to U.S. persons	1 945.5	....
30	Compensation of employees of U.S. affiliates	350.6	....
31	Other	1 594.9	....
32	Less: Sales by U.S. affiliates to other U.S. affiliates of the same parent [2]	n.a.	n.a.
33	Bank affiliates[1]	2.7	2.4
34	**Other income payments**	**248.8**	**210.0**
35	**Unilateral current transfers, net**	**-46.6**	**-58.9**
	Memoranda:		
36	Balance on goods and services	-357.8	-418.0
37	Balance on goods, services, and net receipts from sales by affiliates (line 2 minus line 19)	-251.3	-324.6
38	Balance on current account	-393.7	-480.9

1. Details on underlying sales and expenses are not available for bank affiliates.
2. Not available but, because affiliates are required to report on a consolidated basis, probably immaterial.

Source: Adapted from "An Ownership-Based Framework of the U.S. Current Account, 1992-2002," *Survey of Current Business* 84 (January 2004): 66-68, which contains additional details. The underlying data have subsequently been revised, but certain adjustments needed for this framework will not be made until the presentation is updated in January 2005.

Unduplicated measures of production

BEA's surveys of multinational companies do not directly collect measures of value added, and before BEA began to estimate value added from other data items that are collected, policymakers and others would often use sales or employment as indicators of the scale of operations of the firms covered. While these are useful—even key—measures for many purposes, value added is a preferable measure of activity. Value added indicates the extent to which affiliates' sales result from their own production rather than from production that originates elsewhere, whereas sales data do not distinguish between value added within affiliates and the value that originates in the firms that supply affiliates with intermediate inputs (or in those firms' suppliers). Employment does not suffer from this limitation, but it is limited by its focus on only one factor of production. For example, if one firm has higher employment than another, the difference may reflect either higher production or a lower capital-labour ratio on the part of one firm than on the part of another. Value added estimates for multinational companies also are important because they can be compared to total GDP of the home or host economy, to determine their unduplicated contribution to national production.

In recognition of the need for duplication-free measures of production, BEA developed a methodology for estimating value added by parents and affiliates from items collected on its benchmark and annual surveys of direct investment. It first published estimates of the value added of foreign affiliates of U.S. companies for 1966 and first published estimates of the value added of the U.S. affiliates of foreign companies for 1974. Its first estimates of value added for U.S. parent companies covered 1977. For all three groups of companies, the estimates were initially provided only for years covered by a benchmark survey, but subsequently annual series were introduced.

BEA's estimation methodology for value added exploits the national income identity that draws an equivalence between gross product and the sum of various charges against production. The estimates are derived as the sum of the following five factor and nonfactor charges: Compensation of employees, net interest paid, capital consumption allowances, indirect business taxes, and profit-type return. An alternative method of computation would be to subtract purchases of intermediate inputs from gross output. However, purchases data are not requested on the BEA surveys, and a number of respondents have indicated that such data would be difficult to provide.[9]

Services delivered via commercial presence

To meet the needs associated with growth in the value of trade in services, trade negotiations, and the development of new and more detailed international guidelines for statistical compilation, BEA has taken a variety of steps over roughly the past two decades to improve the coverage, specificity, and international comparability of its statistics on trade in services. Included among them have been improvements in data on both trade in the conventional sense of exchanges between residents and nonresidents and services delivered through locally established affiliates, the latter corresponding broadly to the General Agreement on Trade in Services commercial presence mode of supply (or "Mode 3") and commonly referred to as "foreign affiliates trade in services", or FATS. As set forth in the *Manual on Statistics of International Trade in Services (MSITS)*, the

---

9   Although the collection of data on purchases has not proved feasible, once value added has been estimated, an estimate of purchases can be derived residually, as the difference between sales (plus inventory change) and value added.

domain of FATS statistics encompasses a variety of indicators of affiliate operations, organized in a way that highlights the role of services. BEA's approach to providing data on services delivered through affiliates is consistent with this perspective. As explained earlier, BEA has for many years collected statistics on the operations of foreign affiliates. In response to the demand for more services-oriented information, it built upon this existing system of data collection.

As interest in services grew and as it became apparent that services would be included in negotiations, a key adjustment was made to accommodate this new emphasis. In particular, questions on sales were expanded to request that sales be broken down into separate components for goods and services, and definitions were provided to distinguish between the two. In addition, when industry classifications were revised, additional detail was provided for services industries.

Perhaps the most important change was requesting that sales of services be reported separately from sales of goods. Because the data on affiliate operations are classified according to the primary industry of the affiliate, all of an affiliate's sales are recorded in a single industry, even if the affiliate has operations in multiple industries. Many manufacturing firms and other goods producers have secondary operations in services, but these operations would not be recognized as services in a breakdown by primary industry alone, thus leading to an understatement in the role and importance of services.[10] The breakdown of sales into goods and services avoids this understatement. It would be better still if sales could be broken down by product–that is, by type of good or service– but from the standpoints of respondent burden and processing costs, BEA did not feel justified in requesting this detail. Disaggregating sales as between goods and services thus served as a compromise solution, which avoided misstatement without imposing a large increase in reporting burden or processing costs.

In an annual article on international services, BEA has presented the following two items: (1) sales of services to foreign persons by majority-owned nonbank foreign affiliates of U.S. companies, and (2) sales of services to U.S. persons by majority-owned nonbank U.S. affiliates of foreign companies. The foreign affiliates' sales to U.S. customers, and U.S. affiliates' sales to foreign customers, are excluded from this integrated presentation because they are already reflected in the data on cross-border trade.[11] The data are for nonbank affiliates only, because the surveys from which the data are derived exclude banks from coverage.[12]

In addition to the sales variable, BEA's data on affiliate operations include a variety of other indicators, as described elsewhere in this paper. Although they are sometimes presented using different nomenclature, the variables covered include both the "basic" and the optional "additional" FATS variables suggested in the *MSITS*.

---

10   It is, of course, also possible for services firms to have secondary operations in goods, but this tends to be less common than for goods producers to have secondary services operations.

11   However, data on these sales are made available separately, as are data on total sales (including sales of goods).

12   However, sales of services by U.S. affiliates in banking were collected for the first time in the 2002 benchmark survey of inward direct investment. Also collected were data on interest income and interest expense, which may provide a basis for estimating the value of unpriced services provided by banks. Bank affiliates continue to be excluded from the annual surveys.

A Current Challenge: Offshore outsourcing

Over about the last year, there have been widespread reports in the U.S. business press about what has come to be described as "offshore outsourcing" (or often, simply "offshoring") of production by U.S. companies, either to affiliated or unaffiliated foreign firms. BEA's data on multinational company (MNC) operations have played an important role in informing the public dialog with regard to offshoring that involves the use of foreign affiliates. Here BEA has not—at least thus far—collected any new data. Rather it has taken a number of steps to bring existing data to bear on the issue. These have included accelerating the release of key indicators, organizing and analysing the data with a view to better informing public dialog, and giving a number of presentations on patterns and trends in MNC operations.

Although there has been some examination of the U.S. operations of foreign-owned firms in connection with the debate over offshoring, most of the attention has focused on the domestic and foreign operations of U.S.-headquartered MNCs. The following highlights illustrate the kinds of information that have proved of interest in this context.[13]

- The measures of value added, capital expenditures, and employment have consistently shown that U.S.-MNC operations are concentrated in the United States, but the distributions of capital expenditures and employment have changed over time. For value added, U.S. parents accounted for the same share—75 percent—of the worldwide MNC total in 2002 as in 1977 (table 4). For capital expenditures and employment, the U.S. parent share has decreased: The U.S.-parent share of capital expenditures decreased from 79 percent in 1977 to 75 percent in 2002, and the U.S.-parent share of employment decreased from 78 percent in 1977 to 73 percent in 2002. The decrease in the parent share of capital expenditures was concentrated in 2002, and it may reflect a short-term fluctuation rather than a trend that will be sustained. However, the decrease in the parent share of employment was sustained throughout 1987-2002.

- Employment by foreign affiliates remains concentrated in high-wage countries, but in recent years it has grown faster in low-wage countries. In 1991-2002, affiliate employment grew at an average annual rate of 6 percent in a selected group of "low-wage" countries, which was double the 3-percent rate in "high-wage" countries. It is not clear to what extent these differences in employment growth reflect wage differentials, but the differences probably occurred at least partly for other reasons. Some of the low-wage countries where affiliate employment has grown the most have had rapidly growing domestic markets and have liberalized policies toward direct investment; some of the differences in growth rates may reflect these factors, rather than wage differentials.

---

13   These highlights were drawn from Raymond J. Mataloni, Jr., "U.S. Multinational Companies: Operations in 2002," Survey of Current Business 84 (July 2004): 10-29. See also "A Note on Patterns of Production and Employment by U.S. Multinational Companies," Survey 84 (March 2004): 52-56.

Table 4.   U.S. Parent Share of Selected Measures of the Operations of U.S. Multinational Companies, 1977-2002

(Percent)

	Value added	Capital expenditures[1]	Employment
1977	75.3	79.8	77.9
1978	n.a.	n.a.	n.a.
1979	n.a.	n.a.	n.a.
1980	n.a.	n.a.	n.a.
1981	n.a.	n.a.	n.a.
1982	78.1	80.8	78.8
1983	n.a.	81.3	79.1
1984	n.a.	82.8	78.9
1985	n.a.	83.5	79.0
1986	n.a.	83.0	79.1
1987	n.a.	81.4	79.4
1988	n.a.	79.2	78.8
1989	76.6	77.5	78.6
1990	n.a.	77.6	77.5
1991	n.a.	76.6	76.9
1992	n.a.	76.8	76.8
1993	n.a.	76.4	77.1
1994	76.5	76.4	76.5
1995	74.6	76.6	75.8
1996	74.8	76.4	75.6
1997	75.1	77.7	75.4
1998	75.9	77.1	74.5
1999	77.2	76.5	74.8
2000	77.9	78.2	74.5
2001	76.4	78.9	73.5
2002	75.2	75.1	73.3

[1]Expenditures made to acquire, add to, or improve property, plant, and equipment.

Note. In this table, a U.S. multinational company is defined as a U.S. parent company and its majority-owned foreign affiliates.

- An aspect of the production pattern for U.S. parent companies that has changed significantly is the degree to which these firms rely on purchased goods and services rather than their own production. During 1977-2002, purchases from outside suppliers as a percentage of total sales for U.S. parent companies in all industries except wholesale and retail trade increased from 63 percent to 69 percent, indicating an increasing reliance on purchased inputs. Some of these outside purchases were obtained from domestic suppliers, and some were obtained from both affiliated and unaffiliated foreign suppliers. The share of purchases that were imported directly from foreign suppliers has been essentially unchanged, at 9 percent in both 1977 and 2002. However, it must be recognized that in many cases, the goods and services purchased domestically have some imported content, which may be considered "indirect imports"; attempting to gauge these indirect imports by combining its data on MNC operations with data from its input-output accounts is on BEA's agenda for future research.

While BEA's data on the operations of U.S. MNCs indicate a relatively stable mix of domestic and foreign operations, the inferences that can be drawn from these data about the production strategies of MNCs and about the ultimate effects of U.S.-MNC activity on the U.S. economy and on foreign economies are limited. The U.S.-parent share of U.S.-MNC activity can change for a number of reasons, and these changes do not uniformly correspond to either additions to, or subtractions from, production and employment in the United States.

To illustrate the difficulty in linking cause and effect, it might be expected that new direct investment abroad by U.S. MNCs would cause the share of U.S. parent companies in worldwide MNC employment to fall and that of foreign affiliates to rise, but its impact on employment in the United States and abroad could vary, depending on the form of the investment and the reasons why it was undertaken. For example, a new investment might represent the establishment of a new company (or "greenfield" investment), the acquisition of a successful existing company, or the acquisition of a failing company. In each case, the employment by affiliates would rise, but the impact on host-country employment would likely differ. Furthermore, this impact cannot be discerned from information on MNC operations alone. Instead, the impact will be determined by a wide range of factors, including the overall level of employment in the economy and the types of jobs involved.

To illustrate the significance of the *reasons* for the investment, affiliate employment shares might rise either because of the shifting of production from parents to affiliates or because of the opening of new overseas markets—such as those for meals or lodging— that can be served only through a locally established enterprise. In the case of production shifting, the rise in employment by affiliates might be expected to come partly or wholly at the expense of employment by the parents. In contrast, in the example of new overseas markets, the rise in employment by foreign affiliates would not affect employment in the United States by parent companies, or it could even cause U.S. employment to rise, because of the need to provide headquarters services to the newly established affiliates.

In sum, statistics on MNC operations can help to inform discussions of offshoring, but they alone cannot provide all the answers. Many of the questions are not only questions of fact, but analytical questions that must take into account a variety of factors—such as exchange rates, rates of economic growth in home and host economies, and policies toward foreign direct investment—in addition to statistics on the domestic and foreign operations of the firms that make foreign direct investments. Finally, given the impossibility of conducting controlled experiments that would compare worlds with and without direct investment, realism requires us to acknowledge that some uncertainty about the interactions and mutual dependencies between domestic and foreign operations of MNCs will remain even with the best of data and economic analysis.

Future Tasks

I would like to close this paper with a brief discussion of two situations that have created difficulties in the interpretation of data on direct investment and that BEA would like to make progress in addressing in the future. The first of these is the growing practice by U.S. parent companies of interposing holding company affiliates between themselves and their foreign affiliates that are engaged in the production of goods and services. The second is the phenomenon of corporate inversions, which results in the creation of inward direct investments that in some sense may not be regarded as having true foreign ownership.

Holding companies

For the past two decades, U.S. parent companies have been funnelling an increasing share of their direct investments abroad through holding companies.[14] In 1982, foreign affiliates classified as holding companies accounted for only 9 percent of the U.S. direct investment position abroad, but by 2003, they accounted for 33 percent. This trend reflects a variety of factors. Some holding-company affiliates are established primarily to coordinate management and administration of activities—such as marketing, distribution, or financing—worldwide or in a particular geographic region. In addition, the presence of holding-company affiliates in countries where the effective income tax rate faced by affiliates is relatively low suggests that tax considerations may also have played a role in their growth.

One consequence of the increasing use of holding companies has been a reduction in the degree to which the estimates of the U.S. direct investment position abroad (and of related flows of income and capital) reflect the industries and countries in which the production of goods and services by affiliates occurs. This is because the estimates are classified according to the countries and industries of the affiliates with which the U.S. parent companies have direct transactions and positions, rather than according to the countries and industries of the affiliates whose operations the parents ultimately own or control.

Partly in response to the growing impact of holding companies on the distribution of the estimates, BEA has added presentations of position and income for U.S. direct investment abroad classified by industry of U.S. parent. Although the industry of the parent does not in all cases reflect the industries of its foreign operating affiliates, in many cases it can be expected to provide a more reliable indicator of those industries than the industries of the affiliates—which often are holding companies—with which the parent firms have direct transactions and positions.

To demonstrate the differences in the distribution of data classified on these two basis, table 5 shows position and income estimates for U.S. direct investment abroad for 2003 both by industry of foreign affiliate and by industry of U.S. parent. As can be seen, in some cases the differences are substantial. For example, manufacturing accounts for only 21 percent of the position by industry of affiliate, but it accounts for 59 percent of the position by industry of parent. "Other industries," where holding companies are classified, in contrast, accounts for a much higher share of the position when classified by industry of affiliate than when classified by industry of parent—39 percent compared to 8 percent.

Another approach to coping with the problems of interpretation caused by holding companies is simply to use the financial and operating data instead of the direct investment position data. Because these data are uniformly classified according to the country where the affiliate's physical assets are located or where its primary activity is carried out, they accurately reflect the industries and countries in which the production of goods and services by foreign affiliates occurs. However, as measures of operations, they are not adjusted for the percentage of U.S. ownership and therefore cannot substitute for the position as measures of U.S. direct investments. In addition, some items in the financial and operating data may contain duplication among affiliates that, if not adjusted out, could allow users to arrive at misleading conclusions. The potential for this to occur

---

14   A holding company is a company whose primary activity is holding the securities or financial assets of other companies. The increased use of holding-company affiliates is part of a broader trend in which the U.S. parents own foreign affiliates that, in turn, own other foreign affiliates. However, holding companies have contributed the most to this trend.

is particularly great where holding companies are involved. For example, assets of the holding company will be duplicated in the assets of the affiliates that it holds. The same is true of profits, which will be recorded as profits both of the holding company and of the affiliates whose productive activities generate the profits.[15]

Table 5. U.S. Direct Investment Position Abroad on a Historical-Cost Basis and Direct Investment Income, by Industry of Affiliate and by Industry of U.S. Parent, 2003

	By industry of foreign affiliate		By industry of U.S. parent	
	Position[1]	Income[2]	Position[1]	Income[2]
	Billions of dollars			
All industries	1 789	165	1 789	165
Mining	99	13	43	5
Utilities	27	2	51	2
Manufacturing	378	37	1 058	99
Wholesale trade	141	20	66	7
Information	48	5	82	9
Depository institutions	64	2	61	4
Finance (except depository institutions) and insurance	300	19	221	16
Professional, scientific, and technical services	41	5	65	8
Other industries	693	62	141	14
	Percent of total			
All industries	100	100	100	100
Mining	5.5	7.8	2.4	3.1
Utilities	1.5	1.2	2.8	1.4
Manufacturing	21.1	22.2	59.1	60.1
Wholesale trade	7.9	11.9	3.7	4.2
Information	2.7	3.3	4.6	5.8
Depository institutions	3.6	1.4	3.4	2.1
Finance (except depository institutions) and insurance	16.8	11.6	12.3	9.8
Professional, scientific, and technical services	2.3	2.8	3.7	5.1
Other industries	38.7	37.8	7.9	8.4

[1] At historical cost.

[2] In this table, unlike tables 1 and 3, income is shown net of withholding taxes and without a current-cost adjustment.

Still another approach to dealing with holding companies would be to reallocate flows and positions from the countries of the holding companies (and of any other companies through which indirectly owned affiliates may be held) to the countries of the operating affiliates. Because of the fungibility of money and the multiplicity of uses to which the funds made available by a direct investor to given holding company may be put, it is not clear that this could always be successfully accomplished. However, by following ownership chains, it might be possible to reallocate certain components of the position, such as that accounted for by equity capital.

As the share of U.S. direct investment abroad that is channelled through holding companies has grown, BEA has become more aware of the need to consider alternative or

15   BEA's data allow these sources of duplication to be identified, in most cases. For example, balance sheet data for affiliates separately identify equity investments in other foreign affiliates, and income statement data separately identify income from such investments. In building up value added estimates from charges against production, BEA makes an adjustment to exclude income from equity investments from the profit-type-return component, so that profits are attributed to only one affiliate, which is the affiliate whose productive activities generate the profits.

supplemental presentations that would better deal with these investments. In the months ahead, it hopes to explore the possibilities that may be available.

Corporate inversions

Corporate inversions are business reorganizations that occur when a U.S. corporation—most typically multinational—forms a corporation in a foreign tax haven and simultaneously "inverts" the corporate chain of ownership so that the new foreign corporation replaces the U.S. corporation as the parent of the global corporate group. Once this structure is in place, the U.S. company may choose to transfer the ownership of its foreign assets to the new foreign parent company, protecting them from U.S. tax. The inverted structure may also introduce opportunities to shift profits generated by domestic (U.S.) activities to the new foreign parent, thus further reducing U.S. taxes. A recent U.S. Treasury Department study observed that "while the so-called corporate inversion transactions are not new, there has been a marked increase recently in the frequency, size, and profile of the transactions."[16]

While the development of tax or regulatory policies regarding these transactions falls outside BEA's sphere of responsibility, the agency does have an obligation to consider their implications for economic statistics. In particular, some users have expressed a concern that these transactions—by creating U.S. affiliates whose ownership chain does not end abroad but leads back to the United States—could lead to an overestimate of the extent of foreign control in the business sector of the economy. When an inversion occurs, it often is through an exchange of stock, in which shares in the newly created foreign corporation are exchanged for shares in the domestic corporation. These self-financing transactions result in large, but offsetting, financial flows in the U.S. international transactions accounts and large, offsetting entries in the international investment position accounts. The large financial account inflows on direct investment that result from the newly formed foreign corporation's acquisition of shares in the domestic corporation are offset by outflows on foreign securities accounts that result from the U.S. shareholders receiving the stock of the foreign corporation.

These procedures properly account for all transactions and positions, yet the usefulness of the data on inward direct investment may suffer due to the fact that investment in these inverted U.S. corporations, which are ultimately U.S.-owned, is commingled with investments by firms that have more bona fide foreign ownership.[17] At present, BEA is unable to segregate transactions and positions that involve inverted firms from those that do not. However, it is aware of the potential for these transactions to create problems of interpretation, and when large transactions occur. It generally takes note of them and explains the method of accounting for them in interpretive commentary that accompanies data releases. It will continue to monitor and study this phenomenon. International copyright 2005, all rights reserved.

---

16   "Corporate Inversion Transactions: Tax Policy Implications," U.S. Department of the Treasury, Office of Tax Policy (May 2002).

17   Despite the fact that most or all of the shares in the offshore parent corporations are typically held by U.S. persons (specifically, the former U.S. shareholders of the U.S. corporation), these corporations generally would not be identified in statistics as having U.S. "ultimate beneficial owners" (UBOs), since the U.S. ownership usually is dispersed among many investors, each having a claim on only a small share of the total. (In U.S. statistics, the UBO of a U.S. affiliate of a foreign company is that person, proceeding up a U.S. affiliate's ownership chain, beginning with and including the foreign parent, that is not owned more than 50 percent by another person. Unlike the foreign parent (i.e., the first foreign person in the affiliate's ownership chain), the UBO of an affiliate may be located in the United States.)

Agricultural Support Indicators: Measurement, Meaning and Use

Wilfrid Legg

Head of Policies and Environment Division, Agriculture Directorate

Introduction

OECD governments have a long history of pursuing agricultural policies, with objectives ranging from supporting farm incomes to securing safe food and environmental quality. Policy measures are equally varied, including instruments such as import tariffs, export subsidies and a host of different government payments to farmers. Many of these policies share the common feature that they transfer money to farmers, and thereby impact on production decisions, incomes, international trade and the environment.

Governments of OECD member countries have an interest in learning more about each others' policies, to benefit from best practice experience and minimize negative spillover effects of policies both domestically and internationally. In order to support them in these efforts, the OECD invests heavily in policy analysis. One basic ingredient into any such analysis is the ability to describe agricultural policy developments over time, in a way that is accurate and comparable across countries.

What is required is a common yardstick that can measure the "size" and "shape" of the transfers from the many disparate agricultural policy instruments, in order to assess the progress made in achieving policy goals in more effective and efficient ways. The monetary value of the transfers to agriculture through the various policy instruments is one such yardstick. Each year since the mid-1980s, the OECD has been measuring the monetary transfers associated with agricultural policies in OECD countries (and some non-OECD countries), using a standard method. The results are published annually by the OECD, and are the only available source of internationally comparable and transparent information on support levels in agriculture. They have established a sound basis for international policy dialogue on agriculture, and contributed significantly to the formulation of internationally binding commitments on domestic support in the WTO following the Agreement on Agriculture concluded in the Uruguay Round.

Over the years many questions have been asked about the way in which the OECD builds its yardstick to measure agricultural support, what the data mean, and how it is used and interpreted. Most of the content of this paper is taken from an OECD *Policy Brief* (available on the OECD website), which was prepared to give a response to those frequently asked questions, addressed primarily to the non-technical reader. For those who want more information, a selected list of publications and contact points is given at the end of this paper.

What is meant by agricultural support?

In public discussion, words such as support, subsidy, assistance, and aid to producers are often used interchangeably to describe the transfers provided to farmers or the agricultural sector as a whole, which result from government policies that raise farmers' revenues or reduce their costs. The OECD uses the neutral term "support" to estimate the monetary value of transfers resulting from agricultural policies – whatever the intended objectives of those policies.

The OECD produces several indicators of agricultural support. The most important and central one is the **Producer Support Estimate** (PSE), which shows the annual monetary transfers to *farmers* from policy measures that:

- maintain domestic prices for farm goods at levels higher (and occasionally lower) than those at the country's border (*market price support*);

- provide payments to farmers, based on criteria such as the quantity of a commodity produced, the amount of inputs used, the number of animals kept, the area farmed, or the revenue or income received by farmers (*budgetary payments*).

The key point is that contrary to popular opinion, support not only comprises *budgetary* payments that appear in government accounts, but also the *price gap* for farm goods between domestic and world markets, as measured at a country's border. In fact, the latter constitutes the lion's share of support in most countries. The OECD indicators of support are described in Box 1, while Box 2 briefly compares the OECD's PSE with the World Trade Organization's Aggregate Measurement of Support (AMS) used in multilateral trade negotiations. The focus of this paper is the PSE.

Box 1. Other OECD Indicators of Support

Consumer Support Estimate (CSE) is the annual monetary transfers to consumers from policy measures that:

- maintain domestic prices paid by first consumers (measured at the farm gate) at levels higher (and sometimes lower) than those on world markets at the country's border, which is an implicit tax on consumers as it is the mirror image of market price support to farmers; and

- provide subsidies to keep prices of commodities consumed by certain groups in the economy lower than would otherwise be the case, such as cheap food for poor people, public institutions and some processors.

In general the CSE is negative because the implicit tax on consumers from market price support more than offsets consumer food subsidies.

General Services Support Estimate (GSSE) is the annual monetary transfers to agriculture but not to individual producers that:

- provide budgetary-financed expenditures for the provision of such services as research, development, training, inspection, marketing and promotion.

Total Support Estimate (TSE) is the overall monetary cost of the transfers in a country from policy measures calculated by:

- adding the PSE, the taxpayer cost of consumption subsidies and the provision of general services, and subtracting import tariff receipts.

Nominal Protection Coefficient (NPC) is the ratio between producer and border prices.

Nominal Assistance Coefficient (NAC) is the ratio between farm receipts (including support) and those generated in the market without support.

Box 2. PSE and AMS

The purpose of the PSE is to monitor and evaluate progress in agricultural policy reform, whereas the AMS is the basis for a legal commitment to reduce domestic support in the WTO Agreement on Agriculture. The PSE and AMS are closely related, but there are important differences.

The PSE covers all transfers to farmers from agricultural policies, whereas the AMS covers only domestic policies deemed to have the greatest production and trade effects (amber box), and excludes trade policies that are covered under the WTO market access and export subsidy disciplines. The AMS also excludes production-limiting policies (blue box), those policies deemed non or least trade distorting (green box) and certain trade distorting policies (*e.g.* input subsidies) when the level of domestic support is smaller than a specified de minimis level.

Market price support in the PSE is measured at the farm gate level using actual producer and reference (border) prices for commodities in a given year, whereas in the AMS market price support is calculated by the difference between annual prices fixed by policy makers (administered prices) and world prices in the base period (1986-88).

How is farm support expressed?

PSEs are calculated and shown by OECD country (the European Union with its Common Agricultural Policy is treated as one country) and by commodity. Increasingly PSE calculations are also produced for selected countries outside the OECD area. Market Price Support, the largest component of the PSE, is based on calculations for commodities accounting for around 70% of overall commodity production in the OECD area, with some differences in shares across countries. The PSE indicators are expressed in both absolute monetary terms, such as billions of dollars, and in relative terms – as a percentage of the value of gross farm receipts (%PSE), per hectare of farmland and per full time farmer equivalents.

The monetary value of the PSE is influenced by the size and structure of the country's agricultural sector, as well as the country's rate of inflation. The PSE expressed per farmer or hectare is also influenced by differences in farm structures across countries. Support expressed as a percentage of gross farm receipts shows the amount of support to farmers irrespective of the sectoral structure and inflation rate of a country, making the %PSE the most widely acceptable and useful indicator for comparisons of support across countries, commodities and time.

This paper concentrates on the measurement and interpretation of support, rather than on the actual results. But, by way of illustration, Figure 1 shows the trend in OECD agricultural support in current monetary terms and as a percentage of farm receipts. It is clear that while there has been little change in the value of support at *current prices* since the mid-1980s – with producer support in the aggregate of the 30 OECD countries currently amounting to about 240 billion USD per year – there has been a modest reduction in the %PSE. Even so, a PSE of 31% means that only 69 cents of every dollar of farmers' gross receipts for the average OECD farmer comes from sales of products valued at world market prices.

Figure 1. Producer support has only marginally declined since mid-1980s

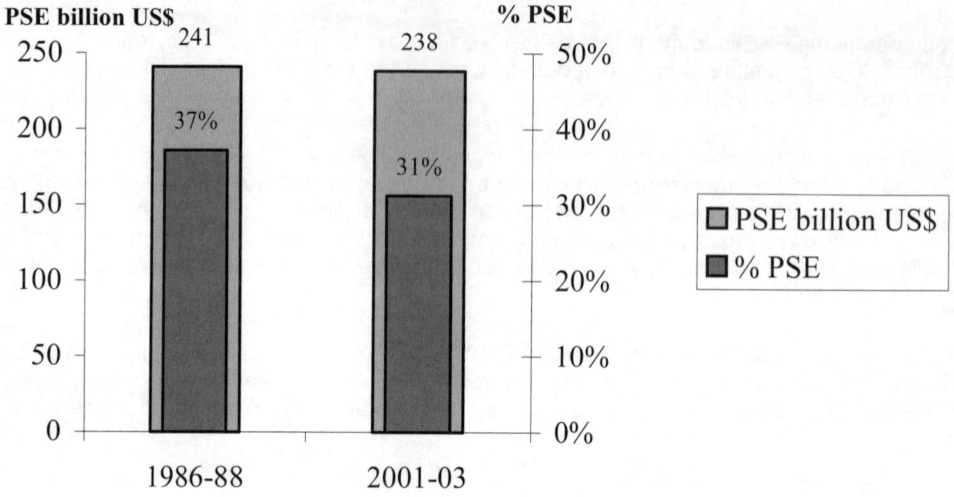

Source: OECD Secretariat.

How is farm support measured?

Farm support is measured by adding up two elements: the difference between domestic and world prices for commodities multiplied by the amount produced, and budgetary transfers. Budgetary transfers include payments to farmers and budgetary revenue foregone through lowering the cost of farm inputs. Tariffs, quotas and other restrictions on imports as well as subsidies on exports, together with government intervention to boost domestic prices through for example stock-building, create a gap between domestic market prices and world prices for commodities at the border. Multiplying that price gap by the amount of domestic production gives the market price support to producers in the PSE. At the same time that domestic producers receive higher prices for commodities, consumers also have to pay those higher prices. In other words, *market price support* channels transfers from consumers to farmers.

Budgetary payments may be granted to farmers, based on such factors as what they produce or the area of land farmed, or to input suppliers to compensate them for charging lower prices to farmers. These are taken from published budgets in OECD countries and included in the PSE. However, some countries make payments to farmers to hold stocks of farm goods on their farms or to public purchasing agencies to accumulate such stocks. The operational costs of acquiring, holding and disposing of public stocks are a budgetary cost to implement market price support policy but do not provide support to farmers over and above market price support, and so are not included in the PSE, but in the TSE.

Energy tax rebates, subsidised irrigation water and interest concessions are examples of potential *revenue foregone* by the government. These are measured by the gap between the tax, water charge or interest rates paid by farmers and those paid by others in the domestic market.

Why are transfers to farmers from consumers through higher prices added to taxpayer transfers?

Policies come in many different forms, but often have much the same effect. For example, the US is a net exporter of wheat and support to wheat farmers is delivered by (among other ways) a government *payment* for each tonne of wheat produced, which raises the price farmers receive but not the price paid by consumers. Japan, by contrast, is a net importer of wheat and applies import tariffs (*market price support*) which raise both the price paid by consumers and received by farmers. In both cases, the result for farmers is that they receive prices higher than the market would generate. Whether provided through a government payment or a border measure, a given price increase delivers the same amount of support and has the same effect on domestic production and farm income. This is illustrated in Figure 2.

Figure 2. Payments per tonne and tariffs have equivalent effect on producer price

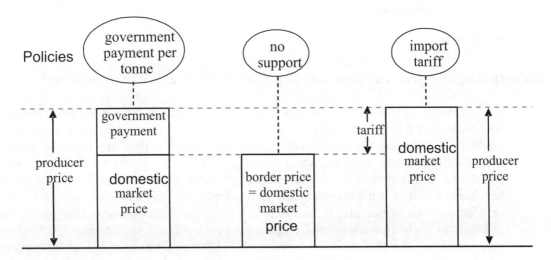

Note: for simplicity, marketing margins are not considered in this graph.

Source: OECD Secretariat.

As both payments per tonne and market price support raise farm commodity prices by the same amount and both affect production, trade and income, the PSE as a yardstick would do a poor job if only payments were included. After all, as Figure 3 shows (in a simplified form, excluding the year-on-year fluctuations), market price support still remains the largest part of overall support, accounting for nearly two thirds of the PSE in the OECD area.

Figure 3. A large part of farm support comes through price support

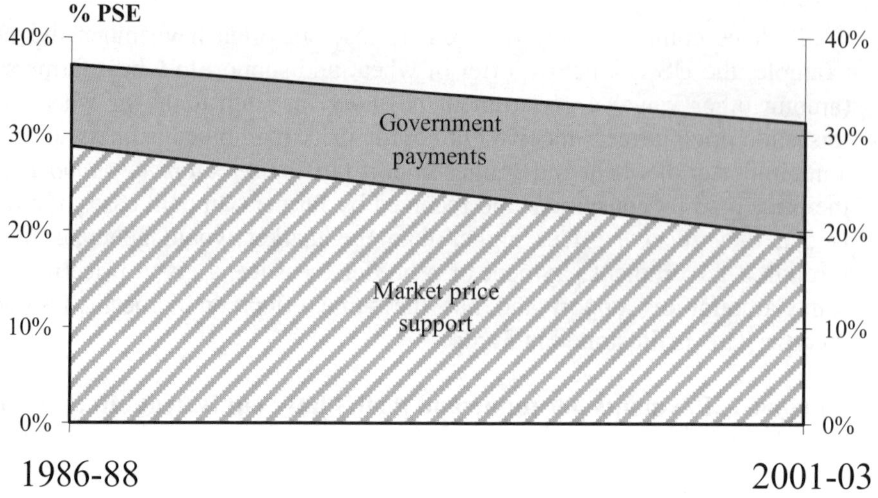

Source: OECD Secretariat.

Are actual border prices appropriate benchmarks to measure price support?

In calculating market price support, the OECD estimates the gap between domestic and world prices at each country's border. However, it is sometimes argued that actual world prices are not the appropriate benchmarks because they are distorted through production enhancing policies, import barriers and export subsidies. Therefore, world prices that might prevail in the absence of all such policies should be used as the benchmarks. Which is the correct approach to adopt here? As in so many cases it depends on what we want to measure. If the aim is to provide an overall picture of the global state of affairs in world agriculture, then calculating world prices in the absence of all policies may have merit. But that is not the purpose of OECD's evaluation of agricultural policies, which is to compare the interventions governments make in pursuit of their policy objectives. How much effort a government makes to ensure its farmers obtain a particular level of domestic price obviously depends on the actual world price. After all, this is the basis on which governments choose tariff levels and other price support instruments.

More specifically, the focus of OECD analysis is to monitor progress in policy reform and to assess whether current policies are best serving countries in achieving their objectives. Therefore, the OECD calculation of support must be an indicator able to say something about the efforts made to support its farmers and progress in the reform of current policies. The market price support element of the PSE would not be able to do this and would therefore provide the wrong guidance to policy makers, were it to be based on world prices that do not exist in reality.

Governments and stakeholders are, however, interested in knowing what might happen to domestic and world prices in the process of agricultural policy reform. The OECD, as well as others, has examined this issue, but the analysis must start from the actual prices that exist in domestic and world markets. Thus the measured price gap is a crucial input into modelling what might happen under different assumptions about policy reform. What these models show is that reforming policies and removing trade barriers changes both domestic and world prices, narrowing the price gap. But the extent of changes in world prices will depend on whether such reform occurs in one or several or all countries. Moreover, not only will reforming policies have effects on market price support, but also on budgetary payments that bridge the gap between world prices and those that governments consider farmers should receive.

Isn't the gap between domestic and world prices caused by factors other than farm policies?

The PSE provides a snapshot of support provided in a given time period due to agricultural policies, in the context of given macro-economic conditions and economy wide policies. The benchmark is the absence of agricultural policies of the country concerned, *i.e.* a situation where farm receipts are entirely generated in the market. In that case, prices received by farmers would reflect changes in world market conditions and exchange rates. When world prices decline, domestic producer prices in a well functioning market follow, and vice versa.

In many cases the PSE tends to fluctuate with changing world market conditions. This is typically the case where governments pursue policies that insulate domestic producer prices against swings in world market prices. Under these conditions, when world market prices decline, say because of abundant world supplies, then the PSE tends to rise. Is this therefore a non-policy effect, which should be excluded from PSE calculations?

Where a government deliberately shields domestic producer prices from such changes in world markets, it effectively alters market signals, even though seemingly only through doing nothing, *i.e.* by keeping the domestic support price constant behind trade barriers. In a situation like that, the relative stability of the domestic price is clearly an effect of farm policy. The government provides more support to domestic farmers the further the world market price declines, and vice versa. The PSE should pick this up – and it does.

Similarly, even if world prices do not change, a country's exchange rate might appreciate or depreciate. In a well functioning market without government interference, this would result in a decrease or increase in domestic prices in national currency. As in the previous example, if a government blocks this price adjustment through its policies, this results in a change in the value of market price support, even though the only "visible" change that has occurred is in the exchange rate.

These simple examples serve to demonstrate that when there are border measures that impede the transmission of world prices to domestic markets, changes in market price support that result from a change in world prices at the border can legitimately be assigned to policy measures that are in place. In evaluating policy developments the OECD deals with this by identifying and measuring the contribution of the various factors included in the measured price gap, thereby providing information that helps policy makers in interpreting year-on-year changes in the PSE.

What do farm support indicators tell about agricultural policy reform?

Countries pursue a variety of goals with their policies. Although they use different mixes of policy measures to do so, it is the way in which the measures are implemented in the context of the conditions in each country that determines the impacts on production, consumption, income, trade and the environment. In order to provide a basis for more in-depth policy analysis, the OECD not only calculates overall support levels, but also reports their composition using different categories of policy measures that reflect how the policies are implemented. The implementation criteria tell us something about how different policies may affect farmers' decisions to produce farm goods.

Some policy measures deliver support directly related to the amount of a specific commodity produced (market price support and payments based on commodity production) or inputs used. These policy measures are the ones that have the strongest influence on production incentives, although this incentive can be weakened in those countries that place constraints on output produced or inputs used. Policy measures that deliver support based on the current area planted or animal numbers, but are not dependant on the amount of a specific commodity produced have somewhat less influence on production incentives. Other policy measures provide support based on criteria such as past production history, the overall farm area, the income situation of the farmer, or for the provision of environmental services, for example. Such measures have the least influence on production incentives.

This classification of policy measures highlights the different production and trade incentives of various policy categories. In assessing policy developments, the OECD takes care to highlight the trends in the policy mix, with particular emphasis on the most production and trade distorting measures – market price support, and output and input payments. It is thus possible to assess policy reform in terms of the trends in the level of support and the shift towards less production and trade distorting policies.

Agricultural policy measures in many OECD countries have become more diverse and complex. Policies not only influence production through their effects on prices but also on their effects on wealth and risks facing farmers. At present the OECD is in the process of revising the PSE classification to accommodate these developments. This mainly involves better classifying policy measures that provide support based on a mixture of current and past production variables and those that deliver support not based on farm commodity production – which will help to evaluate progress in policy reform.

So what do the support indicators say about the extent of policy reform? Figure 4 shows that some reform has occurred in the shift away from the most distorting policy measures (market price support, input and output based payments), which have fallen since the mid-1980s. Nevertheless, such measures still account for about three quarters of support to farmers.

Figure 4. Progress towards reform of farm policies is slow

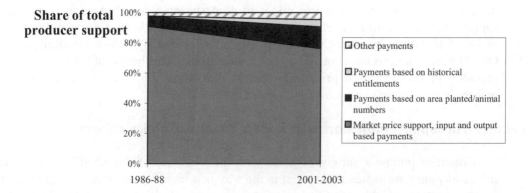

Source: OECD Secretariat.

How much does support increase farm incomes?

The PSE measures transfers from taxpayers and consumers that raise farm receipts. This transfer does not mean that farmers' incomes change by the same amount. In order to receive a transfer, farmers usually have to produce a commodity or service, or use an input, and thus they incur extra costs. The transfer is greater than the farm income generated by the amount of these extra costs. Other work in the OECD calculates the "transfer efficiency" of a policy measure, which is the share of support that translates into extra farm income. In fact, one extra dollar of market price support actually results in a rise in farm incomes of no more than 25 cents, while the share for payments based on historical entitlements is about one-half. Only in the case of a transfer that does not require the farmer to incur any extra costs (such as a lump sum payment) is support translated entirely into extra farm income. It would also be wrong to assume that the amount of support provided to farmers in the rich countries is an indicator of the extra income that developing country farmers might gain if agricultural policies in the OECD countries were eliminated. Certainly, farmers in many developing countries would be better of if OECD countries no longer pursued policies that distort trade and depress world market prices. But the current level of OECD farm support would not necessarily translate into extra income for farmers in poor countries.

Should payments for environmental services provided by farmers be included in farm support?

Some farmers provide environmental services for which markets are lacking. For example they may plant trees or change tillage practices in a way that can contribute to alleviating climate change or flood risk. A farmer may cut a meadow later than usual in order to allow rare birds to nest, thus making a contribution to preserving biodiversity. But farmers also generate harmful environmental effects, such as off-farm water pollution. The objectives of some agricultural policies are to provide environmental services or reduce pollution, through granting payments to farmers. Should payments made under such policies be included in a support estimate such as the PSE?

The PSE does not measure the effects of policy measures, including those on the environment, but can be the basis of such measurement. The intended objectives (environmental services) and unintended effects (externalities) of policy measures depend not only on the characteristics of the measure itself, but also on the overall policy mix. In order to form the basis for policy evaluation, the PSE needs to include all policy measures, including those that address externalities and public goods.

Where do we go from here?

If different policy instruments have different objectives and effects, does it make sense to add up the associated transfers to a single number, as does the PSE for each country? The answer is "yes" because the total value of transfers provided by a set of policy measures to the agricultural sector is a good indicator of the overall intervention of governments to shape developments in that sector. The accuracy of the PSE as a yardstick of support depends not only on the care with which it is constructed, but also on how it is used. For this reason, a great effort is made to complement the measurement of transfers provided by the PSE with the analysis necessary to provide a comprehensive evaluation of policies with respect to how effective and efficient they are at meeting their goals.

Work is underway or planned in the OECD that involve improving the measurement, coverage, classification and use of PSEs in policy evaluation: analysing the impacts of policy measures on production, trade, income and welfare (using the Policy Evaluation Model); analysing policy measures that decouple support from farmers' production decisions; analysing the linkages between policy measures (as measured by categories within the PSE) and environmental outcomes (as measured by agri-environmental indicators); examining the effect of policy changes on land use; and undertaking agricultural policy studies on Brazil, China, India and South Africa.

2 November 2004

More information on measuring support to agriculture and support data can be found in the following publications and papers on the OECD website:

www.oecd.org/agr/support

www.oecd.org/agr/policy

Agricultural Policies in OECD countries at a Glance (2004)

Methodology for the Measurement of Support and Use in Policy Evaluation (2003) (website only)

Is the Concept of the Producer Support Estimate in Need of Revision? (2003) (website only)

China in the Global Economy: Agricultural Policies in China after WTO Accession (2002) (Chapter on the Measurement of Agricultural Support)

Agricultural Policies in OECD Countries: A Positive Reform Agenda (2002)

The 2003 Presidential Address to the Agricultural Economics Society by Wilfrid Legg, "Agricultural Subsidies: Measurement and Use in Policy Evaluation", published in the *Journal of Agricultural Economics* (July 2003), provides a more technical treatment of the issues in a historical perspective.

OECD PUBLICATIONS, 2, rue André-Pascal, 75775 PARIS CEDEX 16
PRINTED IN FRANCE
(30 2005 06 1 P) ISBN 92-64-00900-0 – No. 54413 2005